ISLAMIC LAWS

ISLAMIC LAWS

According to the Fatwas of His Eminence
al-Sayyid Ali al-Husayni al-Sistani

FOURTH EDITION

translated and annotated by
Mohammed Ali Ismail

with a new foreword and biography

THE WORLD FEDERATION

BRITISH LIBRARY CATALOGUING IN PUBLICATION DATA
A catalogue record for this book is available from the British Library

ISBN: 978-1-78991-071-1 (hbk)
ISBN: 978-1-78991-081-0 (pbk)
ISBN: 978-1-78991-082-7 (digital)

Fourth Edition

10 9 8 7 6 5 4 3 2 -

PUBLISHED BY
The World Federation of Khoja Shia Ithna-Asheri Muslim Communities
Registered Charity in the UK No. 282303
The World Federation is an NGO in Special Consultative Status with the Economic and Social Council (ECOSOC) of the United Nations
Islamic Centre, Wood Lane, Stanmore, Middlesex, United Kingdom, HA7 4LQ
www.world-federation.org

Design and layout by Advent Publishing Services, Leeds.

THE WORLD
FEDERATION
OF KSIMC

Contents in Brief

Foreword to the Fourth Edition xix
Translator's Preface to the Third Edition xxi
Translator's Preface to the Fourth Edition xxv
Transliteration xxvii

1. Following a Jurist (*Taqlīd*) 1
2. Purification (*Ṭahārah*) 11
3. Prayer (*Ṣalāh*) 179
4. Fasting (*Ṣawm*) 367
5. Spiritual Retreat (*Iʿtikāf*) 409
6. The One-Fifth Tax (*Khums*) 423
7. Enjoining Good and Forbidding Evil 447
8. Alms Tax (Zakat) 453
9. Hajj 491
10. Buying and Selling 497
11. Partnership (*Shirkah*) 525
12. Settlement (*Ṣulḥ*) 533
13. Hiring/Renting (*Ijārah*) 539
14. Sleeping Partnership (*Muḍārabah*) 551
15. Reward (*Juʿālah*) 557
16. Sharecropping (*Muzāraʿah*) 561
17. Tree Tending Contract (*Musāqāh*) and Tree Planting Contract (*Mughārasah*) 567
18. Those Prohibited from having Disposal over their Property 573
19. Agency (*Wikālah*) 577
20. Loan (*Qarḍ*) 583
21. Transfer of Debt (*Ḥawālah*) 589
22. Security (*Rahn*) 593
23. Suretyship (*Ḍamān*) 597
24. Surety for the Appearance of a Debtor (*Kafālah*) 603
25. Deposit (*Wadīʿah*) and Trust (*Amānah*) 607
26. Gratuitous Loan (*ʿĀriyah*) 613
27. Marriage 619
28. Breastfeeding 647
29. Divorce 659

30. Usurpation (*Ghaṣb*) 675
31. Found Property 681
32. Slaughtering and Hunting Animals 687
33. Eating and Drinking 703
34. Vow (*Nadhr*) and Covenant (*ʿAhd*) 711
35. Oath (*Qasam*) 721
36. Charitable Endowment (*Waqf*) 727
37. Will (*Waṣiyyah*) 735
38. Inheritance (*Irth*) 747

Glossary 765
Appendix 1: Table of Weights, Measures, Values, and Quantities 777
Appendix 2: Biography of His Eminence al-Sayyid Ali al-Husayni al-Sistani 779
Appendix 3: List of Updated Rulings 787
Works Consulted 789

Contents

Foreword to the Fourth Edition xix
Translator's Preface to the Third Edition xxi
Translator's Preface to the Fourth Edition xxv
Transliteration xxvii

1. **Following a Jurist (*Taqlīd*)** 1

2. **Purification (*Ṭahārah*)** 11
Unmixed (*muṭlaq*) and mixed (*muḍāf*) water 13
1. *Kurr* water 13
2. *Qalīl* water 15
3. Flowing water 16
4. Rainwater 17
5. Well water 18
Laws relating to the different types of water 19
Laws relating to emptying the bowels and the bladder 20
Clearing the male urethra of urine (*istibrā'*) 23
Recommended (*mustaḥabb*) and disapproved (*makrūh*) acts when emptying the bowels and the bladder 25
Impurities (*najāsāt*) 26
1. & 2. Urine and faeces 26
3. Semen 27
4. Corpse 27
5. Blood 28
6. & 7. Dog and pig 29
8. Disbeliever (*kāfir*) 29
9. Wine 31
10. Sweat of an excrement-eating animal 31
Ways of establishing impurity (*najāsah*) 32
How a pure (*ṭāhir*) object becomes impure (*najis*) 33
Laws of impurities (*najāsāt*) 35
Things that purify an impure object (*muṭahhirāt*) 38
1. Water 38
2. Earth 45
3. The sun 46

4. Transformation (*istiḥālah*) ... 47
5. Change (*inqilāb*) ... 48
6. Transfer (*intiqāl*) ... 49
7. Islam ... 50
8. Subsequence (*tabaʿiyyah*) ... 50
9. Removal of intrinsic impurity (*ʿayn al-najāsah*) ... 52
10. *Istibrāʾ* of an excrement-eating animal ... 53
11. Absence of a Muslim ... 53
12. Flowing out of blood [of a slaughtered animal] in a normal quantity ... 54
Laws of utensils ... 55
Ablution (*wuḍūʾ*) ... 56
Immersive ablution (*al-wuḍūʾ al-irtimāsī*) ... 60
Recommended supplication (*duʿāʾ*) while performing *wuḍūʾ* ... 61
Conditions for the validity of *wuḍūʾ* ... 64
Laws of *wuḍūʾ* ... 71
Things for which one must perform *wuḍūʾ* ... 74
Things that invalidate *wuḍūʾ* ... 76
Laws of *jabīrah wuḍūʾ* ... 76
Obligatory (*wājib*) ritual bathing (*ghusl*) ... 81
Laws of ritual impurity (*janābah*) ... 81
Things that are unlawful (*ḥarām*) for a *junub* ... 83
Things that are disapproved (*makrūh*) for a *junub* ... 84
The *ghusl* for *janābah* ... 85
Sequential ritual bathing (*al-ghusl al-tartībī*) ... 85
Immersive ritual bathing (*al-ghusl al-irtimāsī*) ... 86
Laws of performing *ghusl* ... 87
Irregular blood discharge (*istiḥāḍah*) ... 91
Laws of *istiḥāḍah* ... 92
Menstruation (*ḥayḍ*) ... 100
Laws of a woman in menstruation (*ḥāʾiḍ*) ... 103
Categories of women in menstruation ... 107
1. A woman with a habit of time and duration ... 108
2. A woman with a habit of time ... 114
3. A woman with a habit of duration ... 116
4. A woman with a disordered habit (*muḍṭaribah*) ... 118
5. A menarcheal woman (*mubtadiʾah*) ... 118
6. A forgetful woman (*nāsiyah*) ... 119
Miscellaneous rulings on *ḥayḍ* ... 120

Lochia (*nifās*) ... 122
The *ghusl* for touching a corpse (*mass al-mayyit*) ... 125
Laws relating to a dying person (*muḥtaḍar*) ... 127
Laws relating to after death ... 129
The obligation to give *ghusl*, shroud (*takfīn*), pray over, camphorate (*taḥnīṭ*), and bury (*dafn*) ... 129
Method of performing the ghusl given to a corpse (*mayyit*) ... 131
Laws of shrouding (*takfīn*) a corpse ... 135
Laws of camphorating (*taḥnīṭ*) a corpse ... 138
Laws of the funeral prayer (*ṣalāt al-mayyit*) ... 139
Method of performing *ṣalāt al-mayyit* ... 141
Recommended (*mustaḥabb*) acts of *ṣalāt al-mayyit* ... 146
Laws of burial (*dafn*) ... 147
Recommended (*mustaḥabb*) acts of burial (*dafn*) ... 149
The prayer of loneliness (*ṣalāt al-waḥshah*) ... 157
Exhumation of a grave ... 158
Recommended (*mustaḥabb*) *ghusls* ... 160
Dry ablution (*tayammum*) ... 163
1. Not having water ... 163
2. Not having access to water ... 165
3. Using water is harmful ... 166
4. Hardship (*ḥaraj*) and excessive difficulty (*mashaqqah*) ... 167
5. Needing water to quench thirst ... 167
6. Performing *wuḍūʾ* or *ghusl* conflicts with another legal responsibility that is more important or just as important ... 168
7. Shortage of time ... 168
Things with which performing *tayammum* is valid (*ṣaḥīḥ*) ... 169
Method of performing *tayammum* in place of *wuḍūʾ* or *ghusl* ... 172
Laws of *tayammum* ... 173

3. **Prayer (*Ṣalāh*)** 179
The obligatory (*wājib*) prayers ... 182
The obligatory daily prayers ... 182
The time for the midday (*ẓuhr*) and afternoon (*ʿaṣr*) prayers ... 182
The Friday prayer (*ṣalāt al-jumuʿah*) and its laws ... 183
Some laws concerning the Friday prayer ... 186
The time for the prayer after sunset (*maghrib*) and the evening (*ʿishāʾ*) prayer ... 187

The time for the morning (*ṣubḥ*) prayer ... 188
Laws relating to the time of prayers ... 188
Prayers that must be performed in order ... 192
Recommended (*mustaḥabb*) prayers ... 193
Timings for the daily supererogatory (*nāfilah*) prayers ... 194
The *ghufaylah* prayer ... 196
Rules of qibla ... 197
Covering the body in prayers ... 200
Conditions of clothing worn by someone performing prayers ... 202
Cases when it is not necessary for the body and clothing of someone performing prayers to be pure ... 212
Things that are recommended (*mustaḥabb*) for the clothing of someone performing prayers ... 215
Things that are disapproved (*makrūh*) for the clothing of someone performing prayers ... 216
The place where prayers are performed ... 216
Places where performing prayers is recommended (*mustaḥabb*) ... 222
Places where performing prayers is disapproved (*makrūh*) ... 223
Laws of a mosque ... 224
The call to prayer (*adhān*) and the call to stand for prayer (*iqāmah*) ... 227
Translation of the sentences of *adhān* and *iqāmah* ... 228
Obligatory components of the prayer ... 233
Intention (*niyyah*) ... 234
Takbīrat al-iḥrām ... 235
Standing (*qiyām*) ... 237
Recitation (*qirā'ah*) ... 240
Bowing (*rukūʿ*) ... 250
Prostrating (*sujūd*) ... 254
Things on which *sajdah* is permitted (*jā'iz*) ... 261
Recommended (*mustaḥabb*) and disapproved (*makrūh*) acts of *sajdah* ... 263
Obligatory (*wājib*) prostrations of the Qur'an ... 265
Testifying (*tashahhud*) ... 267
Salutation (*salām*) ... 269
Sequence (*tartīb*) ... 270
Close succession (*muwālāh*) ... 271
Qunūt ... 271

Translation of prayers ... 273
1. Translation of Sūrat al-Ḥamd ... 273
2. Translation of Sūrat al-Ikhlāṣ ... 274
3. Translation of the *dhikr* of *rukūʿ* and *sujūd*, and the *dhikr*s that are recommended to be said after them ... 274
4. Translation of *qunūt* ... 275
5. Translation of *al-tasbīḥāt al-arbaʿah* ... 276
6. Translation of the complete *tashahhud* and *salām* ... 276
Supplications after prayers (*taʿqībāt*) ... 277
Ṣalawāt ... 278
Things that invalidate (*mubṭilāt*) prayers ... 278
Things that are disapproved (*makrūh*) in prayers ... 286
Instances of when it is permitted (*jāʾiz*) to break an obligatory (*wājib*) prayer ... 287
Doubts that arise in prayers (*shakkiyāt*) ... 288
Doubts that invalidate prayers ... 288
Doubts that must be dismissed ... 289
1. A doubt about an act for which the time of performance has passed ... 289
2. Doubt after *salām* ... 291
3. Doubt after the time of prayers ... 292
4. An excessive doubter (*kathīr al-shakk*) ... 293
5. Doubt of an imam and a follower in congregational prayers ... 294
6. Doubts in recommended prayers ... 295
Doubts that are valid (*ṣaḥīḥ*) ... 296
Method of performing the precautionary prayer (*ṣalāt al-iḥtiyāṭ*) ... 301
The two prostrations for inadvertence (*sajdatā al-sahw*) ... 305
Method of performing *sajdatā al-sahw* ... 308
Making up (*qaḍāʾ*) a forgotten *sajdah* ... 309
Omitting or adding components or conditions of the prayer ... 310
Prayers of a traveller ... 312
Miscellaneous rulings on the prayer of a traveller ... 328
Lapsed (*qaḍāʾ*) prayers ... 331
Lapsed (*qaḍāʾ*) prayers of a father that are obligatory (*wājib*) on the eldest son ... 334
Congregational prayers (*ṣalāt al-jamāʿah*) ... 335
Conditions of the imam of congregational prayers ... 345

Rules of congregational prayers 346
Duties of the imam and the follower in congregational prayers 350
Things that are disapproved (*makrūh*) in congregational prayers 351
The prayer of signs (*ṣalāt al-āyāt*) 352
Method of performing *ṣalāt al-āyāt* 355
The Eid al-Fiṭr & Eid al-Aḍḥā prayers 358
Hiring someone to perform prayers 363

4. **Fasting (*Ṣawm*)** 367
Intention (*niyyah*) 369
Things that invalidate (*mubṭilāt*) a fast 374
1. Eating and drinking 375
2. Sexual intercourse 377
3. Masturbation 377
4. Ascribing something false to Allah the Exalted, the Most Noble Prophet (Ṣ), or the Infallible Imams (ʿA) 378
5. Causing thick dust to reach the throat 380
6. Remaining in a state of *janābah*, *ḥayḍ*, or *nifās* until the time of *ṣubḥ* prayers 381
7. Applying enema 385
8. Vomiting 385
Laws of things that invalidate a fast 386
Things that are disapproved (*makrūh*) for a fasting person to do 387
Times when it is obligatory (*wājib*) to both make up (*qaḍāʾ*) and give recompense (*kaffārah*) 388
Recompense (*kaffārah*) of a fast 389
Times when it is obligatory (*wājib*) to only make up (*qaḍāʾ*) a fast 393
Laws of a lapsed (*qaḍāʾ*) fast 395
Laws of fasting for a traveller 399
Those on whom fasting is not obligatory (*wājib*) 401
Ways of establishing the first of the month 403
Unlawful (*ḥarām*) and disapproved (*makrūh*) fasts 405
Recommended (*mustaḥabb*) fasts 406
Times when it is recommended (*mustaḥabb*) for one to abstain from things that invalidate a fast 408

5. **Spiritual Retreat (*Iʿtikāf*)** 409
Conditions for the validity of *iʿtikāf* 411
Leaving the place of *iʿtikāf* 417
Miscellaneous rulings on *iʿtikāf* 420

6. **The One-Fifth Tax (*Khums*)** 423
1. Surplus income from earnings and gains 425
2. Mined products 435
3. Treasure troves 436
4. Lawful property that has become mixed with unlawful property 438
5. Gems acquired by underwater diving 440
6. Spoils of war 441
7. Land that a *dhimmī* purchases from a Muslim 442
Distribution of *khums* 443

7. **Enjoining Good and Forbidding Evil** 447

8. **Alms Tax (Zakat)** 453
Conditions for zakat to become obligatory (*wājib*) 455
Zakat of wheat, barley, and raisins 457
The taxable limit (*niṣāb*) for gold 462
The *niṣāb* for silver 463
Zakat of camels, cows, and sheep 465
The *niṣāb* for camels 466
The *niṣāb* for cows 467
The *niṣāb* for sheep 468
Zakat on business goods 470
Distribution of zakat 470
Criteria for being entitled (*mustaḥiqq*) to receive zakat 475
Intention (*niyyah*) for giving zakat 477
Miscellaneous rulings on zakat 478
The *fiṭrah* alms tax (*zakāt al-fiṭrah*) 483
Distribution of *zakāt al-fiṭrah* 486
Miscellaneous rulings on *zakāt al-fiṭrah* 488

9. **Hajj** 491

10. **Buying and Selling** 497

Recommended (*mustaḥabb*) acts of buying and selling 499
Disapproved (*makrūh*) transactions 500
Unlawful (*ḥarām*) transactions 500
Conditions relating to the seller and the buyer 508
Conditions relating to the commodity and the payment in exchange 510
The transaction formula (*ṣīghah*) 512
Buying and selling fruit 513
Immediate exchange (*naqd*) and credit (*nasī'ah*) transactions 514
Prepayment (*salaf*) transaction and its conditions 515
Laws relating to prepayment (*salaf*) transactions 517
Selling gold and silver for gold and silver 518
Cases when a person can annul a transaction 518
Miscellaneous rulings 524

11. Partnership (*Shirkah*) 525

12. Settlement (*Ṣulḥ*) 533

13. Hiring/Renting (*Ijārah*) 539
Conditions for property given on rent 543
Conditions relating to the use of the property which is given on rent 544
Miscellaneous rulings on hiring/renting 546

14. Sleeping Partnership (*Muḍārabah*) 551

15. Reward (*Ju'ālah*) 557

16. Sharecropping (*Muzāra'ah*) 561

17. Tree Tending Contract (*Musāqāh*) and Tree Planting Contract (*Mughārasah*) 567

18. Those Prohibited from having Disposal over their Property 573

19. Agency (*Wikālah*) 577

20. Loan (*Qarḍ*) 583

21. **Transfer of Debt (*Ḥawālah*)** 589

22. **Security (*Rahn*)** 593

23. **Suretyship (*Ḍamān*)** 597

24. **Surety for the Appearance of a Debtor (*Kafālah*)** 603

25. **Deposit (*Wadīʿah*) and Trust (*Amānah*)** 607

26. **Gratuitous Loan (*ʿĀriyah*)** 613

27. **Marriage** 619
The marriage contract 621
Method of saying the marriage contract formula (*ṣīghah*) 622
Conditions of a marriage contract 624
Situations in which a man and a woman can annul the marriage contract 628
Women with whom marriage is unlawful (*ḥarām*) 630
Laws of permanent marriage 635
Laws of temporary marriage (*mutʿah*) 638
Looking at non-*maḥram* 640
Miscellaneous rulings on marriage 642

28. **Breastfeeding** 647
Conditions for breastfeeding to cause someone to become *maḥram* 651
Etiquettes of breastfeeding 655
Miscellaneous rulings on breastfeeding 656

29. **Divorce** 659
The prescribed waiting period (*ʿiddah*) of a divorce 664
The *ʿiddah* of a woman whose husband has died 666
Irrevocable (*bāʾin*) and revocable (*rijʿī*) divorce 668
Laws of returning to one's wife 668
Khulʿ divorce 670
Mubārāh divorce 671
Miscellaneous rulings on divorce 672

30. Usurpation (*Ghaṣb*) 675

31. Found Property 681

32. Slaughtering and Hunting Animals 687
Method of slaughtering an animal..........690
Conditions of slaughtering an animal..........691
Method of slaughtering a camel..........693
Recommended (*mustaḥabb*) acts when slaughtering an animal..........694
Disapproved (*makrūh*) acts when slaughtering an animal..........695
Laws relating to hunting with weapons..........695
Hunting with a hunting dog..........698
Fishing and hunting locusts..........700

33. Eating and Drinking 703
Etiquettes of eating..........708
Things that are discouraged (*madhmūm*) when eating..........709
Etiquettes of drinking..........710
Things that are discouraged (*madhmūm*) when drinking..........710

34. Vow (*Nadhr*) and Covenant (*ʿAhd*) 711

35. Oath (*Qasam*) 721

36. Charitable Endowment (*Waqf*) 727

37. Will (*Waṣiyyah*) 735

38. Inheritance (*Irth*) 747
Inheritance of the first group..........750
Inheritance of the second group..........752
Inheritance of the third group..........758
Inheritance of husband and wife..........760
Miscellaneous rules of inheritance..........762

Glossary 765
Appendix 1: Table of Weights, Measures, Values, and Quantities 777

Foreword to the Fourth Edition

By the grace of Allah (swt), The World Federation of KSIMC is pleased to present to our community a fourth edition of *Islamic Laws*, an edition which includes many revisions to the third edition published in 2017.

The World Federation first had the honour of publishing an English translation of the Persian manual of the rulings of His Eminence al-Sayyid Ali al-Husayni al-Sistani (may Allah (swt) protect him) in 1994. It was in accordance with the wishes of His Eminence that the first edition of *Islamic Laws* was published by The World Federation, the result of Mulla Asgharali M. M. Jaffer's translation completed in a remarkably short space of time. All subsequent editions of the work – including this present fourth edition – have been translated by Dr Shaykh Mohammed Ali Ismail. The second edition was originally published as two separate volumes: volume one, *Ritual Acts of Worship*, was published in 2015; and volume two, *Transactions*, was published in 2017. Also in 2017, a combined edition of the entire work was published as one volume.

However, considering that the Qum Office of His Eminence has published five further editions of the Persian manual of his rulings since our last English edition (that is, since the third edition of *Islamic Laws*, which was based on the thirty-first edition of the Persian manual of rulings), we felt it necessary to publish a fourth updated English edition, which would be in accordance with the latest thirty-sixth Persian edition, published in 2021.

In this fourth edition, the reader will find changes to over 100 rulings, six of which pertain to frequently faced situations. These updates, therefore, may potentially have a major impact on the English-speaking followers of His Eminence.[1] Additionally, this new edition, having gone through a robust review process, includes an updated glossary, clearer phrasing of language, and corrections to the Arabic text, making *Islamic Laws* more accurate and user-friendly. So as to bring our *marja*ʿ closer to our community, we have included a new biography of His Eminence and have redesigned the cover with a

[1] These six rulings are: 597, 1498, 1562, 1694, 1699, and 1803. A list of all the updated rulings can be found in Appendix 3.

new look and a photograph of His Eminence, in line with the teaching that looking at the face of an *ʿālim* is an act of worship.

The Islamic Education Department of The World Federation strives towards the goal of making religious education material digitally accessible. As a consequence of our embracing technological changes in education, the fourth edition of *Islamic Laws* is freely available via both our 'OneStopFiqh' dynamic online portal (fiqh.world-federation.org) and mobile application.

I am extremely grateful to Dr Shaykh Mohammed Ali Ismail, as are all the office bearers of The World Federation. Since the second edition of *Islamic Laws*, Shaykh Ismail has accompanied us on a blessed journey to make Islamic rulings more accessible to English readers. His proficiency as a translator combined with his meticulous and efficient approach to his work serve to assist readers to better understand the *fiqhī* rulings of our *marjaʿ*, and practice them as intended. We would also like to thank Shaykh Abbas Ismail for copy-editing this updated translation with utmost efficiency as well as Shaykh Muhammad Mahdi Kassamali for drafting an insightful biography of His Eminence, especially for this volume, which appears here in revised form.

I also acknowledge and appreciate the efforts of the proof-readers, as well as the constant support and guidance received from the offices of His Eminence.

Finally, I would like to express our gratitude to the Islamic Education Department's team, led by Shaykh Murtadha Alidina and Shaykh Afzal Merali, for their constant guidance and project management of this publication. May Allah (swt) reward them and everyone who has contributed to this work.

SAFDER JAFFER
President, The World Federation of KSIMC
London, UK
Shaʿbān al-Muaẓẓam 1444 / March 2023

Translator's Preface to the Third Edition

In the name of Allah, the All-Beneficent, the Ever-Merciful.
All praise is for Allah, Lord of the worlds.
May Allah bless Muḥammad and his pure progeny.

This work is a translation of the Persian *Tawḍīḥ al-Masā'il* (literally, *Explanation of Issues*) of His Eminence al-Sayyid Ali al-Husayni al-Sistani. The text used for this translation is the thirty-first edition, published in 2014 by the Qum Office of His Eminence. The following is a list of the most important conventions that have been adopted in this work.

1. The particular wording employed by a jurist in his rulings is highly significant; sometimes, even small differences in expression can impact greatly on people's lives. With this in mind, and given that the present work is a translation of a manual of jurisprudential rulings, the aim has been to produce a translation that is as close to the original wording as possible. However, where this approach would have produced unfamiliar or unclear expressions in English, a more idiomatic style has been adopted.
2. Annotations and glosses have been added in an effort to enhance the reader's understanding of the rulings and to facilitate cross-referencing with other parts of the work. Many of these annotations and glosses have been based on al-Sayyid al-Sistani's other works on Islamic law, particularly *Minhāj al-Ṣāliḥīn*.
3. In order for all aspects of the work to be accessible to as many English-speaking people around the world as possible, the standard Arabic spelling and pronunciation has been used as a model for the transliteration of legal terminology; for example, '*amānah*' and '*awwal*' have been preferred to '*amānat*' and '*avval*'. For the same reason, in the case of compound terms,

the Arabic form has been preferred; for example, '*ahl al-kitāb*' and '*al-iḥtiyāṭ al-wājib*' have been used instead of '*ahl-i kitāb*' and '*iḥtiyāṭ-i wājib*'.

4. The transliteration of those Arabic parts of the text that in practice are meant to be articulated verbally has aimed to facilitate a more natural and uninterrupted pronunciation of the words and sentences. For example, in the section on the translation of prayers, '*ihdinaṣ ṣirāṭal mustaqīm*' has been preferred to '*ihdinā al-ṣirāṭ al-mustaqīm*'.
5. To avoid making the text longer and more complex than necessary by constantly stating 'he/she' in rulings common to both genders, the word 'he' is used to refer to both a man and a woman in those rulings.
6. The words 'should' and 'should not' are used in the context of recommendations and disapprovals, whereas 'must' and 'must not' refer to instructions that are obligatory to follow.
7. In the original work, many parts of the text that are in Arabic – including nearly all the supplications – are not translated into Persian. However, it was felt that all the Arabic text should be translated into English and included in the current work for the benefit of readers with little or no knowledge of Arabic.
8. In order to produce a more fluid text, the use of square brackets to indicate the inclusion of words that are not in the original work has been kept to a minimum.
9. Legal terminology has been translated into English on the first occasion in each chapter. Upon subsequent use of these terms, only the original Arabic word or its English equivalent is given, depending on which one was deemed to be more familiar to the majority of English-speaking Shia Muslims, or in some cases, more suited to the particular context. In the main headings, however, both the key Arabic and English terms have been mentioned. Original terms and their translations can also be found in the glossary and appendix at the end of the book.
10. The translation of nearly all the Qur'anic passages are from Ali Quli Qara'i's *The Qur'an: With a Phrase-by-Phrase English Translation* (London: ICAS Press, 2005).
11. The invocation '*ṣallal lāhu 'alayhi wa ālih*' (may Allah bless him and his progeny) after the mention of Prophet Muḥammad has been indicated by the abbreviation 'Ṣ';

similarly, the invocation '*ʿalayhis/ʿalayhas/ʿalayhimus salām*' (peace be upon him/her/them) after the mention of one or all of the Imams, or Lady Fāṭimah, has been indicated by the abbreviation 'ʿA'.

I would like to take this opportunity to thank Shaykh Abbas Mohamed Husein Ismail and Dr Amir Dastmalchian for copy-editing and proofreading this work. I am also grateful to Mohammad Mehdi Baghi for his assistance with the meaning of certain words and phrases in the original text, and to Dr Haider Bhogadia for his help with anatomical terms. Warm thanks are due to Shaykh Kumail Rajani, The World Federation's Head of Islamic Education, for his perceptive observations in the final draft of the text. I am grateful to the offices of His Eminence al-Sayyid al-Sistani in Qum and in London for providing clarification on certain rulings. My appreciation also goes to Sayyid Aliraza Naqvi, formerly The World Federation's Assistant Secretary General responsible for Islamic Education, for initiating the project which has resulted in this translation and for his support throughout. For this combined edition, some of the revisions I have made are based on the feedback and suggestions I received from various members of the community, particularly Shaykh Rizwan Arastu; I am grateful to them all. Finally, I am thankful to my wife for all her valuable contributions, and to my children for their patience during the course of this work.

I beseech Allah, without whose grace nothing can come to fruition, to accept the efforts of all those who have been His agents in this project, and to bless us all with the success to worship Him and to live our lives as His true servants.

MOHAMMED ALI ISMAIL
London, UK
Rajab al-Murajjab 1438 / April 2017

Translator's Preface to the Fourth Edition

In the name of Allah, the All-Beneficent, the Ever-Merciful.
All praise is for Allah, Lord of the worlds.
May Allah bless Muḥammad and his pure progeny.

Since the publication of the third edition of *Islamic Laws* in 2017, His Eminence al-Sayyid Ali al-Husayni al-Sistani (may Allah grant him a long and healthy life) has published five further editions of his Persian manual of rulings. As the last of these, the thirty-sixth edition published in 2021, contains many revisions, The World Federation saw it necessary to publish a new, fully updated edition of its English translation of the manual.

For this fourth edition, all the revisions in the latest Persian edition were first identified. The translation was then updated to reflect the changes. The entire work underwent a thorough review during this process, and improvements were made to every chapter. In particular, more rulings and terms were explained through footnotes and glosses in square brackets, and the wording was revised in places for better readability.

All the changed rulings have been marked with an asterisk [*]. Furthermore, a new appendix listing all the updated rulings has been added. The revisions to six rulings, namely 597, 1498, 1562, 1694, 1699, and 1803, are particularly significant as they concern commonly encountered situations and could have important implications for His Eminence's followers. These revisions have been explained in the footnotes.

Two related projects have come to fruition since the publication of the third edition of *Islamic Laws*. The first, 'OneStopFiqh', has made *Islamic Laws* freely available via a mobile device application as well as a dynamic online portal (fiqh.world-federation.org). The second focused on His Eminence's new ruling on *khums* (Ruling 1803 in the present work) and culminated in a booklet titled *Khums: A Brief Guide*, also available from the aforementioned website.

I would like to express my gratitude to everyone who has assisted me in this updated translation. A special word of appreciation goes to my brother, Shaykh Abbas Mohamed Husein Ismail, for copy-editing the work, and to Sayyid Mahmud Marashi of His Eminence's Qum Office, for answering my questions about the rulings.

I pray Allah accepts the contributions everyone has made to this work and its related projects.

MOHAMMED ALI ISMAIL
Hemel Hempstead, UK
Shaʿbān al-Muʿaẓẓam 1444 / March 2023

Transliteration

Arabic terms which do not have standard spellings in English have been transliterated according to the system set out on this page.

ء	a, i, or u (initial form)	ل	l
ء	ʾ (medial or final form)	م	m
ا	a	ن	n
ب	b	ه	h
ت	t	و	w
ث	th	ي	y
ج	j	ة	h (without *iḍāfah*)
ح	ḥ	ة	t (with *iḍāfah*)
خ	kh	~	~
د	d	الـ	al- **
ذ	dh	ـَ	a
ر	r	ـِ	i
ز	z	ـُ	u
س	s	ـَا / آ / ىٰ	ā
ش	sh	ـِي	ī
ص	ṣ	ـُو	ū
ض	ḍ	آ	ʾā (medial form)
ط	ṭ	ـَيْ	ay
ظ	ẓ	ـَيّ	ayy
ع	ʿ	ـِيّ	iyy (medial form)
غ	gh	ـِيّ	ī (final form)
ف	f	ـَوْ	aw
ق	q	ـَوّ	aww
ك	k	ـُوّ	uww

** This does not apply, however, to those Arabic parts of the text that in practice are meant to be articulated verbally. See the fourth convention mentioned in the Translator's Preface to the Third Edition.

CHAPTER ONE

Following a Jurist (*Taqlīd*)

In the name of Allah, the All-Beneficent, the Ever-Merciful.
All praise is for Allah, Lord of the worlds. May there be blessings and peace upon the most noble of the Prophets and Messengers, Muḥammad, and his good and pure progeny. May there be a perpetual curse upon all of their enemies from now until the resurrection on the Day of Retribution.

Ruling 1. A Muslim's belief in the fundamentals of religion (*uṣūl al-dīn*) must be based on personal insight [i.e. grounded in reason], and he cannot follow anyone in the fundamentals of religion; i.e. he cannot accept the word of someone who knows about the fundamentals of religion simply because that person says so. However, in the event that a person has certainty (*yaqīn*) in the rightful beliefs of Islam and expresses them – even though this certainty may not be based on insight – then that person is a Muslim and a believer and all the laws (*aḥkām*) of Islam and the faith are applicable to him.

However, in matters concerning the laws of religion – apart from those that are indispensable and indisputable [such as the obligation to perform prayers (*ṣalāh*)] – a person must either be a jurist (*mujtahid*)[1] who is capable of ascertaining laws based on proof, or he must follow a *mujtahid* [i.e. do *taqlīd*], or he must exercise precaution (*iḥtiyāṭ*) by performing his duty in a way that he is certain to have fulfilled his responsibility (*taklīf*).

An example of exercising precaution [is the following]: if a group of *mujtahid*s consider an act unlawful (*ḥarām*) and another group say it is not unlawful, the person must not perform that act.

Another example of exercising precaution [is as follows]: if a group of *mujtahid*s consider an act obligatory (*wājib*) and another group consider it recommended (*mustaḥabb*), the person must perform it.

Therefore, it is obligatory for those who are not *mujtahid*s and cannot act on precaution to follow a *mujtahid*.

Ruling 2. Following a jurist in Islamic laws means acting according

[1] A *mujtahid* is a person who has attained the level of *ijtihād*, qualifying him to be an authority in Islamic law. *Ijtihād* is the process of deriving Islamic laws from authentic sources.

to a *mujtahid*'s instructions. Only a *mujtahid* who is male, of the age of legal responsibility (*bāligh*), sane (*ʿāqil*), a Twelver (Ithnā ʿAsharī) Shia, of legitimate birth, living, and dutiful (*ʿādil*), can be followed.

A 'dutiful' person is someone who does the things that are obligatory for him and refrains from doing the things that are unlawful for him. The sign of being 'dutiful' is that one appears to be a good person, such that if [religious, trustworthy Shia Muslims who are] local to him, his neighbours, or associate with him were to be asked about him, they would confirm his good character.

In cases where a person knows, albeit vaguely, that there are differences in the fatwas [as defined in Ruling 4 below] of *mujtahids* in matters that are commonly encountered, even though he may not know what these differences are, it is necessary for him to follow the *mujtahid* who is the most learned (*aʿlam*), i.e. the one most capable of understanding the law (*ḥukm*) of Allah the Exalted from among all the *mujtahids* of his time.

Ruling 3. A *mujtahid* or the most learned can be identified in one of three ways:

1. a duty-bound person (*mukallaf*)[2] is certain himself [that someone is a *mujtahid* or the most learned]. For example, the person is a scholar himself and is able to identify a *mujtahid* and the most learned;
2. two learned and dutiful people who are able to distinguish a *mujtahid* and the most learned confirm that someone is a *mujtahid* or the most learned, provided that two other learned and dutiful people do not disagree with their statement. In fact, being a *mujtahid* or the most learned is also established by even one expert (*ahl al-khibrah*) whom one trusts;
3. a *mukallaf* attains confidence (*iṭmiʾnān*) that a person is a *mujtahid* or the most learned by rational means. For example, a group of scholars who are able to distinguish a *mujtahid* and the most learned and from whose statements one gains confidence confirm that someone is a *mujtahid* or the most learned.

[2] A *mukallaf* is someone who is legally obliged to fulfil religious duties.

Ruling 4. There are four ways to obtain a fatwa, i.e. an edict issued by a *mujtahid*:

1. hearing it from the *mujtahid* himself;
2. hearing it from two dutiful people who narrate the *mujtahid*'s fatwa;
3. hearing it from someone whose word one trusts;
4. reading it in the manual of Islamic rulings (*risālah*) of the *mujtahid*, on condition that one has confidence in the manual being correct.

Ruling 5. As long as a person is not certain that the *mujtahid*'s fatwa has changed, he can act according to what is written in his manual of Islamic rulings. Furthermore, if a person deems it probable that a fatwa has changed, it is not necessary for him to investigate.

Ruling 6. If the most learned *mujtahid* gives a fatwa on any matter, a follower (*muqallid*) of his cannot act upon another *mujtahid*'s fatwa in that matter.

However, if he does not give a fatwa and says that based on precaution, such and such action must be taken – for example, he says: 'Based on precaution, in the first and second units (*rakʿah*) of a prayer, a complete chapter (surah) of the Qur'an must be recited after Sūrat al-Ḥamd' – then the follower must either act according to this precaution, which is known as 'obligatory precaution' (*al-iḥtiyāṭ al-wājib*) or 'necessary precaution' (*al-iḥtiyāṭ al-lāzim*),[3] or he must act according to the fatwa of the next most learned *mujtahid*;[4] and if the next most learned *mujtahid* regards the recitation of only Sūrat al-Ḥamd as being sufficient, he can choose not to recite the other surah.

The same applies [i.e. it amounts to saying the ruling is based on obligatory precaution] when the most learned *mujtahid* says the matter is one of 'deliberation' (*maḥall al-taʾammul*) or 'problematic' (*maḥall al-ishkāl*).

[3] To avoid over-complicating the text, and given that '*al-iḥtiyāṭ al-wājib*' and '*al-iḥtiyāṭ al-lāzim*' refer to the same thing, both terms have been translated in the present work as 'obligatory precaution'.

[4] In the terminology of Islamic jurisprudence, acting on the fatwa of the next most learned *mujtahid* when one's *marjaʿ* has stated that a ruling is based on obligatory precaution is known as '*rujūʿ*'.

Ruling 7. If before or after giving a fatwa on a matter, the most learned *mujtahid* expresses precaution – for example, he says: 'An impure (*najis*) utensil that is washed once in *kurr*[5] water becomes pure (*ṭāhir*), although based on precaution it should be washed three times' – his follower does not have to perform this precautionary measure [but is recommended to]. This is called 'recommended precaution' (*al-iḥtiyāṭ al-mustaḥabb*).

Ruling 8.* If a *mujtahid* whom a *mukallaf* is following [i.e. doing *taqlīd* of] dies, his authority after his death is the same as his authority when he was alive. Therefore, if he is more learned than a living *mujtahid*, a *mukallaf* who has a general notion about there being a difference of opinion between the two *mujtahids* in rulings (*masā'il*) that he commonly encounters, even though he may not know what these differences are, must continue following him. However, in the event that a living *mujtahid* is more learned than him, he must refer to the living *mujtahid*.

If it is not known who the most learned among the *mujtahids* is, or if they are equal [in knowledge], in case it is established that one of them is more cautious than the other – i.e. he exercises more caution in matters pertaining to giving fatwas, deriving legal opinions, and is a person who thoroughly researches and investigates – then that *mujtahid* must be followed. However, if it is not established which one is more cautious, then the follower has the choice to act according to the fatwa of whichever *mujtahid* he wants, except in cases of 'non-specific knowledge' (*al-ʿilm al-ijmālī*) or the arising of 'non-specific authority' (*al-ḥujjah al-ijmāliyyah*) over responsibility. For example, in case there is a difference of opinion with regard to performing the shortened (*qaṣr*) or complete (*tamām*) form of the prayer [in a particular situation], he must, based on obligatory precaution, observe the fatwa of both *mujtahids*.[6]

[5] A quantity of water greater or equal to approximately 384 litres. See Ruling 14.

[6] The terms mentioned in this part of the ruling refer to concepts discussed in the Islamic science known as the 'Principles of Jurisprudence' (*uṣūl al-fiqh*). Although the scope of the present work does not allow for a detailed explanation of these concepts, it would be appropriate to expand a little on the example used in the text concerning 'non-specific knowledge'. Suppose a person finds himself in a situation where he is certain that he must perform prayers but he does not know whether his duty is to perform prayers in their shortened form – as a traveller would be

‘*Taqlīd*’ simply means an undertaking to follow the fatwa of a particular *mujtahid*; it does not mean acting according to his instructions.[7]

Ruling 9. It is necessary for a *mukallaf* to learn those rulings that he considers he probably needs to learn in order to avoid sinning. ‘Sinning’ means not performing obligatory acts or performing unlawful acts.

Ruling 10. If a *mukallaf* comes across a matter for which he does not know the Islamic ruling, it is necessary for him to act with caution or to follow a *mujtahid* according to the aforementioned conditions. However, in the event that a person does not have access to the fatwa of the most learned *mujtahid*, it is permitted (*jā’iz*) for him to follow the next most learned *mujtahid*.

Ruling 11. If someone relates a *mujtahid*’s fatwa to a second person, in the event that the *mujtahid*’s fatwa changes, it is not necessary for him to inform that second person that the fatwa of the *mujtahid* has changed. However, if after relating a fatwa, a person realises that he has made a mistake and his statement will cause that second person to act against his legal duty, he must, based on obligatory precaution, rectify his mistake if possible.

Ruling 12.* If for some time a *mukallaf* performs his actions without following a *mujtahid*, there are two situations to consider: the first is that his actions were in actual fact correctly performed, or they happened to be in accordance with the fatwa of a *mujtahid* who at

---

required to – or in their complete form. This state of knowledge (i.e. the certainty of the general duty to perform prayers) that is accompanied by doubt concerning one’s exact duty (i.e. whether to perform the shortened or the complete form of the prayer) is known as ‘non-specific knowledge’. In this example, the person would need to perform both possibilities – i.e. the shortened *and* complete forms of the prayer – in order to be certain that he has fulfilled his duty.

As for ‘non-specific authority’ (*al-ḥujjah al-ijmāliyyah*), this is similar to ‘non-specific knowledge’ except that the *mukallaf* is not certain himself about there being a duty in general but comes to know it though other authoritative evidence that he is obligated to follow (*Tawḍīḥ al-Masā’il-i Jāmi*ʿ, vol. 1, p. 47, Ruling 12, footnotes 1 and 2).

[7] Therefore, one is considered a *muqallid* from the time he makes the intention to follow a particular *mujtahid*, even if he has not yet acted according to that *mujtahid*’s fatwas.

present could be his *marjaʿ*;[8] in this case, his actions are valid (*ṣaḥīḥ*). The second is that he was inculpably ignorant (*al-jāhil al-qāṣir*),[9] and his defective actions were not elemental actions (*arkān*)[10] and suchlike; in this case as well, his actions are valid.

Similarly, [one's actions are deemed to be valid] if he was culpably ignorant (*al-jāhil al-muqaṣṣir*)[11] and his defective actions were of the type that if performed unknowingly they are valid, such as reciting [Sūrat al-Ḥamd and the second surah in prayers] aloud (*jahr*) instead of reciting them in a whisper (*ikhfāt*), or vice versa.[12]

Similarly, if a person does not know how he performed his actions, they are deemed to have been performed correctly, apart from a few cases that are mentioned in *Minhāj al-Ṣāliḥīn*.[13]

It is worth mentioning that with regard to many of the recommended acts (*mustaḥabbāt*) mentioned in this manual, their recommendation is based on the 'principle of leniency in evidence for recommended acts' (*qāʾidat al-tasāmuḥ fī adillat al-sunan*).[14] As we do not regard this to be an established principle, if a *mukallaf* wishes to perform these acts, it is necessary he does so '*rajāʾan*', i.e. in the hope that they are desired by Allah. The rule regarding many disapproved acts (*makrūhāt*) is the same, meaning that the *mukallaf* should avoid doing them '*rajāʾan*', i.e. in the hope that their avoidance is desired by Allah.[15]

[8] A *marjaʿ* is a jurist who has the necessary qualifications to be followed in matters of Islamic jurisprudence (*fiqh*). See Ruling 2.

[9] 'Inculpably ignorant' is a term used to refer to someone who has a valid excuse for not knowing; for example, he relied upon something that he thought was authoritative but in fact was not.

[10] *Arkān* is plural of *rukn* and refers to the elemental components of ritual acts of worship. Specific rules govern the validity of ritual acts of worship if a *rukn* is omitted or added. For example, with regard to prayers, the omission of a *rukn* renders the prayer invalid (*bāṭil*). See Ruling 928.

[11] 'Culpably ignorant' is a term used to refer to someone who does not have a valid excuse for not knowing; for example, he was careless in learning religious laws.

[12] See Ruling 981.

[13] *Minhāj al-Ṣāliḥīn* is al-Sayyid al-Sistani's more detailed work on Islamic law.

[14] According to this principle, traditions attributed to an Infallible (*maʿṣūm*) whose chains of transmission are weak can be relied upon if they state a certain act merits reward and there is no evidence to indicate it is not permitted.

[15] In Islamic jurisprudence, when a jurist declares something '*mustaḥabb*' or '*makrūh*', it means that in his or her opinion the action has an established legal status, i.e. it is something that the sharia has legislated as being 'recommended' or

'disapproved'. A jurist will only make such a declaration if he or she is convinced that there is sufficiently strong evidence to support it. If on the other hand the jurist deems the evidence weak but finds no reason to suggest the act should not be performed/avoided, then he or she may say, just as al-Sayyid al-Sistani has done here, that it can still be enacted but with the intention of '*rajā*'' (shorter form of '*rajā' al-maṭlūbiyyah*'), i.e. in the hope that it is desired by Allah. In this way, the jurist has not attributed something to the sharia that may not have actually been sanctioned by it, nor has he or she dissuaded their followers from performing/avoiding the action just in case in reality it is something that has been divinely legislated and carries with it abundant blessings and rewards.

CHAPTER TWO

Purification (*Ṭahārah*)

UNMIXED (*MUṬLAQ*) AND MIXED (*MUḌĀF*) WATER

Ruling 13. Water is either 'unmixed' or 'mixed'. 'Mixed' water is either water obtained from something, such as watermelon juice or rose water; or it is water that has been mixed with something else, such as water that has been mixed with some mud etc., such that it can no longer be called 'water'. If water is not of the above type, it is 'unmixed'; and unmixed water is of five types:

1. *kurr* water;
2. *qalīl* water;
3. flowing water;
4. rainwater;
5. well water.

1. *Kurr* water

Ruling 14. *Kurr* water is an amount of water that fills a container with dimensions [i.e. length, breadth, and depth] totalling thirty-six cubic hand spans,[1] which is equivalent to approximately 384 litres.

Ruling 15. If an intrinsic impurity (*'ayn al-najāsah*) – such as urine or blood – or something that has become impure (*mutanajjis*) – such as impure clothing – comes into contact with *kurr* water, in the event that *kurr* water acquires the smell, colour, or taste of that impurity, it becomes impure; but if the *kurr* water does not change [in its smell, colour, or taste], it does not become impure.

Ruling 16. If the smell, colour, or taste of *kurr* water changes by means of something that is not impure, it does not become impure.

Ruling 17. If an intrinsic impurity like blood comes into contact with water that is more than *kurr* and changes part of its smell, colour, or taste, in the event that the amount that has not changed is less than *kurr*, all the water becomes impure. If [the amount that has not changed] is equal to *kurr* or more, only the amount that has changed its smell, colour, or taste is impure.

[1] An average span is approximately 22 centimetres. [Author]

Ruling 18. The water of a fountain that is connected to *kurr* water purifies impure water. However, if it falls on impure water drop by drop, it does not purify it unless something is held over the fountain so that before the water begins to fall drop by drop, it connects to the impure water; and for the fountain water to purify the impure water, it must mix with the impure water.

Ruling 19. If an impure object is washed under a tap that is connected to *kurr* water, the water that drips from the object is pure (*ṭāhir*) if it is connected to *kurr* water and has not acquired the smell, colour, or taste of the impurity and does not contain an intrinsic impurity.

Ruling 20. If some part of *kurr* water freezes and the remaining water does not amount to *kurr*, in the event that an impurity comes into contact with it, it becomes impure; and however much of the ice melts is also impure.

Ruling 21. With regard to water that had been equivalent to *kurr*, if one doubts whether it has become less than *kurr* or not, it is to be treated as *kurr* water, meaning that it can still purify an impure object and if an impurity makes contact with it, it does not become impure [as long as its smell, colour, or taste does not change]. As for water that had been less than *kurr*, if one doubts whether it has become equal to *kurr* or not, it is ruled to be (i.e. it has the *ḥukm* of) less than *kurr*.

Ruling 22. There are two ways to establish that a quantity of water is *kurr*:

1. one is certain (i.e. he has *yaqīn*) or confident (i.e. he has *iṭmiʾnān*) about it, even if that is because of what someone has said;
2. two dutiful (*ʿādil*) men report it as so. If one dutiful or trustworthy person, or someone who has possession of the *kurr* water, reports it as so but his report does not give one confidence as to it being true, then based on obligatory precaution (*al-iḥtiyāṭ al-wājib*), the water being *kurr* will not be established.

2. *Qalīl* water

Ruling 23. *Qalīl* water is water that does not gush from the earth and is less than *kurr.*

Ruling 24. If *qalīl* water is poured onto an impure object or an impure object comes into contact with *qalīl* water, the *qalīl* water becomes impure. However, if *qalīl* water is poured over an impure object from above, then the amount that comes into contact with the object is impure, and the amount that does not come into contact with it is pure.

Ruling 25.* *Qalīl* water that separates from an impure object by itself or as a result of pressure and suchlike when that object is washed or after it has been washed is called 'waste water' (*ghusālah*) and is impure (*najis*). If before pouring water onto the object that had become impure there was no intrinsic impurity on it, the impurity (*najāsah*) of the waste water is based on obligatory precaution. There is no difference if that object is from among those things that becomes pure by washing once[2] or by washing more than once. If the object is from among those things that must be washed more than once, there is no difference if the waste water is from the final wash or before the final wash.

Ruling 26. *Qalīl* water with which the urinary outlet or the anus are washed does not make anything it comes into contact with impure, provided that five conditions are met:

1. it does not acquire the smell, colour, or taste of the impurity;
2. another impurity has not come into contact with it;
3. another impurity, such as blood, has not come out with the urine or faeces;
4. particles of faeces do not appear in the water;
5. a more than usual amount of impurity has not spread around the urinary outlet or the anus.

[2] Such as the impure inside of a utensil. See Ruling 144.

3. Flowing water

Flowing water is water that: (1) has a natural source, such as a spring, stream, subterranean canal, or meltwater; (2) flows, even if it is made to flow by some means; (3) is continuous, generally speaking. It is not necessary that the water be connected to a natural source; therefore, if it is naturally disconnected from it – such as water falling from above in the form of drops – then as long as it flows on the earth, it is considered to be flowing water. However, if something becomes an obstacle to the water connecting to the source – for example, something becomes an obstacle to the water falling or gushing, or disconnects it from the source – then the remaining water is not ruled to be flowing water even if it flows on the earth.

Ruling 27. In the event that an impurity makes contact with flowing water – even if it is less than *kurr* – then as long as the smell, colour, or taste of the water does not change by means of the impurity, it is pure.

Ruling 28. If an impurity makes contact with flowing water, the amount of flowing water that changes in smell, colour, or taste by means of the impurity is impure. Flowing water that is connected to a spring is pure even if it is less than *kurr*; and if the water that is on the other side of the stream is equal to *kurr* or it is connected to the spring by means of water that has not changed, it is pure; otherwise, it is impure.

Ruling 29. The water of a spring that is not flowing but is such that if water is taken from it water gushes out again is not ruled to be flowing water, meaning that if an impurity comes into contact with it and the water is less than *kurr*, it becomes impure.

Ruling 30. Water that is stagnant at the side of a stream and is connected to flowing water is not ruled to be flowing water.

Ruling 31. A spring that, for example, gushes in winter but does not gush in summer is ruled to be flowing water only when it gushes.

Ruling 32. If the water of a basin in a public bath is less than *kurr*, and the water is connected to the water of a tank which together with the water of the basin equals *kurr*, in the event that the water of the basin comes into contact with an impurity but its smell, colour, or taste does not change, the water does not become impure.

Ruling 33. With regard to water that pours out from taps and showers and flows in the pipes of bathrooms and buildings, if it is connected to a source that is equal to or greater than *kurr*, it is ruled to be *kurr*.

Ruling 34. With regard to water that flows on the earth but does not gush from it, in the event that it is less than *kurr* and an impurity comes into contact with it, it becomes impure. However, if the water flows from above and an impurity reaches its lower part, its upper part does not become impure.

4. Rainwater

Ruling 35.* If rain falls once on an impure object that does not contain an intrinsic impurity, the area that comes into contact with the rain becomes pure. However, if a person's body or some clothing has become impure by urine, then based on obligatory precaution, rain must fall on it twice for it to become pure. As for the impure inside of a utensil, rain must fall on it three times for it to become pure based on obligatory precaution. With carpets, clothing, and similar things, wringing out the rainwater is not necessary. Of course, a few drops of rainfall does not suffice; rather, it must be such that it can be commonly said to be raining.

Ruling 36. If rain falls on an intrinsic impurity and the water splashes, in the event that none of the intrinsic impurity is included in the splashed water and the water does not acquire the smell, colour, or taste of the impurity, the water is pure. Therefore, if rain falls on blood and the water splashes, in the event that particles of blood are present in the water or it acquires the smell, colour, or taste of blood, it is impure.

Ruling 37. If there is an intrinsic impurity on the roof of a building, then as long as it keeps raining on the roof, any water that comes into contact with the impure object and then falls down from the roof or gutter is pure. However, after it stops raining, if the water that falls from the roof or gutter is known to have made contact with the impure object, the water is impure.

Ruling 38. Ground that is impure becomes pure if rain falls on it; and if rainwater begins to flow on the ground and while it is still raining it comes into contact with an impure area under a roof [on which rain cannot fall directly], it purifies that area as well.

Ruling 39. If impure soil is completely soaked by rainwater, it becomes pure on condition that it is not known whether the water has turned into mixed water by means of it coming into contact with the soil.

Ruling 40. Whenever rainwater collects in a place – even if its quantity is less than *kurr* – in the event that an impure object is washed in it while it is raining and the water does not acquire the smell, colour, or taste of the impurity, the impure object becomes pure.

Ruling 41. If rain falls on a carpet that is pure and which is spread on ground that is impure, and if while it is raining the water soaks through the carpet and comes into contact with the ground, the carpet does not become impure and the ground becomes pure.

5. Well water

Ruling 42. With regard to well water that gushes from the ground – even if its quantity is less than *kurr* – in the event that an impurity comes into contact with it, it is pure as long as its colour, smell, or taste does not change.

Ruling 43. If an impurity falls into a well and changes the water's smell, colour, or taste, in the event that the change in the water disappears, it becomes pure. However, based on obligatory precaution, the water becoming pure is conditional on it mixing with the water that gushes from the well.

LAWS RELATING TO THE DIFFERENT TYPES OF WATER

Ruling 44. Mixed water – the meaning of which was mentioned in Ruling 13 – does not purify an impure object, and ritual bathing (*ghusl*) and ablution (*wuḍūʾ*) performed with it are invalid (*bāṭil*).

Ruling 45. Even if its quantity equals *kurr*, mixed water becomes impure if a particle of an impurity comes into contact with it. However, in the event that it is poured from above onto an impure object, the amount that comes into contact with the impurity is impure, and the amount that does not come into contact with it is pure. For example, if rose water is poured from a rose water bottle onto an impure hand, the amount that makes contact with the hand is impure, and the amount that does not make contact with the hand is pure.

Ruling 46. If impure mixed water is mixed with *kurr* water or flowing water in a way that it can no longer be commonly called 'mixed water', it becomes pure.

Ruling 47. Water that was unmixed and it is not known whether that water has become mixed is deemed to be unmixed, meaning that it purifies an impure object, and *wuḍūʾ* and *ghusl* performed with it are valid (*ṣaḥīḥ*). Furthermore, water that was mixed and it is not known whether that water has become unmixed is deemed to be mixed, meaning that it does not purify an impure object, and *wuḍūʾ* and *ghusl* performed with it are invalid.

Ruling 48. If it is not known whether some water is unmixed or mixed, or whether it was previously unmixed or mixed, then such water does not purify an impure object, and *wuḍūʾ* and *ghusl* performed with it are invalid. In the event that an impurity makes contact with it and the water is less than *kurr*, it becomes impure; and if it is equal to or more than *kurr*, then based on obligatory precaution, it also becomes impure.

Ruling 49. If an intrinsic impurity like blood or urine comes into contact with water and changes its smell, colour, or taste, it becomes impure even if it is *kurr* or flowing water. In fact, based on obligatory precaution, the water also becomes impure even if the smell, colour, or taste of the water changes by means of an impurity that is outside it; for example, an impure carcass that is lying by the side of the water changes the water's smell.

Ruling 50. With regard to water into which an intrinsic impurity like blood or urine has fallen and there is a change in its smell, colour, or taste, in the event that it is connected to *kurr* or flowing water, or it rains on it, or wind makes the rain fall on it, or rainwater flows on it from a gutter while it is raining, in all of these cases, if the change disappears, it becomes pure. However, the rainwater, *kurr* water, or flowing water must become mixed with it for it to be considered pure.

Ruling 51. If an impure object is purified in *kurr* or flowing water, the water that drips from the object after the final wash that makes the object pure,[3] and after the object has been taken out of the water, is pure.

Ruling 52. Water that was pure, and it is not known whether it has become impure or not, is pure. Water that was impure, and it is not known whether it has become pure or not, is impure.

LAWS RELATING TO EMPTYING THE BOWELS AND THE BLADDER

Ruling 53. It is obligatory (*wājib*) for one to cover his private parts when emptying his bowels and/or bladder, and at other times, from people who are duty-bound (*mukallaf*),[4] even if they are his *maḥram*,[5]

[3] The number of times a particular object has to be washed for it to be purified depends on the type of object it is, the thing that made it impure, and the type of water it is washed with. For example, a utensil that has become impure with wine is purified by washing it three times with *kurr* water, flowing water, or suchlike. See Ruling 147.

[4] A *mukallaf* is someone who is legally obliged to fulfil religious duties.

[5] A *maḥram* is a person one is never permitted to marry on account of be-

like his mother and sister. Similarly, it is obligatory for one to cover his private parts from an insane person and from a child who is *mumayyiz*, i.e. someone who is able to discern between right and wrong. However, it is not necessary for a husband and wife to cover their private parts from each other.

Ruling 54. It is not necessary for one to cover his private parts with a particular object, and if, for example, he covers his private parts with his hand, it is sufficient.

Ruling 55. Based on obligatory precaution, when one is emptying his bowels and/or bladder, neither the front of the body – i.e. the stomach and chest – nor the back must face qibla.[6]

Ruling 56. When one is emptying his bowels and/or bladder, if the front or back of his body faces qibla and he turns his private parts away from qibla, it will not suffice. Furthermore, the obligatory precaution is that when one is emptying his bowels and/or bladder, he must not sit in a way that his private parts face qibla, nor must he sit in a way that his private parts face in the direction that is directly opposite qibla.

Ruling 57. The recommended precaution (*al-iḥtiyāṭ al-mustaḥabb*) is that the front or back of one's body should not face qibla while performing *istibrā'*[7] – the laws (*aḥkām*) of which will be mentioned later – nor while purifying the urinary outlet and the anus.

Ruling 58. If a person is obliged to face his front or back to qibla so that someone who is not his *maḥram* does not see him, then based on obligatory precaution, he must sit with his back facing qibla.

Ruling 59. The recommended precaution is that a child should not be made to sit in a way that his front or back faces qibla when he is emptying his bowels and/or bladder.

---

ing related to them in a particular way, such as being their parent or sibling.

[6] Qibla is the direction towards the Ka'bah in Mecca.

[7] *Istibrā'* here refers to the process of clearing the male urethra after urinating.

Ruling 60. It is unlawful (*ḥarām*) for one to empty his bowels and/or bladder in four places:

1. in dead-end alleys without the owner's consent. The same applies to public alleys and roads in the event that it causes harm to pedestrians;
2. on the property of someone who has not given his consent for one to empty his bowels and/or bladder on it;
3. in a place that is a charitable endowment (*waqf*) for use by particular groups, such as some schools;
4. on the graves of believers, whether it is disrespectful to them or not, except if the land is *al-mubāḥāt al-aṣliyyah*.[8] The same applies to any place where emptying one's bowels and/or bladder causes dishonour to one of the sacred things of the religion or faith.

Ruling 61. In three cases, the anus can be purified with water only:[9]

1. another impurity like blood comes out with the faeces;
2. an external impurity comes into contact with the anus, except if urine comes into contact with the anus in the case of women;
3. if the area around the anus has become impure by an amount that is more than usual.

In cases other than these three, the anus can be purified with water, or, in accordance with the instructions that will be mentioned later, it can be purified with cloth, stone, or a similar thing, although it is better to wash it with water.

Ruling 62. The urinary outlet does not become pure with anything other than water and washing it once is sufficient, although the recommended precaution is that it should be washed twice, and it is even better to wash it three times.

[8] This is property that does not belong to anyone in particular and can be used by people in general.

[9] Rulings 61–68 concern a matter that is referred to in Islamic law as '*istinjā*'', i.e. purification of the anus and the urinary outlet.

Ruling 63. If the anus is washed with water, no trace of faeces must remain on it. However, there is no problem if the colour and smell remain. If no particle of faeces remains after the first time it is washed, it is not necessary to rewash it.

Ruling 64. The anus can be purified with stone, a clod of earth, cloth, or a similar thing if they are dry and pure; and there is no problem if they have a little moisture that does not wet the outlet.

Ruling 65. It suffices if the anus is completely purified once with stone, a clod of earth, or cloth. However, it is better to purify it three times by using three pieces; and if it does not become purified after three times, one must keep trying to purify it until it becomes completely purified. However, there is no problem if traces remain that are not normally removed except by washing.

Ruling 66. It is unlawful to purify the anus with things that must be respected, such as paper on which the name of Allah the Exalted and the Prophets are written. There is no problem in purifying the anus with a bone or dung.

Ruling 67. If a person doubts whether or not he has purified the anus or urinary outlet, it is necessary that he purify it even if he habitually purifies it immediately after emptying his bowels and/or bladder.

Ruling 68. If after performing prayers (*ṣalāh*) one doubts whether or not he had purified the anus or urinary outlet before performing prayers, the prayers that he performed are valid but he must purify the anus or urinary outlet for the next prayer.

CLEARING THE MALE URETHRA OF URINE (*ISTIBRĀʾ*)

Ruling 69. *Istibrāʾ* is a recommended (*mustaḥabb*) act performed by men after urinating in order to be confident that no urine is left in the urethra. It is performed in a number of ways; one way is as follows: after urinating, the anus is first purified if it has become impure; then, the middle finger of the left hand is slid three times from the anus up to the scrotum; then, the thumb is placed on the penis, and the forefinger is placed under the penis, and the thumb and forefinger are pulled three times along the penis up to the point of circumcision; finally, the end of the penis is pressed three times.

Ruling 70. The fluid that sometimes comes out of the penis due to sexual arousal, called '*madhī*', is pure. The fluid that sometimes comes out after the ejaculation of semen, called '*wadhī*', is also pure. As for fluid that sometimes comes out after urinating and which is called '*wadī*', it is pure if it has not come into contact with urine. Furthermore, in the event that a man performs *istibrāʾ* after urinating and then fluid comes out and he doubts whether it is urine or one of these three fluids, it is pure.

Ruling 71. If a man doubts whether he has performed *istibrāʾ* or not and fluid comes out and he does not know whether it is pure or not, it is impure; and in the event that he performed *wuḍūʾ*, his *wuḍūʾ* becomes void (*bāṭil*). However, if a man doubts whether the *istibrāʾ* he performed was correct or not and fluid comes out and he is unsure whether it is pure or not, it is pure and it does not invalidate his *wuḍūʾ* either.

Ruling 72. If someone who has not performed *istibrāʾ* becomes confident that no urine is left in the urethra due to the passing of time since he urinated, and if he then sees some fluid and doubts whether it is pure or not, that fluid is pure and it does not invalidate his *wuḍūʾ* either.

Ruling 73. If a man performs *istibrāʾ* after urinating and then performs *wuḍūʾ*, in the event that after *wuḍūʾ* he sees fluid that he knows to be either urine or semen, it is obligatory that as a precaution he perform *ghusl* as well as *wuḍūʾ*. However, if he had not performed *wuḍūʾ*, it is sufficient for him to perform *wuḍūʾ* only.

Ruling 74. There is no *istibrāʾ* for women after urinating; if a woman sees fluid and doubts whether it is urine or not, it is pure and it does not invalidate her *wuḍūʾ* or *ghusl*.

RECOMMENDED (*MUSTAḤABB*) AND DISAPPROVED (*MAKRŪH*) ACTS WHEN EMPTYING THE BOWELS AND THE BLADDER

Ruling 75. When one is emptying his bowels and/or bladder, it is recommended that he sit in a place where no one sees him; and when entering the lavatory, to enter with the left foot first; and when exiting, to exit with the right foot first. Furthermore, when one is emptying his bowels and/or bladder, it is recommended for him to cover his head and to place the weight of his body onto his left leg.

Ruling 76. It is disapproved for one to face the sun or the moon when he is emptying his bowels and/or bladder. However, if he covers his private parts by some means, it is not disapproved. It is also disapproved to empty one's bowels and/or bladder while facing the wind, on roads and streets, in alleyways, in front of the door of a house, and under fruit-yielding trees. Furthermore, while one is emptying his bowels and/or bladder, it is disapproved to eat, take a long time, and wash with the right hand. It is also disapproved to talk while one is emptying his bowels and/or bladder; there is no problem, however, if one is compelled to talk or if one is remembering Allah the Exalted (saying *dhikr*).

Ruling 77. It is disapproved to urinate while standing, on hard ground, in the nests and dens of animals, and in water – particularly stagnant water.

Ruling 78. It is disapproved to withhold passing faeces and urine. If withholding it is in a general sense harmful for the person, it is unlawful.

Ruling 79. It is recommended that one urinate before offering prayers, before sleeping, before sexual intercourse, and after ejaculation.

IMPURITIES (*NAJĀSĀT*)

Ruling 80. Ten things are impure [intrinsically]:[10]

1. urine;
2. faeces;
3. semen;
4. corpse;
5. blood;
6. dog;
7. pig;
8. disbeliever (*kāfir*);
9. wine;
10. the sweat of an excrement-eating animal.

1. & 2. Urine and faeces

Ruling 81. The urine and faeces of a human being and every animal whose meat is unlawful to eat and whose blood gushes out – meaning that if its jugular vein is cut, blood runs out with a gush – is impure. The faeces of an animal whose meat is unlawful but whose blood does not gush out, like fish that are unlawful to eat, as well as the droppings of small animals, like mosquitoes and flies that do not have flesh, are pure. Furthermore, the urine of an animal whose meat is unlawful and whose blood does not gush out must be avoided[11] [i.e. it is ruled to be impure], based on obligatory precaution.

Ruling 82. The urine and droppings of birds whose meat is unlawful are pure, but it is better to avoid them [i.e. it is better not to treat them as being pure].

Ruling 83. The urine and faeces of an animal that eats excrement are impure. The same applies to the urine and faeces of a kid [i.e. a baby goat] that has drunk the milk of a pig – as per the details that will be mentioned in the laws relating to types of food and drink. And

[10] Each of these things is also known as an 'intrinsic impurity' (*'ayn al-najāsah*).
[11] The term 'avoided' (*ijtināb*) here means it cannot be used for anything that is conditional on being pure, such as eating, drinking, and *wuḍū'*.

[the same applies to the urine and faeces of] an animal with which a human being has had sexual intercourse.

3. Semen

Ruling 84. The semen of a man and every male animal whose meat is unlawful and whose blood gushes out is impure. The fluid that comes out of a woman following sexual arousal and causes her to be in a state of ritual impurity (*janābah*) – as per the details that will be mentioned in Ruling 345 – has the ruling of semen. Furthermore, based on obligatory precaution, the semen of an animal whose meat is lawful (*ḥalāl*) and whose blood gushes out must be avoided [i.e. it is ruled to be impure].

4. Corpse

Ruling 85. The corpse of a human being is impure, as is the carcass of an animal whose blood gushes out, irrespective of whether it died naturally or was killed in a manner that is not in accordance with Islamic law. As for fish, as they do not have blood that gushes out, they are pure even if they die in the water.

Ruling 86. Those parts of a corpse or a carcass of an animal [as defined in the previous ruling] that do not contain life – such as wool, fur, fine wool, bones, and teeth – are pure.

Ruling 87. If flesh or something else that contains life is separated from the body of a human being or an animal whose blood gushes out while it is alive, it is impure.

Ruling 88. If small pieces of skin from the lips or other parts of the body are peeled off, in the event that they do not contain life and are easily peeled off, they are pure.

Ruling 89. An egg that comes out of the stomach of a dead hen is pure even if the skin around it has not hardened; however, its exterior must be washed with water.

Ruling 90. If a lamb or a kid dies before it starts to graze, the rennet in its stomach is pure. However, in the event that the rennet is not liquid, its exterior that has come into contact with the body of the dead animal must be washed.

Ruling 91. If a person is not certain whether medicine, perfume, oil, wax, or soap that has been imported from a non-Islamic country is impure, it is pure.

Ruling 92. If there is a probability that some meat, fat, or hide has come from an animal that has been killed according to Islamic law, it is pure. However, if it is obtained from a disbeliever or from a Muslim who obtained it from a disbeliever without investigating whether or not it was from an animal that was killed according to Islamic law, then the meat or fat is unlawful to eat but performing prayers with the hide is permitted (*jāʾiz*). If it is obtained from a Muslim market or a Muslim but it is not known whether or not he obtained it from a disbeliever, or there is a probability that he has investigated even though he obtained it from a disbeliever, then in all of these cases, eating the meat or fat is permitted on condition that the Muslim had right of disposal over it that is particular to lawful meat, such as selling it for eating.

5. Blood

Ruling 93. The blood of a human being and every animal whose blood gushes out (i.e. an animal whose blood runs out with a gush when its jugular vein is cut) is impure. Therefore, the blood of an animal whose blood does not gush out, such as fish or mosquitoes, is pure.

Ruling 94. If an animal whose meat is lawful to eat is killed according to the instructions of Islamic law, and a sufficient amount of the animal's blood runs out, the blood that remains in its body is pure. However, the blood that goes back into the animal's body as a result of the animal breathing or because its head was at a high level is impure.

Ruling 95. The recommended precaution is that the yolk of an egg with a particle of blood should be avoided [i.e. it is better not to consume it].

Ruling 96. The blood that is sometimes seen when milking an animal is impure and makes the milk impure.

Ruling 97. If blood that comes from between the teeth disappears by becoming mixed with saliva, it is not necessary to avoid swallowing the saliva [i.e. it is not ruled to be impure].

Ruling 98. If dead blood forms under the nail or skin as a result of a blow and it becomes such that it can no longer be called 'blood', it is pure; but, if it can be called 'blood' and it becomes evident, it is impure. Furthermore, in the event that the nail or skin is pierced such that the blood is considered to be an outer part of the body, and if bringing out the blood and purifying the area for the purposes of *wuḍū'* or *ghusl* would cause one excessive difficulty (*mashaqqah*), then one must perform *tayammum* (dry ablution).

Ruling 99. If a person does not know whether some blood under the skin is dead blood or if the flesh has become like that as a result of a blow to it, it is pure.

Ruling 100.* If at the time of boiling some food, a particle of blood falls into the food, all the food and the pot become impure. And based on obligatory precaution, boiling, heat, and fire do not purify it.

Ruling 101. If it is not known whether pus that is found around a wound while it is healing is mixed with blood, it is pure.

6. & 7. Dog and pig

Ruling 102. Dogs and pigs are impure, even their hair, bones, paws, nails, and the moisture from their body.

8. Disbeliever (*kāfir*)

Ruling 103. A person who does not believe in Allah or His oneness is impure. Similarly, the following are impure: extremists (*ghulāt*) (i.e. those who regard one of the Infallible Imams ('A) as Allah, or say that

Allah has immanence (*ḥulūl*) in the Imam (ʿA)),[12] Kharijites (*khawārij*), and *nawāṣib* (i.e. those who display enmity towards the Infallible Imams (ʿA)). The same applies to a person who rejects prophethood or any one of the indispensable aspects of the religion – such as prayers (*ṣalāh*) and fasting (*ṣawm*) – if it is in a way that it amounts to refuting Prophet Muḥammad (Ṣ), albeit in a general manner. As for the People of the Book (*ahl al-kitāb*) (i.e. Jews, Christians, and Zoroastrians), they are ruled to be pure.

Ruling 104.* Based on obligatory precaution, the entire body of a disbeliever who is not *kitābī* [i.e. not from among the People of the Book] is impure; this includes his hair, nails, and the moisture from his body. As for an apostate (i.e. someone who is no longer a Muslim), the rule that applies to him is determined by his new religious status. Therefore, if the apostate person becomes a *kitābī* disbeliever, he is pure; and if he becomes a non-*kitābī* disbeliever, he is impure based on obligatory precaution.

Ruling 105.* If the father, mother, paternal grandfather, and paternal grandmother of a child who is not of the age of legal responsibility (*bāligh*) are non-*kitābī* disbelievers, that child is also impure based on obligatory precaution, unless he is *mumayyiz* and professes Islam, in which case he is pure. If he turns away from his father and mother and inclines towards Muslims, or if he is in the process of researching and investigating, then ruling him as being impure is problematic [and therefore, based on obligatory precaution, the requisite precautionary action must be taken].[13] If either his father, mother, paternal grandfather, or paternal grandmother is a Muslim, then as per the details that will be mentioned in Ruling 210, the child is pure.

Ruling 106. If it is not known whether someone is a Muslim and there is no indication of him being a Muslim, he is pure. However, other rules of being a Muslim do not apply to him; for example, he cannot marry a Muslim woman nor be buried in a Muslim cemetery.

[12] This refers to those who believe in the infusion or indwelling of Allah in the Imam (ʿA).

[13] See *Tawḍīḥ al-Masāʾil-i Jāmiʿ*, vol. 1, p. 69, Ruling 122.

Ruling 107.* Based on obligatory precaution, a person who abuses any of the Infallible Imams (ʿA) on account of his enmity towards them is impure.

9. Wine

Ruling 108. Wine is impure. Apart from wine, other things that intoxicate a human being are not impure.

Ruling 109.* Alcohol, whether industrial or medicinal, in all its types, is pure unless it is known and ascertained that the alcohol has been obtained from the vaporisation and distillation of grape wine, in which case it is impure.

Ruling 110. If grape juice bubbles by itself [through fermentation] or by cooking, it is pure; however, it is unlawful to drink. Similarly, based on obligatory precaution, boiled grapes are unlawful to consume but they are not impure.

Ruling 111.* Dates, currants, raisins, and their juice, even if they bubble, are pure and it is lawful to consume them. However, if date juice, currant juice, or raisin juice bubbles and it is known that it will intoxicate, then it is unlawful to consume but it is not impure.

Ruling 112.* Beer (*fuqqāʿ*), which is made from barley and causes a low level of intoxication, is unlawful to consume; and based on obligatory precaution, it is impure. However, barley water derived from barley for medicinal purposes and does not cause any intoxication whatsoever is pure and lawful to consume.

10. Sweat of an excrement-eating animal

Ruling 113. The sweat of a camel that habitually eats human impurity is impure, as is the sweat of other animals that do the same, based on obligatory precaution.

Ruling 114. The sweat of a person who becomes *junub*[14] by unlawful means is pure, and prayers performed with that sweat are valid.

WAYS OF ESTABLISHING IMPURITY (*NAJĀSAH*)

Ruling 115. There are three ways to establish the impurity of an object:

1. one is certain, or is confident by rational means, that the object is impure. If one only supposes (i.e. has a *ẓann*) that an object is impure, it is not necessary for him to avoid it and it is ruled to be pure. Therefore, there is no problem in eating in public places, restaurants, and guesthouses where the people who eat there are unconcerned about religious matters and who do not observe laws relating to what is pure and what is impure, as long as one is not confident that the food brought to him is impure;
2. someone who is in possession of an object says it is impure; for example, one's spouse or domestic worker says that a utensil or something else that they have in their possession is impure;
3. two dutiful men say that an object is impure, on condition that they give the reason for its impurity; for example, they say that the object has come into contact with blood or urine. If one dutiful man, or another reliable person, says something is impure but one does not attain confidence in what he says, the obligatory precaution is that one must avoid that thing [i.e. it is ruled to be impure].

Ruling 116. If on account of not knowing the Islamic ruling one does not know whether an object is impure or pure – for example, he does not know whether the droppings of a mouse are pure or not – he must inquire about the ruling. However, if despite knowing the ruling one doubts whether an object is pure or not – for example, he doubts whether something is blood, or he does not know whether it is the blood of a mosquito or the blood of a human being – then in these

[14] *Junub* is the term used to refer to a person who is in the state of ritual impurity (*janābah*). *Janābah* is explained in Ruling 344.

cases, the object is pure and it is not necessary for him to investigate or ask about it.

Ruling 117. An impure object about which one doubts whether it has become pure or not is impure. And a pure object about which one doubts whether it has become impure or not is pure. Even if one is able to know whether the object is really impure or pure, it is not necessary for him to investigate.

Ruling 118. If someone knows that one of two utensils or one of two items of clothing that he uses has become impure but does not know which one, he must avoid both of them [i.e. they are ruled to be impure]. However, if, for example, one does not know whether it is his own clothing that has become impure or clothing that he does not have any right of disposal over and which is the property of someone else, it is not necessary for him to avoid it [i.e. it is ruled to be pure].

HOW A PURE (*ṬĀHIR*) OBJECT BECOMES IMPURE (*NAJIS*)

Ruling 119. If a pure object touches an impure object and both or one of them is wet – such that the wetness of one transfers onto the other – the pure object also becomes impure; however, it does not become impure through multiple intermediaries [i.e. the spread of impurity is limited to two intermediaries].

An example: if the right hand has become impure (*mutanajjis*) with urine, and [after drying,] that hand touches the left hand with a new wetness, this touching causes the left hand to become impure; and if after drying, the left hand touches something else, such as some clothing, with a new wetness, the clothing also becomes impure; but, if the clothing touches some other object with a new wetness, that other object is not ruled to be impure. Therefore, the third intermediary [the clothing in the example above] is impure but it does not make anything impure. Furthermore, if the wetness is so little that it does not transfer onto another object, the pure object does not become impure even if it touches an intrinsic impurity.

Ruling 120. If a pure object touches an impure object and one doubts whether both or one of them was wet or the wetness was enough to spread onto the other object, the pure object is not considered to have become impure.

Ruling 121. If there are two objects and a person does not know which one is pure and which one is impure, and afterwards a pure object that is wet touches one of them, it is not necessary to avoid it [i.e. it is ruled to be pure], except in some cases, like when both objects were previously impure or when a pure object that is wet touches both objects.

Ruling 122. If the ground, some cloth, or a similar thing is wet, only that part of it that an impurity touches becomes impure and its other parts remain pure, even if the pure part is connected to the impure part. The same applies to a cucumber, melon, etc.

Ruling 123. Whenever syrup, oil, or a similar thing is of a consistency such that when some quantity of it is removed, it does not leave an empty space [due to the space refilling], then even if one part of it becomes impure, the entire quantity becomes impure. However, if it is such that when a part of it is removed it leaves an empty space – even if afterwards it becomes filled – then only the part that the impurity touches is impure. Therefore, if [in the latter scenario] mouse droppings fall into it, only the part that the droppings touch is impure and the rest is pure.

Ruling 124. If a fly or similar insect sits on an impure object that is wet and afterwards it sits on a pure object that is also wet, in the event that one knows that impurity was carried along with the insect, the pure object becomes impure. If one does not know, the pure object remains pure.

Ruling 125. If a part of the body perspires and that part becomes impure, and the sweat goes from that part to another part, then whichever part the sweat touches becomes impure. If the sweat does not go to any other part, the rest of the body is pure.

Ruling 126. If thick phlegm from the nose or throat contains blood, the part containing blood is impure and the rest is pure. Therefore, if the phlegm touches the outer mouth or nose, the area about which one is certain the impure phlegm touched is impure, and the area about which one is doubtful whether the impure phlegm touched or not is pure.

Ruling 127. If a pitcher that has a hole in the bottom of it is placed on impure earth, in the event that water from the pitcher stops flowing, collects under it, and is considered to be one with the pitcher's water, the pitcher's water becomes impure. However, if the pitcher's water flows with pressure, it does not become impure.

Ruling 128. If an object enters the body and comes into contact with some impurity, in the event that after coming out it is not tainted with the impurity, it is pure. Therefore, if an apparatus for inserting enema or the water from it enters the anus, or if a needle, knife, or similar thing is inserted into the body and after coming out it is not tainted with any impurity, it is not impure. The same applies to saliva or mucus of the nose if it comes into contact with blood while inside the body and is not tainted with blood after coming out.

LAWS OF IMPURITIES (*NAJĀSĀT*)

Ruling 129. It is unlawful to make the script of the Qur'an and its pages impure in the event that this amounts to disrespect; and if they become impure, one must wash them immediately. In fact, based on obligatory precaution, it is unlawful to make them impure even if it does not amount to disrespect, and washing them would be obligatory.

Ruling 130. If the cover of the Qur'an becomes impure, in the event that this is disrespectful to the Qur'an, one must wash it.

Ruling 131. Placing the Qur'an on an intrinsic impurity such as blood or a corpse – even if the intrinsic impurity is dry – is unlawful in the event that it is disrespectful to the Qur'an.

Ruling 132. Writing the Qur'an with impure ink, even one letter of it, has the ruling of making it impure; and if it is written in this way, one must wash it off with water or something else to the extent that the impure ink substance is removed.

Ruling 133.* Based on obligatory precaution, selling the Qur'an to a disbeliever is not a valid transaction. Giving the Qur'an to a disbeliever is unlawful if it amounts to disrespect or insult to the Qur'an or places it at risk of being disrespected. However, there is no problem if giving [or selling] the Qur'an to a disbeliever is for guiding him, for example, and it would not amount to disrespect or insult to the Qur'an.

Ruling 134.* If a page of the Qur'an or an object that is necessary to respect – such as paper on which is written the name of Allah the Exalted, Prophet Muḥammad (Ṣ), or one of the Infallibles (ʿA), or an epithet (*laqab*) or *kunyah*[15] of these great personalities – falls into a lavatory, it is obligatory to take it out and wash it even if it costs money to do so. If it is not possible to take it out, the lavatory must not be used by those who know about the fallen paper until they are certain the page has decomposed. Telling others about this is not obligatory. Furthermore, if a *turbah*[16] of Imam al-Ḥusayn (ʿA) falls into a lavatory and it is not possible to take it out, the lavatory must not be used until one is certain the *turbah* has completely dissolved.

Ruling 135. It is unlawful to eat or drink something that has become impure, and the same applies to feeding that thing to someone. However, it is permitted to feed that thing to a child or an insane person. Furthermore, if a child or an insane person eats impure food himself or makes food impure with his impure hand and eats it, it is not necessary to prevent him from doing so.

Ruling 136. There is no problem in selling or lending an impure thing that can be made pure. However, it is necessary to tell the other party about the thing being impure on two conditions:

1. the other party is at risk of opposing a legal responsibility; for

[15] This is an appellation given to someone as the father or mother of someone.
[16] A *turbah* is a piece of earth or clay on which one places his forehead when prostrating.

example, he will use the impure thing in his food or drink, or it will invalidate the *wuḍū'* or *ghusl* with which he will perform an obligatory prayer. However, if this is not the case, it is not necessary to inform him; for example, it is not necessary to inform him about impure clothing with which he performs prayers because wearing pure clothing is not an absolute condition (*al-sharṭ al-wāqiʿī*)[17] for the prayer to be valid;

2. one deems it probable that the other party will heed what he says. Therefore, if one knows that what he says will have no effect, it is not necessary to tell him.

Ruling 137. If a person sees someone eating or drinking something impure or performing prayers with impure clothing, it is not necessary to tell him.

Ruling 138. If a place in someone's house, or if someone's carpet, is impure and one sees that the wet body, dress, or another object of people who are entering his house touches the impure object, in the event that it was he who was responsible for this state of affairs, he must tell them provided that the two conditions mentioned in Ruling 136 are fulfilled.

Ruling 139. If the owner of a house finds out during a meal that the food is impure, he must tell the guests about it provided that the second condition mentioned in Ruling 136 is fulfilled. However, if one of the guests finds out, it is not necessary for him to tell the others about it. Furthermore, in the event that his dealings with the other guests are such that if they became impure he would also become impure and this would result in him doing something that was contrary to an obligatory religious ruling, he must tell them.

Ruling 140. If a borrowed object becomes impure, the person who

[17] An absolute condition is one that must be fulfilled for an action to be valid irrespective of the performer's state of knowledge with regard to that condition. For example, performing *rukūʿ* in prayers is an absolute condition for the prayer to be valid because even if a person omits it unknowingly and realises this afterwards, his prayer is void and he must repeat it. However, wearing pure clothing in prayers is not an absolute condition because if one performs prayers with impure clothing and realises this afterwards, his prayer is deemed to be valid.

borrowed the object must inform the owner about this provided that the two conditions mentioned in Ruling 136 are fulfilled.

Ruling 141. If a child says an object is impure or he has washed something with water, his word is not to be accepted. However, if a child who is *mumayyiz* and understands well what purity and impurity are, says he has washed something with water, then in the event that the object is at his disposal or one attains confidence in what he says, his word is to be accepted. The same applies if he says an object is impure.

THINGS THAT PURIFY AN IMPURE OBJECT (*MUṬAHHIRĀT*)

Ruling 142. Twelve things make an impure object pure; these are known as '*muṭahhirāt*': (1) water; (2) earth; (3) the sun; (4) transformation (*istiḥālah*); (5) change (*inqilāb*); (6) transfer (*intiqāl*); (7) Islam; (8) subsequence (*tabaʿiyyah*); (9) removal of the intrinsic impurity; (10) *istibrāʾ* of an excrement-eating animal; (11) absence of a Muslim; and (12) draining of blood from a slaughtered animal. The rules about these things will be mentioned in detail in the forthcoming rulings (*masāʾil*).

1. Water

Ruling 143. Water makes an impure object pure provided that four conditions are met:

1. the water must be unmixed; therefore, mixed water such as rose water and willow essence does not make an impure object pure;
2. the water must be pure;
3. when an impure object is washed, the water must not turn into mixed water before the object has become pure; and in cases where only one wash is required,[18] the water must not attain the smell, colour, or taste of the impurity. However, in other

[18] See, for example, Ruling 156.

cases, there is no problem if the water changes; for example, if a person washes an object with *kurr* or *qalīl* water and it is necessary to wash that object twice,[19] then even if in the first wash the water changes its colour, smell, or taste because of the impurity, if in the second wash he purifies the object with water that does not change, the object becomes pure;

4. after washing an impure object, small particles of the intrinsic impurity must not remain on the object. Purifying an impure object with *qalīl* water – i.e. water that is less than *kurr* – has other conditions, which will be mentioned later.

Ruling 144. The impure inside of a utensil must be washed three times with *qalīl* water. Similarly, [it must be washed three times] with *kurr*, flowing, or rainwater, based on obligatory precaution. A utensil that a dog has licked or drank water or some other liquid out of must first be scrubbed with pure soil; then, that soil must be discarded and the utensil washed twice with *qalīl*, *kurr*, or flowing water. If a dog's saliva falls into a utensil or its sweat, urine, or excrement touches the inside of it, or if a wet part of a dog's body touches the inside of a utensil, then based on obligatory precaution, the utensil must first be scrubbed with soil and then washed three times with water. If a dog licks something other than a utensil, such as a person's hand, the rule for utensils does not apply and scrubbing it with soil is not necessary; instead, washing it once is sufficient.

Ruling 145. If the mouth of a utensil that a dog has licked is narrow, soil must be poured into it and the utensil must be shaken vigorously so that the soil reaches all parts of it; after that, it must be washed in the manner mentioned above.

Ruling 146. The inside of a utensil that a pig has licked or drank some liquid out of, or in which a field mouse has died, must be washed seven times with *qalīl*, *kurr*, or flowing water, and it is not necessary to scrub it with soil.

Ruling 147. A utensil that has become impure with wine must be washed three times, even with *kurr* water, flowing water, or suchlike. And the

[19] See, for example, Ruling 153.

recommended precaution is that it should be washed seven times.

Ruling 148. If a pitcher made from impure clay, or a pitcher which impure water has permeated, is placed in *kurr* or flowing water, wherever the water reaches becomes pure. If a person wants its inside to become pure as well, it must stay in *kurr* or flowing water for such a length of time that the water permeates all of it. Furthermore, if a utensil has some liquid that prevents water from reaching its inside, it must be dried and then placed in *kurr* or flowing water.

Ruling 149. An impure utensil can be washed with *qalīl* water in two ways:

1. by filling it three times with water and emptying it out each time;
2. by pouring some water in it three times and each time swirling the water around in a manner that it reaches all the impure parts and then emptying it out.

Ruling 150. If a large container like a cauldron or barrel becomes impure, in the event that it is filled and emptied three times, it becomes pure. The same applies if water is poured into it from above three times in a manner that it reaches all its sides and each time the water that collects at the bottom is emptied out; and the recommended precaution is that on the second and third time, the container that is used to empty out the water should be washed with water.

Ruling 151. If some impure metal, plastic, or suchlike is melted, and in the melting process the inside of it also becomes impure, then in the event that it is washed with water after it has solidified, its exterior becomes pure.

Ruling 152.* A *tanūr*,[20] a pool of water, and suchlike do not have the rule of utensils and therefore become pure with one washing. If a *tanūr* or pool of water do not have holes or outlets through which water can drain and water collects at the bottom, then in the event that one wants to purify the area with *qalīl* water, he must

[20] A *tanūr* is a fire-heated oven for baking bread.

take out the water with a cloth, sponge, container, and suchlike.

Ruling 153. If an impure object is immersed once in *kurr* or flowing water such that water reaches all its impure areas, it becomes pure. In the case of a rug, clothing, or a similar thing, it is not necessary to squeeze or wring it or stamp on it. Furthermore, in case a person's body or clothing becomes impure with urine, then based on obligatory precaution, it is necessary to wash it twice with *kurr* water and the like; however, if flowing water is used, it becomes pure by washing it once.

Ruling 154. If a person wants to wash with *qalīl* water an object that has become impure with urine, in the event that water is poured over it once and separates from it and urine does not remain on the object, it becomes pure. However, with clothing and a person's body, water must be poured over it twice for it to become pure. As for washing clothing, rugs, and similar things with *qalīl* water, one must wring them until the remaining water comes out. (The meaning of 'the remaining water' is water that usually drips out by itself or by wringing at the time of washing and after washing.)

Ruling 155. If an object becomes impure with the urine of a breast-feeding boy or a girl who has not started weaning, in the event that some water, however little, is poured over it once so that it reaches the whole of the impure area, it becomes pure. However, the recommended precaution is that water should be poured over it a second time. In the case of clothing, rugs, and similar things, wringing is not necessary.

Ruling 156. If an object becomes impure by something other than urine, in the event that the impurity is removed and *qalīl* water is poured over it once and separates from it, it becomes pure. However, clothing and similar things must be wrung so that the remaining water comes out.

Ruling 157. If a *ḥaṣīr*[21] that has been woven with thread becomes

[21] A *ḥaṣīr* is a mat that is made by plaiting or weaving straw, reed, or similar materials of plant origin.

impure and is immersed in *kurr* or flowing water, it becomes pure after the intrinsic impurity has been removed. However, if a person wants to wash it with *qalīl* water, it must be squeezed in whatever way possible, even by stamping on it, so that the remaining water separates from it.

Ruling 158. If the exterior of wheat, rice, and suchlike becomes impure and it is immersed in *kurr* or flowing water, it becomes pure. It is also possible to purify it with *qalīl* water. If their interior becomes impure, in the event that *kurr* or flowing water reaches the interior, it becomes pure.

Ruling 159. If the exterior of soap becomes impure, it is possible to purify it; however, if its interior becomes impure, it is not possible to purify it. If a person doubts whether impure water has reached the soap's interior or not, its interior is pure.

Ruling 160. If the exterior of rice, meat, and suchlike becomes impure, in the event that it is placed in a pure bowl or something similar, and water is poured over it once and emptied, it becomes pure. If it is placed in an impure utensil, this procedure must be carried out three times for the utensil to become pure. If a person wants to place a cloth or something similar that needs to be squeezed in a utensil and wash it with water, he must squeeze the object each time water is poured over it and tilt the utensil so that the remaining water that has gathered pours out.

Ruling 161. If impure clothing that has been dyed with indigo or something similar is immersed in *kurr* or flowing water, it becomes pure if the water reaches all parts of it before the water becomes mixed with the colour of the clothing. If it is washed with *qalīl* water, in the event that at the time of wringing the mixed water does not come out, it becomes pure.

Ruling 162. If clothing is washed with *kurr* or flowing water and afterwards some sludge, for example, is found on it, in the event that one does not deem it probable for it to have prevented the water from reaching the clothing, the clothing is pure.

Ruling 163. If after washing clothing or something similar some mud or soap is seen on it, in the event that one does not deem it probable for it to have prevented the water from reaching the clothing, the clothing is pure. However, if impure water reaches the inside of the mud or soap, the outside of the mud or soap is pure and the inside is impure.

Ruling 164. An impure object does not become pure until the intrinsic impurity is removed from it. There is no problem, however, if the smell or colour of the impurity remains on it; for example, if clothing that has become impure with blood is washed with water and the blood substance is removed but the colour of the blood remains, the clothing is pure. And even if the colour of the blood could be removed by using a cleaning product, it is not necessary to do so.

Ruling 165. If impurity on the body is removed by immersion in *kurr* or flowing water, the body becomes pure except if it has become impure with urine, in which case, based on obligatory precaution, it does not become pure by washing it once with *kurr* water. However, it is not necessary for one to come out of the water and then go back in; rather, it will suffice if the person wipes the impure part underwater with his hand such that the water separates from that part and then goes over it once again.

Ruling 166. With regard to impure bits of food that have remained in between the teeth, if water (albeit *qalīl* water) is gargled and it reaches all the bits of impure food, they become pure.

Ruling 167. If the hair on one's head and face [become impure and] is washed with *qalīl* water, in case there is not a lot of hair, it is not necessary to apply pressure to take out the remaining water because a regular amount of water will come out of its own accord.

Ruling 168. If an area of the body or clothing is washed with *qalīl* water, both the impure area and the area around it where water usually reaches during washing become pure. Therefore, it is not necessary to wash those adjoining areas separately. The same applies if a pure object is placed by the side of an impure object and water is poured over both of them. For example, to wash one impure finger with water, if water is poured on all the fingers and impure water as well as pure water reaches all of them, then by the impure finger becoming pure, all the fingers become pure.

Ruling 169. Meat or fat that has become impure is washed with water like any other object. The same applies if the body, clothing, or a utensil has a little fat on it that does not prevent water from reaching it.

Ruling 170. If a utensil or a body is impure and afterwards it becomes greasy such that water is prevented from reaching it, in the event that one wishes to wash the utensil or the body with water, he must first remove the grease so that water can reach it.

Ruling 171. Tap water that is connected to *kurr* is ruled to be *kurr*.

Ruling 172.* If a person washes an object with water and he becomes certain that it has become pure, but afterwards he doubts whether he removed the intrinsic impurity from it or not, he must rewash it with water until he is certain or confident that the intrinsic impurity has been removed. However, if he suffers from obsessive doubting (*waswās*), he must not heed his doubt.

Ruling 173. If ground that absorbs water – such as ground on which there is sand or pebbles – becomes impure, it can be purified with *qalīl* water.

Ruling 174. If ground paved with stone or brick, or hard ground that does not absorb water, becomes impure, it can be purified with *qalīl* water; however, one must pour water over it to the extent that it flows. If the water poured over it does not disappear down holes in the ground but instead gathers somewhere, then to purify that place, the gathered water must be removed with a cloth or a utensil.

Ruling 175. If the exterior of rock salt and suchlike becomes impure, it can be purified with *qalīl* water.

Ruling 176. If impure melted sugar is turned into sugar cubes and placed in *kurr* or flowing water, it does not become pure.

2. Earth

Ruling 177. Earth purifies the sole of one's foot or shoe on four conditions:

1. the earth is pure;
2. the earth is dry; however, there is no problem if there is some wetness or moisture on the earth that does not spread;
3. based on obligatory precaution, the impurity has spread onto the sole of one's foot or shoe from impure earth;
4. an intrinsic impurity – such as blood and urine – or an object that has become impure – such as mud that has become impure and is on the sole of one's foot or shoe – is removed by walking or rubbing the foot on earth; and in the event that the intrinsic impurity had previously been removed, then based on obligatory precaution, the sole of one's foot or shoe does not become pure by walking or rubbing the foot on earth. Furthermore, the earth must be of soil, stone, brick, or something similar; therefore, walking on a rug, *ḥaṣīr*, and grass does not purify the impure sole of one's foot or shoe.

Ruling 178.* Based on obligatory precaution, the impure sole of one's foot or shoe does not become pure by walking on asphalt or ground paved with wood. Similarly, it does not become pure by rubbing it against or drawing it along a wall.

Ruling 179. In order to purify the sole of one's foot or shoe, it is better to walk a distance of fifteen cubits (*dhirāʿ*s)[22] or more, even if the impurity is removed by walking less than fifteen cubits or by rubbing the sole of one's foot or shoe on earth.

Ruling 180. It is not necessary for the impure sole of one's foot or shoe to be wet – it becomes pure by walking even if it is dry.

Ruling 181. After the impure sole of one's foot or shoe has become pure by walking, the area on the sides of the sole that usually becomes dirty with mud also becomes pure.

[22] Fifteen cubits is equivalent to approximately seven metres. [Author]

Ruling 182. Based on obligatory precaution, if the palms or knees of someone who moves around on his hands and knees become impure, they do not become pure as a result of him moving around on them. The same applies to the bottom of a walking stick, the bottom of an artificial leg, the shoe of a quadruped animal, the wheel of a motorcycle or car, and similar things.

Ruling 183. After walking, there is no problem if the smell, colour, or small particles of impurity that cannot be seen remain on the sole of one's foot or shoe. However, the recommended precaution is that one should walk to the extent that this is also removed.

Ruling 184. The inside of a shoe does not become pure by walking. Furthermore, based on obligatory precaution, the soles of socks do not become pure as a result of walking unless the sole is made of leather and suchlike and walking on them on earth is considered normal.

3. The sun

Ruling 185. The sun purifies earth, buildings, and walls on five conditions:

1. the impure object is sufficiently wet, such that were something else to come into contact with it, the latter would become wet. Therefore, if the object is dry, it must be wetted by some means so that the sun can then dry it;
2. no intrinsic impurity remains on the impure object;
3. nothing prevents the sun from shining on the impure object. Therefore, if the sun shines on the impure object from behind a curtain or cloud etc. and makes it dry, the object does not become pure. However, there is no problem if the cloud is so thin that it does not prevent the sun from shining on the object;
4. the sun must dry the impure object by itself. Therefore, if, for example, an impure object is dried by both the wind *and* the sun, it does not become pure. However, there is no problem if the drying of the object can be commonly attributed to the sun shining on it;
5. the sun must dry the building that is impure in one go. Therefore, if one time the sun shines on impure earth or a

building and it dries its surface and another time it dries its underside, then only its surface becomes pure and its underside remains impure.

Ruling 186. The sun can purify an impure *ḥaṣīr* mat; but if it is woven with thread, the sun does not purify the threads. Furthermore, based on obligatory precaution, trees, grass, doors, and windows do not become pure by means of the sun.

Ruling 187. If the sun shines on impure earth and afterwards a person doubts whether or not the earth was wet when the sun shone on it, or whether or not the wetness of the earth has dried by means of the sun, then that earth is impure. The same applies if one doubts whether or not the intrinsic impurity has been removed. If a person doubts whether or not something prevented the sun from shining on the impure object, then based on obligatory precaution, it must not be considered pure.

Ruling 188. If the sun shines on one side of an impure wall and as a result the other side of the wall – on which the sun did not shine – also becomes dry, both sides become pure. However, if one day the sun dries the exterior of a wall or some earth and another day its interior, then only its exterior becomes pure.

4. Transformation (*istiḥālah*)

Ruling 189. If the essence of an impure object changes in such a way that it transforms into a pure object, it becomes pure. For example, if impure wood burns and transforms into ash, or a dog falls into a salt marsh and transforms into salt [the ash and the salt are pure]. However, if the essence of the object does not change – for example, impure wheat is turned into flour or made into bread – then it does not become pure.

Ruling 190. A clay pitcher or something similar made from impure clay is impure. As for charcoal made from impure wood, in the event that none of the former physical properties is in it, it is pure. If impure clay is changed by fire into crockery or bricks, then based on obligatory precaution, it remains impure.

Ruling 191. An impure object about which it is not known whether it has undergone a transformation is impure.

5. Change (*inqilāb*)

Ruling 192. If wine turns into vinegar by itself or by pouring something like vinegar or salt into it, it becomes pure. This is called 'change'.

Ruling 193. Wine made from impure grapes and suchlike, or wine that has come into contact with some other impurity, does not become pure by turning into vinegar.

Ruling 194. Vinegar made from impure grapes, raisins, or dates is impure.

Ruling 195. There is no problem if the stalks of grapes or dates remain on them and vinegar is produced. Similarly, there is no problem in adding cucumber, carrot, aubergine, and suchlike even before it turns into vinegar unless it becomes an intoxicant before turning into vinegar.

Ruling 196. Grape juice becomes unlawful to drink if it bubbles either by heating or by itself [through fermentation]. If grape juice bubbles so much that two-thirds of it reduces and only one-third of it remains, it becomes lawful to drink. Furthermore, if it is established that the grape juice is intoxicating, as some [jurists (*fuqahāʾ*)] have said with regard to when it bubbles by itself, it can only become lawful to drink if it turns into vinegar. As mentioned in Ruling 110, grape juice does not become impure by bubbling unless it turns into wine.

Ruling 197. If two-thirds of grape juice reduces without bubbling, in the event that the remainder bubbles and is commonly called 'grape juice' and not 'grape syrup', then based on obligatory precaution, it is unlawful to drink.

Ruling 198. Grape juice about which it is not known whether it has bubbled is lawful to drink. However, if it bubbles, it does not become lawful to drink until one is certain that two-thirds of it has been reduced.

Ruling 199. If, for example, there are some ripe grapes in a bunch of unripe grapes and the juice extracted from the bunch is not regarded as grape juice and it bubbles, then drinking it is lawful.

Ruling 200. If a grape falls into something that is boiling by means of heat and it boils and does not dissolve, then based on obligatory precaution, only eating that grape is unlawful.

Ruling 201. If a person wants to cook grape syrup in several pots, it is permitted to use the spatula that was previously used in a pot that has boiled, in a pot that has not boiled.

Ruling 202. Unripe grape juice does not have the ruling of grape juice; it is therefore pure and lawful to drink if it bubbles. Furthermore, if it is not known whether something is an unripe grape or a ripe grape and it bubbles, then eating it is lawful.

6. Transfer (*intiqāl*)

Ruling 203. If the blood of a human being, or of an animal whose blood gushes out [when its vein is cut], is sucked by an animal that is commonly known to have no blood, such that it may be absorbed in that animal's body – like when a mosquito sucks blood from a human being or an animal – then that blood is pure. This is called 'transfer'. As for the blood that a leech sucks from a human being for treatment, as it is not known whether or not that blood becomes part of its body, it is impure.

Ruling 204. If a person kills a mosquito that had sat on his body and the blood sucked by the mosquito comes out of it, that blood is pure – even if the time that elapsed between the sucking of the blood and killing the mosquito was very little – because the blood was in the process of becoming food for the mosquito. However, the recommended precaution is that in this situation, one should avoid the blood [i.e. it is better not to treat it as being pure].

7. Islam

Ruling 205. If a disbeliever declares in any language the *shahādatayn* (two testimonies) – i.e. he testifies to the oneness of Allah the Exalted and to the prophethood of the Seal of the Prophets [Prophet Muḥammad (Ṣ)] – he becomes a Muslim. In the event that he was previously ruled to be impure based on obligatory precaution,[23] then, after becoming a Muslim, his body, saliva, nasal mucus, and sweat are pure. However, if at the time of becoming a Muslim an intrinsic impurity is on his body, it must be removed and that part of his body must be washed; and if the intrinsic impurity is removed before he becomes a Muslim, then based on obligatory precaution, that part of his body must be washed.

Ruling 206. If when someone was a disbeliever any clothes of his that were wet made contact with his body – irrespective of whether those clothes were on his body at the time he became a Muslim or not – then based on obligatory precaution, one must avoid them [i.e. they are ruled to be impure].

Ruling 207. If a disbeliever says the *shahādatayn* but one does not know whether he has sincerely become a Muslim or not, he is pure. The same applies if a disbeliever says the *shahādatayn* and one knows he has not sincerely become a Muslim but he does not do anything that contradicts his saying of the *shahādatayn*.

8. Subsequence (*tabaʿiyyah*)

Ruling 208. Subsequence means that an impure object becomes pure by means of the purity of another object.

Ruling 209. If wine turns into vinegar, its container also becomes pure up to the level where the wine reached at the time of fermentation; and any piece of cloth or object that is usually placed on top of it also becomes pure if it had become impure by the wine. However, if the outside of the container had become impure by the wine due

[23] See Rulings 104, 105, and 107.

to its fermenting, then it does not become pure by subsequence based on obligatory precaution.

Ruling 210. The child of a disbeliever becomes pure by subsequence in two cases:

1. if a disbeliever becomes a Muslim, his child follows him in becoming pure. The same applies if the child's paternal grandfather, mother, or paternal grandmother becomes a Muslim. However, ruling the child as being pure in this case is conditional upon the child being with the person who has newly become a Muslim and upon the child being under his guardianship; furthermore, a disbeliever who is a closer relative than the person who has newly become a Muslim must not be with the child;
2. if a disbeliever is captured by a Muslim, the disbeliever's child becomes pure if his father or one of his grandparents is not with the child.

In both cases, in the event that the child is *mumayyiz*, his becoming pure by subsequence is conditional upon the child not expressing disbelief (*kufr*).

Ruling 211. The plank or stone [or other such surfaces] on which a corpse is given *ghusl*, and the cloth with which the private parts of a corpse are covered, and the hands of the person who gives *ghusl* – all of these things that usually come into contact with the corpse and the water that is poured on the corpse – become pure once the *ghusl* is complete. However, based on obligatory precaution, the clothing and body of the person who gives *ghusl* and other instruments used for giving *ghusl* do not become pure by subsequence and need to be washed separately.

Ruling 212. With regard to someone who washes an object to make it pure, after that object has become pure, his hands – which were washed along with the object – also become pure. Similarly, when clothes are washed in a washing machine, after the clothes have become pure, the drum of the washing machine as well as the inside of the door (which are commonly deemed to be among the means for washing the clothes) become pure by subsequence and do not need to be washed.

Ruling 213. If clothing or something similar is washed with *qalīl* water and is wrung to a normal extent so that the water with which it was washed separates from it, the water that remains in it is pure.

Ruling 214. With regard to an impure utensil that is washed with *qalīl* water, after the water with which it was washed separates from it, the small amount of water that remains in it is pure.

9. Removal of intrinsic impurity (*ʿayn al-najāsah*)

Ruling 215. If the body of an animal becomes impure with an intrinsic impurity like blood, or with something that has become impure, such as impure water, in the event that the impurity is removed, the animal's body becomes pure. Similarly, the inner parts of a human body – like the inside of the mouth, nose, and ears – become impure by coming into contact with an external impurity, but by removing the impurity they become pure. As for internal impurity – such as blood that comes out from in between the teeth – this does not cause the inner parts of the body to become impure. Similarly, if an external object inside the body comes into contact with internal impurity, it does not make the object impure. Therefore, if dentures come into contact with blood that comes out from in between the teeth, it is not necessary to wash the dentures; but if the dentures come into contact with impure food, it is necessary to wash them.

Ruling 216. If some food has remained between the teeth and blood comes in the mouth, the food does not become impure by coming into contact with the blood.

Ruling 217. Those parts of the lips and eyelids that overlap when shut are ruled to be inner parts of the body. Therefore, in the event that they come into contact with some external impurity, it is not necessary to wash them with water.[24] However, with regard to those

[24] In light of Ruling 215, they become pure by removing the impurity from them, so if this is done, there is no need to wash them with water.

parts that one does not know whether they are outer or inner parts of the body, it is necessary to wash them if they come into contact with external impurity.

Ruling 218. If impure dust settles on dry clothing, a carpet, or similar thing, in the event that the object is shaken in a way that the amount of dust that is certain to have been impure falls off, the clothing, carpet, or similar thing is pure and it is not necessary to wash it.

10. *Istibrāʾ*[25] of an excrement-eating animal

Ruling 219. The urine and faeces of an animal that habitually eats human excrement are impure. For the urine and faeces of such an animal to be considered pure, the animal must be put through a process of *istibrāʾ*, meaning that it must be prevented from eating impurity for some time and be fed pure food so that after that period, it is no longer considered an excrement-eating animal. The recommended precaution is to prevent an excrement-eating camel from eating excrement for forty days, a cow twenty days, a sheep ten days, a duck seven or five days, and a domestic hen three days, even if before these periods are over the animal in question ceases to be considered an excrement-eating animal.

11. Absence of a Muslim

Ruling 220.* If the body, clothing, or something else like a utensil or carpet becomes impure, and if it is in the possession of a Muslim who is *bāligh* – or a non-*bāligh mumayyiz* child who is able to discern between what is pure and what is impure – and that Muslim moves out of sight [with the impure object], then in the event that one deems it rationally probable that he has washed it, it is pure. This rule also applies to a non-*bāligh* child who is not *mumayyiz* as the child's affairs are looked after by such a [Muslim] person entrusted with its affairs. Furthermore, things that a person cannot see because of

[25] The meaning of *istibrāʾ* here is different to that mentioned in two other places in this work: firstly, in Ruling 69, where it refers to the process of clearing the male urethra of urine after urinating; and secondly, in Ruling 495, where it refers to the method of checking whether or not menstruation has stopped.

a lack of light or being blind fall under the rule of becoming absent. Therefore, if the body or clothing of a Muslim becomes impure and someone does not see it being purified due to a lack of light or being blind, then in the event that he deems it rationally probable that it has been washed, it is ruled to be pure.

Ruling 221. If a person is certain or confident that an impure object has become pure, or two dutiful (*ʿādil*) people testify to it having become pure and their testimony concerns the reason for it having become pure, then the object is pure; for example, they testify that an item of clothing that had become impure with urine has been washed twice. The same applies if a person who is in possession of an impure object says that it has become pure, and he is not suspected to be someone whose word in this case cannot be accepted; or, if a Muslim washes an impure object with the intention of making it pure, even if it is not known whether he has washed it properly or not.

Ruling 222. If a person who has been appointed to wash someone's clothes says that he has washed them and one is confident of the truthfulness of what he says, then those clothes are pure.

Ruling 223.* If an obsessively doubtful person (*muwaswis*) who does not attain certainty like normal people do in the washing of an impure object washes it in the same way that normal people wash it, his actions are sufficient to deem the object pure. From an Islamic law perspective, being abnormally cautious in matters of purity and impurity is not approved, and there is no need for any person, obsessively doubtful or not, to investigate and see if his body, clothing, or something else has become impure or not. Furthermore, it is not necessary to carefully see if something impure has made contact with something else, and if it has, whether wetness has spread to it or not. In all of these cases, the objects are ruled to be pure.

12. Flowing out of blood [of a slaughtered animal] in a normal quantity

Ruling 224. Blood that remains inside the body of an animal that has been slaughtered according to Islamic law is pure if a normal amount of blood has already come out, as stated in Ruling 94.

Ruling 225. Based on obligatory precaution, the previous ruling only applies to animals whose meat is lawful to eat; it does not apply to animals whose meat is unlawful to eat.

LAWS OF UTENSILS

Ruling 226. If a utensil has been made from the hide of a dog, pig, or carcass [of an animal that has not been slaughtered according to Islamic law], it is unlawful to eat or drink out of it if the food or drink has become impure [as a result of wetness from the food or drink touching the utensil (see Ruling 119)]. Furthermore, the utensil must not be used for *wuḍūʾ*, *ghusl*, or any other purpose for which only pure objects must be used. And the recommended precaution is that the hide of a dog, pig, or carcass [as defined above] should not be used for any other purposes.

Ruling 227. Eating and drinking from gold or silver utensils are unlawful. In fact, based on obligatory precaution, using these utensils in general is unlawful. However, there is no problem in using them for decorating a room and suchlike, or keeping them, although the recommended precautionary measure is not to [decorate with them and/or keep them]. The same applies to making gold and silver utensils or buying and selling them for decoration or keeping.

Ruling 228. If the handle of a tea cup made of gold or silver can be called a 'utensil', it has the ruling of a gold or silver tea cup; however, if it cannot be called a 'utensil', there is no problem in using it.

Ruling 229. There is no problem in using a gold-plated or silver-plated utensil.

Ruling 230. If metal is mixed with gold or silver and made into a utensil, in the event that the amount of metal is such that the utensil cannot be called a 'gold utensil' or a 'silver utensil', there is no problem in using it.

Ruling 231. If a person places food from a utensil made of gold or silver into another utensil, in the event that the second utensil cannot be commonly considered an intermediary utensil for eating from the first utensil, there is no problem [in eating from the second utensil].

Ruling 232. There is no problem in using the mouthpiece of a shisha pipe, the scabbard of a sword, a knife, or the frame of the Qur'an if they are made of silver or gold. However, the recommended precaution is not to use perfume and kohl containers made of gold or silver.

Ruling 233. There is no problem in eating or drinking from a gold or silver utensil if one is compelled to, but only to the extent that his need is alleviated; more than that is not permitted.

Ruling 234. There is no problem in using a utensil about which one does not know whether it is made of gold, silver, or something else.

ABLUTION (*WUḌŪʾ*)

Ruling 235. In *wuḍūʾ*, it is obligatory to wash (*ghasl*) the face and arms, and to wipe (*masḥ*) the front part of the head and upper part of the feet.

Ruling 236. The length of the face that must be washed is the area from the top of the forehead where the hair grows to the bottom of the chin; and the breadth of the face that must be washed is the area that is covered by the tip of the middle finger to the tip of the thumb. If even a small amount of this area is not washed, the *wuḍūʾ* is invalid; and if one is not certain of having washed this area completely, he must also wash a little extra around this area to be certain.

Ruling 237. If someone's face is longer than normal from the chin, he must wash his entire face. If hair grows on one's forehead or one does not have hair on the front part of his head, he must wash the same amount of his forehead that people with normal foreheads wash. Someone whose face is wider or narrower than normal, or has longer or shorter fingers and thumbs than normal, must take into account an area between the middle finger and thumb that would be proportionate to the size of his face and wash that amount.

Ruling 238. If a person deems it probable that there is dirt or something else in his eyebrows or in the corners of his eyes or lips which would prevent water from reaching those areas, in the event that his deeming this probable would be considered by people to be reasonable, he must examine this before performing *wuḍūʾ*, and if there really is such an obstacle, he must remove it.

Ruling 239. If the skin of one's face is visible from in between his facial hair, he must ensure that the water reaches the skin. If it is not visible, then washing his facial hair is sufficient and it is not necessary for him to ensure that water reaches under his facial hair.

Ruling 240. If a person doubts whether or not the skin of his face is visible from in between his facial hair, then based on obligatory precaution, he must wash his facial hair and ensure that water reaches the skin.

Ruling 241. It is not obligatory to wash inside the nose or those parts of the lips and eyes that cannot be seen when closed. However, if a person is not certain that everything that must be washed has been washed, it is obligatory that he wash a little of those parts as well to be certain. Furthermore, with regard to someone who did not know this rule, if having performed *wuḍūʾ* he does not know whether he washed the required area or not, the prayers he performed with that *wuḍūʾ* are valid and it is not necessary for him to perform *wuḍūʾ* again for the next prayer.

Ruling 242. The direction in which one must wash the arms is from top to bottom [i.e. in a direction towards the fingertips]. The same applies, based on obligatory precaution, to washing the face [i.e. it must be washed in a direction towards the chin]. If a person washes from bottom to top, the *wuḍūʾ* is invalid.

Ruling 243. If a person wets his hand with water and wipes it on his face and arms, in the event that the wetness of his hand is to the extent that by wiping his face and arms the water covers them, it is sufficient, and it is not necessary for the water to flow over them.

Ruling 244. After washing the face, one must wash his right arm from the elbow to the tips of the fingers, and he must then proceed to wash his left arm in the same way.

Ruling 245. If a person is not certain that the elbow has been washed completely, he must also wash a little above it to be certain.

Ruling 246. If someone washes his hands up to his wrists before washing his face, then when he performs *wuḍūʾ* he must still wash his arms up to the tips of his fingers; if he washes his arms only up to his wrists, his *wuḍūʾ* is invalid.

Ruling 247. In *wuḍūʾ*, washing the face and arms once is obligatory, twice recommended, and three times or more unlawful. The first washing is complete when one pours – with the intention (*qaṣd*) of performing *wuḍūʾ* – an amount of water onto the face or arms that covers them completely, such that there is no need to take any further measures to ensure that the water has reached the required area. Therefore, if, for example, one pours water ten times onto his face until the water covers his face completely, and he does this with the intention of the first wash, there is no problem [i.e. the first wash will be deemed to have taken place correctly]. Until he does not make the intention of performing *wuḍūʾ* and washing his face, for example, the first wash is not deemed to have taken place. Therefore, he can pour water onto his entire face a number of times and on the last time he pours water, he can make the intention of a *wuḍūʾ* washing. However, the validity of such an intention for the second washing is problematic, and the obligatory precaution is that one must not pour water onto his face and arms more than one time after the first washing, even if it is not with the intention of performing *wuḍūʾ*.

Ruling 248. After washing both arms, one must wipe the front part of his head with the wetness of the water that has remained on his hand. And the recommended precaution is that one should wipe with the palm of his right hand and wipe from top to bottom [i.e. in a direction towards his forehead].

Ruling 249. The area that must be wiped is the front quarter of the head, i.e. the quarter immediately above the forehead. It is sufficient to wipe any part of this area and to any extent, although the recommended precaution is that the length of the wiping should be at least the length of one finger, and the width of the wiping should be at least the width of three fingers joined together.

Ruling 250. It is not necessary that the wiping of the head be on its skin; rather, it is also correct (*ṣaḥīḥ*) to wipe the hair on the front of one's head. However, if the length of someone's hair at the front of his head is so long that, for example, were he to comb it, it would fall onto his face or it would reach other parts of his head, then he must wipe the roots of the hair. If he gathers at the front of his head the hair which falls on his face or which reaches the other parts of his head and then wipes it, or if he wipes the hair that has come to the front part of his head from other parts of his head, then such a wiping is invalid.

Ruling 251. After wiping the head, one must wipe the upper part of the feet with the wetness of the *wuḍūʾ* water that has remained on his hands. The area that must be wiped is from the tip of one of the toes to the ankle; and based on obligatory precaution, wiping the feet up to the raised part in the middle of the foot [before the ankle] will not suffice. And the recommended precaution is that one should wipe the right foot with the right hand and the left foot with the left hand.

Ruling 252. The wiping of the feet can be of any width; however, it is better that the width be the width of three fingers joined together; and it is even better for the whole of the upper foot to be wiped with the whole palm.

Ruling 253. With regard to the wiping of the feet, it is not necessary for one to place his hand on the tips of the toes and to then draw his hand to the back of the foot; rather, one can place his whole hand on his foot and draw it back a little.

Ruling 254. With regard to the wiping of the head and feet, one must draw his hand over them; therefore, if one keeps his hand still and draws his head or foot along it, the wiping is invalid. However, there is no problem if the head or foot moves slightly when one draws his hand over them.

Ruling 255. The area to be wiped must be dry; if it is wet to the extent that the wetness of the hand has no effect on it, the wiping is invalid. However, there is no problem if the area to be wiped is merely damp, or its wetness is so little that it becomes absorbed in the wetness of the hand.

Ruling 256. If for the purposes of wiping, no moisture is left on the hand such that both arms are dry from the elbow to the tips of the fingers, one cannot wet his hands with additional water; rather, one must take moisture from his beard and perform the wiping with that. Taking moisture from anything other than one's beard and wiping with it is problematic [i.e. based on obligatory precaution, such a wiping does not suffice].

Ruling 257. If the moisture on one's hand is only sufficient for wiping his head, the obligatory precaution is that he must wipe his head with that moisture, and for the wiping of his feet, he must take moisture from his beard.

Ruling 258. Wiping performed on socks or shoes is invalid. However, if one is unable to remove his socks or shoes on account of severe cold, or fear of thieves or predatory animals etc., then the obligatory precaution is that after he has wiped on his shoes or socks, he must also perform *tayammum*. If it is a matter of *taqiyyah*,[26] it is sufficient if he only wipes over his socks or shoes.

Ruling 259. If the upper part of one's foot is impure and it cannot be washed [and made pure] so that it can be wiped, then *tayammum* must be performed.

IMMERSIVE ABLUTION (*AL-WUḌŪʾ AL-IRTIMĀSĪ*)

Ruling 260. Immersive *wuḍūʾ* means that one immerses his face and arms in water with the intention of performing *wuḍūʾ*. And what is

[26] *Taqiyyah* refers to dissimulation or concealment of one's beliefs in the face of danger.

apparent (*ẓāhir*)[27] is that there is no problem in wiping the head and feet with the wetness of the hands that were washed by immersion, although this goes against precaution.[28]

Ruling 261. In immersive *wuḍūʾ*, one must also wash his face and arms from top to bottom. Therefore, if at the time of immersing his face and arms in the water one makes the intention of *wuḍūʾ*, he must immerse his face forehead-first, and his arms elbow-first.

Ruling 262. There is no problem if one performs immersive *wuḍūʾ* for some parts [i.e. face/arms] and non-immersive for others.

RECOMMENDED SUPPLICATION (*DUʿĀʾ*) WHILE PERFORMING *WUḌŪʾ*[29]

Ruling 263. It is recommended for one who is performing *wuḍūʾ* to say the following when his eyes fall on the water:

بِسْمِ اللّٰهِ وَبِاللّٰهِ وَالْحَمْدُ لِلّٰهِ الَّذِيْ جَعَلَ الْمَاءَ طَهُوْرًا وَلَمْ يَجْعَلْهُ نَجِسًا

bismil lāhi wa billāh, wal ḥamdu lillāhil ladhī jaʿalal māʾa ṭahūran wa lam yajʿalhu najisā

In the name of Allah and by Allah, all praise is for Allah who made water pure and did not make it impure.

[27] For practical purposes in jurisprudential rulings, expressing an 'apparent' ruling equates to giving a fatwa.

[28] In another of his works on Islamic law, al-Sayyid al-Sistani hypothetically discusses different ways by which a person could wash his arms by combining the method of performing *wuḍūʾ* by immersion with the method of performing it in the normal (non-immersive) manner, and thereby be able to perform the wiping of his head and feet with the wetness that is on his hand from having washed the arm in the normal manner. One of these ways is as follows: as washing a second time is recommended, a person could – after washing his left arm by immersion – wash it again in the normal way with his right hand and then wipe his head and feet (*Taʿlīqāt ʿalā al-ʿUrwah al-Wuthqā*, vol. 1, p. 160, Ruling 511).

[29] This supplication is based on a tradition in which Imam ʿAlī (ʿA) supplicates to Allah while performing *wuḍūʾ* in the presence of his son, Muḥammad ibn al-Ḥanafiyyah. See, for example, Shaykh al-Ṭūsī's *Tahdhīb al-Aḥkām*, vol. 1, p. 53.

When washing his hands before performing *wuḍū'*, he should say:

بِسْمِ اللّٰهِ وَبِاللّٰهِ، اَللّٰهُمَّ ٱجْعَلْنِيْ مِنَ التَّوَّابِيْنَ وَٱجْعَلْنِيْ مِنَ الْمُتَطَهِّرِيْنَ

bismil lāhi wa billāh, allāhummaj 'alnī minat tawwābīna waj 'alnī minal mutaṭahhirīn

In the name of Allah and by Allah. O Allah! Make me of those who often repent and make me of those who purify themselves.

When rinsing the mouth, he should say:

اَللّٰهُمَّ لَقِّنِّيْ حُجَّتِيْ يَوْمَ أَلْقَاكَ، وَأَطْلِقْ لِسَانِيْ بِذِكْرِكَ

allāhumma laqqinnī ḥujjatī yawma alqāk, wa aṭliq lisānī bidhikrik

O Allah! Inculcate in me my proof on the day I meet You, and make my tongue fluent with Your remembrance.

When rinsing the nose, he should say:

اَللّٰهُمَّ لَا تُحَرِّمْ عَلَيَّ رِيْحَ الْجَنَّةِ، وَٱجْعَلْنِيْ مِمَّنْ يَشَمُّ رِيْحَهَا وَرَوْحَهَا وَطِيْبَهَا

allāhumma lā tuḥarrim 'alayya rīḥal jannah, waj 'alnī mimmay yashammu rīḥahā wa rawḥahā wa ṭībahā

O Allah! Do not deprive me of the fragrance of Paradise, and make me of those who smell its fragrance, its breeze, and its perfume.

When washing the face, he should say:

اَللّٰهُمَّ بَيِّضْ وَجْهِيْ يَوْمَ تَسْوَدُّ فِيْهِ الْوُجُوْهُ، وَلَا تُسَوِّدْ وَجْهِيْ
يَوْمَ تَبْيَضُّ الْوُجُوْهُ

allāhumma bayyiḍ wajhī yawma taswaddu fīhil wujūh, wa lā tusawwid wajhī yawma tabyaḍḍul wujūh

O Allah! Brighten my face on the day when [some] faces shall darken, and do not darken my face on the day when [some] faces shall brighten.

When washing the right arm, he should say:

اَللّٰهُمَّ أَعْطِنِيْ كِتَابِيْ بِيَمِيْنِيْ، وَالْخُلْدَ فِي الْجِنَانِ بِيَسَارِيْ، وَحَاسِبْنِيْ حِسَابًا يَسِيْرًا

allāhumma aʿṭinī kitābī biyamīnī, wal khulda fil jināni biyasārī, wa ḥāsibnī ḥisābay yasīrā

O Allah! Give me my book [of deeds] in my right hand, and a permanent stay in Paradise with ease, and account me [for my deeds] with an easy accounting.

When washing the left arm, he should say:

اَللّٰهُمَّ لَا تُعْطِنِيْ كِتَابِيْ بِشِمَالِيْ، وَلَا مِنْ وَرَاءِ ظَهْرِيْ، وَلَا تَجْعَلْهَا مَغْلُوْلَةً إِلٰى عُنُقِيْ، وَأَعُوْذُ بِكَ مِنْ مُقَطَّعَاتِ النِّيْرَانِ

allāhumma lā tuʿṭinī kitābī bishimālī, wa lā min warāʾi ẓahrī, wa lā tajʿalhā maghlūlatan ilā ʿunuqī, wa aʿūdhu bika mim muqaṭṭaʿātin nīrān

O Allah! Do not give me my book [of deeds] in my left hand, nor from behind my back, and do not chain it to my neck. I seek refuge with You from the garments of hellfire.

When wiping the head, he should say:

اَللّٰهُمَّ غَشِّنِيْ بِرَحْمَتِكَ وَبَرَكَاتِكَ وَعَفْوِكَ

allāhumma ghashshinī biraḥmatika wa barakātika wa ʿafwik

O Allah! Envelop me in Your mercy, Your blessings, and Your pardon.

When wiping the feet, he should say:

اَللّٰهُمَّ ثَبِّتْنِيْ عَلَى الصِّرَاطِ يَوْمَ تَزِلُّ فِيْهِ الْأَقْدَامُ، وَاجْعَلْ سَعْيِيْ فِيْمَا يُرْضِيْكَ عَنِّيْ يَا ذَا الْجَلَالِ وَالْإِكْرَامِ

allāhumma thabbitnī ʿalaṣ ṣirāti yawma tazillu fīhil aqdām, waj ʿal saʿyī fīmā yurḍīka ʿannī, yā dhal jalāli wal ikrām

O Allah! Keep me firmly on the path on the day when feet shall stumble, and let my efforts be in those things that make You pleased with me, O Possessor of Majesty and Bounty!

CONDITIONS FOR THE VALIDITY OF *WUḌŪʾ*

There are a number of conditions for *wuḍūʾ* to be valid.

The first condition: the water used for *wuḍūʾ* must be pure, and based on obligatory precaution, it must not be tainted with anything that human beings find disgusting – such as the urine of an animal whose meat is lawful to eat, a carcass that is pure, or pus from an injury – even if it is pure in Islamic law.

The second condition: the water must not be mixed.

Ruling 264. *Wuḍūʾ* performed with impure or mixed water is invalid, even if one did not know at the time that it was impure or mixed, or he had forgotten about it; and if one has performed prayers with that *wuḍūʾ*, he must perform them again with a valid *wuḍūʾ*.

Ruling 265. If apart from mixed muddy water one does not have any other water with which to perform *wuḍūʾ*, in the event that the time remaining for prayers is short, he must perform *tayammum*. If one has sufficient time, he must wait for the water to become clear or make it clear by some means and perform *wuḍūʾ* with it. Muddy water is considered mixed water only when it can no longer be called 'water'.

The third condition: the water must be permissible (*mubāḥ*) to use [i.e. it must not be usurped].

Ruling 266. Performing *wuḍūʾ* with usurped (*ghaṣbī*) water, or with water about which it is not known if its owner consents to its use or not, is unlawful and invalid. Furthermore, if *wuḍūʾ* water drips from one's face or arms onto a usurped place, or if the place in which one performs *wuḍūʾ* is usurped, in the event that he cannot perform *wuḍūʾ* in any other place, his responsibility (*taklīf*) is to perform *tayammum*; and if he can perform *wuḍūʾ* in another place, it is necessary for him to perform *wuḍūʾ* in that other place. However, in the event that he performs *wuḍūʾ* in the usurped place, thus committing a sin, his *wuḍūʾ* is still valid.[30]

[30] Two scenarios are envisaged here: in the first, the person's duty is to perform

Ruling 267.* There is no problem in performing *wuḍūʾ* in the place designated for *wuḍūʾ* in a school or with water from a school's pool when one does not know whether the *wuḍūʾ* place or pool is a charitable endowment (*waqf*) to the general public or only to the students of the school, as long as people usually perform *wuḍūʾ* in that place or with water from the pool and no one prohibits them from doing so.

Ruling 268. If someone does not want to perform prayers in a mosque and does not know whether the place designated for *wuḍūʾ* in the mosque or its pool is a charitable endowment to the general public or only to those who perform prayers in the mosque, he cannot perform *wuḍūʾ* there. However, there is no problem if people who do not usually pray in that mosque perform *wuḍūʾ* in that place or with water from the pool and no one prohibits them from doing so.

Ruling 269. Performing *wuḍūʾ* with water belonging to hostels, hotels, shopping arcades, motorway restaurants, and similar places is valid only if people who do not reside there usually perform *wuḍūʾ* with water belonging to that place and no one prohibits them from doing so.

Ruling 270. There is no problem in performing *wuḍūʾ* with water from streams that rational people would consider permissible to use without the owner's consent – irrespective of whether the owner is an adult or a child – even if one does not know that the owner consents to it. In fact, it is permitted to use a stream's water even if the owner forbids performing *wuḍūʾ* with it, or if one knows that the owner does not consent, or if the owner is a minor (*ṣaghīr*) or insane.

Ruling 271. If a person forgets that some water is usurped and performs *wuḍūʾ* with it, his *wuḍūʾ* is valid. However, if someone usurps some water himself and then having forgotten that it is usurped performs *wuḍūʾ* with it, then to consider his *wuḍūʾ* valid is problematic [i.e. based on obligatory precaution, it must not be considered valid].

---

tayammum as he cannot perform *wuḍūʾ* except in a place that is usurped. In the second, his duty is to perform *wuḍūʾ* in a place that is not usurped as that is a viable option for him. In either scenario, if he does not act according to his duty and goes ahead and performs *wuḍūʾ* in the usurped place, he will have sinned. Nevertheless, the *wuḍūʾ* he performed there will be valid.

Ruling 272. If a person owns the *wuḍūʾ* water but the water is in a usurped utensil and no other water is available, then in case he can empty the water in a lawful manner into another utensil, it is necessary for him to do so and then perform *wuḍūʾ*; and in the event that this is not possible, he must perform *tayammum*. If he has some other water, it is necessary for him to perform *wuḍūʾ* with that other water. In both cases, if he acts contrary to the above and performs *wuḍūʾ* with water from a usurped utensil, his *wuḍūʾ* is valid.

Ruling 273. If a brick or stone of a pool, for example, is usurped, in the event that drawing water from the pool is not commonly regarded as using the brick or stone, there is no problem. However, in the event that it is regarded as using the brick or stone, then drawing water from the pool is unlawful but the *wuḍūʾ* is valid.

Ruling 274. If a pool or a stream is built in the courtyard of the shrine (*ḥaram*) of one of the Infallible Imams (ʿA) or one of the children of the Infallible Imams (ʿA), and that courtyard had previously been a graveyard, in the event that one does not know that the ground of the courtyard was a charitable endowment for the graveyard, there is no problem in performing *wuḍūʾ* with the water from that pool or stream.

The fourth condition: the parts of the body on which *wuḍūʾ* is performed must be pure at the time of washing and wiping, even if one purifies them during *wuḍūʾ* before he washes or wipes.[31] If the washing during *wuḍūʾ* is performed with *kurr* water or suchlike, then purifying an impure part before washing is not necessary [as it will become pure during the *wuḍūʾ*].

Ruling 275. If a place that has been washed or wiped becomes impure before the *wuḍūʾ* has been completely performed, the *wuḍūʾ* is valid.

Ruling 276. If a part of the body on which *wuḍūʾ* is not performed is impure, the *wuḍūʾ* is valid. However, if one has not purified the

[31] For example, if one's arm is impure and at the time of performing *wuḍūʾ* he pours water on it and purifies it, and if this is done before he wipes his arm down with his hand, then the fourth condition will have been fulfilled.

urinary outlet or the anus, the recommended precaution is that one should first purify it and then perform *wuḍūʾ*.

Ruling 277. If one of the parts of the body on which *wuḍūʾ* is performed is impure, and after performing *wuḍūʾ* one doubts whether or not he washed it with water before performing *wuḍūʾ*, the *wuḍūʾ* is valid. However, he must still wash the part that was impure with water.

Ruling 278. If there is a cut or a wound on one's face or arms, and blood from it does not stop, and water is not harmful to it, he must – having first washed that area in the correct order of *wuḍūʾ* – immerse the cut or wound in *kurr* or flowing water and then put pressure on it so that the blood stops; then, under the water, he must draw his finger along the cut or wound from top to bottom so that water flows over it and then wash the lower parts. If he does this, his *wuḍūʾ* is valid.

The fifth condition: there must be sufficient time for performing *wuḍūʾ* and prayers.

Ruling 279. If there is so little time [before the end of the prescribed time for prayers] that by performing *wuḍūʾ* the entire prayer or part of it would have to be performed after its time, then one must perform *tayammum*. However, if the time required for performing *tayammum* and *wuḍūʾ* is the same, then one must perform *wuḍūʾ*.

Ruling 280. If due to the shortage of time for prayers one's duty is to perform *tayammum*, but instead he performs *wuḍūʾ* with the intention of attaining proximity to Allah (*qaṣd al-qurbah*), or [he performs *wuḍūʾ*] for a recommended act like reciting the Qur'an, then the *wuḍūʾ* he performed is valid [despite the fact that his duty was to perform *tayammum*]. Similarly, the *wuḍūʾ* would still be valid if he performed it with the intention of performing that prayer unless he did so without the intention of attaining proximity to Allah the Exalted.

The sixth condition: one must perform *wuḍūʾ* with the intention of attaining proximity to Allah the Exalted, and it is sufficient to perform it with the intention of following the command of Allah the Exalted. If one performs *wuḍūʾ* to cool down or with some other intention, it is invalid.

Ruling 281. It is not necessary for one to actually utter the intention (*niyyah*) of performing *wuḍūʾ* or feel it in his heart; rather, it is sufficient if he performs all the acts of *wuḍūʾ* in compliance with the command of Allah the Exalted.

The seventh condition:* *wuḍūʾ* must be performed in the sequence (*tartīb*) mentioned earlier, i.e. first the face must be washed, then the right arm, and then the left arm; following that, the head must be wiped and then the feet. And based on obligatory precaution, one must wipe the left foot after the right foot.

The eighth condition: the acts of *wuḍūʾ* must be performed in close succession (*muwālāh*).

Ruling 282. If there is a gap in between the acts of *wuḍūʾ* to the extent that the acts of *wuḍūʾ* cannot be commonly regarded as being performed in close succession, the *wuḍūʾ* is invalid. However, this does not apply if a legitimate excuse (*ʿudhr*) arises; for example, one forgets that he is performing *wuḍūʾ*, or the water runs out. In fact, when one wants to wash or wipe a place, if the moisture on all the places he has already washed or wiped has dried up, the *wuḍūʾ* is invalid. If only the moisture on the place that comes before the area he wants to wash or wipe has dried up – for example, when he wants to wash his left arm, the moisture on his right arm has dried up but his face is still wet – then his *wuḍūʾ* is valid.

Ruling 283. If a person performs the acts of *wuḍūʾ* in close succession but the moisture on the previous places has dried up by means of hot weather or on account of excess body heat and suchlike, his *wuḍūʾ* is valid.

Ruling 284. There is no problem in walking while performing *wuḍūʾ*; therefore, if after washing the face and arms one walks a few steps and then wipes his head and feet, his *wuḍūʾ* is valid.

The ninth condition: washing the face and arms and wiping the head and feet must be performed by the person himself; if someone else performs *wuḍūʾ* on him or helps him in getting the water to his face and arms, or in wiping his head and feet, his *wuḍūʾ* is invalid.

Ruling 285. If a person cannot perform *wuḍūʾ* by himself, he must get assistance from someone else even if this results in the two of them washing and wiping jointly. In the event that the helper wants payment, the *mukallaf* must pay him, provided that he is able to do so and it does not harm him financially. However, in such a case, the *mukallaf* must himself make the intention of performing *wuḍūʾ* and wipe with his own hands. If the *mukallaf* cannot perform *wuḍūʾ* jointly with the helper, he must ask the helper to perform *wuḍūʾ* on him, in which case the obligatory precaution is that both of them must make the intention of performing *wuḍūʾ*. If it is possible, the helper must take the hand of the *mukallaf* and draw it over the place of wiping; but if that is not possible, the helper must take some moisture from the *mukallaf*'s hands and with that moisture wipe the *mukallaf*'s head and feet.

Ruling 286. One must not get assistance from someone else in performing those acts of *wuḍūʾ* that he can perform by himself.

The tenth condition: using the water must not be harmful for the person.

Ruling 287. If someone fears that by performing *wuḍūʾ* he will fall ill, or that if he uses water for performing *wuḍūʾ* he will remain thirsty, he does not have any obligation to perform *wuḍūʾ*. If one does not know that water is harmful for him and he performs *wuḍūʾ* and the water really was harmful for him, his *wuḍūʾ* is void.

Ruling 288. If a person would not be harmed by washing his face and arms with the minimum amount of water with which performing *wuḍūʾ* is valid but he would be harmed by using an amount more than that, he must perform *wuḍūʾ* with the minimum amount.

The eleventh condition: there must not be an obstruction for water to reach the parts of the body on which *wuḍūʾ* is performed.

Ruling 289. If a person knows that something is stuck to a part of the body on which *wuḍūʾ* is performed but he doubts whether or not it would prevent water from reaching that part, he must remove it or make the water go underneath it.

Ruling 290. There is no problem if there is dirt under one's nails. However, if the nails are clipped, in the event that the dirt is an obstruction for water to reach the skin, one must remove the dirt for the purposes of *wuḍū'*. Furthermore, if one's nails are unusually long, then dirt collected under the length that is longer than normal must be removed.

Ruling 291. If there is swelling on one's face, arms, front of head, or feet as a result of being burnt or due to some other reason, it is sufficient to wash and wipe over it; and in the event that the swelling is pierced, it is not necessary to make water go underneath the skin. If part of the skin has peeled, it is not necessary to make water go underneath the unpeeled part; however, in the event that the peeled skin is such that it sometimes sticks to the body and at other times it hangs loose, one must cut it off or make water go underneath it.

Ruling 292.* If a person doubts whether or not something is stuck to a part of the body on which *wuḍū'* is performed, in the event that his deeming this probable would be considered by people to be reasonable – for example, after plastering or painting one doubts whether or not plaster or paint is stuck to his hands – he must examine that part or rub his hands to the extent that it would normally give one confidence that it has been removed or water has gone underneath it.

Ruling 293. If a place on the body that must be washed or wiped is dirty but the dirt is not an obstruction to water reaching the body, there is no problem. Similarly, there is no problem if after plastering and suchlike, something white remains on one's hand that does not prevent water from reaching the skin. However, if one doubts whether or not its presence will prevent water from reaching that part of the body, he must remove it.

Ruling 294. If before performing *wuḍū'* one knows that on some parts of the body on which *wuḍū'* is performed there is an obstruction for water to reach those parts, and after *wuḍū'* he doubts whether at the time of performing *wuḍū'* he made water reach those parts, his *wuḍū'* is valid.

Ruling 295. If on some parts of the body on which *wuḍū'* is performed there is an obstruction under which water sometimes manages to go by itself and at other times does not, and if one doubts after performing *wuḍūʾ* whether water went under it or not, then in the event that he knows that while he was performing *wuḍūʾ* he was not aware of water going under it, the recommended precaution is that he should perform *wuḍūʾ* again.

Ruling 296. If after performing *wuḍūʾ* someone sees on a part of the body on which *wuḍūʾ* is performed something that is an obstruction to water reaching that part, and if he does not know whether it was present at the time of performing *wuḍūʾ* or it appeared afterwards, his *wuḍūʾ* is valid. However, if he knows that at the time of performing *wuḍūʾ* he was not aware of the obstruction, then the recommended precaution is that he should perform *wuḍūʾ* again.

Ruling 297. If a person doubts after performing *wuḍūʾ* whether or not there was something that was an obstruction to water reaching those parts of the body on which *wuḍūʾ* is performed, the *wuḍūʾ* is valid.

LAWS OF *WUḌŪʾ*

Ruling 298. Someone who frequently doubts about the acts of *wuḍūʾ* and its conditions – such as the water being pure and not being usurped – must not heed his doubts.

Ruling 299. If someone doubts whether his *wuḍūʾ* has become void or not, he must treat it as still being valid. However, if after urinating one does not perform *istibrāʾ* and performs *wuḍūʾ*, and after performing *wuḍūʾ* some fluid is discharged about which he does not know if it is urine or something else, his *wuḍūʾ* is void.

Ruling 300. If a person doubts whether he has performed *wuḍūʾ* or not, he must [deem that he has not and] perform *wuḍūʾ*.

Ruling 301. If someone knows he has performed *wuḍūʾ* and also knows that he has done something that invalidates *wuḍūʾ* – for example, he has urinated – but he does not know which one was first [i.e. he does not know whether he performed *wuḍūʾ* and then urinated, for example, or he urinated and then performed *wuḍūʾ*], then in the event that he has this doubt before prayers, he must perform *wuḍūʾ* for those prayers. If he has this doubt during prayers, he must break his prayer and perform *wuḍūʾ*. And if he has this doubt after prayers, the prayer he performed is valid but he must perform *wuḍūʾ* for subsequent prayers.

Ruling 302. If a person becomes certain after or while performing *wuḍūʾ* that he has not washed or wiped some necessary places, in the event that the moisture on the previous parts has dried up due to the passing of time, he must perform *wuḍūʾ* again. If the moisture has not dried up, or it has dried up on account of hot weather and suchlike, he must wash or wipe the part that he forgot and the parts that follow it. If during *wuḍūʾ* one doubts whether or not he has washed or wiped a place, he must follow the same instructions.

Ruling 303. If a person doubts after prayers whether he had performed *wuḍūʾ* or not, his prayers are valid but he must perform *wuḍūʾ* for subsequent prayers.

Ruling 304. If a person doubts during prayers whether or not he had performed *wuḍūʾ*, then based on obligatory precaution, he must perform *wuḍūʾ* and perform the prayer again.

Ruling 305. If a person realises after prayers that his *wuḍūʾ* has become void but doubts whether his *wuḍūʾ* became void before or after prayers, the prayers performed by him are valid.

Ruling 306. If a person suffers from an illness that causes urine to be discharged drop by drop [i.e. urinary incontinence], or if he cannot control faeces from being discharged [i.e. faecal incontinence], in the event that he is certain he will have some respite from a discharge between the beginning and the end of the prayer time such that he will be able to perform *wuḍūʾ* and the prayers during the period of respite, he must perform prayers at the time he has the respite. If the respite is long enough to perform only the obligatory acts of prayers, then at the time he has the respite, he must perform only those acts of the prayer that are obligatory and leave the recommended acts, such as the call to prayer (*adhān*), the call to stand up for prayer (*iqāmah*), and the supplication that is recited with the hands placed in front of the face (*qunūt*).

Ruling 307.* If a person finds respite [from the illness mentioned in the previous ruling] to perform *wuḍūʾ* and only part of the prayer, and during prayers some urine or faeces is discharged once or a few times, the obligatory precaution is that in the respite period he must perform *wuḍūʾ* and prayers. Furthermore, it is not necessary that he renew his *wuḍūʾ* on account of a discharge of urine or faeces during or after prayers; rather, one *wuḍūʾ* will suffice for several prayers unless he does something else that invalidates his *wuḍūʾ*, such as sleeping, or he discharges urine or faeces in a normal manner. However, it is better that he perform *wuḍūʾ* for the next prayer.

Ruling 308. If urine or faeces is discharged with such frequency that the person does not find a long enough respite to perform *wuḍūʾ* and part of the prayer, then one *wuḍūʾ* will be sufficient for several prayers unless he does something else that invalidates his *wuḍūʾ* – such as urinating or defecating in a normal manner, or sleeping – although it is better that he perform *wuḍūʾ* for every prayer. However, for a lapsed (*qaḍāʾ*) prostration (*sajdah*), a *qaḍāʾ tashahhud* (testifying), and the precautionary prayer (*ṣalāt al-iḥtiyāṭ*), performing another *wuḍūʾ* is not necessary.

Ruling 309. If urine or faeces are discharged continuously, it is not necessary for the person to perform prayers immediately after performing *wuḍūʾ*, although it is better that he make haste to perform the prayers.

Ruling 310. If urine or faeces are discharged continuously, it is permitted for the person – after he has performed *wuḍūʾ* – to touch the writing of the Qur'an even if he is not in the state of performing prayers.

Ruling 311. Someone whose urine is discharged drop by drop must use a bag in which there is some cotton or something else that prevents the urine from splashing onto other areas; and the obligatory precaution is that before every prayer, he must wash with water the urinary outlet that has become impure. If someone cannot control the discharge of faeces, he must prevent the faeces from spreading onto other areas during prayers if it is possible for him to do so; and the obligatory precaution is that if it is not excessively difficult, he must wash the anus with water before every prayer.

Ruling 312. If someone cannot control the discharge of urine or faeces, he must prevent their discharge during prayers if it is possible for him to do so; and it is better that he prevents it even if he incurs an expense in doing so. If his illness can be treated easily, it is better that he is treated.

Ruling 313. If someone cannot control the discharge of urine or faeces, then after recovering from his illness, it is not necessary for him to repeat the prayers he performed in accordance with his religious duty while he was ill. However, if he recovers from his illness during the time of prayers, then based on obligatory precaution, he must repeat the prayer he performed at that time.

Ruling 314. If someone suffers from an illness that does not allow him to stop passing wind [i.e. excessive flatulence], he must act in accordance with the duty of those who cannot control the discharge of urine and faeces.

THINGS FOR WHICH ONE MUST PERFORM *WUḌŪʾ*

Ruling 315. It is obligatory to perform *wuḍūʾ* for six things:

1. for obligatory prayers – except the funeral prayer (*ṣalāt al-mayyit*) – and for recommended prayers;
2. for a *sajdah* and *tashahhud* that have been forgotten if between them and the prayer one has done something that invalidates *wuḍūʾ*; for example, he has urinated. It is not obligatory, however, to perform *wuḍūʾ* for the two prostrations for inadvertence (*sajdatā al-sahw*);
3. for the obligatory circumambulation (*ṭawāf*) of the Kaʿbah that is part of hajj or *ʿumrah*;[32]
4. if one had made a vow (*nadhr*) or a covenant (*ʿahd*) or had taken an oath (*qasam*) that he would perform *wuḍūʾ*;

[32] *ʿUmrah* refers to the pilgrimage to Mecca that has fewer rituals than the hajj pilgrimage. It is sometimes referred to as the 'minor pilgrimage'.

5. if one had made a vow that, for example, he would kiss the writing of the Qur'an;
6. for washing a copy of the Qur'an that has become impure or for taking it out from a lavatory and such places, in the event that he is obliged to touch the writing of the Qur'an with his hand or with some other part of his body. However, in the event that the delay that would be caused by performing *wuḍūʾ* would result in further disrespect to the Qur'an, one must take the Qur'an out from the lavatory and such places – or wash it if it has become impure – without performing *wuḍūʾ*.

Ruling 316. Touching the writing of the Qur'an – i.e. making a part of the body come into contact with the writing of the Qur'an – for someone who does not have *wuḍūʾ* is unlawful. However, if the Qur'an is translated into another language, then touching the translation is not a problem.

Ruling 317. It is not obligatory to prevent a child or an insane person from touching the writing of Qur'an. However, if their touching the Qur'an is deemed to be disrespectful to it, then one must prevent them from touching it.

Ruling 318. Based on obligatory precaution, it is unlawful for someone who does not have *wuḍūʾ* to touch the name of Allah the Exalted or His special attributes in whatever language they happen to be written. Furthermore, it is better also to avoid touching the blessed names of the Most Noble Prophet (Ṣ), the Infallible Imams (ʿA), and Her Eminence [Fāṭimah] al-Zahrāʾ (ʿA) without *wuḍūʾ*.

Ruling 319. At whatever time a person performs *wuḍūʾ* with the intention of attaining proximity to Allah, it is valid; and it does not matter whether he performs it shortly before the time for prayers, or well in advance of it, or after it has set in. Furthermore, it is not necessary for one to make the intention of performing an obligatory or recommended *wuḍūʾ*. In fact, even if one mistakenly makes the intention of performing an obligatory *wuḍūʾ* and afterwards realises that it was not obligatory, his *wuḍūʾ* is valid.

Ruling 320. If someone is certain that the time for prayers has set in and makes the intention of performing an obligatory *wuḍūʾ*, and after performing *wuḍūʾ* he realises that the time has not set in yet, the *wuḍūʾ* is valid.

Ruling 321. It is recommended for someone who has *wuḍūʾ* to perform *wuḍūʾ* again for every prayer. According to some jurists, it is recommended that one should perform *wuḍūʾ* for *ṣalāt al-mayyit*, visiting graves, going to a mosque and the shrines of the Infallible Imams (ʿA), carrying the Qur'an, reading and writing it, touching its margins, and before sleeping. However, *wuḍūʾ* being recommended in these cases is not established. Of course, if one performs *wuḍūʾ* on the basis that it being recommended is probable, his *wuḍūʾ* is valid and he can perform any act that requires *wuḍūʾ* with that *wuḍūʾ*; for example, he can perform prayers with that *wuḍūʾ*.

THINGS THAT INVALIDATE *WUḌŪʾ*

Ruling 322. Seven things invalidate *wuḍūʾ*:

1. urinating; and apparently included in the ruling of urinating is the similar moisture that comes out after urinating and before performing *istibrāʾ*;
2. defecating;
3. passing wind of the stomach and the intestine from the anus;
4. sleeping, which means that simultaneously one's eyes do not see and one's ears do not hear; however, if one's eyes do not see but his ears hear, his *wuḍūʾ* does not become invalid;
5. things that cause one to lose his mind, such as insanity, intoxication, and unconsciousness;
6. *istiḥāḍah* of a woman, which will be discussed later;
7. *janābah*; and based on recommended precaution, all things for which one must perform *ghusl*.

LAWS OF *JABĪRAH WUḌŪʾ*

'*Jabīrah*' refers to the thing with which a wound or a break in a bone is bandaged, and to medication applied to a wound and suchlike.

Ruling 323. If on one of the parts of the body on which *wuḍūʾ* is performed there is a wound, boil, or broken bone, in the event that it is uncovered and water is not harmful for the person, he must perform *wuḍūʾ* in the normal manner.

Ruling 324. If a wound, boil, or broken bone is on one's face or arms, and it is uncovered, and pouring water over it is harmful, then the area around the wound or boil must be washed from top to bottom in the manner that was explained regarding *wuḍūʾ*. If drawing a wet hand over it is not harmful, it is better that one draw a wet hand over it, place a pure cloth over it, and then draw a wet hand over the cloth as well. As for the case of a broken bone, it is necessary to perform *tayammum* [instead of *jabīrah wuḍūʾ*].

Ruling 325. If a wound, boil, or broken bone is on the front part of the head or on the feet, and it is uncovered, then in the event that one is unable to wipe it – meaning that the wound, for example, covers the entire area that is to be wiped, or for some reason he is unable to wipe even the unaffected areas – in such a case, it is necessary for him to perform *tayammum*. And based on recommended precaution, he should also perform *wuḍūʾ* and place a pure cloth over it and wipe over the cloth with the wetness of the *wuḍūʾ* water left on his hand.

Ruling 326. If a boil, wound, or broken bone is covered, and uncovering it is possible without causing excessive difficulty, and water is not harmful for the person, then he must uncover it and perform *wuḍūʾ*, irrespective of whether the wound and suchlike is on the face, arms, the front part of the head, or the feet.

Ruling 327. If a wound, boil, or broken bone that is covered is on the face or arms, in the event that it is harmful to uncover and pour water over it, one must wash as much of the area around it as possible. And based on obligatory precaution, one must also wipe over the *jabīrah*.

Ruling 328. If it is not possible to uncover a wound but the wound and the thing that has been placed over it are pure, and if making water reach the wound is possible and not harmful, then one must make water go over the wound from top to bottom. If the wound or the thing that has been placed over it is impure, in the event that it is possible to wash that thing with water and make the water go over the wound, one must wash it with water and at the time of performing *wuḍū'* he must make the water reach the wound. In the event that water is not harmful for the person but washing it with water is not possible, or if uncovering the wound causes excessive difficulty or is harmful for him, he must perform *tayammum*.

Ruling 329. If the *jabīrah* completely covers one of the parts of the body on which *wuḍū'* is performed, then performing *jabīrah wuḍū'* is sufficient. However, if the *jabīrah* covers all or most of the parts of the body on which *wuḍū'* is performed, then based on obligatory precaution, one must perform *tayammum* and *jabīrah wuḍū'*.

Ruling 330. It is not necessary for the *jabīrah* to be made of something that one is permitted to wear when performing prayers. Therefore, if the *jabīrah* is made of silk or pure parts of an animal whose meat is unlawful to eat, it is permitted to wipe over it.

Ruling 331. If someone has a *jabīrah* on the palm of his hand or on his fingers, and at the time of performing *wuḍū'* he draws his wet hand over it, he must wipe his head and feet with the same moisture [that has gathered on the *jabīrah*].

Ruling 332. If the *jabīrah* covers the entire surface of the top of the foot except for an area over the toes and at the top of the foot, one must wipe the places that are uncovered and over the *jabīrah* that is covering the other parts.

Ruling 333. If there are several *jabīrah*s on one's face or arms, he must wash between them; and if the *jabīrah*s are on the head or the feet, he must wipe between them. As for those places covered by the *jabīrah*, he must act according to the rules of *jabīrah*.

Ruling 334. If the *jabīrah* has covered more than the normal area around the wound and it is not possible to remove it without causing excessive difficulty, one must perform *tayammum* unless the *jabīrah* is on a place of the body that *tayammum* is performed on, in which case based on obligatory precaution, it is necessary to perform both *wuḍū'* and *tayammum*. In both cases, if it is possible to remove the *jabīrah* without causing excessive difficulty, the *jabīrah* must be removed. Therefore, if the wound is on the face or arms, the area around it must be washed; and if it is on the head or top of the feet, the area around that must be wiped; and for the place of the wound, one must act according to the rules of *jabīrah*.

Ruling 335. If there is no wound, cut, or broken bone on a part of the body on which *wuḍūʾ* is performed but water is harmful for the person for some other reason, he must perform *tayammum*.

Ruling 336.* If phlebotomy[33] has been performed on one of the parts of the body on which *wuḍūʾ* is performed and water is not harmful for it but the person is unable to wash it because the blood does not congeal and suchlike, then it is necessary for him to perform *tayammum*. However, if one can wash it with water but water is harmful for it, then he must act according to the rules of *jabīrah*.

Ruling 337. If something is stuck on a part of one's body on which *wuḍūʾ* or *ghusl* is performed and it is not possible to remove it, or the difficulty involved in removing it is such that it cannot be endured, then the person's responsibility is to perform *tayammum*. However, if the thing that is stuck is on a part of the body on which *tayammum* is performed, it is necessary to perform both *wuḍūʾ* and *tayammum*. Furthermore, if the thing that is stuck is some form of treatment, it is ruled to be *jabīrah*.

Ruling 338.* For all *ghusls* – apart from the *ghusl* given to a corpse – *jabīrah ghusl* is performed like *jabīrah wuḍūʾ*; however, based on obligatory precaution, one must perform it in sequence. If there is a wound or boil on the body, one has the choice of performing *ghusl* or *tayammum*; and in the event that one chooses to perform *ghusl* and the wound is not covered, the recommended precaution is that he should place a pure cloth over the wound or the uncovered boil and wipe over the cloth. However, if there is a broken bone in the body, one must perform *ghusl*, and as a precautionary measure, he must also wipe over the *jabīrah*; and in the event that it is not possible to

[33] Phlebotomy is the practise of bloodletting, i.e. a treatment in which a vein is cut to release blood.

wipe over the *jabīrah* or the place of the broken bone is uncovered, it is necessary to perform *tayammum*. Therefore, if the place of the broken bone is uncovered, he must perform *tayammum*, and if it is covered, he must perform *ghusl* and wipe over the *jabīrah*. If wiping over the *jabīrah* is not possible, then in the event that the *jabīrah* is not on a part of the body on which *tayammum* is performed, he must perform *tayammum*. If the *jabīrah* is on a part of the body on which *tayammum* is performed, then based on obligatory precaution, he must perform both *ghusl* (without wiping over the injured area) and *tayammum*.

Ruling 339. If someone's responsibility is to perform *tayammum* but on some of the parts of his body on which *tayammum* is performed he has a wound, boil, or broken bone, he must perform *jabīrah tayammum* in accordance with the rules of *jabīrah wuḍūʾ*.

Ruling 340. If someone must perform prayers with *jabīrah wuḍūʾ* or *ghusl*, in the event that he knows his legitimate excuse for not performing normal *wuḍūʾ* or *ghusl* will remain valid until the end of the time for prayers, he can perform prayers at the beginning of their time. However, if he has hope that his legitimate excuse will expire before the end of the time for prayers, it is better that he wait; and in the event that his legitimate excuse remains valid, he must perform prayers with *jabīrah wuḍūʾ* or *ghusl* at the end of the time for prayers. If he performed prayers at the beginning of their time and his legitimate excuse expired by the end of the time for prayers, the recommended precaution is that he should perform *wuḍūʾ* or *ghusl* and repeat the prayers.

Ruling 341.* If there is a dressing over one's eye and the illness is in his eye, he must perform *tayammum*.

Ruling 342.* If someone does not know whether his duty is to perform *tayammum* or *jabīrah wuḍūʾ*, he must perform both of them.

Ruling 343.* The prayers that one performs with *jabīrah wuḍūʾ* are valid, and he can perform subsequent prayers with that *wuḍūʾ* as well. However, if his duty was to perform both *jabīrah wuḍūʾ* and *tayammum*, then after his legitimate excuse has expired, he must perform *wuḍūʾ* for subsequent prayers.

OBLIGATORY (*WĀJIB*) RITUAL BATHING (*GHUSL*)

There are seven obligatory *ghusls*:

1. the *ghusl* for ritual impurity (*janābah*);
2. the *ghusl* for menstruation (*ḥayḍ*);
3. the *ghusl* for lochia[34] (*nifās*);
4. the *ghusl* for irregular blood discharge (*istiḥāḍah*);
5. the *ghusl* for touching a corpse (*mass al-mayyit*);
6. the *ghusl* given to a corpse (*mayyit*);
7. a *ghusl* that becomes obligatory on account of a vow (*nadhr*), oath (*qasam*), or suchlike.

If there is a total solar eclipse or a total lunar eclipse and a *mukallaf* intentionally (*ʿamdan*) does not perform the prayer of signs (*ṣalāt al-āyāt*) in its prescribed time, then based on obligatory precaution, he must perform *ghusl* before he makes it up [i.e. when he performs *ṣalāt al-āyāt* belatedly (*qaḍāʾ*), he cannot do so with *wuḍūʾ*; rather, he must perform *ghusl* first and then perform the prayer with that *ghusl*].

LAWS OF RITUAL IMPURITY (*JANĀBAH*)

Ruling 344. A person becomes *junub*[35] in two ways:

1. sexual intercourse;
2. ejaculation of semen, whether he is asleep or awake, and whether it is a little or a lot, with or without lust, voluntarily or involuntarily.

Ruling 345. If some fluid comes out of the penis and the man does not know whether it is semen, urine, or something else – in the event that it comes out with three characteristics: it is accompanied by lust, it comes out with a gush, and one's body feels weak after it has come out – then that fluid is ruled to be semen; and if none of these three characteristics is present or if even one of them is not, it is not ruled

[34] Lochia refers to blood discharge after childbirth.

[35] *Junub* is the term used to refer to a person who is in the state of *janābah*.

to be semen. However, in the case of a sick person, it is not necessary that the fluid comes out with a gush or that at the time of coming out his body feels weak; rather, if the only characteristic present is that it comes out with lust, it is ruled to be semen.

As for the fluid that is discharged from the vagina when a woman engages in foreplay or imagines lustful thoughts and which is not enough to dirty other places [such as her clothing], it is pure and does not require *ghusl* to be performed, nor does it invalidate *wuḍū'*. However, if the discharged fluid is a lot – to the extent that it can be called an 'ejaculation' and it dirties clothing – then in case it is discharged when the woman reaches sexual climax and complete sexual satisfaction (orgasm), it is impure and causes *janābah*. In fact, even if it is not discharged at that moment, based on obligatory precaution, it is impure and causes *janābah*. Whenever a woman doubts whether or not a discharge of fluid was to this extent, or she doubts whether or not fluid was discharged at all, performing *ghusl* is not obligatory for her nor does it invalidate *wuḍū'* and *ghusl*.

Ruling 346. If some fluid is discharged by a man who is not sick and that fluid has one of the three characteristics mentioned in the previous ruling, but the man does not know whether it had any of the other characteristics, he is not considered *junub* and performing *ghusl* is not obligatory for him.

Ruling 347. It is recommended that one urinate after ejaculation; if he does not urinate, and after performing *ghusl* some fluid comes out about which he does not know whether it is semen or some other fluid, it is ruled to be semen.

Ruling 348. If a person has sexual intercourse with a woman and penetration occurs up to or more than the circumcised part of the penis – irrespective of whether the penetration was in the vagina or the anus, and whether the man had reached the age of legal responsibility (*bulūgh*) or not – then, even if semen is not ejaculated, both the man and the woman become *junub*.

Ruling 349. If a person doubts whether or not penetration has occurred up to the circumcised part of the penis, *ghusl* is not obligatory for him.

Ruling 350. If, God forbid, a man has sexual intercourse with an animal and the man ejaculates, *ghusl* is sufficient. If he does not ejaculate and he had *wuḍūʾ* before penetration, again *ghusl* is sufficient; but if he did not have *wuḍūʾ*, the obligatory precaution is that he must perform *ghusl* and *wuḍūʾ*. The ruling is the same in the case of a man having sexual intercourse with another man or with a boy [God forbid].

Ruling 351. If a person feels the movement of semen but does not ejaculate, or if one doubts whether semen has been ejaculated or not, *ghusl* is not obligatory for him.

Ruling 352. If someone cannot perform *ghusl* but can perform *tayammum*, he can still have sexual intercourse with his wife even after the time for prayers has set in.

Ruling 353. If a person sees semen on his clothes and knows that it has come from himself and he has not performed *ghusl*, he must perform *ghusl* and make up [i.e. perform as *qaḍāʾ*] those prayers that he is certain of having performed while he was *junub*. However, it is not necessary for him to make up those prayers that he deems only probable of having performed before ejaculation of the semen.

THINGS THAT ARE UNLAWFUL (*ḤARĀM*) FOR A *JUNUB*

Ruling 354. Five things are unlawful for a *junub*:

1. touching the writing of the Qur'an or the name of Allah the Exalted with any part of the body as per the details that were mentioned in the section on *wuḍūʾ*;[36]
2. entering Masjid al-Ḥarām and the Mosque of the Prophet (Ṣ), even to the extent of entering from one door and exiting from another;
3. staying in other mosques; and similarly, based on obligatory

[36] See Ruling 318.

precaution, staying in the shrines of the Infallible Imams (ʿA). However, there is no problem if a *junub* passes through a mosque; for example, by entering from one door and exiting from another;

4. entering a mosque to take something from it; and similarly, based on obligatory precaution, placing something in it even if he does not enter the mosque himself [but places something in it from outside];
5. reciting any of the verses for which *sajdah* is obligatory. These verses are found in four chapters (surahs) of the Qur'an:
   a. Sūrat al-Sajdah (Chapter 32), verse 15;
   b. Sūrat Fuṣṣilat (Chapter 41), verse 37;
   c. Sūrat al-Najm (Chapter 53), verse 62;
   d. Sūrat al-ʿAlaq (Chapter 96), verse 19.

THINGS THAT ARE DISAPPROVED (*MAKRŪH*) FOR A *JUNUB*

Ruling 355. Nine things are disapproved for a *junub*:

1.–2. eating and drinking; however, if one washes his face and hands and rinses his mouth, then eating and drinking are not disapproved; and if one only washes his hands, then the disapproval is lessened;

3.* reciting more than seven verses of the Qur'an that do not contain an obligatory *sajdah*; this is the opinion held by most jurists (*mashhūr*);

4. touching the cover, margins, or spaces between the writing of the Qur'an with any part of the body;
5. keeping the Qur'an with oneself;
6. sleeping; however, if one performs *wuḍūʾ*, or on account of not having water one performs *tayammum* in place of *ghusl*, it is not disapproved;
7. dyeing hair with henna or something similar;
8. rubbing oil on the body;
9. having sexual intercourse after having a wet dream, i.e. after semen has been ejaculated in one's sleep.

THE *GHUSL* FOR *JANĀBAH*

Ruling 356. The *ghusl* for *janābah* is obligatory for obligatory prayers and suchlike, but it is not necessary for *ṣalāt al-mayyit*, *sajdatā al-sahw*, the prostration for offering thanks (*sajdat al-shukr*), and for the obligatory prostrations of the Qur'an.

Ruling 357. It is not necessary that at the time of performing *ghusl* one make the intention of performing an obligatory *ghusl*; rather, it is sufficient if one performs *ghusl* with only the intention of *qurbah*, i.e. in humility to the Lord of the worlds.

Ruling 358. If a person is certain that the time for prayers has set in and he makes the intention of performing an obligatory *ghusl*, and afterwards he realises that actually he performed *ghusl* before the time for prayers had set in, his *ghusl* is valid.

Ruling 359. Two types of *ghusls* for *janābah* can be performed: sequential (*tartībī*) and immersive (*irtimāsī*).

SEQUENTIAL RITUAL BATHING (*AL-GHUSL AL-TARTĪBĪ*)

Ruling 360. In sequential *ghusl*, one must – based on obligatory precaution – first wash with the intention of *ghusl* the entire head and neck and then the entire body with the intention of *ghusl*; and it is better to first wash the right side of the body, then the left. In the event that one intentionally or due to being negligent in learning the laws of *ghusl* does not wash the entire head and neck before washing the body, then based on obligatory precaution, his *ghusl* is invalid. Furthermore, based on obligatory precaution, when performing *ghusl*, it is not sufficient to make the intention of *ghusl* when moving the head, neck, or body while they are already under the flow of water; rather, the part that one wants to perform *ghusl* on – in the event that it is already under the flow of water – must be taken out from under the flow of water and then washed with the intention of *ghusl*.

Ruling 361. In case one washes his body before his head and neck, it is not necessary for him to repeat the *ghusl*; rather, in the event that one rewashes his body, his *ghusl* will be valid.

Ruling 362. In case a person is not certain that he has completely washed both parts – i.e. his head and neck, and his body – for him to be certain that he has washed both parts, when he washes one part, he must wash an area of the other part as well.

Ruling 363. If after performing *ghusl* one realises that he has not washed an area of his body but he does not know which area it is, it is not necessary for him to rewash his head and neck; rather, he must only wash that area of his body that he deems probable he had not washed.

Ruling 364. If after performing *ghusl* one realises that he has not washed an area of his body, in the event that the unwashed area happens to be on the left side of his body, it is sufficient for him to wash only the unwashed area. If the unwashed area happens to be on the right side of one's body, the recommended precaution is that after washing the unwashed area, he should rewash the entire left side. Furthermore, if the unwashed area happens to be on one's head and neck, then based on obligatory precaution, he must rewash his body after he has washed the unwashed area.

Ruling 365. If before completing *ghusl* one doubts whether or not he has washed a particular area on the left or right side of his body, it is necessary that he wash that area. If a person doubts whether or not he has washed an area that is on his head or neck, then based on obligatory precaution, after he has washed that area, he must rewash his body.

IMMERSIVE RITUAL BATHING (*AL-GHUSL AL-IRTIMĀSĪ*)

Two types of immersive *ghusl* can be performed: instantaneous (*dafʿī*) and gradual (*tadrījī*).

Ruling 366. In instantaneous immersive *ghusl*, water must cover the entire body in one go. However, it is not necessary for the entire body to be out of the water before starting the *ghusl*; rather, it is sufficient if part of the body is out of the water and the person goes under the water completely with the intention of performing *ghusl*.[37]

Ruling 367. In gradual immersive *ghusl*, one must gradually – but in a way that can be commonly considered one single action – immerse his body in water with the intention of *ghusl*. In this type of *ghusl*, it is necessary for each part of the body to be out of the water before it is washed.[38]

Ruling 368. If after performing immersive *ghusl*, one realises that water has not reached all the parts of his body, he must perform *ghusl* again, irrespective of whether or not he knows which parts of his body the water did not reach.

Ruling 369. If someone does not have time for performing sequential *ghusl* but has time for performing immersive *ghusl*, he must perform immersive *ghusl*.

Ruling 370. A person in the state of *iḥrām*[39] for hajj or *ʿumrah* must not perform immersive *ghusl*. However, if he forgetfully performs immersive *ghusl*, his *ghusl* is valid.

LAWS OF PERFORMING *GHUSL*

Ruling 371. In immersive and sequential *ghusl*, it is not necessary

[37] An example of instantaneous immersive *ghusl* is when a person, with the intention of performing *ghusl*, dives/jumps into a swimming pool and in doing so completely immerses himself in the water; or, when a person who is already partially immersed in the water completely immerses himself with the intention of *ghusl*.
[38] An example of gradual immersive *ghusl* is when a person, with the intention of performing *ghusl*, immerses part of his body into a bathtub of water and then takes that part out of the water; he then immerses another part of his body and takes it out, and so on until all the parts of his body have been immersed.
[39] *Iḥrām* here refers to the state of ritual consecration of pilgrims during hajj and *ʿumrah*.

for the entire body to be pure before performing *ghusl*; rather, if the body becomes pure by immersing the body in water or by pouring water with the intention of *ghusl*, then *ghusl* will have taken place on condition that the water used to perform *ghusl* remains pure; for example, one performs *ghusl* with *kurr* water.[40]

Ruling 372. If someone who has become *junub* by unlawful means performs *ghusl* with hot water, his *ghusl* is valid even if he sweats [during the *ghusl*].

Ruling 373. If in *ghusl* any part of the outer area of the body is left unwashed, the *ghusl* is invalid. However, washing inside the ears, nose, and whatever is considered an inner part of the body is not obligatory.

Ruling 374. If a person doubts whether a part of the body is considered an outer or inner part, he must wash it.

Ruling 375. If earring holes and suchlike have become so stretched that their inner areas are considered outer parts of the body, then those areas must be washed; otherwise, it is not necessary to wash them.

Ruling 376. Anything that is an obstacle for water to reach the body must be removed; if one performs *ghusl* before becoming confident that the obstacle has been removed, the *ghusl* is invalid.

Ruling 377. While performing *ghusl*, if one rationally deems it probable that there is something on his body that may be an obstacle for water to reach the body, he must examine it and become confident that it is not an obstacle.

Ruling 378. In *ghusl*, short hair that is considered part of the body must be washed. It is not obligatory to wash long hair. In fact, if one makes water reach the skin in a way that the hair does not become wet, the *ghusl* is valid. However, if it is not possible for water to reach

[40] As mentioned in Ruling 15, as long as *kurr* water does not acquire the smell, colour, or taste of an impurity with which it has come into contact, it does not become impure.

the skin without the hair becoming wet, then one must wash the hair in a way that water reaches the body.

Ruling 379. All the conditions mentioned for *wuḍūʾ* to be valid – such as the water being pure and not being usurped – are also conditions for *ghusl* to be valid. However, in *ghusl*, it is not necessary for the body to be washed from top to bottom. Furthermore, in sequential *ghusl*, it is not necessary for the body to be washed immediately after washing the head and neck; therefore, there is no problem if after one has washed his head and neck he waits and after some time he washes his body. In fact, it is not necessary for the entire head and neck to be washed in one go; therefore, it is permitted, for example, for one to wash his head and after a while to wash his neck. Furthermore, if someone who cannot control the discharge of urine or faeces does not discharge urine or faeces for the length of time it takes him to perform *ghusl* and prayers, he must immediately perform *ghusl* then immediately perform prayers.

Ruling 380. If someone wants to pay on credit for using a public bath without knowing whether or not the owner consents [to this form of payment, but still performs *ghusl* there], then even if afterwards the owner accepts, his *ghusl* is void.

Ruling 381. If the owner of a public bath consents for the money owed to him for using the public bath to be paid on credit, but the person who performs *ghusl* does not intend to pay the debt he owes him, or he intends to pay him from unlawful money, his *ghusl* is void.

Ruling 382. If someone pays the owner of a public bath from money on which the one-fifth tax (*khums*) has not been paid, then although he has committed an unlawful act, the apparent ruling is that his *ghusl* is valid but he remains indebted to those entitled (*mustaḥiqqūn*) to receive *khums*.

Ruling 383.* Someone who doubts whether or not he has performed *ghusl* must perform it. However, if after performing *ghusl*, when the *ghusl* would commonly be considered finished, one doubts whether or not part of his head and neck or body has been washed, then in case he habitually performs the acts of *ghusl* in close succession and knows that he has washed most parts of his body, he must not heed his doubt.

Ruling 384. If while one is performing *ghusl* he has a minor occurrence (*al-ḥadath al-aṣghar*)[41] – for example, he urinates – it is not necessary for him to stop performing the *ghusl* and start another *ghusl* [all over again]; rather, he can complete his *ghusl* but based on obligatory precaution, he will require *wuḍūʾ* [for performing acts that require *wuḍūʾ*]. However, if [one has a minor occurrence while performing a sequential *ghusl* and] he changes from performing a sequential *ghusl* to an immersive one, or [if one has a minor occurrence while performing an immersive *ghusl* and he changes from performing] an immersive *ghusl* to a sequential one, then it is not necessary for him also to perform *wuḍūʾ*.

Ruling 385. If due to shortage of time one's duty was to perform *tayammum* but thinking that he had enough time to perform both *ghusl* and the prayer, he performed *ghusl* instead and his prayers became *qaḍāʾ* [i.e. they were not performed in their prescribed time], then in case he had performed *ghusl* with the intention of attaining proximity to Allah, his *ghusl* is valid even if he had performed the *ghusl* to perform prayers.

Ruling 386. If after performing prayers a person who had become *junub* doubts whether he had performed *ghusl* or not, the prayers he performed are valid; however, for future prayers he must perform *ghusl*. If after prayers he has a minor occurrence, it is necessary for him also to perform *wuḍūʾ*; and if there is time, he must, based on

[41] *Ḥadath* (literally, 'occurrence') is a term used in Islamic law to refer to something that invalidates *wuḍūʾ*; it can be of two types: *al-ḥadath al-aṣghar* (minor occurrence) and *al-ḥadath al-akbar* (major occurrence). A minor occurrence is something that requires one to perform *wuḍūʾ* in order to engage in an act of worship that requires *wuḍūʾ*, such as prayers. These things are: urinating, defecating, passing wind, sleeping, things that cause one to lose his mind (such as insanity, intoxication, and unconsciousness), and slight irregular blood discharge (*al-istiḥāḍah al-qalīlah*). As for a major occurrence, this is something that requires one to perform *ghusl* in order to perform an act of worship that requires *wuḍūʾ*; under this category come the following: ritual impurity (*janābah*), menstruation (*ḥayḍ*), lochia (*nifās*), medium and excessive irregular blood discharge (*al-istiḥāḍah al-mutawassiṭah* and *al-kathīrah*), and touching a corpse (*mass al-mayyit*).

obligatory precaution, repeat the prayers he had performed.

Ruling 387. Someone who must perform a number of obligatory *ghusl*s can perform one *ghusl* with the intention of all of them. Similarly, if he makes the intention of one of the *ghusl*s, it is sufficient for the others [and he does not have to make separate intentions].

Ruling 388. If a verse of the Qur'an or a name of Allah the Exalted is written on part of one's body, in the event that he wants to perform *ghusl* in its sequential form, he must make water reach the area in a way that his hand does not touch the writing. The same applies if he wants to perform *wuḍūʾ* and a verse of the Qur'an is written on one of the parts of his body on which *wuḍūʾ* is performed; and [in case he wants to perform *wuḍūʾ*] and a name of Allah is written, the same applies, albeit based on obligatory precaution.

Ruling 389. Someone who has performed the *ghusl* for *janābah* must not perform *wuḍūʾ* for prayers. He can perform prayers without performing *wuḍūʾ* after other obligatory *ghusl*s as well, except the *ghusl* for medium *istiḥāḍah*. Furthermore, [he can perform prayers without performing *wuḍūʾ*] with recommended *ghusl*s – which will be discussed in Ruling 633 – although the recommended precaution is that [if he has performed a recommended *ghusl*], he should also perform *wuḍūʾ*.

IRREGULAR BLOOD DISCHARGE (*ISTIḤĀḌAH*)

One of the types of blood that women discharge is the blood of *istiḥāḍah*. A woman at the time of experiencing *istiḥāḍah* is called a '*mustaḥāḍah*'.

Ruling 390. Most of the time, the blood of *istiḥāḍah* is yellow in colour, cold, comes out without pressure or a burning sensation, and is not thick. However, it is possible, sometimes, for it to be black or red, warm, thick, and to come out with pressure and a burning sensation.

Ruling 391. There are three types of *istiḥāḍah*: slight (*qalīlah*), medium (*mutawassiṭah*), and excessive (*kathīrah*).

Slight *istiḥāḍah* is when the blood only stains a piece of cotton [or the top layer of a sanitary pad/another absorbent item] and does not seep into it.

Medium *istiḥāḍah* is when the blood seeps into a piece of cotton [or top layer of a sanitary pad/another absorbent item] that a woman would normally use to absorb the discharge of blood – albeit into only one side of it – but it does not reach the bottom of it.

Excessive *istiḥāḍah* is when the blood soaks a piece of cotton [or sanitary pad/another absorbent item] and reaches the bottom of it.

LAWS OF *ISTIḤĀḌAH*

Ruling 392. For slight *istiḥāḍah*, a woman must perform one *wuḍūʾ* for every prayer and she must wash the outside of the vagina with water if there is blood there. And based on recommended precaution, she should purify the piece of cotton [or sanitary pad/another absorbent item] with water or change it for every prayer.

Ruling 393.* For medium *istiḥāḍah*, a woman must, based on obligatory precaution, perform one *ghusl* daily for her prayers, and she must do the things that were mentioned in the previous ruling with regard to slight *istiḥāḍah*. Therefore, if she experiences medium *istiḥāḍah* before or during morning (*ṣubḥ*) prayers, she must perform *ghusl* for *ṣubḥ* prayers based on obligatory precaution. If she intentionally or forgetfully does not perform *ghusl* for *ṣubḥ* prayers, she must perform *ghusl* for midday (*ẓuhr*) and afternoon (*ʿaṣr*) prayers. And if she does not perform *ghusl* for *ẓuhr* and *ʿaṣr* prayers, she must perform *ghusl* before prayers after sunset (*maghrib*) and evening (*ʿishāʾ*) prayers, whether the bleeding has stopped or not.

Ruling 394.* For excessive *istiḥāḍah*, a woman must, based on obligatory precaution, change or purify with water the piece of cotton [or sanitary pad/another absorbent item]. It is also necessary for her to perform one *ghusl* for *ṣubḥ* prayers, one for *ẓuhr* and *ʿaṣr* prayers, and one for *maghrib* and *ʿishāʾ* prayers. Furthermore, she must not delay between *ẓuhr* and *ʿaṣr* prayers nor between *maghrib* and *ʿishāʾ* prayers; if she delays between them, she must perform *ghusl* again for *ʿaṣr* and *ʿishāʾ* prayers.

All of this applies when blood continuously soaks the piece of cotton [or sanitary pad/another absorbent item] and reaches the bottom of it. However, in the event that there is a delay in the blood soaking the piece of cotton [or sanitary pad/another absorbent item] and reaching the bottom of it to the extent that the woman can perform one or more prayers in that time, the obligatory precaution is that whenever the blood soaks the piece of cotton [or sanitary pad/another absorbent item] and reaches the bottom of it, she must change or purify it with water and perform *ghusl*. Therefore, if a woman performs *ghusl* and, for example, she performs *ẓuhr* prayers but before *ʿaṣr* prayers or during *ʿaṣr* prayers blood soaks the piece of cotton [or sanitary pad/another absorbent item] and reaches the bottom of it, then again, she must perform *ghusl* for *ʿaṣr* prayers based on obligatory precaution. However, in the event that the delay is to the extent that in that time, the woman can perform two or more prayers – for example, she can perform *maghrib* and *ʿishāʾ* prayers before blood reaches the bottom of it again – then for those prayers [i.e. *maghrib* and *ʿishāʾ*], it is not necessary for her to perform another *ghusl*. In each case, for excessive *istiḥāḍah*, *ghusl* suffices in place of *wuḍūʾ*.

Ruling 395. If the blood of *istiḥāḍah* is discharged before the time for prayers, in the event that a woman has not performed *wuḍūʾ* or *ghusl* [depending on her duty] for it, she must perform *wuḍūʾ* or *ghusl* at the time of prayers, even if she is not *mustaḥāḍah* at that moment.

Ruling 396. A woman who has medium *istiḥāḍah* and must perform *wuḍūʾ* as well as *ghusl*, must, based on obligatory precaution, first perform *ghusl* and then perform *wuḍūʾ*. However, if a woman who has excessive *istiḥāḍah* wants to perform *wuḍūʾ*, she must perform it before she performs *ghusl*.

Ruling 397. If the slight *istiḥāḍah* of a woman becomes medium after *ṣubḥ* prayers, she must perform *ghusl* for *ẓuhr* and *ʿaṣr* prayers. If it becomes medium after *ẓuhr* and *ʿaṣr* prayers, she must perform *ghusl* for *maghrib* and *ʿishāʾ* prayers.

Ruling 398. If the slight or medium *istiḥāḍah* of a woman becomes excessive after *ṣubḥ* prayers and she remains in this state, she must observe the laws mentioned in Ruling 394 regarding *ẓuhr*, *ʿaṣr*, *maghrib*, and *ʿishāʾ* prayers.

Ruling 399. For excessive *istiḥāḍah*, in case it is necessary for there not to be a delay between performing *ghusl* and prayers – as mentioned in Ruling 394 – then, if performing *ghusl* before the time for prayers has set in causes delay, that *ghusl* will be of no use for the purposes of performing the prayer and a *mustaḥāḍah* must perform *ghusl* again for the prayer. This ruling also applies to a woman who has medium *istiḥāḍah*.

Ruling 400. A woman who has slight or medium *istiḥāḍah* must perform *wuḍūʾ* for every prayer – including the daily prayers, for which the ruling has already been mentioned – be it an obligatory prayer or a recommended one. However, if she wants to perform again one of the daily prayers that she has already performed as a precautionary measure, or if she wants to repeat in congregation (*jamāʿah*) the prayer she previously performed alone, she must do all the things that were mentioned with regard to *istiḥāḍah*. However, for performing *ṣalāt al-āyāt* or for a *sajdah* or *tashahhud* that has been forgotten, if she performs these immediately after prayers – and for *sajdatā al-sahw* in any condition [i.e. whether she performs them immediately after prayers or not] – it is not necessary for her to do those things that were mentioned with regard to *istiḥāḍah*.

Ruling 401. After a *mustaḥāḍah* has stopped bleeding, she must do the things required of a *mustaḥāḍah* for only the first prayer she performs. For subsequent prayers, it is not necessary for her to do those things.

Ruling 402. If a woman does not know which type of *istiḥāḍah* she has, then based on obligatory precaution, she must examine herself when she wants to perform prayers. For example, she must insert some cotton into the vagina, wait a little while, and then take it out. After discovering which of the three types of *istiḥāḍah* she has, she must do the things that have been instructed for that particular type. However, if she knows that until the time she wants to perform prayers her *istiḥāḍah* will not change, she can examine herself before the time for prayer has set in.

Ruling 403.* If a *mustaḥāḍah* is able to examine herself but starts performing prayers without examining herself, then in the event that she had the intention of attaining proximity to Allah and acted in accordance with her duty – for example, her *istiḥāḍah* was slight and she acted according to the rules of someone who has slight *istiḥāḍah* – in such a case, her prayers are valid. However, if she did not have the intention of attaining proximity to Allah or her actions were not according to her duty – for example, her *istiḥāḍah* was excessive but she acted according to the rules of someone who has slight *istiḥāḍah* – then her prayers are void.

Ruling 404. If a *mustaḥāḍah* cannot examine herself, she must act according to what is undoubtedly her responsibility. For example, if she does not know whether her *istiḥāḍah* is slight or medium, she must do the things required of a woman with slight *istiḥāḍah*; and if she does not know whether she has medium or excessive *istiḥāḍah*, she must do the things required of a woman with medium *istiḥāḍah*.[42] However, if she knows which one of the three types it was previously, she must act according to the duties for that type.

Ruling 405. If when the blood of *istiḥāḍah* is first discharged, it remains inside and does not come out, this does not invalidate a woman's *wuḍūʾ* or *ghusl*; but if it comes out – however little it may be – then this invalidates her *wuḍūʾ* and *ghusl*.

Ruling 406. If a *mustaḥāḍah* examines herself after prayers and does not see any blood, then even if she knows that bleeding will start again, she can perform prayers with the *wuḍūʾ* she already has.

Ruling 407. If a *mustaḥāḍah* knows that from the time she started performing *wuḍūʾ* or *ghusl* no blood has come out, nor is it in the vagina, she can delay performing prayers until the time she knows she will not experience *istiḥāḍah*.

Ruling 408. If a *mustaḥāḍah* knows that before the end of the time for prayers her *istiḥāḍah* will completely stop or that it will stop for

[42] In these two examples, the *mustaḥāḍah* knows for sure that her *istiḥāḍah* is *at least* the lesser type. It could possibly be more than this, but as that is only a possibility, she must act according to what she knows is certain, i.e. the lesser type.

long enough for her to perform prayers, then based on obligatory precaution, she must wait and perform prayers when her *istiḥāḍah* has stopped.

Ruling 409. If after performing *wuḍūʾ* and *ghusl* the bleeding appears to have stopped and a *mustaḥāḍah* knows that if she delays the prayer her *istiḥāḍah* will stop for long enough for her to perform *wuḍūʾ*, *ghusl*, and prayers, then based on obligatory precaution, she must delay the prayer; and when her *istiḥāḍah* completely stops, she must perform *wuḍūʾ* and *ghusl* again and perform the prayer. Furthermore, if when the bleeding appears to have stopped, the time for prayers is short, it is not necessary for her to perform *wuḍūʾ* and *ghusl* again; rather, she can perform prayers with the *wuḍūʾ* and *ghusl* that she already has.

Ruling 410. When the bleeding of a woman with excessive *istiḥāḍah* completely stops, if she knows that from the time she became engaged in performing *ghusl* for the previous prayer there has not been any discharge of blood, it is not necessary for her to perform *ghusl* again. Apart from this case, she must perform *ghusl* based on obligatory precaution. As for a woman who has medium *istiḥāḍah*, it is not necessary for her to perform *ghusl* if her *istiḥāḍah* has completely stopped.

Ruling 411. After a woman who has slight *istiḥāḍah* performs *wuḍūʾ*, and after a woman who has medium *istiḥāḍah* performs *ghusl* and *wuḍūʾ*, and after a woman who has excessive *istiḥāḍah* performs *ghusl*, she must immediately engage in performing her obligatory prayers [for which the time is due] except in the two cases that were mentioned in Rulings 394 and 407. However, there is no problem if she says *adhān* and *iqāmah* before prayers, and [when she is performing prayers,] she can also perform recommended acts of the prayer, such as *qunūt*.

Ruling 412. If the duty of a *mustaḥāḍah* is that she must not delay in performing *wuḍūʾ*, *ghusl*, and prayers but she does not act according to her duty, she must perform *wuḍūʾ* or *ghusl* again and engage in performing the prayer without further delay.

Ruling 413. If the blood of a *mustaḥāḍah* is continuous and does not stop, in the event that it is not harmful for her, she must, based on obligatory precaution, prevent the blood from coming out before performing *ghusl*. In the event that she is negligent in doing this and blood comes out, and she has performed prayers, she must perform them again. And the recommended precaution is that she should perform *ghusl* again [before performing these prayers].

Ruling 414. If bleeding does not stop at the time of performing *ghusl*, the *ghusl* is valid. However, if while performing *ghusl*, medium *istiḥāḍah* becomes excessive, it is necessary to start the *ghusl* all over again.

Ruling 415. The recommended precaution is that during the entire day that a *mustaḥāḍah* is fasting, she should prevent the blood from coming out as much as she can.

Ruling 416. Based on the opinion held by most jurists (*mashhūr*), the fast of a woman who has excessive *istiḥāḍah* is valid if she performs *ghusl* for *maghrib* and *ʿishāʾ* prayers the night before the day she wants to fast and if she performs the *ghusl*s that are obligatory for the prayers of the day. However, it is not farfetched to consider the validity of her fast as not being conditional on her performing *ghusl*, just as it is not conditional – based on a stronger opinion (*aqwā*)[43] – for a woman who has medium *istiḥāḍah*.[44]

Ruling 417. If a fasting woman becomes *mustaḥāḍah* after *ʿaṣr* prayers and she does not perform *ghusl* until sunset (*ghurūb*), her fast is valid without any problem.

Ruling 418. If before prayers the slight *istiḥāḍah* of a woman becomes medium or excessive, she must do the things required of a woman with medium or excessive *istiḥāḍah*, which were mentioned earlier. If the medium *istiḥāḍah* of a woman becomes excessive, she must do the things required of a woman with excessive *istiḥāḍah*; and in the event that she has performed *ghusl* for medium *istiḥāḍah*, it is

[43] For practical purposes, where an opinion is stated to be 'stronger', a fatwa is being given.
[44] This rule is clearly stated in Ruling 1613.

of no use and she must perform *ghusl* again for excessive *istiḥāḍah*.

Ruling 419.* If during prayers the medium *istiḥāḍah* of a woman becomes excessive, she must break her prayer, perform *ghusl* for excessive *istiḥāḍah*, do the other things required of a woman with excessive *istiḥāḍah*, and then perform that prayer; and based on recommended precaution, she should perform *wuḍūʾ* before *ghusl*. If she does not have time to perform *ghusl*, it is necessary for her to perform *tayammum* in place of *ghusl*; and if she does not have time to perform *tayammum* either, then based on recommended precaution, she should not break her prayer but instead complete it in the state that she is in; however, it is necessary for her to make it up after its prescribed time. Similarly, if during prayers the slight *istiḥāḍah* of a woman becomes excessive, she must break her prayer and do the things required of a woman with excessive *istiḥāḍah*. Based on obligatory precaution, the same rule applies if the slight *istiḥāḍah* of a woman becomes medium.

Ruling 420. If bleeding stops during prayers and a *mustaḥāḍah* does not know whether the bleeding has also stopped internally, or whether her *istiḥāḍah* will stop for long enough for her to obtain ritual purity (*ṭahārah*) [i.e. to perform *wuḍūʾ* or *ghusl*, according to her duty] and to perform all or part of the prayer, then based on obligatory precaution, she must perform *wuḍūʾ* or *ghusl* – according to her duty – and perform the prayer again.

Ruling 421. If the excessive *istiḥāḍah* of a woman becomes medium, she must do the things required of a woman with excessive *istiḥāḍah* for the first prayer; and for subsequent prayers, she must do the things required of a woman with medium *istiḥāḍah*. For example, if before *ẓuhr* prayers her excessive *istiḥāḍah* becomes medium, she must perform *ghusl* for *ẓuhr* prayers; and for *ʿaṣr*, *maghrib*, and *ʿishāʾ* prayers, she must perform *wuḍūʾ* only. However, if she does not perform *ghusl* for *ẓuhr* prayers and she has time only to the extent of performing *ʿaṣr* prayers, she must perform *ghusl* for *ʿaṣr* prayers; and if she does not perform *ghusl* for *ʿaṣr* prayers either, she must perform *ghusl* for *maghrib* prayers; and if she does not perform *ghusl* for even those prayers and she has time only for *ʿishāʾ* prayers, she must perform *ghusl* for *ʿishāʾ* prayers.

Ruling 422. If before each prayer the bleeding of a woman with excessive *istiḥāḍah* stops and starts again, she must perform one *ghusl* for each prayer.

Ruling 423. If the excessive *istiḥāḍah* of a woman becomes slight, she must do the things required of a woman with excessive *istiḥāḍah* for the first prayer; and for subsequent prayers, she must do the things required of a woman with slight *istiḥāḍah*. Furthermore, if medium *istiḥāḍah* becomes slight, a *mustaḥāḍah* must do the things required of a woman with medium *istiḥāḍah* for the first prayer, if she has not done so already.

Ruling 424. If a *mustaḥāḍah* does not perform any of the acts that are obligatory for her, her prayers are invalid.

Ruling 425. If a woman with slight or medium *istiḥāḍah* wants to perform an act – other than prayers – that is conditional on having *wuḍūʾ* – for example, she wants to touch the writing of the Qur'an with a part of her body – then, in the event that this is after finishing prayers, she must, based on obligatory precaution, perform *wuḍūʾ*, and the *wuḍūʾ* that she had performed for prayers will not suffice.

Ruling 426. It is lawful for a *mustaḥāḍah* who has performed her obligatory *ghusl*s to go to a mosque and stay in it, and to recite a verse with an obligatory *sajdah*,[45] and for her husband to have sexual intercourse with her, even if she has not done the other things that she would have done for prayers, such as changing the piece of cotton [or sanitary pad/another absorbent item]. In fact, these acts are permitted even if she has not performed *ghusl*.

Ruling 427. If a woman with excessive or medium *istiḥāḍah* wants to recite a verse with an obligatory *sajdah* before the time for prayers, or if she wants to go to a mosque, then based on recommended precaution, she should perform *ghusl*. The same applies if her husband wants to have sexual intercourse with her.

Ruling 428. *Ṣalāt al-āyāt* is obligatory for a *mustaḥāḍah*. In order for

[45] These verses are mentioned in the fifth part of the list mentioned in Ruling 354.

a *mustaḥāḍah* to perform *ṣalāt al-āyāt*, she must do all the things that were mentioned with regard to performing the daily prayers.

Ruling 429. Whenever *ṣalāt al-āyāt* becomes obligatory for a *mustaḥāḍah* during the time of the daily prayers and she wants to perform both of them one after the other, then based on obligatory precaution, she cannot perform both of them with one *ghusl* and *wuḍūʾ* [and she would need to perform an additional *ghusl* or *wuḍūʾ*].

Ruling 430. If a *mustaḥāḍah* wants to make up *qaḍāʾ* prayers, then for each prayer she must do everything that is obligatory for her for performing prayers within their prescribed time (*adāʾ*); and based on obligatory precaution, for *qaḍāʾ* prayers, she cannot suffice with the things that she has done for *adāʾ* prayers.

Ruling 431. If a woman knows that the blood being discharged is not blood from an injury but she is uncertain whether it is the blood of *istiḥāḍah*, *ḥayḍ*, or *nifās*, then in the event that the blood is not legally (*sharʿan*) ruled to be of *ḥayḍ* or *nifās*, she must act according to the instructions pertaining to *istiḥāḍah*. In fact, if she doubts whether it is the blood of *istiḥāḍah* or another type of blood, then in the event that it does not have the attributes of other types of blood, she must, based on obligatory precaution, consider the blood to be *istiḥāḍah*.

MENSTRUATION (*ḤAYḌ*)

Ḥayḍ is blood that is usually discharged from the uterus of women every month for a few days. A woman in menstruation is called a '*ḥāʾiḍ*'.

Ruling 432. Most of the time, the blood of *ḥayḍ* is thick and warm, its colour is black or red, and it comes out with a little pressure and a burning sensation.

Ruling 433. The bleeding that women above the age of sixty experience is not ruled to be *ḥayḍ*; however, a woman can experience *ḥayḍ* between the age of fifty and sixty, although the recommended precaution is that women who are not Qurayshi (*sayyidah*)[46] and who experience bleeding which would previously have been ruled to be *ḥayḍ* [i.e. had they experienced it before the age of fifty, it would have been ruled to be *ḥayḍ*], should refrain from doing the things that are unlawful for a *ḥā'iḍ* to do and perform the duties of a *mustaḥāḍah*.

Ruling 434. Bleeding that a girl experiences before the age of nine is not *ḥayḍ*.

Ruling 435. It is possible for a pregnant woman and a breastfeeding woman to menstruate. The ruling of a pregnant woman and a non-pregnant woman is the same except that if a pregnant woman who has a habit of time[47] experiences bleeding with the attributes of *ḥayḍ* after the passing of twenty days from the first day of her habit, it is necessary for her, based on obligatory precaution, to do the things that a *mustaḥāḍah* must do and refrain from doing the things that are unlawful for a *ḥā'iḍ* to do.

Ruling 436. If a girl who does not know whether she has completed nine years of age experiences bleeding that does not have the attributes of *ḥayḍ*, it is not *ḥayḍ*. If it has the attributes of *ḥayḍ*, then considering it to be *ḥayḍ* is problematic [i.e. based on obligatory precaution, it must not be considered to be *ḥayḍ*], unless one is confident that it is *ḥayḍ*, in which case the girl will be considered to have reached the age of nine.

Ruling 437. If a woman who doubts whether she has reached the age of sixty experiences bleeding but does not know if it is *ḥayḍ*, she must assume that she has not reached the age of sixty.

Ruling 438. *Ḥayḍ* cannot last for less than three days or more than ten days; if bleeding lasts for even a little less than three days, it is not *ḥayḍ*.

Ruling 439. The first three days of *ḥayḍ* must be continuous; therefore,

[46] A *sayyidah* is a female descendant of Hāshim, the great grandfather of Prophet Muḥammad (Ṣ).

[47] This is explained in Ruling 468.

if, for example, a woman experiences bleeding for two days, and then the bleeding stops for one day, and then she experiences bleeding again for one day, it is not *ḥayḍ*.

Ruling 440. At the beginning of *ḥayḍ*, it is necessary for the blood to come out. However, it is not necessary for the blood to come out on all three days, and it is sufficient if the blood remains inside the vagina. In the event that during the three days a woman's bleeding stops for a short time in a manner that is common among all or some women, it is still counted as *ḥayḍ*.

Ruling 441. It is not necessary for a woman to experience bleeding on the eve of the first and fourth day. However, the bleeding must not stop on the eve of the second and third day. Therefore, if from the start of the morning of the first day the bleeding continues until sunset of the third day and does not stop at all, it is *ḥayḍ*. The same applies if it starts during the first day and stops at the same time on the fourth day.

Ruling 442. If a woman experiences bleeding for three consecutive days and then her bleeding stops, in the event that she experiences bleeding again and the days on which she experiences bleeding plus the days on which her bleeding stops in between altogether do not exceed ten, then the blood on all the days that she experienced bleeding is *ḥayḍ*. However, the obligatory precaution is that on the days that her bleeding stops in between, she must do the things that are obligatory for a non-*ḥāʾiḍ* and refrain from doing the things that are unlawful for a *ḥāʾiḍ*.

Ruling 443. If a woman experiences bleeding for more than three and less than ten days, but she does not know whether the bleeding is from a boil, wound, or due to *ḥayḍ*, she must not consider it to be *ḥayḍ*.

Ruling 444. If a woman experiences bleeding but does not know whether it is from a wound or due to *ḥayḍ*, she must perform her ritual acts of worship (*ʿibādāt*) [as normal], unless prior to this she was in the state of *ḥayḍ* [in which case she would consider it to be *ḥayḍ*].

Ruling 445. If a woman experiences bleeding and doubts whether it is *ḥayḍ* or *istiḥāḍah*, in the event that it has the conditions of *ḥayḍ*, it must be considered to be *ḥayḍ*.

Ruling 446. If a woman experiences bleeding and does not know whether it is *ḥayḍ* or bleeding caused by her hymen tearing, she must examine herself; i.e. she must insert some cotton in the vagina, wait a while, and then take it out. If she finds that blood has stained only the sides of the cotton, it is bleeding caused by her hymen tearing, but if it has reached all parts of the cotton, it is *ḥayḍ*.

Ruling 447. If a woman experiences bleeding for less than three days, and then her bleeding stops, and afterwards she experiences bleeding again for three days, the second bleeding is *ḥayḍ* and the first bleeding – even if she experiences it during her habitual period – is not *ḥayḍ*.

LAWS OF A WOMAN IN MENSTRUATION (*ḤĀʾIḌ*)

Ruling 448. Certain things are unlawful for a *ḥāʾiḍ*:

1. to perform those ritual acts of worship that must be performed with *wuḍūʾ*, *ghusl*, or *tayammum* – such as prayers – if she does so with the intention of performing a valid act. However, there is no problem if she performs ritual acts of worship for which *wuḍūʾ*, *ghusl*, or *tayammum* is not necessary, such as *ṣalāt al-mayyit*;
2. all the things that are unlawful for a *junub*, as mentioned in the rules of *janābah*;
3. vaginal intercourse, which is unlawful for both the man and the woman even if the penis penetrates only to the point of circumcision and the man does not ejaculate. In fact, the obligatory precaution is that the penis must not penetrate even less than the point of circumcision. This law does not apply to anal intercourse; however, based on obligatory precaution, anal intercourse with a woman without her consent – whether she is *ḥāʾiḍ* or not – is not permitted.

Ruling 449. Sexual intercourse is unlawful on the days when even though *ḥayḍ* is not certain, the woman must still regard herself as being *ḥāʾiḍ*. Therefore, a husband cannot have intercourse with his wife on the days when she experiences bleeding for more than ten days and who must – according to the instructions that will be mentioned later – regard the days of her close relatives' habitual pattern as her *ḥayḍ* days.

Ruling 450. If a man has sexual intercourse with his wife while she is in the state of *ḥayḍ*, it is obligatory for him to seek forgiveness from Allah. However, giving recompense (*kaffārah*) is not obligatory for him, even though it is better that he give *kaffārah*. The *kaffārah* for sexual intercourse at the beginning of *ḥayḍ* is one legal (*sharʿī*) *mithqāl*[48] of coined gold, at the middle of *ḥayḍ* it is half a legal *mithqāl*, and at the end of *ḥayḍ* it is one-quarter of a legal *mithqāl*. A legal *mithqāl* is eighteen *nukhuds*.[49]

Ruling 451. Apart from having sexual intercourse with a *ḥāʾiḍ*, there is no problem in deriving other forms of sexual pleasure with her, such as kissing and foreplay.

Ruling 452. As per the laws relating to divorce, divorcing a woman who is in the state of *ḥayḍ* is invalid.

Ruling 453. If a woman says she is *ḥāʾiḍ* or that her *ḥayḍ* has stopped, in the event that she is not suspected to be someone whose word in this case cannot be accepted, her statement must be accepted. However, if she is suspected to be someone whose word in this case cannot be accepted, then accepting her statement is problematic [i.e. based on obligatory precaution, her statement must not be accepted].

Ruling 454. If a woman becomes *ḥāʾiḍ* during prayers, her prayers are invalid; and based on obligatory precaution, this applies even if *ḥayḍ* occurs after the last *sajdah* and before the last word of the salutation (*salām*) of the prayer.

Ruling 455. If a woman doubts during prayers whether or not she has become *ḥāʾiḍ*, her prayers are valid. However, if after prayers she realises that she had actually become *ḥāʾiḍ* during prayers, then the

[48] A legal *mithqāl* is a measure of weight equal to 3.456 grams.
[49] A *nukhud* is a measure of weight equivalent to 0.192 grams.

prayers she performed are void, as mentioned in the previous ruling.

Ruling 456. After a woman's *ḥayḍ* has stopped, it is obligatory for her to perform *ghusl* for prayers and for other ritual acts of worship that must be performed with *wuḍūʾ*, *ghusl*, or *tayammum*. The *ghusl* for *ḥayḍ* is performed in the same way as the *ghusl* for *janābah*, and the *ghusl* for *ḥayḍ* suffices in place of *wuḍūʾ*, although it is recommended to also perform *wuḍūʾ* before performing *ghusl*.

Ruling 457. If a woman is divorced after her *ḥayḍ* has stopped, the divorce is valid even if she has not yet performed *ghusl*. Furthermore, [after her *ḥayḍ* has stopped but before she has performed *ghusl*,] her husband can have sexual intercourse with her. However, the obligatory precaution is that intercourse must take place after washing the vagina; and the recommended precaution is that having sexual intercourse with her should be avoided before she has performed *ghusl*. However, other acts that were unlawful for the woman during *ḥayḍ* on account of them being conditional on her being in a state of ritual purity – such as touching the writing of the Qur'an – do not become lawful for her until she performs *ghusl*. Similarly, based on obligatory precaution, acts that have not been established as being unlawful for a *ḥāʾiḍ* on account of them being conditional on her being in a state of ritual purity, such as staying in a mosque [also do not become lawful for her until she performs *ghusl*].

Ruling 458. If the amount of water that is available is not sufficient for performing both *wuḍūʾ* and *ghusl* and it is sufficient for performing only *ghusl*, a woman must perform *ghusl*, and it is better that she perform *tayammum* in place of *wuḍūʾ*. If the water is sufficient for performing only *wuḍūʾ* and not for performing *ghusl*, it is better that she perform *wuḍūʾ* with the water and then she must perform *tayammum* in place of *ghusl*. If she does not have sufficient water for performing *wuḍūʾ* or *ghusl*, she must perform *tayammum* in place of *ghusl*, and it is better that she perform another *tayammum* in place of *wuḍūʾ* as well.

Ruling 459. A woman does not have to make up those prayers that she did not perform while she was in the state of *ḥayḍ*; however, she does have to make up those fasts of the month of Ramadan that she did not keep while she was in the state of *ḥayḍ*. Similarly, based on obligatory precaution, she must make up any fasts that were obligatory for her at a particular time on account of a vow and which she did not keep while she was in the state of *ḥayḍ*.

Ruling 460. Whenever the time for prayers sets in and a woman knows that if she delays performing prayers she will become *ḥāʾiḍ*, she must perform those prayers immediately. Similarly, based on obligatory precaution, she must perform prayers immediately even if she merely deems it probable that she will become *ḥāʾiḍ* if she delays performing them.

Ruling 461. If a woman delays performing prayers and from the start of the time of prayers there elapses a length of time – equivalent to the time it takes to perform one prayer with all its prerequisites, including obtaining clean clothes and performing *wuḍūʾ* – and if she becomes *ḥāʾiḍ* after that, it is obligatory for her to make up those prayers. In fact, if the time for prayers had set in and she could have performed one prayer with *wuḍūʾ*, *ghusl*, or even *tayammum* but she did not, she must, based on obligatory precaution, make up those prayers even if there was not sufficient time for all the other prerequisites. However, she must take into account her own situation in terms of performing prayers quickly or slowly and other things. For example, if a woman who is not a traveller [and therefore must perform the four-unit (*rakʿah*) prayers in their complete (*tamām*) form] does not perform the *ẓuhr* prayer at the start of its prescribed time, it becomes obligatory for her to make it up only if before she became *ḥāʾiḍ*, there was time equivalent to performing a four *rakʿah* prayer with *wuḍūʾ* or *tayammum* from the start of the time for *ẓuhr* prayers. However, for a traveller [who must perform the four *rakʿah* prayers in their shortened form], it is sufficient if there was time equivalent to obtaining ritual purity and performing a two *rakʿah* prayer.

Ruling 462. If at the end of the time for prayers a woman's *ḥayḍ* stops and she has time equivalent to performing *ghusl* and one *rakʿah* or more of the prayer, she must perform that prayer; if she does not, she must make it up.

Ruling 463. If after her bleeding stops a *ḥāʾiḍ* does not have time equivalent to performing *ghusl* but she can perform the prayer during its prescribed time by performing *tayammum*, the obligatory precaution is that she must perform the prayer with *tayammum*; and in case she does not perform the prayer, she must make it up. Furthermore, apart from shortage of time, if for some other reason her duty is to perform *tayammum* – for example, because water is harmful for her – then she must perform *tayammum* and the prayer; and in case she does not perform the prayer, it is necessary for her to make it up.

Ruling 464. If after her *ḥayḍ* has stopped, a woman is unsure whether or not she has time to perform prayers, she must perform those prayers.

Ruling 465. If a woman does not perform prayers thinking that she does not have sufficient time to become ritually pure from an occurrence (*ḥadath*)[50] and to perform one *rakʿah*, and afterwards she realises that actually she did have time, she must make up that prayer.

Ruling 466.* It is recommended that at the time of prayers, a *ḥāʾiḍ* should clean herself of the blood, change the piece of cotton [or sanitary pad/another absorbent item that a woman would normally use to absorb the discharge of blood], and perform *wuḍūʾ*; and if she cannot perform *wuḍūʾ*, she should perform *tayammum*. It is also recommended for her to sit in the place of prayers facing qibla and to engage in remembering Allah (*dhikr*), reciting *duʿā*'s, and invoking blessings (*ṣalawāt*) upon Prophet Muḥammad (Ṣ) and his progeny, and it is better that she recite the four glorifications (*al-tasbīḥāt al-arbaʿah*).

Ruling 467.* According to some jurists, it is disapproved for a *ḥāʾiḍ* to read the Qur'an, keep the Qur'an with herself, touch in between the writing of the Qur'an or the margins of the Qur'an, and dye her hair with henna or something similar.

CATEGORIES OF WOMEN IN MENSTRUATION

Ruling 468. There are six categories of women in menstruation:

[50] See the footnote pertaining to Ruling 384 for an explanation of this term.

1. a woman with a habit of time and duration: this is a woman who on two consecutive months starts her period at a fixed time, and the number of days on which she has her period is the same in each of the two months. For example, in two consecutive months she experiences bleeding from the first of the month until the seventh;
2. a woman with a habit of time: this is a woman who on two consecutive months starts her period at a fixed time but the number of days on which she has her period is not the same in each of the two months. For example, in two consecutive months she experiences bleeding on the first of the month, but in the first month her bleeding stops on the seventh day and in the second month it stops on the eighth day;
3. a woman with a habit of duration: this is a woman who has her period for the same number of days on two consecutive months but the time when her bleeding starts in each of the two months is not the same. For example, in the first month she experiences bleeding from the fifth to the tenth of the month and in the second month from the twelfth to the seventeenth;
4. a woman with a disordered habit (*muḍṭaribah*): this is a woman who, for several months, experiences a period but does not have a fixed habit with regard to this [neither of time nor duration], or her habit has been disturbed and she has not yet formed a new habit;
5. a menarcheal woman (*mubtadi'ah*): this is a woman who experiences bleeding for the first time;
6. a forgetful woman (*nāsiyah*): this is a woman who has forgotten the habit of her period.

Specific rules apply to each of these categories, which will be discussed in the following rulings.

1. A woman with a habit of time and duration

Ruling 469. Women who have a habit of time and duration are of two types:

1. a woman who on two consecutive months has her period at a fixed time, and her period also stops at a fixed time. For

example, on two consecutive months she experiences bleeding on the first day of the month and it stops on the seventh. Therefore, her habit of *ḥayḍ* is from the first of the month to the seventh;

2. a woman who on two consecutive months has her period at a fixed time, and after she experiences bleeding for three or more days, it stops for one or more days, and then she experiences bleeding again; and the total number of days on which she experiences bleeding plus the days on which it stops in between do not exceed ten; and in both months, all the days on which she experiences bleeding and all the days on which it stops in between are the same. In such a case, her habit is the number of days on which she experienced bleeding without the addition of the number of days on which it stopped. Therefore, it is necessary that the days on which she experiences bleeding and the number of days on which it stops in between in both months be the same. For example, if in both months she experiences bleeding from the first day to the third, then it stops for three days, and then she experiences bleeding for another three days, her habit is six separated days. Furthermore, for the three days in between on which her period stops, she must, based on obligatory precaution, refrain from doing the things that are unlawful for a *ḥāʾiḍ* and do the things required of a *mustaḥāḍah*. In the event that the days on which she experiences bleeding in the second month are more or less than in the first month, she has a habit of time and not of duration.

Ruling 470. If a woman with a habit of time – irrespective of whether she also has a habit of duration or not – experiences bleeding during the time of her habit, or on one or more days earlier than the time of her habit such that it can be said that her habit has moved forward, then even if the bleeding does not have the attributes of *ḥayḍ*, she must act according to the rules that were mentioned for a *ḥāʾiḍ*. In the event that afterwards, she realises that it was not *ḥayḍ* – for example, her bleeding stops in less than three days – she must make up the ritual acts of worship that she did not perform [when she considered her bleeding to be *ḥayḍ*].

Ruling 471. If a woman with a habit of time and duration experiences bleeding on all the days of her habit and a few days before and after her habit, and if the total number of days does not exceed ten, then the bleeding on all of those days is considered to be *ḥayḍ*. If the number of days exceeds ten, only the bleeding during her habit is *ḥayḍ* and the bleeding before and after that is *istiḥāḍah*, and she must make up the ritual acts of worship that she did not perform before and after her habit.

If a woman experiences bleeding on all the days of her habit and a few days before her habit, and if the total number of days does not exceed ten, then the bleeding on all of those days is considered to be *ḥayḍ*. If it exceeds ten days, only the bleeding on the days of her habit is considered to be *ḥayḍ* – even if the bleeding does not have the attributes of *ḥayḍ* and the days before her habit had the attributes of *ḥayḍ* – and the bleeding before her habit is considered to be *istiḥāḍah*. In the event that she did not perform ritual acts of worship on those days, she must make them up.

If a woman experiences bleeding on all the days of her habit and a few days after her habit, and if the total number of days does not exceed ten, then the bleeding on all of those days is considered to be *ḥayḍ*. If the total is more than ten days, only the bleeding on the days of her habit is considered to be *ḥayḍ* and the rest is considered to be *istiḥāḍah*.

Ruling 472. If a woman with a habit of time and duration experiences bleeding on some of the days of her habit and a few days before her habit, and if the total number of days does not exceed ten, then the bleeding on all those days is considered to be *ḥayḍ*. If the bleeding exceeds ten days, the bleeding on the days of her habit plus the few days before that – which total the number of days of her habit – is *ḥayḍ*, and the bleeding on the first few days is considered to be *istiḥāḍah*. If she experiences bleeding on some days of her habit and a few days after her habit, and the total number of days does not exceed ten, then the bleeding on all the days is *ḥayḍ*. If it exceeds ten days, the bleeding on the days of her habit plus a few days after that – which total the number of days of her habit – is *ḥayḍ*, and the bleeding on the remaining days is considered to be *istiḥāḍah*.

Ruling 473. If a woman with a habit experiences bleeding for three or more days and after that her bleeding stops, and if she then experiences bleeding again and the gap between the two bleedings is less than ten days, and if all the days on which she experiences bleeding plus the days on which her bleeding stops total more than ten – for example, she experiences bleeding for five days, then her bleeding stops for five days, and then she experiences bleeding again for five days – in such a case, there are a few scenarios to consider:

1. all or some of the woman's first bleeding was on the days of her habit and her second bleeding was not on the days of her habit; in this case, she must consider all of her first bleeding to be *ḥayḍ* and her second bleeding to be *istiḥāḍah*. However, if her second bleeding has the attributes of *ḥayḍ*, she must add together the number of days of her first bleeding and the number of days on which her bleeding stopped after her first bleeding; then, to that figure, she must add a number of days from her second bleeding such that the total number of days does not exceed ten. Having done this, she must consider her first bleeding and the bleeding on the days she added from her second bleeding to be *ḥayḍ* and the rest to be *istiḥāḍah*. For example, if she experiences bleeding for three days, then her bleeding stops for three days, and then she experiences bleeding again for five days and her second bleeding has the attributes of *ḥayḍ*, the first three days plus four days from her second bleeding is *ḥayḍ*. For the days in between when her bleeding stops, she must, based on obligatory precaution, perform the obligatory acts that are required of a non-*ḥāʾiḍ* and refrain from doing the things that are unlawful for a *ḥāʾiḍ*;
2. the woman's first bleeding is not on the days of her habit, and all or some of her second bleeding is on the days of her habit. In this case, she must consider all of her second bleeding to be *ḥayḍ* and her first bleeding to be *istiḥāḍah*;
3. some of the woman's first and second bleeding is on the days of her habit, and her first bleeding that was on the days of her habit lasts for not less than three days, and the number of days on which her bleeding stops in between and some of the days of her second bleeding that was also on the days of her habit does not exceed ten. In this case, both bleedings are *ḥayḍ*. The obligatory precaution is that on the days that her bleeding stops in between, she must do the things that are obligatory for a

non-*ḥā'iḍ* and refrain from doing the things that are unlawful for a *ḥā'iḍ*. The days of the second bleeding after the days of her habit are considered to be *istiḥāḍah*. As for the amount of the first bleeding that she experiences before the days of her habit, in the event that it can commonly be said that her habit has moved forward, it is ruled to be *ḥayḍ* unless considering it as *ḥayḍ* results in some or all the days of her second bleeding that was also on the days of her habit to exceed ten days, in which case it is ruled to be *istiḥāḍah*. For example, if a woman's habit is from the third of the month to the tenth, and she experiences bleeding from the first to the sixth in one month, then her bleeding stops on two days, and then she experiences bleeding again until the fifteenth, in such a case, the bleeding that she experiences from the first to the tenth is *ḥayḍ*, and the bleeding that she experiences from the eleventh to the fifteenth is *istiḥāḍah*;

4. the woman experiences some of her first and second bleeding on the days of her habit but the part of her first bleeding that she experiences on the days of her habit is less than three days. In this case, she must consider the last three days of her first bleeding to be *ḥayḍ*. Similarly, her second bleeding – which together with the first three days and the days on which her bleeding stops in between total ten days – must also be considered to be *ḥayḍ*, and whatever is more than that is *istiḥāḍah*. If the number of days on which her bleeding stops is seven, all of her second bleeding is *istiḥāḍah*. In some cases, she must consider all of her first bleeding to be *ḥayḍ*, and this is when two conditions are fulfilled:
   a. all of her first bleeding has moved ahead to such an extent that her habit can be said to have moved forward;
   b. if all of her first bleeding were to be considered *ḥayḍ*, the number of days of her second bleeding that she experienced on the days of her habit would not exceed ten. For example, if the habit of a woman was from the third of the month to the tenth and she now experiences bleeding from the first of the month until the end of the fourth day, then her bleeding stops for two days, and then she experiences bleeding again until the fifteenth,

in such a case, all of her first bleeding is *ḥayḍ*. Similarly, the second bleeding until the end of the tenth day is *ḥayḍ*.

Ruling 474. If a woman with a habit of time and duration does not experience bleeding on the days of her habit, and at another time she experiences bleeding for the same number of days as her *ḥayḍ*, she must consider it to be *ḥayḍ* irrespective of whether she experienced it before the time of her habit or after it.

Ruling 475. If a woman with a habit of time and duration experiences bleeding on the days of her habit for three days or more, and the number of days are more or less than the days of her habit, and if after her bleeding stops she experiences bleeding again on the same number of days as her habit, then in such a case, there are a few scenarios to consider:

1. the total number of days of the two bleedings plus the number of days when her bleeding stops in between does not exceed ten. In this case, the two bleedings together are considered to be one *ḥayḍ*;
2. the number of days that her bleeding stops in between the two bleedings exceeds ten. In this case, each of the two bleedings is considered to be a separate *ḥayḍ*;
3. the number of days that her bleeding stops in between the two bleedings is less than ten, and the total of the two bleedings plus the days on which her bleeding stops in between is more than ten. In this case, the first bleeding must be considered to be *ḥayḍ* and the second bleeding *istiḥāḍah*.

Ruling 476. If a woman with a habit of time and duration experiences bleeding for more than ten days, the bleeding that she experiences on the days of her habit – even if it does not have the attributes of *ḥayḍ* – is *ḥayḍ*; and the bleeding that she experiences after the days of her habit – even if it has the attributes of *ḥayḍ* – is *istiḥāḍah*. For example, if a woman whose habit is from the first of the month to the seventh experiences bleeding from the first of the month to the twelfth, the first seven days are *ḥayḍ* and the next five days are *istiḥāḍah*.

2. A woman with a habit of time

Ruling 477. Women who have a habit of time and whose habit has a fixed start date are of two types:

1. a woman who on two consecutive months has her period at a fixed time and whose period stops after a few days but the number of days in each month is not the same. For example, on two consecutive months she experiences bleeding on the first of the month but in the first month the bleeding stops on the seventh, and in the second month the bleeding stops on the eighth. This woman must consider the first of the month to be the first day of her habit of *ḥayḍ*;
2. a woman who on two consecutive months has her period at a fixed time for three or more days, then her period stops, and then she experiences bleeding again, and all the days on which she experiences bleeding plus the days in between on which her bleeding stops do not exceed ten; but in the second month, this figure is more or less than the first month. For example, in the first month it is eight days and in the second month nine days, but in both months she experiences bleeding from the first of the month. Such a woman must also consider the first of the month to be the first day of her habit of *ḥayḍ*.

Ruling 478. If a woman with a habit of time experiences bleeding on the days of her habit or two or three days before her habit, she must act according to the rules mentioned for a *ḥāʾiḍ* as per the details in Ruling 470. In cases other than these two – for example, when a woman experiences bleeding so much in advance of her habit that it could not be said her habit has moved forward; rather, it would be said that she has experienced bleeding outside the days of her habit; or, she experiences bleeding after the days of her habit – then, in the event that the bleeding has the attributes of *ḥayḍ*, she must act according to the rules mentioned for a *ḥāʾiḍ*. Similarly, if it does not have the attributes of *ḥayḍ* but she knows that the bleeding will continue for three days [she must act according to the rules mentioned for a *ḥāʾiḍ*]. However, if she does not know whether it will continue for three days, the obligatory precaution is that she must do the things that are obligatory for a *mustaḥāḍah* and refrain from doing the things that are unlawful for a *ḥā'iḍ*.

Ruling 479. If a woman with a habit of time experiences bleeding on the days of her habit and the number of days that her bleeding lasts for is more than ten, and if on some of the days her bleeding has the attributes of *ḥayḍ* and on some other days it does not, and if the number of days that her bleeding has the attributes of *ḥayḍ* is not less than three nor more than ten, then in such a case, she must consider her bleeding on those days when it has the attributes of *ḥayḍ* to be *ḥayḍ* and the rest to be *istiḥāḍah*. If this type of bleeding is repeated – for example, four days with the attributes of *ḥayḍ*, followed by four days with the attributes of *istiḥāḍah*, followed by four days with the attributes of *ḥayḍ* again – she must consider only the first four days to be *ḥayḍ* and all the rest to be *istiḥāḍah*. If the bleeding with the attributes of *ḥayḍ* lasts for less than three days, she must consider it to be *ḥayḍ* and determine the number of days of it in one of two ways: either by referring to her close relatives or by selecting the number of days. If it is more than ten days, she must consider part of it to be *ḥayḍ* by one of these two ways. If a woman cannot distinguish the amount of *ḥayḍ* by means of its attributes – i.e. she finds that all the blood has the same attributes, or the blood that has the attributes of *ḥayḍ* lasts for more than ten days or less than three days – then she must consider it to be *ḥayḍ* according to the number of days of the habit of some of her close relatives, whether they be her paternal or maternal relatives, alive or dead. However, in this case, two conditions must be fulfilled:

1. the woman does not know that her close relative's habit is different to the duration of her *ḥayḍ*. For example, she is youthful and healthy and the other woman is approaching the age of menopause, when usually the duration of a woman's habit is shorter. The same applies if the situation is the other way round or the woman has an incomplete habit, the meaning and rules of which will be mentioned in Ruling 488.
2. the woman does not know that the habit of the other woman differs from the habit of her other close relatives who meet the first condition. However, there is no problem if the difference is very little such that it cannot really be counted. The same rule applies to a woman who has a habit of time and does

not experience bleeding at all on the days of her habit but experiences bleeding at other times which lasts for more than ten days, and she cannot distinguish the duration of *ḥayḍ* by means of its attributes.

Ruling 480. A woman with a habit of time cannot consider her bleeding to be *ḥayḍ* at times other than the time of her habit. Therefore, if the start of her habit is known – for example, she used to experience bleeding every month from the first of the month, and sometimes her bleeding would stop on the fifth day and at other times on the sixth – then, in the event that in one month she experiences bleeding for twelve days and she cannot determine her duration by means of the attributes of *ḥayḍ*, she must consider the first of the month to be the beginning of *ḥayḍ*. For the duration, she must refer to what was said in the previous ruling; and if the middle or end of her habit is known, then in the event that her bleeding exceeds ten days she must consider the duration to be such that the end or middle of it is in accordance with the time of her habit.

Ruling 481. A woman with a habit of time who experiences bleeding for more than ten days and cannot determine it according to what was said in Ruling 479 can choose any number of days from three to ten that she feels is appropriate for the duration of her *ḥayḍ*; and it is better that she consider it to be seven days if she feels it appropriate for herself. Of course, the number of days that she considers to be *ḥayḍ* must be in accordance with the time of her habit, as mentioned in the previous ruling.

3. A woman with a habit of duration

[Women with a habit of duration are of two types:]

1. a woman whose duration of *ḥayḍ* is the same on two consecutive months but the time of her bleeding is not the same in each. In this case, her habit is considered to be however many days she experiences bleeding. For example, if in the first month she experiences bleeding from the first of the month to the fifth, and in the second month from the eleventh to the fifteenth, her habit will be five days.

2. a woman who on two consecutive months experiences bleeding for three days or more, then her period stops for one or more days, and then she experiences bleeding again, and the time of bleeding in the first month differs from that of the second, such that all the days on which she experiences bleeding plus all the days on which her period stops in between do not exceed ten, and the number of days on which she experiences bleeding is the same. In this case, all the days on which she experiences bleeding is her habit of *ḥayḍ*, and on the days that her bleeding stops, she must, as a precautionary measure, do the things that are obligatory for a non-*ḥāʾiḍ* and refrain from doing the things that are unlawful for a *ḥāʾiḍ*. For example, if in the first month she experiences bleeding from the first to the third of the month, then her bleeding stops for two days, and then she experiences bleeding again for three days, and in the second month she experiences bleeding from the eleventh to the thirteenth, then her bleeding stops for two days, and then she experiences bleeding for three days, in such a case, her habit will be six days. However, if in one month, for example, she experiences bleeding for eight days and in the second month for four days, then her bleeding stops, and then she experiences bleeding again, and the total number of the days on which she experiences bleeding plus the days on which her bleeding stops in between is eight, then in this case, the woman does not have a habit of duration; rather, she is considered to be a *muḍṭaribah* (i.e. a woman with a disordered duration), the ruling for which will come later.

Ruling 482. If a woman with a habit of duration experiences bleeding for more or less than the number of days of her habit and it does not exceed ten days, she must consider it all to be *ḥayḍ*. If it exceeds ten days, then in the event that all the blood is similar, the days from the start of bleeding until the number of days of her habit is considered to be *ḥayḍ* and the rest *istiḥāḍah*. If all the bleeding is not the same, rather, on some days it has the attributes of *ḥayḍ* and on others the attributes of *istiḥāḍah*, and if the number of days on which it has the attributes of *ḥayḍ* is the same as the number of days of her habit, she must consider those days to be *ḥayḍ* and the rest *istiḥāḍah*. If the days on which the bleeding has the attributes of *ḥayḍ* are more than the days of her habit, then only the same number of days as her habit is *ḥayḍ* and the rest is *istiḥāḍah*. If the days on which the bleeding has the attributes of *ḥayḍ* are less than the days of her habit, she must consider those days with a few more days that together total the duration of her habit to be *ḥayḍ* and the rest *istiḥāḍah*.

4. A woman with a disordered habit (*muḍṭaribah*)

Ruling 483. A *muḍṭaribah* is a woman who experiences bleeding on two consecutive months but there is a difference in the time and duration of her bleeding. If a *muḍṭaribah* experiences bleeding for more than ten days and all the blood is the same – i.e. all of it either has the attributes of *ḥayḍ* or the attributes of *istiḥāḍah* – then based on obligatory precaution, the rules that apply to her are the same as those that apply to a woman with a habit of time who experiences bleeding at a time other than that of her habit, and who cannot distinguish *ḥayḍ* from *istiḥāḍah* by the attributes of the bleeding and so must consider the habit of some of her close relatives to be her habit of *ḥayḍ*. In case this is not possible, she must choose a number of days between three and ten and consider that to be her *ḥayḍ*, as per the explanation mentioned in Rulings 479 and 481.

Ruling 484. If a *muḍṭaribah* experiences bleeding for more than ten days, and the blood on some of those days has the attributes of *ḥayḍ* and on other days the attributes of *istiḥāḍah*, she must act according to the instructions mentioned at the beginning of Ruling 479.

5. A menarcheal woman (*mubtadi'ah*)

Ruling 485. A *mubtadi'ah* is a woman who experiences bleeding for the first time. If a woman experiences bleeding for more than ten days and all the blood is the same, she must consider the duration of the habit of one of her close relatives to be the number of days of her *ḥayḍ* and the rest to be *istiḥāḍah*, provided that she fulfils the two conditions mentioned in Ruling 479. If this is not possible, she must choose a number of days between three and ten and consider that to be the duration of her *ḥayḍ*, according to the instructions explained in Ruling 481.

Ruling 486. If a *mubtadi'ah* experiences bleeding for more than ten days, and on some of the days the bleeding has the attributes of *ḥayḍ* and on others the attributes of *istiḥāḍah*, then in the event that the bleeding with the attributes of *ḥayḍ* does not last for less than three days or more than ten, it is all *ḥayḍ*. However, if she experiences bleeding again before the passing of ten days from the time she experienced bleeding with the attributes of *ḥayḍ*, and this bleeding also has the attributes of *ḥayḍ* – for example, the bleeding is black for five days, yellow for nine days, and then it is black again for five days – then, in this case, she must consider the first bleeding to be *ḥayḍ* and the other two bleedings to be *istiḥāḍah*, as is the case with a *muḍṭaribah*.

Ruling 487. If a *mubtadi'ah* experiences bleeding for more than ten days, and on some of the days the bleeding has the attributes of *ḥayḍ* and on others the attributes of *istiḥāḍah*, but the bleeding that has the attributes of *ḥayḍ* lasts for less than three days or more than ten, then, in this case, she must act according to the instructions mentioned in Ruling 479.

6. A forgetful woman (*nāsiyah*)

Ruling 488. A *nāsiyah* is a woman who has forgotten the duration and/or time of her habit. If such a woman experiences bleeding for three days or more but less than ten, then all of it is *ḥayḍ*. However, if her bleeding lasts for more than ten days, then there are some scenarios to consider:

1. the woman had a habit of time or duration or both but she has completely forgotten it, such that she cannot remember its time or duration, even in general. For this type of woman, the rules of a *mubtadi'ah* that were mentioned earlier apply;
2. the woman had a habit of time and may or may not also have had a habit of duration, and she remembers something in general about the time of her habit. For example, she knows that a particular day is part of her habit or that her habit is in the first half of the month. For this type of woman, the rules of a *mubtadi'ah* apply as well; however, she must not consider *ḥayḍ* to be at a time that is definitely contrary to her habit. For example, if

she knows that the seventeenth day of the month is part of her habit or that her habit is in the second half of the month, and if she experiences bleeding from the first to the twentieth of the month, then she cannot consider her habit to be in the first ten days of the month even if it has the attributes of *ḥayḍ* and the bleeding in the second ten days has the attributes of *istiḥāḍah*;

3. the woman had a habit of duration but she has forgotten the duration of her habit. For this type of woman, the rules of a *mubtadi'ah* also apply; however, she must not knowingly underestimate the duration of her *ḥayḍ* [for example, if she knows that the number of days of her habit is at least seven days, she cannot consider her *ḥayḍ* to be less than seven days]. Similarly, she cannot knowingly overestimate the duration of her *ḥayḍ* to be more than her habit.

A similar rule must be observed by a woman with an incomplete habit of duration, i.e. a woman whose habit of duration fluctuates between two figures that are more than three days and less than ten. For example, a woman who experiences bleeding for either six or seven days every month cannot consider her *ḥayḍ* to be less than six days or more than seven days by means of the attributes of *ḥayḍ*, or by the habit of her close relatives, or by choosing a number in case she experiences bleeding for more than ten days.

MISCELLANEOUS RULINGS ON *ḤAYḌ*

Ruling 489. If a *mubtadi'ah, muḍṭaribah, nāsiyah*, or a woman with a habit of duration experiences bleeding and the blood has the attributes of *ḥayḍ*, or if she is certain that her bleeding will last for three days, she must refrain from engaging in ritual acts of worship. In the event that she realises afterwards that it was not *ḥayḍ*, she must make up the ritual acts of worship that she did not perform.

Ruling 490. If on two consecutive months a woman with a habit of *ḥayḍ* – whether it be a habit of time, duration, or both – experiences bleeding that is contrary to her habit and her bleeding in both months is the same in terms of its time, duration, or both, her habit will change to what she has observed in these two months. For example, if she used to experience bleeding from the first day of the month to the seventh and then her bleeding would stop, then in the event that in two consecutive months she experiences bleeding from the tenth to the seventeenth of the month and then her bleeding stops, her habit will change and be from the tenth to the seventeenth.

Ruling 491. The meaning of 'one month' – except with regard to determining the habit of time – is the passing of thirty days from the start of bleeding and not from the first day of the month to the last. With regard to determining the habit of time, the lunar month is intended, not the solar.

Ruling 492. If a woman who usually experiences bleeding once a month experiences bleeding twice in one month, then in the event that the number of days on which her bleeding stops in between is not less than ten, she must consider both bleedings to be *ḥayḍ* even if one of them does not have the attributes of *ḥayḍ*.

Ruling 493. With regard to a woman who must distinguish *ḥayḍ* by means of differences observed in the attributes of her bleeding, if she experiences bleeding for three or more days and it has the attributes of *ḥayḍ*, and if afterwards she experiences bleeding for ten days or more and it has the attributes of *istiḥāḍah*, and if she then experiences bleeding again for three days and this has the attributes of *ḥayḍ*, then she must consider the first and last bleeding – which had the attributes of *ḥayḍ* – to be *ḥayḍ*. However, if she experiences one of the two bleedings during her habit and it is not known whether the ten days in between are all *istiḥāḍah* or partly *ḥayḍ*, then the bleeding that she experiences during her habit is *ḥayḍ* and the rest is *istiḥāḍah*.

Ruling 494. If a woman's bleeding stops before ten days and she knows that there is no blood inside, she must perform *ghusl* for her ritual acts of worship even if she supposes that she will experience bleeding again before the completion of ten days. If she is certain that she will experience bleeding again before the completion of ten days, she must, as stated previously, perform *ghusl* as a precautionary measure, perform her ritual acts of worship, and refrain from doing the things that are unlawful for a *ḥā'iḍ*.

Ruling 495. If a woman's bleeding stops before ten days and she deems it probable that there is blood inside, she must either perform ritual acts of worship as a precautionary measure or perform *istibrāʾ*; and it is not permitted for her to refrain from worshipping without performing *istibrāʾ*. *Istibrāʾ* here means she must insert some cotton inside the vagina and wait for a short while – and if her habit is such that her bleeding stops for a short while in the middle of *ḥayḍ*, as it has been said of some women, she must wait for a longer time – then, she must bring the cotton out. If it is clean, she must perform *ghusl* and perform her ritual acts of worship; and if it is not clean – even if it is stained with a yellow-coloured liquid – then, in the event that she does not have a habit of *ḥayḍ*, or her habit is ten days, or the days of her habit have not yet finished, she must wait. If her bleeding stops before ten days, she must perform *ghusl*; and if her bleeding stops on the tenth day or her bleeding lasts for more than ten days, she must perform *ghusl* on the tenth day. If her habit is less than ten days, then in case she knows that her bleeding will stop before the completion of ten days or on the tenth day, she must not perform *ghusl*.

Ruling 496. If a woman considers her bleeding on some days to be *ḥayḍ* and does not perform ritual acts of worship, and afterwards she realises that it was not *ḥayḍ*, she must make up the prayers and fasts that she missed on those days. If she worships on some days supposing that her bleeding on those days is not *ḥayḍ*, and afterwards she realises that it was *ḥayḍ*, then in the event that she had also kept obligatory fasts on those days, she must make them up.

LOCHIA (*NIFĀS*)

Ruling 497. From the time the first part of a baby's body comes out of its mother's womb, the bleeding that a woman experiences for ten days is the bleeding of *nifās*, on condition that it can be called 'the bleeding of childbirth'. A woman in the state of *nifās* is called a '*nufasāʾ*'.

Ruling 498. Blood discharged before the first part of a baby's body comes out is not *nifās*.

Ruling 499. It is not necessary for the baby to be fully developed; even if it is born under-developed, as long as its development has passed the stage of an *ʿalaqah*, which is a clot of blood, and a *muḍghah*, which is a lump of flesh [embryo], and it is miscarried, then the bleeding of the woman for ten days is considered to be *nifās*.

Ruling 500. It is possible that the blood of *nifās* lasts no longer than a moment; however, it is not considered to be *nifās* if the blood continues for more than ten days.

Ruling 501. Whenever a person doubts whether something is miscarried, or whether the thing that is miscarried is a child, it is not necessary to investigate; and the blood that comes out is not legally ruled to be *nifās*.

Ruling 502. The things that are obligatory for a *ḥāʾiḍ* are also obligatory for a *nufasāʾ*. And based on obligatory precaution, the following are unlawful for a *nufasāʾ*: entering a mosque (however, merely passing through a mosque is permitted), staying in a mosque, passing through the 'Two Mosques' (i.e. Masjid al-Ḥarām and the Mosque of the Prophet (Ṣ)), reciting the verses that have obligatory *sajdah*,[51] and touching the writing of the Qur'an and the name of Allah the Exalted.

Ruling 503.* A divorce given to a woman who is in the state of *nifās* is invalid, and having sexual intercourse with a woman who is in the state of *nifās* is unlawful but it does not require one to give *kaffārah*.

Ruling 504. If the bleeding of a woman who does not have a habit of duration of *ḥayḍ* does not exceed ten days after giving birth, then all of it is considered to be *nifās*. Therefore, if her bleeding stops before ten days, she must perform *ghusl* and ritual acts of worship. If after that she experiences bleeding on one or more occasions, then in the event that the total number of days on which she experiences bleeding plus the days on which her bleeding stops in between is ten or less, all the blood is considered to be *nifās*; and on the days that her bleeding stops, she must, as an [obligatory] precaution, perform ritual acts of worship and refrain from doing the things that are unlawful for a

[51] These verses are mentioned in the fifth part of the list mentioned in Ruling 354.

nufasā'. Therefore, in the event that she had kept any obligatory fasts, she must make them up. Furthermore, if the last bleeding continues for more than ten days, she must consider the first ten days to be *nifās* and the bleeding after ten days to be *istiḥāḍah*.

Ruling 505.* If a woman with a habit of duration of *ḥayḍ* experiences bleeding more than once and the total number of her bleeding exceeds the number of days of her habit and is more than ten days, she must consider the number of days of her habit to be *nifās*, and based on obligatory precaution, in the days after the number of days of her habit until the tenth day, she must refrain from doing the things that are unlawful for a *nufasā'* and perform the things that are obligatory for a *mustaḥāḍah*.

Ruling 506. If a woman's *nifās* stops and she deems it probable that there is blood inside, she must perform *ghusl* as a precautionary measure and the ritual acts of worship, or she must perform *istibrā'*; it is not permitted for her to refrain from performing the ritual acts of worship without performing *istibrā'*. The method of performing *istibrā'* was mentioned in Ruling 495.

Ruling 507. If a woman's *nifās* exceeds ten days, then in the event that she has a habit of duration for *ḥayḍ*, the same number of days of her habit is *nifās* and the rest is *istiḥāḍah*. If she does not have a habit, it is *nifās* for the duration of ten days and the rest is *istiḥāḍah*. If she has forgotten her habit, she must consider her habit to be the highest number of days that she deems probable. Furthermore, the recommended precaution is that a woman with a habit should perform the things required for a *mustaḥāḍah* and refrain from doing the things that are unlawful for a *nufasā'*, starting from the day after her habit. A woman who does not have a habit should do this after the tenth day until the eighteenth day after childbirth.

Ruling 508. If a woman with a habit of duration for *ḥayḍ* continuously experiences bleeding for one or more months after giving birth, the same number of days of her habit is *nifās* and the bleeding for ten days after *nifās* is *istiḥāḍah*, even if she has a habit of time and the bleeding is experienced on the days of her habit. For example, if a woman whose habit of *ḥayḍ* is from the twentieth to the twenty-seventh of every month gives birth on the tenth, and she continuously experiences bleeding for one or more months, the bleeding until the seventeenth day is *nifās* and the bleeding for ten days from the seventeenth is *istiḥāḍah*, even if she experiences bleeding on the days of her habit, i.e. from the twentieth to the twenty-seventh. After the passing of ten days, if she has a habit of time and does not experience bleeding on the days of her habit, she must wait for the days of her habit, even if her waiting lasts for one or more months and even if the bleeding during this period has the attributes of *ḥayḍ*. However, if she does not have a habit of time, she must determine her *ḥayḍ* by its attributes in the event that this is possible (the method for doing this was mentioned in Ruling 479). If this is not possible – for example, all the bleeding after ten days of *nifās* is the same, and it continues with the same attributes for one or more months – then in every month, she must consider the *ḥayḍ* of her close relatives to be her *ḥayḍ*, as per the details mentioned in Ruling 479. If this is not possible either, she must choose a figure that she considers appropriate for herself, the explanation of which was given in Ruling 481.

Ruling 509. If a woman who does not have a habit of duration for *ḥayḍ* experiences bleeding for one or more months after giving birth, the bleeding on the first ten days is *nifās* and the bleeding on the second ten days is *istiḥāḍah*. As for the bleeding after that, it is possible that it could be *ḥayḍ* or *istiḥāḍah*; to determine whether it is *ḥayḍ* or not, she must act according to the instructions mentioned in the previous ruling.

THE *GHUSL* FOR TOUCHING A CORPSE (*MASS AL-MAYYIT*)

Ruling 510. If someone touches – i.e. makes part of his body come into contact with – the body of a dead person after it has become cold but before it has been given *ghusl*, he must perform the *ghusl* for touching a corpse, irrespective of whether he touches it while he is asleep or awake, voluntarily or involuntarily. Even if one's nail or bone touches a nail or bone of the corpse, he must perform this *ghusl*. However, if one touches a dead animal, performing *ghusl* is not obligatory for him.

Ruling 511. Performing this *ghusl* is not obligatory for touching a deceased person whose entire body has not yet become cold, even if one touches a part that has become cold.

Ruling 512. If a person makes his hair touch a corpse, or he makes his body touch the hair of a corpse, or he makes his hair touch the hair of a corpse, then performing this *ghusl* is not obligatory for him.

Ruling 513. If a child is stillborn, his mother must perform this *ghusl* based on obligatory precaution. If [a child is born alive but] his mother dies, the child must perform this *ghusl* before reaching the age of legal responsibility based on obligatory precaution.

Ruling 514. If a person touches a corpse that has been given the three *ghusls*[52] completely, then performing this *ghusl* does not become obligatory for him. However, if one touches part of a corpse before the completion of the third *ghusl*, then even if that particular part of the corpse has been given the third *ghusl*, he must perform the *ghusl* for touching a corpse.

Ruling 515. If an insane person or a child who has not reached the age of legal responsibility touches a corpse, then after the insane person becomes sane or the child reaches the age of legal responsibility, he must perform the *ghusl* for touching a corpse. If the child is *mumayyiz* [and performs this *ghusl*], his *ghusl* is valid.

Ruling 516. If part of the body of a living person, or part of the body of a dead person who has not been given *ghusl*, becomes separated and one touches it before it is given *ghusl*, it is not necessary for him to perform the *ghusl* for touching a corpse even if the separated part contains a bone. However, if a corpse is cut into pieces and one touches all or most of them, this *ghusl* becomes obligatory.

Ruling 517. Performing this *ghusl* is not obligatory for touching a bone that has not been given *ghusl* and has separated from a dead or living person. Similarly, [performing this *ghusl* is not obligatory] for touching a tooth that has separated from a dead or living person.

[52] See Ruling 538.

Ruling 518. The *ghusl* for touching a corpse is like the *ghusl* for *janābah*, and it suffices in place of *wuḍūʾ*.

Ruling 519. If a person touches a number of corpses or one corpse a number of times, then performing one *ghusl* is sufficient.

Ruling 520. There is no problem for someone who has touched a corpse but has not performed the *ghusl* for touching a corpse to stay in a mosque, have sexual intercourse with his wife, or recite verses of the Qur'an that contain an obligatory *sajdah*.[53] However, for prayers and suchlike, he must perform *ghusl*.

LAWS RELATING TO A DYING PERSON (*MUḤTAḌAR*)

Ruling 521. Based on obligatory precaution, a believer who is dying – i.e. breathing his last breaths – must be laid on his back if possible, in a way that the soles of his feet face qibla, whether the believer is male or female, an adult or a child.

Ruling 522. It is better that until the *ghusl* given to a corpse has not been completely performed, a dying person should be laid in the manner mentioned in the previous ruling [with the soles of his feet] facing qibla. After a corpse has been given *ghusl*, it is better to lay it in the same position as it will be when people perform *ṣalāt al-mayyit* for it.

Ruling 523. Based on obligatory precaution, laying a dying person in a way that the soles of his feet face qibla is obligatory for every Muslim. In the event that Muslims know that the dying person consents [to being laid like this] and he is not incapacitated, it is not necessary to get the consent of his guardian (*walī*) [to lay him like this]; otherwise [i.e. if he is incapacitated], it is necessary to get the consent of his guardian based on obligatory precaution.

[53] These verses are mentioned in the fifth part of the list mentioned in Ruling 354.

Ruling 524. It is recommended to perform *talqīn*[54] on a dying person with the *shahādatayn* (two testimonies),[55] the avowal (*iqrār*) of the Most Noble Prophet (Ṣ) and the Infallible Imams (ʿA), and other rightful beliefs of the faith in a manner that he understands. It is also recommended that the things mentioned above be repeated until the time of death.

Ruling 525. It is recommended that this *duʿāʾ* be impressed upon the dying person in a manner that he understands:

اَللّٰهُمَّ ٱغْفِرْ لِيَ الْكَثِيْرَ مِنْ مَعَاصِيْكَ، وَٱقْبَلْ مِنِّيَ الْيَسِيْرَ مِنْ طَاعَتِكَ،
يَا مَنْ يَقْبَلُ الْيَسِيْرَ وَيَعْفُوْ عَنِ الْكَثِيْرِ، اِقْبَلْ مِنِّيَ الْيَسِيْرَ وَٱعْفُ عَنِّيَ الْكَثِيْرَ،
إِنَّكَ أَنْتَ الْعَفُوُّ الْغَفُوْرُ، اَللّٰهُمَّ ٱرْحَمْنِيْ فَإِنَّكَ رَحِيْمٌ

allāhummagh fir liyal kathīra min maʿāṣīk, waqbal minniyal yasīra min ṭāʿatik, yā man yaqbalul yasīra wa yaʿfū ʿanil kathīr, iqbal minniyal yasīra waʿfu ʿanniyal kathīr, innaka antal ʿafuwwul ghafūr, allāhummar ḥamnī faʾinnaka raḥīm

O Allah! Pardon the many times I have disobeyed You, and accept the few instances when I have obeyed You. O You Who accepts the few and pardons the many! Accept from me what are few and pardon me for the many. Indeed, You are the All-Pardoning, the All-Forgiving. O Allah! Have mercy on me, for You are the Ever-Merciful.

Ruling 526. If someone is experiencing a painful death, it is recommended that he be taken to the place where he used to perform prayers, as long as this does not upset him.

Ruling 527. In order to comfort a dying person, it is recommended to recite at his side the blessed surahs of Yāsīn,[56] al-Ṣāffāt,[57] and al-Aḥzāb;[58] and to recite Āyat al-Kursī,[59] verse fifty-four of Sūrat

[54] *Talqīn* refers to impressing principle beliefs upon a dying person or corpse.

[55] As explained in Ruling 205, 'the two testimonies' refers to testifying to the oneness of Allah and the prophethood of Prophet Muḥammad (Ṣ).

[56] Chapter 36 of the Qur'an. [57] Chapter 37 of the Qur'an. [58] Chapter 33 of the Qur'an.

[59] Verse 255 of Chapter 2 of the Qur'an.

al-Aʿrāf,[60] and the last three verses of Sūrat al-Baqarah.[61] In fact, [it is recommended] to recite as much of the Qur'an as possible.

Ruling 528. It is disapproved to leave a dying person alone, place a weighty object on his stomach, be *junub* or *ḥāʾiḍ* near him, talk excessively near him, cry near him, or leave women alone next to him.

LAWS RELATING TO AFTER DEATH

Ruling 529. After someone has died, it is recommended to close his lips, eyes, and mouth, straighten his hands and legs, and cover him with a piece of cloth. If someone dies at night, [it is recommended] to keep the place where he died lighted, inform the believers about the funeral, and hasten in burying his body. However, if his death is not certain, people must wait until it is certain. If the deceased is a pregnant woman and the child in her womb is alive, the burial must be delayed so that the woman's stomach can be cut open, the baby removed, and the woman's stomach stitched up.

THE OBLIGATION TO GIVE *GHUSL*, SHROUD (*TAKFĪN*), PRAY OVER, CAMPHORATE (*TAḤNĪṬ*), AND BURY (*DAFN*)

Ruling 530. It is obligatory for the guardian of a Muslim who has died to give him *ghusl* and to camphorate, shroud, perform prayers over, and bury him, even if the deceased is not a Twelver (Ithnā ʿAsharī) Shia. The guardian must either do these things himself or instruct someone else to do them; and in the event that someone else does these things with the guardian's consent, the responsibility is lifted from the guardian. In fact, even if the burial and suchlike is carried out without the guardian's consent, the responsibility is still lifted from him and there is no need to repeat those things. If the deceased does not have a guardian or the guardian refuses to do those things, it is obligatory for every *mukallaf* to do them as a collective obligation

[60] Chapter 7 of the Qur'an.

[61] Chapter 2 of the Qur'an.

(*al-wājib al-kifāʾī*), meaning that if someone or some people do those things, the responsibility is lifted from everyone else, and in the event that no one does them, then everyone will have committed a sin. In case the guardian refuses [to do those things or instruct someone else to do them], it is not necessary to obtain his permission.

Ruling 531. If a person is engaged in attending to the duties relating to a deceased person, it is not obligatory for others to start doing them. However, if the person leaves the duties half-finished, others must complete them.

Ruling 532. If a person is confident that others are engaged in attending to the duties relating to a deceased person, it is not obligatory for him to start doing those things. However, if one doubts or merely supposes [that others are engaged in attending to those duties], he must start doing them.

Ruling 533. If someone knows that the *ghusl*, shrouding, prayers, or burial of a deceased person has been performed incorrectly, he must perform that act again. However, if one merely supposes that it was performed incorrectly or doubts whether it was performed correctly or not, then it is not necessary for him to perform it again.

Ruling 534. The guardian of a woman is her husband. In other cases, the guardian of a deceased person is the heir in accordance with the order of the tiers of inheritance, which will be mentioned later. In each tier, men take precedence over women; however, it is problematic to consider [certain members of the family as having precedence over others, such as] the father of the deceased over the deceased's son; his paternal grandfather over his brother; his brother over his paternal half-brother or his maternal half-brother; his paternal half-brother over his maternal half-brother; and his paternal uncle over his maternal uncle. Therefore, in these cases, the requisite precautionary action must be taken. Furthermore, if there are a number of guardians, the permission of one of them suffices.

Ruling 535. The guardian of a deceased person must not be a non-*bāligh* child nor a person who is insane. Similarly, a person who is absent and cannot personally undertake the duties or instruct someone else to do them cannot be a guardian.

Ruling 536. If someone says he is the guardian of a deceased person or that the guardian of the deceased has given his consent to give *ghusl*, shroud, and bury the deceased, or if with regard to preparing the corpse he says that he is his executor (*waṣī*), then in the event that one is confident that what he says is the truth, or the deceased's body is at his disposal, or two dutiful people testify to the veracity of what he says, his word must be accepted.

Ruling 537.* If a person specifies in his will (*waṣiyyah*) that an individual other than his guardian is to personally perform his *ghusl*, shroud him, or pray over him, it is not necessary for that individual to accept the request. However, if he does accept, he must perform those duties and there is no need for him to get the guardian's consent. If a person specifies in his will that an individual has authority over these matters and is responsible for and in charge of matters concerning his body after his death, such that the individual may choose to perform the duties himself or appoint someone else to do them, then, in this case, the obligatory precaution is that the individual must accept the request. However, if accepting the request would be extraordinarily difficult for him, or if he rejects the request while the person who made the will is still alive and the news of his rejection reaches him and he is able to specify someone else in his will, then in these cases, it is not obligatory for him to accept.

METHOD OF PERFORMING THE GHUSL GIVEN TO A CORPSE (*MAYYIT*)

Ruling 538. It is obligatory to give a corpse three *ghusls* in the following order:

1. a *ghusl* with water that has been mixed with lote tree (*sidr*) leaves;
2. a *ghusl* with water that has been mixed with camphor (*kāfūr*);
3. a *ghusl* with ordinary water.

Ruling 539. The amount of *sidr* leaves and camphor in the water must not be so great that they turn the water into mixed (*muḍāf*) water, neither must the amount be so little that it cannot be said that *sidr* leaves and camphor have been mixed in the water.

Ruling 540. If the necessary amount of *sidr* leaves and camphor cannot be found, then based on recommended precaution, the amount to which one has access should be mixed in the water.

Ruling 541. If someone dies in the state of *iḥrām*, he must not be given *ghusl* with camphor water; instead, he must be given *ghusl* with ordinary water unless he was in the state of *iḥrām* for *ḥajj al-tamattuʿ*[62] and he had completed the *ṭawāf*,[63] its prayer, and *saʿy*;[64] or, he was in the state of *iḥrām* for *ḥajj al-qirān* or *ḥajj al-ifrād*[65] and he had performed *ḥalq*;[66] in these two cases, he must be given *ghusl* with camphor water.

Ruling 542. If *sidr* leaves and camphor, or one of them, cannot be found, or if using them is not permitted – for example, they are usurped – then based on obligatory precaution, a person must perform one *tayammum* on the deceased; and in place of whichever one was not possible [i.e. in place of the *sidr* leaves and/or camphor that could not be found or its use was not permitted], *ghusl* must be given with ordinary water.

Ruling 543. One who gives *ghusl* to a corpse must be sane, Muslim, and, based on obligatory precaution, a Twelver Shia; furthermore, he must know the rulings of *ghusl*. If a *mumayyiz* child performs *ghusl* correctly, it is acceptable [for him to perform the *ghusl*]. In the event that the deceased is not a Twelver Shia and someone from the deceased's religious denomination (*madhhab*) gives him *ghusl* – albeit

[62] *Ḥajj al-tamattuʿ* is the pilgrimage to Mecca performed by Muslims who reside further than 88 kilometres from Mecca.

[63] *Ṭawāf* refers to the circumambulation of the Kaʿbah.

[64] *Saʿy* refers to the hajj and *ʿumrah* ritual of traversing to and from the mountains of Ṣafā and Marwah.

[65] These are two types of pilgrimage to Mecca performed by Muslims who reside within 88 kilometres of Mecca.

[66] *Ḥalq* is the shaving of the head performed by men as part of the hajj rituals.

according to the laws of his denomination – the responsibility is lifted from Twelver believers unless a Twelver believer is the guardian of the deceased, in which case the responsibility is not lifted from him.

Ruling 544. One who gives *ghusl* to a corpse must have the intention of attaining proximity to Allah the Exalted, and it is sufficient if he has an intention to follow the command of Allah the Exalted.

Ruling 545. Giving *ghusl* to a Muslim child is obligatory even if the child is of illegitimate birth. Giving *ghusl*, shrouding, and burying a disbeliever and his offspring is not obligatory; however, if the child of a disbeliever is *mumayyiz* and expresses belief in Islam, he is a believer. As for someone who was insane from childhood and reached the age of legal responsibility while he was insane, in the event that his father or his mother is Muslim, he must be given *ghusl*.

Ruling 546. A miscarried child of four months or more must be given *ghusl*. In fact, based on obligatory precaution, even a miscarried child of fewer than four months whose body formation is complete must be given *ghusl*. In cases other than these two, based on obligatory precaution, one must wrap the child in cloth and bury him without giving it *ghusl*.

Ruling 547. A man cannot give *ghusl* to a woman who is not his *maḥram*. Similarly, a woman cannot give *ghusl* to a man who is not her *maḥram*. A husband and wife can give *ghusl* to one another.

Ruling 548. A man can give *ghusl* to a young girl who cannot discern between right and wrong. A woman can give *ghusl* to a young boy who cannot discern between right and wrong.

Ruling 549. Those who are *maḥram* can give *ghusl* to one another, whether they are *maḥram* by being biological/blood relatives – for example, a mother and a sister – or by way of breastfeeding, or by marriage. Except for the private parts, it is not necessary to cover a corpse and give it *ghusl* from under the cover, although it is better to do so. However, based on obligatory precaution, a man can only give *ghusl* to a *maḥram* woman when he cannot find a woman who can give *ghusl* to her, and vice versa [i.e. a woman can only give *ghusl* to a *maḥram* man when she cannot find a man who can give *ghusl* to him].

Ruling 550. If a corpse and the person giving *ghusl* to it are both male or both are female, it is permitted for the corpse to be naked, except for the private parts. However, it is better to give it *ghusl* from under a cover.

Ruling 551. Looking at the private parts of a corpse is unlawful, except in the case of a husband and wife. If the person giving *ghusl* looks [at the private parts], he commits a sin but the *ghusl* does not become invalid.

Ruling 552. If there is an intrinsic impurity on any part of a corpse, it must be removed before *ghusl* is given to that part; and it is better to remove impurities from the entire body before starting the *ghusl*.

Ruling 553. [The method of performing] the *ghusl* given to a corpse is the same as that of the *ghusl* for *janābah*; and the obligatory precaution is that one must not give a corpse immersive *ghusl* if it is possible to give it sequential *ghusl*. If sequential *ghusl* is given, the right side must be washed before the left side.

Ruling 554. If someone dies while in the state of *ḥayḍ* or *janābah*, it is not necessary to give that person the *ghusl* for *ḥayḍ* or the *ghusl* for *janābah*; rather, the *ghusl* given to a corpse is sufficient.

Ruling 555. Based on obligatory precaution, it is unlawful to take a fee for giving *ghusl* to a corpse; if someone gives *ghusl* to a corpse with the intention of earning a fee such that it conflicts with him having an intention to attain proximity to Allah, the *ghusl* is invalid. However, it is not unlawful to take a fee for preliminary matters relating to giving *ghusl* [such as getting the three types of water ready].

Ruling 556. Giving *jabīrah ghusl* to a corpse has not been sanctioned in Islamic law (i.e. it is not *mashrūʿ*). Furthermore, if one does not find water or there is an obstacle to using water, he must perform one *tayammum* on the corpse instead of giving it *ghusl*; and the recommended precaution is to perform three *tayammums* on it.

Ruling 557. Someone who performs *tayammum* on a corpse must strike his own palms on the earth and then wipe them on the face and the back of the hands of the corpse; and if it is possible, the recommended precaution is to perform *tayammum* using the hands of the corpse.

LAWS OF SHROUDING (*TAKFĪN*) A CORPSE

Ruling 558. The body of a dead Muslim must be shrouded with three pieces of cloth: a loincloth, a shirt, and a full cover.

Ruling 559. Based on obligatory precaution, the loincloth must cover the area from the navel to the knees; and it is better that it cover the area from the chest to over the feet. Furthermore, based on obligatory precaution, the shirt must cover the area from the top of the shoulders to the middle of the calf; and it is better that it reach over the feet. As for the full cover, this must be long enough to cover the entire body; and the obligatory precaution is that its length must be long enough for both ends to be tied, and its width must be wide enough for one side to overlap the other.

Ruling 560.* The obligatory quantity of the shroud (*kafan*) mentioned in the previous ruling must be taken from the estate of the deceased if someone has not donated it. In fact, even the recommended quantity of the *kafan* – up to a limit that is common and normal, and taking into consideration the status of the deceased – can also be taken from the estate of the deceased. However, in case the deceased's heir is not *bāligh*, the recommended precaution is that one should not take more than the obligatory quantity of the *kafan* from the estate.

Ruling 561. If someone makes a will stipulating that the recommended amount of his *kafan* should be paid for from the one-third of his estate,[67] or, if he makes a will that one-third of his estate should be spent on himself but does not specify how it should be spent or he specifies how only part of it should be spent, then in these cases, the

[67] This refers to the maximum amount of one's estate over which he has discretion in a will for it to be disposed of in accordance with his wishes after his death.

recommended quantity of the *kafan* can be taken from the one-third of his estate even if the quantity is more than the amount that is commonly used.

Ruling 562. If a deceased person has not made a will stipulating that the cost of his *kafan* must be taken from the one-third of his estate, and if one wants to take it out from his estate, he must not take more than what was mentioned in Ruling 560. For example, the recommended quantity of the *kafan* must not be taken from the deceased's estate in an amount that is uncommon and more than what is appropriate to the deceased's status. Similarly, if one pays more than the usual price for the *kafan*, he must not pay the extra amount from the deceased's estate. However, he can pay for it from the share of the heirs who are *bāligh* with their consent.

Ruling 563. It is the husband's responsibility to provide the *kafan* for his wife even if she has her own wealth. Similarly, if a woman is given a revocable divorce (*al-ṭalāq al-rijʿī*) – which will be explained in the section on the rules of divorce – and she dies before the expiry of her prescribed waiting period (*ʿiddah*), her husband must provide the *kafan* for her. In the event that her husband is not *bāligh* or is insane, the guardian of the husband must provide the wife's *kafan* from the husband's estate.

Ruling 564. Providing the *kafan* for a deceased person is not obligatory for his relatives, even if it was obligatory for them to pay for his living expenses while he was alive.

Ruling 565. If a deceased person does not have an estate from which his *kafan* can be purchased, it is not permitted to bury him naked; rather, based on an obligatory precaution, it is obligatory for the Muslims [who come to know about this] to shroud him. It is permitted to pay for the *kafan* from alms tax (zakat).

Ruling 566.* The recommended precaution is that each of the three pieces of the *kafan* must not be so thin that the corpse can be seen through them. However, if the pieces are such that all three of them together prevent the corpse from being seen, it will suffice.

Ruling 567. It is not permitted to shroud a corpse with something that has been usurped even if nothing else can be procured; and in the event that the *kafan* of a corpse has been usurped and the owner does not consent, it must be removed from the corpse even if it has already been buried, except in a few cases – but space does not allow for the details of these cases to be mentioned here.

Ruling 568. It is not permitted to shroud a corpse with anything impure or with pure silk cloth; and based on obligatory precaution, [it is not permitted to shroud a corpse] with cloth that has been woven with gold. However, there is no problem in using these if no other option is available.

Ruling 569. It is not permitted to shroud a corpse with the hide of an impure carcass when other options are available. Similarly, based on obligatory precaution, shrouding with the hide of a pure carcass and with cloth made of the wool or fur of an animal whose meat is unlawful to eat is also not permitted when there are other options available. However, there is no problem if the *kafan* is made of the fur or wool of an animal whose meat is lawful to eat, although the recommended precaution is that a corpse should not be shrouded with either of these.

Ruling 570. If the *kafan* of a corpse becomes impure with an impurity – irrespective of whether the impurity was from the corpse itself or something else – then, in the event that the *kafan* would not be destroyed, the impure part must be washed or cut out even if this takes place after the corpse has been placed in the grave; and if washing or cutting it out is not possible but it is possible to replace the *kafan*, then it must be replaced.

Ruling 571. If someone in the state of *iḥrām* for hajj or *ʿumrah* dies, he must be shrouded in the same manner as other people [who die while not in the state of *iḥrām*]; and there is no problem in covering his head and face.

Ruling 572. It is recommended that while someone is healthy, he should prepare his *kafan*, *sidr* leaves, and camphor.

LAWS OF CAMPHORATING (*TAḤNĪṬ*) A CORPSE

Ruling 573. After *ghusl* has been given to a corpse, it is obligatory to camphorate it – i.e. to apply camphor on its forehead, palms, knees, and the tips of the big toes – such that a little of the camphor remains on them even if by means other than rubbing. It is recommended that camphor also be applied to the tip of the nose of the corpse. The camphor must be powdered, fresh, and *mubāḥ* (not usurped); and if it has lost its fragrance on account of it being old, it is not sufficient.

Ruling 574. The recommended precaution is that camphor should be first applied to the forehead of the corpse; after that, there is no particular order in applying camphor to the other parts of the body.

Ruling 575. It is better that camphorating be done before shrouding, although there is no problem in doing it during or after shrouding.

Ruling 576. If someone dies while in the state of *iḥrām* for *ʿumrah* or hajj, it is not permitted to camphorate his body except in the case mentioned in Ruling 541.

Ruling 577. Although applying perfume is unlawful for someone engaged in a spiritual retreat (*iʿtikāf*)[68] and for a woman whose *ʿiddah* has not yet finished following the death of her husband, when such a person dies, it is obligatory to camphorate his or her body.

Ruling 578. The recommended precaution is that a corpse should not be perfumed with musk, ambergris (*ʿanbar*), aloes-wood (*ʿūd*), and other fragrances, nor should these be mixed with the camphor.

Ruling 579. It is recommended to mix some *turbah* from the grave of His Eminence Sayyid al-Shuhadāʾ [Imam al-Ḥusayn] (ʿA) with the camphor. However, the camphor must not be applied to places on the body that would cause disrespect to that earth. Furthermore, the amount of *turbah* should not be so great that when mixed with the camphor, it can no longer be called 'camphor'.

[68] *Iʿtikāf* refers to the act of staying in a mosque under particular conditions with the intention of worshipping Allah. The laws of *iʿtikāf* are stated in Chapter 5.

Ruling 580. If camphor cannot be procured, or if the quantity that can be procured is sufficient only for *ghusl*, then camphorating is not necessary. In the event that after *ghusl* an amount of camphor is left over but it is not sufficient for it to be applied to all seven parts of the body, then based on recommended precaution, it must first be applied to the forehead and then to the other parts if any is left over.

Ruling 581. It is recommended to place two freshly cut twigs in the grave with the corpse.

LAWS OF THE FUNERAL PRAYER (*ṢALĀT AL-MAYYIT*)

Ruling 582. It is obligatory to perform *ṣalāt al-mayyit* for a Muslim who has died, and for every child who is considered a Muslim and has completed six years of age.

Ruling 583. Based on obligatory precaution, it is necessary to perform *ṣalāt al-mayyit* for a child who has not completed six years of age but could understand prayers. If the child could not understand prayers, there is no problem in performing the prayer with the intention of *rajā᾿* [i.e. with the intention of performing it in the hope that it is desired by Allah]. There is no recommendation to perform the prayer for a stillborn child.

Ruling 584. *Ṣalāt al-mayyit* must be performed after giving *ghusl*, camphorating, and shrouding. If it is performed before or while performing these – albeit forgetfully or on account of not knowing the ruling – it is not sufficient.

Ruling 585.* It is not necessary for someone who wants to perform *ṣalāt al-mayyit* to have *wuḍū᾿*, *ghusl*, or *tayammum*, or for his body and clothes to be pure. In fact, even if his clothes are usurped there is no problem, although it is better that he observe all the rules that apply to other prayers. One must refrain from doing anything that breaks the form of *ṣalāt al-mayyit*, and based on obligatory precaution, one must abstain from talking, laughing, and turning their back to the qibla.

Ruling 586. The person who performs *ṣalāt al-mayyit* must face qibla. It is also obligatory to place the corpse in a way that it lies on its back in front of the person performing the prayer with its head on the person's right-hand side and its feet on his left.

Ruling 587. The place where one performs the prayers must not be higher or lower than the corpse; however, being a little higher or lower is not a problem. The recommended precaution is that the place where the prayers are being performed should not be usurped.

Ruling 588. The person performing the prayer must not be far away from the corpse. However, there is no problem in him being far away if the prayer is performed in congregation and the rows are connected to one another.

Ruling 589. The person performing the prayer must stand with the corpse in front of him. However, if the prayer is being performed in congregation, there is no problem if some of the people do not stand in front of the corpse.

Ruling 590. There must not be a curtain, wall, or a similar thing between the corpse and the person performing the prayer. However, there is no problem if the corpse is in a coffin or something similar.

Ruling 591. During the prayer, the private parts of the corpse must be covered. If it has not been possible to shroud the corpse, the private parts must still be covered, albeit with a board, brick, or something similar.

Ruling 592. *Ṣalāt al-mayyit* must be performed while standing and with the intention of attaining proximity to Allah. At the time of making the intention, the corpse must be specified; for example, one may make the intention: 'I am performing the prayer for this corpse *qurbatan ilal lāh* (to attain proximity to Allah)'. And the obligatory precaution is that the type of stillness of body required in the daily prayers must be observed [in this prayer as well].

Ruling 593. If there is no one who can perform *ṣalāt al-mayyit* while standing, it can be performed while sitting.

Ruling 594. If the deceased person had made a will stipulating that a particular person must perform the prayer for him, it is not necessary for that nominated person to get the consent of the guardian of the deceased, although it is better that he does.

Ruling 595. The opinion of some jurists is that it is disapproved to perform *ṣalāt al-mayyit* a number of times. However, this matter is not established, and if the deceased is a learned and God-wary person, there is no problem in considering it not disapproved.

Ruling 596. If a corpse is intentionally, forgetfully, or for some other reason buried without the prayer being performed for it, or if after burying a corpse it becomes known that the prayer performed for it was invalid, it is not permitted to exhume the body to perform the prayer for it. However, there is no problem if, before the body decomposes, the prayer is performed at the grave-side with the intention of *rajāʾ* while observing the conditions mentioned earlier for this prayer.

METHOD OF PERFORMING *ṢALĀT AL-MAYYIT*

Ruling 597.* *Ṣalāt al-mayyit* has five *takbīrs*.[69] It is sufficient if one who is performing the prayer says five *takbīrs* as follows:[70]

After making the intention and saying the first *takbīr*, the person says:

أَشْهَدُ أَنْ لَا إِلٰهَ إِلَّا اللّٰهُ وَأَنَّ مُحَمَّدًا رَسُوْلُ اللّٰهِ

ashhadu an lā ilāha illal lāhu wa anna muḥammadan rasūlul lāh

I testify that there is no god but Allah and that Muḥammad is the messenger of Allah.

After the second *takbīr*, he says:

[69] *Takbīr* is a proclamation of Allah's greatness by saying '*allāhu akbar*'.

[70] The changes in this ruling relate to the *duʿāʾ* that is recited after the fourth *takbīr*. Some words which were not there in the previous edition of *Islamic Laws* have been added. These words are underlined.

اَللّٰهُمَّ صَلِّ عَلَىٰ مُحَمَّدٍ وَآلِ مُحَمَّدٍ

allāhumma ṣalli ʿalā muḥammdin wa āli muḥammad

O Allah! Bless Muḥammad and the progeny of Muḥammad.

After the third *takbīr*, he says:

اَللّٰهُمَّ ٱغْفِرْ لِلْمُؤْمِنِيْنَ وَالْمُؤْمِنَاتِ

allāhummagh fir lilmu'minīna wal mu'mināt

O Allah! Forgive the believers, men and women alike.

After the fourth *takbīr*, if the deceased is male, he says:

اَللّٰهُمَّ ٱغْفِرْ لِهٰذَا الْمَيِّتِ

allāhummagh fir lihādhal mayyit

O Allah! Forgive this deceased man.

If the deceased is female, he says:

اَللّٰهُمَّ ٱغْفِرْ لِهٰذِهِ الْمَيِّتَةِ

allāhummagh fir lihādhihil mayyitah

O Allah! Forgive this deceased woman.

Then he says the fifth *takbīr* [to conclude the prayer].

It is better that after the first *takbīr*, he says:

أَشْهَدُ أَنْ لَا إِلٰهَ إِلَّا اللّٰهُ وَحْدَهُ لَا شَرِيْكَ لَهُ، وَأَشْهَدُ أَنَّ مُحَمَّدًا عَبْدُهُ وَرَسُوْلُهُ،
أَرْسَلَهُ بِالْحَقِّ بَشِيْرًا وَنَذِيْرًا بَيْنَ يَدَيِ السَّاعَةِ

ashhadu an lā ilāha illal lāhu waḥdahu lā sharīka lah, wa ashhadu anna muḥammadan ʿabduhu wa rasūluh, arsalahu bilḥaqqi bashīran wa nadhīran bayna yadayis sāʿah

I testify that there is no god but Allah, He alone, for whom there is no partner; and I testify that Muḥammad is His servant and His messenger, whom He sent with the truth as a giver of glad tidings and a warner before the advent of the Hour [i.e. the Day of Judgement.]

[And it is better that] after the second *takbīr*, he says:

اَللّٰهُمَّ صَلِّ عَلَىٰ مُحَمَّدٍ وَآلِ مُحَمَّدٍ، وَبَارِكْ عَلَىٰ مُحَمَّدٍ وَآلِ مُحَمَّدٍ، وَٱرْحَمْ مُحَمَّدًا وَآلَ مُحَمَّدٍ، كَأَفْضَلِ مَا صَلَّيْتَ وَبَارَكْتَ وَتَرَحَّمْتَ عَلَىٰ إِبْرَاهِيْمَ وَآلِ إِبْرَاهِيْمَ، إِنَّكَ حَمِيْدٌ مَجِيْدٌ، وَصَلِّ عَلَىٰ جَمِيْعِ الْأَنْبِيَاءِ وَالْمُرْسَلِيْنَ وَالشُّهَدَاءِ وَالصِّدِّيْقِيْنَ وَجَمِيْعِ عِبَادِ اللّٰهِ الصَّالِحِيْنَ

allāhumma ṣalli ʿalā muḥammadin wa āli muḥammad, wa bārik ʿalā muḥammadin wa āli muḥammad, warḥam muḥammadan wa āla muḥammad, ka'afḍali mā ṣallayta wa bārakta wa taraḥḥamta ʿalā ibrāhīma wa āli ibrāhīm, innaka ḥamīdun majīd, wa ṣalli ʿalā jamīʿil anbiyā'i wal mursalīna wash shuhadā'i waṣ ṣiddīqīna wa jamīʿi ʿibādil lāhiṣ ṣāliḥīn

O Allah! Bless Muḥammad and the progeny of Muḥammad, and bestow Your bounty upon Muḥammad and the progeny of Muḥammad, and have mercy on Muḥammad and the progeny of Muḥammad, with the best blessing, bestowal of bounty, and mercy that You showered upon Ibrāhīm and the progeny of Ibrāhīm. Indeed, You are the All-Laudable, All-Glorious. Bless all the Prophets and Messengers and witnesses and the truthful and all Allah's righteous servants.

[And it is better that] after the third *takbīr*, he says:

اَللّٰهُمَّ ٱغْفِرْ لِلْمُؤْمِنِيْنَ وَالْمُؤْمِنَاتِ، وَالْمُسْلِمِيْنَ وَالْمُسْلِمَاتِ، الْأَحْيَاءِ مِنْهُمْ وَالْأَمْوَاتِ، تَابِعْ بَيْنَنَا وَبَيْنَهُمْ بِالْخَيْرَاتِ، إِنَّكَ مُجِيْبُ الدَّعَوَاتِ، إِنَّكَ عَلَىٰ كُلِّ شَيْءٍ قَدِيْرٌ

allāhummagh fir lilmu'minīna wal mu'mināt, wal muslimīna wal muslimāt, al'aḥyā'i minhum wal amwāt, tābiʿ baynanā wa baynahum bilkhayrāt, innaka mujībud daʿawāt, innaka ʿalā kulli shay'in qadīr

O Allah! Forgive the believers, men and women alike, and the Muslims, men and women alike, the living among them and the dead. Shower us and them with blessings. Indeed, You are the Answerer of Supplications. Indeed, You are powerful over everything.

[And it is better that] after the fourth *takbīr*, if the deceased is male, he says:

اَللّٰهُمَّ إِنَّ هٰذَا الْمُسَجَّىٰ قُدَّامَنَا عَبْدُكَ وَٱبْنُ عَبْدِكَ وَٱبْنُ أَمَتِكَ، نَزَلَ بِكَ وَأَنْتَ خَيْرُ مَنْزُوْلٍ بِهِ، اَللّٰهُمَّ إِنَّا لَا نَعْلَمُ مِنْهُ إِلَّا خَيْرًا، وَأَنْتَ أَعْلَمُ بِهِ مِنَّا، اَللّٰهُمَّ إِنْ كَانَ مُحْسِنًا فَزِدْ فِيْ إِحْسَانِهِ، وَإِنْ كَانَ مُسِيْئًا فَتَجَاوَزْ عَنْ سَيِّئَاتِهِ وَٱغْفِرْ لَهُ، اَللّٰهُمَّ ٱجْعَلْهُ عِنْدَكَ فِيْ أَعْلَىٰ عِلِّيِّيْنَ، وَٱخْلُفْ عَلَىٰ أَهْلِهِ فِي الْغَابِرِيْنَ، وَٱرْحَمْهُ بِرَحْمَتِكَ يَا أَرْحَمَ الرَّاحِمِيْنَ

allāhumma inna hādhāl musajjā quddāmanā ʿabduka wabnu ʿabdika wabnu amatik, nazala bika wa anta khayru manzūlin bih, allāhumma innā lā naʿlamu minhu illā khayra, wa anta aʿlamu bihi minnā, allāhumma in kāna muḥsinan fazid fī iḥsānih, wa in kāna musīʾan fatajāwaz ʿan sayyiʾātihi waghfir lah, allāhummaj ʿalhu ʿindaka fī aʿlā ʿilliyyīn, wakh luf ʿalā ahlihi fil ghābirīn, warḥamhu biraḥmatika yā arḥamar rāhimīn

O Allah! Indeed, this shrouded corpse in front of us is Your servant, son of Your servant, and son of Your maidservant. He has taken abode with You and You are the best of those who are taken abode with. O Allah! We do not know from him anything but good, and You are more knowing of him than we. O Allah! If he was benevolent, then increase his benevolent deeds, and if he was sinful, then overlook his sins and forgive him. O Allah! Place him near You in the highest of the high ranks, and be his replacement for his family while they remain, and have mercy on him, by Your mercy, O Most Merciful!

Then he says the fifth *takbīr* [to conclude the prayer].

However, if the deceased is female, [it is better that] after the fourth *takbīr*, he says:

اَللّٰهُمَّ إِنَّ هٰذِهِ الْمُسَجَّاةَ قُدَّامَنَا أَمَتُكَ وَٱبْنَةُ عَبْدِكَ وَٱبْنَةُ أَمَتِكَ، نَزَلَتْ بِكَ وَأَنْتَ خَيْرُ مَنْزُوْلٍ بِهِ، اَللّٰهُمَّ إِنَّا لَا نَعْلَمُ مِنْهَا إِلَّا خَيْرًا، وَأَنْتَ أَعْلَمُ بِهَا مِنَّا، اَللّٰهُمَّ إِنْ كَانَتْ مُحْسِنَةً فَزِدْ فِيْ إِحْسَانِهَا، وَإِنْ كَانَتْ مُسِيْئَةً فَتَجَاوَزْ عَنْ سَيِّئَاتِهَا وَٱغْفِرْ لَهَا، اَللّٰهُمَّ ٱجْعَلْهَا عِنْدَكَ فِيْ أَعْلَىٰ عِلِّيِّيْنَ، وَٱخْلُفْ عَلَىٰ أَهْلِهَا فِي

الْغَابِرِيْنَ، وَٱرْحَمْهَا بِرَحْمَتِكَ يَا أَرْحَمَ الرَّاحِمِيْنَ

allāhumma inna hādhihil musajjāta quddāmanā amatuka wabnatu ʿabdika wabnatu amatik, nazalat bika wa anta khayru manzūlin bih, allāhumma innā lā naʿlamu minhā illā khayra, wa anta aʿlamu bihā minnā, allāhumma in kānat muḥsinatan fazid fī iḥsānihā, wa in kānat musīʾatan fatajāwaz ʿan sayyiʾātihā wagh fir lahā, allāhummaj ʿalhā ʿindaka fī aʿlā ʿilliyyīn, wakh luf ʿalā ahlihā fil ghābirīn, war ḥamhā biraḥmatika yā arḥamar rāhimīn

O Allah! Indeed, this shrouded corpse in front of us is Your maidservant, daughter of Your servant, and daughter of Your maidservant. She has taken abode with You and You are the best of those who are taken abode with. O Allah! We do not know from her anything but good, and You are more knowing of her than we. O Allah! If she was benevolent, then increase her benevolent deeds, and if she was sinful, then overlook her sins and forgive her. O Allah! Place her near You in the highest of the high ranks, and be her replacement for her family while they remain, and have mercy on her, by Your mercy, O Most Merciful!

It is worth noting that the supplication mentioned after the fourth *takbīr* is exclusively for people who are *bāligh*. For a prayer conducted for believing children, the following is said after the fourth *takbīr*:

اَللّٰهُمَّ ٱجْعَلْهُ لِأَبَوَيْهِ وَلَنَا سَلَفًا وَفَرَطًا وَأَجْرًا

allāhummaj ʿalhu liabawayhi wa lanā salafan wa faraṭan wa ajrā

O Allah! Make him for his parents and for us a good deed sent beforehand, a cause of recompense prepared in advance, and a cause of reward.

Ruling 598. The *takbīr*s and *duʿāʾ*s must be performed one after another such that the prayer does not lose its form.

Ruling 599. Someone who performs *ṣalāt al-mayyit* in congregation must also perform the *takbīr*s and recite the *duʿāʾ*s even if he is a follower in the prayer [as opposed to being the imam of the prayer].

RECOMMENDED (*MUSTAḤABB*) ACTS OF *ṢALĀT AL-MAYYIT*

Ruling 600. The following are recommended acts of *ṣalāt al-mayyit*:

1. the person performing the prayer should have *wuḍūʾ*, *ghusl*, or *tayammum*; and the recommended precaution is that he should perform *tayammum* only when it is not possible for him to perform *wuḍūʾ* or *ghusl*, or he fears that were he to perform *wuḍūʾ* or *ghusl* he would not reach the prayer in time;
2. if the deceased is male, the imam of the congregation or the person who is performing the prayer on his own should stand and face the middle part of the corpse; and if the deceased is female, they should stand and face her chest;
3. performing the prayer bare-footed;
4. raising one's hands for each *takbīr*;
5. the distance between the person who is performing the prayer and the corpse should be so little that if a wind were to blow any loose clothing that the person happened to be wearing, it would touch the coffin;
6. performing the prayer in congregation;
7. the imam of the congregation should say the *takbīr*s and *duʿāʾ*s aloud, and those who are following him in the prayer should say them quietly;
8. if the prayer is being performed in congregation, the person following the imam should stand behind him even if he is the only one following the imam;
9. praying a lot for the deceased and the believers;
10. if the prayer is being performed in congregation, '*aṣṣalāh*' should be said three times before commencing the prayer;
11. performing the prayer in a place where people go more often for performing *ṣalāt al-mayyit*;
12. if a *ḥāʾiḍ* woman wants to perform *ṣalāt al-mayyit* in congregation, she should stand alone and not in the rows with other people who are performing the prayer.

Ruling 601. Performing *ṣalāt al-mayyit* in mosques is disapproved. Performing it in Masjid al-Ḥarām, however, is not disapproved.

LAWS OF BURIAL (*DAFN*)

Ruling 602. It is obligatory to bury a corpse in a manner that its smell does not come out and predatory animals cannot dig it out. If there is a danger that an animal will dig it out, the grave must be strengthened with bricks or similar things.

Ruling 603. If it is not possible to bury a corpse in the ground, it can be placed in a building or a coffin instead.

Ruling 604. A corpse must be laid in the grave on its right side in a way that the front of the body faces qibla.

Ruling 605. If someone dies on a ship, in the event that the corpse will not decompose and there is no problem with it being on the ship, the people must wait until the ship reaches land and then bury it in the ground; otherwise, the *ghusl*, camphorating, and shrouding must be performed on the corpse while it is on the ship. After performing *ṣalāt al-mayyit*, the corpse must be placed in a large barrel, the lid must be closed, and the barrel must then be thrown into the sea; or, a heavy object must be tied to the feet of the corpse and it must then be thrown into the sea. If possible, the corpse must be thrown in a place where it will not immediately become food for animals.

Ruling 606. If there is a danger that an enemy will dig up the grave of a deceased person, exhume the body, and cut off its ears, nose, or some other part, then in the event that it is possible to do so, the body must be thrown into the sea in the way mentioned in the previous ruling.

Ruling 607. If necessary, the expenses of throwing a corpse into the sea and strengthening the grave can be taken from the deceased's estate.

Ruling 608. If a [pregnant] disbelieving woman dies and the baby in her womb has also died, in the event that the father of the child is a Muslim, the woman must be laid on her left side with her back facing qibla so that the front of the baby faces qibla. The same applies, based on recommended precaution, if the spirit (*rūḥ*) has not yet entered the foetus.

Ruling 609. It is not permitted to bury a Muslim in the graveyard of disbelievers or to bury a disbeliever in the graveyard of Muslims.

Ruling 610. It is not permitted to bury a Muslim in a place that is disrespectful to him, such as a place where rubbish and dirt are thrown.

Ruling 611.* It is not permitted to bury a corpse in a place that is usurped nor in the ground of a place like a mosque, *ḥusayniyyah*,[71] or religious school that has been given as a charitable endowment (*waqf*) for purposes other than burial if it causes damage to the endowment or inconveniences the purpose of the endowment. In fact, based on obligatory precaution, it is not permitted even if it does not cause damage or inconvenience.

Ruling 612.* It is not permitted to exhume a grave for another corpse to be buried there unless the grave is very old, the first corpse has completely decomposed, and the act would not necessitate sinning, such as encroaching on the right of another person.

Ruling 613. If a part of the corpse becomes separated – even if it is its hair, nail, or tooth – it must be buried with the body. In the event that the separated part is found after the body has been buried, then based on obligatory precaution, even if it is its hair, nail, or tooth, it must be buried in a different place. Furthermore, it is recommended to bury nails and teeth that were separated from a person's body when he was alive.

Ruling 614. If someone dies in a well and it is not possible to bring him out of it, the well must be sealed and it will be considered his grave.

Ruling 615. If a child dies in his mother's womb, and were he to remain in the womb he would be dangerous for the mother, he must be taken out in the easiest way possible; and there is no problem if one is compelled to cut the child's body into pieces. Furthermore, if her husband is skilled [in this matter], he must take the child out. If

[71] A *ḥusayniyyah* is a congregation hall used by Shia Muslims for religious ceremonies.

this is not possible, a woman who is skilled [in this matter] must take him out. The mother can also refer this matter to someone who can better perform this task and is more suited to her condition, even if that person is not her *maḥram*.

Ruling 616. Whenever a woman dies with a living child in her womb, if there is hope in the child surviving – albeit for a short time – then the woman must be cut open from wherever it is best suited for the health of the child and the child must be taken out; the mother's body must then be stitched up. However, if one knows or is confident that if this were done the child would die, then it is not permitted.

RECOMMENDED (*MUSTAḤABB*) ACTS OF BURIAL (*DAFN*)

Ruling 617. The following are recommended acts of burial:

1. the depth of the grave should be equal to the height of an average person or be at the level of an average person's shoulders;
2. the corpse should be buried in the nearest graveyard unless a further graveyard is better for some reason; for example, righteous people are buried there, or because people visit there more often to recite Sūrat al-Fātiḥah etc. for those buried there;
3. the corpse should be placed on the ground at a short distance from the grave and be taken slowly towards the grave in three stages; and at each stage, the corpse should be placed on the ground and then lifted; and the fourth time the corpse is put down should be when it is lowered into the grave;
4. if the deceased is male, then on the third time that the corpse is put down, it should be placed on the ground in a way that the head is at the feet end of the grave; and on the fourth time, it should be lowered into the grave head-first. If the deceased is female, then on the third time that the corpse is put down, it should be placed at the side of the grave facing qibla and then lowered into the grave sideways; and a cloth should be held over the grave while it is being lowered into the grave;

5. the corpse should be taken out of the coffin and lowered into the grave gently;
6. the recommended *duʿā*'s should be recited before and during the burial;
7.* after the corpse has been placed in a niche in the side of the grave [as is done in some countries], the ties of the *kafan* should be unfastened. It is better that first the tie of the *kafan* at the head of the corpse be opened and the face of the corpse be placed on soil. An earthen headrest should be formed and placed under its head;
8. unbaked bricks or clods of earth should be placed behind the back of the corpse so that it does not come to lie flat on its back;
9. before the niche is covered, a person should hold the right shoulder of the corpse with his right hand, firmly take its left shoulder with his left hand, place his mouth near the ear of the corpse, vigorously shake the corpse, and say three times:[72]

إِسْمَعْ إِفْـهَمْ (إِسْمَعِيْ إِفْـهَمِيْ) يَا ___ أَبْنَ (بِنْتَ) ___

isma' ifham (isma'ī ifhamī) yā ___ ibna (binta) ___

Listen and understand, O ___ son (daughter) of ___.

In the blank spaces, one should say the name of the deceased person and the name of his father. For example, if his name is Muḥammad and his father's name is ʿAlī, he should say three times:

إِسْمَعْ إِفْـهَمْ يَا مُحَمَّدَ بْنَ عَلِيٍّ

isma' ifham yā muḥammadab na 'alī

Listen and understand, O Muḥammad son of ʿAlī.

Then, he should say:

هَلْ أَنْتَ (أَنْتِ) عَلَى الْعَهْدِ الَّذِيْ فَارَقْتَـنَا (فَارَقْتِنَا) عَلَيْهِ مِنْ شَهَادَةِ

[72] In the following text, the words inside parentheses do not appear in the original work. They have been added here to facilitate the speaker when the deceased is female.

أَنْ لَا إِلٰهَ إِلَّا اللّٰهُ وَحْدَهُ لَا شَرِيْكَ لَهُ، وَأَنَّ مُحَمَّدًا صَلَّى اللّٰهُ عَلَيْهِ وَآلِهِ عَبْدُهُ وَرَسُوْلُهُ وَسَيِّدُ النَّبِيِّيْنَ وَخَاتَمُ الْمُرْسَلِيْنَ، وَأَنَّ عَلِيًّا أَمِيْرُ الْمُؤْمِنِيْنَ وَسَيِّدُ الْوَصِيِّيْنَ وَإِمَامٌ افْتَرَضَ اللّٰهُ طَاعَتَهُ عَلَى الْعَالَمِيْنَ، وَأَنَّ الْحَسَنَ وَالْحُسَيْنَ، وَعَلِيَّ بْنَ الْحُسَيْنِ، وَمُحَمَّدَ بْنَ عَلِيٍّ، وَجَعْفَرَ بْنَ مُحَمَّدٍ، وَمُوْسَى بْنَ جَعْفَرٍ، وَعَلِيَّ بْنَ مُوْسَىٰ، وَمُحَمَّدَ بْنَ عَلِيّ، وَعَلِيَّ بْنَ مُحَمَّدٍ، وَالْحَسَنَ بْنَ عَلِيٍّ، وَالْقَائِمَ الْحُجَّةَ الْمَهْدِيَّ، صَلَوَاتُ اللّٰهِ عَلَيْهِمْ أَئِمَّةُ الْمُؤْمِنِيْنَ، وَحُجَجُ اللّٰهِ عَلَى الْخَلْقِ أَجْمَعِيْنَ، وَأَئِمَّتُكَ (أَئِمَّتُكِ) أَئِمَّةُ هُدىً بِكَ (بِكِ) أَبْرَارٌ يَا ___

hal anta (anti) ʿalal ʿahdil ladhī fāraqtanā (fāraqtinā) ʿalayhi min shahādati an lā ilāha illal lāhu waḥdahu lā sharīka lah, wa anna muḥammadan ṣallal lāhu ʿalayhi wa ālihi ʿabduhu wa rasūluhu wa sayyidun nabiyyīna wa khātamul mursalīn, wa anna ʿaliyyan amīrul muʾminīna wa sayyidul waṣiyyīna wa imāmunif taraḍal lāhu ṭāʿatahu ʿalal ʿālamīn, wa annal ḥasana wal ḥusayn, wa ʿaliyyabnal ḥusayn, wa muḥammadabna ʿalī, wa jaʿfarabna muḥammad, wa mūsabna jaʿfar, wa ʿaliyyabna mūsā, wa muḥammadabna ʿalī, wa ʿaliyyabna muḥammad, wal ḥasanabna ʿalī, wal qāʾimal ḥujjatal mahdī, ṣalawātullāhi ʿalayhim aʾimmatul muʾminīn, wa ḥujajul lāhi ʿalal khalqi ajmaʿīn, wa aʾimmatuka (aʾimmatuki) aʾimmatu hudan bika (biki) abrārun yā ___

Do you hold true to the covenant to which you held when you parted from us? Whereby you testify that there is no god but Allah, He alone, for whom there is no partner; that Muḥammad – may Allah bless him and his progeny – is His servant and His messenger and the foremost of all the Prophets and the seal of all the Messengers; that ʿAlī is the Commander of the Faithful and the master of all the successors and an Imam whose obedience Allah has made obligatory for the worlds; that al-Ḥasan, and al-Ḥusayn, and ʿAlī son of al-Ḥusayn, and Muḥammad son of ʿAlī, and Jaʿfar son of Muḥammad, and Mūsā son of Jaʿfar, and ʿAlī son of Mūsā, and Muḥammad son of ʿAlī, and ʿAlī son of Muḥammad, and al-Ḥasan son of ʿAlī, and the

> Upriser, the Proof, al-Mahdī – may Allah's blessings be upon them all – are Imams of the faithful and Allah's proofs over the whole of creation, and your Imams are Imams of guidance for you and are pious, O ___ .

In the blank space, he should say the name of the deceased person and the name of his father. Then, he should say:

إِذَا أَتَاكَ (أَتَاكِ) الْمَلَكَانِ الْمُقَرَّبَانِ رَسُوْلَيْنِ مِنْ عِنْدِ اللّٰهِ تَبَارَكَ وَتَعَالَىٰ وَسَأَلَاكَ (سَأَلَاكِ) عَنْ رَبِّكَ (رَبِّكِ) وَعَنْ نَبِيِّكَ (نَبِيِّكِ) وَعَنْ دِيْنِكَ (دِيْنِكِ) وَعَنْ كِتَابِكَ (كِتَابِكِ) وَعَنْ قِبْلَتِكَ (قِبْلَتِكِ) وَعَنْ أَئِمَّتِكَ (أَئِمَّتِكِ) فَلَا تَخَفْ (تَخَافِيْ) وَلَا تَحْزَنْ (تَحْزَنِيْ) وَقُلْ (قُوْلِيْ) فِيْ جَوَابِهِمَا اللّٰهُ رَبِّيْ، وَمُحَمَّدٌ صَلَّى اللّٰهُ عَلَيْهِ وَآلِهِ وَسَلَّمَ نَبِيِّيْ، وَالْإِسْلَامُ دِيْنِيْ، وَالْقُرْآنُ كِتَابِيْ، وَالْكَعْبَةُ قِبْلَتِيْ، وَأَمِيْرُ الْمُؤْمِنِيْنَ عَلِيُّ ابْنُ أَبِيْ طَالِبٍ إِمَامِيْ، وَالْحَسَنُ بْنُ عَلِيٍّ الْمُجْتَبَىٰ إِمَامِيْ، وَالْحُسَيْنُ بْنُ عَلِيٍّ الشَّهِيْدُ بِكَرْبَلَاءَ إِمَامِيْ، وَعَلِيٌّ زَيْنُ الْعَابِدِيْنَ إِمَامِيْ، وَمُحَمَّدٌ الْبَاقِرُ إِمَامِيْ، وَجَعْفَرٌ الصَّادِقُ إِمَامِيْ، وَمُوْسَى الْكَاظِمُ إِمَامِيْ، وَعَلِيٌّ الرِّضَا إِمَامِيْ، وَمُحَمَّدٌ الْجَوَادُ إِمَامِيْ، وَعَلِيٌّ الْهَادِيْ إِمَامِيْ، وَالْحَسَنُ الْعَسْكَرِيُّ إِمَامِيْ، وَالْحُجَّةُ الْمُنْتَظَرُ إِمَامِيْ، هٰؤُلَاءِ صَلَوَاتُ اللّٰهِ عَلَيْهِمْ أَئِمَّتِيْ وَسَادَتِيْ وَقَادَتِيْ وَشُفَعَائِيْ، بِهِمْ أَتَوَلَّىٰ وَمِنْ أَعْدَائِهِمْ أَتَبَرَّأُ فِي الدُّنْيَا وَالْآخِرَةِ، ثُمَّ اعْلَمْ (اعْلَمِي) يَا ___

idhā atākal (atākil) malakānil muqarrabāni rasūlayni min ʿindillāhi tabāraka wa taʿālā, wa saʾalāka (saʾalāki) ʿan rabbika (rabbiki), wa ʿan nabiyyika (nabiyyiki), wa ʿan dīnika (dīniki), wa ʿan kitābika (kitābiki), wa ʿan qiblatika (qiblatiki), wa ʿan aʾimmatika (aʾimmatiki), falā takhaf (takhāfī) wa lā taḥzan (taḥzanī), wa qul (qūlī) fī jawābihimal lāhu rabbī, wa muḥammadun ṣallal lāhu ʿalayhi wa ālihi wa sallam nabiyyī, wal islāmu dīnī, wal qurʾānu kitābī, wal

> ka'batu qiblatī, wa amīrul mu'minīna 'aliyyubnu abī ṭālib imāmī, wal ḥasanubnu 'aliyyinil mujtabā imāmī, wal ḥusaynubnu 'aliyyinish shahīdu bikarbalā'a imāmī, wa 'alliyyun zaynul 'ābidīna imāmī, wa muḥammadunil bāqiru imāmī, wa ja'faruniṣ ṣādiqu imāmī, wa mūsal kāẓimu imāmī, wa 'aliyyunir riḍā imāmī, wa muḥammadunil jawādu imāmī, wa 'aliyyunil hādī imāmī, wal ḥasanul 'askariyyu imāmī, wal ḥujjatul muntaẓaru imāmī, hā'ulā'i ṣalawātul lāhi 'alayhim a'immatī wa sādatī wa qādatī wa shufa'ā'ī, bihim atawallā wa min a'dā'ihim atabarra'u fid dunyā wal ākhirah, thumma' lam (lamī) yā ___
>
> When the two angels who are close [to Allah], come to you as messengers from Allah – the Blessed, the Exalted – and ask you about your Lord, your Prophet, your religion, your book, your qibla, and your Imams, then do not fear nor grieve, but say in response to them: Allah is my Lord, Muḥammad – may Allah's blessing and peace be upon him and his progeny – is my Prophet, Islam is my religion, the Qur'an is my book, and the Ka'bah is my qibla. The Commander of the Faithful 'Alī ibn Abī Ṭālib is my Imam, al-Ḥasan al-Mujtabā is my Imam, al-Ḥusayn the Martyr of Karbala is my Imam, 'Alī Zayn al-'Ābidīn is my Imam, Muḥammad al-Bāqir is my Imam, Ja'far al-Ṣādiq is my Imam, Mūsā al-Kāẓim is my Imam, 'Alī al-Riḍā is my Imam, Muḥammad al-Jawād is my Imam, 'Alī al-Hādī is my Imam, al-Ḥasan al-'Askarī is my Imam, and al-Ḥujjah al-Muntaẓar is my Imam. All of them – may Allah's blessings be upon them – are my Imams, my masters, my leaders, and my intercessors. I befriend only them and I have hatred only for their enemies in this world and the Hereafter. Then know, O ___.

In the blank space, he should say the name of the deceased person and the name of his father. Then, he should say:

أَنَّ اللّٰهَ تَبَارَكَ وَتَعَالَىٰ نِعْمَ الرَّبُّ، وَأَنَّ مُحَمَّدًا صَلَّى اللّٰهُ عَلَيْهِ وَآلِهِ وَسَلَّمَ نِعْمَ الرَّسُوْلُ، وَأَنَّ عَلِيَّ ابْنَ أَبِيْ طَالِبٍ وَأَوْلَادَهُ الْمَعْصُوْمِيْنَ الْأَئِمَّةَ الْإِثْنَيْ عَشَرَ نِعْمَ الْأَئِمَّةُ، وَأَنَّ مَا جَاءَ بِهِ مُحَمَّدٌ صَلَّى اللّٰهُ عَلَيْهِ وَآلِهِ وَسَلَّمَ حَقٌّ، وَأَنَّ الْمَوْتَ حَقٌّ، وَسُؤَالَ مُنْكَرٍ وَنَكِيْرٍ فِي الْقَبْرِ حَقٌّ، وَالْبَعْثَ حَقٌّ، وَالنُّشُوْرَ حَقٌّ، وَالصِّرَاطَ حَقٌّ، وَالْمِيْزَانَ حَقٌّ، وَتَطَايُرَ

الْكُتُبِ حَقٌّ، وَأَنَّ الْجَنَّةَ حَقٌّ، وَالنَّارَ حَقٌّ، وَأَنَّ السَّاعَةَ آتِيَةٌ لَا رَيْبَ فِيْهَا، وَأَنَّ اللّٰهَ يَبْعَثُ مَنْ فِي الْقُبُوْرِ

annal lāha tabāraka wa taʿālā niʿmar rabb, wa anna muḥammadan ṣallal lāhu ʿalayhi wa ālihi wa sallama niʿmar rasūl, wa anna ʿaliyyabna abī ṭālib wa awlādahul maʿsūmīnal aʾimmatal ithnay ʿashara niʿmal aʿimmah, wa anna mā jāʾa bihi muḥammadun ṣallal lāhu ʿalayhi wa ālihi wa sallama ḥaqq, wa annal mawta ḥaqq, wa suʾāla munkarin wa nakīrin fil qabri ḥaqq, wal baʿtha ḥaqq, wan nushūra ḥaqq, waṣ ṣirāṭa ḥaqq, wal mīzāna ḥaqq, wa taṭāʾural kutubi ḥaqq, wa annal jannata ḥaqq, wan nāra ḥaqq, wa annas sāʿata ātiyatun lā rayba fīhā, wa annal lāha yabʿathu man fil qubūr

Allah, the Blessed, the Exalted, is the best Lord, and Muḥammad – may Allah's blessing and peace be upon him and his progeny – is the best messenger, and ʿAlī ibn Abī Ṭālib and his infallible descendants, [together being] the twelve Imams, are the best Imams. What Muḥammad – may Allah's blessing and peace be upon him and his progeny – brought is true; death is real; the questioning of Munkar and Nakīr in the grave is real; the raising [from the graves] is real; the resurrection is real; the Path is real, the Scale is real; the disclosure of the book of deeds is real; Paradise is real; the Fire is real; the Hour is coming, there is no doubt about it; and Allah will raise those who are in the graves.

Then, he should say:

أَفَهِمْتَ (أَفَهِمْتِ) يَا ___

afahimta (afahimti) yā

Do you understand, O ___?

In the blank space, he should mention the name of the deceased. Then, he should say:

ثَبَّتَكَ (ثَبَّتَكِ) اللّٰهُ بِالْقَوْلِ الثَّابِتِ، وَهَدَاكَ (هَدَاكِ) اللّٰهُ إِلَىٰ صِرَاطٍ مُسْتَقِيْمٍ، عَرَّفَ اللّٰهُ بَيْنَكَ (بَيْنَكِ) وَبَيْنَ أَوْلِيَائِكَ (أَوْلِيَائِكِ) فِي

مُسْتَقَرٍّ مِنْ رَحْمَتِهِ

thabbatakal (thabbatikil) lāhu bilqawlith thābit, wa hadākal (hadākil) lāhu ilā ṣirāṭin mustaqīm, ʿarrafal lāhu baynaka (baynaki) wa bayna awliyāʾika (awliyāʾiki) fī mustaqarrin min raḥmatih

May Allah keep you steadfast with the firm beliefs, and may He guide you on the right path. May Allah foster acquaintance between you and your guardians in the abode of His mercy.

Then, he should say:

اَللّٰهُمَّ جَافِ الْأَرْضَ عَنْ جَنْبَيْهِ (جَنْبَيْهَا)، وَٱصْعَدْ بِرُوْحِهِ (بِرُوْحِهَا) إِلَيْكَ، وَلَقِّهِ (لَقِّهَا) مِنْكَ بُرْهَانًا، اَللّٰهُمَّ عَفْوَكَ عَفْوَكَ

allāhumma jāfil arḍa ʿan jambayh (jambayhā), waṣʿad birūḥihi (birūḥihā) ilayk, wa laqqihi (laqqihā) minka burhāna, allāhumma ʿafwaka ʿafwak

O Allah! Make the ground spacious for him (her) on both of his (her) sides, and elevate his (her) soul to You, and direct Your proof to him (her). O Allah! Bestow Your pardon! Bestow Your pardon!

Ruling 618. It is recommended that the person who places the corpse in the grave should have *wuḍūʾ* or *ghusl*, be bare-headed and bare-footed, and climb out of the grave from the feet-side of the corpse. Persons other than the relatives of the deceased should put the soil into the grave with the back of their hands and say:

﴿إِنَّا لِلّٰهِ وَإِنَّا إِلَيْهِ رَاجِعُوْنَ﴾

innā lillāhi wa innā ilayhi rājiʿūn

Indeed we belong to Allah, and to Him do we indeed return.[73]

If the deceased is a woman, someone who is her *maḥram* should lower her in the grave. If a *maḥram* is not present, her other relatives should do this.

Ruling 619. It is recommended that the grave be four-sided and raised to the height of four fingers from the ground. A sign should be kept

[73] Al-Baqarah (Chapter 2), verse 156.

over it so that it is not mistaken, and water should be splashed over it. After splashing water over it, those who are present should place their hands on the grave, spread their fingers, press them into the soil, recite the blessed Sūrat al-Qadr[74] seven times, ask forgiveness for the deceased, and recite this *duʿāʾ*:

اَللّٰهُمَّ جَافِ الْأَرْضَ عَنْ جَنْبَيْهِ (جَنْبَيْهَا)، وَأَصْعِدْ إِلَيْكَ رُوْحَهُ (رُوْحَهَا)، وَلَقِّهِ (لَقِّهَا) مِنْكَ رِضْوَانًا، وَأَسْكِنْ قَبْرَهُ (قَبْرَهَا) مِنْ رَحْمَتِكَ مَا تُغْنِيْهِ (تُغْنِيْهَا) بِهِ عَنْ رَحْمَةِ مَنْ سِوَاكَ

allāhumma jāfil arḍa ʿan jambayh (jambayhā), wa aṣʿid ilayka ruḥahu (ruḥahā), wa laqqihi (laqqihā) minka riḍwānā, wa askin qabrahu (qabrahā) min raḥmatika mā tughnīhi (tughnīhā) bihi ʿan raḥmati man siwāk

O Allah! Make the ground spacious for him (her) on both of his (her) sides, and elevate his (her) soul, and direct Your pleasure to him (her), and settle Your mercy in his (her) grave, which will make him (her) needless of the mercy of anyone other than You.

Ruling 620. It is recommended that after the people who attended the funeral have departed, the guardian of the deceased or the person to whom the guardian has given permission should recite the recommended *duʿā*'s for the deceased.

Ruling 621. After burial, it is recommended that the grieving family be given condolences. However, if after the passing of some time, giving condolences would cause them to remember their grief, it is better to avoid it. It is also recommended to send food to the grieving family for three days, and during this time, it is disapproved to eat food with them and in their house.

Ruling 622. It is recommended for one to be patient on the death of his near ones, especially on the death of a child; and whenever he remembers the deceased, he should say:

﴿إِنَّا لِلّٰهِ وَإِنَّا إِلَيْهِ رَاجِعُوْنَ﴾

[74] Chapter 97 of the Qur'an.

innā lillāhi wa innā ilayhi rāji'ūn
Indeed we belong to Allah, and to Him do we indeed return.[75]

Furthermore, he should recite the Qur'an for the deceased, and at the grave of his father and mother, he should pray to Allah the Exalted for his needs and make the grave solid so that it is not easily ruined.

Ruling 623. Based on obligatory precaution, it is not permitted for a person to scratch his face and body or to cut his hair in mourning someone. However, it is permitted to slap one's head and face.

Ruling 624. Based on obligatory precaution, it is not permitted for one to tear his collar in mourning the death of anyone except his father and brother. And the recommended precaution is that one should not tear his collar even in mourning their death.

Ruling 625. If a woman scratches her face in mourning a deceased person and makes it bleed, or if she pulls out her hair, then based on recommended precaution, she should free one slave, or feed ten poor people (*fuqarā'*), or clothe them. The same applies to a man who tears his collar or his clothes in mourning the death of his wife or child.

Ruling 626. The recommended precaution is that one should not raise his voice very much when crying for a deceased person.

THE PRAYER OF LONELINESS (*ṢALĀT AL-WAḤSHAH*)

Ruling 627. It is recommended that on the first night of burial, the two *rak'ah* prayer known as '*ṣalāt al-waḥshah*' be performed for the deceased. The method of performing this prayer is as follows: in the first *rak'ah* after reciting Sūrat al-Ḥamd, Āyat al-Kursī[76] is recited once; and in the second *rak'ah* after reciting Sūrat al-Ḥamd, Sūrat al-Qadr is recited ten times; and after the *salām* of the prayer [i.e. after completing the prayer], the following is said:

[75] Al-Baqarah (Chapter 2), verse 156.

[76] With regard to reciting Āyat al-Kursī, the obligatory precaution is to recite verses 255–257 of Chapter 2 of the Qur'an (*Minhāj al-Ṣāliḥīn*, vol. 1, p. 346, Ruling 964).

اَللّٰهُمَّ صَلِّ عَلَىٰ مُحَمَّدٍ وَآلِ مُحَمَّدٍ، وَٱبْعَثْ ثَوَابَهَا إِلَىٰ قَبْرِ ___

allāhumma ṣalli ʿalā muḥammadin wa āli muḥammad, wab ʿath thawābahā ilā qabri ___

O Allah! Bless Muḥammad and the progeny of Muḥammad, and send the reward of this [prayer] to the grave of ___.

In the blank space, one should say the name of the deceased person.

Ruling 628. *Ṣalāt al-waḥshah* can be performed at any time on the first night of burial. However, it is better to perform it at the start of the evening after *ʿishāʾ* prayers.

Ruling 629. If people want to take the corpse to another town that is far away, or if the burial is delayed for some other reason, *ṣalāt al-waḥshah* should be delayed until the first night of burial.

EXHUMATION OF A GRAVE

Ruling 630. Exhuming the grave of a believer – i.e. opening his grave – is unlawful, even if the grave belongs to a child or an insane person. However, there is no problem if the body has completely decomposed and become dust.

Ruling 631. It is unlawful to destroy the graves of the descendants of the Infallible Imams (ʿA), martyrs, and scholars, in any way that is considered disrespectful, even if many years have passed since the person was buried and the body has completely decomposed.

Ruling 632.* Exhuming a grave is not unlawful in the following cases:

1. when the corpse has been buried in usurped land and the owner of the land does not consent to the body remaining there, and exhuming the body does not cause hardship (*ḥaraj*). In such a case, exhuming a grave is not unlawful on condition that there is not a more important reason for not exhuming the body – for example, it would remain without being reburied or would fall apart – in which case it is not permitted to exhume the body. In fact, if exhuming a grave causes disrespect to the deceased

and the deceased was not the one to usurp the land, then permission to exhume the grave is problematic, and in such a scenario, the obligatory precaution is that the usurper must get the consent from the owner of the land for the deceased to remain buried there even if this entails paying the owner;

2. when the *kafan* or something else buried with the corpse is usurped and the owner does not consent to it remaining in the grave. The same applies if something from the deceased's own estate that his heir has inherited is buried with the corpse and the heir does not consent to the object remaining in the grave. However, if the deceased had stipulated in his will that a certain *duʿāʾ*, copy of the Qur'an, or ring must be buried with him and his will is valid, then one cannot exhume the grave to take the object out. In this case, the exception that was mentioned in the previous case also applies;
3. when opening the grave does not cause disrespect and the corpse had been buried without having been given *ghusl*, or it was buried without a *kafan* or having been camphorated, or it becomes known that the *ghusl* was invalid, or the corpse had not been shrouded or camphorated according to religious instruction, or it had not been placed in the grave facing qibla;
4. to see the body in order to establish a right that is more important than, or equal to, not exhuming the grave;
5. when the corpse has been buried in a place that is disrespectful to it, such as in the graveyard of disbelievers or a place where dirt and rubbish are thrown;
6. for a religious matter that is more important than not exhuming the grave; for example, to bring out a living child from the womb of a pregnant woman who has been buried;
7. when there is fear that a predatory animal will tear the body apart, or a flood will carry it away, or an enemy will exhume it;
8. when the deceased had stipulated in his will that his body must be transferred to a place where a holy person is buried in the event that there was no legal reason for not transferring the corpse and yet he was still buried elsewhere, either intentionally, unknowingly, or forgetfully. In such a case, the grave can be exhumed and the body transferred to a sacred place as long as it does not cause disrespect to it and there is no legal reason for not transferring it to the place where the

holy person is buried. In fact, in this case, exhuming the grave and transferring the body is obligatory.

RECOMMENDED (*MUSTAḤABB*) GHUSLS

Ruling 633.* In the sacred law of Islam, there are many recommended *ghusl*s, including:

1. the Friday *ghusl*. The time for performing this *ghusl* is from *ṣubḥ* prayers until sunset, and it is better to perform it near *ẓuhr*. If a person does not perform it until after *ẓuhr*, it is better that he perform it before sunset without specifying an intention of *adāʾ* or *qaḍāʾ* [i.e. without specifying whether it is being performed within its prescribed time or not]. If a person does not perform this *ghusl* [before sunset] on Friday, it is recommended that he perform it as *qaḍāʾ* on Friday evening or before sunset on Saturday. If someone knows that he will not procure water on Friday, he can perform this *ghusl* on Thursday or the night before Friday with the intention of *rajāʾ*. When one performs this *ghusl*, it is recommended that he say:

أَشْهَدُ أَنْ لَا إِلٰهَ إِلَّا اللّٰهُ وَحْدَهُ لَا شَرِيْكَ لَهُ، وَأَنَّ مُحَمَّدًا عَبْدُهُ وَرَسُوْلُهُ، اَللّٰهُمَّ صَلِّ عَلَىٰ مُحَمَّدٍ وَآلِ مُحَمَّدٍ، وَٱجْعَلْنِيْ مِنَ التَّوَّابِيْنَ وَٱجْعَلْنِيْ مِنَ الْمُتَطَهِّرِيْنَ

ashhadu an lā ilāha illal lāhu waḥdahu lā sharīka lah, wa anna muḥammadan ʿabduhu wa rasūluh, allāhumma ṣalli ʿalā muḥammadin wa āli muḥammad, wajʿalnī minat tawwābīna wajʿalnī minal mutaṭahhirīn

I testify that there is no god but Allah, He alone; and I testify that Muḥammad is His servant and His messenger. O Allah! Bless Muḥammad and the progeny of Muḥammad. Make me of those who often repent and make me of those who purify themselves.

2–7. the *ghusl* for the night of the 1st, 17th, 19th, 21st, 23rd, and 24th of the month of Ramadan;

8–9. the *ghusl* for the day of Eid al-Fiṭr[77] and Eid al-Aḍḥā.[78] The time for performing these *ghusls* is from *ṣubḥ* prayers until sunset, and it is better to perform them before the Eid prayers;

10–11. the *ghusl* for the day of the 8th and 9th of Dhū al-Ḥijjah,[79] and it is better to perform the *ghusl* on the day of the 9th at the time of *ẓuhr* prayers;

12. the *ghusl* of someone who has touched a corpse after it has been given *ghusl*;
13. the *ghusl* for *iḥrām*;
14. the *ghusl* for entering the sacred precinct (*ḥaram*) of Mecca;
15. the *ghusl* for entering Mecca;
16. the *ghusl* for visiting the Kaʿbah;
17. the *ghusl* for entering the Kaʿbah;
18. the *ghusl* for slaughtering a camel (*naḥr*) and for slaughtering an animal (*dhabḥ*);
19. the *ghusl* for shaving one's hair (*ḥalq*);
20. the *ghusl* for entering the *ḥaram* of Medina;
21. the *ghusl* for entering Medina;
22. the *ghusl* for bidding farewell to the holy grave of Prophet Muḥammad (Ṣ);
23. the *ghusl* for *mubāhalah* (mutual imprecation) with an opponent;
24. the *ghusl* for the *ṣalāh* of *istikhārah* (the practice of seeking from Allah the best choice between two or more options);
25. the *ghusl* for the *ṣalāh* of *istisqā*ʾ (invocation for rain).

Ruling 634. In the course of explaining recommended *ghusls*, jurists have mentioned many other *ghusls*, including:

1. the *ghusl* for each of the odd nights of the month of Ramadan, the *ghusl* for each of the last ten nights of the month of Ramadan, and another *ghusl* at the end of the 23rd night of the month of Ramadan;
2. the *ghusl* for the 24th of Dhū al-Ḥijjah;[80]

[77] The 1st of Shawwāl. [78] The 10th of Dhū al-Ḥijjah. [79] These days are known as the days of Tarwiyah and ʿArafah. [80] The day of Mubāhalah.

3. the *ghusl* for the Eid of Nawrūz,[81] 15th of Shaʿbān,[82] 9th of Rabīʿ al-Awwal,[83] 17th of Rabīʿ al-Awwal,[84] and the 25th day of Dhū al-Qaʿdah;[85]
4. the *ghusl* for a woman who has used fragrance for other than her husband;
5. the *ghusl* for someone who slept while intoxicated;
6. the *ghusl* for someone who went to see a hanging and actually saw it; however, if he happened to see it by chance, or he had no choice but to see it, or, for example, he had gone to give evidence and saw it, then in these cases, this *ghusl* is not recommended;
7. the *ghusl* for the visitation (*ziyārah*) of the Infallibles (*maʿṣūmīn*) from near or far.

It is worth noting, however, that the recommendation for these *ghusls* is not established, and someone who wants to perform them must do so with the intention of *rajāʾ*.

Ruling 635. If someone performs one of the *ghusls* that has been legally established as being a recommended *ghusl* – such as those mentioned in Ruling 633 – he can perform acts that require *wuḍūʾ*, such as prayers, with that *ghusl*. As for *ghusls* that are performed with the intention of *rajāʾ* – such as those mentioned in Ruling 634 – these do not suffice in place of *wuḍūʾ*.

Ruling 636. It is sufficient for one to perform one *ghusl* with the intention of several different recommended *ghusls*, except for those *ghusls* that have become recommended for one to perform on account of having done something, such as the *ghusl* for having touched a corpse that has been given *ghusl*. For this type of *ghusl*, the obligatory precaution is that one must not suffice with performing one *ghusl* for several *ghusls*.

[81] The day of the spring equinox. [82] The birthday of the Twelfth Holy Imam (ʿA). [83] Eid al-Zahrāʾ (ʿA). [84] The birthday of Prophet Muḥammad (Ṣ) and Imam Jaʿfar al-Ṣādiq (ʿA). [85] The day of Dahw al-Arḍ.

DRY ABLUTION (*TAYAMMUM*)

Tayammum must be performed in place of *wuḍūʾ* or *ghusl* in seven situations [which are set out below].

1. Not having water

Ruling 637. If a person happens to be in a populated area, he must search for water for performing *wuḍūʾ* and *ghusl* until such time that he loses hope in finding water. The same applies if one happens to be staying in a desert, like those who stay in tents. If a person is on a journey in a desert, he must search for water on the way and in the places near where he is staying. The obligatory precaution is that if the ground is uneven, or if due to some other reason the road is difficult to traverse – for example, because it has a lot of trees – one must go in search of water in the area around him as far as the distance that a shot arrow travels as it would have been shot from a bow in the past.[86] If the land is even, however, one must go in search of water in the area around him up to the distance that two shot arrows travel.[87]

Ruling 638. If some of the area around a person is even and some uneven, he must search for water in the even area up to a distance that two shot arrows travel, and in the uneven area up to a distance that one shot arrow travels.

Ruling 639. It is not necessary to search for water in any area in which one is certain there is no water.

Ruling 640. If the time for performing prayers is not short and one has time to procure water, and he is certain or confident that there is water in a place that is further than the distance he is obliged to go up to in search of water, he must go there to procure water unless it is so far that he would commonly be considered to be someone who

[86] There is a difference of opinion [among jurists] regarding the distance a shot arrow travels. The most often quoted distance is 480 cubits, which is equivalent to approximately 220 metres (*Minhāj al-Ṣāliḥīn*, vol. 1, p. 141, Ruling 342). [Author]
[87] Based on the distance quoted in the previous footnote, this would equate to approximately 440 metres.

does not have water. However, if he merely supposes that there is water in a place, it is not necessary for him to go there.

Ruling 641. It is not necessary for a person to go in search of water himself; rather, he can suffice with the statement of someone who has searched for water and whose word he trusts.

Ruling 642. If someone deems it probable that there is water in his travel luggage, or in his house, or with the group of people he is travelling with, he must search for water in those places until he becomes confident that there is no water or he loses hope in finding some, except if previously in a particular situation there was no water and now he deems it probable that water will be found, in which case it is not necessary for him to search.

Ruling 643. If a person searches for water before the time for prayers and does not find any, and he remains in that place until the time for prayers, in the event that he deems it probable that he will find water, the recommended precaution is that he should go in search of water again.

Ruling 644. If a person searches for water after the time for prayers has set in and does not find any, and he remains in that place until the time for the next prayers, in the event that he deems it probable that water will be found, the recommended precaution is that he should go in search of water again.

Ruling 645. If the time for performing prayers is short, or there is a fear of thieves and predatory animals, or searching for water is so difficult for someone that usually people in his situation would not be able to endure it, it is not necessary to search for water.

Ruling 646. If a person does not search for water until the time for performing prayers becomes short, and if he had gone he would have found some, he will have sinned; however, the prayer he performed with *tayammum* is valid.

Ruling 647. If someone is certain that he will not find water and does not go in search of it, and he performs prayers with *tayammum* and afterwards realises that if he had searched for water he would have found some, then based on obligatory precaution, it is necessary for him to perform *wuḍūʾ* and to perform the prayer again.

Ruling 648. If a person does not find water after searching for it and loses hope in finding some and performs prayers with *tayammum*, and afterwards he realises that there was water in the place where he had searched, his prayer is valid.

Ruling 649. If someone who is certain that the time for performing prayers is short does not search for water and performs prayers with *tayammum*, and after his prayers – but before the time for the prayer ends – he realises that he had time to search, the obligatory precaution is that he must perform the prayer again.

Ruling 650. If a person has *wuḍūʾ* and knows that if he invalidates his *wuḍūʾ* it will not be possible to find water or he will not be able to perform *wuḍūʾ*, then in the event that he can keep his *wuḍūʾ*, based on obligatory precaution, he must not invalidate his *wuḍūʾ*, whether that be before or after the time for prayers has set in. However, one can have sexual intercourse with his wife even if he knows that he will not be able to perform *ghusl*.

Ruling 651. If a person has water that is only sufficient for performing *wuḍūʾ* or *ghusl* with, and he knows that were he to spill the water he would not be able to find any more, in the event that the time for prayers has set in, it is unlawful for him to spill the water; and the obligatory precaution is that he must not spill it even before the time for prayers has set in.

Ruling 652. If someone who knows he will not find water invalidates his *wuḍūʾ* or spills the water he has, he commits a sin but his prayer performed with *tayammum* is valid. However, the recommended precaution is that he should make up that prayer afterwards.

2. Not having access to water

Ruling 653. If a person does not have access to water on account of old age, weakness, fear of a thief or an animal and suchlike, or on account of not having the means to draw water out from a well, he must perform *tayammum*.

Ruling 654. If a bucket, rope, or a similar thing is needed for drawing water out from a well and one would need to purchase or hire it, he must do so even if he has to pay much more than the usual price for it. Similarly, if water is being sold at a much higher price [he must purchase it]. However, if purchasing these requires so much money that it would harm him financially and cause him extraordinary difficulty, it is not obligatory for him to purchase them.

Ruling 655. If a person has to borrow money to procure water, he must do so. However, it is not obligatory to borrow money if one knows or supposes that he will not be able to repay the loan.

Ruling 656. One must dig a well to obtain water as long as it is not excessively difficult to do so.

Ruling 657. One must accept water if it is given to him without any obligation.

3. Using water is harmful

Ruling 658. If using water would result in a person dying, or it would make him ill, inflict him with some defect, prolong an illness he has, or make his illness worse or difficult to treat, then in all these cases, he must perform *tayammum*. However, if one can reduce the harm of using water – for example, by heating it – he must do so and thereby perform *wuḍūʾ* or *ghusl* as required.

Ruling 659. It is not necessary for one to be certain that water is harmful for him; rather, if he deems it probable that it is harmful, in the event that his deeming it probable would be considered by people to be reasonable, he must perform *tayammum*.

Ruling 660. If someone is certain or deems it probable that water is harmful for him and performs *tayammum*, and before prayers he realises that water is not harmful for him, his *tayammum* is void. If he realises this after prayers, he must perform the prayer again with *wuḍū'* or *ghusl* unless performing *wuḍū'* or *ghusl* while being certain of harm, or deeming it probable, would cause anxiety which would be difficult to endure.

Ruling 661. If someone who is certain that water is not harmful for him performs *ghusl* or *wuḍū'* and afterwards realises that water was harmful for him, his *wuḍū'* or *ghusl* is void.

4. Hardship (*ḥaraj*) and excessive difficulty (*mashaqqah*)

Ruling 662. If procuring water or using it causes someone hardship or excessive difficulty that cannot normally be endured, he can perform *tayammum*. However, if he endures it and performs *wuḍū'* or *ghusl*, his *wuḍū'* or *ghusl* is valid.

5. Needing water to quench thirst

Ruling 663. A person must perform *tayammum* if he needs water to quench his thirst. It is permitted to perform *tayammum* for this reason in two cases:

1. if one uses water for *wuḍū'* or *ghusl*, he fears he will presently or later on become thirsty which will cause him to die or become ill, or it will require him to endure excessive difficulty;
2. one fears for someone dependent on him – even if the person is not among those whose life is legally protected – if the affairs of the person's life matter to him because of his intense affection for the person, or because if the person dies it will harm him financially, or because it is commonly considered necessary to care for the person as is the case with a friend or a neighbour.

Apart from these two cases, it is possible for thirst to be a valid reason for performing *tayammum*, but not from the perspective mentioned above; rather, from the perspective that preserving life is obligatory, or because the death or restlessness of someone [due to thirst] would assuredly cause one hardship.

Ruling 664. If apart from having pure water for *wuḍū'* or *ghusl* a person also has impure water that is sufficient only for drinking, he must keep the pure water for drinking and perform prayers with *tayammum*. However, in the event that one wants the pure water for those who are dependent on him, he can perform *wuḍūʾ* or *ghusl* with the pure water even if his dependants are compelled to quench their thirst with the impure water. In fact, if they are unaware of the water being impure, or they do not refrain from drinking impure water, it is necessary for him to use the pure water for *wuḍūʾ* or *ghusl*. Similarly, if one wants water for his animal or for a child who is not *bāligh*, he must give them the impure water and perform *wuḍūʾ* or *ghusl* with the pure water.

6. Performing *wuḍūʾ* or *ghusl* conflicts with another legal responsibility that is more important or just as important

Ruling 665. If someone has a little water and his body or clothing is impure, and were he to perform *wuḍūʾ* or *ghusl* with that water there would not be enough left over with which he could wash his body or clothing, he must wash his body or clothing with the water and perform prayers with *tayammum*. However, if one does not have anything with which he can perform *tayammum*, he must use the water for *wuḍūʾ* or *ghusl* and perform prayers with his impure body or clothing.

Ruling 666. If a person only has water or a utensil [in which there is water] that is unlawful to use – for example, the water or utensil is usurped and he does not have any other water or utensil – he must perform *tayammum* in place of *wuḍūʾ* and *ghusl*.

7. Shortage of time

Ruling 667. Whenever the time remaining [to perform prayers within their prescribed time] is so little that if one were to perform *wuḍūʾ* or *ghusl* he would have to perform the entire prayer or part of it after its time, he must perform *tayammum*.

Ruling 668. If someone intentionally delays the prayer to the extent that he does not have time to perform *wuḍūʾ* or *ghusl*, he commits a sin but his prayers performed with *tayammum* are valid. However, the recommended precaution is that he should make up that prayer afterwards.

Ruling 669. If a person doubts whether or not he will have time to perform prayers if he performs *wuḍū᾿* or *ghusl*, he must perform *tayammum*.

Ruling 670. If someone performs *tayammum* due to shortage of time and after the prayer he is able to perform *wuḍū᾿* but does not, and now he does not have the water he had previously, in such a case, if his duty now is to perform *tayammum*, he must perform *tayammum* again for subsequent prayers even if he has not done anything that invalidates *tayammum*.

Ruling 671. If someone has water but due to shortage of time he starts performing prayers with *tayammum*, and during prayers the water he had is lost, in the event that his duty now is to perform *tayammum*, it is not necessary for him to perform *tayammum* again for subsequent prayers although it is better that he does.

Ruling 672. If a person has just enough time to perform *wuḍū᾿* or *ghusl* and to perform prayers without doing the recommended acts, such as *iqāmah* and *qunūt*, he must perform *ghusl* or *wuḍū᾿* and perform prayers without doing the recommended acts. In fact, if one does not have time to recite even the surah [of the Qur'an, following the recitation of Sūrat al-Ḥamd], he must perform *ghusl* or *wuḍū᾿* and perform the prayer without reciting the surah.

THINGS WITH WHICH PERFORMING *TAYAMMUM* IS VALID (*ṢAḤĪḤ*)

Ruling 673. Performing *tayammum* with soil, pebbles, a clod of earth, and stone is valid. However, the recommended precaution is that if it is possible to perform *tayammum* with soil, one should not perform it with any other thing; and if soil is not available, [the recommended precaution is to perform *tayammum*] with fine sand that is very soft, such that it can be called 'soil'; and if that is not possible, with a clod of earth; and if that is not possible, with pebbles; and in the event that pebbles and a clod of earth are not available, one must perform *tayammum* with a stone.

Ruling 674. *Tayammum* performed with gypsum or limestone is valid. Similarly, *tayammum* performed with dust that gathers on carpets, clothing, and similar things is also valid provided that its quantity is such that it can commonly be considered to be very fine soil, although the recommended precaution is that if alternatives are available, one should not perform *tayammum* with dust. Similarly, based on recommended precaution, if alternatives are available, one should not perform *tayammum* with gypsum and limestone that have been baked, nor with brick that has been baked, nor with mineral stones such as agate (*ʿaqīq*).

Ruling 675. If a person cannot find soil, pebbles, a clod of earth, or stone, he must perform *tayammum* with mud; and if one cannot find any mud, he must perform *tayammum* on top of a carpet, clothing, or similar thing that has gathered dust or on which dust has settled but not to the extent that it can commonly be considered soil. If none of these can be found, the recommended precaution is that one should perform prayers without performing *tayammum*; however, it is obligatory for him to make them up afterwards.

Ruling 676. If a person can gather soil by shaking a carpet and similar things, then performing *tayammum* with something that is merely dusty is invalid. Similarly, if one can dry some mud and procure soil from it, then performing *tayammum* with mud [that has not been dried] is invalid.

Ruling 677. If someone does not have water but does have snow or ice, in the event that it is possible, he must melt it and perform *wuḍūʾ* or *ghusl* with it; and if it is not possible and he does not have anything with which *tayammum* can be validly performed, it is necessary for him to make up the prayer after its time. Furthermore, it is better that with the snow or ice he wet those parts of the body on which *wuḍūʾ* or *ghusl* is performed, and in the case of *wuḍūʾ*, he should wipe his head and feet with the wetness on his hands. If this is not possible, he should perform *tayammum* with snow or ice and perform the prayer within its time. In both cases, it is necessary for him to make up the prayer afterwards.

Ruling 678. If something like straw – with which performing *tay-*

ammum is invalid – becomes mixed with soil or pebbles, one cannot perform *tayammum* with it. However, if the quantity of that thing [such as straw] is so little that it is considered to have disappeared in the soil or pebbles, then performing *tayammum* with the soil or pebbles is valid.

Ruling 679. If a person does not have anything with which to perform *tayammum*, in the event that it is possible, he must procure it by purchasing it and suchlike.

Ruling 680. Performing *tayammum* with a mud wall is valid. The recommended precaution is that if there is dry earth or soil, one should not perform *tayammum* with damp earth or soil.

Ruling 681. The thing with which a person performs *tayammum* must be pure (*ṭāhir*); and based on obligatory precaution, it must also be commonly considered clean, meaning that it must not be tainted with anything that causes disgust. If one does not have a pure thing with which *tayammum* can be validly performed, then performing prayers at that time is not obligatory for him; however, he must make up that prayer; and it is better that he also perform the prayer within its time except if the situation has reached the point whereby he must perform *tayammum* with a dusty carpet or similar thing.[88] If it is impure, the obligatory precaution is that he must perform *tayammum* with it, perform the prayer, and make up the prayer afterwards.

Ruling 682. If someone is certain that performing *tayammum* with a particular thing is valid and he does so, and afterwards he realises that performing *tayammum* with that thing is invalid, he must perform the prayers he had performed with that *tayammum* again.

Ruling 683. The thing with which one performs *tayammum* must not be usurped; therefore, if one performs *tayammum* with usurped soil, his *tayammum* is invalid.

Ruling 684. *Tayammum* performed in a usurped area is not invalid; therefore, if a person strikes his hands on soil belonging to him, and

[88] See Ruling 675.

then enters the property of another person without his consent and wipes his hands on his forehead, his *tayammum* is valid even though he will have sinned.

Ruling 685. If a person forgetfully or neglectfully performs *tayammum* with a usurped thing, his *tayammum* is valid. However, if he has usurped that thing and he forgets that he has usurped it, then based on obligatory precaution, his *tayammum* is invalid.

Ruling 686.* If a person is imprisoned in a usurped place and both the water and the soil of that place are usurped, he must perform prayers with *tayammum*; however, when he performs *tayammum*, he must not strike his hands on the ground; rather, he must suffice with placing them on the ground.

Ruling 687. Based on obligatory precaution, the thing with which one performs *tayammum* must have dust on it that will stay on the palms; and after striking his hands on it, he must not shake his hands vigorously, causing all the dust to fall off.

Ruling 688. It is disapproved to perform *tayammum* with the earth of a pit, the soil of a road, and the ground of a salt marsh on which salt has not settled; and if salt has settled on it, the *tayammum* is invalid.

METHOD OF PERFORMING *TAYAMMUM* IN PLACE OF *WUḌŪʾ* OR *GHUSL*

Ruling 689. Three things are obligatory when performing *tayammum* in place of *wuḍūʾ* or *ghusl*:

1. striking or placing the palms of both hands on something with which *tayammum* can be validly performed; and based on obligatory precaution, the striking of both palms must be done simultaneously;
2. wiping the palms of both hands over the entire forehead – and based on obligatory precaution, over the two sides of the forehead as well – from the place where the hair of the head grows

to the eyebrows and above the nose; and the recommended precaution is that the palms should be wiped over the eyebrows as well;

3. wiping the palm of the left hand over the whole of the back of the right hand from the wrist to the fingertips, and wiping the palm of the right hand over the whole of the back of the left hand from the wrist to the fingertips; and the obligatory precaution is that that the order mentioned above must be observed [i.e. first the back of the right hand must be wiped, then the back of the left].

It is necessary that *tayammum* be performed with the intention of attaining proximity to Allah, just as was mentioned with regard to performing *wuḍūʾ*.[89]

Ruling 690. The recommended precaution is that *tayammum* – whether it be in place of *wuḍūʾ* or *ghusl* – should be performed in this manner: (1) the palms are struck on the ground once and wiped over the forehead and the back of the hands; and (2) they are then struck again on the ground and wiped over the back of the hands.

LAWS OF *TAYAMMUM*

Ruling 691. If a person fails to wipe even a small area of his forehead or the back of his hands, his *tayammum* is invalid, irrespective of whether he fails to wipe the area intentionally, or because he did not know the ruling or had forgotten to wipe it. However, it is not necessary to be very particular either, and it is sufficient if it can be said that the entire forehead and back of the hands have been wiped.

Ruling 692. If someone is not certain that he has wiped all of the back of his hand, then, to be certain, he must wipe an area a little higher than his wrist as well. However, it is not necessary to wipe in between the fingers.

Ruling 693. Based on obligatory precaution, the forehead and the back

[89] See the sixth condition for the validity of *wuḍūʾ* and Ruling 281.

of the hands must be wiped from top to bottom [i.e. the forehead must be wiped in a direction towards the eyebrows and above the nose, and the back of the hands must be wiped in a direction towards the fingertips]. These actions must be performed one after the other; if there is a delay between performing them such that it cannot be said that one is performing *tayammum*, then the *tayammum* is invalid.

Ruling 694. When making the intention to perform *tayammum,* it is not necessary for one to specify whether the *tayammum* is in place of *ghusl* or *wuḍūʾ*. However, in cases where two *tayammums* must be performed, it is necessary to specify each of them [in one's intention]. In the event that one *tayammum* is obligatory for a person and he makes the intention that he is performing his current duty, then even if he makes a mistake in determining his duty, his *tayammum* is valid.

Ruling 695. In *tayammum* it is not necessary for one's forehead, the palms of his hands, and the back of his hands to be pure. Therefore, if the parts of the body on which *tayammum* is performed have become impure but are dry, the *tayammum* is valid, although it is better that the parts of the body on which *tayammum* is performed be completely pure.

Ruling 696. One must remove any rings from his fingers when wiping over his hands; and if there is any obstruction on his forehead, the back of his hands, or on his palms – for example, something is stuck on them – he must remove it.

Ruling 697. If there is a wound on one's forehead or the back of his hands, and the cloth or something else that is tied over it cannot be untied, he must wipe his hands over it. If there is a wound on the palms of his hands and the cloth or something else that is tied over it cannot be untied, one must strike his hands on something with which *tayammum* can be validly performed with the same cloth tied over the wound and wipe over his forehead and the back of his hands. However, if part of the cloth is open, then striking and wiping with that open part is sufficient.

Ruling 698. There is no problem if there is a normal amount of hair on one's forehead and the back of his hands. However, if the hair of one's head drops over onto his forehead, he must draw it back.

Ruling 699. If a person deems it probable that there is an obstruction on his forehead, palms, or the back of his hands, then in the event that his deeming it probable would be considered by people to be reasonable, he must look into this until he becomes certain or confident that there is no obstruction.

Ruling 700. If someone's duty is to perform *tayammum* but he cannot perform it on his own, he must get help from someone else. The helper must take the *mukallaf*'s hands and strike them on something with which *tayammum* can be validly performed; then, the helper must place the *mukallaf*'s hands on the *mukallaf*'s forehead and the back of the *mukallaf*'s hands so that the *mukallaf* himself wipes the palms of his two hands over his forehead and the back of his hands, if it is possible for him to do so. If it is not possible, the helper must perform *tayammum* on the *mukallaf* with the *mukallaf*'s own hands [i.e. after the helper has placed the *mukallaf*'s hands on the *mukallaf*'s forehead and the back of the *mukallaf*'s hands, the helper must draw the *mukallaf*'s hands over his forehead and the back of his hands]. If this is not possible, the helper must strike his own hands on something with which *tayammum* can be validly performed and wipe them over the *mukallaf*'s forehead and the back of the *mukallaf*'s hands. In these two cases, based on obligatory precaution, both of them must make the intention of *tayammum*. However, in the first case [where the *mukallaf*'s own hands are used], it is sufficient if only the *mukallaf* makes this intention.

Ruling 701. If while performing *tayammum* one doubts whether or not he has forgotten a certain part of it, in the event that he has passed that stage [i.e. he has performed that particular part of *tayammum*], he must not heed his doubt; and if he has not passed that stage, he must perform that stage.

Ruling 702. If one doubts whether or not he has correctly performed tayammum after wiping the left hand, his *tayammum* is valid. In the event that one's doubt is about the wiping of the left hand, it is necessary for him to wipe it unless it can commonly be said that he has finished performing *tayammum*; for example, he has started to perform an act that requires purification [such as prayers], or the close succession (*muwālāh*) [in performing *tayammum*] has not been maintained.

Ruling 703. If someone whose duty is to perform *tayammum* loses hope in his legitimate excuse [for performing *tayammum* in place of *wuḍū'* or *ghusl*] expiring during the entire length of time for prayers, or if he deems it probable that if he delays performing *tayammum* he will not be able to perform *tayammum* in time, he can perform *tayammum* before the time for prayers has set in. If one performs *tayammum* for another obligatory or recommended act and his legitimate excuse remains valid until the time of prayer has set in, he can perform the prayer with that *tayammum*.

Ruling 704. If someone whose duty is to perform *tayammum* knows that his legitimate excuse will remain valid until the end of the time for prayers, or if he loses hope in his legitimate excuse expiring, he can perform prayers with *tayammum* at any point during the entire length of time for the prayer. However, if one knows that his legitimate excuse will expire by the end of the time for prayers, he must wait and perform the prayer with *ghusl* or *wuḍū'*. If a person does not lose hope in his legitimate excuse expiring by the end of the time for prayers, he cannot perform *tayammum* and perform the prayer until he loses hope, unless he deems it probable that if he does not perform the prayer with *tayammum* earlier, he will not be able to perform the prayer by the end of its time even with *tayammum*.

Ruling 705. If someone who cannot perform *wuḍū'* or *ghusl* loses hope in his legitimate excuse expiring, he can perform his *qaḍā'* prayers with *tayammum*. However, if afterwards his legitimate excuse expires, the obligatory precaution is that he must perform his *qaḍā'* prayers again with *wuḍū'* or *ghusl*. If he does not lose hope in his legitimate excuse expiring, then based on obligatory precaution, he cannot perform *tayammum* for *qaḍā'* prayers.

Ruling 706. It is permitted for someone who cannot perform *wuḍū'* or *ghusl* to perform recommended prayers that have a specific time – such as the daily supererogatory (*nāfilah*) prayer – with *tayammum*. However, if one does not lose hope in his legitimate excuse expiring before the end of the time for such prayers, the obligatory precaution is that he must not perform them at the start of their time. Recommended prayers that do not have a specific time can be performed with *tayammum* at any time.

Ruling 707. If someone performs *jabīrah ghusl* and *tayammum* as a precautionary measure, and after performing *jabīrah ghusl* and *tayammum* he performs a prayer, and after performing the prayer he has a minor occurrence[90] – for example, he urinates – then in such a case, for subsequent prayers he must perform *wuḍū'*. In the event that the occurrence happens before prayers, he must perform *wuḍū'* for that prayer as well.

Ruling 708. If someone performs *tayammum* because he did not have water or some other legitimate excuse, then once that excuse expires, his *tayammum* becomes void.

Ruling 709. The things that invalidate *wuḍū'* also invalidate *tayammum* performed in place of *wuḍū'*. The things that invalidate *ghusl* also invalidate *tayammum* performed in place of *ghusl*.

Ruling 710. If someone cannot perform *ghusl* and a few *ghusl*s are obligatory for him, it is permitted for him to perform one *tayammum* in place of all of them. However, the recommended precaution is that he should perform one *tayammum* in place of each *ghusl*.

Ruling 711. If someone who cannot perform *ghusl* wants to perform an act for which *ghusl* is obligatory, he must perform *tayammum* in place of *ghusl*. If someone who cannot perform *wuḍū'* wants to perform an act for which *wuḍū'* is obligatory, he must perform *tayammum* in place of *wuḍū'*.

Ruling 712.* If someone performs *tayammum* in place of the *ghusl* for *janābah*, it is not necessary for them to perform *wuḍū'* for prayers. Similarly, [it is not necessary for them to perform *wuḍū'* for prayers] if the *tayammum* is in place of other *ghusl*s – except the *ghusl* for medium *istiḥāḍah* – although in such a case, the recommended

[90] See the footnote pertaining to Ruling 384 for an explanation of this term.

precaution is that they should perform *wuḍūʾ* as well; and if they cannot perform *wuḍūʾ*, they should perform another *tayammum* in place of *wuḍūʾ*.

Ruling 713. If someone performs *tayammum* in place of *ghusl* and afterwards something happens that invalidates *wuḍūʾ*, in the event that he cannot perform *ghusl* for subsequent prayers, he must perform *wuḍūʾ*. And the recommended precaution is that he should also perform *tayammum*; and if he cannot perform *wuḍūʾ*, he must perform *tayammum* instead.

Ruling 714. If someone's duty is to perform *tayammum* and he performs it for some act, then as long as his *tayammum* and the legitimate excuse remain valid, he can perform those acts that must be performed with *wuḍūʾ* or *ghusl*. However, if his legitimate excuse was a shortage of time, or despite having water he performed *tayammum* for *ṣalāt al-mayyit* or sleeping, then with that *tayammum* he can perform only those acts for which he performed *tayammum*.

Ruling 715. In some cases, it is better for one to make up the prayers he performed with *tayammum*:

1. he was fearful of using water and intentionally became *junub* and performed prayers with *tayammum*;
2. he knew or supposed he would not find water by the end of the time for prayers and intentionally became *junub* and performed prayers with *tayammum*;
3. he intentionally did not go in search of water until the end of the time for prayers and performed prayers with *tayammum* and afterwards realised that if he had searched for water, he would have found it;
4. he intentionally delayed performing prayers and performed them with *tayammum* at the end of their time;
5. he knew or supposed that water would not be found, spilt the water he had, and performed prayers with *tayammum*.

CHAPTER THREE

Prayer (*Ṣalāh*)

Prayer is the best act of worship. If it is accepted by the Lord of the worlds, then all other ritual acts of worship (*ʿibādāt*) are accepted. If it is not accepted, then all other acts of worship are not accepted. In the same way that no dirt would remain on one's body if he were to wash himself in a stream five times a day, performing the five daily prayers cleanses a person of sins. It is befitting for one to perform prayers at the start of their prescribed time (*awwal al-waqt*), and one who considers prayers lowly and unimportant is like one who does not perform prayers. It has been reported that the Most Noble Messenger (Ṣ) said, 'One who does not give importance to prayers and considers them unimportant deserves chastisement in the Hereafter.' It has also been reported that once, when His Eminence (Ṣ) was in the mosque, a man entered and began performing prayers but did not perform the bowing (*rukūʿ*) and prostration (*sajdah*) properly. His Eminence (Ṣ) said, 'If this man dies while his prayers are like this, he will not leave this world adhering to my religion.'

Therefore, one must be careful not to perform prayers in a hurry. While performing prayers, one should remember Allah the Exalted, be humble, submissive, dignified, and mindful of whom he is communicating with. He should consider himself extremely low and insignificant in relation to the greatness and grandeur of the Lord of the worlds. If a person is completely mindful of this matter while performing prayers, he will become oblivious to his own self, just as the Commander of the Faithful, ʿAlī (ʿA), was reported to have been when an arrow was pulled out from his blessed foot while he was performing prayers. Furthermore, one must repent and seek forgiveness and not commit sins that are obstacles to prayers being accepted; sins such as jealousy, pride, backbiting, eating unlawful (*ḥarām*) things, drinking intoxicating beverages, and not paying the one-fifth tax (*khums*) or the alms-tax (zakat). In fact, one must refrain from all sins. Similarly, it is befitting that one does not do anything that diminishes the reward of prayers; for example, one should not perform prayers while sleepy or needing to go to the toilet, nor should one look at the sky while performing prayers. Instead, one should do things that increase the reward of prayers; for example, one should wear a ring with an agate (*ʿaqīq*) stone, wear clean clothes, comb his hair, brush his teeth, and apply perfume.

THE OBLIGATORY (*WĀJIB*) PRAYERS

There are six obligatory prayers in the period of the Imam of the Time's (ʿA) occultation (*ghaybah*):

1. the daily prayers;
2. the prayer of signs (*ṣalāt al-āyāt*);
3. the funeral prayer (*ṣalāt al-mayyit*);
4. the prayer for the obligatory circumambulation (*ṭawāf*) of the Kaʿbah;
5. the lapsed (*qaḍāʾ*) prayers of one's father that, based on obligatory precaution (*al-iḥtiyāṭ al-wājib*), are obligatory for the eldest son to perform;
6. prayers that become obligatory on account of hire (*ijārah*), vow (*nadhr*), oath (*qasam*), and covenant (*ʿahd*).

The Friday prayer (*ṣalāt al-jumuʿah*) is regarded as one of the daily prayers.

THE OBLIGATORY DAILY PRAYERS

There are five obligatory daily prayers: (1) midday (*ẓuhr*) and (2) afternoon (*ʿaṣr*) prayers – each of these consists of four units (*rakʿah*s); (3) after sunset (*maghrib*), which is three *rakʿah*s; (4) evening (*ʿishāʾ*), which is four *rakʿah*s; and (5) morning (*ṣubḥ*), which is two *rakʿah*s.

Ruling 716. While travelling, one must perform the four *rakʿah* prayers as two *rakʿah*s in accordance with the conditions that will be mentioned later.

THE TIME FOR THE MIDDAY (*ẒUHR*) AND AFTERNOON (*ʿAṢR*) PRAYERS

Ruling 717. The time for *ẓuhr* and *ʿaṣr* prayers is from *zawāl* [i.e. the time after midday when the sun begins to decline] (known as the 'legal midday' (*al-ẓuhr al-sharʿī*))[1] until sunset (*ghurūb*). However, in the event that one intentionally (*ʿamdan*) performs the *ʿaṣr* prayer before the *ẓuhr* prayer, his prayer is invalid (*bāṭil*), except if this happens at the end of the prescribed time and there is scope for performing only one prayer, in which case if someone has not performed the *ẓuhr* prayer by then, his *ẓuhr* prayer is deemed to have become *qaḍāʾ* and he must perform the *ʿaṣr* prayer. If before this time someone mistakenly performs the whole of the *ʿaṣr* prayer before the *ẓuhr* prayer, his prayer is valid (*ṣaḥīḥ*), and he must then perform the *ẓuhr* prayer. And the recommended precaution (*al-iḥtiyāṭ al-mustaḥabb*) is that he should perform the second set of four *rakʿah*s with the intention (*niyyah*) to fulfil whatever his legal obligation happens to be (*mā fī al-dhimmah*).

Ruling 718. If someone inadvertently (*sahwan*) starts performing the *ʿaṣr* prayer before he has performed the *ẓuhr* prayer and realises this mistake in the middle of the prayer, he must change his intention to *ẓuhr* prayers, i.e. he must make the intention that whatever I have performed until now, and whatever I am performing right now, and whatever I will perform, is all part of the *ẓuhr* prayer. After completing the prayer, he must perform the *ʿaṣr* prayer.

THE FRIDAY PRAYER (*ṢALĀT AL-JUMUʿAH*) AND ITS LAWS

Ruling 719.* The Friday prayer consists of two *rakʿah*s like the *ṣubḥ* prayer, with the difference that in the Friday prayer, two sermons must be delivered before it. The Friday prayer is an optional obligation (*al-wājib al-takhyīrī*), meaning that on Fridays, someone who is duty-bound (*mukallaf*)[2] has the option to either perform the Friday prayer – if all its conditions are fulfilled – or the *ẓuhr* prayer; and if he performs the Friday prayer, it will suffice in place of the *ẓuhr* prayer.

[1] The legal midday is defined as the passing of the midway point of the day. For example, if the day is twelve hours long, the legal midday is after the passing of six hours from the time of sunrise. If the day is thirteen hours long, the legal midday is after the passing of six and a half hours from the time of sunrise. [Author]

[2] A *mukallaf* is someone who is legally obliged to fulfil religious duties.

Some conditions must be met for the Friday prayer to be obligatory:

1. the time for the prayer must have set in. This refers to the time of *zawāl*, or in other words, the time of *ẓuhr*.[3] Furthermore, the time for the Friday prayer is that which is commonly regarded to be the beginning of *zawāl*; therefore, if the Friday prayer is delayed beyond this time, its time will be deemed over and the *ẓuhr* prayer must be performed instead;
2. the number of people must be at least five, including the imam. If five Muslims do not gather, the Friday prayer does not become obligatory;
3. there must be an imam who meets all the conditions, such as being dutiful (*ʿādil*) and all the other qualities that are required of an imam, which will be mentioned in the section on congregational (*jamāʿah*) prayers.[4] In the absence of an imam, the Friday prayer does not become obligatory.

Some conditions must be met for the Friday prayer to be valid:

1. it must be performed in congregation; therefore, it is not correct (*ṣaḥīḥ*) to perform the Friday prayer on one's own (*furādā*). If the follower (*maʾmūm*) of an imam in congregational prayers joins the prayer before the *rukūʿ* of the second *rakʿah* of the Friday prayer and performs one more *rakʿah* on his own, his Friday prayer is valid. However, if one joins in the *rukūʿ* of the second *rakʿah*, then based on obligatory precaution, he cannot suffice with this Friday prayer and must perform *ẓuhr* prayers;
2. the imam must deliver two sermons before the prayer. In the first sermon, he must praise (*ḥamd*) and eulogise (*thanāʾ*) Allah, exhort the congregation to God-wariness (*taqwā*), and recite a short chapter (surah) from the Qur'an. In the second sermon, again he must praise and eulogise Allah and invoke blessings (*ṣalawāt*) upon the Most Noble Messenger (Ṣ) and the Infallible Imams (ʿA); and the recommended precaution is that he should also seek forgiveness for the believers. Furthermore, it is necessary that the sermons be delivered before the prayer; therefore, if the imam starts the prayer before the two sermons,

[3] See Ruling 717.

[4] See Rulings 1433–1439.

it is incorrect. Delivering the sermons before *ẓuhr* time is problematic (*maḥall al-ishkāl*) [i.e. based on obligatory precaution, it is not correct].[5] In addition, it is necessary that the person delivering the sermons be in a standing position; therefore, if he delivers the sermons in a sitting position, it is incorrect. It is also necessary that he sit down a little between the two sermons and that his sitting be short and light. Furthermore, it is necessary that the imam of the congregation deliver the sermons himself, and based on obligatory precaution, he must praise Allah and pray for blessings to be showered upon the Most Noble Messenger (Ṣ) and the Infallible Imams (ʿA) in the Arabic language; however, saying other parts of the sermons in Arabic, such as eulogising Allah and exhorting the congregation to God-wariness, is not a requirement. Indeed, if most of the congregation do not understand Arabic, then the obligatory precaution is that exhorting the congregation to God-wariness must be said in the language of the attendees;

3. the distance between two Friday prayers must not be less than one *farsakh*;[6] therefore, if another Friday prayer takes place at a distance of less than 3.4 miles, then in the event that both prayers commenced together, both are invalid. If one of them commences before the other – even to the extent of the *takbīrat al-iḥrām*[7] – it is valid and the second one is invalid. However, if after a Friday prayer has taken place it becomes known that another Friday prayer took place at the same time or before it at a distance of less than 3.4 miles, it is not obligatory to perform the *ẓuhr* prayer. Furthermore, a Friday prayer can only have a prohibitive effect on another one taking place within the stipulated distance if it is a valid Friday prayer and fulfils all the conditions; otherwise, it does not have any prohibitive effect.

Ruling 720. Whenever the Friday prayer takes place with all its conditions fulfilled, if the one establishing it is the infallible Imam (ʿA) or his specific representative, it is obligatory to attend it; otherwise,

[5] As mentioned in Ruling 6, the term 'problematic' (*maḥall al-ishkāl*) amounts to saying the ruling is based on obligatory precaution.

[6] A *farsakh* is a measure of distance equivalent to approximately 5.5 kilometres, or 3.4 miles.

[7] Saying '*allāhu akbar*' at the beginning of the prayer.

it is not obligatory. In the first situation, however, it is not obligatory for the following groups of people to attend:

1. women;
2. slaves;
3. travellers, even those travellers whose duty is to perform the complete (*tamām*) form of the prayer, such as those who have made an intention to stay [at their destination for ten or more days];
4. the sick, blind, and aged;
5. those who are more than two *farsakhs* [6.8 miles] from a place of Friday prayer;
6. those who find it difficult and hard to attend the Friday prayer on account of rain, severe cold, and suchlike.

Ruling 721. If the Friday prayer is obligatory for someone but he performs the *ẓuhr* prayer instead, his prayer is valid.

SOME LAWS CONCERNING THE FRIDAY PRAYER

1. Taking into consideration what was mentioned above – namely that the Friday prayer is not a fixed obligation (*al-wājib al-taʿyīnī*)[8] during the time of the occultation – it is permitted (*jāʾiz*) to hasten for performing the *ẓuhr* prayer at the start of its prescribed time.
2. Talking while the imam is delivering the sermons is disapproved (*makrūh*); and if it prevents others from listening to the sermons, then based on obligatory precaution, it is not permitted.
3. Based on obligatory precaution, listening to the two sermons is obligatory; however, it is not obligatory for those who do not understand the sermons to listen to them.
4. It is not obligatory to be present at the time of the imam's sermons.

[8] This is an act of worship for which there is no alternative act that a *mukallaf* can perform instead. The Friday prayer is not a fixed obligation during the time of the occultation because the *ẓuhr* prayer can be performed in its place.

THE TIME FOR THE PRAYER AFTER SUNSET (*MAGHRIB*) AND THE EVENING (*ʿISHĀʾ*) PRAYER

Ruling 722. If a person doubts whether the sun has set and deems it probable that it is hidden behind mountains, buildings, or trees, he must not perform the *maghrib* prayer before the redness of the sky in the east – which appears after sunset – has passed overhead. Even if one does not have such a doubt, he must, based on obligatory precaution, wait until the aforementioned time.

Ruling 723. For a person under normal circumstances, the time for the *maghrib* prayer is until midnight, but for a helpless person – who due to forgetfulness, oversleeping, menstruation (*ḥayḍ*), or suchlike did not perform prayers before midnight – the time for *maghrib* and *ʿishāʾ* prayers is extended until dawn. However, in both cases, the proper order between the two prayers must be observed, meaning that if the *ʿishāʾ* prayer is knowingly performed before the *maghrib* prayer, it is invalid unless the time remaining is sufficient for performing only the *ʿishāʾ* prayer, in which case it is necessary that one perform the *ʿishāʾ* prayer before the *maghrib* prayer.

Ruling 724. If someone mistakenly performs the *ʿishāʾ* prayer before the *maghrib* prayer and realises his mistake after the prayer, his prayer is valid and he must perform the *maghrib* prayer after it.

Ruling 725. If before performing the *maghrib* prayer one inadvertently engages in performing the *ʿishāʾ* prayer and realises during the prayer that he has made a mistake, in the event that he has not performed the *rukūʿ* of the fourth *rakʿah*, he must change his intention to the *maghrib* prayer, complete the prayer, and then perform the *ʿishāʾ* prayer. However, if he has performed the *rukūʿ* of the fourth *rakʿah*, he can complete the *ʿishāʾ* prayer and then perform the *maghrib* prayer.

Ruling 726. As previously mentioned, the time for the *ʿishāʾ* prayer for a person under normal circumstances ends at midnight. The night is the period from the beginning of sunset until dawn.

Ruling 727. If someone wilfully does not perform *maghrib* or *ʿishāʾ*

prayers by midnight, he must, based on obligatory precaution, perform them before the time of the morning call to prayer (*adhān*) without making the intention of performing them in their prescribed time (*adāʾ*) or belatedy (*qaḍāʾ*).

THE TIME FOR THE MORNING (*ṢUBḤ*) PRAYER

Ruling 728. Near the time of the morning call to prayer, a whiteness in the sky moves upwards from the east; this is known as 'the first dawn'. When this whiteness spreads, it is called 'the second dawn', which is the start of the prescribed time for the morning prayer.[9] The end of the time for the morning prayer is when the sun rises.

LAWS RELATING TO THE TIME OF PRAYERS

Ruling 729. One can start performing prayers when he attains certainty (*yaqīn*) that the time has set in or when two dutiful men inform him that the time has set in. In fact, one can conclude that the time for the morning prayer has set in if he hears the *adhān* said by someone whom he knows is extremely careful in observing the time of prayers, or if he is informed by such a person, provided that he derives confidence (*iṭmiʾnān*) from it.

Ruling 730. If due to a personal impediment, such as blindness or being imprisoned, a person cannot perform prayers at the start of their prescribed time on account of being unable to attain certainty in the time having set in, he must delay his prayers until he is certain or confident that the time has set in. And based on obligatory precaution, the same applies if the impediment to one attaining certainty in the time having set in is due to non-personal hindrances, such as clouds, dust, and similar things.

Ruling 731. If through one of the ways mentioned previously it becomes established for someone that the time for prayers has set in

[9] 'The first dawn' is also known as the 'the false dawn' (*al-fajr al-kādhib*), and 'the second dawn' is also known as 'the true dawn' (*al-fajr al-ṣādiq*).

and he starts to perform his prayer, and during the prayer he realises that the time has not yet set in, his prayer is invalid. The same applies if he realises after the prayer that he performed the entire prayer before the time had set in. However, if during the prayer he realises that the time has set in, or if he realises after the prayer that during the prayer the time had set in, his prayer is valid.

Ruling 732. If a person is unaware of the fact that he must be certain that the time for prayers has set in and he starts performing the prayer, in the event that after the prayer he realises that he had performed the entire prayer within its time, his prayer is valid. However, if he realises that he performed the prayer before the time had set in, or he does not know whether he had performed the prayer within its time or before it, his prayer is invalid. In fact, if he realises after the prayer that the time had set in during the prayer, he must perform that prayer again.

Ruling 733. If a person is certain that the time has set in and starts his prayer, and during the prayer he doubts whether the time has set in or not, his prayer is invalid. However, if during the prayer he was certain that the time had set in and doubts after completing the prayer whether the prayer he performed was within the time or not, his prayer is valid.

Ruling 734. If the time remaining for prayers is so little that by performing some of the recommended (*mustaḥabb*) acts of the prayer a part of the prayer would have to be performed after its prescribed time, one must not perform those recommended acts. For example, if by performing *qunūt*[10] a part of the prayer would have to be performed after its prescribed time, he must not perform *qunūt*. Furthermore, if he does perform that recommended act, his prayer is valid only if at least one *rakʿah* of it was performed within the prescribed time.

Ruling 735. Someone who has time to perform one *rakʿah* of the prayer must perform the prayer with the intention of *adāʾ*; however, he must not intentionally delay the prayer until this time.

[10] This is the act of supplicating in prayers with the hands placed in front of the face.

Ruling 736. If someone who is not a traveller has time until sunset to perform five *rakʿahs*, he must perform the *ẓuhr* and *ʿaṣr* prayers in sequence. If he has less time than this, he must first perform the *ʿaṣr* prayer and after that the *ẓuhr* prayer with the intention of *qaḍāʾ*. Similarly, if one has time until midnight to perform five *rakʿahs*, he must perform the *maghrib* and *ʿishāʾ* prayers in sequence. If he has less time than this, he must first perform the *ʿishāʾ* prayer and after that the *maghrib* prayer without making the intention of *adāʾ* or *qaḍāʾ*.

Ruling 737. If someone who is a traveller has time until sunset to perform three *rakʿahs*, he must perform the *ẓuhr* and *ʿaṣr* prayers in sequence. If he has less time than this, he must first perform the *ʿaṣr* prayer and after that the *ẓuhr* prayer with the intention of *qaḍāʾ*. If a person has time until midnight to perform four *rakʿahs*, he must perform the *maghrib* and *ʿishāʾ* prayers in sequence. If he has time to perform only three *rakʿahs*, he must first perform the *ʿishāʾ* prayer and then the *maghrib* prayer so that he has performed one *rakʿah* of the *maghrib* prayer within its time. If he has time for less than three *rakʿahs*, he must first perform the *ʿishāʾ* prayer and after that the *maghrib* prayer without making the intention of *adāʾ* or *qaḍāʾ*. In the event that after performing the *ʿishāʾ* prayer he realises that there is still time until midnight for one or more *rakʿahs*, he must immediately perform the *maghrib* prayer with the intention of *adāʾ*.

Ruling 738. It is recommended that one perform prayers at the start of their prescribed time; this is something that has been highly advised. The nearer to the start of the prescribed time, the better, unless delaying the prayer is better for some reason; for example, someone waits a little to perform the prayer in congregation, on condition that it does not pass the prime time (*waqt al-faḍīlah*).[11]

Ruling 739. Whenever someone has a legitimate excuse (*ʿudhr*) that obliges him to perform his prayer with dry ablution (*tayammum*), if he wants to perform his prayer at the start of its prescribed time, then in the event that he is not hopeful of his excuse expiring, or he deems it probable that even if he delays performing *tayammum* he will still be

[11] This refers to the early period of the prescribed time for a prayer during which there is more reward for performing it.

unable [to perform his prayer with ablution (*wuḍūʾ*)], in such a case, he can perform *tayammum* at the start of its prescribed time and perform his prayer. However, if he is hopeful [of his excuse expiring], he must wait until his excuse expires or he loses hope; and in the event that his excuse does not expire, he must perform his prayer at the end of its prescribed time. Furthermore, it is not necessary that he wait until he has time to perform only the obligatory acts of the prayer; rather, if he has time, he can perform *tayammum* and perform his prayer with the recommended acts, such as *adhān*, the call to stand for prayer (*iqāmah*), and *qunūt*. In the case of excuses other than those for which one can perform *tayammum*, even if one is hopeful of the excuse expiring, it is permitted to perform prayers at the start of their prescribed time; however, in the event that the excuse expires within the prescribed time, it is necessary to repeat the prayer in some cases.

Ruling 740. If someone does not know the rulings (*masāʾil*) of prayers and cannot perform prayers correctly without learning the rulings, or if he does not know what to do about doubts that arise in prayers (*shakkiyāt*) or acts that are inadvertently left out (*sahwiyāt*), and if he deems it probable that one of these issues will arise in his prayer and on account of not learning the rulings he will not perform an obligatory act or will commit an unlawful act, then in these cases, he must delay his prayer from the start of its prescribed time to learn the rulings. However, if he begins to perform his prayer at the start of its prescribed time with the hope that he will perform it correctly, and if during the prayer a problem for which he does not know the rule does not arise, his prayer is valid. However, if a problem for which he does not know the rule arises, it is permitted for him to act according to the more probable of two possibilities [concerning what he thinks the correct ruling is] in the hope that his responsibility is fulfilled and then complete the prayer. After the prayer, he must find out about the ruling; if his prayer was invalid, he must perform it again, and if it was valid, it is not necessary for him to repeat it.

Ruling 741. If there is ample time for prayers and a creditor asks to be paid what he is owed, one must first pay his debt and then perform his prayer, if this is possible. Similarly, if some other obligation arises that must be performed immediately – for example, one sees that the mosque has become impure – he must first purify the mosque and then perform his prayer. In both cases, in the event that he first performs his prayer, he commits a sin but his prayer is valid.

PRAYERS THAT MUST BE PERFORMED IN ORDER

Ruling 742. One must perform the *ʿaṣr* prayer after the *ẓuhr* prayer, and the *ʿishāʾ* prayer after the *maghrib* prayer. If someone intentionally performs *ʿaṣr* before *ẓuhr* or *ʿishāʾ* before *maghrib*, the prayer is invalid.

Ruling 743. If a person starts to perform prayers with the intention of the *ẓuhr* prayer and while performing it realises that he has already performed the *ẓuhr* prayer, he cannot change his intention to the *ʿaṣr* prayer. Instead, he must break his prayer and perform the *ʿaṣr* prayer. The same applies to *maghrib* and *ʿishāʾ* prayers.

Ruling 744. If a person becomes certain during the *ʿaṣr* prayer that he has not performed the *ẓuhr* prayer and he changes his intention to the *ẓuhr* prayer, in the event that he remembers that he has actually performed the *ẓuhr* prayer, he can revert his intention to the *ʿaṣr* prayer and complete the prayer provided that he has not performed any obligatory components of the prayer with the intention of the *ẓuhr* prayer; if he has, he must perform them again with the intention of the *ʿaṣr* prayer. However, if the act is an obligatory component of the *rakʿah*, his prayer in both cases is invalid. Similarly, if the act is a *rukūʿ*, or two *sajdah*s in one *rakʿah*, then based on obligatory precaution, his prayer is invalid.

Ruling 745. If a person doubts during the *ʿaṣr* prayer whether he has performed the *ẓuhr* prayer or not, he must complete the prayer with the intention of the *ʿaṣr* prayer and after that perform the *ẓuhr* prayer. However, if the time is so little that after completing the *ʿaṣr* prayer the time for prayers ends and there is not enough time remaining to perform even one *rakʿah*, it is not necessary to make up the *ẓuhr* prayer.

Ruling 746. If a person doubts during the *ʿishāʾ* prayer whether he has performed the *maghrib* prayer or not, he must complete the prayer with the intention of the *ʿishāʾ* prayer and after that perform the *maghrib* prayer. However, if the time is so little that after completing the prayer the time for prayers ends and there is not enough time remaining to perform even one *rakʿah*, it is not necessary to make up the *maghrib* prayer.

Ruling 747. If a person doubts during the *ʿishāʾ* prayer after reaching the *rukūʿ* of the fourth *rakʿah* whether he has performed the *maghrib* prayer or not, he must complete the prayer and after that perform the *maghrib* prayer provided that there is enough time remaining to do so.

Ruling 748. If a person performs a prayer and then performs it again as a precautionary measure, and during the prayer he remembers that he has not performed the prayer that was necessary for him to perform before it, he cannot change his intention to that prayer. For example, if when he performs the *ʿaṣr* prayer as a precautionary measure he remembers he has not performed the *ẓuhr* prayer, he cannot change his intention to the *ẓuhr* prayer.

Ruling 749. Changing one's intention from a *qaḍāʾ* prayer to an *adāʾ* prayer, or from a recommended prayer to an obligatory prayer, is not permitted.

Ruling 750. If there is ample time for an *adāʾ* prayer, one can, during the prayer – in the event that he remembers he has an outstanding *qaḍāʾ* prayer to perform – change his intention to the *qaḍāʾ* prayer. However, [for this to be valid,] it must be possible to change the intention to a *qaḍāʾ* prayer; for example, if he has started to perform the *ẓuhr* prayer, he can change his intention to a *qaḍāʾ ṣubḥ* prayer only if he has not yet reached the *rukūʿ* of the third *rakʿah*.

RECOMMENDED (*MUSTAḤABB*) PRAYERS

Ruling 751. There are many recommended prayers; they are called 'supererogatory' (*nāfilah*) prayers. From among the recommended prayers, the daily *nāfilah* prayers have been recommended more. These number thirty-four *rakʿahs* (on days other than Friday): eight *rakʿahs* are the *nāfilah* of *ẓuhr*, eight of *ʿaṣr*, four of *maghrib*, two of *ʿishāʾ*, eleven of the night, and two of *ṣubḥ*. As the two *rakʿahs* of the *nāfilah* of *ʿishāʾ* must be performed in a sitting position, they are counted as one *rakʿah*, based on obligatory precaution. On Fridays, four *rakʿahs* are added to the sixteen *rakʿahs* of *ẓuhr* and *ʿaṣr*. It is better that all twenty *rakʿahs* be performed before *zawāl*, except for two *rakʿahs* – it is better to perform these at the time of *zawāl*.

Ruling 752. From among the eleven *rakʿahs* of the night *nāfilah*,[12] eight *rakʿahs* must be performed with the intention of *nāfilah* of the night, two *rakʿahs* with the intention of the *shafʿ* prayer, and one *rakʿah* with the intention of the *witr* prayer. Full instructions on how to perform the *nāfilah* of the night are mentioned in the books of supplications (*duʿāʾs*).

Ruling 753. *Nāfilah* prayers can be performed in a sitting position even if one does so voluntarily, and [if someone performs these prayers in a sitting position,] it is not necessary to count two *rakʿahs* as one *rakʿah*. However, it is better to perform them in a standing position, except for the *nāfilah* of *ʿishāʾ*, which based on obligatory precaution must be performed in a sitting position.

Ruling 754. A traveller must not perform the *nāfilah* of *ẓuhr* and *ʿaṣr*. There is no problem if a traveller performs the *nāfilah* of *ʿishāʾ* with the intention of *rajāʾ* [i.e. in the hope that it is desired by Allah].

TIMINGS FOR THE DAILY SUPEREROGATORY (*NĀFILAH*) PRAYERS

Ruling 755. The *nāfilah* of *ẓuhr* is performed before the *ẓuhr* prayer, and its time commences from the time of *ẓuhr* and continues until the time it is possible to perform it before performing the *ẓuhr* prayer. However, if one delays performing the *nāfilah* of *ẓuhr* until the time that the shadow of an indicator (*shākhiṣ*), which is visible after the time of *ẓuhr*, becomes two-sevenths the length of the indicator – meaning that if the length of the indicator is seven spans, the shadow becomes two spans in length – then in such a case, it is better to

[12] These eleven *rakʿahs* are collectively referred to as '*ṣalāt al-layl*' (the night prayer) or '*ṣalāt al-tahajjud*' (the night vigil prayer).

perform the *ẓuhr* prayer before the *nāfilah* prayer unless one has performed one *rakʿah* of the *nāfilah* prayer before [the shadow of the indicator becomes two-sevenths the length of the indicator], in which case it is better to complete the *nāfilah* prayer before the *ẓuhr* prayer.

Ruling 756. The *nāfilah* of *ʿaṣr* is performed before the *ʿaṣr* prayer, and its time continues until the time it is possible to perform it before performing the *ʿaṣr* prayer. However, if one delays performing the *nāfilah* of *ʿaṣr* until the time that the shadow of an indicator becomes four-sevenths the length of the indicator, it is better to perform the *ʿaṣr* prayer before the *nāfilah* prayer, except in the case mentioned in the previous ruling.

Ruling 757.* The time for the *nāfilah* of *maghrib* starts after performing the *maghrib* prayer and continues until the time it is possible to perform it after performing the *maghrib* prayer within its prescribed time. However, if one delays performing the *nāfilah* of *maghrib* until the redness of the western sky – which is visible after the sun sets – disappears, it is better that he first perform the *ʿishāʾ* prayer.

Ruling 758. The time for the *nāfilah* of *ʿishāʾ* is after performing the *ʿishāʾ* prayer until midnight, and it is better that it be performed immediately after the *ʿishāʾ* prayer.

Ruling 759. The *nāfilah* of the *ṣubḥ* prayer is performed before the *ṣubḥ* prayer. Its time commences after the time it takes to perform the night prayer (*ṣalāt al-layl*) at its earliest time, and continues until there is still time to perform it before the *ṣubḥ* prayer. However, if one delays performing the *nāfilah* of *ṣubḥ* until the redness of the eastern sky becomes visible, it is better that he first perform the *ṣubḥ* prayer.

Ruling 760. Based on the opinion held by most jurists (*mashhūr*), the commencement of the *nāfilah* of the night is midnight. Although this is accordant with recommended precaution and better, it is not farfetched (*baʿīd*)[13] that its commencement be the start of the night and its time continue until the time of the morning call to prayer. It

[13] For practical purposes, a legal opinion that is termed 'not farfetched' equates to a fatwa.

is better that the *nāfilah* of the night be performed near the time of the morning call to prayer.

Ruling 761. If a person wakes up at the appearance of daybreak, he can perform *ṣalāt al-layl* without making the intention of *adāʾ* or *qaḍāʾ*.

THE *GHUFAYLAH* PRAYER

Ruling 762. The *ghufaylah* [literally, 'a brief state of unmindfulness'] prayer is one of the recommended prayers that is performed between *maghrib* and *ʿishāʾ* prayers. In the first *rakʿah* after Sūrat al-Ḥamd, these verses are recited instead of a surah:

﴿وَذَا النُّوْنِ إِذْ ذَهَبَ مُغَاضِبًا فَظَنَّ أَنْ لَنْ نَقْدِرَ عَلَيْهِ فَنَادَىٰ فِي الظُّلُمَاتِ أَنْ لَا إِلٰهَ إِلَّا أَنْتَ سُبْحَانَكَ إِنِّيْ كُنْتُ مِنَ الظَّالِمِيْنَ ۞ فَاسْتَجَبْنَا لَهُ وَنَجَّيْنَاهُ مِنَ الْغَمِّ وَكَذٰلِكَ نُنْجِي الْمُؤْمِنِيْنَ﴾

wa dhan nūni idh dhahaba mughāḍiban faẓanna an lan naqdira ʿalayhi fanādā fiẓ ẓulumāti an lā ilāha illā anta subḥānaka innī kuntu minaẓ ẓālimīn. fastajabnā lahu wa najjaynāhu minal ghammi wa kadhālika nunjil muʾminīn

And the Man of the Fish [Prophet Yūnus], when he left in a rage, thinking that We would not put him to hardship. Then he cried out in the darkness, 'There is no god except You! You are immaculate! I have indeed been among the wrongdoers!' So We answered his prayer and delivered him from the agony; and thus do We deliver the faithful.[14]

In the second *rakʿah* after Sūrat al-Ḥamd, this verse is recited instead of a surah:

﴿وَعِنْدَهُ مَفَاتِحُ الْغَيْبِ لَا يَعْلَمُهَا إِلَّا هُوَ وَيَعْلَمُ مَا فِي الْبَرِّ وَالْبَحْرِ وَمَا تَسْقُطُ مِنْ وَرَقَةٍ إِلَّا يَعْلَمُهَا وَلَا حَبَّةٍ فِيْ ظُلُمَاتِ الْأَرْضِ وَلَا رَطْبٍ وَلَا يَابِسٍ إِلَّا فِيْ كِتَابٍ مُبِيْنٍ﴾

wa ʿindahu mafātiḥul ghaybi lā yaʿlamuhā illā huwa wa yaʿlamu mā fil barri

[14] Sūrat al-Anbiyāʾ (Chapter 21), verses 87 & 88.

wal baḥri wa mā tasquṭu min waraqatin illā ya'lamuhā wa lā ḥabbatin fī ẓulumātil arḍi wa lā raṭbin wa lā yābisin illā fī kitābin mubīn

With Him are the treasures of the Unseen; no one knows them except Him. He knows whatever there is in land and sea. No leaf falls without His knowing it, nor is there a grain in the darkness of the earth, nor anything fresh or withered but it is in a manifest Book.[15]

In *qunūt*, this is recited:

اَللّٰهُمَّ إِنِّيْ أَسْأَلُكَ بِمَفَاتِحِ الْغَيْبِ الَّتِيْ لَا يَعْلَمُهَا إِلَّا أَنْتَ، أَنْ تُصَلِّيَ عَلَىٰ مُحَمَّدٍ وَآلِ مُحَمَّدٍ، وَأَنْ تَفْعَلَ بِيْ ___

allāhumma innī as'aluka bimafātiḥil ghaybil latī lā ya'lamuhā illā ant, an tuṣalliya 'alā muḥammadin wa āli muḥammad, wa an taf'ala bī ___

O Allah! I ask You by the treasures of the Unseen that no one knows except You, to bless Muḥammad and the progeny of Muḥammad and to fulfil for me ___.

In the blank place, one should ask for his needs (*ḥājāt*) to be fulfilled and then recite:

اَللّٰهُمَّ أَنْتَ وَلِيُّ نِعْمَتِيْ وَالْقَادِرُ عَلَىٰ طَلِبَتِيْ، تَعْلَمُ حَاجَتِيْ فَأَسْأَلُكَ بِحَقِّ مُحَمَّدٍ وَآلِ مُحَمَّدٍ عَلَيْهِ وَعَلَيْهِمُ السَّلَامُ، لَمَّا قَضَيْتَهَا لِيْ

allāhumma anta waliyyu ni'matī wal qādiru 'alā ṭalibatī, ta'lamu ḥājatī fa'as'aluka biḥaqqi muḥammadin wa āli muḥammadin 'alayhi wa 'alayhimus salām, lammā qaḍaytahā lī

O Allah! You are the Patron of my blessings and the One Powerful to respond to my request. You know my needs, so I ask You by the right of Muḥammad and the progeny of Muḥammad, peace be upon him and them, to fulfil them for me.

He should then ask Allah the Exalted to fulfil his needs.

RULES OF QIBLA

Ruling 763. Qibla is the place of the Ka'bah in Mecca, and prayers

[15] Sūrat al-An'ām (Chapter 6), verse 59.

must be performed facing it. However, for someone who is far away, it is sufficient to stand in such a manner that it can be said he is performing prayers facing qibla. The same applies to other acts – such as slaughtering animals – that must be performed facing qibla.

Ruling 764. Someone who performs the obligatory prayers in a standing position must do so with his chest and stomach facing qibla, and his face must not divert a lot from qibla. And the recommended precaution is that his toes should also face qibla.

Ruling 765. Someone who must perform prayers in a sitting position must do so with his chest and stomach facing qibla, and his face must not divert a lot from qibla.

Ruling 766. Someone who cannot perform prayers in a sitting position must perform them lying on his side in a way that the front of his body faces qibla. Furthermore, as far as it is possible for him to lie on his right side, he must not lie on his left side, based on obligatory precaution. If both of these positions are not possible for him, he must lie on his back in a way that the soles of his feet face qibla.

Ruling 767. The precautionary prayer (*ṣalāt al-iḥtiyāṭ*) and a forgotten *sajdah* or *tashahhud* (testifying) must be performed facing qibla. And based on recommended precaution, the two prostrations for inadvertence (*sajdatā al-sahw*) should also be performed facing qibla.

Ruling 768. A recommended prayer can be performed while walking and riding, and if a person performs a recommended prayer in either of these ways, it is not necessary that he face qibla.

Ruling 769. Someone who wants to perform prayers must make efforts to find out the direction of qibla to the extent that he attains certainty about its direction, or that which comes under the rule (*ḥukm*) of certainty, such as the testimony of two dutiful people if their testimony is based on sensory perception and suchlike. If he cannot [find out its direction to this extent], he must act according to what he supposes to be the direction of qibla based on the position of the *miḥrāb*[16] of a mosque, or the graves of believers, or by some other way. Even if he bases his supposition (*ẓann*) on the words of an immoral person or a disbeliever who knows the direction of qibla by employing scientific principles, it is sufficient.

Ruling 770. If someone who has a supposition about the direction of qibla arrives at a stronger supposition, he cannot act on his first supposition. For example, if a guest has a supposition about the direction of qibla through the words of his host but he arrives at a stronger opinion by another way, he must not act on the words of his host.

Ruling 771. If someone does not have any means to find the direction of qibla, or despite his efforts he cannot arrive at a supposition as to its direction, it is sufficient for him to perform prayers facing a direction that he thinks could be qibla. Furthermore, the recommended precaution is that if there is enough time, he should perform prayers four times, each time facing one of the four compass directions [i.e. what he supposes to be north, east, south, and west].

Ruling 772. If a person is certain or supposes that qibla is in one of two directions, he must perform prayers in both of those directions.

Ruling 773. If someone who has to perform prayers in different directions wants to perform two prayers that must be performed one after the other, such as the *ẓuhr* and *ʿaṣr* prayers, the recommended precaution is that he perform the first prayer in those different directions and then the second prayer in those different directions as well.

Ruling 774. If someone wants to do something, other than perform prayers, that must be done facing qibla – for example, he wants to slaughter an animal – but he is neither certain nor has knowledge that comes under the rule of certainty about the direction of qibla, he must act on his supposition. If acting on his supposition is not possible, then it will be correct for him to perform the act facing any direction.

[16] This is a niche, chamber, or slab in a mosque that faces the direction of Mecca and where the imam usually stands for congregational prayers.

COVERING THE BODY IN PRAYERS

Ruling 775. While performing prayers, a man must cover his private parts even if no one sees him; and it is better that he cover his body from the navel to the knees.

Ruling 776. While performing prayers, a woman must cover her entire body, even her head and hair; and based on obligatory precaution, she must cover her body in a way that even she cannot see it. Therefore, if she wears a chador in a way that she can see her body, it is problematic [i.e. based on obligatory precaution, a woman must not wear a chador in such a way]. However, it is not necessary for a woman to cover her face, her hands below the wrists, or her feet below the ankles. To be certain that she has covered the obligatory areas, she must also cover a little of the sides of her face and a little of the area below her wrists and ankles.

Ruling 777. When someone makes up a forgotten *sajdah* or *tashahhud*, he must cover himself in the same manner as when he performs prayers. And the recommended precaution is that he should cover himself in this manner when he performs *sajdatā al-sahw* as well.

Ruling 778. When performing prayers, if one intentionally does not cover his private parts,[17] his prayers are invalid. If he does this on account of not knowing the ruling, then in the event that he was negligent in not learning the ruling, he must, based on obligatory precaution, perform the prayers again.

Ruling 779. If someone realises during his prayers that his private parts are visible, he must cover them but it is not necessary for him to repeat his prayers. However, the obligatory precaution is that while he realises his private parts are visible, he must not continue with any component of the prayer. If he realises after his prayer that during the prayer his private parts were visible, his prayer is valid.

[17] With regard to a woman, 'private parts' in this and in subsequent rulings pertaining to covering the body in prayers refers to all the parts of the body that a woman must cover in prayers; i.e. her entire body – apart from her face, her hands below the wrists, and her feet below the ankles (*Tawḍīḥ al-Masāʾil-i Jāmiʿ*, vol. 1, p. 288, Ruling 933).

Ruling 780. If some clothing covers one's private parts while he is standing but it is possible that it would not cover them in other positions – for example, in the position of *rukūʿ* and *sujūd* (prostrating) – then, in the event that when his private parts are visible he covers them by some means, his prayer is valid. However, the recommended precaution is that he should not perform prayers with such clothing.

Ruling 781. When performing prayers, one can cover himself using grass and tree leaves. However, the recommended precaution is that he should only use these when he does not have clothing.

Ruling 782. If a person is in a helpless situation whereby he does not have anything with which to cover his private parts, he can cover them with mud and suchlike so that they are not visible.

Ruling 783. If a person does not have anything with which to cover himself while performing prayers, in the event that he has not lost hope in finding something to cover himself with, the obligatory precaution is that he must delay performing prayers. If he does not find anything, he must perform his prayer according to his duty at the end of the prescribed time. However, if he has lost hope, he can perform his prayer according to his duty at the start of the prescribed time; and in this case, if he performs prayers at the start of the prescribed time and afterwards his excuse expires, it is not necessary for him to repeat his prayer.

Ruling 784. If someone who wants to perform prayers does not even have tree leaves, grass, mud, or sludge with which to cover himself, and if he is not hopeful of finding something with which he could cover himself before the end of the prayer's prescribed time, then, in case he is confident that someone from whom it is obligatory to cover his private parts will not see him, he must perform his prayer in a standing position and perform *rukūʿ* and *sujūd* normally. Furthermore, in the event that he deems it probable that an onlooker (*al-nāẓir al-muḥtaram*)[18] will see him, he must perform his prayer in

[18] *Al-nāẓir al-muḥtaram* (literally, a 'respected onlooker') is someone who is sane (*ʿāqil*), able to discern between right and wrong (*mumayyiz*), of the age of legal responsibility (*bāligh*), and not married to the person being seen.

such a manner that his private parts are not visible; for example, by performing it in a sitting position. If to prevent himself from being seen by an onlooker in each of these three states he is obliged to perform his prayer in a sitting position and to leave out *rukūʿ* and *sujūd*, he must sit and perform *rukūʿ* and *sujūd* by indicating; and if he is obliged to leave out only one of these three acts, he must leave out only that one. Therefore, if he can, he must stand and perform *rukūʿ* and *sujūd* by indicating; and if standing results in him being seen, he must sit and perform *rukūʿ* and *sujūd*. And the recommended precaution is that when performing the prayer in the sitting or standing position, he should perform *rukūʿ* and *sujūd* by indicating. Furthermore, the obligatory precaution is that a naked person performing prayers must cover his private parts using some part of his body, such as his thighs in a sitting position and his hands in a standing position.

CONDITIONS OF CLOTHING WORN BY SOMEONE PERFORMING PRAYERS

Ruling 785. The clothing worn by someone performing prayers must meet six conditions:

1. it must be pure (*ṭāhir*);
2. it must be permissible (*mubāḥ*) [i.e. it must not be usurped], as an obligatory precaution;
3. it must not be made from the parts of the carcass [of an animal that has not been slaughtered according to Islamic law];
4. it must not be from a predatory animal; and based on obligatory precaution, nor must it be from an animal whose meat is unlawful to eat;

5.–6 if the person performing prayers is male, it must not be made from pure silk nor embroidered with gold.

The details of these conditions will be explained in the following rulings.

Ruling 786. The first condition: the clothing worn by a person performing prayers must be pure. If someone voluntarily performs prayers with an impure body or with impure clothing, his prayers are invalid.

Ruling 787. If on account of being negligent in learning the religious ruling a person does not know that prayers performed with an impure body or with impure clothing are invalid, or that, for example, semen is impure, and he performs prayers with it, the obligatory precaution is that he must perform the prayer again; and if the prescribed time has expired, he must make it up.

Ruling 788. If on account of not knowing the ruling a person performs prayers with an impure body or with impure clothing, and if he was not negligent in learning the ruling, then it is not necessary for him to perform the prayer again or make it up.

Ruling 789. If someone is certain that his body or clothing is not impure and after prayers he realises it was impure, his prayers are valid.

Ruling 790.* If someone forgets that his body or clothing is impure and remembers it during or after prayers, in the event that his forgetfulness was due to carelessness and heedlessness, he must perform the prayer again based on obligatory precaution. If the prescribed time for the prayer has expired, he must make it up. [If his forgetfulness was not due to carelessness and heedlessness and] he remembers after prayers [that his body or clothing was impure], it is not necessary for him to perform the prayer again. However, if he remembers this during prayers, he must act according to the instructions that will be mentioned in the next ruling.

Ruling 791. If a person starts performing a prayer when there is ample time, and during it he becomes aware that his body or clothing has become impure, and he deems it probable that it became impure after he started his prayer, then, in case his prayer would not be broken up by washing his body, changing his clothes, or taking them off, he must during the prayer wash his body or clothes, change his clothes, or take them off, as long as another thing covers his private parts. However, in the event that washing his body or clothes, or changing or removing his clothes, would break up the prayer, or if by removing his clothes he would become naked, then based on obligatory precaution, he must perform his prayer again with pure clothes.

Ruling 792. If a person starts performing a prayer when time is short, and during it he realises that his clothing has become impure, and he deems it probable that it had become impure after he started the prayer, then, in case his prayer would not be broken up by washing or changing his clothes or taking them off, and he can remove them, he must wash his clothes, change them, or take them off – as long as another thing covers his private parts – and he must then complete his prayer. However, if nothing else covers his private parts and he cannot wash nor change his clothes, he must complete his prayer with the impure clothing.

Ruling 793. If a person starts performing a prayer when time is short, and during it realises that his body has become impure, and he deems it probable that it became impure after he started his prayer, then, in case washing his body would not break up the prayer, he must wash his body. If it would break up the prayer, he must complete it just as he is and it will be valid.

Ruling 794. If someone has a doubt about his body or clothing being pure, in the event that he investigates and does not see anything on it and performs prayers, and after prayers he realises that his body or clothing was impure, his prayers are valid. However, if he does not investigate, then based on obligatory precaution, he must perform his prayer again; and in the event that the time has expired, he must make it up.

Ruling 795. If a person washes his clothing and is certain that it has become pure and performs prayers with it, and afterwards he realises that it had not become pure, his prayers are valid.

Ruling 796. If someone sees some blood on his body or clothing and is certain that it is not impure blood – for example, he is certain that it is the blood of a mosquito – then, in the event that after prayers he realises that it was a type of impure blood with which prayers cannot be performed, his prayers are valid.

Ruling 797. If someone is certain that the blood on his body or clothing is impure blood with which prayers can be performed – for example, he is certain that it is the blood of a wound or a boil – then, in the event that he realises after prayers that the blood was of the type with which prayers cannot be performed, his prayers are valid.

Ruling 798. If a person forgets that something is impure and his wet body or clothing touches it, and while he is in the state of forgetfulness he performs prayers with it and remembers it after prayers, his prayers are valid. However, if his wet body touches an impure object that he had forgotten was impure, and without washing himself he performs ritual bathing (*ghusl*) and prayers, his *ghusl* and prayers are invalid unless by performing *ghusl* his body also becomes pure and the water does not become impure, like when *ghusl* is performed in running water. Furthermore, if a wet part of the body on which *wuḍūʾ* is performed touches an impure object that he had forgotten was impure, and before washing it he performs *wuḍūʾ* and prayers, his *wuḍūʾ* and prayer are invalid unless by performing *wuḍūʾ* the impure part on which *wuḍūʾ* is performed also becomes pure and the water does not become impure, like when *wuḍūʾ* is performed with *kurr*[19] or running water.

Ruling 799.* If someone possesses only one piece of clothing and his body and clothing become impure, and the water in his possession is enough to wash only one of them, the obligatory precaution is to wash the body and perform prayers with the impure clothing. And based on obligatory precaution, it is not permitted to wash the clothing and perform prayers with an impure body. However, in case the impurity on his clothing is more than what is on his body, or there is an impurity on his clothing that has an additional prohibitive element, such as the blood of a predatory animal,[20] then in such a case, he has the choice of washing whichever one he wants.

Ruling 800. Someone who does not have any other clothing apart

[19] A quantity of water greater or equal to approximately 384 litres. See Ruling 14.
[20] The blood of a predatory animal has two prohibitive elements: 1) it is impure; and 2) it is from an animal whose meat is unlawful to eat (*Tawḍīḥ al-Masāʾil-i Jāmiʿ*, vol. 1, p. 291, Ruling 941, part b).

from impure clothing must perform prayers with impure clothing, and his prayers will be valid.

Ruling 801. If someone who has two sets of clothing knows that one of them is impure but he does not know which one it is, in the event that he has sufficient time, he must perform prayers with each of them. For example, if he wants to perform the *ẓuhr* and *ʿaṣr* prayers, he must perform one *ẓuhr* prayer and one *ʿaṣr* prayer with each. However, if time is short and neither of them can be preferred based on the strength of probability, then whichever one he performs his prayer with will be sufficient.

Ruling 802. The second condition: based on obligatory precaution, the clothing with which a person performing prayers covers his private parts must be permissible (*mubāḥ*) [i.e. it must not be usurped (*ghaṣbī*)]. If a person knows that wearing usurped clothing is unlawful, or he does not know the ruling due to his negligence, and he intentionally performs prayers with that clothing, then based on obligatory precaution, his prayers are invalid. However, with regard to usurped things that do not on their own cover the private parts, and things that the person performing prayers is not currently wearing – such as a big handkerchief or a loincloth in his pocket, even though they could cover his private parts – and things that he is currently wearing but under which he has some other clothes that are not usurped and which cover his private parts, in all of these cases, the fact that these things are usurped do not affect the validity of the prayer, although as a recommended precaution using such things should be avoided.

Ruling 803. If someone knows that wearing usurped clothing is unlawful but does not know the ruling on performing prayers with it, and he intentionally performs prayers with usurped clothing, then as per the details mentioned in the previous ruling his prayers are invalid based on obligatory precaution.

Ruling 804. If someone does not know his clothing is usurped or forgets that it is and performs prayers with it, his prayers are valid. However, if someone usurps some clothing himself and forgets that he has usurped it and performs prayers with it, then based on obligatory precaution, his prayers are invalid.

Ruling 805. If someone does not know or forgets that his clothing is usurped and realises this during prayers, in the event that something else covers his private parts and he can immediately or without breaking the close succession (*muwālāh*) – i.e. by maintaining continuity in the prayer – remove the clothing and continue praying, he must do so. If there is nothing else that covers his private parts from an onlooker [as defined in the footnote pertaining to Ruling 784] or he cannot remove the usurped clothing, he must continue the prayer with that clothing and the prayer will be valid.

Ruling 806. If someone performs prayers with usurped clothing to protect his life, then in case he cannot perform prayers with other clothing by the end of the prescribed time, or he has to wear it out of necessity due to no fault of his own – for example, he did not usurp it himself – his prayers are valid. Similarly, if he performs prayers in usurped clothing so that a thief does not steal it and he cannot perform prayers before the end of the prescribed time with other clothing, or he keeps it with the intention of returning it to its owner as soon as possible, his prayers are valid.

Ruling 807.* If a person purchases clothing with money on which the one-fifth tax (*khums*) has not been paid, and the purchase is a non-specified undertaking (*al-kullī fī al-dhimmah*),[21] as most purchases are, the clothing will be lawful (*ḥalāl*) for him. However, because he used money on which *khums* had not been paid, and he delayed paying the *khums* that was due on it, he will have sinned and must pay *khums* on the money he gave to the seller. However, if a person purchases clothing with the actual money on which *khums* has not been paid,[22] then performing prayers with that clothing without the authorisation of a fully qualified jurist (*al-ḥākim al-sharʿī*) is ruled to be the same as performing prayers with usurped clothing.

[21] This refers to a purchase in which the actual thing with which the payment is made is not specified. For example, a buyer purchases some goods for £20 without specifying to the seller that he is purchasing the goods with a particular £20 note.

[22] This is known as a 'specified' (*shakhṣī*) purchase and is not common. Here, the transaction takes place over money that has been singled out for that purchase. For example, a buyer tells the seller that he is purchasing the goods with such and such £20.

Ruling 808. The third condition: the clothing that is large enough to cover the private parts on its own of someone performing prayers must not be made from the carcass [of an animal that has not been slaughtered according to Islamic law] and whose blood gushes out when its jugular vein is cut. Based on obligatory precaution, this condition also applies to clothing that cannot cover the private parts on its own. And the recommended precaution is that one should not perform prayers with clothing that has been made from an animal whose blood does not gush out, such as a snake.

Ruling 809. If a person performs prayers while he has with him something from an impure carcass that contained life – such as a piece of meat or skin – his prayers are valid.

Ruling 810. If a person performs prayers while he has with him something from the carcass of an animal whose meat is lawful to eat, and that thing is not something that contains life – such as fur or wool – or, if he performs prayers with clothing made from it, his prayers are valid.

Ruling 811. The fourth condition: the clothing of a person performing prayers – apart from things that do not cover the private parts on their own, such as socks – must not be made from a predatory animal; in fact, based on obligatory precaution, it must not be made from an animal whose blood gushes out when its jugular vein is cut. Similarly, a person's body and clothing must not be tainted with the urine, faeces, sweat, milk, or hair of such an animal. However, there is no problem if, for example, one strand of hair of such an animal is on his clothing, and the same applies if he carries something on his person from that animal; for example, in a container or box.

Ruling 812. If saliva, nasal mucus, or any other moisture from an animal whose meat is unlawful to eat, such as a cat, is on the body or clothing of someone performing prayers and it is wet, his prayers are invalid. However, his prayers are valid if it has dried up and the actual substance has been removed.

Ruling 813. There is no problem if someone's hair, sweat, or saliva is on the body or clothing of a person performing prayers, and the same applies to pearls, wax, and honey.

Ruling 814. If a person doubts whether some clothing is made from an animal whose meat is lawful or unlawful to eat – irrespective of whether it was made in an Islamic country or not – it is permitted to perform prayers with it.

Ruling 815. It is not known if seashells are from the parts of animals whose flesh is unlawful to eat; therefore, it is permitted for one to perform prayers with them.

Ruling 816. Wearing the fur of a squirrel in prayers is not a problem, although the recommended precaution is that prayers should not be performed with it.

Ruling 817. If a person performs prayers with clothing about which he does not know or has forgotten that it was made from an animal whose meat is unlawful, his prayers are valid.

Ruling 818. The fifth condition: wearing clothing embroidered with gold for men is unlawful, and prayers performed with it are invalid. However, for women, wearing it in prayers and at other times is not a problem.

Ruling 819. Wearing gold, such as a gold necklace, ring, and wristwatch, is unlawful for men, and performing prayers with it is invalid. However, for women, wearing it in prayers and at other times is not a problem.

Ruling 820.* If a man does not know the previous ruling, or he does not know that his ring or clothing is made from gold, or he forgets or doubts [that it is made from gold], and he performs prayers with it, his prayers are valid. However, if he was culpably ignorant (*al-jāhil al-muqaṣṣir*)[23] about the ruling, his prayers are invalid and he must perform them again.

[23] 'Culpably ignorant' is a term used to refer to someone who does not have a valid excuse for not knowing; for example, he was careless in learning religious laws.

Ruling 821. The sixth condition: the clothing of a man performing prayers that can cover the private parts on its own must not be made of pure silk. Furthermore, it is unlawful for a man to wear such clothing at other times.

Ruling 822. If an entire sleeve or part of it is made out of pure silk, it is unlawful for a man to wear it, and prayers performed with it are invalid.

Ruling 823. It is permitted for one to wear clothing about which he does not know whether it is made out of pure silk or something else, and there is no problem in performing prayers with it.

Ruling 824. There is no problem if a silk handkerchief or similar item is in a man's pocket, and it does not invalidate prayers.

Ruling 825. For women, there is no problem in wearing silk clothing in prayers and at other times.

Ruling 826. [For a man,] there is no problem in wearing pure silk clothing or clothing embroidered with gold if he is compelled to. Also, someone who is compelled to wear clothing and does not have any clothing except this type can perform prayers with it.

Ruling 827. If a person does not have clothing other than clothing that is usurped, or made of pure silk, or embroidered with gold, and if he is not compelled to wear clothes, he must perform prayers according to the instructions that were mentioned regarding a naked person.[24]

Ruling 828. If a person does not have clothing other than that made from a predatory animal, in the event that he is compelled to wear it, he can perform prayers with it provided that the necessity for him to do so remains until the end of the prescribed time. However, if he is not compelled, he must perform prayers according to the instructions that were mentioned regarding a naked person. If a person does not have clothing other than that made from an animal whose meat is unlawful to eat but is not a predatory animal, in the event that he is

[24] See Rulings 781–784.

not compelled to wear it, the obligatory precaution is that he must perform prayers twice: once with that clothing, and once according to the instructions that were mentioned regarding a naked person.

Ruling 829.* If a person does not have anything with which he can cover his private parts in prayers, it is obligatory for him to procure such a thing even if he has to hire or purchase it. However, if procuring it would cause him excessive difficulty due to his poor financial situation, or the item being expensive, or him suffering some injustice – then it is not necessary for him to procure it and he can perform prayers according to the instructions that were mentioned regarding a naked person.

Ruling 830. If someone who does not have clothing is gifted or loaned some clothing by someone else, in the event that accepting it does not cause him excessive difficulty (*mashaqqah*), he must accept it. In fact, if borrowing or asking for clothing is not difficult for him, he must borrow or ask for it from someone who has it.

Ruling 831. Wearing clothing made of a material, colour, or style that is not normal for someone who wants to wear it is unlawful if it would cause him disrespect and humiliation. However, his prayers are valid if he performs prayers in that clothing, even if that is his only covering.

Ruling 832. It is not unlawful for a man to wear a woman's clothing, nor for a woman to wear a man's clothing, and performing prayers with such clothing does not invalidate the prayer. However, based on obligatory precaution, it is not permitted for a man to appear in the form of a woman, and similarly vice versa.

Ruling 833. With regard to the bed sheet or quilt that is used by someone who must perform prayers while lying down, it is not necessary for it to fulfil the conditions of clothing of someone performing prayers unless it is used in such a way that it can be said to be worn, like if he were to wrap himself in it.

CASES WHEN IT IS NOT NECESSARY FOR THE BODY AND CLOTHING OF SOMEONE PERFORMING PRAYERS TO BE PURE

Ruling 834. In three cases – the details of which will follow afterwards – if the body or clothing of someone performing prayers is impure, his prayers are valid:

1. if due to a wound, sore, or boil on his body the clothing or his body has become impure with blood;
2. if the amount of blood that has made his body or clothing impure is less than the area covered by a dirham. Based on obligatory precaution, a dirham is equal to the size of the upper joint of the thumb;
3. if he is compelled to perform prayers with an impure body or clothing.

In one case, [despite not falling under any of the three cases above,] if the clothing of someone performing prayers is impure, his prayers are valid, and that is when his small items of clothing – such as his socks and cap – are impure.

The laws (*aḥkām*) of these four situations will be explained in detail in the following rulings.

Ruling 835. If blood from a wound, sore, or boil is on the body or clothing of someone performing prayers, he can perform prayers with that blood as long as the wound, sore, or boil has not healed. The same applies to pus that comes out with blood or any medicine that is applied to the wound and becomes impure.

Ruling 836. If blood from a cut or wound that heals quickly and is easy to wash is on the body or clothing of someone performing prayers, and the amount of blood is equal to or more than the area covered by a dirham, his prayers are invalid.

Ruling 837. If a part of one's body or clothing that is distant from a wound becomes impure by means of the moisture from the wound, it is not permitted to perform prayers with it. However, if part of one's body or clothing around the wound becomes impure by means of the moisture from the wound, there is no problem in performing prayers with it.

Ruling 838. If a person's body or clothing has blood on it from piles or a wound that is inside one's mouth or nose etc., he can perform prayers with it; and it makes no difference whether the swollen haemorrhoid vessels are internal or external.

Ruling 839. If there is a wound on one's body, and on his body or clothing he sees blood that is equal to or more than the area covered by a dirham but does not know whether it is blood from the wound or not, the obligatory precaution is that he must not perform prayers with it.

Ruling 840. If there are several wounds on one's body and they are so close to each other that they are considered one wound, there is no problem in performing prayers with that blood until the time all the wounds heal. However, if the wounds are so far apart from one another that each of them is considered a separate wound, then whenever one of them heals, he must wash the blood from his body and clothing to perform prayers.

Ruling 841. If there is even the tiniest amount of *ḥayḍ* blood on the body or clothing of someone performing prayers, the prayers are invalid. Furthermore, based on obligatory precaution, the same applies with regard to blood from an intrinsic impurity (*ʿayn al-najāsah*) – such as a pig or a corpse – and blood from an animal whose meat is unlawful to eat, the blood of lochia (*nifās*), and the blood of an irregular blood discharge (*istiḥāḍah*). However, there is no problem in performing prayers if there are other types of blood on one's body or clothing – such as blood from a human being or an animal whose meat is lawful to eat – even if it is on a number of areas of the body or clothing, provided that their combined area is less than that of a dirham.

Ruling 842. If blood spills on clothing that does not have a lining and it reaches the other side, it is considered to be one blood; and the side on which the blood has spread more must be taken into account [when determining its amount in relation to the area covered by a dirham]. However, if the other side of the clothing becomes bloody separately, then each side must be considered separately. Therefore, if the combined area of blood on the front and back of the clothing is less than the area covered by a dirham, prayers with it are valid; but if it is equal to or more than the area covered by a dirham, then prayers performed with it are invalid.

Ruling 843. If blood spills on clothing that has a lining and reaches the lining, or it spills on the lining and reaches the upper layer of the clothing, or from one piece of clothing it reaches another piece, then, in each of these cases, the blood must be considered to be separate. Therefore, if the combined area of blood is less than the area covered by a dirham, the prayers are valid; otherwise, they are invalid unless the areas are joined together such that they would be commonly considered to be one area of blood, in which case if the area of blood on the side that has spread more is less than the area covered by a dirham, prayers with it are valid; but if the amount of blood is equal to or more than the area covered by a dirham, then prayers performed with it are invalid.

Ruling 844. If the area of blood on one's body or clothing is less than the area covered by a dirham, and some moisture reaches it and spreads it further, prayers performed with it are invalid even if the area of the blood and the moisture is not equal to the area covered by a dirham. However, if moisture only reaches the blood without spreading it, there is no problem in performing prayers with it.

Ruling 845. If a person's body or clothing has not become bloody but on account of moisture reaching the blood it becomes impure, he cannot perform prayers with it even if the area that has become impure is less than the area covered by a dirham.

Ruling 846. If the area of blood on one's body or clothing is less than the area covered by a dirham and another impurity reaches it – for example, a drop of urine falls on it – then in case it reaches a pure part of the body or clothing, it is not permitted to perform prayers with it. In fact, even if it does not reach a pure part of the body or clothing, it is not correct to perform prayers with it based on obligatory precaution.

Ruling 847. If the small items of clothing of someone performing prayers that cannot cover the private parts – such as socks or a cap – become impure, in the event that they are not made from an impure carcass or an animal that is an intrinsic impurity – such as a dog – prayers performed with them are valid. However, if they are made from an impure carcass or an impure animal, then based on obligatory precaution, prayers performed with them are invalid. However, there is no problem in performing prayers with an impure ring.

Ruling 848. It is permitted for someone performing prayers to have with him an impure object like an impure handkerchief, key, or knife. Similarly, there is no problem in having impure clothing with him [that is not worn].

Ruling 849. If a person knows that the area of blood on his body or clothing is less than the area covered by a dirham, but he deems it probable that the blood may be of a type that is not excusable in prayers, it is permitted for him to perform prayers with that blood.

Ruling 850. If the area of blood on one's body or clothing is less than the area covered by a dirham, but he does not know that it is a type of blood that is not excusable in prayers and performs prayers, and afterwards he realises that it was a type of blood that is not excusable in prayers, it is not necessary for him to perform the prayer again. Similarly, if he believes that the amount of blood is less than the area covered by a dirham and performs prayers, and afterwards he realises that it was equal to or more than the area covered by a dirham, it is not necessary for him to perform the prayer again.

THINGS THAT ARE RECOMMENDED (*MUSTAḤABB*) FOR THE CLOTHING OF SOMEONE PERFORMING PRAYERS

Ruling 851. The jurists (*fuqahāʾ*) – may Allah sanctify their souls –

have known some things to be recommended for the clothing of someone performing prayers. These include: wearing a turban (*ʿamāmah*) with its final fold passing under the chin (*taḥt al-ḥanak*), wearing a cloak that rests on the shoulders (*ʿabā*), wearing white clothes, wearing very clean clothing, applying perfume, and wearing an agate (*ʿaqīq*) ring.

THINGS THAT ARE DISAPPROVED (*MAKRŪH*) FOR THE CLOTHING OF SOMEONE PERFORMING PRAYERS

Ruling 852. The jurists – may Allah sanctify their souls – have known some things to be disapproved for the clothing of someone performing prayers. These include: wearing black clothes, wearing dirty or tight clothes, wearing the clothes of someone who drinks alcohol, wearing the clothes of someone who does not refrain from impure things, wearing clothes that have a picture of a face on them, leaving buttons open, and wearing a ring that has a picture of a face on it.

THE PLACE WHERE PRAYERS ARE PERFORMED

The place where prayers are performed must fulfil seven conditions.

The first condition: it must be permissible to use [i.e. it must not be usurped], based on obligatory precaution.

Ruling 853. If someone performs prayers on usurped property, even if it is a carpet, couch, or something similar, then based on obligatory precaution, his prayers are invalid. However, there is no problem in performing prayers under a usurped roof or in a usurped tent.

Ruling 854. Performing prayers on property whose benefit belongs to someone else without the consent of the one who benefits from the property is ruled to be the same as performing prayers on usurped property. For example, if in a rented house the landlord or someone else performs prayers without the tenant's consent, then based on obligatory precaution, his prayers are invalid.

Ruling 855. If someone is sitting in a mosque and another person takes his place and without his consent performs prayers there, his prayers are valid although he has sinned.

Ruling 856. If a person does not know or has forgotten that a certain place is usurped and performs prayers there, and after his prayers he realises or remembers it is usurped, his prayers are valid. However, if someone has usurped a place himself but forgets and performs prayers there, then based on obligatory precaution, his prayers are invalid.

Ruling 857. If someone knows that a certain place is usurped and that using it is unlawful, but he does not know that there is a problem in performing prayers in a usurped place and performs prayers there, then based on obligatory precaution, his prayers are invalid.

Ruling 858.* If someone is compelled to perform an obligatory prayer while he is on or in a mode of transport, or if he wishes to perform a recommended prayer while he is in such a position, then the seat he performs his prayers on, and the wheels of that mode of transportation, fall under the rules of this first condition, i.e. they must not be ruled to be usurped.

Ruling 859. If someone owns a property in partnership with someone else, and if his share is not separately defined, he cannot use that property without his partner's consent; and based on obligatory precaution, prayers performed there are invalid.

Ruling 860. If a person purchases property with money on which *khums* has not been paid and the purchase is a non-specified undertaking,[25] as most purchases are, then using it is lawful for him and he owes *khums* on the money he paid for the property. However, if a person purchases property with the actual money on which *khums*

[25] See the first footnote pertaining to Ruling 807 for an explanation of this term.

has not been paid,[26] then using that property without the authorisation of a fully qualified jurist is unlawful; and based on obligatory precaution, prayers performed there are invalid.

Ruling 861. If the owner of a property verbally gives his consent to perform prayers there but one knows that in reality he does not consent, then performing prayers on his property is not permitted. If he does not give his consent but one is certain that in reality he consents, performing prayers there is permitted.

Ruling 862. If a dead person owes money in alms tax (zakat) or to people, there is no problem in using his property with the consent of his heirs provided that the use does not conflict with the paying of his debt; for example, [there would be no problem in] performing prayers in his house. Similarly, if the heirs pay his debt, take it upon themselves to pay his debt, or keep aside the amount of his debt from his estate, there is no problem in using his property even if this causes it to be ruined.

Ruling 863. If some of the heirs of a dead person are minors (*ṣaghīr*), insane, or absent, then using the property without the consent of the guardian (*walī*) of those heirs is unlawful, and performing prayers there is not permitted. However, there is no problem in using it in a normal way to start preparations for the burial of the corpse.

Ruling 864. Performing prayers on someone else's property is permitted only when the owner clearly gives his consent to do so, or he says something that indicates he has given permission – such as giving someone his consent to sit and sleep on his property, by which it can be understood that he has given permission for prayers to be performed there as well – or when one derives confidence by some other way that the owner consents.

Ruling 865. It is permitted to perform prayers on a vast expanse of land even if its owner is a minor or insane, or he does not consent to prayers being performed there. Similarly, it is permitted to perform

[26] This is known as a 'specified' (*shakhṣī*) purchase. See the second footnote pertaining to Ruling 807 for an explanation of this term.

prayers without the owner's consent in gardens and on land that do not have gates or walls. However, in this case, if one knows that the owner does not consent, he must not use it. If the owner is a minor or insane, or if one supposes that he does not consent, the obligatory precaution is that he must not use it nor perform prayers there.

Ruling 866. The second condition: the place where obligatory prayers are performed must not move so vigorously that it would prevent the person from performing prayers from standing and performing *rukūʿ* and *sujūd* normally; in fact, based on obligatory precaution, the movement must not prevent his body from being steady. If one is compelled to perform prayers in such a place due to shortage of time or any other reason – for example, in certain types of cars or on a ship or train – he must remain still and face qibla as much as possible. If the vehicle moves away from the direction of qibla, he must turn and face the qibla again; and if it is not possible to face qibla precisely, he must try to ensure that the difference is less than ninety degrees; and if this is not possible, he must face qibla at least while performing *takbīrat al-iḥrām*; and if even this is not possible, it is not necessary for him to face qibla.

Ruling 867. Performing prayers in a car, ship, train etc. is permitted while it is standing still. The same applies when it is moving, provided that it does not move to such an extent that it prevents the person's body from being steady.

Ruling 868. Prayers performed on a pile of wheat, barley, and similar things on which one cannot remain still are invalid.

The third condition: one must perform prayers in a place where he deems it probable that he will complete them. However, if one is confident that he will not be able to complete his prayers in a place on account of wind, rain, or there being a lot of people around and suchlike, he must perform prayers with the intention of *rajāʾ*; and if he happens to complete his prayer, it will be valid.

Ruling 869. If a person performs prayers at a place where it is unlawful to stay – for example, under a roof that is close to collapsing – his prayers are valid although he will have sinned.

Ruling 870. Performing prayers on something that is unlawful to stand or sit on – such as a place on a mat that has the name of Allah the Exalted written on it – is not correct in the event that it prevents one from establishing an intention to attain proximity to Allah (*qaṣd al-qurbah*).

The fourth condition: the ceiling of the place where one performs prayers must not be so low that he cannot stand up straight; and the place must not be so small that there is no room to perform *rukūʿ* and *sujūd*.

Ruling 871. If a person is compelled to perform prayers in a place where it is not at all possible to stand up straight, it is necessary that he perform prayers in a sitting position; and if performing *rukūʿ* and *sujūd* is not possible either, he must perform them by indications of the head.

Ruling 872. In prayers and other situations, it is unlawful to turn one's back to the grave of the Prophet (Ṣ) or the Infallible Imams (ʿA) if it amounts to disrespecting them. However, if it would not amount to disrespecting them due to there being a large distance or an obstacle like a wall between the person and the grave, then there is no problem. Of course, on its own, the distance between the person and the sacred coffin, or the cloth that is placed over it, or the sacred lattice enclosure of the tomb (*ḍarīḥ*), would not be sufficient for discounting any disrespectful behaviour towards them; but in either case, if the person establishes an intention to attain proximity to Allah, his prayer will be valid.

The fifth condition: If the place where a person performs prayers is impure, it must not be so wet that its moisture reaches his body or clothing in case the impurity is of the type that invalidates prayers. However, if the place where one places his forehead is impure, the prayers are invalid even if the place is dry. And the recommended precaution is that the place where one performs prayers should not be impure at all.

The sixth condition: Based on obligatory precaution, a woman must stand behind a man at least to the extent that the place of her *sajdah* is level with the place of his knees when he performs *sajdah*.

Ruling 873. If a woman stands level with or in front of a man and they both start prayers together, then based on obligatory precaution, they must perform the prayer again. If one of them starts prayers before the other, then based on obligatory precaution, the prayer of the one who performed *takbīrat al-iḥrām* second is invalid, and the prayer of the one who performed *takbīrat al-iḥrām* first is valid provided that what is mentioned in the next ruling is observed; if it is not observed, the prayer of the first person who performed *takbīrat al-iḥrām* will also be invalid. However, if observing what is mentioned in the next ruling is not possible, then the person should continue with the prayer and it will be valid.

Ruling 874. If a man and a woman stand level with each other or a woman stands in front and they perform prayers, and if there is a wall, curtain, or something else between them so that they cannot see one another, or the distance between them is more than ten cubits (*dhirāʿ*s) (equivalent to approximately four and a half metres), then in these cases, the prayers of both of them are valid.

The seventh condition: The place of one's forehead must not be higher or lower than the height of four fingers closed together in relation to the place of his knees and big toes. The details of this ruling will be mentioned in the section on *sajdah*.

Ruling 875. It is unlawful for a man and a woman who are not *maḥram*[27] to be in a secluded place together if there is a probability of a sin taking place. And the recommended precaution is that [in such a situation] they should not perform prayers there.

Ruling 876. It is not unlawful to perform prayers in a place where there is singing and unlawful music, even though listening to it and playing it is sinful.

Ruling 877. The obligatory precaution is that obligatory prayers must

[27] A *maḥram* is a person one is never permitted to marry on account of being related to them in a particular way, such as being their parent or sibling.

not be wilfully performed inside the Kaʿbah or on its roof. There is no problem, however, if one is compelled.

Ruling 878. There is no problem in performing recommended prayers inside the Kaʿbah or on its roof. In fact, it is recommended to perform a two *rakʿah* recommended prayer inside the Kaʿbah in front of each corner.

PLACES WHERE PERFORMING PRAYERS IS RECOMMENDED (*MUSTAḤABB*)

Ruling 879. In the sacred law of Islam, it has been highly advised to perform prayers in a mosque. The best of all mosques is Masjid al-Ḥarām, and after that the Mosque of the Prophet (Ṣ), and after that the Mosque of Kufa, and after that the al-Aqsa Mosque, and after that the *jāmiʿ* mosque[28] of every town, and after that one's local mosque, and after that a mosque in the bazaar.

Ruling 880. It is better that women perform their prayers in a place where it is more likely that they will not be seen by those who are not *maḥram* to them, whether that place be at home, in a mosque, or somewhere else.

Ruling 881. Performing prayers in the shrines (*ḥarams*) of the Infallible Imams (ʿA) is recommended; indeed, it is better than performing them in a mosque. It has been reported that a prayer in the sacred shrine of His Eminence, the Commander of the Faithful [Imam ʿAlī] (ʿA), is equal to 200,000 prayers.

Ruling 882. It is recommended to go to a mosque frequently, and to go to a mosque that does not have people performing prayers there. Furthermore, it is disapproved for the neighbours of a mosque to perform prayers in any place other than in the mosque without a legitimate excuse.

[28] As defined in Ruling 1728, a *jāmiʿ* mosque is one that is not particular to a specific group of people but is frequented by people from different areas of the town.

Ruling 883. It is recommended that one should not sit to eat with someone who does not attend a mosque, nor should one seek his advice on matters, be his neighbour, take his daughter in marriage, or give him a daughter in marriage.

PLACES WHERE PERFORMING PRAYERS IS DISAPPROVED (*MAKRŪH*)

Ruling 884. Performing prayers is disapproved in a number of places, including:

1. a public bath;
2. on saliferous land;
3. facing a person;
4. facing an open door;
5. on a street, road, and in an alley, in the event that it does not cause trouble for passers-by; if it does cause them trouble, it is unlawful;
6. facing a fire or lamp;
7. in a kitchen and in every place where there is a furnace;
8. facing a pit or ditch where people urinate;
9. facing a picture or statue of a living thing, unless it is covered;
10. in a room where a *junub*[29] is present;
11. in a place where there is a picture, even if it is not facing the person performing prayers;
12. facing a grave;
13. on a grave;
14. in between two graves;
15. in a graveyard.

Ruling 885. If a person performs prayers in a place where people pass by, or if someone is in front of him, it is recommended that he place something in front of him; and it is sufficient if that thing is some wood or rope.

[29] *Junub* is the term used to refer to a person who is in the state of ritual impurity (*janābah*). *Janābah* is explained in Ruling 344.

LAWS OF A MOSQUE

Ruling 886. It is unlawful to make impure a mosque's floor, ceiling, roof, and inside walls, as well as fixtures and fittings that are deemed to be part of the building, such as doors and windows.

Whoever finds out that it has become impure must immediately purify it. The recommended precaution is that the outside walls of the mosque should not be made impure either, but if they become impure, it is not necessary to purify them. However, if making the outside walls of a mosque impure amounts to disrespecting the mosque, it would, of course, be unlawful and make it necessary to purify them to the extent that it would no longer be considered disrespectful.

Ruling 887. If someone cannot make a mosque pure or needs help to do so but does not find it, it is not obligatory for him to make it pure. However, in the event that he knows that if he informs someone else it would be done, then, if leaving the impurity as it is would cause disrespect to the mosque, he must inform the other person.

Ruling 888. If a place in a mosque becomes impure and it cannot be made pure without digging it up or demolishing it, the impure place must be dug up or demolished provided that it is only a little area, or if rectifying the disrespect caused to the mosque is dependent on digging up or demolishing a large area; otherwise, demolishing it is problematic [i.e. based on obligatory precaution, it must not be demolished]. Furthermore, it is not obligatory to fill the place that has been dug up or rebuild the place that has been demolished. However, if something like a brick of the mosque becomes impure, then after it has been washed, it must be put back in its original position, if possible.

Ruling 889. If someone usurps a mosque and builds a house or something similar in its place, or if it becomes ruined to the extent that it can no longer be called a mosque, then making it impure is not unlawful, nor is it obligatory to purify it.

Ruling 890. It is unlawful to make the shrines of the Infallible Imams (ʿA) impure. If one of the shrines becomes impure, in the event that it remaining impure is disrespectful, it is obligatory to make it pure. In fact, the recommended precaution is that even if it is not disrespectful, it should be made pure.

Ruling 891. If the *ḥaṣīr*[30] or carpet of a mosque becomes impure, it must be washed; and if cutting out the impure part is better, it must be cut out. However, cutting out a considerable amount, or making it pure by causing damage to it, is problematic [i.e. based on obligatory precaution, it must not be done], unless leaving it causes disrespect.

Ruling 892. Taking something that is an intrinsic impurity, or something that has become impure by secondary means (*mutanajjis*), into a mosque is unlawful if it causes disrespect to the mosque. In fact, the recommended precaution is that even if it is not disrespectful, an intrinsic impurity should not be taken into a mosque unless it is something that naturally comes in with a person when he enters a mosque, such as the blood of a wound that is on his body or clothing.

Ruling 893. If for the purposes of holding mourning ceremonies a mosque is draped in curtains and covered in rugs and black cloth, and if utensils for serving tea are brought into it, then as long as these actions do not damage the mosque or obstruct the performing of prayers in it, there is no problem.

Ruling 894. The obligatory precaution is that a mosque must not be decorated with gold. And the recommended precaution is that it should not be decorated with things that have the form of a human being, an animal, or anything else that has a soul.

Ruling 895. Even if a mosque is ruined, it is not permitted to sell it or make it part of another property or road.

Ruling 896. Selling the doors, windows, and other things of a mosque is unlawful; and if a mosque becomes ruined, these things must be used solely for the renovation of the same mosque. In the event that they are of no use to that mosque, they must be used in another mosque. If they are of no use to other mosques, they can be sold and

[30] A *ḥaṣīr* is a mat that is made by plaiting or weaving straw, reed, or similar materials of plant origin.

the proceeds must be used solely for the renovation of that same mosque, if possible. If this is not possible either, the proceeds must be used on the renovation of another mosque.

Ruling 897. It is recommended to build a mosque and to renovate one that is close to ruin. If a mosque is ruined to the extent that it is not possible to renovate it, it can be demolished and rebuilt. In fact, to meet the needs of the people, a mosque that is not ruined can be demolished and a bigger mosque built.

Ruling 898. It is recommended for one to clean a mosque and to turn on its lights. For someone who wants to visit a mosque, it is recommended to apply perfume, wear clean and good clothes, and ensure that the soles of his shoes do not contain any impurity. When entering a mosque, it is recommended for one to place his right foot in first, and when leaving it, to put his left foot out first. It is also recommended that one come to the mosque earlier than everyone else and leave it later than everyone else.

Ruling 899. It is recommended that when a person enters a mosque, he should perform a two *rakʿah* prayer with the intention of saluting (*taḥiyyah*) and respecting (*iḥtirām*) the mosque; and if he performs an obligatory prayer or another recommended prayer, it is sufficient.

Ruling 900. The following are disapproved for a person to do in a mosque: sleep (unless he is compelled to), talk about worldly affairs, engage in craft, recite poetry (unless it exhorts people to good), and similar things. It is also disapproved to discharge nasal mucus, saliva, and phlegm in a mosque; in fact, this is unlawful in some cases. Furthermore, it is disapproved to look for something lost or raise one's voice in a mosque; however, there is no problem in raising one's voice for *adhān*.

Ruling 901. It is disapproved to give access to an insane person to enter a mosque, and similarly, to a child if it causes trouble for those performing prayers there or there is a probability that the child would make the mosque impure. Apart from these two reasons, there is no problem in allowing a child to enter a mosque; indeed, sometimes it is preferable to do so. Furthermore, if someone has eaten onions, garlic, or something similar, and his breath would thereby annoy people, it is disapproved for him to go to a mosque.

THE CALL TO PRAYER (*ADHĀN*) AND THE CALL TO STAND FOR PRAYER (*IQĀMAH*)

Ruling 902. It is recommended for both men and women to say *adhān* and then *iqāmah* before the daily obligatory prayers; however, they have not been sanctioned in Islamic law (they are not *mashrūʿ*) for other obligatory prayers or for recommended prayers. If Eid al-Fiṭr[31] and Eid al-Aḍḥā[32] prayers are performed in congregation, it is recommended to say '*aṣṣalāh*' three times before commencing them.

Ruling 903. It is recommended that on the day a child is born, or before his umbilical cord falls off, *adhān* should be said in his right ear and *iqāmah* in his left.

Ruling 904. *Adhān* consists of the following eighteen sentences:

×4	اَللّٰهُ أَكْبَرُ	allāhu akbar
×2	أَشْهَدُ أَنْ لَا إِلٰهَ إِلَّا اللّٰهُ	ashhadu an lā ilāha illal lāh
×2	أَشْهَدُ أَنَّ مُحَمَّدًا رَسُوْلُ اللّٰهِ	ashhadu anna muḥammadan rasūlul lāh
×2	حَيَّ عَلَى الصَّلَاةِ	ḥayya ʿalaṣ ṣalāh
×2	حَيَّ عَلَى الْفَلَاحِ	ḥayya ʿalal falāḥ
×2	حَيَّ عَلَىٰ خَيْرِ الْعَمَلِ	ḥayya ʿalā khayril ʿamal
×2	اَللّٰهُ أَكْبَرُ	allāhu akbar
×2	لَا إِلٰهَ إِلَّا اللّٰهُ	lā ilāha illal lāh

Iqāmah consists of the following seventeen sentences:

[31] The 1st of Shawwāl.

[32] The 10th of Dhū al-Ḥijjah.

×2	اَللّٰهُ أَكْبَرُ	allāhu akbar
×2	أَشْهَدُ أَنْ لَا إِلٰهَ إِلَّا اللّٰهُ	ashhadu an lā ilāha illal lāh
×2	أَشْهَدُ أَنَّ مُحَمَّدًا رَسُوْلُ اللّٰهِ	ashhadu anna muḥammadan rasūlul lāh
×2	حَيَّ عَلَى الصَّلَاةِ	ḥayya ʿalaṣ ṣalāh
×2	حَيَّ عَلَى الْفَلَاحِ	ḥayya ʿalal falāḥ
×2	حَيَّ عَلٰى خَيْرِ الْعَمَلِ	ḥayya ʿalā khayril ʿamal
×2	قَدْ قَامَتِ الصَّلَاةُ	qad qāmatiṣ ṣalāh
×2	اَللّٰهُ أَكْبَرُ	allāhu akbar
×1	لَا إِلٰهَ إِلَّا اللّٰهُ	lā ilāha illal lāh

Ruling 905. The sentence:

أَشْهَدُ أَنَّ عَلِيًّا وَلِيُّ اللّٰهِ

ashhadu anna ʿaliyyan waliyyul lāh

...is not a part of *adhān* and *iqāmah*, but it is good to say it after the sentence '*ashhadu anna muḥammadar rasūlul lāh*' with the intention of attaining proximity to Allah.

Translation of the sentences of *adhān* and *iqāmah*

اَللّٰهُ أَكْبَرُ	allāhu akbar	Allah is greater [than what He is described as].
أَشْهَدُ أَنْ لَا إِلٰهَ إِلَّا اللّٰهُ	ashhadu an lā ilāha illal lāh	I testify that there is no god but Allah.
أَشْهَدُ أَنَّ مُحَمَّدًا رَسُوْلُ اللّٰهِ	ashhadu anna muḥammadan rasūlul lāh	I testify that Muḥammad is the messenger of Allah.

أَشْهَدُ أنَّ عَلِيًّا أَمِيرُ الْمُؤْمِنِينَ وَوَلِيُّ اللهِ	ashhadu anna ʿaliyyan amīrul mu'minīna wa waliyyul lāh	I testify that ʿAlī is the Commander of the Faithful and the vicegerent of Allah.
حَيَّ عَلَى الصَّلَاةِ	ḥayya ʿalaṣ ṣalāh	Hasten to prayers.
حَيَّ عَلَى الْفَلَاحِ	ḥayya ʿalal falāḥ	Hasten to prosperity.
حَيَّ عَلَىٰ خَيْرِ الْعَمَلِ	ḥayya ʿalā khayril ʿamal	Hasten to the best act.
قَدْ قَامَتِ الصَّلَاةُ	qad qāmatiṣ ṣalāh	Certainly, the prayer has been established.
لَا إِلٰهَ إِلَّا اللّٰهُ	lā ilāha illal lāh	There is no god but Allah.

Ruling 906. There must not be a long interval between the sentences of *adhān* and *iqāmah*. If there is an interval between them that is longer than usual, they must be repeated from the beginning.

Ruling 907. If *adhān* and *iqāmah* are said in a manner that amounts to singing, i.e. in a manner that is in common with gatherings of entertainment and amusement, it is unlawful. If it does not amount to singing [but is somewhat similar to singing], it is disapproved.

Ruling 908. Whenever a person performs two prayers that share a common time one after the other, if he says *adhān* for the first prayer, then saying it for the second prayer is excepted. This is irrespective of whether or not it is better to join the two prayers together, such as joining *ẓuhr* and *ʿaṣr* prayers on the Day of ʿArafah – which is the ninth day of the month of Dhū al-Ḥijjah – [when it is better to join the two prayers together] if one performs them within the prime time (*waqt al-faḍīlah*) of the *ẓuhr* prayer even if he is not in ʿArafāt. [Another example is] joining *maghrib* and *ʿishā'* prayers on the eve of Eid al-Aḍḥā for one who is in Mashʿar al-Ḥarām and he joins them within the prime time of the *ʿishā'* prayer.

Adhān being excepted in these cases is conditional upon there not being a long interval between the two prayers. There is no problem if an interval occurs on account of performing *nāfilah* prayers or reciting *duʿā'*s after prayers (*taʿqībāt*). In these cases, the obligatory precaution is that *adhān* must not be said with the intention of it being an act that has been sanctioned in Islamic law; in fact, saying *adhān* in the two cases mentioned above on the Day of ʿArafah and in Mashʿar while observing the conditions mentioned above is contrary to obligatory precaution [and therefore, *adhān* must not be said], even without the intention of it being an act that has been sanctioned in Islamic law.

Ruling 909. If *adhān* and *iqāmah* have been said for a congregational prayer, a person joining that congregation must not say *adhān* and *iqāmah* for his own prayers.

Ruling 910. If a person goes to the mosque to perform prayers and finds that congregational prayers are over, he does not have to say *adhān* and *iqāmah* for his own prayers as long as the rows have not broken up and the people have not dispersed; in other words, saying them in such a situation is not an emphasised recommended act. In fact, if he wants to say *adhān*, it is better that he does so in a very low voice. If he wants to establish another congregational prayer, he must not say *adhān* and *iqāmah*.

Ruling 911. Apart from the case mentioned in the previous ruling, *adhān* and *iqāmah* become excepted if six conditions are fulfilled:

1. congregational prayers are performed in a mosque; if they are not performed in a mosque, then *adhān* and *iqāmah* are not excepted;
2. *adhān* and *iqāmah* have already been said for that prayer;
3. the congregational prayer is not invalid;
4. his prayer and the congregational prayer take place in one place; therefore, if the congregational prayer is performed inside a mosque and he wants to perform prayers on the mosque's rooftop, it is recommended that he say *adhān* and *iqāmah*;
5. the congregational prayer is performed within its prescribed time; but it is not a condition that his prayer also be one that is performed within its prescribed time if he is performing it on his own;
6. his prayer and the congregational prayer are performed in a

time that is common to both; for example, both perform *ẓuhr* prayers or both perform *ʿaṣr* prayers, or the prayer that is performed in congregation is *ẓuhr* and he performs *ʿaṣr* prayers, or he performs *ẓuhr* prayers and the congregational prayer is *ʿaṣr*. However, if the congregational prayer is *ʿaṣr* and it is being performed at the end of its prescribed time [and the rows have not yet broken up] and he wants to perform *maghrib* within its prescribed time, then *adhān* and *iqāmah* are not excepted.

Ruling 912. If a person has a doubt about the third condition mentioned above, i.e. he doubts whether or not the congregational prayer is valid, then saying *adhān* and *iqāmah* is excepted for him. However, if he has a doubt about one of the five other conditions, it is better that he say *adhān* and *iqāmah*; but if his prayer is in congregation, he must say them with the intention of *rajāʾ*.

Ruling 913. If someone hears another *adhān* that is said as an announcement or as a call to congregational prayers, it is recommended that he quietly repeat whichever part he hears.

Ruling 914. If someone hears another *adhān* and *iqāmah* – irrespective of whether he repeats after them or not – then, in the event that the interval between that *adhān* and *iqāmah* and the prayer that he wants to perform is not long, and he had the intention to perform prayers from the time he started hearing them, he can suffice with that *adhān* and *iqāmah*. However, if only the imam or only the followers of a congregational prayer hear the *adhān*, this rule is problematic [i.e. based on obligatory precaution, he cannot suffice with it].

Ruling 915. If a man listens to an *adhān* said by a woman with the intention of deriving lustful pleasure, then saying *adhān* is not excepted for him; in fact, *adhān* being excepted by listening to the *adhān* of a woman in general is a problem [i.e. based on obligatory precaution, it is not excepted].

Ruling 916. The *adhān* and *iqāmah* of congregational prayers must be said by a man. However, in congregational prayers of women, if a woman says *adhān* and *iqāmah*, it is sufficient. Sufficing with the *adhān* and *iqāmah* said by a woman in a congregational prayer in which the men present are her *maḥram* is problematic [i.e. based on obligatory precaution, it does not suffice].

Ruling 917. *Iqāmah* must be said after *adhān*, and it is a requirement that *iqāmah* be said while one is standing and in the state of ritual purity, i.e. while one has *wuḍū'*, *ghusl*, or *tayammum*.

Ruling 918. If a person says the sentences of *adhān* and *iqāmah* in the wrong order – for example, he says '*ḥayya 'alal falāḥ*' before '*ḥayya 'alaṣ ṣalāh*' – he must repeat them from the place where the order was disturbed.

Ruling 919. There must not be an interval between *adhān* and *iqāmah*, and if an interval occurs to the extent that the *adhān* that was said cannot be regarded as being the *adhān* of that *iqāmah*, then the *adhān* is invalid. Also, if there is an interval between the *adhān* and *iqāmah* and the prayer to the extent that the *adhān* and *iqāmah* cannot be regarded as being those of that prayer, then the *adhān* and *iqāmah* are invalid.

Ruling 920. *Adhān* and *iqāmah* must be said in correct Arabic; therefore, if they are said in incorrect Arabic, or instead of one of the letters another letter is said, or, for example, the English translation is said, it is not correct.

Ruling 921. *Adhān* and *iqāmah* must be said after the time for prayer has set in. If a person says them before that time – whether intentionally or forgetfully – they are invalid, except in the case when the time of prayer sets in during a prayer and the prayer is ruled to be valid, as explained in Ruling 731.

Ruling 922. If before saying *iqāmah* one doubts whether he said *adhān* or not, he must say *adhān*; but if while saying *iqāmah* he doubts whether he said *adhān* or not, then saying *adhān* is not necessary.

Ruling 923. If a person has started *adhān* or *iqāmah* and before saying some [particular] part of it he doubts whether he said the previous part or not, he must say the part about which he doubts; but if while saying some part of *adhān* and *iqāmah* he doubts whether he said the previous part or not, then saying it is not necessary.

Ruling 924. It is recommended that while saying *adhān*, one stands facing qibla, has *wuḍūʾ* or *ghusl*, places his hands on his ears, raises and extends his voice, briefly pauses between the sentences, and does not talk in between them.

Ruling 925. It is recommended that at the time of saying *iqāmah*, one's body should be still and he should say it quieter than *adhān* and not join the sentences together. However, the pauses in between the sentences of *iqāmah* should not be as long as they are in *adhān*.

Ruling 926. It is recommended that between *adhān* and *iqāmah*, one should take a step forward, or sit down briefly, or perform *sajdah*, or engage in remembering Allah the Exalted (*dhikr*), or recite a *duʿāʾ*, or be silent briefly, or talk, or perform a two *rakʿah* prayer. However, talking between *adhān* and *iqāmah* of *ṣubḥ* prayers is not recommended.

Ruling 927. It is recommended that a person who is appointed to say *adhān* be dutiful (*ʿādil*), know the timings, and have a loud voice. And it is recommended that *adhān* be said from an elevated place.

OBLIGATORY COMPONENTS OF THE PRAYER

There are eleven obligatory components of the prayer:

1. intention (*niyyah*);
2. standing (*qiyām*);
3. *takbīrat al-iḥrām*, i.e. saying '*allāhu akbar*' at the beginning of the prayer;
4. bowing (*rukūʿ*);
5. prostrating (*sujūd*);
6. recitation (*qirāʾah*);
7. declaring in *rukūʿ* and *sujūd* that Allah is free from imperfections (*dhikr*);
8. testifying (*tashahhud*);
9. salutation (*salām*);
10. sequence (*tartīb*);
11. close succession (*muwālāh*).

Ruling 928. Some of the obligatory components of the prayer are elemental (*rukn*), i.e. if one does not perform them – whether intentionally or mistakenly – the prayer is invalid. Some other obligatory components are not elemental, i.e. if they are omitted mistakenly, the prayer is not invalid. There are five *rukn*s of the prayer:

1. intention;
2. *takbīrat al-iḥrām* while standing;
3. standing that is joined to *rukūʿ*, i.e. standing before *rukūʿ*;
4. *rukūʿ*;
5. two *sajdah*s in one *rakʿah*.

If a *rukn* is intentionally performed more than the prescribed number of times, the prayer is invalid. If it is done mistakenly, and if the additional act is a *rukūʿ* or two *sajdah*s in one *rakʿah*, then based on obligatory precaution, the prayer is invalid; otherwise [i.e. if the additional act is not a *rukūʿ* or two *sajdah*s in one *rakʿah*], it is not invalid.

INTENTION (*NIYYAH*)

Ruling 929. One must perform prayers with the intention of *qurbah*, i.e. in humility and obedience to the Lord of the worlds. It is not necessary to make the intention pass through his heart or, for example, for him to say 'I am performing four *rakʿah*s of the *ẓuhr* prayer *qurbatan ilal lāh* [to attain proximity to Allah]'.

Ruling 930. If a person makes the intention in *ẓuhr* or *ʿaṣr* prayers that 'I am performing a four *rakʿah* prayer' but does not specify if it is the *ẓuhr* or *ʿaṣr* prayer, his prayer is invalid. However, it is sufficient if he specifies the *ẓuhr* prayer as the first prayer and the *ʿaṣr* prayer as the second prayer. With regard to someone for whom it is obligatory, for example, to make up a *ẓuhr* prayer, if he wants to make up that prayer or perform the *ẓuhr* prayer within the prescribed time for *ẓuhr* prayers, he must specify in his intention which prayer he is performing.

Ruling 931. One must maintain the intention from the beginning of the prayer until its end; therefore, if during the prayer he becomes unmindful to the extent that were he to be asked 'What are you doing?' he would not know what to reply, his prayer would be invalid.

Ruling 932. One must only perform prayers in humility to the Lord of the worlds; therefore, if one performs prayers ostentatiously – i.e. to show off to people – his prayer is invalid, irrespective of whether he does so solely for people or partly for Allah the Exalted and partly for people.

Ruling 933. If someone performs part of the prayer for other than Allah the Exalted – irrespective of whether that part is an obligatory one, such as the recitation of Sūrat al-Ḥamd, or a recommended one, such as *qunūt* – and if that intention permeates the entire prayer – for example, his ostentatious intention in the performance of an act is to show off his prayer – or, if to redress that part it would mean adding an act that invalidates the prayer [for example, to redress the *rukūʿ* that he performed ostentatiously, he would need to perform another *rukūʿ*, which would invalidate the prayer, as mentioned in Ruling 928], then in these cases, his prayer is invalid. If one performs prayers for Allah the Exalted but to show off to people he performs it in a specific place such as a mosque, or at a particular time such as at the start of its prescribed time, or in a particular manner such as in congregation, then his prayer is invalid in these cases as well.

TAKBĪRAT AL-IḤRĀM

Ruling 934. Saying '*allāhu akbar*' at the beginning of every prayer is obligatory and an elementary part of the prayer. The letters in '*allāh*' and '*akbar*', as well as the two words '*allāh*' and '*akbar*', must be said in succession. Furthermore, these two words must be pronounced in correct Arabic; if someone pronounces them in incorrect Arabic or, for example, says their translation in English, it is not correct.

Ruling 935. The recommended precaution is that *takbīrat al-iḥrām* should not be joined to anything that was said before it, such as the *iqāmah* or a *duʿā'* that was recited before the *takbīr*.

Ruling 936. If a person wants to join '*allāhu akbar*' with something after it, for example, with '*bismil lāhir raḥmānir raḥīm*', it is better that the letter '*r*' in '*akbar*' be given a *ḍammah* [i.e. it would be pronounced '*akbaru*']. However, the recommended precaution is that one should not join it in obligatory prayers.

Ruling 937. When saying *takbīrat al-iḥrām* in an obligatory prayer, the body must be still; if one intentionally says *takbīrat al-iḥrām* while his body is moving, it is invalid.

Ruling 938. One must say *takbīr*, Sūrat al-Ḥamd, the other surah, *dhikr*, and *duʿā*'s in a manner that he at least hears his own voice. If he cannot hear it on account of being hard of hearing or deaf or there being too much noise, he must say them in a manner that he would have been able to hear them were there no impediment.

Ruling 939. If due to some reason one has become dumb or has some speech impediment that prevents him from saying '*allāhu akbar*', he must say it in whatever way he can. If he cannot say the *takbīr* at all, he must say it in his heart and indicate with his finger in a manner that suitably conveys the words, and he must also move his tongue and lips if he can. As for someone born dumb, he must move his tongue and lips in a manner that resembles someone pronouncing the *takbīr* while also indicating with his finger.

Ruling 940. Before *takbīrat al-iḥrām*, it is good that one says the following with the intention of *rajā*ʾ:

يَا مُحْسِنُ قَدْ أَتَاكَ الْمُسِيْءُ، وَقَدْ أَمَرْتَ الْمُحْسِنَ أَنْ يَتَجَاْوَزَ عَنِ الْمُسِيْءِ، أَنْتَ الْمُحْسِنُ وَأَنَا الْمُسِيْءُ، بِحَقِّ مُحَمَّدٍ وَآلِ مُحَمَّدٍ، صَلِّ عَلَىٰ مُحَمَّدٍ وَآلِ مُحَمَّدٍ، وَتَجَاوَزْ عَنْ قَبِيْحِ مَا تَعْلَمُ مِنِّيْ

yā muḥsinu qad atākal musīy', wa qad amartal muḥsina an yatajāwaza 'anil musīy', antal muḥsinu wa anal musīy', biḥaqqi muḥammadin wa āli muḥammad, ṣalli 'alā muḥammadin wa āli muḥammad, wa tajāwaz 'an qabīḥi mā ta'lamu minnī

O the Benevolent! A sinful person has come to You, and You have instructed the benevolent to overlook the sinner. You are the Benevolent and I am the sinner. By the right of Muḥammad and the progeny of Muḥammad, bless Muḥammad and the progeny of Muḥammad, and overlook my ugly acts of which You are aware.

Ruling 941. When saying *takbīrat al-iḥrām* of the prayer and the *takbīr*s during the prayer, it is recommended for one to raise his hands up to his ears.

Ruling 942. If a person doubts whether he has said *takbīrat al-iḥrām* or not, in the event that he has started *qirā'ah*, he must not pay any attention to his doubt; but if he has not yet recited anything, he must say the *takbīr.*

Ruling 943. If after saying *takbīrat al-iḥrām* one doubts whether he said it correctly or not, he must not pay any attention to his doubt, whether he has already started saying something or not.

STANDING (*QIYĀM*)

Ruling 944. Standing while saying *takbīrat al-iḥrām* and standing before *rukūʿ* – which is called 'the standing that is connected to the *rukūʿ*' (*al-qiyām al-muttaṣil bil-rukūʿ*) – is a *rukn*. However, standing while reciting Sūrat al-Ḥamd and the other surah, and standing after *rukūʿ*, are not *rukn*s; and if one omits these forgetfully, his prayer is valid.

Ruling 945. It is obligatory to stand a short while before and after saying *takbīrat al-iḥrām* to be certain that *takbīr* has been said while standing.

Ruling 946. If a person forgets to perform *rukūʿ* and sits down [for *sajdah*] after Sūrat al-Ḥamd and the other surah and then remembers that he has not performed *rukūʿ*, he must stand up and then perform *rukūʿ*. If he does not stand up but instead performs *rukūʿ* while bending forward [as he gets up], it will not be sufficient as he will not have performed the standing that is connected to the *rukūʿ*.

Ruling 947. When one stands for *takbīrat al-iḥrām* or *qirā'ah*, he must not walk nor incline to one side. And based on obligatory precaution, he must not move his body or voluntarily lean on anything; however, there is no problem if he is compelled to.

Ruling 948. While standing, if one forgetfully walks a little, inclines to one side, or leans on something, there is no problem.

Ruling 949. The obligatory precaution is that both feet must be on the ground while standing. However, it is not necessary for the weight of one's body to be on both feet; and if the weight is on one foot, there is no problem.

Ruling 950. If someone who can stand properly spreads his feet so wide that it cannot be called [normal] standing, his prayer is invalid. In fact, based on obligatory precaution, one must not spread his feet very wide, even if it can be called standing.

Ruling 951. While one is engaged in saying obligatory *dhikr* in prayers, his body must be still; and based on obligatory precaution, [the same applies] while he is engaged in saying recommended *dhikr* in prayers. If a person wants to move a little forwards or backwards or move his body a little to the right or left, he must not say any *dhikr* [at the moment of moving].

Ruling 952. If a person says recommended *dhikr* while moving – for example, he says *takbīr* while going into *rukūʿ* or *sajdah* – in the event that he says it with the intention of it being a *dhikr* that has been prescribed in prayers, that *dhikr* is not valid but his prayer is valid.

The [recommended] sentence:

بِحَوْلِ اللّٰهِ وَقُوَّتِهِ أَقُومُ وَأَقْعُدُ

biḥawlil lāhi wa qūwwatihi aqūmu wa aqʿud

By Allah's power and His strength I stand and sit.

...should be said while getting up [after the completion of a *rakʿah*].

Ruling 953. There is no problem in moving one's hands and fingers while reciting Sūrat al-Ḥamd, although the recommended precaution is that one should not move them.

Ruling 954. If while reciting Sūrat al-Ḥamd and the other surah, or while saying the four glorifications (*al-tasbīḥāt al-arbaʿah*), one's body involuntarily moves a little such that the body is no longer still, the recommended precaution is that after his body becomes still again, he should repeat whatever he said while his body was moving.

Ruling 955. If a person is unable to stand while performing prayers, he must sit down; and if he is unable to sit down, he must lie down. However, he must not say any of the obligatory *dhikr*s until his body becomes still.

Ruling 956. As long as a person is able to perform prayers in a standing position, he must not sit down. For example, someone whose body shakes when he stands or is compelled to lean on something or incline his body a little, must perform prayers in a standing position in whatever way he can. However, if he cannot stand at all, he must sit straight and perform prayers in a sitting position.

Ruling 957. As long as one can sit, he must not perform prayers in a lying position, and if he cannot sit straight, he must sit in whatever way he can. If he cannot sit at all, he must – as mentioned in the rules relating to qibla – lie on his side in a way that the front part of his body faces qibla. Furthermore, as long as it is possible for him to lie on his right side, he must not – based on obligatory precaution – lie on his left side. If neither of these is possible, he must lie on his back with the soles of his feet facing qibla.

Ruling 958. With regard to someone who performs prayer in a sitting position, if after reciting Sūrat al-Ḥamd and the other surah he can stand and perform *rukūʿ* in a standing position, he must stand up and from a standing position go into *rukūʿ*; but if he cannot stand and perform *rukūʿ* in a standing position, he must perform *rukūʿ* sitting.

Ruling 959. With regard to one who performs prayers lying down, if he can sit during prayers, he must do so as much as he is able to. Similarly, if he can stand, he must do so as much as he is able to.

However, as long as his body is not still, he must not say any of the obligatory *dhikr*s. If he knows that he can stand for only a short while, he must do so specifically for the standing that is connected to the *rukūʿ*.

Ruling 960. If someone who performs prayers in a sitting position can stand during prayers, he must perform prayers in a standing position as much as he is able to. However, as long as his body is not still, he must not say any of the obligatory *dhikr*. If he knows that he can stand for only a short while, he must do so for the standing that is connected to the *rukūʿ*.

Ruling 961. If someone who can stand fears that by standing he will become ill or that he will be harmed, he can perform prayers in a sitting position. If he also fears [illness or harm] from sitting, he can perform prayers in a lying position.

Ruling 962. If a person has not lost hope in being able to perform prayers in a standing position by the end of the prescribed time for the prayer, in the event that he performs prayers at the beginning of the prescribed time [sitting] and he is able to stand at the end of the prescribed time, he must perform the prayer again [standing]. However, if he has lost hope in being able to perform prayers in a standing position and performs prayers at the beginning of the prescribed time [sitting] and then he is able to stand, it is not necessary for him to repeat the prayer.

Ruling 963. It is recommended that while standing, one stands upright, lowers his shoulders, places his hands on his thighs, closes his fingers together, looks at the place of *sajdah*, places the weight of his body equally on both feet, stands humbly and submissively, and keeps both his feet in line. Furthermore, it is recommended for men to spread their feet between the measure of three open fingers and one hand span, and for women to keep their feet together.

RECITATION (*QIRĀʾAH*)

Ruling 964. In the first and second *rakʿah*s of the daily obligatory prayers, one must recite Sūrat al-Ḥamd followed by another surah; and based on obligatory precaution, [the second surah] must be a complete surah. Also based on obligatory precaution, 'Sūrat al-Ḍuḥā' and 'Sūrat al-Sharḥ', and similarly 'Sūrat al-Fīl' and 'Sūrah Quraysh', are counted as one surah in prayers.

Ruling 965. If the time for prayers is short or one is compelled to not recite the other surah – for example, he fears that if he recites the other surah, a thief, predatory animal, or something else will harm him – or if one has some urgent matter to attend to, then in these cases, he can leave out reciting the other surah. In fact, when time is short and in some cases where a person is fearful, he must not recite the other surah.

Ruling 966. If a person intentionally recites the other surah before Sūrat al-Ḥamd, his prayers are invalid. If he mistakenly recites the other surah before Sūrat al-Ḥamd and realises his mistake while he is reciting it, he must stop reciting it, recite Sūrat al-Ḥamd, and then recite the other surah from the beginning.

Ruling 967. If a person forgets to recite Sūrat al-Ḥamd and the other surah, or one of them, and realises this after going into *rukūʿ*, his prayers are valid.

Ruling 968. If before bending for *rukūʿ* one realises that he has not recited Sūrat al-Ḥamd and the other surah, he must recite them. If he realises that he has [recited Sūrat al-Ḥamd but] not the other surah, he must recite only the other surah. However, if he realises that he has not recited Sūrat al-Ḥamd only, he must first recite Sūrat al-Ḥamd and then the other surah again. Similarly, if one bends forward but before getting into the *rukūʿ* position he realises that he has not recited Sūrat al-Ḥamd and the other surah, or only the other surah, or only Sūrat al-Ḥamd, he must stand up straight and act according to what has been mentioned earlier in this ruling.

Ruling 969. If during obligatory prayers one intentionally recites one of the four surahs that contain an obligatory *sajdah* – as mentioned in Ruling 354 – it is obligatory that he perform *sajdah* after reciting the verse of *sajdah*. However, based on obligatory precaution, by performing the *sajdah* his prayer becomes invalid, and it is obligatory that he perform the prayer again unless he performed the *sajdah* forgetfully. If he does not perform the *sajdah*, he can continue with the prayer but he will have sinned for not performing the *sajdah*.

Ruling 970. If a person starts to recite a surah that contains an obligatory *sajdah* – whether he does so intentionally or inadvertently – in the event that he realises this before reciting the verse that contains the obligatory *sajdah*, he can stop reciting that surah and recite another surah instead. If he realises after reciting the verse that contains the obligatory *sajdah*, he must act according to the instructions mentioned in the previous ruling.

Ruling 971. If one listens to a verse that contains an obligatory sajdah during prayers, his prayer is valid. And based on obligatory precaution, if this happens during an obligatory prayer, he must make an indication for *sajdah*, and after the prayer he must perform the *sajdah*.

Ruling 972. In recommended prayers, it is not necessary to recite the other surah even if that prayer has become obligatory on account of a vow. However, in some recommended prayers, such as the prayer of loneliness (*ṣalāt al-waḥshah*), that require a specific surah to be recited, if one wants to act according to the rules of that prayer, he must recite the specified surah.

Ruling 973. It is recommended that in the Friday prayer, and in *ṣubḥ*, *ẓuhr*, and *ʿaṣr* prayers on Friday, and in *ʿishāʾ* prayers on Thursday night, one should recite Sūrat al-Jumuʿah in the first *rakʿah* after Sūrat al-Ḥamd, and Sūrat al-Munāfiqūn in the second *rakʿah* after Sūrat al-Ḥamd. If a person begins reciting one of these surahs in prayers on Friday, then based on obligatory precaution, he cannot leave it and recite another surah.

Ruling 974.* If after Sūrat al-Ḥamd one begins reciting Sūrat al-Ikhlāṣ or Sūrat al-Kāfirūn, he cannot leave it and recite another surah instead. This rule applies to the *nāfilah* prayers as well based on obligatory precaution. However, in the Friday prayer and the prayers on Friday, if one forgetfully recites one of these two surahs instead of Sūrat al-Jumuʿah and Sūrat al-Munāfiqūn, he can leave it and recite Sūrat al-Jumuʿah and Sūrat al-Munāfiqūn instead; however, the recommended precaution is that one should not leave it [i.e. Sūrat al-Ikhlāṣ or Sūrat al-Kāfirūn] after having recited half of it.

Ruling 975. If in the Friday prayer or prayers on Friday one intentionally recites Sūrat al-Ikhlāṣ or Sūrat al-Kāfirūn, then even if he has not reached half of it, he cannot, based on obligatory precaution, leave it and recite Sūrat al-Jumuʿah and Sūrat al-Munāfiqūn instead.

Ruling 976.* If in the obligatory or *nāfilah* prayers a person recites a surah other than Sūrat al-Ikhlāṣ and Sūrat al-Kāfirūn, and if he has not recited up to half of it, he can leave it and recite another surah instead. However, if he has recited half of it, then based on obligatory precaution, it is not permitted for him to leave it and change to another surah.

Ruling 977. If a person forgets a part of the other surah or is unable to complete it due to some compelling reason, such as shortness of time, he can leave that surah and recite another surah instead even if he has reached half of it and even if the surah he is reciting is al-Ikhlāṣ or al-Kāfirūn. In the case of forgetfulness, he can suffice with the amount he has recited [and he does not need to recite another full surah].

Ruling 978. Based on obligatory precaution, it is obligatory for a man to recite Sūrat al-Ḥamd and the other surah aloud (*jahr*) in *ṣubḥ*, *maghrib*, and *ʿishāʾ* prayers. And based on obligatory precaution, it is obligatory for a man and a woman to recite Sūrat al-Ḥamd and the other surah in *ẓuhr* and *ʿaṣr* in a whisper (*ikhfāt*).

Ruling 979. Based on obligatory precaution, in *ṣubḥ*, *maghrib*, and *ʿishāʾ* prayers, a man must be careful that he recites all the words of Sūrat al-Ḥamd and the other surah aloud, even their last letters.

Ruling 980. A woman can recite Sūrat al-Ḥamd and the other surah in *ṣubḥ*, *maghrib*, and *ʿishāʾ* prayers aloud or in a whisper. However, if someone who is not her *maḥram* is able to hear her voice and the situation is such that it would be unlawful for her to make her voice heard by a non-*maḥram* man, then she must recite them in a whisper.

And if she intentionally recites them aloud, her prayer will be invalid based on obligatory precaution.

Ruling 981. If when one must recite aloud he intentionally recites in a whisper, or when one must recite in a whisper he intentionally recites aloud, his prayer is invalid based on obligatory precaution. However, his prayer is valid if he does this due to forgetfulness or not knowing the ruling. While reciting Sūrat al-Ḥamd or the other surah, if he realises that he has made a mistake [in not reciting aloud or in a whisper as per his duty], it is not necessary for him to repeat what he has already recited.

Ruling 982. While reciting Sūrat al-Ḥamd and the other surah, if one raises his voice higher than what is normal, as if he is shouting, his prayer is invalid.

Ruling 983. One must correctly recite *qirāʾah* of the prayer. If someone cannot in any way recite the whole of Sūrat al-Ḥamd correctly, he must recite it in the way he can, provided that the amount he recites correctly is significant. However, if that amount is insignificant, then based on obligatory precaution, he must add to it an amount of the Qur'an that he can recite correctly. If he cannot do this, he must add to it *tasbīḥ* [i.e. saying '*subḥānal lāh*']. However, if someone cannot recite the other surah correctly at all, it is not necessary for him to recite something else in its place. In all the above cases, the recommended precaution is that such a person should perform prayers in congregation.

Ruling 984. One who does not know Sūrat al-Ḥamd well must try to perform his duty, whether by learning it, inculcating it in himself, following in congregational prayers, or repeating the prayer whenever he doubts the correctness of his recitation. If time is short and he performs the prayer as stated in the previous ruling, his prayer is valid. However, if he has been negligent in learning and if possible, he must perform his prayers in congregation to escape punishment.

Ruling 985. Based on obligatory precaution, taking wages for teaching obligatory acts of the prayer is unlawful. However, taking wages for teaching recommended acts of the prayer is permitted.

Ruling 986. If a person intentionally or on account of culpable ignorance (*al-jahl al-taqṣīrī*) does not recite one of the words of Sūrat al-Ḥamd or the other surah, or in place of one of the letters he utters another letter – for example, instead of 'ض', he says 'ذ' or 'ز', or he does not correctly observe the *fatḥah* [َـ] and *kasrah* [ِـ] of words such that his recitation is considered wrong, or he does not pronounce with *tashdīd* [ّـ] [when he is supposed to] – then in these cases, his prayer is invalid.

Ruling 987. If a person considers a word that he has learned to be correct and recites it in the same way in prayers, and he later realises that it was wrong, it is not necessary for him to repeat his prayers.

Ruling 988.* If a *mukallaf* does not know the *fatḥah* and *kasrah* of a particular word, or, for example, he does not know whether a particular word is spelt with a 'ه' or a 'ح', then he must perform his duty in some way; for example, he must learn it, or perform prayers in congregation, or recite it in two or more ways so that he is certain that he has recited it correctly. However, in such a case, his prayer is deemed to be valid only if that wrong sentence can be commonly considered part of the Qur'an or a *dhikr*.

Ruling 989. The scholars of *tajwīd* have said that if a word contains the letter *wāw* [و], and the letter before the *wāw* has a *ḍammah* [ُـ], and the letter after the *wāw* is a *hamzah* [ء] – as in the word سُوء [*sū'*] – then the *wāw* must be given a *madd* [~]; i.e. its recitation must be prolonged. Similarly, if a word contains the letter *alif* [ا], and the letter before the *alif* has a *fatḥah*, and the letter after the *alif* is a *hamzah* – as in the word جَآءَ [*jā'a*] – then the recitation of the *alif* must be prolonged. Furthermore, if a word contains the letter *yā'* [ي], and the letter before the *yā'* has a *kasrah*, and the letter after the *yā'* is a *hamzah* – as in the word جِيءَ [*jī'a*] – then the *yā'* must be pronounced with a *madd*. If after these letters (*wāw*, *alif*, and *yā'*) there is a letter other than *hamzah* that has a *sākin* [ْـ], i.e. it does not have a *fatḥah*, *kasrah*, or *ḍammah*, then again these letters must be recited with a *madd*. However, apparently, the validity of the *qirā'ah* in such cases does not depend on reciting such words with a *madd*, so in the event that one does not follow the above rules, his prayer is still valid. However, in a case like ﴿وَلَا الضَّآلِّينَ﴾ [*wa laḍ ḍāllīn*] where correctly pronouncing the *tashdīd* and the *alif* is dependent on prolonging to some extent, the *alif* must be prolonged to that extent.

Ruling 990. The recommended precaution is that in prayers one should not stop on a letter that has a vowel nor join a letter that has a *sukūn*. The meaning of stopping on a letter that has a vowel is that one pronounces the *fatḥah*, *kasrah*, or *ḍammah* of the last letter in a word and then pauses between that word and the next. For example, when he recites ﴿الرَّحْمَـٰنِ ٱلرَّحِيـمِ﴾ [*arraḥmānir raḥīm*], he pronounces the *kasrah* of the letter *mīm* [م] in الرَّحِيْم [*arraḥīm*, so that it is pronounced *'arraḥīmi'*], and then pauses briefly before reciting the next verse ﴿مٰلِكِ يَوْمِ الدِّيْنِ﴾ [*māliki yawmid dīn*]. The meaning of joining a letter that has a *sukūn* is that one does not pronounce the *fatḥah*, *kasrah*, or *ḍammah* of the last letter in a word and then joins that word with the next. For example, when he recites ﴿الرَّحْمَـٰنِ ٱلرَّحِيْمِ﴾ [*arraḥmānir raḥīm*], he does not pronounce the *kasrah* of the letter *mīm* [م] in الرَّحِيْم [*arrahīm*], and then immediately recites ﴿مٰلِكِ يَوْمِ الدِّيْنِ﴾ [*māliki yawmid dīn*].

Ruling 991. In the third and fourth *rakʿah*s of prayers, a person can either recite one Sūrat al-Ḥamd or say one *al-tasbīḥāt al-arbaʿah*, i.e. he can say once:

سُبْحَانَ اللّٰهِ وَالْحَمْدُ لِلّٰهِ وَلَا إِلٰهَ إِلَّا اللّٰهُ وَاللّٰهُ أَكْبَرُ

subḥānal lāhi wal ḥamdu lillāhi wa lā ilāha illal lāhu wallāhu akbar

I declare emphatically that Allah is free from imperfections, and all praise is for Allah, and there is no god but Allah, and Allah is greater [than what He is described as].

...and it is better that he says this three times. A person can recite Sūrat al-Ḥamd in one *rakʿah* and say *al-tasbīḥāt al-arbaʿah* in the second *rakʿah*, although it is better that he says *al-tasbīḥāt al-arbaʿah* in both the *rakʿah*s.

Ruling 992. If time is short, one must say *al-tasbīḥāt al-arbaʿah* once. If one does not have time for even that, it is sufficient to say *subḥānal lāh* once.

Ruling 993. Based on obligatory precaution, it is obligatory for men and women to recite Sūrat al-Ḥamd and to say *al-tasbīḥāt al-arbaʿah* in a whisper in the third and fourth *rakʿah*s of the prayer.

Ruling 994. If a person recites Sūrat al-Ḥamd in the third and fourth *rakʿah*s, it is not obligatory for him to also recite its *bismillāh* in a whisper except if he is a follower in congregational prayers, in which case the obligatory precaution is that he must also recite *bismillāh* in a whisper.

Ruling 995. A person who cannot learn *al-tasbīḥāt al-arbaʿah* or cannot say it correctly must recite Sūrat al-Ḥamd in the third and fourth *rakʿah*s.

Ruling 996. If a person says *al-tasbīḥāt al-arbaʿah* in the first two *rakʿah*s of prayers thinking that he is performing the last two *rakʿah*s, in the event that he realises this before *rukūʿ*, he must recite Sūrat al-Ḥamd and the other surah. If he realises this during or after *rukūʿ*, his prayer is valid.

Ruling 997. If a person recites Sūrat al-Ḥamd in the last two *rakʿah*s of prayers thinking that he is performing the first two *rakʿah*s, or if one recites it in the first two *rakʿah*s supposing that he is performing the last two *rakʿah*s, his prayer is valid whether he realises this before or after *rukūʿ*.

Ruling 998. If a person wants to recite Sūrat al-Ḥamd in the third or fourth *rakʿah*s but happens to say *al-tasbīḥāt al-arbaʿah* instead, or if one wants to say *al-tasbīḥāt al-arbaʿah* but happens to recite Sūrat al-Ḥamd instead, then in the event that he did not have the intention of prayers at all, not even subconsciously, he must leave whatever it was he was saying and recite Sūrat al-Ḥamd or say *al-tasbīḥāt al-arbaʿah* again. However, if it was not the case that he did not have the intention of prayers, rather it was his habit to say that thing, then he can complete what he was saying and his prayer will be valid.

Ruling 999. With regard to someone who has a habit of saying *al-tasbīḥāt al-arbaʿah* in the third and fourth *rakʿah*s, if he ignores his habit and with the intention of performing his duty starts reciting

Sūrat al-Ḥamd, it will suffice and it is not necessary for him to recite Sūrat al-Ḥamd or to say *al-tasbīḥāt al-arbaʿah* again.

Ruling 1000. In the third and fourth *rakʿahs*, it is recommended that after *al-tasbīḥāt al-arbaʿah* one seeks forgiveness by saying, for example:

أَسْتَغْفِرُ اللّٰهَ رَبِّيْ وَأَتُوْبُ إِلَيْهِ

astaghfirul lāha rabbī wa atūbu ilayh

I seek forgiveness from Allah, My Lord, and I turn to Him in repentance.

...or:

اَللّٰهُمَّ ٱغْفِرْ لِيْ

allāhummagh fir lī

O Allah! Forgive me.

If before seeking forgiveness and bending for *rukūʿ* one doubts whether or not he has recited Sūrat al-Ḥamd or said *al-tasbīḥāt al-arbaʿah*, he must recite Sūrat al-Ḥamd or say *al-tasbīḥāt al-arbaʿah*. If he doubts it while seeking forgiveness or after it, then again he must, based on obligatory precaution, recite Sūrat al-Ḥamd or say *al-tasbīḥāt al-arbaʿah*.

Ruling 1001. If in the *rukūʿ* of the third or fourth *rakʿahs* or while going into *rukūʿ* one doubts whether or not he has recited Sūrat al-Ḥamd or said *al-tasbīḥāt al-arbaʿah*, he must not heed his doubt.

Ruling 1002. Whenever one doubts whether or not he has pronounced a verse or a word correctly – for example, he doubts whether or not he recited ﴿قُلْ هُوَ اللّٰهُ أَحَدٌ﴾ [*qul huwal lāhu aḥad*][33] correctly – he can ignore his doubt. However, if he repeats that verse or word in a correct manner as a precautionary measure, there is no problem; and even if he doubts it several times, he can repeat it several times. However, if it becomes obsessive, it is better not to repeat it.

[33] The first verse of Sūrat al-Ikhlāṣ (Chapter 112).

Ruling 1003. It is recommended that in the first *rakʿah* before reciting Sūrat al-Ḥamd, one says:

أَعُوْذُ بِاللّٰهِ مِنَ الشَّيْطَانِ الرَّجِيْمِ

aʿūdhu billāhi minash shayṭānir rajīm

I seek refuge in Allah from the outcast Satan.

And [it is recommended that] in the first and second *rakʿah*s of *ẓuhr* and *ʿaṣr* prayers, one recites '*bismillāh*' aloud, and recites Sūrat al-Ḥamd and the other surah distinctly, and pauses at the end of every verse – i.e. he does not join it with the next verse – and while reciting Sūrat al-Ḥamd and the other surah, [it is recommended that] he pays attention to the meaning of the verses. Furthermore, if he is performing prayers in congregation, then after the imam has completed the recitation of Sūrat al-Ḥamd, or if he is performing prayers on his own, after he has completed the recitation of Sūrat al-Ḥamd, [it is recommended that] he says:

اَلْحَمْدُ لِلّٰهِ رَبِّ الْعَالَمِيْنَ

alḥamdu lillāhi rabbil ʿālamīn

All praise is for Allah, Lord of the worlds.

...and after completing the recitation of Sūrat al-Ikhlāṣ, [it is recommended that] he either says:

كَذٰلِكَ اللّٰهُ رَبِّيْ

kadhālikal lāhu rabbi

Such is Allah my Lord.

...or:

كَذٰلِكَ اللّٰهُ رَبُّنَا

kadhālikal lāhu rabbunā

Such is Allah our Lord.

...once, twice, or three times. And [it is also recommended that] after reciting the other surah, he should pause for a short while and then say the *takbīr* before *rukūʿ* or *qunūt.*

Ruling 1004. It is recommended that in all the prayers, one should recite Sūrat al-Qadr[34] in the first *rakʿah* and Sūrat al-Ikhlāṣ in the second.

Ruling 1005. It is disapproved for one not to recite Sūrat al-Ikhlāṣ [at least once] in any of the daily prayers.

Ruling 1006. Reciting Sūrat al-Ikhlāṣ in one breath is disapproved.

Ruling 1007. It is disapproved to recite the same surah in the second *rakʿah* that one has recited in the first *rakʿah*; however, it is not disapproved if one recites Sūrat al-Ikhlāṣ in both *rakʿah*s.

BOWING (*RUKŪʿ*)

Ruling 1008. In every *rakʿah* after *qirāʾah*, one must bend forward to the extent that he can place all his fingertips, including his thumb, on his knees. This action is called '*rukūʿ*'.

Ruling 1009. There is no problem if a person bends forward to the extent of *rukūʿ* but does not place his fingertips on his knees.

Ruling 1010. If a person performs *rukūʿ* in an unusual manner – for example, he bends towards the left or right side, or he bends his knees forward – then even if his hands reach his knees, it is invalid.

Ruling 1011. The bending forward must be done with the intention of performing *rukūʿ*; therefore, if it is done with some other intention – for example, to kill an animal – then one cannot consider it as *rukūʿ*. Instead, he must stand up straight and then bend forward again for *rukūʿ*; by doing this, a *rukn* is not added and the prayer does not become invalid.

[34] Chapter 97 of the Qur'an.

Ruling 1012. If a person's arms or knees are different to those of others – for example, his arms are very long such that if he bends a little his hands reach his knees, or his knees are lower than those of others such that he must bend a lot for his hands to reach his knees – then in these cases, he must bend forward to the usual extent [as other people do].

Ruling 1013. One who performs *rukūʿ* while sitting must bend forward to the extent that his face is positioned directly opposite his knees; and it is better that he bends forward to the extent that his face is positioned directly opposite the place of *sajdah*.

Ruling 1014. It is better that when one has the option to, he says in *rukūʿ*:

×3 سُبْحَانَ اللّٰهِ subḥānal lāh

...or:

×1 سُبْحَانَ رَبِّيَ الْعَظِيْمِ وَبِحَمْدِهِ subḥāna rabbiyal ʿaẓīmi wa biḥamdih

...although saying any *dhikr* suffices; and based on obligatory precaution, [the other *dhikr*] must be of this length. However, if time is short or one is compelled, then saying *subḥānal lāh* once suffices. Someone who cannot say *subḥāna rabbiyal ʿaẓīmi wa biḥamdih* properly must say another *dhikr*, such as *subḥānal lāh*, three times.

Ruling 1015. The *dhikr* of *rukūʿ* must be said consecutively and in correct Arabic; and it is recommended that one says it three, five, seven, or even more times.

Ruling 1016. While performing *rukūʿ*, the body must be still and one must not intentionally move his body in a manner that it is no longer still, even when – based on obligatory precaution – he is not saying an obligatory *dhikr*. If a person intentionally does not observe this requirement to be still, then based on obligatory precaution, his prayer is invalid even if he says *dhikr* while his body is still.

Ruling 1017. If at the time of saying the obligatory *dhikr* of *rukūʿ* one's body moves inadvertently or unintentionally to the extent that it is no longer still, it is better that after his body has become still once more, he says the *dhikr* again. However, there is no problem if his body moves a little such that it does not stop becoming still, or if he moves his fingers.

Ruling 1018. If a person, before bending all the way forward to the position of *rukūʿ* and before his body becomes still, intentionally says the *dhikr* of *rukūʿ*, his prayer is invalid unless he says the *dhikr* of *rukūʿ* again while his body is still. If he does this inadvertently, it is not necessary to say it again.

Ruling 1019. If a person intentionally raises his head from *rukūʿ* before completing the obligatory *dhikr*, his prayer is invalid. However, if he inadvertently raises his head, repeating the *dhikr* is not necessary.

Ruling 1020. If a person cannot remain in the position of *rukūʿ* for the length of the *dhikr* – not even for saying one *subḥānal lāh*, even without being still – then it is not obligatory for him to say it. However, the recommended precaution is that he say the *dhikr* even if he says the rest of it while rising from *rukūʿ* with a general intention of attaining proximity to Allah (*qaṣd al-qurbah al-muṭlaqah*) [i.e. with the intention of attaining proximity to Allah without specifying it is an obligatory *dhikr* of the prayer]. Alternatively, he should start before that [i.e. he should start saying the *dhikr* before reaching the position of *rukūʿ* with a general intention of attaining proximity to Allah].

Ruling 1021. If due to some illness or suchlike one cannot become still in *rukūʿ*, his prayer is valid. However, before coming out of the *rukūʿ* position, he must say the obligatory *dhikr* in the manner mentioned in the previous ruling.

Ruling 1022. If a person cannot bend forward to the extent of *rukūʿ*, he must lean on something and perform *rukūʿ*. If when he leans on something he still cannot perform *rukūʿ* in a normal manner, he must bend forward to the extent that it can be commonly considered to be *rukūʿ*. If he cannot bend forward to even this extent, he must perform *rukūʿ* by indicating with his head.

Ruling 1023. If someone whose duty is to make an indication with his head for *rukūʿ* cannot do so, he must close his eyes with the intention of performing *rukūʿ* and say the *dhikr* and then open his eyes with the intention of rising from *rukūʿ*. If he is unable to do this, he must make an intention in his heart of performing *rukūʿ*; and based on obligatory precaution, he must make an indication with his hand for *rukūʿ* and say the *dhikr*. In this case, if it is possible, he must – based on obligatory precaution – combine this act with indicating for *rukūʿ* while sitting [i.e. he must perform prayers while standing and perform the *rukūʿ*s by making an intention in his heart of performing *rukūʿ*, indicate with his hand, and say the *dhikr*; and he must also perform prayers again and perform the *rukūʿ*s while sitting and indicate with his head].

Ruling 1024. Someone who cannot perform *rukūʿ* in a standing position but can bend forward for *rukūʿ* while sitting must perform prayers in a standing position, and for *rukūʿ*, he must indicate with his head. And the recommended precaution is that he should perform another prayer in which, for the *rukūʿ*s, he should sit down and bend forward.

Ruling 1025. If a person intentionally raises his head after reaching the position of *rukūʿ* and again bends forward to the extent of *rukūʿ*, his prayer is invalid.

Ruling 1026. After completing the *dhikr* of *rukūʿ*, one must stand straight; and based on obligatory precaution, he must go into *sajdah* after his body has become still. If he intentionally goes into *sajdah* before standing, his prayer is invalid; and the same applies, based on obligatory precaution, if he intentionally goes into *sajdah* before his body has become still.

Ruling 1027. If a person forgets to perform *rukūʿ* and remembers this before he performs *sajdah*, he must stand upright and then perform *rukūʿ*. It will not suffice if he performs *rukūʿ* while in the state of bending forward [not having stood upright].

Ruling 1028. If after one's forehead touches the ground he remembers that he did not perform *rukūʿ*, it is necessary that he stand up and perform *rukū*ʿ. In case he remembers in the second *sajdah*, his prayer is invalid based on obligatory precaution.

Ruling 1029. It is recommended that one say *takbīr* while standing straight before going into *rukū*ʿ, and for men to push back their knees when they are in *rukū*ʿ. It is also recommended for one to keep his back flat, stretch his neck forward and keep it in line with his back, look between his feet, invoke blessings (*ṣalawāt*) upon Prophet Muḥammad (Ṣ) and his progeny before or after the *dhikr*; and after rising from *rukū*ʿ and standing straight, while his body is still, he should say:

سَمِعَ اللّٰهُ لِمَنْ حَمِدَهُ

samiʿal lāhu liman ḥamidah

Allah hears the one who praises Him.

Ruling 1030. It is recommended that when a woman performs *rukū*ʿ, she should place her hands above her knees and not push back her knees.

PROSTRATING (*SUJŪD*)

Ruling 1031. In every *rak*ʿ*ah* of the obligatory and recommended prayers, one must perform two *sajdah*s after *rukū*ʿ. A *sajdah* is performed when one places his forehead on the ground in a particular manner with the intention of humility [before Allah]. While performing a *sajdah* in prayers, it is obligatory that the palms of both hands, both knees, and both big toes be placed on the ground. Based on obligatory precaution, [for the purposes of *sajdah*] the 'forehead' refers to its middle area, i.e. the rectangular area when two imaginary lines are drawn between the place where the eyebrows begin[35] in the middle of the forehead up to the point where the hair grows.

Ruling 1032. Two *sajdah*s together comprise one *rukn*, and if someone

[35] This refers to the ends of the eyebrows that are nearest to the nose, not the ends that are nearest to the temples (*Tawḍīḥ al-Masāʾil-i Jāmi*ʿ, vol. 1, p. 361, Ruling 1235).

does not perform both of them in obligatory prayers in one *rakʿah* – even if this is due to forgetfulness or not knowing the ruling – his prayer is invalid. The same applies, based on obligatory precaution, if one adds two *sajdah*s in one *rakʿah* forgetfully or due to inculpable ignorance (*al-jahl al-quṣūrī*). (Inculpable ignorance is when someone has a valid excuse for not knowing.)

Ruling 1033. If a person intentionally does not perform a *sajdah* or adds a *sajdah*, his prayer becomes invalid; but if he inadvertently does not perform a *sajdah* or adds one, his prayer does not become invalid. The rule relating to when a *sajdah* is not performed will be mentioned later.

Ruling 1034. If someone who can place his forehead on the ground intentionally or inadvertently does not place it on the ground, he has not performed *sajdah* even if the other parts of his body touch the ground. However, if he places his forehead on the ground and inadvertently does not place the other parts of his body on the ground or inadvertently does not say *dhikr*, his *sajdah* is valid.

Ruling 1035. When one has the option to, it is better that in *sajdah* he says:[36]

×3 سُبْحَانَ اللّٰهِ subḥānal lāh

...or:

×1 سُبْحَانَ رَبِّيَ الْأَعْلَىٰ وَبِحَمْدِهِ subḥāna rabbiyal aʿlā wa biḥamdih

...and these words must be said consecutively and in correct Arabic. Saying any *dhikr* suffices, but it must be of this length based on obligatory precaution. And it is recommended that one say *subḥāna rabbiyal aʿlā wa biḥamdih* three, five, seven, or even more times.

Ruling 1036. While performing *sujūd*, one's body must be still, and he must not intentionally move his body in a manner that it is no

[36] For the translation of these phrases, see the third section of 'Translation of prayers' after Ruling 1107.

longer still, even when – based on obligatory precaution – he is not saying an obligatory *dhikr*.

Ruling 1037. If a person intentionally says the *dhikr* of *sajdah* before his forehead touches the ground and before his body becomes still, his prayer is invalid unless he says the *dhikr* again when his body is still. If he intentionally raises his head from *sajdah* before completing the *dhikr*, his prayer is invalid.

Ruling 1038. If a person inadvertently says the *dhikr* of *sajdah* before his forehead touches the ground, and before he lifts his head from *sajdah* he realises he has made a mistake, he must remain still and say the *dhikr* again. However, if his forehead touches the ground and he inadvertently says the *dhikr* before his body is still, it is not necessary to repeat the *dhikr*.

Ruling 1039. If after one raises his head from *sajdah* he realises that he raised his head before he completed the *dhikr* of *sajdah*, his prayer is valid.

Ruling 1040. If while saying the *dhikr* of *sajdah* one intentionally raises one of the seven parts of the body from the ground, and if this is inconsistent with the requirement for the body to be still in *sujūd*, the prayer is invalid. The same applies, based on obligatory precaution, when he is not saying the *dhikr*.

Ruling 1041. If before completing the *dhikr* of *sajdah* one inadvertently raises his forehead from the ground, he must not place it on the ground again, and he must count it as one *sajdah*. However, if he inadvertently raises another part of his body from the ground, he must place it back on the ground and say the *dhikr*.

Ruling 1042. After completing the *dhikr* of the first *sajdah*, one must sit until his body becomes still and then go into *sajdah* again.

Ruling 1043. In *sajdah*, the difference in height between the place where one places his forehead and where he places his knees and toes must not be more than the height of four closed fingers. In fact, the obligatory precaution is that the difference in height between the place where he places his forehead and the place where he stands must also not be more than four closed fingers.

Ruling 1044. On sloping ground, even if the incline is not very evident, if the difference in height between the place of one's forehead and the place of his knees and toes is more than four closed fingers, his prayer is problematic [i.e. based on obligatory precaution, it is not valid].

Ruling 1045. If a person mistakenly places his forehead on something higher than the place of his knees and toes by more than the height of four closed fingers, in the event that the height of the object is such that it cannot be said he is performing *sajdah*, he must raise his head and place it on something that is not higher than the height of four closed fingers. If the height of the object is such that it can be said he is performing *sajdah*, in the event that he becomes aware of this after saying the obligatory *dhikr*, he can raise his head from *sajdah* and complete the prayer. However, if he becomes aware of this before saying the obligatory *dhikr*, he must slide his head from it and place it on something equal to or lower than the height of four closed fingers and then say the obligatory *dhikr*. If it is not possible for him to slide his forehead in this manner, he can say the obligatory *dhikr* in the position that he is in and complete the prayer, and it is not necessary for him to perform the prayer again.

Ruling 1046. There must not be a barrier between one's forehead and the thing on which it is permitted to perform *sajdah*. Therefore, if the *turbah*[37] is so dirty that his forehead does not make contact with the *turbah* itself, the *sajdah* is invalid. However, if, for example, only the colour of the *turbah* has changed, there is no problem.

Ruling 1047. In *sajdah*, one must place his two palms on the ground; and based on obligatory precaution, one must place the whole of his palms on the ground if possible. However, if it is not possible, there is no problem in him placing the back of his hand on the ground. If placing the back of the hand is not possible either, he must place his wrists on the ground based on obligatory precaution. In the event that

[37] A *turbah* is a piece of earth or clay on which one places his forehead in *sajdah*.

this is not possible, he must place any part of his forearm up to his elbows on the ground. And if even this is not possible, then placing the upper arm on the ground is sufficient.

Ruling 1048. In *sajdah*, one must place his two big toes on the ground. However, it is not necessary to place the tips of the toes on the ground; rather, placing the back or front of them also suffices. If a person does not place his big toe on the ground but instead places his other toes or the top of his foot on the ground, or if on account of having long nails his big toe does not make contact with the ground, his prayer is invalid. If one has performed prayers in this manner while not knowing the ruling due to his own fault, he must perform them again.

Ruling 1049. If part of one's big toe has been cut off, he must place the rest of it on the ground; and if nothing of it remains or the remaining part is very short and cannot in any way be placed on the ground or something else, then based on obligatory precaution, he must place his other toes on the ground. If he does not have any toes, he must place whatever is remaining of his foot on the ground.

Ruling 1050. If a person performs *sajdah* in an unusual manner – for example, he places his chest and stomach on the ground, or he stretches his legs a little – in the event that it can be said that he has performed *sajdah*, his prayer is valid. However, if it is said that he lay down and it cannot be called a *sajdah*, his prayer is invalid.

Ruling 1051. The part of the *turbah* or the thing on which it is permitted to perform *sajdah* must be pure. However, if, for example, one places a *turbah* on an impure carpet, or if one side of the *turbah* is impure and he places his forehead on its pure side, or if one part of the *turbah* is pure and another impure, then as long as it does not make the forehead impure, there is no problem.

Ruling 1052. If there is a boil, wound, or suchlike on one's forehead that cannot be placed on the ground even without him exerting any pressure on it, in the event that the boil, for example, does not cover his entire forehead, he must perform *sajdah* with the unaffected part of his forehead. If performing *sajdah* with the unaffected part is dependent on him digging a hole in the ground and placing his boil in the hole and placing the unaffected part on the ground to the extent that is sufficient for *sajdah*, then he must do this. (The explanation of what is meant by 'forehead' was mentioned at the beginning of this section.)

Ruling 1053. If a boil or wound covers one's entire forehead as previously defined, then based on obligatory precaution, he must place either side of it – i.e. the rest of his forehead – or one side of it, on the ground in whatever way he can. If he cannot do this, he must perform *sajdah* with a part of his face; and the obligatory precaution is that if he can, he must perform *sajdah* with his chin. If he cannot perform *sajdah* with one of the two sides of his forehead, and if performing *sajdah* with his face is not possible at all, he must perform *sajdah* by indication.

Ruling 1054. With regard to someone who can sit but cannot make his forehead touch the ground, if he can bend forward to the extent that it can be commonly called *sajdah*, he must bend forward to that extent and place the *turbah* (or something else on which it is permitted to perform *sajdah*) on an object in order raise it, and then he must place his forehead on it. However, he must place his palms, knees, and toes on the ground in the usual manner if possible.

Ruling 1055. In the situation mentioned in the previous ruling, if there is nothing on which the *turbah* (or something else on which it is permitted to perform *sajdah*) can be placed to raise it, and there is no one who can, for example, raise the *turbah* and hold it so that he can perform *sajdah* on it, then in such a case, he must raise the *turbah* or the other thing with his hand and perform *sajdah* on it.

Ruling 1056. If a person cannot perform *sajdah* at all and the extent to which he can bend forward is not sufficient for it to be called *sajdah*, he must perform *sajdah* by indicating with his head. If he cannot do this, he must indicate with his eyes. If he cannot even indicate with his eyes, he must make the intention of performing *sajdah* in his heart; and based on obligatory precaution, he must indicate with his hands and suchlike and say the obligatory *dhikr*.

Ruling 1057. If a person's forehead is raised involuntarily from the place of *sajdah*, in the event that it is possible to do so, he must not let it touch the place of *sajdah* again; this is considered to be one *sajdah*, whether he has said the *dhikr* of *sajdah* or not. If he cannot keep check of his head's movements and his forehead involuntarily touches the place of *sajdah* again, this is still considered to be one *sajdah*. However, if he has not said the *dhikr*, the obligatory precaution is that he must say it but he must do so with a general intention of attaining proximity to Allah and not with a specific intention [i.e. not with the intention of it being an obligatory *dhikr* of the prayer].

Ruling 1058. In a situation where one must observe *taqiyyah*,[38] he can perform *sajdah* on a rug or something similar, and it is not necessary he go to another place to perform prayers or delay prayers to perform them in that place once the reason for observing *taqiyyah* is no longer valid. However, if in the same place he can perform *sajdah* on *ḥaṣīr* or something else that is valid to perform *sajdah* on in a manner that does not contravene *taqiyyah*, then he must not perform *sajdah* on a rug or something similar.

Ruling 1059. If a person performs *sajdah* on a feather mattress or a similar thing and his body does not stay still, it is invalid.

Ruling 1060. If a person is compelled to perform prayers on muddy ground, in the event that it does not cause him excessive difficulty (*mashaqqah*) for his body and dress to become soiled with mud, he must perform *sajdah* and say *tashahhud* in the normal manner. However, if it does cause him excessive difficulty, he must indicate with his head for *sajdah* while he is standing and say *tashahhud* standing as well. In such a situation, his prayer is valid.

Ruling 1061. In the first and third *rakʿahs* which do not have *tashahhud* – as is the case in the third *rakʿah* of *ẓuhr*, *ʿaṣr*, and *ʿishāʾ* prayers – the obligatory precaution is that after the second *sajdah*, one must sit still for a moment and then stand up.

[38] *Taqiyyah* refers to dissimulation or concealment of one's beliefs in the face of danger.

THINGS ON WHICH *SAJDAH* IS PERMITTED (*JĀ'IZ*)

Ruling 1062. One must perform *sajdah* on earth and on those things that grow from the earth but are neither edible nor worn, such as wood and the leaves of trees. It is not permitted to perform *sajdah* on edible things, nor on things that are worn, such as wheat, barley, and cotton. Furthermore, it is not permitted to perform *sajdah* on things that are not considered parts of the earth, such as gold, silver, and suchlike. However, when one is compelled, performing *sajdah* on tar and asphalt (which is a lower grade of tar) take precedence over other things on which it is not permitted to perform *sajdah*.

Ruling 1063. Performing *sajdah* on grapevine leaves when they are delicate and edible is not permitted; otherwise, there is no problem.

Ruling 1064. It is permitted to perform *sajdah* on something that originates from the ground and is food for animals, such as grass and straw.

Ruling 1065. It is permitted to perform *sajdah* on flowers that are not edible. In fact, it is also permitted to perform *sajdah* on edible medicinal foliage and suchlike that grows from the ground and is steamed or boiled and its water drunk, such as violets and borage.

Ruling 1066. Regarding plants that are commonly eaten in some towns but not in others, it is not permitted to perform *sajdah* on them if they are considered edible in those other towns [in which they are not commonly eaten]. Furthermore, it is not permitted to perform *sajdah* on unripe fruit based on obligatory precaution.

Ruling 1067. It is permitted to perform *sajdah* on limestone and gypsum. Moreover, there is no problem in performing *sajdah* on baked gypsum, baked lime, brick, and a clay pitcher.

Ruling 1068. It is permitted to perform *sajdah* on writing paper made from something on which it is permitted to perform *sajdah*, such as wood and grass; the same applies if it is made out of cotton or flax. However, if it is made out of silk and suchlike, performing *sajdah* on it is not permitted. As for performing *sajdah* on tissue paper, it is only permitted if one knows that it is made out of something on which it is permitted to perform *sajdah.*

Ruling 1069. The best thing on which to perform *sajdah* is the *turbah* of His Eminence Sayyid al-Shuhadā᾽ [Imam al-Ḥusayn] (ʿA), and after that, earth, then stone, and then grass.

Ruling 1070. If a person does not have anything on which it is permitted to perform *sajdah*, or if he does have something but cannot perform *sajdah* on it on account of severe heat or cold and suchlike, then performing *sajdah* on tar and asphalt takes precedence over performing *sajdah* on other things. However, if it is not possible to perform *sajdah* on them, one must perform *sajdah* on his clothes or any other thing on which performing *sajdah* is not permitted in normal circumstances. However, the recommended precaution is that as long as it is possible for one to perform *sajdah* on his clothes, he should not perform *sajdah* on anything else.

Ruling 1071. Performing *sajdah* on mud and soft soil on which one's forehead cannot remain still is invalid.

Ruling 1072. If the turbah sticks to one's forehead in the first *sajdah*, he must remove it for the second *sajdah.*

Ruling 1073. If while performing prayers the thing on which one performs *sajdah* is lost, and he does not have anything else on which performing *sajdah* is permitted, and he is unable to obtain such an item without invalidating his prayer, he can act according to the sequence mentioned in Ruling 1070, irrespective of whether time is short or sufficient for him to break his prayer and perform it again.

Ruling 1074. If while performing *sajdah* one realises that he has placed his forehead on something that invalidates a *sajdah*, in the event that he becomes aware of this after saying the obligatory *dhikr*, he can raise his head from *sajdah* and continue with the prayer. However, if he becomes aware of this before saying the obligatory *dhikr*, he must slide his forehead onto something on which it is permitted to perform *sajdah* and then say the obligatory *dhikr*. If it is not possible for him to slide his forehead, he can say the obligatory *dhikr* as he is. In both cases, his prayer is valid.

Ruling 1075. If a person realises after performing *sajdah* that he had placed his forehead on a thing that is not valid for performing *sajdah* on, there is no problem.

Ruling 1076. It is unlawful to perform *sajdah* for any being other than Allah the Exalted. Some people place their forehead on the ground in front of the graves of the Infallible Imams (ʿA); if they do this for offering thanks to Allah the Exalted, there is no problem; otherwise, it is problematic [i.e. based on obligatory precaution, it must not be done].

RECOMMENDED (*MUSTAḤABB*) AND DISAPPROVED (*MAKRŪH*) ACTS OF *SAJDAH*

Ruling 1077. The following things are recommended when performing *sajdah*:

1. saying *takbīr* before going into *sajdah*. For someone who performs prayers standing, this should be performed after he has raised his head from *rukūʿ* and stood perfectly straight. For someone who performs prayers sitting, this should be performed after he has sat perfectly upright;
2. when going into *sajdah*, a man should place his hands on the ground first and a woman her knees first;
3. one should also place his nose on a *turbah* or on something on which it is permitted to perform *sajdah*;
4. when in *sajdah*, one should join his fingers together and place them in line with his ears such that the tips of his fingers face qibla;
5. one should supplicate in *sajdah* and seek from Allah the Exalted that He fulfil his needs (*ḥājāt*), and he should recite this *duʿāʾ*:

يَا خَيْرَ الْمَسْؤُوْلِيْنَ وَيَا خَيْرَ الْمُعْطِيْنَ، اُرْزُقْنِيْ وَٱرْزُقْ عِيَالِيْ مِنْ فَضْلِكَ، فَإِنَّكَ ذُو الْفَضْلِ الْعَظِيْمِ

yā khayral mas'ūlīn wa yā khayral mu'ṭīn, urzuqnī war zuq 'iyālī min faḍlik, fa'innaka dhūl faḍlil 'aẓīm

O Best of those who are asked! O Best of givers! Provide for me and provide for my family out of Your grace, for surely You possess tremendous grace.

6. after *sajdah*, one should sit with his weight placed on his left thigh and place the top part of his right foot on the sole of his left foot;
7. after each *sajdah*, when one sits and his body is still, he should say *takbīr*;
8. after the first *sajdah*, when one's body is still, he should say:

أَسْتَغْفِرُ اللّٰهَ رَبِّيْ وَأَتُوْبُ إِلَيْهِ

astaghfirul lāha rabbī wa atūbu ilayh

I ask Allah my Lord forgiveness for my sins, and I turn to him in repentance.

9. one should prolong his *sajdah*, and when sitting, he should place his hands on his thighs;
10. before going into the second *sajdah*, one should say *allāhu akbar* while his body is still;
11. one should invoke blessings (*ṣalawāt*) upon Prophet Muḥammad (Ṣ) and his progeny in *sajdah*;
12. when getting up, one should lift his hands from the ground after lifting his knees;
13. men should not make their elbows touch the ground. They should keep their stomachs raised higher from the ground (compared to women) and keep their arms detached from their sides. Women should place their elbows on the ground, keep their stomachs closer to the ground, and tuck in their limbs.

Other recommended acts of *sajdah* are mentioned in more detailed books.

Ruling 1078. It is disapproved to recite the Qur'an while in *sajdah*. Furthermore, it is disapproved to blow on the place of *sajdah* to remove dust from it; and if as a result of blowing two words intentionally come out of one's mouth, then based on obligatory precaution, the prayer is invalid.

Apart from these instances, there are other disapproved acts mentioned in more detailed books.

OBLIGATORY (*WĀJIB*) PROSTRATIONS OF THE QUR'AN

Ruling 1079. In each of the four surahs al-Sajdah, Fuṣṣilat, al-Najm, and al-ʿAlaq, there is a verse of *sajdah*,[39] which means that if one recites this verse or listens to it, he must immediately perform *sajdah* after the verse has finished. If he forgets to do this, he must perform *sajdah* whenever he remembers. Performing *sajdah* is not obligatory if one hears such a verse involuntarily, although it is better that he does.

Ruling 1080. When listening to a verse of *sajdah*, if one recites along with it, he must perform two *sajdah*s.

Ruling 1081. If a person is performing a *sajdah* that is not part of prayers and he recites or listens to a verse of *sajdah*, he must raise his head from *sajdah* and perform *sajdah* again.

Ruling 1082. If a person hears or listens to a verse of *sajdah* being recited by a person who is asleep or insane, or by a child who does not recognise the verses of the Qur'an, then *sajdah* becomes obligatory for him. However, if he hears it from a gramophone or a tape recorder [or some other sound-playing device], then *sajdah* is not obligatory. The same applies [i.e. *sajdah* is not obligatory] to hearing it from a radio if it is pre-recorded. However, if someone recites a verse of *sajdah* live on the radio and one listens to it live, then *sajdah* is obligatory.

[39] In Sūrat al-Sajdah (Chapter 32), the verse is number 15; in Sūrat Fuṣṣilat (Chapter 41), it is verse 37; in Sūrat al-Najm (Chapter 53), it is verse 62; and in Sūrat al-ʿAlaq (Chapter 96), it is verse 19.

Ruling 1083. Based on obligatory precaution, for an obligatory *sajdah* of the Qur'an, the place where one performs *sajdah* must not be usurped. And based on recommended precaution, the place of his forehead in relation to the place of his knees and the tips of his toes should not be higher or lower than the height of four closed fingers. However, it is not necessary for him to have *wuḍū'* or *ghusl*, face qibla, or cover his private parts, nor for his body and the place of his forehead to be pure. Furthermore, the conditions relating to the clothing of someone performing prayers do not apply.

Ruling 1084. The obligatory precaution is that for an obligatory *sajdah* of the Qur'an, one must place his forehead on a *turbah* or something else on which it is permitted to perform *sajdah*. And based on recommended precaution, one should place the other parts of his body on the ground according to the instructions that were mentioned with regard to performing *sajdah* in prayers.

Ruling 1085. If one does not say any *dhikr* when he places his forehead on the ground with the intention of performing an obligatory *sajdah* of the Qur'an, it is sufficient. However, saying a *dhikr* is recommended, and it is better to say the following:

لَا إِلٰهَ إِلَّا اللّٰهُ حَقًّا حَقًّا، لَا إِلٰهَ إِلَّا اللّٰهُ إِيمَانًا وَتَصْدِيْقًا، لَا إِلٰهَ إِلَّا اللّٰهُ عُبُوْدِيَّةً وَرِقًّا، سَجَدْتُ لَكَ يَا رَبِّ تَعَبُّدًا وَرِقًّا، لَا مُسْتَنْكِفًا وَلَا مُسْتَكْبِرًا، بَلْ أَنَا عَبْدٌ ذَلِيْلٌ ضَعِيْفٌ خَائِفٌ مُسْتَجِيْرٌ

lā ilāha illal lāhu ḥaqqan ḥaqqa, lā ilāha illal lāhu iymānan wa taṣdīqa, lā ilāha illal lāhu 'ubūdiyyatan wa riqqa, sajadtu laka yā rabbi ta'abbudan wa riqqa, lā mustankifan wa lā mustakbira, bal anā 'abdun dhalīlun ḍa'īfun khā'ifun mustajīr

There is no god but Allah, truly, truly. There is no god but Allah, I believe in this certainly and I affirm it certainly. There is no god but Allah, I testify this in servitude and as a slave. I prostrate to You, O my Lord, in servitude and as a slave, not disdainfully nor arrogantly. Rather, I am a servant lowly, weak, fearing, and seeking refuge.

TESTIFYING (*TASHAHHUD*)

Ruling 1086. In the second *rakʿah* of all obligatory and recommended prayers, and in the third *rakʿah* of *maghrib* prayers, and in the fourth *rakʿah* of *ẓuhr*, *ʿaṣr* and *ʿishāʾ* prayers, one must sit [in a kneeling type of position] after the second *sajdah*; and while his body is still, he must say *tashahhud*, i.e.:

أَشْهَدُ أَنْ لَا إِلٰهَ إِلَّا اللّٰهُ وَحْدَهُ لَا شَرِيْكَ لَهُ، وَأَشْهَدُ أَنَّ مُحَمَّدًا عَبْدُهُ وَرَسُوْلُهُ،
اَللّٰهُمَّ صَلِّ عَلَىٰ مُحَمَّدٍ وَآلِ مُحَمَّدٍ

ashhadu an lā ilāha illal lāhu waḥdahu lā sharīka lah, wa ashhadu anna muḥammadan ʿabduhu wa rasūluh, allāhumma ṣalli ʿalā muḥammadin wa āli muḥammad

I testify that there is no god but Allah, He alone, for whom there is no partner. And I testify that Muḥammad is His servant and His messenger. O Allah! Bless Muḥammad and the progeny of Muḥammad.

And it is sufficient for one to say:

أَشْهَدُ أَنْ لَا إِلٰهَ إِلَّا اللّٰهُ، وَأَشْهَدُ أَنَّ مُحَمَّدًا صَلَّى اللّٰهُ عَلَيْهِ وَآلِهِ عَبْدُهُ وَرَسُوْلُهُ

ashhadu an lā ilāha illal lāh, wa ashhadu anna muḥammadan ṣallal lāhu ʿalayhi wa ālihi ʿabduhu wa rasūluh

I testify that there is no god but Allah. And I testify that Muḥammad – may Allah shower His blessings upon him and his progeny – is His servant and His messenger.

Tashahhud is also necessary in the *witr* prayer.[40]

Ruling 1087. The words of *tashahhud* must be said in correct Arabic, consecutively, and in a normal manner.

Ruling 1088. If a person forgets *tashahhud*, stands up, and remembers before going into *rukūʿ* that he has not performed it, he must sit down,

[40] This is the one *rakʿah* prayer that is performed as part of the night prayer. See Ruling 752.

say *tashahhud*, stand up again, recite everything that must be recited in that *rakʿah*, and complete the prayer. And based on recommended precaution, after completing the prayer, he should perform *sajdatā al-sahw* for standing without due reason. However, if he remembers [that he has not said *tashahhud*] during or after performing *rukūʿ*, then he must complete the prayer. And based on recommended precaution, after the *salām* of the prayer, he should perform *qaḍāʾ* of the *tashahhud*, and he must perform *sajdatā al-sahw* for the forgotten *tashahhud*.

Ruling 1089. It is recommended that while saying *tashahhud*, one should sit with his weight placed on his left thigh and place the front of his right foot on the sole of his left; and before *tashahhud*, he should say:

اَلْحَمْدُ لِلّٰهِ

alḥamdu lillāh

...or he should say:

بِسْمِ اللّٰهِ وَبِاللّٰهِ وَالْحَمْدُ لِلّٰهِ وَخَيْرُ الْأَسْمَاءِ لِلّٰهِ

bismil lāhi wa billāh, wal ḥamdu lillāh, wa khayrul asmāʾi lillāh
In the name of Allah and by Allah. All praise is for Allah, and the best names belong to Allah.

It is also recommended that one place his hands on his thighs, close his fingers together, look at his lap, and say after reciting *ṣalawāt* in *tashahhud*:

وَتَقَبَّلْ شَفَاعَتَهُ وَٱرْفَعْ دَرَجَتَهُ

wa taqabbal shafāʿatahu war faʿ darajatah
And accept his [i.e. the Prophet's] intercession and raise his rank.

Ruling 1090. It is recommended that women keep their thighs closed together when saying *tashahhud*.

SALUTATION (*SALĀM*)

Ruling 1091. After completing *tashahhud* of the last *rakʿah* of the prayer, it is recommended that while one is sitting and his body is still, he should say:

اَلسَّلَامُ عَلَيْكَ أَيُّهَا النَّبِيُّ وَرَحْمَةُ اللّٰهِ وَبَرَكَاتُهُ

assalāmu ʿalayka ayyuhan nabiyyu wa raḥmatul lāhi wa barakātuh

Peace be upon you O Prophet, and Allah's mercy and His blessings (be upon you too).

And after that, he must say:

اَلسَّلَامُ عَلَيْكُمْ

assalāmu ʿalaykum

Peace be upon you.

And the recommended precaution is that [after saying *assalāmu ʿalaykum*,] one adds the sentence:

وَرَحْمَةُ اللّٰهِ وَبَرَكَاتُهُ

wa raḥmatul lāhi wa barakātuh

And Allah's mercy and His blessings (be upon you too).

Or [i.e. instead of saying *assalāmu ʿalaykum*], one must say:

اَلسَّلَامُ عَلَيْنَا وَعَلَىٰ عِبَادِ اللّٰهِ الصَّالِحِيْنَ

assalāmu ʿalaynā wa ʿalā ʿibādil lāhiṣ ṣāliḥīn

Peace be upon us and upon the righteous servants of Allah.

However, if he says this, then the obligatory precaution is that he must also say after it:

اَلسَّلَامُ عَلَيْكُمْ

assalāmu ʿalaykum

Peace be upon you.

Ruling 1092. If a person forgets the *salām* of the prayer and remembers it before the form of the prayer has broken up, and if he has neither intentionally nor inadvertently done something that would invalidate his prayer – such as turning his back to qibla – then he must say the *salām* and his prayer is valid.

Ruling 1093. If a person forgets the *salām* of the prayer and remembers it after the form of the prayer has broken up, or if he has intentionally or inadvertently done something that would invalidate his prayer – such as turning his back to qibla – then his prayer is valid.

SEQUENCE (*TARTĪB*)

Ruling 1094. If a person intentionally breaks the sequence of prayers – for example, he recites the other surah before Sūrat al-Ḥamd, or he performs *sajdah* before *rukūʿ* – his prayer becomes invalid.

Ruling 1095. If a person forgets a *rukn* of the prayer and performs the *rukn* that comes after it – for example, before performing *rukūʿ* he performs two *sajdah*s – then based on obligatory precaution, his prayer is invalid.

Ruling 1096. If a person forgets a *rukn* and performs the act after it which is not a *rukn* – for example, before performing two *sajdah*s he says *tashahhud* – he must perform the *rukn* and then perform again what he mistakenly performed before it.

Ruling 1097. If a person forgets something that is not a *rukn* and performs the *rukn* that comes after it – for example, he forgets Sūrat al-Ḥamd and starts performing *rukūʿ* – his prayer is valid.

Ruling 1098. If a person forgets something that is not a *rukn* and performs the act that comes after it that is not a *rukn* either – for example, he forgets Sūrat al-Ḥamd and recites the other surah – he must perform the act he forgot and then perform the act he mistakenly performed before it.

Ruling 1099. If a person performs the first *sajdah* thinking that it is the second *sajdah*, or if he performs the second *sajdah* thinking that it is the first, his prayer is valid. [The *sajdah* he deems as] his first *sajdah* is counted as the first *sajdah*, and [the *sajdah* he deems as] his second *sajdah* is counted as the second *sajdah*.

CLOSE SUCCESSION (*MUWĀLĀH*)

Ruling 1100. One must perform [the parts of the] prayer in close succession, i.e. he must perform acts such as *rukūʿ*, *sujūd*, and *tashahhud* one after the other, and he must say those things that are said in prayers one after the other in a normal manner. If a person delays between the acts to the extent that it cannot be said he is performing prayers, his prayer is invalid.

Ruling 1101. If during prayers one inadvertently pauses between letters and words but the pause is not long enough for it to break up the form of the prayer, in the event that he has not started performing the *rukn* after it, he must say those letters or words in the normal manner. If he has said something after it, it is necessary that he repeat it, and if he has started performing the *rukn* after it, his prayer is valid.

Ruling 1102. Prolonging *rukūʿ* and *sujūd* and reciting long surahs does not break *muwālāh*.

QUNŪT

Ruling 1103. In all the obligatory and recommended prayers, it is recommended to perform *qunūt* before the *rukūʿ* of the second *rakʿah*. However, in the *shafʿ* prayer, one must perform *qunūt* with the intention of *rajāʾ*. In the *witr* prayer – despite it being only one *rakʿah* – it is recommended to perform *qunūt* before *rukūʿ*. In the Friday prayer, each *rakʿah* has a *qunūt*. *Ṣalāt al-āyāt* has five *qunūt*s. The Eid al-Fiṭr and Eid al-Aḍḥā prayers each have a number of *qunūts* in the two *rakʿahs*, details of which will be explained in their own place.

Ruling 1104. It is recommended that in *qunūt* one places his hands in front of his face with his palms facing the sky and with both hands kept next to each other; and apart from his thumb, he should close his other fingers together and look at the palms of his hands. In fact, based on obligatory precaution, *qunūt* is incorrect without raising the hands unless it is necessary for one not to [raise his hands].

Ruling 1105. In *qunūt*, it is sufficient to say any *dhikr*, even if it is one '*subḥānal lāh*', and it is better if one says the following:

لَا إِلٰهَ إِلَّا اللّٰهُ الْحَلِيْمُ الْكَرِيْمُ، لَا إِلٰهَ إِلَّا اللّٰهُ الْعَلِيُّ الْعَظِيْمُ، سُبْحَانَ اللّٰهِ رَبِّ السَّمَاوَاتِ السَّبْعِ، وَرَبِّ الْأَرَضِيْنَ السَّبْعِ، وَمَا فِيْهِنَّ وَمَا بَيْنَهُنَّ وَرَبِّ الْعَرْشِ الْعَظِيْمِ، وَالْحَمْدُ لِلّٰهِ رَبِّ الْعَالَمِيْنَ

lā ilāha illal lāhul ḥalīmul karīm, lā ilāha illal lāhul ʿaliyyul ʿaẓīm, subḥānal lāhi rabbis samāwātis sabʿ, wa rabbil araḍīnas sabʿ, wa mā fīhinna wa mā baynahunna wa rabbil ʿarshil ʿaẓīm, wal ḥamdu lillāhi rabbil ʿālamīn

There is no god but Allah, the Forbearing, the Generous. There is no god but Allah, the High, the Great. I declare emphatically that Allah is free from imperfections, [Allah,] Lord of the seven skies and all that is in them and all that is between them, and Lord of the Great Throne. And all praise is for Allah, Lord of the worlds.

Ruling 1106. It is recommended that one say the *dhikr* in *qunūt* aloud. However, with regard to someone who is performing prayers in congregation, if the imam would be able to hear him, then saying it aloud is not recommended.

Ruling 1107. If a person intentionally does not perform *qunūt*, it cannot be made up. If he forgets to perform it and remembers it before bending forward to the extent required for *rukūʿ*, it is recommended that he stand up and perform it. If he remembers it in *rukūʿ*, it is recommended that he make it up after the *rukūʿ*. If he remembers it in *sajdah*, it is recommended that he make it up after the *salām*.

TRANSLATION OF PRAYERS

1. Translation of Sūrat al-Ḥamd

﴿بِسْمِ اللهِ الرَّحْمٰنِ الرَّحِيْمِ﴾

bismil lāhir raḥmānir raḥīm

In the Name of Allah, the All-Beneficent, the Ever-Merciful.

﴿اَلْحَمْدُ لِلّٰهِ رَبِّ الْعَالَمِيْنَ﴾

alḥamdu lillāhi rabbil ʿālamīn

All praise is for Allah, Lord of the worlds,

﴿الرَّحْمٰنِ الرَّحِيْمِ﴾

arraḥmānir raḥīm

the All-Beneficent, the Ever-Merciful,

﴿مَالِكِ يَوْمِ الدِّيْنِ﴾

māliki yawmid dīn

Master of the Day of Retribution.

﴿إِيَّاكَ نَعْبُدُ وَإِيَّاكَ نَسْتَعِيْنُ﴾

iyyāka naʿbudu wa iyyāka nastaʿīn

You [alone] do we worship, and to You [alone] do we turn for help.

﴿اِهْدِنَا الصِّرَاطَ الْمُسْتَقِيْمَ﴾

ihdinaṣ ṣirāṭal mustaqīm

Guide us on the straight path,

﴿صِرَاطَ الَّذِيْنَ أَنْعَمْتَ عَلَيْهِمْ غَيْرِ الْمَغْضُوْبِ عَلَيْهِمْ وَلَا الضَّالِّيْنَ﴾

ṣirāṭal ladhīna anʿamta ʿalayhim ghayril maghḍūbi ʿalayhim wa laḍ ḍāllīn

the path of those whom You have blessed – such as have not incurred Your wrath, nor are astray.

2. Translation of Sūrat al-Ikhlāṣ

﴿بِسْمِ اللّٰهِ الرَّحْمٰنِ الرَّحِيْمِ﴾

bismil lāhir raḥmānir raḥīm

In the Name of Allah, the All-Beneficent, the Ever-Merciful.

﴿قُلْ هُوَ اللَّهُ أَحَدٌ﴾

qul huwal lāhu aḥad

Say, 'He is Allah, One.'

﴿اللَّهُ الصَّمَدُ﴾

allāhuṣ ṣamad

'Allah, the Referent for All Needs.'

﴿لَمْ يَلِدْ وَلَمْ يُوْلَدْ﴾

lam yalid wa lam yūlad

'He neither begets nor is He begotten,'

﴿وَلَمْ يَكُنْ لَهُ كُفُوًا أَحَدٌ﴾

wa lam yakun lahu kufuwan aḥad

'and there is no one comparable to Him.'

3. Translation of the *dhikr* of *rukūʿ* and *sujūd*, and the *dhikr*s that are recommended to be said after them

سُبْحَانَ رَبِّيَ الْعَظِيْمِ وَبِحَمْدِهِ

subḥāna rabbiyal ʿaẓīmi wa biḥamdih

I declare emphatically that my great Lord is free from imperfections, and I do so by praising Him.

سُبْحَانَ رَبِّيَ الْأَعْلٰى وَبِحَمْدِهِ

subḥāna rabbiyal aʿlā wa biḥamdih

I declare emphatically that my most high Lord is free
from imperfections, and I do so by praising Him.

سَمِعَ اللّٰهُ لِمَنْ حَمِدَهُ

samiʿal lāhu liman ḥamidah
Allah hears the one who praises Him.

أَسْتَغْفِرُ اللّٰهَ رَبِّيْ وَأَتُوْبُ إِلَيْهِ

astaghfirul lāha rabbī wa atūbu ilayh
I seek forgiveness from Allah, My Lord, and I turn to Him in repentance.

بِحَوْلِ اللّٰهِ وَقُوَّتِهِ أَقُوْمُ وَأَقْعُدُ

biḥawlil lāhi wa quwwatihi aqūmu wa aqʿud
I stand and sit by the strength of Allah and by His power.

4. Translation of *qunūt*

لَا إِلٰهَ إِلَّا اللّٰهُ الْحَلِيْمُ الْكَرِيْمُ

lā ilāha illal lāhul ḥalīmul karīm
There is no god but Allah, the Forbearing, the Generous.

لَا إِلٰهَ إِلَّا اللّٰهُ الْعَلِيُّ الْعَظِيْمُ

lā ilāha illal lāhul ʿaliyyul ʿaẓīm
There is no god but Allah, the High, the Great.

سُبْحَانَ اللّٰهِ رَبِّ السَّمَاوَاتِ السَّبْعِ، وَرَبِّ الْأَرَضِيْنَ السَّبْعِ

subḥānal lāhi rabbis samāwātis sabʿ, wa rabbil araḍīnas sabʿ
I declare emphatically that Allah is free from imperfections,
[Allah,] Lord of the seven skies and Lord of the seven earths,

وَمَا فِيْهِنَّ وَمَا بَيْنَهُنَّ وَرَبِّ الْعَرْشِ الْعَظِيْمِ

wa mā fīhinna wa mā baynahunna wa rabbil ʿarshil ʿaẓīm

and all that is in them and all that is between them, and Lord of the Great Throne.

وَالْحَمْدُ لِلّٰهِ رَبِّ الْعَالَمِيْنَ

wal ḥamdu lillāhi rabbil ʿālamīn

And all praise is for Allah, Lord of the worlds.

5. Translation of *al-tasbīḥāt al-arbaʿah*

سُبْحَانَ اللّٰهِ وَالْحَمْدُ لِلّٰهِ وَلَا إِلٰهَ إِلَّا اللّٰهُ وَاللّٰهُ أَكْبَرُ

subḥānal lāhi wal ḥamdu lillāhi wa lā ilāha illal lāhu wal lāhu akbar

I declare emphatically that Allah is free from imperfections, and all praise is for Allah, and there is no god but Allah, and Allah is greater [than what He is described as].

6. Translation of the complete *tashahhud* and *salām*

اَلْحَمْدُ لِلّٰهِ، أَشْهَدُ أَنْ لَا إِلٰهَ إِلَّا اللّٰهُ وَحْدَهُ لَا شَرِيْكَ لَهُ

alḥamdu lillāh, ashhadu an lā ilāha illal lāhu waḥdahu lā sharīka lah

All praise is for Allah. I testify that there is no god but Allah, He alone, for whom there is no partner.

وَأَشْهَدُ أَنَّ مُحَمَّدًا عَبْدُهُ وَرَسُوْلُهُ

wa ashhadu anna muḥammadan ʿabduhu wa rasūluh

And I testify that Muḥammad is His servant and His messenger.

اَللّٰهُمَّ صَلِّ عَلَىٰ مُحَمَّدٍ وَآلِ مُحَمَّدٍ

allāhumma ṣalli ʿalā muḥammadin wa āli muḥammad

O Allah! Bless Muḥammad and the progeny of Muḥammad.

وَتَقَبَّلْ شَفَاعَتَهُ وَارْفَعْ دَرَجَتَهُ

wa taqabbal shafāʿatahu war faʿ darajatah

And accept his [i.e. the Prophet's] intercession and raise his rank.

اَلسَّلَامُ عَلَيْكَ أَيُّهَا النَّبِيُّ وَرَحْمَةُ اللّٰهِ وَبَرَكَاتُهُ

assalāmu ʿalayka ayyuhan nabiyyu wa raḥmatul lāhi wa barakātuh
Peace be upon you O Prophet, and Allah's mercy
and His blessings (be upon you too).

اَلسَّلَامُ عَلَيْنَا وَعَلَىٰ عِبَادِ اللّٰهِ الصَّالِحِيْنَ

assalāmu ʿalaynā wa ʿalā ʿibādil lāhiṣ ṣāliḥīn
Peace be upon us and upon the righteous servants of Allah.

اَلسَّلَامُ عَلَيْكُمْ وَرَحْمَةُ اللّٰهِ وَبَرَكَاتُهُ

assalāmu ʿalaykum wa raḥmatul lāhi wa barakātuh
Peace be upon you all, and Allah's mercy and
His blessings (be upon you too).

When saying these two *salāms*, it is better that one makes a general intention that the addressees of the *salāms* are those whom the Legislator [Allah] intended.[41]

SUPPLICATIONS AFTER PRAYERS (*TAʿQĪBĀT*)

Ruling 1108. After prayers, it is recommended that one engage himself in *taʿqībāt*, i.e. saying *dhikr*, reciting *duʿā*'s, and reciting the Qur'an. It is better that he recite *taʿqībāt* facing qibla before he moves from his place and before his *wuḍū*ʾ, *ghusl*, or *tayammum* becomes invalid. It is not necessary that the *taʿqībāt* be in Arabic, but it is better to recite what has been instructed in the books of *duʿā*'s. One of the *taʿqībāt* that has been highly recommended is the *tasbīḥ* of Her Eminence [Fāṭimah] al-Zahrāʾ (ʿA), which must be said in this order: thirty-four times '*allāhu akbar*', then thirty-three times '*alḥamdu lillāh*', and then thirty-three times '*subḥānal lāh*'. It is possible to say the '*subḥānal lāh*' before '*alḥamdu lillāh*', but it is better to say it after it.

[41] It is better for one to make such an intention even though according to some traditions, the addressees of these *salāms* are the two angels on the person's right and left, and the believers.

Ruling 1109. It is recommended that one perform the prostration for offering thanks (*sajdat al-shukr*) after prayers, and it is sufficient if he places his forehead on the ground with the intention of offering thanks. However, it is better that he say the following phrase 100 times, or three times, or once: '*shukran lillāh*' ['I am very grateful to Allah']; or: '*shukran*' ['I am very grateful (to You, O Allah)!']; or: '*ʿafwan*' ['Bestow Your pardon (on me, O Allah)!']. It is also recommended that whenever a blessing comes to someone or tribulation is averted from him, he should perform *sajdat al-shukr.*

ṢALAWĀT

Ruling 1110. Whenever one says or hears the blessed name of His Eminence, the Messenger of Allah (Ṣ) – such as 'Muḥammad' and 'Aḥmad' – or an epithet (*laqab*) or *kunyah*[42] of his – such as 'Muṣṭafā' and 'Abū al-Qāsim' – even during prayers, it is recommended that he recite *ṣalawāt.*

Ruling 1111. When writing the blessed name of His Eminence, the Messenger of Allah (Ṣ), it is recommended that one also write *ṣalawāt.* Similarly, it is better that one recite *ṣalawāt* whenever he remembers His Eminence.

THINGS THAT INVALIDATE (*MUBṬILĀT*) PRAYERS

Ruling 1112. Twelve things invalidate prayers. These twelve things are called the '*mubṭilāt*' of prayers.

First: during prayers, one of the required conditions is no longer fulfilled. For example, during prayers one realises that his clothes are impure.

Second: during prayers, one intentionally, inadvertently, or due to helplessness, does something that invalidates *wuḍūʾ* or *ghusl.* For example, he urinates, even if – based on obligatory precaution – this

[42] This is an appellation given to someone as the father or mother of someone.

happens inadvertently or due to helplessness after completing the last *sajdah* of the prayer. However, if one cannot prevent the discharge of urine and faeces, and during prayers urine or faeces is discharged from his body, then in the event that he acts according to the instructions mentioned in the section on *wuḍū'*, his prayer does not become invalid. Similarly, if during prayers, blood is discharged from a woman experiencing an irregular blood discharge (*istiḥāḍah*), in the event that she has acted according to the instructions concerning irregular blood discharge, her prayer is valid.

Ruling 1113. If someone falls asleep involuntarily and does not know whether he fell asleep during prayers or after them, it is not necessary for him to repeat his prayers on condition that he knows that the extent to which he performed the prayers could be commonly regarded as prayers.

Ruling 1114. If a person knows that he slept voluntarily but doubts whether he slept after prayers or he slept during prayers having forgotten that he was performing prayers, his prayer is valid subject to the same condition that was mentioned in the previous ruling.

Ruling 1115. If a person wakes up from the act of performing *sajdah* and doubts whether he is in the last *sajdah* of the prayer or in *sajdat al-shukr*, then, whether he knows he fell asleep intentionally or unintentionally, his prayer is considered valid and it is not necessary for him to repeat it.

Third: a person places his hands on top of one another with the intention of humility and respect. The prayer becoming invalid by this act is based on obligatory precaution; however, there is no doubt that this act is unlawful if performed with the intention that it is sanctioned in Islamic law.

Ruling 1116. There is no problem if a person places one hand on the other forgetfully, helplessly, due to *taqiyyah*, or for some other reason, such as wanting to scratch his hand.

Fourth: after reciting Sūrat al-Ḥamd one says '*āmīn*'. With regard to someone who is not a follower in congregational prayers, his prayer becoming invalid by saying *'āmīn'* is based on obligatory precaution. However, there is no doubt that this act is unlawful if performed with the intention that it is sanctioned in Islamic law. However, there is no problem if one says *'āmīn'* mistakenly or due to *taqiyyah*.

Fifth: one turns away from qibla without a legitimate excuse. However, if one has a legitimate excuse, such as forgetfulness, or something compels him – for example, a mighty wind turns him away from qibla – then, in the event that he does not turn completely to the right or left, his prayer is valid. However, after the legitimate excuse expires, it is necessary that he immediately turn towards qibla. In the event that he does turn completely to the right or left or he has his back towards qibla, then, if he had forgotten or was unmindful of this fact, or he had made a mistake in identifying the direction of qibla and is reminded or becomes aware of this at a time when he is able to break his prayer and perform it again facing the qibla – even if one *rak'ah* is performed within the prescribed time – then in such a case, he must perform the prayer from the start; otherwise, he must continue with the prayer and it is not necessary for him to make it up. The same applies if he is compelled to turn away from qibla, i.e. if without turning away from qibla he can perform the prayer again within its prescribed time – even if one *rak'ah* is performed within the prescribed time – he must perform the prayer from the start; otherwise, he must complete the prayer and it is not necessary for him to perform it again or to make it up.

Ruling 1117. If a person turns only his face away from qibla and his body remains facing qibla, in the event that he turns his neck to such an extent that he can see a little of what is behind him, the rule of turning away from qibla – which was mentioned earlier – applies. However, if his turning is not to this extent but is commonly considered a lot, then based on obligatory precaution, he must perform his prayer again. If he turns his neck a little, his prayer does not become invalid, although this action is disapproved.

Sixth: one intentionally speaks, even if what he says is only one letter, as long as it conveys a meaning; for example, he says 'قِ' (*qi*), which in Arabic means 'keep safe'. The same applies if what he says only means something in a particular context; for example, he says

'باء' (*bāʾ*) in response to someone who asks what the second letter of the Arabic alphabet is. In the event that what he intentionally says conveys no meaning at all but consists of two or more letters, then based on obligatory precaution, it also invalidates prayers.

Ruling 1118. If a person inadvertently says a word that has one or more letters, then even if that word conveys a meaning, his prayer does not become invalid. However, based on obligatory precaution, it is necessary that after prayers he perform *sajdatā al-sahw*, which will be discussed later.

Ruling 1119. There is no problem if one coughs or burps in prayers. The obligatory precaution is that one must not voluntarily sigh or groan in prayers. However, saying 'oh' or 'ah' and suchlike, if said intentionally, invalidates prayers.

Ruling 1120. If a person says a word with the intention of *dhikr* – for example, he says '*allāhu akbar*' with the intention of *dhikr* – and if when saying it he raises his voice to make someone aware of something, there is no problem. Similarly, if a person says a word with the intention of *dhikr*, then even if he knows that by saying it someone will become aware of some matter, there is no problem. However, if he does not make an intention of *dhikr* at all, or he makes an intention for both purposes [i.e. an intention to perform *dhikr and* an intention to make someone aware of something], then his prayer becomes invalid.[43] However, if he makes an intention of *dhikr* but his motive for saying it is to make someone aware of something, his prayer is valid.

Ruling 1121. During prayers, there is no problem in reciting the Qur'an[44] – apart from the four verses of obligatory *sajdah* – and

[43] For example, if during prayers a person realises that someone is knocking on the door of the house, and in order to draw the attention of one of his family members to this, he says '*allāhu akbar*' with the intention of it meaning 'someone is at the door' and not as a *dhikr*, his prayer is invalid. Similarly, if when he says '*allāhu akbar*' he intends it to mean two things: 'someone is at the door' *and* 'Allah is greater', then again his prayer is invalid.

[44] Although as mentioned in Ruling 1078, it is disapproved to recite the Qur'an in *sajdah*.

there is also no problem in supplicating. However, the recommended precaution is that one should not supplicate in a language other than Arabic. (The rule regarding the four verses of obligatory *sajdah* is mentioned in the section on *qirā'ah*, Ruling 969.)

Ruling 1122. There is no problem if a person intentionally or as a precautionary measure repeats parts of Sūrat al-Ḥamd, the other surah, or a *dhikr* of the prayer multiple times.

Ruling 1123. During prayers, one must not say *salām* [the Islamic greeting] to another person; and if someone says *salām* to him, he must reply but in the same way as the person said *salām* to him; i.e. he must not add anything to the initial *salām*. For example, he must not reply '*salāmun ʿalaykum wa raḥmatul lāhi wa barakātuh*' ['peace be upon you, and Allah's mercy and His blessing (be upon you too)']. In fact, based on obligatory precaution, he must not say the words '*ʿalaykum*' ['upon you' (plural form)] or '*ʿalayk*' ['upon you' (singular form)] before the word '*salām*' if the person who said *salām* did not say it in that way either. And the recommended precaution is that one's response should be exactly the same as the *salām* said by the other person. For example, if he said '*salāmun ʿalaykum*', he should reply '*salāmun ʿalaykum*'; and if he said '*salāmun ʿalayk*', he should reply '*salāmun ʿalayk*'. However, in response to '*ʿalaykum salām*', he can say '*ʿalaykum salām*', or '*assalāmu ʿalaykum*', or '*salāmun ʿalaykum*'.

Ruling 1124. One must immediately reply to *salām*, irrespective of whether he is performing prayers or not. If a person intentionally or due to forgetfulness delays his reply to *salām* to the extent that were he to reply to it, it would not be considered a reply to that initial *salām*, then in the event that he is performing prayers, he must not reply; and if he is not performing prayers, replying is not obligatory.

Ruling 1125. One must reply to *salām* in a manner that the person who said *salām* to him hears the reply. However, if the person who said *salām* is deaf or passes by quickly having said *salām*, in the event that it is possible to make that person aware of the reply by indicating and suchlike, it is necessary to do so. In other cases – except during prayers – it is not necessary to reply, and during prayers it is not permitted.

Ruling 1126. It is obligatory for a person who is performing prayers to reply to a *salām* with the intention of greeting (*taḥiyyah*), and there is no problem if he also makes an intention of a *duʿāʾ*, i.e. he asks Allah the Exalted to grant good health to the person who said *salām* to him.

Ruling 1127. If a woman or a man who is neither a *maḥram* nor a *mumayyiz* child – i.e. a child who is able to discern between right and wrong – says *salām* to a person who is performing prayers, that person must reply. If a woman greets him with the words '*salāmun ʿalayka*', he can reply '*salāmun ʿalayki*', i.e. with a *kasrah* on the *kāf.*

Ruling 1128. If a person who is performing prayers does not reply to a *salām*, then even though he commits a sin, his prayer is valid.

Ruling 1129. If someone says *salām* incorrectly to a person performing prayers, he must reply correctly based on obligatory precaution.

Ruling 1130. It is not obligatory to reply to a *salām* that is said mockingly or jokingly, nor to the *salām* of a non-Muslim man or woman who is not a *dhimmī*.[45] If the person is a *dhimmī*, then based on obligatory precaution, the answer must be restricted to the word '*ʿalayk*'.

Ruling 1131. If someone says *salām* to a group of people, replying to his *salām* is obligatory for everyone. However, it is sufficient if one of them replies.

Ruling 1132. If someone says *salām* to a group of people but the person to whom the *salām* was not directed replies, it is still obligatory for the group to reply to his *salām*.

Ruling 1133. If a person says *salām* to a group of people and someone from among them who is performing prayers doubts whether the person who said *salām* intended to address him as well, he must not reply. Based on obligatory precaution, the same applies if he knows

[45] *Dhimmīs* are People of the Book (*ahl al-kitāb*) – i.e. Jews, Christians, and Zoroastrians – who have entered into a *dhimmah* treaty, i.e. an agreement that gives them rights as protected subjects in an Islamic state.

that he intended to address him as well but another person replied. However, if he knows that he intended to address him as well but another person does not reply, or he doubts whether another person replied, he must reply to him.

Ruling 1134. It is recommended to say *salām*. It is reported that a person who is riding should say *salām* to a person who is walking, and a person who is standing should say it to one who is sitting, and the younger of two people should say it to the older person.

Ruling 1135. If two people together say *salām* to each other, then based on obligatory precaution, each of them must reply to the *salām* of the other.

Ruling 1136. Except in prayers, it is recommended that the reply to *salām* be better than the *salām* itself. For example, if one says '*salāmun ʿalaykum*', the other person should reply '*salāmun ʿalaykum wa raḥmatul lāh*'.

Seventh: one intentionally laughs aloud. If one laughs aloud involuntarily but what led him to do so was of his own volition, or, based on obligatory precaution, even if it was not of his own volition, then, if there is enough time for him to perform the prayer again, he must do so. However, if he laughs intentionally but without making any noise, or he inadvertently laughs aloud, his prayer is correct.

Ruling 1137. If on account of refraining oneself from laughing aloud one's condition changes – for example, the colour of his face turns red – the obligatory precaution is that he must perform his prayer again.

Eighth: based on obligatory precaution, intentionally crying loudly or silently over a worldly matter. However, if one cries silently or loudly out of fear of Allah the Exalted, or in eagerness for Him or the Hereafter, there is no problem; indeed, it is among the best actions. If one cries in asking Allah the Exalted for a worldly matter in humility to Him, there is no problem.

Ninth: doing something that breaks the form of the prayer, such as jumping in the air and suchlike, whether intentionally or forgetfully. However, doing something that does not break the form of the prayer, such as indicating with one's hand, is not a problem.

Ruling 1138. If during prayers one remains silent to the extent that it cannot be said he is performing prayers, his prayer becomes invalid.

Ruling 1139. If during prayers one does something or remains silent for a while and doubts whether or not his prayer has broken up, he must perform the prayer again. However, it is better that he first complete that prayer and then repeat it.

Tenth: eating and drinking. If one eats or drinks while performing prayers in a manner that it cannot be said he is performing prayers – irrespective of whether he does this intentionally or forgetfully – his prayer becomes invalid. However, if before the time of *ṣubḥ* prayers a person who wants to fast performs a recommended prayer and becomes thirsty, then in the event that he fears that if he completes the prayer it will be time for *ṣubḥ* prayers, and if there is some water two or three steps in front of him, he can drink the water while performing prayers. However, he must not do anything that invalidates prayers, such as turning away from qibla.

Ruling 1140. Based on obligatory precaution, even if the form of prayer does not break by intentionally eating or drinking, one must perform the prayer again, irrespective of whether or not *muwālāh* is maintained, i.e. irrespective of whether or not it can be said that he is performing [the parts of] the prayer in close succession.

Ruling 1141. If one swallows food that had remained in his mouth or in between his teeth while performing prayers, his prayer does not become invalid. Furthermore, there is no problem if a lump of sugar or sugar granules and suchlike remain in one's mouth and gradually dissolve and are swallowed while one is performing prayers.

Eleventh: one has a doubt about the number of *rakʿah*s he has performed while performing a two *rakʿah* or three *rakʿah* prayer, or while performing the first two *rakʿah*s of a four *rakʿah* prayer, on condition that the doubt remains.

Twelfth: one intentionally or inadvertently does not perform a *rukn* of the prayer, or intentionally does not perform an obligatory component of the prayer that is not a *rukn*, or intentionally adds one of the parts of the prayer. Similarly, if one inadvertently adds a *rukn* like a *rukūʿ* or two *sajdah*s in the same *rakʿah*, his prayer becomes invalid based on obligatory precaution. As for inadvertently adding a *takbīrat al-iḥrām*, this does not invalidate prayers.

Ruling 1142. If after performing prayers one doubts whether or not he has performed an act that invalidates prayers, his prayer is valid.

THINGS THAT ARE DISAPPROVED (*MAKRŪH*) IN PRAYERS

Ruling 1143. It is disapproved for one to turn his face a little to the right or left while performing prayers to the extent that he cannot see what is behind his head; and if he can see what is behind his head, his prayer is invalid, as mentioned previously. It is also disapproved for one to close his eyes, turn them to the right or left, play with his beard and hands, interlock his fingers, spit, look at the writing of the Qur'an or of another book, and to look at the inscription on a ring. Furthermore, when one is reciting Sūrat al-Ḥamd, the other surah, or *dhikr*, it is disapproved for him to become silent in order to hear someone talking. In fact, any act that takes away one's humility and submissiveness is disapproved.

Ruling 1144. It is disapproved for one to perform prayers when drowsy or needing to urinate or defecate. It is also disapproved for one to perform prayers while wearing tight socks that exert pressure on his feet. Apart from these instances, there are other disapproved acts mentioned in more detailed books.

INSTANCES OF WHEN IT IS PERMITTED (*JĀʾIZ*) TO BREAK AN OBLIGATORY (*WĀJIB*) PRAYER

Ruling 1145. Based on obligatory precaution, it is not permitted for one to voluntarily break an obligatory prayer. However, there is no problem if one does so to protect property or prevent financial or physical harm. In fact, there is no problem [if one breaks an obligatory prayer] for any religious or worldly purpose that is of importance to him.

Ruling 1146. If without breaking one's prayers it is not possible for him to protect his life or the life of someone whose life is obligatory for him to protect, or property whose protection is obligatory for him, then he must break his prayers.

Ruling 1147. If there is ample time for prayers and while one is performing prayers a creditor asks him to pay him what he is owed, in the event that he is able to repay his debt while performing prayers, he must do so. If it is not possible for him to repay his debt without breaking his prayers, he must break his prayer, repay the debt, and then perform the prayer.

Ruling 1148. If while performing prayers one realises that the mosque is impure, in the event that the time remaining is short, he must complete his prayers. However, if there is ample time and purifying the mosque would not break up the prayer, he must purify it while in prayers and then perform the rest of the prayer. If the prayer would be broken up, then in case it is possible to purify the mosque, it is permitted to break the prayer to purify it. If purifying the mosque after prayers is not possible, he must break his prayers, purify the mosque, and then perform prayers.

Ruling 1149. If someone who must break his prayer completes it, his prayer is valid even though he has sinned. However, the recommended precaution is that he should perform the prayer again.

Ruling 1150. If before *qirāʾah* or before bowing down to the extent required for *rukūʿ* one remembers that he has forgotten to say *adhān* and *iqāmah*, or only *iqāmah*, in the event that there is ample time, it is recommended that he break his prayer to say them. In fact, if he remembers before completing his prayer that he has forgotten them, it is recommended that he break his prayer to say them.

DOUBTS THAT ARISE IN PRAYERS (*SHAKKIYĀT*)

There are twenty-three types of doubt in prayers; eight invalidate prayers, six must be dismissed, and nine are valid.

DOUBTS THAT INVALIDATE PRAYERS

Ruling 1151. The following are doubts that invalidate prayers:

1. a doubt about the number of *rakʿahs* performed in obligatory prayers consisting of two *rakʿahs*, such as *ṣubḥ* prayers and the prayer of a traveller. However, a doubt about the number of *rakʿahs* performed in recommended prayers and *ṣalāt al-iḥtiyāṭ* does not invalidate them;
2. a doubt about the number of *rakʿahs* performed in prayers consisting of three *rakʿahs*;
3. a doubt about whether one has performed one *rakʿah* or more in a prayer consisting of four *rakʿahs*;
4. in a prayer consisting of four *rakʿahs*, before going into the second *sajdah*, one doubts whether he has performed two *rakʿahs* or more;
5. a doubt about whether one has performed two or five *rakʿahs*, or, two or more than five *rakʿahs*;
6. a doubt about whether one has performed three or six *rakʿahs*, or, three or more than six *rakʿahs*;
7. a doubt about the number of *rakʿahs* when one does not know at all how many *rakʿahs* he has performed;
8. a doubt about whether one has performed four or six *rakʿahs*, or four or more than six *rakʿahs*, as per the details that will be mentioned later.

Ruling 1152. If a person has a doubt that invalidates prayers, it is better that he does not break his prayer as soon as the doubt arises; rather, he should think [about the doubt] to the extent that the form of the prayer breaks up or until he loses hope in attaining certainty or a supposition [about what he has or has not performed].

DOUBTS THAT MUST BE DISMISSED

Ruling 1153. Doubts that must be dismissed are as follows:

1. a doubt about an act for which the time of performance has passed. For example, in *rukūʿ*, one doubts whether he recited Sūrat al-Ḥamd or not;
2. a doubt that arises after the *salām* of the prayer;
3. a doubt that arises after the time of prayers has expired;
4. a doubt of one who doubts excessively (*kathīr al-shakk*);
5. a doubt held by an imam of congregational prayers about the number of *rakʿah*s performed when a follower is sure about it; and similarly, a doubt held by a follower when the imam is sure of the number of *rakʿah*s performed;
6. a doubt in recommended prayers and *ṣalāt al-iḥtiyāṭ*.

These six types of doubt will now be dealt with in sequence.

1. A doubt about an act for which the time of performance has passed

Ruling 1154. If during prayers one doubts whether or not he performed a certain obligatory act of the prayer – for example, he doubts whether or not he recited Sūrat al-Ḥamd – then, in the event that he has started to perform an act that he must not legally (*sharʿan*) perform if he intentionally misses that previous act – for example, while reciting the other surah he doubts whether or not he recited Sūrat al-Ḥamd – in such a case, he must dismiss his doubt;[46] otherwise [i.e.

[46] In normal circumstances, if one intentionally does not recite Sūrat al-Ḥamd, he is not permitted to recite the other surah. However, in a situation where one has not missed Sūrat al-Ḥamd intentionally and while he is saying the other surah he doubts whether or not he recited Sūrat al-Ḥamd, he must dismiss his doubt.

if he has not started to perform the other act], he must perform the act about which he doubts.

Ruling 1155. If while reciting a verse one doubts whether or not he recited the previous verse, or while reciting the end of a verse, one doubts whether or not he recited the beginning of it, he must dismiss his doubt.

Ruling 1156. If after *rukūʿ* or *sajdah* one doubts whether or not he performed its obligatory acts, such as *dhikr* and keeping the body still, he must dismiss his doubt.

Ruling 1157. If while going to *sajdah* one doubts whether or not he performed *rukūʿ*, or he doubts whether or not he stood up after *rukūʿ* [before going into *sajdah*], he must dismiss his doubt.

Ruling 1158. If while standing up one doubts whether or not he performed *sajdah* or said *tashahhud*, he must dismiss his doubt.

Ruling 1159. With regard to someone who performs prayers in a sitting or lying position, if while reciting Sūrat al-Ḥamd or *al-tasbīḥāt al-arbaʿah* he doubts whether or not he performed *sajdah* or said *tashahhud*, he must dismiss his doubt. However, if before one starts to recite Sūrat al-Ḥamd or *al-tasbīḥāt al-arbaʿah* he doubts whether or not he performed *sajdah* or said *tashahhud*, he must perform them.

Ruling 1160. If a person doubts whether or not he performed one of the *rukn*s of prayers, in the event that he has not started to perform the act after it, he must perform it. For example, before saying *tashahhud*, if he doubts whether or not he performed two *sajdah*s, he must perform them. In the event that afterwards he remembers that he had performed that *rukn*, then based on obligatory precaution, his prayer is invalid as he will have performed an additional *rukn*.

Ruling 1161. If a person doubts whether or not he performed an act that is not a *rukn* of the prayer, in the event that he has not started to perform the act after it, he must perform it. For example, if before reciting the other surah he doubts whether or not he recited Sūrat al-Ḥamd, he must recite Sūrat al-Ḥamd. If after performing it he remembers that he had recited it, his prayer is valid as he will not have performed an additional *rukn*.

Ruling 1162. If a person doubts whether or not he performed a *rukn* of the prayer – for example, while saying *tashahhud* he doubts whether or not he performed the two *sajdah*s – and he then dismisses his doubt but later remembers that he had not performed that *rukn*, then in case he has not started to perform the next *rukn*, he must perform it. However, if he has started to perform the next *rukn*, his prayer is invalid based on obligatory precaution. For example, if before he performs the *rukūʿ* of the next *rakʿah* he remembers that he did not perform the two *sajdah*s, he must perform them; but, if he remembers this while performing *rukūʿ* or after it, his prayer is invalid, as mentioned earlier.

Ruling 1163. If a person doubts whether or not he performed an act that is not a *rukn*, in the event that he has started to perform the next act, he must dismiss his doubt. For example, while reciting the other surah, if he doubts whether or not he recited Sūrat al-Ḥamd, he must dismiss his doubt. If he later remembers that he did not perform it, then in case he has not started to perform the next *rukn*, he must perform it and whatever comes after it; but, if he has started to perform the next *rukn*, his prayer is valid. Therefore, if, for example, while performing *qunūt* he remembers that he did not recite Sūrat al-Ḥamd, he must recite Sūrat al-Ḥamd and the other surah, and if he remembers this in *rukūʿ*, [he must continue and] his prayer is valid.

Ruling 1164. If a person doubts whether or not he said the *salām* of the prayer, in the event that he has started reciting *taʿqībāt*, or he has started to perform another prayer, or he has done something that invalidates prayers, he must dismiss his doubt. If his doubt arises before he has performed these, he must say the *salām*. If one doubts whether or not he said the *salām* correctly, he must dismiss his doubt no matter what stage of the prayer he is in.

2. Doubt after *salām*

Ruling 1165. If a person doubts after the *salām* of the prayer whether or not his prayer was valid – for example, he doubts whether or not he performed *rukūʿ*, or after the *salām* of a four *rakʿah* prayer he doubts whether he performed four or five *rakʿahs* – he must dismiss his doubt. However, if both sides of his doubt are such that each possibility would mean his prayer is invalid – for example, after the *salām* of a four *rakʿah* prayer he doubts whether he performed three or five *rakʿahs*, his prayer is invalid.

3. Doubt after the time of prayers

Ruling 1166. If after the time for prayers has expired one doubts whether or not he performed the prayer, or he supposes[47] that he has not, it is not necessary for him to perform that prayer. However, if before the time for prayers has expired he doubts whether or not he performed it, he must perform it even if he supposes he has done so.

Ruling 1167. If after the time for prayers has expired one doubts whether or not he performed the prayer correctly, he must dismiss his doubt.

Ruling 1168. If after the time for *ẓuhr* and *ʿaṣr* has expired one knows that he performed a four *rakʿah* prayer but he does not know whether he performed it with the intention of *ẓuhr* or *ʿaṣr*, he must perform another four *rakʿah* prayer with the intention of making up the prayer that is obligatory for him.

Ruling 1169. If after the time for *maghrib* and *ʿishāʾ* has expired one knows that he has performed a prayer but he does not know whether he performed a three or four *rakʿah* prayer, he must make up both the *maghrib* and *ʿishāʾ* prayers.

[47] In Islamic law, the difference between a 'doubt' (*shakk*) and a 'supposition' (*ẓann*) is as follows: with a doubt, the person regards the two sides of a possibility as having an equal likelihood of being correct. For example, he does not know whether he performed two *rakʿahs* or three and he deems both of these possibilities as having an equal likelihood of being correct. In this situation, his uncertainty is referred to as his doubt. With a supposition, however, the person regards one side of the possibility as having a greater likelihood of being correct than the other. In the example above, if the person deems it more likely that he performed three *rakʿahs* rather than two, then this stronger possibility is his supposition.

4. An excessive doubter (*kathīr al-shakk*)

Ruling 1170. An excessive doubter is someone who doubts excessively, i.e. a person who doubts more than usual when compared with other people like him in terms of having an unsettled mind when subjected to the same factors. An excessive doubter is not only someone who has already made a habit of doubting excessively; rather, it is sufficient for one to be in a state of developing a habit of doubting [for him to be considered an excessive doubter].

Ruling 1171. If someone who doubts excessively doubts whether or not he has performed an obligatory component of the prayer, he must assume he has performed it. For example, if he doubts whether or not he has performed *rukūʿ*, he must assume he has performed *rukūʿ*. If he doubts whether or not he has performed an act that invalidates prayers – for example, he doubts whether he performed *ṣubḥ* prayers as a two *rakʿah* prayer or a three *rakʿah* prayer – he must assume he has performed it correctly.

Ruling 1172. If a person doubts excessively about a particular act of the prayer such that his excessive doubting is considered to be only with regard to that particular act, in the event that he has a doubt about another act of the prayer, he must act according to the instructions that apply to a person who is not an excessive doubter. For example, if someone who doubts excessively about whether or not he has performed *sajdah* also doubts whether he has performed *rukūʿ* or not, he must act according to the instructions concerning that doubt; i.e. if he has not gone into *sajdah*, he must perform *rukūʿ*, and if he has gone into *sajdah*, he must dismiss his doubt.

Ruling 1173. If a person always doubts excessively in a particular prayer – for example, in the *ẓuhr* prayer – such that his excessive doubting is considered to be only with regard to that particular prayer, then, if he doubts in another prayer, such as the *ʿaṣr* prayer, he must act according to the instructions concerning that doubt.

Ruling 1174. If a person doubts excessively only when he performs prayers in a particular place in the same manner mentioned in the previous ruling, then, if he performs prayers in another place and has a doubt, he must act according to the instructions concerning that doubt.

Ruling 1175. If a person doubts whether or not he has become an excessive doubter, he must act according to the instructions concerning doubts [and not consider himself to be an excessive doubter]. Furthermore, as long as someone who is an excessive doubter is not certain that he has returned to a state that is normal among people, then, if his lack of certainty about this stems from being unsure about a change having taken place in his condition rather than from a doubt in the meaning of being an excessive doubter, he must dismiss his doubt [and consider himself to be an excessive doubter].

Ruling 1176. If an excessive doubter doubts whether or not he has performed a *rukn* and dismisses his doubt but later realises that he had not performed it, in the event that he has not started to perform the next *rukn*, he must perform that *rukn* [about which he doubted] and what follows it. However, if he has started to perform the next *rukn*, his prayer is invalid based on obligatory precaution. For example, if he doubts whether he has performed *rukūʿ* or not and dismisses his doubt, in the event that before performing the second *sajdah* he remembers he has not performed *rukūʿ*, he must go back and perform *rukūʿ*; but if he remembers this in the second *sajdah*, then based on obligatory precaution, his prayer is invalid.

Ruling 1177. If a person who doubts excessively doubts whether or not he has performed an act that is not a *rukn* and dismisses it and later realises that he had not performed it, in the event that the time for performing that act has not passed, he must perform it and what follows it. However, if the time for performing it has passed, his prayer is valid. For example, if he doubts whether or not he has recited Sūrat al-Ḥamd and dismisses his doubt, in the event that he remembers in *qunūt* that he has not recited Sūrat al-Ḥamd, he must recite Sūrat al-Ḥamd and the other surah; but if he remembers this in *rukūʿ*, his prayer is valid.

5. Doubt of an imam and a follower in congregational prayers

Ruling 1178. If an imam of a congregational prayer has a doubt about the number of *rakʿahs* – for example, he doubts whether he has performed three *rakʿahs* or four *rakʿahs* – then, in the event that a follower is certain or supposes that he has performed four *rakʿahs* and makes it known to the imam that he has performed four *rakʿahs*,[48] the imam must complete the prayer and it is not necessary for him to perform *ṣalāt al-iḥtiyāṭ*. Similarly, if the imam is certain or supposes that he has performed a certain number of *rakʿahs* and a follower has a doubt about the number of *rakʿahs*, the follower must dismiss his doubt. The same applies with regard to a doubt that they may have about the acts of prayers, such as a doubt about the number of *sajdahs* performed.

6. Doubts in recommended prayers

Ruling 1179. If a person has a doubt about the number of *rakʿahs* he has performed in a recommended prayer, in the event that the greater of the two numbers he is doubtful about would invalidate the prayer, he must assume the lesser number is correct. For example, in the *nāfilah* of *ṣubḥ*, if one doubts whether he has performed two *rakʿahs* or three *rakʿahs*, he must assume he has performed two *rakʿahs*. However, if the greater of the two numbers would not invalidate the prayer – for example, he doubts whether he has performed two *rakʿahs* or one *rakʿah* – then his prayer is valid whichever side of the doubt he acts upon.

Ruling 1180. Not performing a *rukn* invalidates *nāfilah* prayers; however, performing an additional *rukn* does not invalidate them. Therefore, if one forgets one of the acts of *nāfilah* prayers and remembers it when he has started to perform the next *rukn*, he must perform the act and then perform the *rukn* again. For example, if while performing *rukūʿ* he remembers that he has not recited Sūrat al-Ḥamd, he must go back and recite Sūrat al-Ḥamd and then perform *rukūʿ* again.

[48] For example, the follower can make it known to the imam that he has performed four *rakʿahs* by saying '*alḥamdu lillāh*' after the second *sajdah* of the fourth *rakʿah* in a manner that is audible to the imam, thereby alerting him to the fact that he must now start saying the *tashahhud* of the prayer.

Ruling 1181. If a person has a doubt about one of the acts of *nāfilah* prayers – irrespective of whether it is a *rukn* or not – then, in the event that its time of performance has not passed, he must perform it; and if its time of performance has passed, he must dismiss his doubt.

Ruling 1182. If in a two *rakʿah* recommended prayer one supposes that he has performed three *rakʿah*s or more, he must dismiss his doubt and his prayer is valid. However, if he supposes he has performed two *rakʿah*s or less, he must act according to that supposition based on obligatory precaution. For example, if he supposes that he has performed one *rakʿah*, he must as a precautionary measure perform another *rakʿah*.

Ruling 1183. If in a *nāfilah* prayer one does something that would make it obligatory for him to perform *sajdatā al-sahw* were he to do that thing in an obligatory prayer, or if he forgets to perform one *sajdah*, then it is not necessary for him to perform *sajdatā al-sahw* or to perform a *qaḍāʾ sajdah* after the prayer.

Ruling 1184. If a person doubts whether or not he has performed a recommended prayer, in the event that the prayer does not have a specific time for its performance, such as the Prayer of Jaʿfar al-Ṭayyār,[49] he must assume he has not performed it. The same applies if the recommended prayer does have a specific time for its performance, such as the daily *nāfilah* prayers, and before its time has expired one doubts whether or not he has performed it. However, if one doubts whether or not he has performed it after its time has expired, he must dismiss his doubt.

DOUBTS THAT ARE VALID (*ṢAḤĪḤ*)

Ruling 1185. In nine situations, if one has a doubt about the number of *rakʿah*s in a four *rakʿah* prayer, he must think [about the doubt]; then, if he becomes certain or he supposes that a particular possibility is

[49] The Prayer of Jaʿfar al-Ṭayyār is a four *rakʿah* recommended prayer taught by the Holy Prophet (Ṣ) to his cousin, Jaʿfar al-Ṭayyār. See, for example, Shaykh ʿAbbās al-Qummī's *Mafātīḥ al-Jinān*, in the section on the recommended acts for Friday.

correct, he must act according to that possibility and complete the prayer; otherwise, he must act according to the instructions that will be mentioned later. The nine situations are set out below.

First: after starting the second *sajdah*, one doubts whether he has performed two *rakʿahs* or three *rakʿahs*. In this situation, he must assume he has performed three *rakʿahs* and perform one more *rakʿah* and complete the prayer, and after the prayer, he must perform one *rakʿah* of *ṣalāt al-iḥtiyāṭ* in a standing position. Based on obligatory precaution, performing two *rakʿahs* in a sitting position will not suffice.

Second: after starting the second *sajdah*, one doubts whether he has performed two *rakʿahs* or four *rakʿahs*. In this situation, he must assume he has performed four *rakʿahs* and complete the prayer; and after the prayer, he must perform two *rakʿahs* of *ṣalāt al-iḥtiyāṭ* in a standing position.

Third: after starting the second *sajdah*, one doubts whether he has performed two, three, or four *rakʿahs*. In this situation, he must assume he has performed four *rakʿahs*, and after the prayer, he must perform two *rakʿahs* of *ṣalāt al-iḥtiyāṭ* in a standing position followed by two *rakʿahs* in a sitting position.

Fourth: after starting the second *sajdah*, one doubts whether he has performed four or five *rakʿahs*. In this situation, he must assume he has performed four *rakʿahs*, complete the prayer, and after the prayer, he must perform *sajdatā al-sahw*. Similarly, whenever the weaker possibility of a doubt is four *rakʿahs* – for example, he doubts whether he has performed four or six *rakʿahs* – and whenever one doubts whether he has performed four *rakʿahs* or more or less after having started the second *sajdah*, he can assume he has performed four *rakʿahs*, and he must act in accordance with the instructions applicable to both possibilities of his doubt; i.e. he must perform *ṣalāt al-iḥtiyāṭ* based on the possibility that he had performed less than four *rakʿahs*, and he must then perform *sajdatā al-sahw* based on the possibility that he had performed more than four *rakʿahs*.

In each case, if any of these four doubts arise after the first *sajdah* and before performing the second *sajdah*, his prayer is invalid.

Fifth: at any stage of the prayer, one doubts whether he has performed three or four *rakʿahs*. In this situation, he must assume he has performed four *rakʿahs* and complete the prayer; after the prayer, he must perform one *rakʿah* of *ṣalāt al-iḥtiyāṭ* in a standing position or two *rakʿahs* in a sitting position.

Sixth: while standing, one doubts whether he has performed four or five *rakʿahs*. In this situation, he must sit down, say *tashahhud* and the *salām* of the prayer, and perform one *rakʿah* of *ṣalāt al-iḥtiyāṭ* in a standing position or two *rakʿahs* in a sitting position.

Seventh: while standing, one doubts whether he has performed three or five *rakʿahs*. In this situation, he must sit down, say *tashahhud* and the *salām* of the prayer, and perform two *rakʿahs* of *ṣalāt al-iḥtiyāṭ* in a standing position.

Eighth: while standing, one doubts whether he has performed three, four, or five *rakʿahs*. In this situation, he must sit down, say *tashahhud* and the *salām* of the prayer, perform two *rakʿahs* of *ṣalāt al-iḥtiyāṭ* in a standing position, and then perform two *rakʿahs* in a sitting position.

Ninth: while standing, one doubts whether he has performed five or six *rakʿahs*. In this situation, he must sit down, say *tashahhud* and the *salām* of the prayer, and then perform *sajdatā al-sahw*.

Ruling 1186. If a person has a valid doubt, in the event that the time for performing prayers is short such that he cannot perform it from the beginning, he must not break his prayer and must act according to the instructions that were mentioned. However, if there is ample time for prayers, he can break his prayer and perform it from the beginning.

Ruling 1187. If one has a doubt in prayers for which it is obligatory to perform *ṣalāt al-iḥtiyāṭ*, in the event that he completes the prayer, the recommended precaution is that he should perform *ṣalāt al-iḥtiyāṭ*; he should not start performing the prayer again from the beginning without performing *ṣalāt al-iḥtiyāṭ*. If he starts performing the prayer again from the beginning before he does something that invalidates prayers, then based on obligatory precaution, his second prayer is also invalid. However, if he starts performing the prayer again after doing something that invalidates prayers, his second prayer is valid.

Ruling 1188. If a person has a doubt that invalidates prayers and he knows that if he continues to the next stage of the prayer he will either be certain or have a supposition [about the thing he is currently doubting], then in case his doubt arises in the first two *rakʿah*s of the prayer, it is not permitted for him to continue the prayer in the state of doubt. For example, if while standing he doubts whether he has performed one *rakʿah* or more and knows that if he goes into *rukūʿ* one of the possibilities of his doubt will become a certainty or a supposition, it is not permitted for him to perform *rukūʿ* in that state. As for all other doubts that invalidate prayers, one can continue the prayer until he becomes certain or has a supposition.

Ruling 1189. If a person initially inclines more towards one of the two possibilities of his supposition and later both possibilities appear equal to him, he must act according to the instructions concerning that doubt. However, if from the outset both possibilities appear equal to him and he adopts the possibility that is in accordance with his duty but later he inclines towards the other possibility, he must act according to the possibility that he inclines towards and complete his prayer.

Ruling 1190. Someone who does not know if his supposition is inclined more towards one of two possibilities or if both possibilities are equal must act according to the instructions concerning that doubt.

Ruling 1191. If after prayers one realises that he was in a state of doubt during his prayer – for example, he doubted whether he had performed two *rakʿah*s or three *rakʿah*s – and he assumed that he had performed three, but now he does not know whether his supposition was actually inclined towards performing three *rakʿah*s or if both possibilities appeared equal to him, it is not necessary for him to perform *ṣalāt al-iḥtiyāṭ*.

Ruling 1192. If after standing up one doubts whether or not he performed two *sajdah*s, and at the same time a doubt arises, which, were it to have arisen after completing two *sajdah*s it would be valid – for example, he doubts whether he has performed two *rakʿahs* or three *rakʿahs* – then, in the event that he acts according to the instructions concerning that doubt, his prayer is valid. However, if when he is saying *tashahhud* one of these doubts arises, then, if his doubt is about whether he has performed two or three *rakʿahs*, his prayer is invalid, but if it is about whether he has performed two or four *rakʿahs*, or two, three, or four *rakʿahs*, his prayer is valid and he must act according to the instructions concerning that doubt.

Ruling 1193. If before one starts saying *tashahhud*, or before standing up in those *rakʿahs* that do not have *tashahhud*, he doubts whether or not he performed one or two *sajdahs*, and at the same time he has one of the doubts that is valid after completing two *sajdahs*, his prayer is invalid.

Ruling 1194. If while standing one doubts whether he has performed three or four *rakʿahs*, or three, four, or five *rakʿahs*, and he remembers that he did not perform one or two *sajdahs* in the previous *rakʿah*, his prayer is invalid.

Ruling 1195. If someone's doubt is allayed and another doubt arises – for example, he first doubts whether he has performed two *rakʿahs* or three *rakʿahs*, and then he doubts whether he has performed three *rakʿahs* or four *rakʿahs* – he must act according to the instructions concerning the second doubt.

Ruling 1196. If after prayers one doubts that while performing the prayer he doubted about, for example, whether he had performed two or four *rakʿahs*, or three or four *rakʿahs*, then in such a case, he can act according to the instructions relating to both doubts, and after doing something that invalidates prayers, he can perform the prayer again.

Ruling 1197. If after prayers one realises that while performing the prayer he had a doubt but he does not know whether it was a doubt that invalidates the prayer or not, in such a case, he must perform the prayer again. If he knows that it was one of the valid doubts but does not know which one it was, it is permitted for him to perform the prayer again.

Ruling 1198. If someone who performs prayers in a sitting position has a doubt for which he must perform one *rakʿah* of *ṣalāt al-iḥtiyāṭ* in a standing position or two *rakʿahs* in a sitting position, he must perform one *rakʿah* in a sitting position. If he has a doubt for which he must perform two *rakʿahs* of *ṣalāt al-iḥtiyāṭ* in a standing position, he must perform two *rakʿahs* in a sitting position.

Ruling 1199. If someone who performs prayers in a standing position is unable to stand for performing *ṣalāt al-iḥtiyāṭ*, he must perform *ṣalāt al-iḥtiyāṭ* like a person who performs prayers in a sitting position, the rule of which was mentioned in the previous ruling.

Ruling 1200. If someone who performs prayers in a sitting position can stand while performing *ṣalāt al-iḥtiyāṭ*, he must act according to the duty of someone who performs prayers in a standing position.

METHOD OF PERFORMING THE PRECAUTIONARY PRAYER (*ṢALĀT AL-IḤTIYĀṬ*)

Ruling 1201. A person on whom *ṣalāt al-iḥtiyāṭ* is obligatory must make the intention of performing *ṣalāt al-iḥtiyāṭ* immediately after the *salām* of the prayer. He must then say *takbīr*, recite Sūrat al-Ḥamd, and perform *rukūʿ* and two *sajdahs*. If one *rakʿah* of *ṣalāt al-iḥtiyāṭ* is obligatory for him, then after performing the two *sajdahs* he must say *tashahhud* and the *salām*. If two *rakʿahs* of *ṣalāt al-iḥtiyāṭ* are obligatory for him, then after performing the two *sajdahs* he must perform another *rakʿah* in the same way as the first, and after *tashahhud* he must say the *salām*.

Ruling 1202. *Ṣalāt al-iḥtiyāṭ* does not have a second surah or *qunūt*, and one must not speak out the intention for it. Furthermore, based on obligatory precaution, one must recite Sūrat al-Ḥamd in a whisper. And the recommended precaution is that one should also say its *bismillāh* in a whisper.

Ruling 1203. If before performing *ṣalāt al-iḥtiyāṭ* one realises that the prayer he performed was correct, it is not necessary for him to perform *ṣalāt al-iḥtiyāṭ*. If he realises this while performing *ṣalāt al-iḥtiyāṭ*, it is not necessary for him to complete it.

Ruling 1204. If before performing *ṣalāt al-iḥtiyāṭ* one realises that the number of *rakʿahs* he performed was less than the required number, in the event that he has not done anything that invalidates prayers, he must perform whatever he has not performed; then, based on obligatory precaution, he must perform *sajdatā al-sahw* for saying an additional *salām*. However, if he has done something that invalidates prayers – for example, he turned his back to qibla – he must perform the prayer again.

Ruling 1205. If after performing *ṣalāt al-iḥtiyāṭ* one realises that the deficiency in the number of *rakʿahs* in his prayer was the same as the number of *rakʿahs* in his *ṣalāt al-iḥtiyāṭ* – for example, for the doubt between three and four *rakʿahs*, he performs one *rakʿah* of *ṣalāt al-iḥtiyāṭ* and later realises that he had performed three *rakʿahs* – in such a case, his prayer is valid.

Ruling 1206. If after performing *ṣalāt al-iḥtiyāṭ* one realises that the deficiency in the number of *rakʿahs* in his prayer was less than the number of *rakʿahs* in his *ṣalāt al-iḥtiyāṭ* – for example, for the doubt between two and four *rakʿahs*, he performs two *rakʿahs* of *ṣalāt al-iḥtiyāṭ* and later realises that he had performed three *rakʿahs* – in such a case, he must perform the [original] prayer again.

Ruling 1207. If after performing *ṣalāt al-iḥtiyāṭ* one realises that the deficiency in the number of *rakʿahs* in his prayer was more than the number of *rakʿahs* in his *ṣalāt al-iḥtiyāṭ* – for example, for the doubt between three and four *rakʿahs*, he performs one *rakʿah* of *ṣalāt al-iḥtiyāṭ* and later realises that he had performed two *rakʿahs* – then, in the event that after performing *ṣalāt al-iḥtiyāṭ* he did something that invalidates prayers, such as turning his back to qibla, he must perform the prayer again. However, if he did not do anything that invalidates prayers, the obligatory precaution is that he must perform the prayer again, and he must not suffice with joining one *rakʿah* to the prayer.

Ruling 1208. If a person doubts whether he has performed two, three, or four *rakʿahs*, and after performing two *rakʿahs* of *ṣalāt al-iḥtiyāṭ* in a standing position he remembers that he had actually performed two *rakʿahs*, it is not necessary for him to perform two *rakʿahs* of *ṣalāt al-iḥtiyāṭ* from a sitting position.

Ruling 1209. If a person doubts whether he has performed three or four *rakʿahs*, and while performing one *rakʿah* of *ṣalāt al-iḥtiyāṭ* in a standing position he remembers that he had performed three *rakʿahs*, he must abandon his *ṣalāt al-iḥtiyāṭ*; and in the event that he remembers this before going into *rukūʿ*, he must perform one *rakʿah* in a way that it connects with his prayer, and his prayer will be valid. And for performing an additional *salām*, based on obligatory precaution, he must perform *sajdatā al-sahw*. However, if he remembers [that he had performed three *rakʿahs*] after going into *rukūʿ*, he must perform the prayer again; and based on obligatory precaution, he cannot suffice with joining the remaining *rakʿah* to his prayer.

Ruling 1210. If a person doubts whether he has performed two, three, or four *rakʿahs*, and while performing two *rakʿahs* of *ṣalāt al-iḥtiyāṭ* in a standing position he remembers that he has performed three *rakʿahs*, then what was said in the previous ruling applies here as well.

Ruling 1211. If while performing *ṣalāt al-iḥtiyāṭ* one realises that the deficiency in the number of *rakʿahs* in his prayer was more or less than the number of *rakʿahs* in his *ṣalāt al-iḥtiyāṭ*, then what was mentioned in Ruling 1209 applies here as well.

Ruling 1212. If a person doubts whether or not he has performed a *ṣalāt al-iḥtiyāṭ* that was obligatory for him, in the event that the time for prayer has expired, he must dismiss his doubt. However, if there is time, then in case a lot of time has not elapsed between the doubt and the [original] prayer, and he has not started to do something else, and he has not done something that invalidates prayers – such as turning his back to qibla – in such a case, he must perform *ṣalāt al-iḥtiyāṭ*. However, if he has done something that invalidates prayers, or he has started to do something else, or a lot of time has elapsed between the doubt and the [original] prayer, then based on obligatory precaution, he must perform the [original] prayer again.

Ruling 1213. If in *ṣalāt al-iḥtiyāṭ* a person performs two *rakʿah*s instead of one, his *ṣalāt al-iḥtiyāṭ* becomes invalid and he must perform his original prayer again. The same applies, based on obligatory precaution, if one adds a *rukn* to *ṣalāt al-iḥtiyāṭ*.

Ruling 1214. If while performing *ṣalāt al-iḥtiyāṭ* one has a doubt about one of the acts, in the event that its time of performance has not passed, he must perform it; and if its time of performance has passed, he must dismiss his doubt. For example, if he doubts whether or not he has recited Sūrat al-Ḥamd, in the event that he has not yet gone into *rukūʿ*, he must recite it, but if he has gone into *rukūʿ*, he must dismiss his doubt.

Ruling 1215. If a person has a doubt about the number of *rakʿah*s he has performed in *ṣalāt al-iḥtiyāṭ*, in the event that the greater of the two numbers he is doubtful about would invalidate the prayer, he must assume the lesser number is correct. However, if the greater of the two numbers would not invalidate the prayer, he must assume the greater number is correct. For example, if while performing two *rakʿah*s of *ṣalāt al-iḥtiyāṭ* he doubts whether he has performed two or three *rakʿah*s, as the greater of the two numbers would invalidate the prayer, he must assume that he has performed two *rakʿah*s; but if he doubts whether he has performed one or two *rakʿah*s, then as the greater number would not invalidate the prayer, he must assume that he has performed two *rakʿah*s.

Ruling 1216. If in *ṣalāt al-iḥtiyāṭ* something that is not a *rukn* is inadvertently omitted or added, then performing *sajdatā al-sahw* is not required.

Ruling 1217. If after the *salām* of *ṣalāt al-iḥtiyāṭ* one doubts whether or not he has performed a particular component of it or fulfilled all its conditions, he must dismiss his doubt.

Ruling 1218. If in *ṣalāt al-iḥtiyāṭ* one forgets *tashahhud* or one *sajdah* and it is not possible to perform them at their correct time, the obligatory precaution is that after the *salām* of the prayer he must make up the *sajdah*; however, it is not necessary for him to make up the *tashahhud*.

Ruling 1219. If *ṣalāt al-iḥtiyāṭ* and *sajdatā al-sahw* become obligatory for a person, he must first perform *ṣalāt al-iḥtiyāṭ*. The same applies, based on obligatory precaution, if *ṣalāt al-iḥtiyāṭ* and making up a *sajdah* become obligatory for a person.

Ruling 1220.* The rule concerning suppositions (*ẓann*) in the number of *rakʿah*s in obligatory prayers is the same as the rule concerning certainty; and based on obligatory precaution, this also applies to *nāfilah* prayers. For example, if someone does not know whether he has performed one or two *rakʿah*s but has a supposition that he has performed two *rakʿah*s, he must assume he has performed two *rakʿah*s. If in a four *rakʿah* prayer he has a supposition that he has performed four *rakʿah*s, then performing *ṣalāt al-iḥtiyāṭ* is not necessary. As for acts of prayers, the rule concerning suppositions is the same as that for doubts. Therefore, if one has a supposition that he has performed *rukūʿ*, then in case he has not gone into *sajdah*, he must perform *rukūʿ*. If he has a supposition that he has not recited Sūrat al-Ḥamd, in the event that he has started to recite the other surah, he must dismiss his supposition and his prayer is valid.

Ruling 1221. There is no difference in the rules for doubt, inadvertence, and supposition in the daily obligatory prayers and the other obligatory prayers. For example, if in *ṣalāt al-āyāt* one doubts whether he has performed one *rakʿah* or two, then as his doubt is in a two *rakʿah* prayer, his prayer becomes invalid.[50] If he has a supposition that he has performed two *rakʿah*s or that he has performed one *rakʿah*, he must complete his prayer in accordance with his supposition.

THE TWO PROSTRATIONS FOR INADVERTENCE (*SAJDATĀ AL-SAHW*)

Ruling 1222.* In the following two situations, one must perform *sajdatā al-sahw* after the *salām* of the prayer in a manner that will be explained later:

[50] See Ruling 1151.

1. one forgets to say the entire *tashahhud*;
2. in a four *rakʿah* prayer after going into the second *sajdah*, one doubts whether he has performed four or five *rakʿahs*, or he doubts whether he has performed four or six *rakʿahs*, as mentioned earlier in the fourth situation in the section on valid doubts.

Also, performing *sajdatā al-sahw* is necessary in three further situations, based on obligatory precaution:

1. one generally knows that he has mistakenly omitted or added something in a prayer and the prayer is ruled to be valid;
2. one inadvertently talks during prayers;
3. one says the *salām* of the prayer at a time when he must not; for example, in the first *rakʿah* he inadvertently says the *salām*. The recommended precaution is that if he forgets one *sajdah*, or when he must stand – for example, while reciting Sūrat al-Ḥamd and the other surah – he mistakenly sits down, or when he must sit – for example, while saying *tashahhud* – he mistakenly stands up, then in these cases, he should perform *sajdatā al-sahw*. In fact, for anything that is mistakenly omitted or added in prayer, he should perform *sajdatā al-sahw*. The rules of these situations will be explained in the following rulings.

Ruling 1223. If a person talks mistakenly or because he imagines his prayer has finished, then based on obligatory precaution, he must perform *sajdatā al-sahw*.

Ruling 1224. It is not obligatory for one to perform *sajdatā al-sahw* for the sound he makes when coughing; however, if one inadvertently groans, sighs, or says 'oh', then based on obligatory precaution, he must perform *sajdatā al-sahw*.

Ruling 1225. If a person repeats correctly something that he had inadvertently recited incorrectly, it is not obligatory for him to perform *sajdatā al-sahw* for reciting it again.

Ruling 1226. If, while performing prayers, one inadvertently talks for a while and all his talking stems from one mistake, then performing *sajdatā al-sahw* after the *salām* of the prayer is sufficient.

Ruling 1227. If a person inadvertently does not say *al-tasbīḥāt al-arbaʿah*, the recommended precaution is that he should perform *sajdatā al-sahw* after prayers.

Ruling 1228. If at a time when he must not say the *salām* of the prayer one inadvertently says: *assalāmu ʿalaynā wa ʿalā ʿibādil lāhiṣ ṣāliḥīn*, or he says: *assalāmu ʿalaykum* even if after it he does not say: *wa raḥmatul lāhi wa barakātuh*, then based on obligatory precaution, he must perform *sajdatā al-sahw*. However, if he mistakenly says: *assalāmu ʿalayka ayyuhan nabiyyu wa raḥmatul lāhi wa barakātuh*, then the recommended precaution is that he should perform *sajdatā al-sahw*. If he says two or more words of the *salām*, then based on obligatory precaution, he must perform *sajdatā al-sahw*.

Ruling 1229. If a person mistakenly says all three sentences of *salām* at a time when he must not say *salām*, *sajdatā al-sahw* will suffice.

Ruling 1230. If a person forgets one *sajdah* or *tashahhud* and remembers it before performing *rukūʿ* of the next *rakʿah*, he must go back and perform it; and based on recommended precaution, he should perform *sajdatā al-sahw* for the additional standing.

Ruling 1231. If a person remembers in *rukūʿ* or after it that he has forgotten one *sajdah* or *tashahhud* from the previous *rakʿah*, he must make up the *sajdah* after the *salām* of the prayer [for the forgotten *sajdah*]; and for [the forgotten] *tashahhud*, he must perform *sajdatā al-sahw*.

Ruling 1232. If a person intentionally does not perform *sajdatā al-sahw* after the *salām* of the prayer, he commits a sin; and based on obligatory precaution, he must perform it as soon as possible. In the event that he inadvertently does not perform it, he must perform it as soon as he remembers and it will not be necessary for him to perform the prayer again.

Ruling 1233. If a person doubts whether or not, for example, *sajdatā* *al-sahw* have become obligatory for him, it is not necessary for him to perform them.

Ruling 1234. If a person doubts whether, for example, *sajdatā al-sahw* [i.e. two of them] have become obligatory for him or four, it is sufficient if he performs *sajdatā al-sahw*.

Ruling 1235. If a person knows that he has not performed one of the *sajdatā al-sahw*, and it is not possible to perform the other one on account of a long time having elapsed, or he knows that he inadvertently performed three *sajdahs*, then he must perform *sajdatā al-sahw*.

METHOD OF PERFORMING *SAJDATĀ AL-SAHW*

Ruling 1236. The method of performing *sajdatā al-sahw* is that immediately after the *salām* of the prayer, one must make the intention of *sajdatā al-sahw* and place his forehead, based on obligatory precaution, on something on which performing *sajdah* is permitted. The recommended precaution is that one should say *dhikr* in the *sajdah*, and it is better that he say:

بِسْمِ اللّٰهِ وَبِاللّٰهِ، اَلسَّلَامُ عَلَيْكَ أَيُّهَا النَّبِيُّ وَرَحْمَةُ اللّٰهِ وَبَرَكَاتُهُ

bismil lāhi wa billāhi, assalāmu ʿalayka ayyuhan nabiyyu wa raḥmatul lāhi wa barakātuh

In the name of Allah and by Allah. Peace be upon you O Prophet, and Allah's mercy and His blessings (be upon you too).

Then, he must sit up and go into *sajdah* again, and he should say the *dhikr* mentioned above. [He must then sit] and say *tashahhud*, after which he must say:

اَلسَّلَامُ عَلَيْكُمْ

assalāmu ʿalaykum

Peace be upon you all.

And it is preferable that he adds the words:

وَرَحْمَةُ اللّٰهِ وَبَرَكَاتُهُ

wa raḥmatul lāhi wa barakātuh

And Allah's mercy and His blessings (be upon you too).

MAKING UP (*QAḌĀʾ*) A FORGOTTEN *SAJDAH*

Ruling 1237. If a person forgets a *sajdah* in his prayers and is required to make it up after the prayer, he must do so having met all the conditions of prayers, such as his body and clothing being pure, facing qibla, and the other conditions.

Ruling 1238. If a person forgets a few *sajdah*s – for example, he forgets one *sajdah* from the first *rakʿah* and another from the second – then after the prayer, he must make up both *sajdah*s. And the recommended precaution is that he should perform *sajdatā al-sahw* for each forgotten *sajdah*.

Ruling 1239. If a person forgets one *sajdah* and one *tashahhud*, he must perform *sajdatā al-sahw* for the forgotten *tashahhud*, but it is not necessary for him to do so for the forgotten *sajdah*, although it is better that he does.

Ruling 1240. If a person forgets two *sajdah*s from two *rakʿah*s, it is not necessary for him to observe sequence when making them up.

Ruling 1241. If between the *salām* of the prayer and making up the *sajdah* one does something that were he to do it intentionally or inadvertently in prayers it would invalidate the prayer – for example, he turns his back to qibla – the recommended precaution is that after making up the *sajdah*, he should perform the prayer again.

Ruling 1242. If a person remembers after the *salām* of the prayer that he has forgotten one *sajdah* from the last *rakʿah*, in the event that he does not do anything that invalidates prayers, he must perform it and all that follows it, i.e. *tashahhud* and *salām*. And based on obligatory precaution, he must perform *sajdatā al-sahw* for saying an additional *salām*.

Ruling 1243. If between the *salām* of the prayer and making up the *sajdah* a person does something that makes it obligatory for him to perform *sajdatā al-sahw* – for example, he inadvertently speaks – then based on obligatory precaution, he must first make up the *sajdah* and then perform *sajdatā al-sahw*.

Ruling 1244. If a person does not know whether he has forgotten a *sajdah* or *tashahhud* in prayers, he must make up the *sajdah* and perform *sajdatā al-sahw*. And the recommended precaution is that he should also make up the *tashahhud*.

Ruling 1245. If a person doubts whether or not he has forgotten a *sajdah* or *tashahhud*, it is not obligatory for him to make up the *sajdah* or the *sajdatā al-sahw*.

Ruling 1246. If a person knows he has forgotten to perform a *sajdah* but doubts whether or not he remembered before performing *rukūʿ* of the next *rakʿah* and then performed it, the recommended precaution is that he should make it up.

Ruling 1247. With regard to someone who must make up a *sajdah*, if for some reason *sajdatā al-sahw* becomes obligatory for him as well, then based on obligatory precaution, after prayers, he must first make up the *sajdah* and then perform *sajdatā al-sahw*.

Ruling 1248. If after prayers one doubts whether or not he has made up a forgotten *sajdah*, in the event that the time for the prayer has not expired, he must make up the *sajdah*. In fact, even if the time has expired, he must, based on obligatory precaution, make it up.

OMITTING OR ADDING COMPONENTS OR CONDITIONS OF THE PRAYER

Ruling 1249. Whenever a person intentionally omits or adds something that is an obligatory component of the prayer, even to the extent of one word, the prayer is invalid.

Ruling 1250. If, on account of ignorance, a person adds or omits something that is an obligatory *rukn*, the prayer is invalid. As for omitting something that is obligatory, but not a *rukn*, by someone who is inculpably ignorant – such as someone who trusts the words of a reliable person or a credible manual of Islamic rulings (*risālah*), and afterwards he realises that the person or the manual was wrong – this does not invalidate the prayer. Furthermore, in the event that a person does not know the relevant ruling, even if it is his own fault [for not knowing it], and he recites Sūrat al-Ḥamd and the other surah of *ṣubḥ*, *maghrib*, and *ʿishāʾ* prayers in a whisper, or he recites Sūrat al-Ḥamd and the other surah of *ẓuhr* and *ʿaṣr* aloud, or he performs *ẓuhr*, *ʿaṣr*, and *ʿishāʾ* prayers as four *rakʿah* prayers when he is a traveller, in all these cases, his prayer is valid.

Ruling 1251. If during or after prayers one learns that his *wuḍūʾ* or *ghusl* was invalid, or that he started performing prayers without *wuḍūʾ* or *ghusl*, he must perform the prayer again with *wuḍūʾ* or *ghusl*; and if the time for the prayer has expired, he must make it up.

Ruling 1252. If after going into *rukūʿ* one remembers that he forgot to perform the two *sajdah*s in the previous *rakʿah*, then based on obligatory precaution, his prayer is invalid. However, if he remembers this before going into *rukūʿ*, he must go back, perform the two *sajdah*s, stand up, recite Sūrat al-Ḥamd and the other surah or *al-tasbīḥāt al-arbaʿah*, and then complete the prayer. After prayers, based on recommended precaution, he should perform *sajdatā al-sahw* for the additional standing.

Ruling 1253. If before saying '*assalāmu ʿalaynā*' and '*assalāmu ʿalaykum*' [in the *salām* of the prayer] one remembers that he has not performed the two *sajdah*s in the last *rakʿah*, he must perform the two *sajdah*s and then say *tashahhud* and the *salām* of the prayer again.

Ruling 1254. If before the *salām* of the prayer one remembers that he has not performed one *rakʿah* or more from the end of the prayer, he must perform what he had forgotten.

Ruling 1255. If after the *salām* of the prayer one remembers that he has not performed one *rakʿah* or more from the end of the prayer, in the event that he has done something that were he to do it intentionally or inadvertently during prayers it would invalidate the prayer – such as turning his back to qibla – his prayer is invalid. However, if he has not done anything that were he to do it intentionally or inadvertently during prayers it would invalidate the prayer, he must immediately perform what he had forgotten, and for the additional *salām*, he must, based on obligatory precaution, perform *sajdatā al-sahw*.

Ruling 1256. Whenever after the *salām* of the prayer one does something that were he to do it intentionally or inadvertently during prayers it would invalidate them – such as turning his back to qibla – and he later remembers that he has not performed the two last *sajdahs*, his prayer is invalid. However, if he remembers this before doing something that invalidates prayers, he must perform the two *sajdahs* that he had forgotten and say *tashahhud* and the *salām* of the prayer again; and based on obligatory precaution, he must perform *sajdatā al-sahw* for the *salām* that he first said.

Ruling 1257. If a person realises that he has performed a prayer before its prescribed time, he must perform it again; and if its time has expired, he must make it up. If he realises that he performed it with his back to qibla or had turned ninety degrees or more [away from qibla], in the event that its time has not expired, he must perform it again. However, if its time has expired, then in the event that he was uncertain or was ignorant about the rule, it is obligatory for him to make it up; otherwise, it is not. If he realises that he had turned less than ninety degrees, and he did not have a legitimate excuse for turning away from qibla – for example, he was searching for the direction of qibla, or he was negligent in learning the ruling – then based on obligatory precaution, he must perform the prayer again, irrespective of whether there is time or not. However, if he did have a legitimate excuse, it is not necessary for him to perform the prayer again.

PRAYERS OF A TRAVELLER

If the following eight conditions are fulfilled, a traveller must perform *ẓuhr*, *ʿaṣr*, and *ʿishāʾ* prayers in their shortened (*qaṣr*) form; i.e. he must perform them as two *rakʿah* prayers.

First condition: the journey must not be less than eight *farsakhs* (approximately forty-four kilometres) [which is equal to approximately twenty-seven and a half miles].

Ruling 1258. If a person's outward and return journey totals eight *farsakhs* – irrespective of whether or not the outward or the return journey on its own is less than four *farsakhs* – he must perform *qaṣr* prayers. Therefore, if his outward journey is three *farsakhs* and his return is five, or vice versa, he must perform *qaṣr* prayers, i.e. [he must perform the four *rakʿah* prayers] as two *rakʿah* prayers.

Ruling 1259. If a person's outward and return journey totals eight *farsakhs*, then even if he does not return on the same day or night, he must perform *qaṣr* prayers; however, it is better that in this case, as a recommended precaution, he also perform prayers in their complete (*tamām*) form.

Ruling 1260. If a person's journey is a little short of eight *farsakhs*, or if he does not know whether or not his journey is eight *farsakhs*, he must not perform *qaṣr* prayers. In the event that he doubts whether or not his journey is eight *farsakhs*, it is not necessary for him to investigate and he must perform *tamām* prayers.

Ruling 1261. If a dutiful or reliable person informs a person that his journey is eight *farsakhs*, and if he attains confidence in what he says, he must perform *qaṣr* prayers.

Ruling 1262. If someone who is certain that his journey is eight *farsakhs* performs *qaṣr* prayers and later realises that it was not eight *farsakhs*, he must perform them as four *rakʿah* prayers; and if the time has expired, he must make them up.

Ruling 1263. With regard to someone who is certain that the journey he wants to go on is not eight *farsakhs*, or he doubts whether or not it is eight *farsakhs*, in the event that he realises on the way that his journey is eight *farsakhs*, he must perform *qaṣr* prayers even if only a short distance of his journey is left. If he has performed *tamām* prayers, he must perform them again in their shortened form; however, if the time has expired, it is not necessary for him to make them up.

Ruling 1264. If a person comes and goes a number of times between two places which are less than four *farsakhs* apart, he must perform *tamām* prayers even if the total distance travelled by him is eight *farsakhs*.

Ruling 1265. If there are two roads to a place – one of them less than eight *farsakhs* and the other eight or more *farsakhs* – then, in the event that one goes to that place by the road that is eight *farsakhs*, he must perform *qaṣr* prayers. If he goes by the road that is not eight *farsakhs*, he must perform *tamām* prayers.

Ruling 1266.* The start of the eight *farsakhs* on one's journey must be calculated from the point beyond which a person is deemed to be a traveller; this is usually the outskirts of a town. However, in some very big cities, it is possible that it is the outskirts of a particular area. The end of the journey of a traveller who intends to travel to a town or village that is not his home town (*waṭan*) is deemed to be his destination in that town or village, not the point of entry into that town or village.

Second condition: one must have the intention of travelling eight *farsakhs* from the commencement of his journey; i.e. he must know that he will travel eight *farsakhs*. Therefore, if he travels to a place that is less than eight *farsakhs*, and after reaching that place he makes the intention of going to a place that together with the distance he has already travelled totals eight *farsakhs*, then as he did not have the intention of travelling eight *farsakhs* from the commencement of his journey, he must perform *tamām* prayers. However, if he wants to travel eight *farsakhs* from that place, or, for example, he wants to travel a distance that together with the return journey totals eight *farsakhs*, he must perform *qaṣr* prayers.

Ruling 1267. With regard to someone who does not know how many *farsakhs* his journey is – for example, he travels to find a lost person and does not know how far he must go before he finds him – he must perform *tamām* prayers. However, on the return journey, in the event that the distance to his home town or to a place where he intends to stay for ten days is eight or more *farsakhs*, he must perform *qaṣr* prayers. Similarly, if during his journey he makes an intention to travel a distance that together with the return journey totals eight *farsakh*s, he must perform *qaṣr* prayers.

Ruling 1268. A traveller must perform *qaṣr* prayers when he has decided to travel eight *farsakh*s. Therefore, if someone goes out of his town and, for example, his intention is that if he finds a friend he will travel for eight *farsakh*s, then in the event that he is confident that he will find a friend, he must perform *qaṣr* prayers; and if he is not confident about this, he must perform *tamām* prayers.

Ruling 1269. If someone who has the intention of travelling eight *farsakh*s covers even a short distance every day, when he reaches the permitted limit (*ḥadd al-tarakhkhuṣ*) (the meaning of which will be explained in Ruling 1304), he must perform *qaṣr* prayers. However, if he covers a very short distance every day, the obligatory precaution is that he must perform both *qaṣr* and *tamām* prayers.

Ruling 1270. With regard to someone like a prisoner who is travelling under the authority of someone else [i.e. a guard], in the event that he knows the journey will be eight *farsakh*s, he must perform *qaṣr* prayers. However, if he does not know, he must perform *tamām* prayers and it is not necessary for him to inquire [about the distance of the journey], although it is better that he does.

Ruling 1271. With regard to someone who is travelling under the authority of someone else, if he knows or supposes that he will become separated from the other person before reaching four *farsakh*s and that he will not travel any further, he must perform *tamām* prayers.

Ruling 1272. With regard to someone who is travelling under the authority of someone else, if he is not confident that he will become separated from the other person before reaching four *farsakh*s and that he will not travel any further, he must perform *tamām* prayers. However, if he is confident about this, he must perform *qaṣr* prayers.

Third condition: one must not change his intention on the way [i.e. he must not decide against travelling]. If before travelling four *farsakh*s one changes his mind [about travelling] or becomes unsure [about travelling], and the distance he has already travelled together with the return journey totals less than eight *farsakhs*, he must perform *tamām* prayers.

Ruling 1273. If after travelling some of the way, which together with the return journey totals eight *farsakhs*, one abandons the journey, in the event that he decides to remain in that place or to return after ten days, or he is unsure about returning or staying there, he must perform *tamām* prayers.

Ruling 1274. If after travelling some of the way, which together with the return journey totals eight *farsakhs*, one changes his mind and decides to return, he must perform *qaṣr* prayers even if he wants to stay less than ten days in that place.

Ruling 1275. If a person travels towards a place on a journey of eight *farsakhs* and after going some distance he decides to go somewhere else, in the event that the distance between the first place from where he started his journey to the place where he wants to go is eight *farsakhs*, he must perform *qaṣr* prayers.

Ruling 1276. If before travelling eight *farsakhs* one becomes unsure about continuing his journey, and while he is unsure he does not continue with his journey and later decides to continue with it, he must perform *qaṣr* prayers until the end of his journey.

Ruling 1277. If before travelling eight *farsakhs* one becomes unsure about continuing his journey, and while he is unsure he travels some distance and later decides to travel another eight *farsakhs*, or to travel to a place the distance to and from which totals eight *farsakhs*, he must perform *qaṣr* prayers until the end of his journey.

Ruling 1278. If before travelling eight *farsakhs* one becomes unsure about continuing his journey, and while he is unsure he travels some distance and later decides to continue with his journey, then in the event that the total outward and return journey minus the distance he travelled while he was unsure is less than eight *farsakhs*, he must perform *tamām* prayers. If it is not less than eight *farsakhs*, his prayers must be in *qaṣr* form.

Fourth condition: before travelling eight *farsakhs*, one must not intend to pass through his home town and stay there, or to stay in a place for ten or more days. Therefore, if before travelling eight *farsakhs* someone intends to pass through his home town and stay there, or to stay in a place for ten or more days, he must perform *tamām* prayers. If he intends to pass through his home town without staying there, he must, as a precautionary measure, perform both *qaṣr* and *tamām* prayers.

Ruling 1279. If someone does not know whether he will pass through his home town before travelling eight *farsakhs*, or if he will intend to stay in a place for ten days, he must perform *tamām* prayers.

Ruling 1280. If someone wants to pass through his home town and stay there before travelling eight *farsakhs*, or if he wants to stay at a place for ten days, and similarly, if someone is unsure about passing through his home town, or he is unsure about staying at a place for ten days, then, if he changes his mind about staying in a place for ten days or passing through his home town, he must perform *tamām* prayers. However, if the remaining distance, even with the return journey added, is eight *farsakhs*, he must perform *qaṣr* prayers.

Fifth condition: one must not travel for an unlawful purpose. If a person travels for an unlawful purpose, such as theft, he must perform *tamām* prayers. The same applies if the journey itself is unlawful; for example, it is harmful for him in that it can result in death or the loss of a limb, or a wife travels without the consent of her husband on a journey that is not obligatory. However, if it is like a journey for obligatory hajj, she must perform *qaṣr* prayers.

Ruling 1281. A journey that is not obligatory and is a source of annoyance for one's father or mother on the account of their compassion for their child, is unlawful. On such a journey, the child must perform *tamām* prayers and fast [i.e. if he is legally obliged to fast on that day, he is not exempt from fasting as he normally would be].

Ruling 1282. With regard to someone whose journey is not unlawful and who is not travelling for any unlawful purpose, if he commits a sin on his journey – for example, he backbites or drinks alcohol – he must perform *qaṣr* prayers.

Ruling 1283. If a person travels to avoid an obligatory act – irrespective of whether or not he has some other purpose for travelling as well – he must perform *tamām* prayers. Therefore, if a person owes some money and can repay his debt and the creditor demands it from him, in the event that he cannot pay his debt while he is travelling and he travels to escape the repayment of his debt, he must perform *tamām* prayers. However, if the purpose of his travel is something else, then even if he avoids an obligatory act on his journey, he must perform *qaṣr* prayers.

Ruling 1284. If the mode of transport a person uses is usurped and he has travelled to escape from its owner, or if he travels on usurped land, he must perform *tamām* prayers.

Ruling 1285. With regard to someone who travels in compliance with the orders of an oppressor, if he is not compelled to do so and his journey is to help the oppressor in his oppression, he must perform *tamām* prayers. However, if he is compelled, or, for example, he travels with the oppressor to save an oppressed person, his prayers must be performed in *qaṣr* form.

Ruling 1286. If a person travels for recreational and leisure purposes, his journey is not unlawful and he must perform *qaṣr* prayers.

Ruling 1287.* If a person goes hunting for amusement and fun, although it is not unlawful, his prayer during the outward journey must be performed in *tamām* form. As for his return journey, if it is not for recreational hunting, he must perform *qaṣr* prayers, provided it is of the prescribed distance. If the outward journey is not for hunting and the person hunts for food, he must perform his prayers in *qaṣr* form. The same applies if he hunts for the purposes of business and increasing his wealth. If one travels for a purpose that would commonly be regarded as pointless – such as a journey that has no rational purpose – the obligatory precaution is that he must perform both *qaṣr* and *tamām* prayers.

Ruling 1288.* With regard to someone who has travelled for a sinful purpose, he must perform *qaṣr* prayers on his return journey, whether he repents for his sin or not and whether the return journey on its own is eight *farsakh*s or less.

Ruling 1289. With regard to someone whose journey is a sinful one, if on the way he abandons his intention to sin – irrespective of whether or not the remaining distance on its own, or the sum of both the outward and return journey from that point is eight *farsakh*s – he must perform *qaṣr* prayers.

Ruling 1290. With regard to someone who has not travelled for a sinful purpose, if on the way he makes the intention of travelling the rest of the journey for a sinful purpose, he must perform *tamām* prayers. However, the prayers he performed in *qaṣr* form [before he changed his intention] are valid.

Sixth condition: one must not be a nomad, such as the desert dwellers who roam the deserts and stay wherever they find water and food for themselves and their animals, and after a while move to another place. Such people must perform *tamām* prayers on these journeys.

Ruling 1291. If a nomad travels in search of a place to stay and pasture for his animals, for example, in the event that he travels with his possessions and equipment such that it can be said he has his house with him, he must perform *tamām* prayers. Otherwise, in the event that his journey is eight *farsakh*s, he must perform *qaṣr* prayers.

Ruling 1292. If a nomad travels for *ziyārah*,[51] hajj, business, or suchlike, and it cannot be said that he is travelling with his house, he must perform *qaṣr* prayers; and if it can be said, then he must perform *tamām* prayers.

Seventh condition: one must not be a frequent traveller (*kathīr al-safar*). [The frequent traveller is of two kinds:] 1) someone whose profession is travelling – such as a driver and the captain of a ship, or a delivery person or shepherd – and 2) someone who frequently

[51] *Ziyārah* is a visitation to the place of burial of a holy personality or a holy place.

travels even though his work does not require him to do so – such as someone who travels three days in a week even if it is for recreational and touristic purposes – such a person must perform *tamām* prayers.

Ruling 1293. With regard to someone whose profession is travelling, if he travels for another purpose, such as *ziyārah* or hajj, he must perform *qaṣr* prayers unless he is commonly known to be a frequent traveller, such as someone who always travels three days in a week. However, if, for example, a car driver is hired for a *ziyārah* trip and on that trip he also performs *ziyārah*, he must perform *tamām* prayers.

Ruling 1294.* A tour leader (someone who travels to take pilgrims to Mecca) must perform *tamām* prayers if his profession is travelling. However, if his profession is not travelling and he only travels in the hajj season to take pilgrims and stays in his home town for the rest of the year, then in the event that his trip does not exceed two months, he must perform *qaṣr* prayers. If his trip lasts three months or more, he must perform *tamām* prayers. If his trip is in between the two, then as an obligatory precaution, he must perform both *qaṣr* and *tamām* prayers.

Ruling 1295. For someone to be called a 'driver' and suchlike, it is a requirement that he intends to continue driving and his resting time must not be longer than usual for drivers. Therefore, if someone, for example, travels one day a week, he cannot be called a driver. Furthermore, someone can be called a frequent traveller if he travels a minimum of ten times a month and travels on ten days a month, or spends ten days a month travelling, albeit on two or three separate journeys, on condition that he intends to continue doing this for six months in one year or three months every year for two or more years. In such a case, his prayers on all his journeys, even on his non-repetitive ones, must be performed in *tamām* form; and in the first two weeks he must, as an obligatory precaution, perform both *qaṣr* and *tamām* prayers. If the numbers or days of his journey in a month comes to eight or nine, then based on obligatory precaution, he must perform both *qaṣr* and *tamām* prayers on all the journeys. If the number of days is less than this, he must perform his prayers in *qaṣr* form.

Ruling 1296. Someone whose profession is to travel part of the year – such as a driver who is hired for his services only in summer or winter – must perform *tamām* prayers on that journey. And the recommended precaution is that he should perform both *qaṣr* and *tamām* prayers.

Ruling 1297. A driver or a salesperson who comes and goes in distances of two or three *farsakh*s from a town must perform *qaṣr* prayers in the event that he happens to travel eight *farsakh*s.

Ruling 1298. Someone whose profession is travelling – whether he stays in his home town for ten or more days and had an intention from the outset to stay for ten days, or he stays without any such intention – must perform *tamām* prayers on the first journey he goes on after ten days. The same applies if he stays in a place that is not his home town for ten days, whether he had an intention to do so or not. However, with regard to a herdsman or a driver who is hired, the recommended precaution is that on the first journey he goes on after ten days, he should perform both *qaṣr* and *tamām* prayers.

Ruling 1299. With regard to someone whose profession is travelling, it is not a condition that he travel three times for his prayers to be in *tamām* form; rather, whenever the title 'driver' and suchlike can be applied to him, even if it is on his first journey, his prayers must be performed in *tamām* form.

Ruling 1300. With regard to someone whose profession is travelling, such as a herdsman or driver, in case travelling causes him excessive difficulty and exhaustion that is more than usual, he must perform *qaṣr* prayers.

Ruling 1301. Someone who travels around different cities and has not adopted a home town for himself must perform *tamām* prayers.

Ruling 1302. With regard to someone whose profession is not travelling, if, for example, he has to continuously travel to a town or village to pick up a commodity that he transports, he must perform *qaṣr* prayers unless he is a frequent traveller, the criteria for which was explained in Ruling 1295.

Ruling 1303. With regard to someone who has disregarded a place as his home town and wants to adopt another home town, if he cannot be given one of the titles that require a person to perform *tamām* prayers – such as 'frequent traveller' or 'nomad' – he must perform *qaṣr* prayers on his travels.

Eighth condition: one must reach the permitted limit (*ḥadd al-tarakhkhuṣ*) if he starts his journey from his home town. However, if he travels from a place that is not his home town, then the permitted limit does not apply to him and he must perform his prayers in *qaṣr* form from the moment he sets out on his journey from his place of residence.

Ruling 1304. The permitted limit is the place where the people of a town – including those who live on its outskirts and are considered residents of the town – cannot see a traveller due to the distance he has travelled. A traveller would know he has reached this point when he can no longer see the people of the town nor those living on its outskirts.

Ruling 1305. A traveller returning to his home town must perform *qaṣr* prayers until he enters his home town. Similarly, a traveller who wants to stay somewhere for ten days must perform *qaṣr* prayers until the time he reaches that place.

Ruling 1306. If a town's location happens to be elevated such that its residents can be seen from around it, or if it happens to be in a depression such that if one went a short distance away from it he would not see its residents, then, if a resident of that town travels and reaches a distance such that had the town's location been at ground level he would not be able to see its residents, he must perform *qaṣr* prayers. Similarly, if the elevation or depression of the road he is travelling on is more than normal, he must take into account a normal type of road [in determining whether he must perform *qaṣr* or *tamām* prayers].

Ruling 1307. If before reaching the permitted limit a person who is sitting on a ship or train starts performing prayers with the intention of *tamām* prayers, but before performing *rukūʿ* of the third *rakʿah* he reaches the permitted limit, he must perform prayers in *qaṣr* form.

Ruling 1308. If in the situation mentioned above one reaches the permitted limit after performing *rukūʿ* of the third *rakʿah*, he must perform another prayer in *qaṣr* form and it will not be necessary for him to complete the first prayer.

Ruling 1309. If a person is certain that he has reached the permitted limit and performs his prayer in *qaṣr* form, and later he realises that when he performed his prayer he had not actually reached the permitted limit, he must perform the prayer again. When he performs the prayer again, if he has still not reached the permitted limit, he must perform the prayer in *tamām* form, but if he has passed it, he must perform it in *qaṣr* form. If the time for the prayer has expired, he must perform it according to what his duty was when the prescribed time for it expired.

Ruling 1310. If a person's eyesight is not normal, he must perform *qaṣr* prayers from the point where people of average eyesight would not be able to see the residents of the town.

Ruling 1311. If one doubts whether or not he has reached the permitted limit while travelling, he must perform *tamām* prayers.

Ruling 1312. If a traveller who passes his home town on his journey stays there, he must perform *tamām* prayers; otherwise [i.e. if he does not stay there], the obligatory precaution is that he must perform both *qaṣr* and *tamām* prayers.

Ruling 1313. A traveller who reaches his home town on his journey and stays there must perform *tamām* prayers while he is there. However, if he wants to travel eight *farsakh*s from there, or, for example, he wants to travel four *farsakh*s going and four *farsakh*s returning, then when he reaches the permitted limit, he must perform *qaṣr* prayers.

Ruling 1314. A place that one adopts as his permanent residence is his home town, irrespective of whether he was born there or not, or it was the home of his parents, or he selected it himself for his residence.

Ruling 1315. If a person intends to stay for a short time in a location that is not his home town and to later move to another place, that location is not considered his home town.

Ruling 1316. A place that one has adopted as his residence is ruled to be his home town – even if he does not intend to always live there – provided that he cannot be commonly regarded as being a traveller there, such that were he to choose to stay somewhere else for ten days or more temporarily, people would still say the first place is his place of residence.

Ruling 1317. With regard to a person who resides in two places – for example, he resides six months in one town and six months in another – both places are his home towns. Furthermore, if he has chosen to reside in more than two places, then all of them are considered his home towns.

Ruling 1318. Some jurists have said: with regard to a person who owns a residential home somewhere, that place is ruled to be his home town if he stays there for six continuous months with the intention of residing there and as long as that house belongs to him. Therefore, whenever he travels there, he must perform *tamām* prayers. However, this rule is not established.

Ruling 1319. If a person reaches a place that was once his home town but which he now disregards [as being his home town], he must not perform *tamām* prayers there even if he has not adopted another place as his home town.

Ruling 1320. A traveller who has the intention of staying somewhere for ten consecutive days, or knows that he has no choice but to stay somewhere for ten days, must perform *tamām* prayers in that place.

Ruling 1321. It is not necessary for a traveller who wants to stay somewhere for ten days to have the intention to stay there on the first night and the eleventh night. Rather, [it is sufficient if] he makes the intention that he will stay there from sunrise on the first day until sunset of the tenth day, [and if he does so,] he must perform *tamām* prayers. The same applies if, for example, he makes the intention to stay there from noon on the first day until noon on the eleventh day.

Ruling 1322. A traveller who wants to stay somewhere for ten days must perform *tamām* prayers if he wants to stay in one place for ten days. Therefore, if he intends to stay, for example, ten days in Najaf and Hilla, or in Tehran and Karaj, he must perform *qaṣr* prayers.

Ruling 1323. With regard to a traveller who wants to stay somewhere for ten days, if from the outset he intends during the ten days to travel to a surrounding place – which is commonly regarded as being a different place – and if the distance to it is less than four *farsakh*s, then, if the period of his outward and return journeys is such that it does not conflict with him staying for ten days, he must perform *tamām* prayers. However, if it does conflict, he must perform *qaṣr* prayers. For example, if he intends from the outset to travel for one complete day or one complete night, this conflicts with his staying and he must perform *qaṣr* prayers. However, in the event that his intention is, for example, to travel for half a day and return, even if the return is after sunset, then he must perform his prayers in *tamām* form unless this type of travelling happens so often that he is commonly regarded as residing in two or more places.

Ruling 1324. A traveller who has not decided to stay somewhere for ten days but whose intention is, for example, that if his friend comes or he finds a good house then he will stay there for ten days, must perform *qaṣr* prayers.

Ruling 1325. With regard to a person who has decided to stay somewhere for ten days, if he deems it probable that some obstacle to his staying there will arise, and if rational people would consider this probability to be significant, he must perform *qaṣr* prayers.

Ruling 1326. If a traveller knows, for example, that ten days or more remain before the end of the month and he intends to stay somewhere until the end of the month, he must perform *tamām* prayers. However, if he does not know how long is left until the end of the month and makes an intention to stay until the end of the month, he must perform *qaṣr* prayers even if ten days or more remain from the time he made the intention until the last day of the month.

Ruling 1327. If a traveller intends to stay somewhere for ten days, in the event that before he performs a four *rakʿah* prayer within its prescribed time he abandons the idea of staying there, or he becomes unsure of whether to stay there or go to another place, then in such a case, he must perform *qaṣr* prayers. However, if after performing a four *rakʿah* prayer within its prescribed time he abandons the idea of staying there or becomes unsure, he must perform *tamām* prayers as long as he stays there.

Ruling 1328. If a traveller who has made the intention to stay somewhere for ten days keeps a fast and after the time for *ẓuhr* prayers he changes his mind about staying there, in the event that he has performed a four *rakʿah* prayer within its prescribed time, the fasts he keeps there are valid and he must perform *tamām* prayers. However, if he has not performed a four *rakʿah* prayer within its prescribed time, he must, as an obligatory precaution, complete that day's fast and make it up as well. Furthermore, he must also perform *qaṣr* prayers and he cannot fast on the remaining days.

Ruling 1329. If a traveller who has made the intention to stay somewhere for ten days changes his mind about staying but doubts whether he changed his mind about staying after or before he performed a four *rakʿah* prayer within its prescribed time, he must perform *qaṣr* prayers.

Ruling 1330. If a traveller starts performing a prayer with the intention of performing a *qaṣr* prayer and during it he decides to stay in that place for ten days or more, he must complete his prayer as a four *rakʿah* prayer.

Ruling 1331. If a traveller who has made the intention to stay somewhere for ten days changes his mind during his first four *rakʿah* prayer within its prescribed time, in the event that he has not yet started to perform the third *rakʿah*, he must complete his prayer as a two *rakʿah* prayer and perform his remaining prayers in *qaṣr* form. If he has started to perform the third *rakʿah* but has not yet gone into *rukūʿ*, he must sit down and complete the prayer in *qaṣr* form. However, if he has gone into *rukūʿ*, he can either break his prayer or complete it, and he must perform it again in *qaṣr* form.

Ruling 1332. If a traveller who has made the intention to stay somewhere for ten days stays there for more than ten days, he must perform *tamām* prayers as long as he does not travel; and it is not necessary for him to make another intention to stay for ten days.

Ruling 1333. A traveller who has made the intention to stay somewhere for ten days must keep obligatory fasts. He can also keep recommended fasts and perform the *nāfilah* of *ẓuhr*, *ʿaṣr*, and *ʿishāʾ*.

Ruling 1334. With regard to a traveller who has made the intention to stay somewhere for ten days, if after performing a four *rakʿah* prayer within its prescribed time or after staying there for ten days – even if he has not performed one prayer in *tamām* form – he wants to go to a place that is less than four *farsakh*s away and then come back and stay in the first place again for ten days or less, in such a case, he must perform *tamām* prayers from the time he goes until the time he comes back and after coming back as well. However, if his returning to the place of his residence is only because it is on the way, and if the distance of his journey is eight *farsakh*s, then it is necessary for him to perform *qaṣr* prayers while going, returning, and at his place of residence.

Ruling 1335. With regard to a traveller who has made the intention to stay somewhere for ten days, if after performing a four *rakʿah* prayer within its prescribed time he wants to go somewhere else that is less than eight *farsakh*s away and stay there for ten days, he must perform *tamām* prayers while going and at the place where he intends to stay for ten days. However, if he wants to go to a place that is eight *farsakh*s away or further, he must perform *qaṣr* prayers while going. In the event that he does not want to stay there for ten days, he must perform *qaṣr* prayers while he is there.

Ruling 1336. With regard to a traveller who has made the intention to stay somewhere for ten days, if after performing a four *rakʿah* prayer within its prescribed time he wants to go somewhere else that is less than eight *farsakh*s away, then in the event that he is unsure whether or not he will return to his first destination, or he is totally unmindful about returning there, or he wants to return but is unsure whether or not he will stay there for ten days, or he is unmindful about staying there for ten days or travelling from there, then in these cases, he must perform *tamām* prayers from the time he goes until the time he returns and after he returns as well.

Ruling 1337. If someone makes an intention to stay somewhere for ten days because he thinks his friends want to stay there for ten days, and after performing a four *rakʿah* prayer within its prescribed time he realises that they did not have such an intention, then even if he changes his mind to stay there he must perform *tamām* prayers as long as he stays there.

Ruling 1338. If a traveller happens to stay somewhere for thirty days – for example, throughout those thirty days he was unsure about going or staying – he must perform *tamām* prayers after thirty days have passed even if he stays there for a short time [after the thirty days].

Ruling 1339. If a traveller wants to stay somewhere for nine days or less, and if after staying there for nine days or less he wants to stay for another nine days or less, and so on until thirty days, he must perform *tamām* prayers from the thirty-first day.

Ruling 1340. After thirty days, a traveller must perform *tamām* prayers if he has stayed in one place for those thirty days. Therefore, if he stays part of that period in one place and part of it in another, he must perform *qaṣr* prayers even after thirty days.

MISCELLANEOUS RULINGS ON THE PRAYER OF A TRAVELLER

Ruling 1341. A traveller can perform *tamām* prayers in the entire city of Mecca, Medina, and Kufa, and in the shrine (*ḥaram*) of His Eminence Sayyid al-Shuhadāʾ [Imam al-Ḥusayn] (ʿA) up to a distance of approximately 11.5 metres from the sacred grave [i.e. the area known as the '*ḥāʾir*'].

Ruling 1342. With regard to someone who knows he is a traveller and must perform *qaṣr* prayers, if he intentionally performs *tamām* prayers in a place other than the four places mentioned above, his prayers are invalid. The same applies if he forgets that the prayers of a traveller are *qaṣr* and performs them in *tamām* form. However, if he remembers this after the time [for the prayer has expired], it is not necessary for him to make it up.

Ruling 1343. With regard to someone who knows he is a traveller and must perform *qaṣr* prayers, if he inadvertently performs *tamām* prayers, in the event that he becomes aware of this within the prescribed time for the prayer, he must perform the prayer again. However, if he becomes aware after the time has expired, he must make it up based on obligatory precaution.

Ruling 1344. If a traveller who does not know that he must perform *qaṣr* prayers performs *tamām* prayers, his prayers are valid.

Ruling 1345. A traveller who knows that he must perform *qaṣr* prayers but does not know some of its details – for example, he does not know that *qaṣr* prayers must be performed on an eight *farsakh* journey – then, in the event that he performs *tamām* prayers and realises this within the prescribed time for the prayer, he must, based on obligatory precaution, perform it again; and if he does not perform it again, he must make it up. However, if he realises after the time has expired, there is no obligation to make it up.

Ruling 1346. If a traveller who knows that he must perform *qaṣr* prayers performs *tamām* prayers supposing that his journey is less than eight *farsakh*s, then whenever he realises that his journey was eight *farsakh*s, he must perform the prayers he performed in *tamām* form again in *qaṣr* form. If he realises that after the time for prayers has expired, it is not necessary to make it up.

Ruling 1347. If a person forgets that he is a traveller and performs *tamām* prayers, in the event that he remembers this within the time for the prayer, he must perform the prayer in *qaṣr* form. If he remembers this after the time for the prayer, then making it up is not obligatory for him.

Ruling 1348. If someone who must perform *tamām* prayers performs them in *qaṣr* form, his prayers are invalid in all circumstances. And based on obligatory precaution, this rule also applies to a traveller who has an intention of staying somewhere for ten days and performs *qaṣr* prayers there on account of not knowing the ruling.

Ruling 1349. If a person starts performing a four *rakʿah* prayer and during the prayer he remembers that he is a traveller, or he becomes aware that his journey is of eight *farsakh*s, in the event that he has not gone into *rukūʿ* of the third *rakʿah*, he must complete the prayer as a two *rakʿah* prayer. However, if he has completed the third *rakʿah*, his prayer is invalid; and if he has gone into *rukūʿ* of the third *rakʿah*, then based on obligatory precaution, his prayer is also invalid. Furthermore, in case there is enough time to perform even one *rakʿah*, he must perform the prayer again in *qaṣr* form; and if there is no time, he must make it up in *qaṣr* form.

Ruling 1350. If a traveller does not know some of the details of the prayer of a traveller – for example, he does not know that if he travels four *farsakh*s on his outward journey and four *farsakh*s on his return journey he must perform *qaṣr* prayers – then, in the event that he starts performing a prayer with the intention of performing a four *rakʿah* prayer and becomes aware of the ruling before going into *rukūʿ* of the third *rakʿah*, he must complete the prayer as a two *rakʿah* prayer. However, if he becomes aware of this in *rukūʿ*, his prayer is invalid based on obligatory precaution. And in case there is enough time for him to perform even one *rakʿah*, he must perform *qaṣr* prayers.

Ruling 1351. If a traveller who must perform *tamām* prayers on account of not knowing the ruling starts performing prayers with the intention of performing a two *rakʿah* prayer, and he becomes aware of the ruling during prayers, he must complete the prayer as a four *rakʿah* prayer. And the recommended precaution is that after completing the prayer, he should perform that prayer again as a four *rakʿah* prayer.

Ruling 1352. If a traveller who has not performed prayers at the start of their prescribed time arrives at his home town before the time for the prayer has expired, or he arrives at a place where he wants to stay for ten days, then based on obligatory precaution, he must perform *tamām* prayers. If someone who is not a traveller does not perform prayers at the start of their prescribed time and then travels, he must perform *qaṣr* prayers during his journey based on obligatory precaution.

Ruling 1353. With regard to a traveller who must perform *qaṣr* prayers, if his *ẓuhr*, *ʿaṣr*, or *ʿishāʾ* prayers become *qaḍāʾ*, he must perform them as two *rakʿah qaḍāʾ* prayers even if he wants to make them up when he is not travelling. If these prayers become *qaḍāʾ* for someone who is not a traveller, he must perform them as four *rakʿah qaḍāʾ* prayers even if he wants to make them up when he is travelling.

Ruling 1354. After every *qaṣr* prayer, it is recommended that a traveller says thirty times: '*subḥānal lāhi wal ḥamdu lillāhi wa lā ilāha illal lāhu wal lāhu akbar*'.[52] Although it is recommended to recite this *dhikr* after every obligatory prayer as well, in this case [i.e. for a traveller after every *qaṣr* prayer], it is recommended even more, and it is better to say it sixty times after *ẓuhr*, *ʿaṣr*, and *ʿishāʾ* prayers.

LAPSED (*QAḌĀʾ*) PRAYERS

Ruling 1355. With regard to someone who has not performed his daily prayers within their prescribed time, he must make them up even if he slept throughout the prescribed time or did not perform them on account of being intoxicated. The same applies to any other obligatory prayer that was not performed within its prescribed time, even, based on obligatory precaution, those prayers that had become obligatory at a specific time on account of a vow. However, the prayers of Eid al-Fiṭr and Eid al-Aḍḥā cannot be made up, and the prayers that a woman does not perform while experiencing *ḥayḍ* or *nifās* are not required to be made up, irrespective of whether they are the daily prayers or other prayers. The rule concerning *ṣalāt al-āyāt* will be mentioned later.

Ruling 1356. If after the time for the prayers has expired a person

[52] For the translation of this phrase, see the fifth section of 'Translation of prayers' after Ruling 1107.

realises that the prayers he performed were invalid, he must make them up.

Ruling 1357. Someone who has outstanding *qaḍāʾ* prayers must not be negligent about performing them; however, it is not obligatory for him to perform them immediately.

Ruling 1358. Someone who has outstanding *qaḍāʾ* prayers can perform recommended prayers.

Ruling 1359. If a person deems it probable that he has *qaḍāʾ* prayers to perform or that the prayers he performed were not valid, it is recommended that he make them up as a precautionary measure.

Ruling 1360. It is not necessary to make up daily prayers in the order they became *qaḍāʾ*, except for the prayers that must be performed in a particular order when they are performed within their prescribed time, such as *ẓuhr* and *ʿaṣr* prayers, and *maghrib* and *ʿishāʾ* prayers, of the same day.

Ruling 1361. If a person wants to make up prayers that are not the daily prayers – such as *ṣalāt al-āyāt* – or if, for example, he wants to make up one daily prayer and some other prayers, it is not necessary for him to perform them in the order they became *qaḍāʾ*.

Ruling 1362. With regard to someone who knows he has not performed a four *rakʿah* prayer but does not know whether it was *ẓuhr* or *ʿishāʾ* prayers, if he performs a four *rakʿah* prayer with the intention of making up the prayer that he did not perform, it is sufficient; moreover, he has the option of reciting Sūrat al-Ḥamd and the other surah aloud or in a whisper.

Ruling 1363. With regard to someone who has to make up, for example, a number of *ṣubḥ* or *ẓuhr* prayers, but he does not know how many or has forgotten how many – for example, he does not know if it is three, four, or five prayers that he has to make up – then, in the event that he performs the lower number, it is sufficient. However, it is better that he perform prayers up to the extent that he can be certain of having performed all of them. For example, if he has forgotten how many *ṣubḥ* prayers have become *qaḍāʾ* but he is certain that it is not more than ten, then as a recommended precaution he should perform ten *ṣubḥ* prayers.

Ruling 1364. With regard to someone who has only one *qaḍāʾ* prayer from the past, it is better that if the prime time of that day's prayer will not expire, he should first perform the *qaḍāʾ* prayer and then start performing his daily prayer. Similarly, if he does not have any *qaḍāʾ* prayers from the past but on that day one or more of his prayers became *qaḍāʾ*, then, if the prime time of his prayer will not expire, it is better that he perform that day's *qaḍāʾ* prayers before he performs the *adāʾ* prayers.

Ruling 1365. If during prayers one remembers that one or more prayers of that day have become *qaḍāʾ*, or that he has only one *qaḍāʾ* prayer from the past, in the event that there is ample time and it is possible for him to change his intention to *qaḍāʾ* prayers, it is better that he change his intention to *qaḍāʾ* prayers if the prime time for the daily prayer he was performing does not expire. For example, if in *ẓuhr* prayers before the *rukūʿ* of the third *rakʿah* he remembers that the *ṣubḥ* prayer of that day had become *qaḍāʾ*, then in case the prime time remaining for him to perform *ẓuhr* prayers is not tight, he should change his intention to *ṣubḥ* prayers and complete his prayer as a two *rakʿah* prayer and then perform *ẓuhr* prayers. However, if the prime time remaining for *ẓuhr* is tight or he cannot change his intention to *qaḍāʾ* prayers – for example, he remembers in the *rukūʿ* of the third *rakʿah* of *ẓuhr* prayers that he has not performed *ṣubḥ* prayers – then, if he were to change his intention to *ṣubḥ* prayers, it would mean that he will have performed an additional *rukūʿ*, which is a *rukn*; therefore, in such a case, he must not change his intention to the *qaḍāʾ* of *ṣubḥ* prayers.

Ruling 1366. If a person has *qaḍāʾ* prayers from the past and one or more prayers of that day have also become *qaḍāʾ*, in the event that he does not have time to make up all of them or he does not want to perform all of them on that day, it is recommended that he make up that day's *qaḍāʾ* prayer before he performs the *adāʾ* prayers.

Ruling 1367. As long as one is alive, another person cannot make up prayers on his behalf, even if he is unable to perform his *qaḍāʾ* prayers himself.

Ruling 1368. *Qaḍāʾ* prayers can be performed in congregation, irrespective of whether the prayer of the imam of the congregation is a *qaḍāʾ* or *adāʾ* prayer; and it is not necessary that both the follower and the imam perform the same prayer. For example, there is no problem if a follower performs *qaḍāʾ ṣubḥ* prayers with the *ẓuhr* or *ʿaṣr* prayers of the imam.

Ruling 1369. It is recommended that a *mumayyiz* child – i.e. a child who is able to discern between right and wrong – be habituated into performing prayers and other ritual acts of worship; in fact, it is recommended that the child be encouraged to perform *qaḍāʾ* prayers as well.

LAPSED (*QAḌĀʾ*) PRAYERS OF A FATHER THAT ARE OBLIGATORY (*WĀJIB*) ON THE ELDEST SON

Ruling 1370.* If one's father is a believer who has not performed his daily and other obligatory prayers – excluding those prayers that had become obligatory at a specific time on account of a vow – and he could have made them up, in the event that he did not fail to perform them due to outright disobedience, then based on obligatory precaution, after the father's death his eldest son must either perform them himself or hire someone to perform them. However, if his father intentionally did not perform them, it is not obligatory for his eldest son to make them up. The *qaḍāʾ* prayers of one's mother are not obligatory for him to perform, although it is better that he does.

Ruling 1371. If the eldest son doubts whether or not his father had any *qaḍāʾ* prayers, it is not obligatory for him to perform them.

Ruling 1372. If the eldest son knows that his father had *qaḍāʾ* prayers but doubts whether or not he performed them, then based on obligatory precaution, it is obligatory for him to perform them.

Ruling 1373. If it is not known who the eldest son is, it is not obligatory for any of the sons to perform their father's *qaḍā'* prayers. However, the recommended precaution is that they should divide the *qaḍā'* prayers between themselves or draw lots (*qurʿah*) for performing them.

Ruling 1374. If a dying person makes a will that someone must be hired to perform his *qaḍā'* prayers, and if his will is valid, it is not obligatory for the eldest son to perform them.

Ruling 1375. If the eldest son wishes to perform the *qaḍā'* prayers of his mother, he must act according to his own duty with regard to reciting Sūrat al-Ḥamd and the other surah aloud or in a whisper. Therefore, he must perform his mother's *qaḍā' ṣubḥ*, *maghrib*, and *ʿishā'* prayers [by reciting Sūrat al-Ḥamd and the other surah] aloud.

Ruling 1376. With regard to someone who has his own *qaḍā'* prayers to perform, if he wants to perform the *qaḍā'* prayers of his father or mother as well, he can perform any of them first.

Ruling 1377. If at the time of his father's death the eldest son was not of the age of legal responsibility (*bāligh*) or he was insane, then when he becomes *bāligh* and/or sane, it is not obligatory for him to perform his father's *qaḍā'* prayers.

Ruling 1378. If the eldest son dies before performing the *qaḍā'* prayers of his father, it is not obligatory for the second son to perform them.

CONGREGATIONAL PRAYERS (*ṢALĀT AL-JAMĀʿAH*)

Ruling 1379. It is recommended to perform the daily prayers in congregation, and it is recommended more to perform *ṣubḥ*, *maghrib*, and *ʿishā'* prayers in congregation, especially for the neighbours of a mosque and for those who can hear the *adhān* of a mosque. Similarly, it is recommended for the other obligatory prayers to be performed in congregation; however, the legality (*mashrūʿiyyah*) of performing in congregation the prayer for *ṭawāf* and *ṣalāt al-āyāt* – except for lunar and solar eclipses – is not established.

Ruling 1380. It has been reported in authentic traditions that a prayer performed in congregation is better than performing it twenty-five times on one's own.

Ruling 1381. Not attending congregational prayers due to indifference about it is not permitted. And it is not befitting for one not to attend congregational prayers without a valid excuse.

Ruling 1382. It is recommended that one delay his prayer to perform it in congregation. A short congregational prayer is better than a long prayer performed on one's own. Furthermore, a congregational prayer is better than a prayer performed on one's own at the start of its prescribed time; however, it is not known whether performing congregational prayer after the prayer's prime time is better than a prayer performed on one's own within its prime time.

Ruling 1383. When congregational prayers are being performed, it is recommended that a person who has performed his prayers on his own perform them again with the congregation. If he later realises that his first prayer was invalid, his second prayer will suffice.

Ruling 1384. If an imam or follower has performed a prayer in congregation and wants to perform it again in congregation, then although this act is not established as being recommended, there is no problem in him doing so with the intention of *rajāʾ*.

Ruling 1385. If a person is so obsessively doubtful (*muwaswis*) in prayers that it invalidates his prayers, and if he becomes free of doubt only when he performs his prayers in congregation, he must perform his prayers in congregation.

Ruling 1386. If a father or a mother commands their child to perform prayers in congregation, the recommended precaution is that he should perform them in congregation. In fact, if his father or mother's command is due to their compassion for him, and if his opposition to it annoys them, it is unlawful for him to oppose.

Ruling 1387.* Recommended prayers cannot be performed in congregation (in some cases, however, this rule is based on obligatory precaution). [There are some exceptions,] however: *ṣalāt al-istisqāʾ*,

which is performed to invoke rain, can be performed in congregation. The same applies [i.e. they too can be performed in congregation] to the prayers that were obligatory and have become recommended due to some reason, such as the Eid al-Fiṭr and Eid al-Aḍḥā prayers that were obligatory when the Imam (ʿA) was present and are recommended during his occultation.

Ruling 1388. When the imam of a congregational prayer is leading a daily prayer, one can follow him for performing any of the daily prayers.

Ruling 1389. One can follow the imam of a congregational prayer who is performing the *qaḍāʾ* of his own or someone else's daily prayer about which he is certain. However, if he is performing such a *qaḍāʾ* prayer as a precautionary measure [as opposed to being certain about it being a *qaḍāʾ* prayer], then it is not permitted to follow him unless the follower is also performing his prayer as a precautionary measure and the reason for his precaution is the same as that of the imam's;[53] and if the follower has another reason for his precaution as well, he can still follow.

Ruling 1390. If a person does not know whether the prayer of the imam is an obligatory daily prayer or a recommended prayer, he cannot follow him.

Ruling 1391. For a congregational prayer to be valid, it is a condition that there is no obstruction between the imam and the follower, nor between the follower and another follower who is the link between him and the imam. The meaning of 'obstruction' here is something that separates them, irrespective of whether it is an obstruction to seeing, such as a curtain, wall, or similar thing, or it is not an obstruction to seeing, such as glass. Therefore, if there is such an obstruction between the imam and the follower during the entire prayer or a part of it, or the follower and another follower who is the link, the congregation becomes invalid. Women are exempted from this rule, as will be mentioned later.

[53] For example, the imam and the follower have deemed it probable that the place where they both performed a previous prayer was usurped, and so they are now performing that prayer again as a precautionary measure.

Ruling 1392. If on account of the first row being long those who are standing at either end of the row do not see the imam, they can still follow. Furthermore, if on account of any of the other rows being long those standing at either end of it do not see the row in front of them, they can also follow.

Ruling 1393. If the rows of a congregation extend to the mosque's door, the prayer of someone standing in front of the door behind the row is valid. Also, the prayer of those who follow behind him is valid. In fact, the prayer of those standing on either side and are linked to the congregation by means of another follower is also valid.

Ruling 1394. If a person who is standing behind a pillar is not linked to the imam by another follower from either the left side or the right, he cannot follow.

Ruling 1395. The place where the imam stands must not be higher than the place of the follower; however, there is no problem if the difference is insignificant. Similarly, if the land slopes and the imam stands at the end that is higher, there is no problem as long as the slope is not big.

Ruling 1396. There is no problem if the place of the follower is higher than the place of the imam; however, if the difference is such that it cannot be said they are joined, then the congregation is not valid.

Ruling 1397. If the link person in the congregation is a *mumayyiz* child – i.e. a child who is able to discern between right and wrong – then, in the event that the people in the congregation do not know his prayer is invalid, they can join with him. The same applies if the link person is not a Twelver (Ithnā ʿAsharī) Shia, in the event that his prayer is valid according to his religious denomination (*madhhab*).

Ruling 1398. If after the imam says *takbīrat al-iḥrām* those standing in the front row are ready to perform the prayer and are close to saying their *takbīrat al-iḥrām*, then someone standing in the next row can say his *takbīrat al-iḥrām*. However, the recommended precaution is that he should wait until those in the front row have completed their *takbīrat al-iḥrām*.

Ruling 1399. If a person knows that one of the front rows of a congregation is invalid, he cannot follow in the other rows. However, if he does not know whether their prayers are invalid, he can follow.

Ruling 1400. If a person knows that the imam's prayer is invalid – for example, he knows that the imam has not performed *wuḍūʾ* even though the imam himself may not be aware of this – he cannot follow.

Ruling 1401. If after prayers a follower realises that the imam was not a dutiful person, or that he was a disbeliever, or for some reason his prayer was invalid – for example, he performed it without *wuḍūʾ* – his prayer is valid.

Ruling 1402. If during prayers one doubts whether or not he joined the imam, in the event that he becomes confident by means of some indications that he joined, he must complete the prayer in congregation; otherwise, he must complete the prayer with the intention of performing it on his own.

Ruling 1403. If during prayers a follower makes the intention to perform the prayer on his own without any legitimate excuse, the validity of his congregational prayer is problematic [i.e. based on obligatory precaution, his congregational prayer is not valid]. However, his prayer [performed on his own, as opposed to his congregational prayer] is valid unless he does not act in accordance with the duty of one who performs prayers on his own, in which case, based on obligatory precaution, he must perform the prayer again. However, if he has added or omitted something, which if he had a legitimate excuse for doing would not invalidate the prayer, then it is not necessary for him to perform the prayer again. For example, if from the outset of the prayer he did not intend to perform it on his own, and he did not recite *qirāʾah*, and during *rukūʿ* he decided to perform the prayer on his own, then he can complete the prayer with the intention of performing the prayer on his own and it is not necessary for him to perform it again. The same applies if he performed an additional *sajdah* with the intention of following the congregation.

Ruling 1404. If after the imam has recited Sūrat al-Ḥamd and the other surah a follower makes the intention to perform the prayer on his own due to a legitimate excuse, it is not necessary that he recite Sūrat al-Ḥamd and the other surah. However, if he does not have a legitimate excuse or he makes the intention of performing the prayer on his own before the completion of Sūrat al-Ḥamd and the other surah, then based on obligatory precaution, it is necessary that he recite all of Sūrat al-Ḥamd and the other surah.

Ruling 1405. If during congregational prayers one makes the intention of performing the prayer on his own, he cannot change it back to congregational prayers. Based on obligatory precaution, the same applies if he becomes unsure about changing his intention to perform the prayer on his own and later decides to complete his prayer in congregation.

Ruling 1406. If during congregational prayers a person doubts whether or not he has made an intention to perform the prayer on his own, he must assume he has not made such an intention.

Ruling 1407. If a person joins congregational prayers when the imam is in *rukūʿ*, then even if the *dhikr* of the imam has finished, his congregational prayer is valid and he is regarded as being in his first *rakʿah*. However, if he bows down to the extent that is required for *rukūʿ* but the imam is no longer in *rukūʿ*, he can either complete his prayer on his own or break his prayer to join in the next *rakʿah*.

Ruling 1408. If a person joins congregational prayers when the imam is in *rukūʿ* and he bows down to the extent that is required for *rukūʿ* but doubts whether or not he joined when the imam was in *rukūʿ*, in the event that his doubt arises after the completion of *rukūʿ*, his congregational prayer is valid; otherwise, he can either complete his prayer on his own or break his prayer to join in the next *rakʿah*.

Ruling 1409. If a person joins congregational prayers when the imam is in *rukūʿ* and before he bows down to the extent that is required for *rukūʿ* the imam raises his head from *rukūʿ*, he has [three] choices: [one,] to complete the prayer on his own; [two,] to follow the imam and proceed to *sajdah* with a general intention of attaining proximity to Allah (*qaṣd al-qurbah al-muṭlaqah*) [i.e. with the intention of attaining proximity to Allah without specifying any particulars about the *sajdah*, such as it being a *sajdah* of the prayer], and when the imam stands [for the next *rakʿah*] he says *takbīr* again with the intention that the *takbīr* is his *takbīrat al-iḥrām* which he has renewed as well as a general *dhikr*, and he then performs the rest of the prayer in congregation; [three,] to break his prayer in order to join the next *rakʿah*.

Ruling 1410. If a person joins a congregational prayer from the beginning or during Sūrat al-Ḥamd and the other surah, and if it so happens that before he goes to *rukūʿ* the imam raises his head from *rukūʿ*, his congregational prayer is valid.

Ruling 1411. If a person arrives when the imam is saying *tashahhud* at the end of the congregational prayer, in the event that he wants to earn the reward of congregational prayers, he must make the intention, say *takbīrat al-iḥrām*, and sit down; and he can say *tashahhud* with the imam with a general intention of attaining proximity to Allah [i.e. with the intention of attaining proximity to Allah without specifying any particulars about the *tashahhud*, such as it being a *tashahhud* of the prayer]. However, based on obligatory precaution, he must not say the *salām*. He must then wait until the imam has said the *salām*, stand up, and without saying *takbīr* or making the intention again, he must recite Sūrat al-Ḥamd and the other surah and count that *rakʿah* as his first.

Ruling 1412. A follower must not stand in front of the imam. In fact, the obligatory precaution is that if there are a number of followers, they must not stand in line with the imam; however, if the follower is only one person, there is no problem if he stands in line with the imam.

Ruling 1413. If the imam is a man and the follower a woman, there is no problem if there is a curtain or something similar between the woman and the imam, or between the woman and another follower who is a man and who is the link between the woman and the imam.

Ruling 1414. If after a congregational prayer has commenced a curtain or something similar intervenes between a follower and the imam, or between a follower and another follower who is the link between him and the imam, then the congregational prayer becomes invalid [for the follower who is separated from the congregation] and it is necessary that the follower act according to the duty of one who performs prayers on his own.

Ruling 1415. The obligatory precaution is that between the place where a follower performs *sajdah* and the imam stands, there must not be a gap of more than a person's largest normal step.[54] The same applies with regard to a follower who is linked to the imam by another follower in front of him. And the recommended precaution is that between the place where a follower stands and the place where another follower stands in front of him, there should not be a gap of more than the space needed for a person to perform *sajdah*.

Ruling 1416. If a follower is linked to the imam by a person on either his right or left side and he is not linked to the imam from the front, then based on obligatory precaution, there must not be a gap of more than a step [as defined in the previous ruling] between himself and the follower on his right or left side.

Ruling 1417. If during congregational prayers a gap of more than one step [as defined in Ruling 1415] occurs between a follower and the imam, or between a follower and a person who is the link between him and the imam, he can continue his prayer with the intention of performing it on his own.

Ruling 1418. If the prayer of all those standing in the first row comes to an end and they do not immediately join the imam for the next prayer, the congregational prayer of those in the next row becomes invalid. In fact, even if they join immediately, the validity of the congregational prayer of those on the next row is problematic [i.e. based on obligatory precaution, it is not valid].

Ruling 1419.* If a person joins in the second *rakʿah*, it is not necessary that he recite Sūrat al-Ḥamd and the other surah; however, it is

[54] In *Tawḍīḥ al-Masāʾil-i Jāmiʿ*, 'a large step' is defined as 'approximately one metre' (vol. 1, p. 484, Ruling 1710).

recommended that he say *qunūt* and *tashahhud* with the imam. And the obligatory precaution is that when he says *tashahhud* he must sit in a squatted position, such that his fingers and the balls of his feet are on the ground and his knees are off the ground; and after *tashahhud*, he must stand up with the imam and recite Sūrat al-Ḥamd and the other surah. If he does not have enough time to recite the other surah, he must complete Sūrat al-Ḥamd and perform his *rukūʿ* with the imam. And if he does not have enough time to recite all of Sūrat al-Ḥamd, he can discontinue reciting it and perform *rukūʿ* with the imam. However, the recommended precaution in this situation is that he should complete his prayer with the intention of performing it on his own.

Ruling 1420. If a person joins the imam when he is in the second *rakʿah* of a four *rakʿah* prayer, then in his second *rakʿah* – which is the third *rakʿah* of the imam – he must sit after the two *sajdah*s, say *tashahhud* to the extent that is obligatory, and then stand up. In the event that he does not have enough time [in his third *rakʿah*] to say *al-tasbīḥāt al-arbaʿah* three times, he must say it once and join the imam in *rukūʿ*.

Ruling 1421. If the imam is in the third or fourth *rakʿah* and a follower knows that if he joins and recites Sūrat al-Ḥamd he will not be able to join the imam in *rukūʿ*, then based on obligatory precaution, he must wait until the imam goes into *rukūʿ* and then join.

Ruling 1422. If a person joins when the imam is in *qiyām* of the third or fourth *rakʿah*, he must recite Sūrat al-Ḥamd and the other surah. If he does not have enough time to recite the other surah, he must complete Sūrat al-Ḥamd and join the imam in *rukūʿ*. If he does not have enough time to recite all of Sūrat al-Ḥamd, he can discontinue reciting Sūrat al-Ḥamd and go into *rukūʿ* with the imam. However, the recommended precaution is that in this situation, he should make the intention of performing the prayer on his own and complete the prayer.

Ruling 1423. With regard to someone who knows that if he completes the other surah or *qunūt* he will not be able to join the imam in *rukūʿ*, in the event that he intentionally recites the other surah or performs *qunūt* and does not join the imam in *rukūʿ*, his congregational prayer becomes invalid and he must act according to the duty of one who performs prayers on his own.

Ruling 1424. With regard to someone who is confident that if he starts reciting the other surah or completes it he will be able to join the imam in *rukūʿ*, in the event that he does not prolong the other surah a lot, it is better that he starts reciting the other surah or completes it if he has started it. However, if he does prolong it a lot, such that it cannot be said he is following the imam, then he must not start it, or if he has started it, he must not complete it; otherwise, his congregational prayer becomes invalid although his prayer [performed on his own] is valid if he acted according to the duty of one who performs prayers on his own, as per the details mentioned in Ruling 1403.

Ruling 1425. With regard to someone who is certain that if he recites the other surah he will be able to join the imam in *rukūʿ* and he will be able to follow the imam, in the event that he recites the other surah but is unable to join the imam in *rukūʿ*, his congregational prayer is valid.

Ruling 1426. If the imam is standing and the follower does not know which *rakʿah* it is, he can join the congregational prayer; and based on obligatory precaution, he must recite Sūrat al-Ḥamd and the other surah; however, he must recite them with the intention of *qurbah*.

Ruling 1427. If a person does not recite Sūrat al-Ḥamd and the other surah thinking that the imam is in the first or second *rakʿah*, and after *rukūʿ* he realises that it was the third or fourth *rakʿah*, his prayer is valid. However, if he realises this before *rukūʿ*, he must recite Sūrat al-Ḥamd and the other surah; and if he does not have enough time, he must act according to Ruling 1422 mentioned earlier.

Ruling 1428. If a person recites Sūrat al-Ḥamd and the other surah thinking that the imam is in the third or fourth *rakʿah*, and before or after *rukūʿ* he realises that it was the first or second *rakʿah*, his prayer is valid. If he realises this during Sūrat al-Ḥamd or the other surah, it is not necessary that he complete them.

Ruling 1429. If while a person is performing a recommended prayer a congregational prayer commences, in the event that he is not confident that if he completes the recommended prayer he will be able to join the congregational prayer, it is recommended that he abandon his prayer and join the congregational prayer even if it is to join it in the first *rakʿah*.

Ruling 1430. If while a person is performing a three *rakʿah* or four *rakʿah* prayer a congregational prayer commences, in the event that the congregational prayer is for the same prayer that the person is performing, and he has not gone into the *rukūʿ* of the third *rakʿah*, and he is not confident that if he completes the prayer he will be able to join the congregational prayer, it is recommended that he complete the prayer as a two *rakʿah* prayer with the intention of a recommended prayer and join the congregational prayer.

Ruling 1431. If the imam's prayer comes to an end and the follower is saying *tashahhud* or the first *salām* of the prayer, it is not necessary that he make the intention of performing the prayer on his own.

Ruling 1432. With regard to someone who is one *rakʿah* behind the imam, it is better that when the imam says *tashahhud* of the last *rakʿah*, he should sit [in a squatted position] such that his fingers and the balls of his feet are on the ground and his knees are off the ground, and he should wait until the imam has said the *salām* of the prayer and then stand up. If at that point he wants to make an intention of performing the prayer on his own, there is no problem.

CONDITIONS OF THE IMAM OF CONGREGATIONAL PRAYERS

Ruling 1433. The imam of congregational prayers must be *bāligh*, sane (*ʿāqil*), a Twelver Shia, dutiful (*ʿādil*), of legitimate birth, and a person who performs prayers correctly. Furthermore, if the follower is a man, the imam must also be a man. The validity of following a ten year old child, although it has some basis, is problematic [i.e. based on obligatory precaution, one must not follow a ten year old child]. Being 'dutiful' means he does the things that are obligatory for him and refrains from doing the things that are unlawful for him. The sign of being dutiful is that he appears to be a good person, [and this is sufficient] as long as one does not have information that contradicts this.

Ruling 1434. With regard to an imam who was considered dutiful, if a person doubts whether he is still dutiful or not, he can follow him.

Ruling 1435. A person who performs prayers standing cannot follow someone who performs prayers sitting or lying down. And a person who performs prayers sitting cannot follow someone who performs prayers lying down.

Ruling 1436. A person who performs prayers sitting can follow someone who performs prayers sitting. However, it is problematic [i.e. based on obligatory precaution, it is not correct] for someone who performs prayers lying down to join congregational prayers, irrespective of whether the imam performs prayers standing, sitting, or lying down.

Ruling 1437. If due to some legitimate excuse an imam of a congregational prayer performs prayers with impure clothes or with *tayammum* or with *jabīrah wuḍūʾ*, it is permitted to follow him.

Ruling 1438. If an imam of a congregational prayer suffers from an illness whereby he cannot control the discharge of urine or faeces [i.e. incontinence], it is permitted to follow him. Furthermore, a woman who is not a *mustaḥāḍah* is permitted to follow a woman who is a *mustaḥāḍah.*

Ruling 1439. It is better that one who suffers from vitiligo or leprosy does not lead congregational prayers. And based on obligatory precaution, someone who has been punished by Islamic penal law and has repented must not be followed.

RULES OF CONGREGATIONAL PRAYERS

Ruling 1440. When a follower makes the intention [for performing a congregational prayer], he must specify the imam [he is following]; however, it is not necessary for him to know his name. If he makes the intention that he is following the imam of the present congregational prayer, his prayer is valid.

Ruling 1441. A follower must say everything in congregational prayers except the recitation of Sūrat al-Ḥamd and the other surah; however, if the first or second *rakʿah* of the follower is the third or fourth *rakʿah* of the imam, then he must recite Sūrat al-Ḥamd and the other surah.

Ruling 1442. If in the first and second *rakʿah* of the *ṣubḥ*, *maghrib*, and *ʿishāʾ* prayers a follower hears Sūrat al-Ḥamd and the other surah, then even though he is unable to distinguish the individual words, he must not recite Sūrat al-Ḥamd and the other surah. However, if he cannot hear the imam's voice, it is recommended that he recite Sūrat al-Ḥamd and the other surah, but he must recite them in a whisper; and in the event that he inadvertently recites them aloud, there is no problem.

Ruling 1443. If a follower hears some of the words of Sūrat al-Ḥamd and the other surah, he can recite the parts that he does not hear.

Ruling 1444. If a follower inadvertently recites Sūrat al-Ḥamd and the other surah, or he thinks that the voice he is hearing is not the voice of the imam and recites Sūrat al-Ḥamd and the other surah, and he later realises that it was the voice of the imam, his prayer is valid.

Ruling 1445. If a person doubts whether or not he is hearing the voice of the imam, or if he hears a voice but does not know if it is the imam's voice or someone else's, he can recite Sūrat al-Ḥamd and the other surah.

Ruling 1446. Based on obligatory precaution, in the first and second *rakʿah* of *ẓuhr* and *ʿaṣr* prayers, a follower must not recite Sūrat al-Ḥamd and the other surah, and it is recommended that he say *dhikr* instead.

Ruling 1447. A follower must not say *takbīrat al-iḥrām* before the imam. In fact, the recommended precaution is that he should not say *takbīrat al-iḥrām* until the imam has completed saying it.

Ruling 1448. If a follower inadvertently says the *salām* of the prayer before the imam, his prayer is valid and it is not necessary that he say the *salām* again along with the imam. In fact, there is no problem even if he intentionally says the *salām* before the imam.

Ruling 1449. Apart from *takbīrat al-iḥrām*, there is no problem if a follower says other parts of the prayer before the imam. However, if he can hear those other parts or knows when the imam will say them, the recommended precaution is that he should not say them before the imam.

Ruling 1450. Except for those things that are recited in prayers, a follower must perform all other acts of the prayer – such as the *rukūʿ*s and *sajdah*s – either with the imam or a little after him. If he intentionally performs them before the imam or delays them after the imam to such an extent that it cannot be said he is following the imam, his congregational prayer is invalid. However, if he acts according to the duty of one who performs the prayer on his own, his prayer is valid as per the details that were mentioned in Ruling 1403.

Ruling 1451. If a follower inadvertently raises his head from *rukūʿ* before the imam, then based on obligatory precaution, in the event that the imam is in *rukūʿ*, he must go back into *rukūʿ* and raise his head with the imam; in this case, performing the additional *rukūʿ*, which is a *rukn*, does not invalidate the prayer. If he intentionally does not go back into *rukūʿ*, then based on obligatory precaution, his congregational prayer becomes invalid, although his prayer [performed on his own] is valid as per the details mentioned in Ruling 1403. However, if he goes back into *rukūʿ* but before he joins the imam in *rukūʿ* the imam raises his head, then based on obligatory precaution, his prayer is invalid.

Ruling 1452. If a follower inadvertently raises his head and sees that the imam is in *sajdah*, then based on obligatory precaution, he must go back into *sajdah*. In the event that this happens in both *sajdah*s, then performing the two additional *sajdah*s, which constitute a *rukn*, does not invalidate the prayer.

Ruling 1453. If someone inadvertently raises his head from *sajdah* before the imam and goes back into *sajdah*, and then he realises that the imam had raised his head before he went into *sajdah*, his prayer is valid. However, if this happens in both *sajdah*s, then based on obligatory precaution, his prayer is invalid.

Ruling 1454. If a person mistakenly raises his head from *rukūʿ* or *sajdah* and inadvertently or thinking that he will not be able to join the imam does not go back into *rukūʿ* or *sajdah*, his congregational prayer is valid.

Ruling 1455. If a person raises his head from *sajdah* and sees that the imam is in *sajdah*, in the event that he thinks it is the imam's first *sajdah* and he goes into *sajdah* with the intention of performing it with the imam, but then he realises that actually it was the imam's second *sajdah*, in such a case, it will be counted as his second *sajdah*. If he thinks it is the imam's second *sajdah* and he goes into *sajdah*, but then he realises that actually it was the imam's first *sajdah*, in this case, he must complete the *sajdah* with the intention of performing it with the imam and then go into *sajdah* again with the imam. In each case, it is better that he complete the prayer in congregation and perform it again.

Ruling 1456. If a person inadvertently goes into *rukūʿ* before the imam, in the event that after saying the obligatory *dhikr* of *rukūʿ* he can go back and join part of the imam's *rukūʿ*, he must say the *dhikr* and then, based on obligatory precaution, he must go back into *rukūʿ*. And the recommended precaution is that he say *dhikr* in the second *rukūʿ* as well. If he intentionally does not go back into *rukūʿ*, the validity of his congregational prayer is problematic [i.e. based on obligatory precaution, it is not valid]. However, his prayer [performed on his own] is valid as per the details mentioned in Ruling 1403. If he cannot go back to say the obligatory *dhikr* and join the *rukūʿ* of the imam, he must say the *dhikr* and then go into *sajdah* with the imam; if he does this, his congregational prayer is valid.

Ruling 1457. If a person inadvertently goes into *sajdah* before the imam, in the event that after saying the obligatory *dhikr* of *sajdah* he can go back and perform the *sajdah* with the imam, then based on obligatory precaution, he must say the *dhikr* and then go back. And the recommended precaution is that he should say the *dhikr* in the second *sajdah* which he performed to follow the imam. If he intentionally does not go back, the validity of his congregational prayer is problematic [i.e. based on obligatory precaution, it is not valid]. However, his [individual] prayer is valid as per the details mentioned in Ruling 1403. If he cannot go back to say the obligatory *dhikr* and join the imam in *sajdah*, he must say the *dhikr* and then continue with the imam; if he does this, his congregational prayer is valid.

Ruling 1458. If the imam mistakenly performs *qunūt* in a *rakʿah* that does not have *qunūt*, or if he mistakenly starts saying *tashahhud* in a *rakʿah* that does not have *tashahhud*, then the follower must not perform *qunūt* or say *tashahhud*. However, he cannot go into *rukūʿ* before the imam or stand up before the imam; rather, he must wait until the *qunūt* and *tashahhud* of the imam finish and then complete the rest of the prayer with him.

DUTIES OF THE IMAM AND THE FOLLOWER IN CONGREGATIONAL PRAYERS

Ruling 1459.* If the follower is a man, it is recommended that he stand at the right-hand side of the imam. If the follower is a woman, it is recommended that she also stand on the right-hand side of the imam, but based on obligatory precaution, she must stand behind him at least to the extent that the place of her *sajdah* is in line with the place of his knees when he goes into *sajdah*. If the imam is a man and the follower is a woman, or if the followers are a man and some women, it is recommended that the man stand on the right-hand side of the imam and the woman or women stand behind the imam. If the followers are some men and one woman or some women, it is recommended that the men stand behind the imam and the women stand behind the men.

Ruling 1460. If both the imam and the followers are women, the obligatory precaution is that they must all stand in one line, and the imam must not stand in front of the others.

Ruling 1461. It is recommended that the imam stand in the middle of the line and that learned, virtuous, and God-wary people stand in the first row.

Ruling 1462. It is recommended that the rows of the congregation be orderly, that there be no gaps between the persons standing in one row, and that their shoulders be in line with one another.

Ruling 1463. It is recommended that a follower stand up [for the prayer] after '*qad qāmatiṣ ṣalāh*' [of *iqāmah*] has been said.

Ruling 1464. It is recommended that the imam of congregational prayers take into account the condition of the followers who are weaker than others, and not prolong *qunūt*, *rukūʿ*, and *sujūd* unless he knows that all the persons following him prefer him to do so.

Ruling 1465. When reciting Sūrat al-Ḥamd and the other surah, and when saying the *dhikr*s that are said aloud, it is recommended that the imam of congregational prayers raise his voice to the extent that others can hear him; however, he must not raise it more than what is considered to be a normal voice.

Ruling 1466. If while performing *rukūʿ* the imam realises that a person has just arrived and wants to join, it is recommended that he prolong the *rukūʿ* twice as much as normal and then stand up, even if he realises that another person has also arrived and wants to join.

THINGS THAT ARE DISAPPROVED (*MAKRŪH*) IN CONGREGATIONAL PRAYERS

Ruling 1467. If there is space in the rows of congregational prayers, it is disapproved for a person to stand alone.

Ruling 1468. It is disapproved for a follower to say the *dhikr* of prayers in a way that the imam hears it.

Ruling 1469. It is disapproved for a traveller who performs *ẓuhr*, *ʿaṣr*, and *ʿishāʾ* as two *rakʿah* prayers to follow in these prayers someone who is not a traveller. Similarly, it is disapproved for someone who is not a traveller to follow in these prayers someone who is a traveller.

THE PRAYER OF SIGNS (*ṢALĀT AL-ĀYĀT*)

Ruling 1470. *Ṣalāt al-āyāt*, for which the method of performance will be explained later, becomes obligatory when the following three phenomena occur:

1. solar eclipse;
2. lunar eclipse;

and with the occurrence of these two phenomena, *ṣalāt al-āyāt* becomes obligatory even if the eclipse is partial and one is not frightened by it;

3. earthquake, based on obligatory precaution, even if one is not frightened by it.

Based on recommended precaution, *ṣalāt al-āyāt* should be performed when thunder and lightning, gales that make the sky look black or red, and other similar natural celestial phenomena occur, provided that most people are frightened by them. Similarly, [the prayer should be performed] when natural terrestrial phenomena occur that cause most people to fear, such as sinkholes and rock-slides.

Ruling 1471. If more than one phenomenon that makes it obligatory to perform *ṣalāt al-āyāt* occurs, one must perform *ṣalāt al-āyāt* for each one of them. For example, if there is a solar eclipse and an earthquake, one must perform two *ṣalāt al-āyāt*s.

Ruling 1472. If it is obligatory for someone to perform a number of *qaḍāʾ ṣalāt al-āyāt*s, whether they have become obligatory due to the same phenomenon – for example, there were three solar eclipses for which he did not perform *ṣalāt al-āyāt* – or they have become obligatory due to different phenomena – for example, a solar eclipse, a lunar eclipse, and an earthquake – then, when one makes them up, it is not necessary for him to specify the phenomenon for which he is performing the prayer.

Ruling 1473. When a phenomenon occurs for which *ṣalāt al-āyāt* is obligatory, only the people of the area in which the phenomenon occurred must perform *ṣalāt al-āyāt*. It is not obligatory for people in other areas.

Ruling 1474. The time for performing *ṣalāt al-āyāt* for a solar or lunar eclipse commences from the moment the eclipse begins, and it continues until the sun or the moon goes back to its normal state (although it is better not to delay the prayer until the eclipse starts to reverse). However, completing *ṣalāt al-āyāt* can be delayed until after the eclipse is over.[55]

Ruling 1475. If a person delays performing *ṣalāt al-āyāt* until the eclipse begins to reverse, there is no problem if he performs it with the intention of *adāʾ*. However, once the eclipse is over, the prayer becomes *qaḍāʾ*.

Ruling 1476. If an eclipse lasts long enough for one *rakʿah* or less to be performed, one must perform the prayer with the intention of *adāʾ*. The same applies if the eclipse lasts for a longer time. If one does not perform the prayer until the time remaining is enough to perform only one *rakʿah* or less, *ṣalāt al-āyāt* must still be performed with the intention of *adāʾ*.

Ruling 1477. When thunder, lightning, and other similar natural phenomena occur, if one wants to [perform *ṣalāt al-āyāt*] as a precautionary measure, and if these phenomena last a long time, it is not necessary for him to perform the prayer immediately. In other

[55] This means that although a person must start performing *ṣalāt al-āyāt* during the eclipse, he can continue performing it while the eclipse continues and does not need to finish it before the eclipse is over.

cases, such as an earthquake, one must perform it immediately in a way that people would not consider it delayed. If he does delay it, the recommended precaution is that he should perform it later without making an intention of *adāʾ* or *qaḍāʾ*.

Ruling 1478. If a person does not know about the occurrence of an eclipse and after the eclipse is over he realises that there was a total eclipse, he must make up the *ṣalāt al-āyāt*. However, if he realises that it was a partial eclipse, then making it up is not obligatory for him.

Ruling 1479. If a group of people say that an eclipse has occurred, in the event that one does not personally attain certainty or confidence [that an eclipse has occurred] and does not perform *ṣalāt al-āyāt*, and later he realises that they were right, then in case it was a total eclipse, he must perform *ṣalāt al-āyāt*. However, if it was a partial eclipse, it is not obligatory for him to perform *ṣalāt al-āyāt*. The same applies if two people about whom one does not know whether they are dutiful or not say that an eclipse has occurred, and later he realises that they were dutiful.

Ruling 1480. If a person attains confidence that an eclipse has occurred based on the statement of persons who know the time of eclipses by means of scientific principles, he must perform *ṣalāt al-āyāt*. Furthermore, if they say the eclipse will take place at such and such time and that it will last for such and such duration, and one attains confidence in what they say, he must act according to what they say.

Ruling 1481. If a person realises that the *ṣalāt al-āyāt* he performed for a solar or lunar eclipse was invalid, he must perform it again; and if the time for it has passed, he must make it up.

Ruling 1482. If *ṣalāt al-āyāt* becomes obligatory for someone during the time of a daily prayer, in the event that there is enough time for him to perform both of them, it is not a problem whichever one he performs first. However, if the time for performing one of them is short, he must perform that one first; and if the time for both of them is short, he must perform the daily prayer first.

Ruling 1483. If while performing the daily prayer one realises that the time for performing *ṣalāt al-āyāt* is short, in the event that the time for performing the daily prayer is also short, he must complete it and then perform *ṣalāt al-āyāt*. If the time for the daily prayer is not short, he must break his prayer and first perform *ṣalāt al-āyāt* and then perform the daily prayer.

Ruling 1484. If while performing *ṣalāt al-āyāt* one realises that the time for performing the daily prayer is short, he must leave the *ṣalāt al-āyāt* unfinished and without doing anything that invalidates prayers, he must start performing the daily prayer. After completing the prayer but before doing something that invalidates prayers, he must continue performing the rest of *ṣalāt al-āyāt* from the point he left it.

Ruling 1485. If a woman is in the state of *ḥayḍ* or *nifās* and an eclipse or earthquake occurs, it is not obligatory for her to perform *ṣalāt al-āyāt*, nor does she have to make it up.

METHOD OF PERFORMING *ṢALĀT AL-ĀYĀT*

Ruling 1486. *Ṣalāt al-āyāt* consists of two *rakʿah*s, and in each *rakʿah* there are five *rukūʿ*s. The method of performing the prayer is as follows: after one has made the intention [of performing the prayer], he says *takbīr*, recites one Sūrat al-Ḥamd and one other complete surah, goes into *rukūʿ*, and raises his head from *rukūʿ*; then, he again recites one Sūrat al-Ḥamd and one other complete surah, goes into *rukūʿ* again, and so on until he has done this a total of five times. After getting up from the fifth *rukūʿ*, he performs two *sajdah*s, stands up, and proceeds to perform the second *rakʿah* in the same way as the first; he then says *tashahhud* and the *salām* of the prayer.

Ruling 1487. [A shorter method of performing *ṣalāt al-āyāt* is as follows:] after one has made the intention [of performing the prayer], he says *takbīr* and recites Sūrat al-Ḥamd; then, he divides the verses of the other surah into five parts and recites one verse or more, or even less, provided that – based on obligatory precaution – it is a complete sentence. He must start from the beginning of the surah and must not suffice with reciting *bismillāh* [on its own and count that as one verse]. Then, he goes into *rukūʿ*, raises his head, and without reciting Sūrat al-Ḥamd he recites the second part of the other surah. He then goes into *rukūʿ* again, and so on until he completes the other surah before he goes into the fifth *rukūʿ*. For example, if the other surah is Sūrat al-Falaq,[56] he first says:

﴿بِسْمِ اللّٰهِ الرَّحْمٰنِ الرَّحِيْمِ ۞ قُلْ أَعُوْذُ بِرَبِّ الْفَلَقِ﴾

bismil lāhir raḥmānir raḥīm. qul aʿūdhu birabbil falaq

In the Name of Allah, the All-Beneficent, the Ever-Merciful. Say, 'I seek refuge in the Lord of the daybreak,

...and goes into *rukūʿ* [for the first time]; he then stands up and says:

﴿مِنْ شَرِّ مَا خَلَقَ﴾

min sharri mā khalaq

from the evil of what He created,

...and goes into *rukūʿ* again [for the second time]; he then stands up and says:

﴿وَمِنْ شَرِّ غَاسِقٍ إِذَا وَقَبَ﴾

wa min sharri ghāsiqin idhā waqab

and from the evil of the darkness of night when it settles,

...and goes into *rukūʿ* again [for the third time]; he then stands up and says:

﴿وَمِنْ شَرِّ النَّفَّاثَاتِ فِي الْعُقَدِ﴾

wa min sharrin naffāthāti fil ʿuqad

and from the evil of those who blow on knots,

...and goes into *rukūʿ* again [for the fourth time]; he then stands up and says:

[56] Chapter 113 of the Qur'an.

﴿وَمِنْ شَرِّ حَاسِدٍ إِذَا حَسَدَ﴾

wa min sharri ḥāsidin idhā ḥasad

and from the evil of an envier when he envies.'

...and goes into *rukū'* for the fifth time. He then stands up, performs two *sajdahs*, and proceeds to perform the second *rak'ah* in the same way as the first. After the second *sajdah* [of the second *rak'ah*], he says *tashahhud* and the *salām* of the prayer. It is permitted for one to divide the surah into less than five parts, but whenever he completes the surah, it is necessary that he recite Sūrat al-Ḥamd before performing the next *rukū'*.

Ruling 1488. There is no problem if a person recites Sūrat al-Ḥamd and the other surah five times in one *rak'ah* of *ṣalāt al-āyāt*, and in the other *rak'ah* he recites one Sūrat al-Ḥamd and divides the other surah into five parts.

Ruling 1489.* Those things that are obligatory and recommended in the daily prayers are also obligatory and recommended in *ṣalāt al-āyāt*. However, *adhān* and *iqāmah* are not said for *ṣalāt al-āyāt*, and if the prayer is performed in congregation, it is better one say '*aṣṣalāh*' three times with the intention of *rajā'* instead of *adhān* and *iqāmah*; this does not apply if the prayer is not performed in congregation. The legality of performing *ṣalāt al-āyāt* in congregation for phenomena other than solar and lunar eclipses is not established [i.e. it must not be performed in congregation for other than these phenomena].

Ruling 1490. It is recommended that one say *takbīr* before and after *rukū'*, but saying *takbīr* after the fifth and the tenth *rukū'* is not recommended; instead, it is recommended that one say '*sami'al lāhu liman ḥamidah*'.

Ruling 1491. It is recommended that one perform *qunūt* before the second, fourth, sixth, eighth, and tenth *rukū'*; and if one performs *qunūt* before only the tenth *rukū'*, it is sufficient.

Ruling 1492. If in *ṣalāt al-āyāt* one doubts how many *rak'ahs* he has performed, and having thought about it he does not find an answer, his prayer is invalid.

Ruling 1493. If a person doubts whether he is in the last *rukūʿ* of the first *rakʿah* or the first *rukūʿ* of the second *rakʿah*, and having thought about it he does not find an answer, his prayer is invalid. However, if, for example, he doubts whether he has performed four or five *rukūʿ*s, in the event that his doubt arises before he bends down for *sajdah*, he must perform the *rukūʿ* about which he doubts. However, if he has already bent down for *sajdah*, he must dismiss his doubt.

Ruling 1494. Every *rukūʿ* of *ṣalāt al-āyāt* is a *rukn*; therefore, if a *rukūʿ* is intentionally omitted or added, the prayer is invalid. The same applies if a *rukūʿ* is mistakenly omitted or, based on obligatory precaution, if it is mistakenly added.

THE EID AL-FIṬR[57] & EID AL-AḌḤĀ PRAYERS[58]

Ruling 1495. The Eid al-Fiṭr and Eid al-Aḍḥā prayer is obligatory during the presence of the Imam (ʿA) and must be performed in congregation. In our time, when the Imam (ʿA) is in occultation, the prayer is recommended and it can be performed in congregation or on one's own.

Ruling 1496. The time for the Eid al-Fiṭr and Eid al-Aḍḥā prayer is from the start of sunrise to the time of *ẓuhr* prayers on the day of Eid.

Ruling 1497. It is recommended that one perform the Eid al-Aḍḥā prayer after the sun has risen. After the sun has risen on the day of Eid al-Fiṭr, it is recommended that one eat something, pay the *fiṭrah* alms tax (*zakāt al-fiṭrah*),[59] and then perform Eid prayers.

Ruling 1498.* The Eid al-Fiṭr and Eid al-Aḍḥā prayer consists of two *rakʿah*s and is performed as follows: after saying *takbīrat al-iḥrām* at the start of the prayer and reciting Sūrat al-Ḥamd and the other surah in each *rakʿah*, one must say a number of *takbīr*s and perform a *qunūt* between each *takbīr*. Based on obligatory precaution, the number of *takbīr*s and *qunūt*s in each *rakʿah* is three *takbīr*s and two *qunūt*s. After

[57] The 1st of Shawwāl. [58] The 10th of Dhū al-Ḥijjah.

[59] The laws relating to this tax are stated in Ruling 2003 and onwards.

the third *takbīr*, based on obligatory precaution, one must say another *takbīr* before going into *rukūʿ*. Therefore, there will be a total of four *takbīr*s in each *rakʿah*. However, it is better that in the first *rakʿah* one says five *takbīr*s with four *qunūt*s between them, and in the second *rakʿah* four *takbīr*s and three *qunūt*s between them. Here also, based on obligatory precaution, one must perform another *takbīr* before going into *rukūʿ*. The rest of the prayer must then be performed in the same way one would perform other two *rakʿah* prayers, i.e. with two *sajdah*s, *tashahhud*, and *salām*.[60]

Ruling 1499. In the *qunūt* of the Eid al-Fiṭr and Eid al-Aḍḥā prayer, it is sufficient for one to recite any *duʿāʾ* or say any *dhikr*. However, it is better that one recites this *duʿāʾ*:

اَللّٰهُمَّ أَهْلَ الْكِبْرِيَاءِ وَالْعَظَمَةِ، وَأَهْلَ الْجُوْدِ وَالْجَبَرُوْتِ، وَأَهْلَ الْعَفْوِ وَالرَّحْمَةِ،
وَأَهْلَ التَّقْوَىٰ وَالْمَغْفِرَةِ، أَسْأَلُكَ بِحَقِّ هٰذَا الْيَوْمِ، الَّذِيْ جَعَلْتَهُ لِلْمُسْلِمِيْنَ
عِيْدًا، وَلِمُحَمَّدٍ صَلَّى اللّٰهُ عَلَيْهِ وَآلِهِ وَسَلَّمَ، ذُخْرًا وَشَرَفًا وَكَرَامَةً وَمَزِيْدًا، أَنْ
تُصَلِّيَ عَلَىٰ مُحَمَّدٍ وَآلِ مُحَمَّدٍ، وَأَنْ تُدْخِلَنِيْ فِيْ كُلِّ خَيْرٍ أَدْخَلْتَ فِيْهِ مُحَمَّدًا
وَآلَ مُحَمَّدٍ، وَأَنْ تُخْرِجَنِيْ مِنْ كُلِّ سُوْءٍ أَخْرَجْتَ مِنْهُ مُحَمَّدًا وَآلَ مُحَمَّدٍ
صَلَوَاتُكَ عَلَيْهِ وَعَلَيْهِمْ، اَللّٰهُمَّ إِنِّيْ أَسْأَلُكَ خَيْرَ مَا سَأَلَكَ بِهِ عِبَادُكَ الصَّالِحُوْنَ،
وَأَعُوْذُ بِكَ مِمَّا اسْتَعَاذَ مِنْهُ عِبَادُكَ الْمُخْلَصُوْنَ

allāhumma ahlal kibriyāʾi wal aẓamah, wa ahlal jūdi wal jabarūt, wa ahlal ʿafwi war raḥmah, wa ahlat taqwā wal maghfirah, asʾaluka biḥaqqi hādhal yawm, alladhī jaʿaltahu lilmuslimīna ʿīdā, wa limuḥammadin ṣallallāhu

[60] Compared with the previous edition of *Islamic Laws*, only the wording has changed in this ruling, not the actual method of performing Eid Prayers. According to the majority of the *marājiʿ*, five *qunūt*s are performed in the first *rakʿah* and four *qunūt*s are performed in the second *rakʿah*. According to al-Sayyid al-Sistani, however, four *qunūt*s are performed in the first *rakʿah* and three *qunūt*s are performed in the second *rakʿah*. He also says that based on obligatory precaution, one must say another *takbīr* before going into *rukūʿ* in each *rakʿah*.

His Eminence also allows a shorter method in which only three *takbīr*s are said in each *rakʿah* with two *qunūt*s between the *takbīr*s, but he says the method with the four and three *qunūt*s in each *rakʿah* is better.

ʿalayhi wa ālihi wa sallam, dhukhran wa sharafan wa karāmatan wa mazīdā, an tuṣalliya ʿalā muḥammadin wa āli muḥammad, wa an tudkhilanī fī kulli khayrin adkhalta fīhi muḥammadan wa āla muḥammad, wa an tukhrijanī min kulli sū'in akhrajta minhu muḥammadan wa āla muḥammad, ṣalawātuka ʿalayhi wa ʿalayhim, allāhumma innī as'aluka khayra mā sa'alaka bihi ʿibādukaṣ ṣāliḥūn, wa aʿūdhu bika mimmas taʿādha minhu ʿibādukal mukhlaṣūn

O Allah! Worthy of supremacy and greatness, and worthy of magnanimity and omnipotence, and worthy of pardoning and showing mercy, and worthy of being wary of and forgiving: I beseech You by the right of this day – which You have appointed to be an Eid for the Muslims, and to be for Muḥammad, may Allah shower His blessings upon, and extend His salutations to, him and his progeny, [a source for] accumulating [Your blessings], and [a source of] honour, nobility, and increase [in Your blessings] – that You bless Muḥammad and the progeny of Muḥammad, and that You place me in every goodness in which You placed Muḥammad and the progeny of Muḥammad, and that You remove me from every evil from which You removed Muḥammad and the progeny of Muḥammad, may Your blessings be upon him and upon them. O Allah! I indeed beseech You for the good for which Your righteous servants have beseeched You, and I seek protection in You from all that for which Your purified servants have sought Your protection.

Ruling 1500.* During the period of occultation of the Imam (ʿA), if the Eid al-Fiṭr and Eid al-Aḍḥā prayer is performed in congregation, the obligatory precaution is that two sermons must be delivered after the prayer, and the imam must sit down a little between them. It is better that in the sermon of Eid al-Fiṭr the laws of zakat of *fiṭr* be mentioned, and in the sermon of Eid al-Aḍḥā the laws of sacrificing animals be mentioned.

Ruling 1501. The Eid prayer does not have a specified surah [to be recited], but it is better that in the first *rakʿah* Sūrat al-Shams (the ninety-first chapter) be recited, and in the second *rakʿah* Sūrat al-Ghāshiyah (the eighty-eighth chapter) be recited; or, in the first *rakʿah* Sūrat al-Aʿlā (the eighty-seventh chapter) be recited, and in the second *rakʿah* Sūrat al-Shams be recited.

Ruling 1502. It is recommended that Eid prayers be performed in the desert [or in open fields, etc.]. However, in Mecca, it is recommended that they be performed in Masjid al-Ḥarām.

Ruling 1503. It is recommended to walk barefooted and in a dignified manner to Eid prayers, perform ghusl before the prayer, and place a white turban (ʿamāmah) on one's head.

Ruling 1504. It is recommended in Eid prayers to perform *sajdah* on earth, raise one's hands when saying the *takbīr*s, and recite Sūrat al-Ḥamd and the other surah aloud, whether one is the imam of the congregation or performing the prayer on his own.

Ruling 1505. After *maghrib* and *ʿishāʾ* prayers on the eve of Eid al-Fiṭr, and after *ṣubḥ* prayers, and after the Eid al-Fiṭr prayer, it is recommended that one say these *takbīr*s:

اَللّٰهُ أَكْبَرُ، اَللّٰهُ أَكْبَرُ، لَا إِلٰهَ إِلَّا اللّٰهُ وَاللّٰهُ أَكْبَرُ، اَللّٰهُ أَكْبَرُ وَلِلّٰهِ الْحَمْدُ، اَللّٰهُ أَكْبَرُ عَلَىٰ مَا هَدَانَا

allāhu akbar, allāhu akbar, lā ilāha illal lāhu wal lāhu akbar, allāhu akbar wa lillāhil ḥamd, allāhu akbaru ʿalā mā hadānā

Allah is greater;[61] Allah is greater; there is no god but Allah and Allah is greater; Allah is greater and all praise is for Allah; Allah is greater for having guided us.

Ruling 1506. It is recommended that on Eid al-Aḍḥā after ten [consecutive] prayers – the first of which being the *ẓuhr* prayer on the day of Eid and the last being the *ṣubḥ* prayer on the twelfth day [of Dhū al-Ḥijjah] – a person say the *takbīr*s that were mentioned in the previous ruling, and that after each one he says:

اَللّٰهُ أَكْبَرُ عَلَىٰ مَا رَزَقَنَا مِنْ بَهِيْمَةِ الْأَنْعَامِ، وَالْحَمْدُ لِلّٰهِ عَلَىٰ مَا أَبْلَانَا

allāhu akbaru ʿalā mā razaqanā min bahīmatil anʿām, wal ḥamdu lillāhi ʿalā mā ablānā

---

[61] As mentioned in the section on *adhān*, the complete meaning of this statement is 'Allah is greater than what He is described as'.

Allah is greater for having sustained us with [the produce of] cattle livestock, and all praise is for Allah for having tested us.

However, if one is in Mina on Eid al-Aḍḥā, it is recommended that one say these *takbīrs* after fifteen [consecutive] prayers, the first of which being the *ẓuhr* prayer on the day of Eid and the last being the *ṣubḥ* prayer on the thirteenth day of Dhū al-Ḥijjah.

Ruling 1507. The recommended precaution is that women should avoid going to Eid prayers; however, this precaution does not apply to elderly women.

Ruling 1508. In Eid prayers, just like in other prayers, the follower must say everything except the recitation of Sūrat al-Ḥamd and the other surah.

Ruling 1509. If a follower joins [the Eid prayer] when the imam has already said some of the *takbīrs*, then after the imam goes into *rukūʿ*, he must say all the *takbīrs* and perform all the *qunūts* that he missed and then perform *rukūʿ*. It is sufficient if in every *qunūt* he says '*subḥānal lāhi wal ḥamdu lillāh*'. If there is not enough time, he must only say the *takbīrs*; and if there is not enough time to perform the *takbīrs*, it is sufficient if he follows the imam and goes into *rukūʿ*.

Ruling 1510. If a person joins the Eid prayer when the imam is in *rukūʿ*, he can make the intention [of performing the prayer] and say the first *takbīr* of the prayer and then go into *rukūʿ*.

Ruling 1511. If a person forgets a *sajdah* in the Eid prayer, it is necessary that he perform it after the prayer. Similarly, if something happens [in the Eid prayer] that would necessitate *sajdatā al-sahw* to be performed were it to happen in a daily prayer, then it is necessary to perform *sajdatā al-sahw* for it.

HIRING SOMEONE TO PERFORM PRAYERS[62]

Ruling 1512. After someone has died, a person can be hired – i.e. he can be paid – to perform the prayers and other ritual acts of worship that the deceased did not perform during his lifetime. If someone performs them without getting paid, this is also valid.

Ruling 1513. A person can be hired to perform certain recommended acts – such as hajj, *ʿumrah*, and *ziyārah* of the graves of the Most Noble Messenger (Ṣ) and the Infallible Imams (ʿA) – on behalf of someone else. A person can also be hired to perform recommended acts and dedicate their reward to living or deceased persons.

Ruling 1514. A person who is hired to perform the *qaḍāʾ* prayers of a deceased person must either be a *mujtahid*,[63] or he must perform prayers according to the fatwa of someone whom it is valid to follow [i.e. do *taqlīd* of],[64] or he must act on precaution if he knows fully the situations in which one can exercise precaution.

Ruling 1515. A person who is hired must specify the deceased at the time of making the intention, but it is not necessary that he know his name. Therefore, if he makes the intention that 'I am performing prayers on behalf of the person I am hired for', it is sufficient.

Ruling 1516. A person who is hired must perform the act with the intention of discharging the obligation that is on the deceased. Therefore, it is not sufficient if he simply performs an act and dedicates its reward to him.

Ruling 1517. A person who hires someone must be confident that he will perform the act; and he must deem it probable that he will perform it correctly.

[62] The laws stated in this section are sometimes discussed under the heading '*niyābah*', i.e. doing something on behalf of someone else.

[63] A *mujtahid* is a person who has attained the level of *ijtihād*, qualifying him to be an authority in Islamic law. *Ijtihād* is the process of deriving Islamic laws from authentic sources.

[64] The laws of *taqlīd* are mentioned in the first chapter of the present work.

Ruling 1518. If someone realises that the person he hired to perform the prayers of a deceased person has not performed them, or that he has performed them incorrectly, he must hire someone again.

Ruling 1519. If someone doubts whether or not the hired person has performed the act – even if the hired person says, 'I have performed it' but he is not confident in the statement being true – then based on obligatory precaution, he must hire someone again. However, if he doubts whether or not he performed the act correctly, he can assume it was performed correctly.

Ruling 1520. Based on obligatory precaution, a person who has a legitimate excuse [for performing prayers in a certain way] – for example, he performs prayers with *tayammum* or in a sitting position – cannot be hired in any case to perform the prayers of a deceased person, even if the prayers of the deceased became *qaḍāʾ* in the same way. However, hiring someone who performs prayers with *jabīrah wuḍūʾ* or with *jabīrah ghusl* is not a problem. The same applies to hiring someone whose hands or feet have been amputated, although to suffice with the acts he performs on behalf of the person is problematic [i.e. based on obligatory precaution, one must not suffice with the acts he performs].

Ruling 1521. A man can be hired for a woman and a woman for a man. As for performing prayers aloud or in a whisper, the hired person must act according to his or her own duty.[65]

Ruling 1522. It is not necessary to perform the *qaḍāʾ* prayers of a deceased person in the order they became *qaḍāʾ* except for the prayers that must be performed in a particular order when they are performed within their prescribed time, such as *ẓuhr* and *ʿaṣr* prayers, and *maghrib* and *ʿishāʾ* prayers, of the same day, as was mentioned previously. However, if someone is hired to act according to the fatwa of the deceased's *marjaʿ*[66] or according to the *marjaʿ* of the deceased's

[65] Therefore, if, for example, a man has been hired to perform the *qaḍāʾ ṣubḥ* prayers of a deceased woman, he must recite Sūrat al-Ḥamd and the other surah aloud. See Ruling 978.

[66] That is, a jurist who has the necessary qualifications to be followed in matters of Islamic jurisprudence.

guardian (*walī*),[67] and that *marja*ʿ considers it necessary to observe the order, then one must observe the order.

Ruling 1523. If someone makes a condition with the hired person to perform an act in a particular manner, the hired person must do so unless he is certain that the particular manner will invalidate the act. If such a condition is not made with him, he must perform the act according to his own duty. And the recommended precaution is that if there is a difference between his duty and that of the deceased's, he should act according to the duty that is more precautionary; for example, if the duty of the deceased was to say *al-tasbīḥāt al-arbaʿah* three times and his duty is to say it once, then he should say it three times.

Ruling 1524. If a condition has not been made with a hired person as to how many recommended acts must be performed, he must perform prayers with a normal amount of recommended acts.

Ruling 1525. If someone hires a number of people to perform the *qaḍāʾ* prayers of a deceased person, then, as per Ruling 1522, it is not necessary to specify a time for each of them.

Ruling 1526. If a person is hired to, for example, perform the prayers of a deceased person within the period of one year, and if he dies before the end of one year, then another person must be hired to perform the prayers that are known not to have been performed [by the previous hired person]. If it is deemed probable that the hired person did not perform them, another person must still be hired based on obligatory precaution.

Ruling 1527. If someone who is hired to perform the prayers of a deceased person dies before completing the prayers, and if he had taken wages for all of them, in the event that it was a condition that he would perform all the prayers himself, the person who hired him can take back the wages, based on the agreed rate (*al-ujrah al-musammāh*), for the prayers that were not performed. Alternatively, he can annul

[67] This scenario could arise when, for example, the *walī* is the eldest son of the deceased, and it is obligatory on him to perform the *qaḍāʾ* prayers of his late father, and he hires someone to perform them. See Ruling 1370.

(*faskh*) the contract and [for the prayers that were not performed,] he can take back the wages based on the standard rate (*ujrat al-mithl*) for performing such prayers. However, if it was not a condition that he would perform the prayers himself, then his heirs must hire someone from his estate; and if he does not have an estate, then nothing is obligatory for his heirs.

Ruling 1528. If someone who is hired dies before performing all the *qaḍāʾ* prayers of the deceased, and if he has *qaḍāʾ* prayers of his own, then, after acting according to the instructions mentioned in the previous ruling, if anything is left over from his estate, and if he has made a will and his heirs give their consent, then someone must be hired to perform all his prayers. However, if the heirs do not give their consent, then the one-third of his estate[68] must be used for [hiring someone to offer] his prayers.

[68] This refers to the maximum amount of one's estate over which he has discretion in a will for it to be disposed of in accordance with his wishes after his death.

CHAPTER FOUR

Fasting (*Ṣawm*)

'Fasting' means that one abstains from eight things – which will be mentioned later – from the start of the time of morning (*ṣubḥ*) prayers[1] until the time of *maghrib*,[2] in humility and obedience to the Lord of the worlds.

INTENTION (*NIYYAH*)

Ruling 1529. It is not necessary for one to make an intention in his heart to fast, or to say, for example, 'I will fast tomorrow'; rather, it is sufficient for one to decide that in humility to the Lord of the worlds, from the start of the time of *ṣubḥ* prayers until the time of *maghrib* prayers, he will not do anything that invalidates a fast. To be certain [i.e. have *yaqīn*] that one has fasted throughout this time, he must begin abstaining from a short period before the time of *ṣubḥ* prayers, and he must also refrain from doing anything that invalidates the fast for a short period after *maghrib*.

Ruling 1530. On every night of the month of Ramadan, one can make the intention to fast the next day.

Ruling 1531. The latest time available for a conscious person to make the intention to keep a fast of the month of Ramadan is at the time of *ṣubḥ* prayers. This means that, based on obligatory precaution (*al-iḥtiyāṭ al-wājib*), at the time of *ṣubḥ* his abstinence [from the eight things that invalidate a fast] must coincide with his intention to fast, albeit subconsciously.

Ruling 1532. [With regard to a recommended (*mustaḥabb*) fast,] if a person has not done anything that invalidates a fast, then at whatever time of the day he makes the intention to keep a recommended fast – even if there is a short period until *maghrib* – his fast will be valid (*ṣaḥīḥ*).

[1] In the original work, the term 'morning call to prayer (*adhān*)' is used, which practically speaking means the start of the time of the *ṣubḥ* prayer. The legal definition of *ṣubḥ* is given in Ruling 728.

[2] For the legal definition of *maghrib*, see Ruling 722.

Ruling 1533. If someone goes to sleep before the time of *ṣubḥ* prayers in the month of Ramadan – or on any day which he assigned for keeping an obligatory (*wājib*) fast – without making the intention to fast, and he wakes up before midday (*ẓuhr*)[3] and makes the intention to fast, his fast will be valid. However, if he wakes up after *ẓuhr*, he must, as a precautionary measure, abstain [from the eight things that invalidate a fast] for the rest of the day with a general intention of attaining proximity to Allah (*qaṣd al-qurbah al-muṭlaqah*) [i.e. with the intention of attaining proximity to Allah without specifying any particulars about the fast], and he must also keep a *qaḍāʾ* fast for it [i.e. he must make up a fast for it after the month of Ramadan].

Ruling 1534. If someone wants to keep a *qaḍāʾ* fast or a fast for recompense (*kaffārah*), he must specify it. For example, he must make the intention that 'I am keeping a *qaḍāʾ* fast', or 'I am keeping a *kaffārah* fast'. However, in the month of Ramadan, it is not necessary for one to make the intention that 'I am keeping a fast of the month of Ramadan'. In fact, if someone does not know or forgets that it is the month of Ramadan and makes the intention to keep some other fast, it will be considered a fast of the month of Ramadan. Similarly, for a fast of a vow (*nadhr*) and suchlike, it is not necessary to make the intention to keep a fast of a vow.

Ruling 1535. If someone knows that it is the month of Ramadan yet intentionally (*ʿamdan*) makes the intention to keep a fast other than that of the month of Ramadan, then the fast for which he made the intention will not be valid. Similarly, it will not be considered a fast of the month of Ramadan if that intention is inconsistent with attaining proximity to Allah. In fact, even if it is not inconsistent with attaining proximity to Allah, based on obligatory precaution, it will not be considered a fast of the month of Ramadan.

Ruling 1536. If, for example, someone keeps a fast with the intention of the first day of the month of Ramadan and afterwards he realises that it was the second or third of the month, his fast is valid.

Ruling 1537.* If someone who makes the intention before the time

[3] For the legal definition of *ẓuhr*, see Ruling 717.

of *ṣubḥ* prayers to fast the next day but unwillingly becomes unconscious, and during the day he regains consciousness, then based on obligatory precaution, he must complete the fast of that day; and if he does not complete it, he must keep a *qaḍāʾ* fast for it. If he becomes unconscious willingly (for example, in order to have an operation, he consents to a doctor making him unconscious), the obligatory precaution is that he must complete the fast of that day and keep a *qaḍāʾ* fast for it as well.

Ruling 1538. If someone makes an intention before the time of *ṣubḥ* prayers to fast the next day and he becomes intoxicated, and during the day he becomes sober, then based on obligatory precaution, he must complete the fast of that day and keep a *qaḍāʾ* fast for it as well.

Ruling 1539. If someone makes the intention before the time of *ṣubḥ* prayers to fast the next day, goes to sleep, and wakes up after *maghrib*, his fast is valid.

Ruling 1540. If someone does not know or forgets that it is the month of Ramadan and becomes aware of this before *ẓuhr*, in the event that he has done something that invalidates a fast, his fast is invalid (*bāṭil*) and [he must act according to two instructions]: (1) for the rest of that day, he must not do anything else that invalidates a fast until *maghrib*; and (2) after the month of Ramadan, he must keep a *qaḍāʾ* fast for it. If someone becomes aware after *ẓuhr* that it is the month of Ramadan and he has not done anything that invalidates a fast, then based on obligatory precaution, he must fast with the intention of *rajāʾ* [i.e. to keep the fast in the hope that it is desired by Allah]; and after the month of Ramadan, he must also keep a *qaḍāʾ* fast for it. However, if he becomes aware before *ẓuhr* and has not done anything that invalidates a fast, he must make the intention of fasting and his fast will be valid.

Ruling 1541. If a child reaches the age of legal responsibility [i.e. becomes *bāligh*] before the time of *ṣubḥ* prayers in the month of Ramadan, he must fast. If a child becomes *bāligh* after the time of *ṣubḥ* prayers, the fast of that day is not obligatory for him. However, if he had made the intention to keep a recommended fast, the recommended precaution (*al-iḥtiyāṭ al-mustaḥabb*) is that he should complete it.

Ruling 1542.* If someone has been hired to keep the *qaḍā'* fasts of a dead person, or if he has to keep a *kaffārah* fast of his own, there is no problem in him keeping a recommended fast of his own. However, if someone has to keep his own *qaḍā'* fasts of the month Ramadan, he cannot keep a recommended fast [until he has kept his own *qaḍā'* fasts], even if he has vowed to keep that recommended fast. In the event that he forgets and keeps a recommended fast and remembers this before *ẓuhr*, his recommended fast becomes invalid but he can change his intention to an intention of keeping a *qaḍā'* fast. However, if he becomes aware after *ẓuhr*, then based on obligatory precaution, his fast is invalid, but if he remembers after *maghrib*, his fast is valid.

Ruling 1543. If it is obligatory for a person to keep an assigned [i.e. time-specific] fast other than the fast of the month of Ramadan – for example, he had made a vow that he would fast on a particular day – in the event that he intentionally does not make the intention to keep that fast until the time of *ṣubḥ* prayers, his fast is invalid. However, if he does not know that it is obligatory for him to fast on that day, or he forgets and remembers before *ẓuhr*, in the event that he has not done anything that invalidates a fast and consequently makes the intention to fast, his fast will be valid. However, if he remembers after *ẓuhr*, he must exercise the obligatory precautionary measure that was mentioned concerning the fast of the month of Ramadan [in Ruling 1533, which stated that he must abstain for the rest of the day from the eight things that invalidate a fast with a general intention of attaining proximity to Allah and that he must also keep a *qaḍā'* fast for it].

Ruling 1544. There is no problem if someone intentionally does not make the intention to fast until near *ẓuhr* for an obligatory fast that has not been assigned for a particular day, such as a fast for *kaffārah*. If a person decides not to fast or is indecisive as to whether he should fast or not, in the event that he has not done anything that invalidates a fast, he can make the intention before *ẓuhr* to fast and his fast will be valid.

Ruling 1545. If a disbeliever (*kāfir*) becomes a Muslim during the daytime in the month of Ramadan, and from the time of *ṣubḥ* prayers until the time he became a Muslim he did not do anything that invalidates a fast, then based on obligatory precaution, he must abstain [from the eight things that invalidate a fast] until the end of the day with the intention to fulfil whatever his legal obligation happens to be (*mā fī al-dhimmah*). If he does not do this, he must keep a *qaḍāʾ* fast for it.

Ruling 1546. If in the middle of a day in the month of Ramadan a sick person gets well before *ẓuhr* and until that time he did not do anything that invalidates a fast, then based on obligatory precaution, he must make the intention to fast and [he must] keep the fast of that day. In the event that he gets better after *ẓuhr*, it is not obligatory for him to fast on that day but he must keep a *qaḍāʾ* fast for it.

Ruling 1547. If someone doubts whether it is the last day of Shaʿbān or the first day of the month of Ramadan, it is not obligatory for him to fast on that day; and if he wants to fast on that day, he cannot do so with the intention of keeping the fast of the month of Ramadan. However, if he makes the intention that if it is the month of Ramadan, he is keeping the fast of the month of Ramadan, and if it is not the month of Ramadan, he is keeping a *qaḍāʾ* fast or another legitimate fast [including a recommended fast], the fast will be valid. In this situation, it is better that he fast with the intention of keeping a *qaḍāʾ* fast or another legitimate fast, and in the event that afterwards it becomes known that it was the first day of the month of Ramadan, it will be counted as the fast of the month of Ramadan. Furthermore, if a person makes the intention of fasting in general [i.e. with the intention of attaining proximity to Allah without specifying any particulars about the fast] and afterwards it becomes known that it was the month of Ramadan, it is also sufficient.[4]

Ruling 1548. If there is doubt as to whether it is the last day of Shaʿbān or the first day of the month of Ramadan and someone keeps a fast with the intention of a *qaḍāʾ* fast or a recommended fast or suchlike, and if during the day he finds out that it is the month of Ramadan, he must make the intention of the fast of the month of Ramadan [and continue fasting].

[4] This ruling and the next concern a matter that is referred to as '*yawm al-shakk*' (day of doubt).

Ruling 1549. If someone [having no legitimate excuse (*'udhr*)] is indecisive as to whether or not to invalidate an assigned [i.e. time-specific] obligatory fast – such as the fast of the month of Ramadan – or he decides to invalidate his fast [but does not do anything to break his fast] and does not make the intention to fast again, his fast becomes invalid. If he does make the intention to fast again, the obligatory precaution is that he must complete the fast of that day and afterwards keep a *qaḍā'* fast for it.

Ruling 1550. With regard to a recommended fast or an obligatory fast that does not have an assigned time – such as a fast for *kaffārah* – if someone decides to do something that invalidates a fast or is indecisive as to whether or not to invalidate it, then in the event that he does not do so and makes the intention to fast again before *ẓuhr* in the case of an obligatory fast, or before sunset (*ghurūb*) in the case of a recommended fast, his fast will be valid.

THINGS THAT INVALIDATE (*MUBṬILĀT*) A FAST

Ruling 1551. Eight things invalidate a fast:

1. eating and drinking;
2. sexual intercourse;
3. masturbation, meaning that a man – either with himself or by means of something – does something other than having sexual intercourse that results in ejaculation. How this applies to a woman was explained in Ruling 345;
4. based on obligatory precaution, ascribing false things to Allah the Exalted, the Most Noble Messenger (Ṣ), and the successors of the Most Noble Messenger (Ṣ) [i.e. the Infallible Imams ('A)];
5. causing thick dust to reach the throat, based on obligatory precaution;
6. remaining in a state of ritual impurity (*janābah*), menstruation (*ḥayḍ*), or lochia (*nifās*) until the time of *ṣubḥ* prayers;
7. applying liquid enema;
8. vomiting intentionally.

The laws (*aḥkām*) relating to these will be explained in the following rulings (*masāʾil*).

1. Eating and drinking

Ruling 1552. If a fasting person who is aware of the fact that he is fasting intentionally eats or drinks something, his fast becomes invalid, irrespective of whether the thing he ate or drank was something normal – such as bread and water – or not – such as earth and the sap of a tree – and irrespective of whether it was a little or a lot. In fact, even if one takes a toothbrush out of his mouth and then puts it back into his mouth and swallows the moisture, his fast becomes invalid unless the moisture on the toothbrush was so little that it could be said to have disappeared in his saliva.

Ruling 1553. If someone realises while eating that it is the time of *ṣubḥ*, he must take the food out of his mouth; and in the event that he intentionally swallows it, his fast is invalid. Furthermore, according to the rules that will be mentioned later, *kaffārah* also becomes obligatory for him.

Ruling 1554. If a fasting person eats or drinks something inadvertently (*sahwan*), his fast does not become invalid.

Ruling 1555. Injections and intravenous drips do not invalidate a fast even if the former is an energy injection and the latter a glucose-saline drip. Similarly, a spray used for asthma does not invalidate a fast provided that the medicine only enters the lungs. Applying medicine [such as drops] to the eyes and ears does not invalidate a fast either, even if its taste reaches the throat. Likewise, if medicine is applied in the nose, it does not invalidate a fast as long as it does not reach the throat.

Ruling 1556. If a fasting person intentionally swallows something that has remained in between his teeth, his fast becomes invalid.

Ruling 1557. If someone wishes to keep a fast, it is not necessary for him to use a toothpick before the time of *ṣubḥ* prayers. However, if one knows that some food that has remained in between his teeth will be swallowed during the day, he must use a toothpick to remove it.

Ruling 1558. Swallowing saliva does not invalidate a fast even though it may have collected in one's mouth due to thinking about food and suchlike.

Ruling 1559. There is no problem in swallowing the mucus of the head and chest as long as it has not entered the cavity of the mouth. If it enters the mouth cavity and is swallowed, the fast does not become invalid, although the recommended precaution is that one should not swallow it.

Ruling 1560. If a fasting person becomes so thirsty that he fears he may die of thirst, sustain some harm, or fall into hardship that he cannot bear, he can drink water to the extent that his fear of these things is averted; but in this case, his fast becomes invalid. In fact, in the case of fear of death and suchlike, it is obligatory for one to drink. If it is the month of Ramadan, then based on obligatory precaution, the person must not drink an amount that is more than necessary, and for the rest of the day he must refrain from doing anything else that invalidates a fast.

Ruling 1561. Chewing food for feeding a child or a bird, and tasting food [for example, to check that the right amount of salt has been used] and suchlike – which usually does not cause the food to reach the throat – does not invalidate a fast even if the food happens to reach the throat accidentally. However, if one knows from the outset that such food will reach the throat yet intentionally does it, his fast becomes invalid and he must keep a *qaḍā'* fast for it and *kaffārah* is also obligatory for him.

Ruling 1562.* One cannot break his fast in the month of Ramadan on account of feeling weak, even if the weakness caused is severe. However, if one's weakness is to such an extent that normally it could not be endured, then based on obligatory precaution, one is permitted to eat or drink to the extent that is necessary. In such a case, the person must abstain for the rest of the day from the things that invalidate a fast, and he must keep a *qaḍā'* fast for it after the month of Ramadan; however, *kaffārah* will not be obligatory for him.[5]

2. Sexual intercourse

Ruling 1563. Sexual intercourse invalidates a fast even if penetration is as little as the circumcised part of the penis and there is no ejaculation.

Ruling 1564. If penetration is less than the circumcised part of the penis and there is no ejaculation, the fast does not become invalid. However, for a man who has not been circumcised, any amount of penetration – even if it is less than the circumcised part of a penis – invalidates his fast.

Ruling 1565. If someone intentionally decides to have sexual intercourse and then doubts whether or not there was penetration up to the circumcised part of the penis, the rule (*ḥukm*) concerning this matter can be found in Ruling 1549; and if he has not done anything that invalidates a fast, *kaffārah* is not obligatory for him.

Ruling 1566. If someone forgets that he is fasting and has sexual intercourse, or if someone is forced to have sexual intercourse in a manner that is not of his free will, his fast does not become invalid. However, in the event that during sexual intercourse he remembers [that he is fasting], or he is no longer forced to have sexual intercourse, he must immediately stop having sexual intercourse; and if he does not stop, his fast is invalid.

3. Masturbation

Ruling 1567. If a fasting person masturbates (the meaning of masturbation was mentioned in Ruling 1551), his fast becomes invalid.

[5] The underlined words are new to this edition of *Islamic Laws*. In summary, a person may break their fast because of weakness only if its severity is to a level that cannot normally be endured. Even then, the person can only eat or drink to the necessary extent. Furthermore, the person must fast for the rest of the day and keep a *qaḍā'* fast after the month of Ramadan.

Ruling 1568. If a person ejaculates involuntarily, his fast does not become invalid.

Ruling 1569. Whenever a fasting person knows that if he goes to sleep during the day he will have a wet dream [i.e. become *muḥtalim*] – meaning that semen will be ejaculated in his sleep – it is permitted (*jā'iz*) for him to go to sleep even if he will not encounter difficulty by not sleeping; and if he has a wet dream, his fast does not become invalid.

Ruling 1570. If a fasting person wakes up from sleep while ejaculation is taking place, it is not obligatory for him to stop the ejaculation.

Ruling 1571. A fasting person who has a wet dream can urinate even if he knows that by urinating, some of the remaining semen will come out of his penis.

Ruling 1572. If a fasting person who has a wet dream knows that some semen has remained in his penis, and he knows that if he does not urinate before performing ritual bathing (*ghusl*), semen will be discharged after *ghusl*, then the recommended precaution is that he should urinate before performing *ghusl*.

Ruling 1573. If someone intentionally indulges in courtship with the intention of ejaculating but does not ejaculate, and he does not make another intention to fast, his fast is invalid. If he does make another intention to fast, then based on obligatory precaution, he must complete his fast and keep a *qaḍā'* fast as well.

Ruling 1574. If, for example, a fasting person indulges in courtship with his wife without the intention of ejaculating, in the event that he is confident [i.e. he has *iṭmi'nān*] that he will not ejaculate but does ejaculate, his fast is valid. However, if he is not confident that he will not ejaculate and does ejaculate, his fast is invalid.

4. Ascribing something false to Allah the Exalted, the Most Noble Prophet (Ṣ), or the Infallible Imams (ʿA)

Ruling 1575. If a fasting person intentionally ascribes something false to Allah the Exalted, the Most Noble Prophet (Ṣ), or the Infallible Imams (ʿA) – whether he does this verbally, in writing, or by making a sign and suchlike – and even if he immediately says, 'I have lied' or he repents, then based on obligatory precaution, his fast is invalid. The same applies, based on recommended precaution, to ascribing something false to Her Eminence [Fāṭimah] al-Zahrāʾ (ʿA) and the other Prophets and their successors.

Ruling 1576. If someone wishes to report a narration about which he does not have any evidence as to its authenticity, and he does not know whether it is true or false, then based on obligatory precaution, he must report it in such a way that he does not directly attribute it to the Most Noble Prophet (Ṣ) or the Infallible Imams (ʿA).

Ruling 1577. If someone quotes something as the word of Allah the Exalted, the Most Noble Prophet (Ṣ), [or the Infallible Imams (ʿA)] with the belief that it is true, and afterwards he realises that it was false, his fast does not become invalid.

Ruling 1578. If someone ascribes to Allah the Exalted, the Most Noble Prophet (Ṣ), [or the Infallible Imams (ʿA)] something that he knows to be false, and afterwards he realises that what he said was true, and he knew that this act would invalidate his fast, he must, based on obligatory precaution, complete his fast and keep a *qaḍāʾ* fast as well.

Ruling 1579. If someone intentionally ascribes to Allah the Exalted, the Most Noble Prophet (Ṣ), or the Infallible Imams (ʿA) something that has been fabricated by some other person, then as an obligatory precaution, his fast becomes invalid. However, if he simply narrates from the person who fabricated the falsehood without knowing it to be false, there is no problem [and his fast is valid].

Ruling 1580. If a fasting person is asked whether the Most Noble Prophet (Ṣ) [or Allah the Exalted, or one of the Infallible Imams (ʿA)] said such and such thing and he intentionally replies 'Yes' when he should say 'No', or he intentionally replies 'No' when he should say 'Yes', then based on obligatory precaution, his fast becomes invalid.

Ruling 1581. If someone correctly quotes the words of Allah the

Exalted, the Most Noble Prophet (Ṣ), [or the Infallible Imams (ʿA)] and then says, 'I lied', or if at night he ascribes something false to them and on the following day when he is fasting says, 'What I said last night is true', then based on obligatory precaution, his fast becomes invalid unless his intention is to explain the state of his information [i.e. he means to assert that it is true that he *did* actually say that last night, not that *what* he said is true].

5. Causing thick dust to reach the throat

Ruling 1582. On the basis of obligatory precaution, causing thick dust to reach one's throat invalidates a fast, whether the dust is of something lawful (*ḥalāl*) to eat, such as flour, or it is of something unlawful (*ḥarām*) to eat, such as soil.

Ruling 1583. Causing dust that is not thick to reach the throat does not invalidate a fast.

Ruling 1584.* If thick dust appears and a person – despite being aware and able to take care – does not take care and the dust reaches his throat, then based on obligatory precaution, his fast becomes invalid. However, if dust were to appear by means of the wind or a storm and suchlike, and preventing it from reaching one's throat would be considered excessively difficult, then preventing it would not be necessary.

Ruling 1585. The obligatory precaution is that a fasting person must not cause the smoke of cigarettes, tobacco, or something similar to reach his throat.

Ruling 1586. If someone does not take due care and dust, smoke, or suchlike enters his throat, in the event that he was certain or confident that it would not reach his throat, his fast is valid; but if he only supposed (i.e. had *ẓann*) that it would not reach his throat, it is better that he keep a *qaḍāʾ* fast for it.

Ruling 1587. If someone forgets that he is fasting and does not take due care, or if dust or something similar reaches his throat involuntarily, his fast does not become invalid.

Ruling 1588. Immersing the entire head in water does not invalidate the fast but is highly disapproved (*makrūh*).

6. Remaining in a state of *janābah*, *ḥayḍ*, or *nifās* until the time of *ṣubḥ* prayers

Ruling 1589. If in the month of Ramadan a *junub*[6] intentionally does not perform *ghusl* until the time of *ṣubḥ* prayers – or, if his duty is to perform dry ablution (*tayammum*) and he does not perform it – he must complete the fast of that day with the intention of *mā fī al-dhimmah*, and he must also fast another day [after the month of Ramadan]. With regard to the fast on this additional day, as it is not known whether it is a fast of *qaḍā*ʾ or punishment, he must keep it with the intention of *mā fī al-dhimmah*, not with the intention of *qaḍā*ʾ.

Ruling 1590. Whenever someone who wants to keep a *qaḍā*ʾ fast of the month of Ramadan intentionally remains in the state of *janābah* until the time of *ṣubḥ* prayers, he cannot fast on that day. If he does this unintentionally, he can fast on that day, although the recommended precaution is that he should not [fast on that day, and should instead fast on another day].

Ruling 1591. With regard to obligatory or recommended fasts other than the fast of the month of Ramadan and their *qaḍā*ʾ, if a *junub* intentionally remains in the state of *janābah* until the time of *ṣubḥ* prayers, he can fast on that day.

Ruling 1592. In the event that someone who is *junub* on a night of the month of Ramadan does not perform *ghusl* until the time remaining to *ṣubḥ* prayers becomes short, he must perform *tayammum* and keep the fast and his fast will be valid.

Ruling 1593. If a *junub* in the month of Ramadan forgets to perform *ghusl* and remembers after one day, he must keep a *qaḍā*ʾ fast for that day. If he remembers after a few days, he must keep a *qaḍā*ʾ fast for

[6] *Junub* is the term used to refer to a person who is in the state of ritual impurity (*janābah*). *Janābah* is explained in Ruling 344.

all the days he is certain to have been *junub* on. For example, if he does not know whether he was *junub* for three or four days, he must keep *qaḍāʾ* fasts for three days.

Ruling 1594. If on a night of the month of Ramadan someone knows that he will not have time to perform *ghusl* or *tayammum*, yet intentionally becomes *junub*, his fast is invalid and *qaḍāʾ* and *kaffārah* become obligatory for him [i.e. he must keep a fast after the month of Ramadan and give recompense as well].

Ruling 1595. If someone knows that he does not have time to perform *ghusl* and intentionally becomes *junub* and then performs *tayammum*, or if despite having time he intentionally delays performing *ghusl* until the time becomes short and then performs *tayammum*, in these cases, although he commits a sin, his fast is valid.

Ruling 1596. If someone who is *junub* on a night of the month of Ramadan knows that if he goes to sleep he will not wake up until the time of *ṣubḥ* prayers, then as an obligatory precaution, he must not go to sleep without performing *ghusl*. In the event that he chooses to go to sleep before performing *ghusl* and does not wake up until the time of *ṣubḥ* prayers, he must complete the fast of that day and *qaḍāʾ* and *kaffārah* become obligatory for him.

Ruling 1597. Whenever a *junub* goes to sleep on a night of the month of Ramadan, if when he wakes up he deems it probable that were he to go to sleep again he would wake up before the time of *ṣubḥ* prayers, he can go to sleep [without performing *ghusl*].

Ruling 1598. If someone is *junub* on a night of the month of Ramadan and is certain or confident that if he goes to sleep he will wake up before the time of *ṣubḥ* prayers, in the event that he decides to perform *ghusl* after waking up and goes to sleep with this decision but remains asleep until the time of *ṣubḥ* prayers, his fast is valid.

Ruling 1599. If someone is *junub* on a night of the month of Ramadan and is not confident that if he goes to sleep he will wake up before the time of *ṣubḥ* prayers, in the event that he is unmindful of the fact that he must perform *ghusl* after waking up, and he goes to sleep and remains asleep until the time of *ṣubḥ* prayers, then based on precaution, *qaḍāʾ* becomes obligatory for him.

Ruling 1600. If someone is *junub* on a night of the month of Ramadan and is certain or deems it probable that if he goes to sleep he will wake up before the time of *ṣubḥ* prayers, and if he wakes up but does not want to perform *ghusl*, and he goes back to sleep and does not wake up again before the time of *ṣubḥ* prayers, then in such a case, he must complete the fast of that day and *qaḍāʾ* and *kaffārah* become obligatory for him. Based on obligatory precaution, the same applies if he doubts whether he will perform *ghusl* after waking up.

Ruling 1601. If a *junub* on a night of the month of Ramadan goes to sleep, wakes up, and is certain or deems it probable that if he sleeps again he will wake up before the time of *ṣubḥ* prayers, and he decides that he will perform *ghusl* after waking up, then in the event that he goes to sleep again but does not wake up until the time of *ṣubḥ* prayers, he must keep a *qaḍāʾ* fast for the fast of that day. Furthermore, if he wakes up from the second sleep and goes back to sleep for a third time but does not wake up until the time of *ṣubḥ* prayers, he must keep a *qaḍāʾ* fast for the fast of that day; and based on recommended precaution, he should also give *kaffārah*.

Ruling 1602. A sleep in which a wet dream has taken place is considered the first sleep. Therefore, if after waking up from this first sleep someone goes back to sleep and does not wake up until the time of *ṣubḥ* prayers, then, as stated in the previous ruling, he must keep a *qaḍāʾ* fast for the fast of that day.

Ruling 1603. If someone who is fasting has a wet dream during the day, it is not obligatory for him to perform *ghusl* immediately.

Ruling 1604. Whenever someone in the month of Ramadan wakes up after the time of *ṣubḥ* prayers and finds that he has had a wet dream, then, even if he knows he had a wet dream before the time of *ṣubḥ* prayers, his fast is valid.

Ruling 1605. If someone who wants to keep a *qaḍāʾ* fast of the month of Ramadan wakes up after the time of *ṣubḥ* prayers and finds that he has had a wet dream, and if he knows that he had this wet dream before the time of *ṣubḥ* prayers, he can fast on that day with the intention of keeping a *qaḍāʾ* fast of the month of Ramadan.

Ruling 1606. If a woman's *ḥayḍ* or *nifās* stops on a night of the month of Ramadan before the time of *ṣubḥ* prayers and she intentionally does not perform *ghusl*, or if her duty is to perform *tayammum* but she does not do so, she must complete the fast of that day and keep a *qaḍāʾ* fast for that day as well. Furthermore, with regard to a *qaḍāʾ* fast of the month of Ramadan, if she intentionally does not perform *ghusl* or *tayammum* before the time of *ṣubḥ* prayers, then based on obligatory precaution, she cannot fast on that day.

Ruling 1607. If a woman whose *ḥayḍ* or *nifās* stops on a night of the month of Ramadan intentionally does not perform *ghusl* until the time before *ṣubḥ* prayers becomes too short to perform *ghusl*, she must perform *tayammum* and the fast of that day will be valid.

Ruling 1608. If a woman's *ḥayḍ* or *nifās* stops before the time of *ṣubḥ* prayers in the month of Ramadan but she does not have time to perform *ghusl*, she must perform *tayammum*; however, it is not necessary for her to remain awake until the time of *ṣubḥ* prayers. The rule is the same for a *junub* in the event that his duty is to perform *tayammum*.

Ruling 1609. If a woman's *ḥayḍ* or *nifās* stops near the time of *ṣubḥ* prayers in the month of Ramadan but she does not have time to perform *ghusl* or *tayammum*, her fast will be valid.

Ruling 1610. If a woman's *ḥayḍ* or *nifās* stops after the time of *ṣubḥ* prayers, she cannot fast on that day. Furthermore, if she experiences *ḥayḍ* or *nifās* during the day while she is fasting, then even if it is near the time of *maghrib* prayers, her fast is invalid.

Ruling 1611. If a woman forgets to perform *ghusl* for *ḥayḍ* or *nifās* and remembers after a day or few days, the fasts that she kept are valid.

Ruling 1612. If a woman's *ḥayḍ* or *nifās* stops before the time of *ṣubḥ* prayers in the month of Ramadan but she is negligent in performing *ghusl* until the time of *ṣubḥ* prayers, and if in the short time remaining she does not perform *tayammum* either, then, as mentioned previously, she must complete the fast of that day and keep a *qaḍāʾ* fast. However, in the event that she is not negligent – for example, she waits for the public bath to become accessible to women only [or, she cannot access the bathroom due to a legitimate reason] – then even if she sleeps three times and does not perform *ghusl* until the time of *ṣubḥ* prayers, her fast will be valid provided she is not negligent in performing *tayammum*.

Ruling 1613. If a woman has excessive *istiḥāḍah* and does not perform the *ghusls* according to the laws of *istiḥāḍah* mentioned in Ruling 394, her fast is valid. Similarly, if a woman has medium *istiḥāḍah* and does not perform *ghusl*, her fast is valid.

Ruling 1614. Someone who has touched a corpse – i.e. he has brought a part of his own body into contact with the corpse – can fast without performing the *ghusl* for touching a corpse (*mass al-mayyit*). Furthermore, if one touches a corpse while fasting, his fast does not become invalid.

7. Applying enema[7]

Ruling 1615. Applying liquid enema – even if one is obliged to or for the purposes of treatment – invalidates a fast.

8. Vomiting

Ruling 1616. Whenever a fasting person intentionally vomits, his fast becomes invalid even if he vomited out of necessity or because of illness and suchlike. However, if he vomits unintentionally or involuntarily, there is no problem [and his fast remains valid].

Ruling 1617. If at night one eats something that he knows will cause him to vomit unintentionally during the day, his fast will be valid.

Ruling 1618. If a fasting person feels sick and the cause of this is

[7] The injection of water or other fluid into the large intestine by way of the rectum. [Author]

something natural, such that it could not commonly be said that he made himself feel sick, then even if he can restrain himself from vomiting, it is not necessary for him to do so and his fast will be valid.

Ruling 1619. If bits of food or other tiny items enter a fasting person's throat and go down to an extent that it could not be called 'eating', it is not necessary for him to bring it out and his fast is valid. However, if the items do go down to that extent [that it could be called 'eating'], then he must bring them out even if this requires vomiting, unless vomiting is harmful or excessively difficult (*mashaqqah*) for him to the extent that it could not normally be endured. In the event that he does not vomit it but swallows it instead, his fast becomes invalid. Similarly, if he brings it out by vomiting, his fast becomes invalid.

Ruling 1620. If a person unintentionally swallows something and remembers that he is fasting before it reaches his stomach, and if it goes down to such an extent that were he to then make it enter his stomach it could not be called 'eating', it is not necessary for him to bring it out and his fast is valid.

Ruling 1621. If a person is certain that by burping something will come out of his throat, and were he to burp it would be in a manner that could be called 'vomiting', then in such a case, he must not burp intentionally. However, there is no problem [in him burping] if he is not certain about this.

Ruling 1622. If someone burps and something comes up in his throat or mouth, he must spit it out; and if he swallows it involuntarily, his fast is valid.

LAWS OF THINGS THAT INVALIDATE A FAST

Ruling 1623. If a person intentionally and voluntarily does something that invalidates a fast, his fast becomes invalid; and in the event that he does not do it intentionally, there is no problem [and his fast remains valid]. However, if a *junub* goes to sleep and – as per the details mentioned in Ruling 1600 – he does not perform *ghusl* until the time of *ṣubḥ* prayers, his fast is invalid. Furthermore, in the event that one does not know that some of the things mentioned previously invalidate a fast, and he has not been negligent in not knowing, nor does he doubt [that a particular thing may invalidate his fast], or he trusts in something that is legally authoritative (*al-ḥujjah al-sharʿiyyah*) [for example, the statement of a reliable person], and he does that thing, in such a case, his fast does not become invalid except in the case of eating, drinking, and sexual intercourse.

Ruling 1624. If a fasting person inadvertently does something that invalidates a fast, and with the belief that his fast has become invalid he intentionally does one of those things again, then the rule in the previous ruling will apply to him.

Ruling 1625. If something is forced down a fasting person's throat, his fast does not become invalid. However, if he is forced to break his fast by eating, drinking, or having sexual intercourse – for example he is told, 'If you do not eat food, we will inflict some financial or physical harm on you' – and he eats something to prevent the harm from being inflicted, his fast becomes invalid. Furthermore, based on obligatory precaution, his fast also becomes invalid if he is forced to do any of the other things that invalidate a fast.

Ruling 1626. A fasting person must not go to a place where he knows something will be poured down his throat or where he will be forced to break his fast; and if he goes to such a place and he is compelled to do something that breaks his fast, his fast becomes invalid. Based on obligatory precaution, the same applies if something is poured down his throat.

THINGS THAT ARE DISAPPROVED (*MAKRŪH*) FOR A FASTING PERSON TO DO

Ruling 1627. Some things are disapproved for a fasting person to do, including:

1. putting medication in the eyes and applying collyrium in a way that the taste or smell of it reaches the throat;

2. doing anything that causes weakness, such as giving blood or taking a shower;
3. putting medication in the nose, if one does not know that it will reach the throat; and if one knows that it will reach the throat, it is not permitted;
4. smelling aromatic plants;
5. for women, to sit in water;
6. using a suppository;
7. making the clothes that are on the body wet;
8. having teeth extracted or doing anything that causes blood to come out of the mouth;
9. brushing the teeth with a wet piece of wood;
10. putting water or any other fluid in the mouth without due cause;
11. immersing the entire head in water.

It is also disapproved for someone to kiss his wife or do something that arouses him without intending to ejaculate.

TIMES WHEN IT IS OBLIGATORY (*WĀJIB*) TO BOTH MAKE UP (*QAḌĀʾ*) AND GIVE RECOMPENSE (*KAFFĀRAH*)

Ruling 1628. If someone invalidates a fast of the month of Ramadan by eating, drinking, having sexual intercourse, masturbating, or remaining in the state of *janābah* until the time of *ṣubḥ* prayers, in the event that he did one of these things intentionally and voluntarily – and he was not compelled or forced to – then, as well as *qaḍāʾ*, *kaffārah* also becomes obligatory for him [i.e. he must keep a fast after the month of Ramadan and give recompense as well]. As for someone who invalidates a fast by means other than those mentioned, the recommended precaution is that in addition to *qaḍāʾ*, he should also give *kaffārah*.

Ruling 1629. If someone performs one of the things mentioned [in the previous ruling] while believing with certainty that it would not invalidate his fast, then *kaffārah* is not obligatory for him. The same applies to someone who does not know that fasting is obligatory for him, such as a child in the early stages of legal responsibility (*bulūgh*).

RECOMPENSE (*KAFFĀRAH*) OF A FAST

Ruling 1630. The *kaffārah* for breaking a fast (*ifṭār*) unlawfully in the month of Ramadan is that the person must free a slave, or fast for two months in accordance with the instructions that will be mentioned in the next ruling, or feed sixty poor people (*fuqarāʾ*) or give each of them a *mudd* – which is approximately 750 grams – of food, i.e. wheat, barley, bread, and suchlike. In the event that none of these is possible for the person, he must give charity to the extent that he can. If this is not possible either, he must seek forgiveness from Allah the Exalted; and the obligatory precaution is that he must give *kaffārah* whenever he can.

Ruling 1631. Someone who wants to fast for two months for the *kaffārah* of the month of Ramadan must fast one complete month and one day from the next month continuously. Similarly, based on obligatory precaution, he must fast the rest of that second month continuously. If an obstacle arises that would commonly be considered a legitimate excuse, he does not have to fast that particular day, but once his legitimate excuse expires, he must resume his fasts.

Ruling 1632. Someone who wants to fast for two consecutive months for the *kaffārah* of a fast of the month of Ramadan must not start at a time when he knows a day on which fasting is unlawful – such as Eid al-Aḍḥā[8] – will fall within the one month and one day period, nor must he fast at a time when he knows a day on which fasting is obligatory (such as a day of the month of Ramadan) will fall within that period.

Ruling 1633. If someone who must fast continuously does not fast one of the days without a legitimate excuse, he must start the *kaffārah* fasts all over again.

[8] The 10th of Dhū al-Ḥijjah.

Ruling 1634. If during the days that someone must fast continuously a legitimate excuse arises – such as *ḥayḍ*, *nifās*, or a journey on which he has to go – then once the excuse expires, it is not obligatory for him to start the fasts all over again; rather, he will continue the rest of the fasts immediately after the excuse has expired.

Ruling 1635. If a person invalidates his fast by means of something unlawful – whether that thing is fundamentally unlawful, like wine or fornication, or something that has become unlawful due to a particular reason, like eating lawful food that is in a general sense harmful for him, or having intercourse with his wife when she is in the state of *ḥayḍ* – then in these cases, giving one *kaffārah* is sufficient. However, the recommended precaution is that he should give the 'total *kaffārah*', i.e. free one slave, fast for two months, and feed sixty poor people or give each of them one *mudd* of wheat, barley, bread, and suchlike. In the event that all three are not possible for him, he should do the ones that are possible for him.

Ruling 1636. If a fasting person intentionally attributes a lie to Allah the Exalted, the Most Noble Prophet (Ṣ), [or the Infallible Imams (ʿA)], it is not obligatory for him to give *kaffārah*. However, the recommended precaution is that he should give *kaffārah*.

Ruling 1637. If on several occasions on a day of the month of Ramadan a person eats, drinks, has sexual intercourse, or masturbates, then giving one *kaffārah* is sufficient for all of them.

Ruling 1638. If a fasting person does something that invalidates a fast – other than having sexual intercourse or masturbating – and afterwards he has sexual intercourse with his lawful partner, then giving one *kaffārah* is sufficient for both actions.

Ruling 1639. If a fasting person does something that is lawful but invalidates a fast – for example, he drinks water – and afterwards he does something else that is unlawful and invalidates a fast – for example, he eats unlawful food – then giving one *kaffārah* is sufficient.

Ruling 1640. If a fasting person burps and something comes up in his mouth, then based on obligatory precaution, if he intentionally swallows it, his fast is invalid and he must keep a *qaḍā*ʾ fast and give *kaffārah*. If eating that thing is unlawful – for example, when burping, blood or some food-like substance that has lost the form of food reaches his mouth and he intentionally swallows it – then it is better that he give the 'total *kaffārah*' [as defined in Ruling 1635].

Ruling 1641. If someone keeps a vow that he will fast on an assigned day, in the event that he intentionally invalidates his fast on that day, he must give *kaffārah*. The *kaffārah* for this will be mentioned in the laws relating to vows.

Ruling 1642. If a fasting person breaks his fast based on the statement of someone who says it is *maghrib*, despite the fact that he was not confident in the statement being true, and afterwards he finds out that it was not *maghrib*, or if he doubts whether it is *maghrib* or not [but still breaks his fasts], then in these cases, *qaḍā*ʾ and *kaffārah* become obligatory for him. If he was of the belief that the person's statement was authoritative, then only *qaḍā*ʾ is necessary.

Ruling 1643. If someone intentionally invalidates his fast and travels after *ẓuhr*, *kaffārah* is not waived. Similarly, if he intentionally invalidates his fast and then travels before *ẓuhr* to escape *kaffārah* [i.e. if he thinks that by being considered a traveller that day, he will have a legitimate excuse for not fasting and so he will not have to give *kaffārah* for intentionally invalidating his fast], again *kaffārah* is not waived. In fact, even if it becomes necessary for him to travel before *ẓuhr*, *kaffārah* remains obligatory for him.

Ruling 1644. If a person intentionally breaks his fast and afterwards a legitimate excuse arises – such as *ḥayḍ*, *nifās*, or an illness – the recommended precaution is that he should give *kaffārah*, especially if some medication or other such means brought about the *ḥayḍ* or illness.

Ruling 1645. If a person is certain that it is the first day of the month of Ramadan and he intentionally invalidates his fast, and afterwards it becomes known that it was actually the last day of Shaʿbān, *kaffārah* is not obligatory for him.

Ruling 1646. If a person doubts whether it is the last day of the month of Ramadan or the first of Shawwāl and he intentionally invalidates his fast, and afterwards it becomes known that it was the first of Shawwāl, *kaffārah* is not obligatory for him.

Ruling 1647. If a fasting man in the month of Ramadan has sexual intercourse with his wife who is fasting, in the event that he had compelled his wife to do so, he must give *kaffārah* for invalidating his fast; and based on obligatory precaution, he must give *kaffārah* for invalidating his wife's fast as well. If his wife consented to having sexual intercourse, one *kaffārah* becomes obligatory for each of them.

Ruling 1648. If a woman compels her fasting husband to have sexual intercourse with her, it is not obligatory for her to give *kaffārah* for invalidating her husband's fast.

Ruling 1649. If a fasting man in the month of Ramadan compels his wife to have sexual intercourse with him and during the intercourse his wife consents, one *kaffārah* becomes obligatory for each of them; and the recommended precaution is that the man should give two *kaffārah*s.

Ruling 1650. If a fasting man in the month of Ramadan has sexual intercourse with his fasting wife while she is asleep, one *kaffārah* becomes obligatory for him. Furthermore, his wife's fast is valid and *kaffārah* is not obligatory for her.

Ruling 1651. If a man compels his wife or a wife compels her husband to do something that invalidates a fast – other than having sexual intercourse – *kaffārah* is not obligatory for either of them.

Ruling 1652. A man who does not fast due to travelling or illness cannot compel his fasting wife to have sexual intercourse with him; however, if he does compel her, *kaffārah* is not obligatory for him.

Ruling 1653. One must not be negligent in giving *kaffārah* in the sense that him not giving it would be deemed to be carelessness in performing an obligatory act; however, it is not necessary to give it immediately.

Ruling 1654. If *kaffārah* becomes obligatory for someone and he does not give it for a few years, nothing is added to it.

Ruling 1655. If someone who must feed sixty poor people as the *kaffārah* for one day has access to all sixty people, he cannot reduce the number of poor people to feed even if he gives the same amount of *kaffārah*. For example, he cannot give two *mudd*s to thirty people and suffice with that. He can, however, give a poor person (*faqīr*) one *mudd* of food for each of the poor person's family members, even if they are minors (*ṣaghīr*) and the poor person accepts this by way of agency (*wikālah*) for his family, or by way of guardianship (*wilāyah*) if they are minors. If he cannot find sixty poor people but, for example, he finds thirty people, he can give two *mudd*s of food to each of them. However, based on obligatory precaution, he must give one *mudd* of food to another thirty poor people whenever he can.

Ruling 1656. If after *ẓuhr* someone who is keeping a *qaḍā᾽* fast of the month of Ramadan intentionally does something that invalidates his fast, he must give one *mudd* of food to ten poor people, and if he cannot, he must fast for three days.

TIMES WHEN IT IS OBLIGATORY (*WĀJIB*) TO ONLY MAKE UP (*QAḌĀ᾽*) A FAST

Ruling 1657. In some cases – other than those that were indicated previously – only *qaḍā᾽* is obligatory for a person, not *kaffārah*:

1. one is *junub* on a night of the month of Ramadan and – as per the details mentioned in Ruling 1601 – he does not wake up from the second sleep until the time of *ṣubḥ* prayers;
2. one does not do anything that invalidates a fast but does not make the intention to fast, pretends to fast, or intends not to fast; and the same applies if he intends to do something that invalidates a fast, as per the details explained in Ruling 1549;
3. in the month of Ramadan, one forgets to perform *ghusl* of *janābah* and in the state of *janābah* he fasts one day or several days;

4. in the month of Ramadan, one does not investigate whether or not the time for *ṣubḥ* prayers has set in and does something that invalidates a fast, and afterwards it becomes known that the time of *ṣubḥ* prayers had set in;
5. someone says the time of *ṣubḥ* prayers has not set in and based on his statement one does something that invalidates a fast, and afterwards it becomes known that the time of *ṣubḥ* prayers had set in;
6. someone says it is *ṣubḥ* but a fasting person does not have certainty about the validity of the person's statement, or he thinks that the person who made the statement is joking, and he does not investigate, and he does something that invalidates a fast, and afterwards it becomes known that it really was *ṣubḥ*;
7. one breaks his fast based on the statement of someone whose statement is legally (*sharʿan*) authoritative for him [for example, someone whose word he trusts] who tells him it is *maghrib* – or he mistakenly believes that his report is authoritative – and afterwards it becomes known that it was not *maghrib*;
8. one is certain or confident that it is *maghrib* and breaks his fast, and afterwards it becomes known that it was not *maghrib*. However, if he breaks his fast because the weather was cloudy that day and suchlike, and he supposed it had become *maghrib*, and afterwards it becomes known that it was not *maghrib*, then the obligation of *qaḍāʾ* in this instance is based on obligatory precaution;
9. someone who gargles – i.e. he circulates water in his mouth – due to thirst and unintentionally swallows the water. However, if the person forgets that he is fasting and swallows the water, or he gargles for reasons other than thirst – as in cases when gargling is recommended, such as in *wuḍūʾ* – and he unintentionally swallows the water, then there is no obligation for him to keep a *qaḍāʾ* fast;
10. someone who breaks his fast due to compulsion, necessity, or *taqiyyah*;[9] and if he breaks his fast due to compulsion or *taqiyyah*, then *qaḍāʾ* is due only if he was required to eat, drink, or have sexual intercourse. Based on obligatory precaution, the

[9] *Taqiyyah* refers to dissimulation or concealment of one's beliefs in the face of danger.

same applies if he was required to break his fast by means other than eating, drinking, or having sexual intercourse.

Ruling 1658. If a person puts something other than water in his mouth and unintentionally swallows it, or if he puts water in his nose and unintentionally swallows it, then *qaḍā'* is not obligatory for him.

Ruling 1659. Gargling a lot is disapproved for a fasting person, and if after gargling one wants to swallow his saliva, it is better to spit out the saliva three times [before swallowing].

Ruling 1660. If a person knows that by gargling, water will unintentionally or forgetfully enter his throat, he must not gargle; however, if in this case he does gargle but water does not enter his throat, then based on obligatory precaution, *qaḍā'* is necessary.

Ruling 1661. If in the month of Ramadan, after investigating (by looking at the horizon to sight the true dawn),[10] it is not known to someone that the time of *ṣubḥ* prayers has set in, and he does something that invalidates a fast, and afterwards it becomes known that it was *ṣubḥ*, then *qaḍā'* is not necessary.

Ruling 1662. One cannot break his fast if he merely doubts whether it is *maghrib* or not. However, if one doubts whether it is *ṣubḥ* or not, he can do something that invalidates a fast even before investigating.

LAWS OF A LAPSED (*QAḌĀ'*) FAST

Ruling 1663. If an insane person becomes sane, it is not obligatory for him to make up the fasts that he did not keep when he was insane.

Ruling 1664. If a disbeliever becomes a Muslim, it is not obligatory for him to make up the fasts that he did not keep when he was a disbeliever. However, if a Muslim becomes a disbeliever and then becomes a Muslim again, he must make up the fasts that he did not keep while he was a disbeliever.

[10] See Ruling 728.

Ruling 1665. One must make up a fast that he did not keep due to intoxication, even if he consumed the intoxicating thing for the purposes of treatment.

Ruling 1666. If someone does not fast for a few days due to a legitimate excuse and afterwards doubts when his excuse expired, it is not obligatory for him to fast more days than what he deems probable as having missed. For example, someone who travelled before the month of Ramadan and who does not know whether he returned on the fifth of the month of Ramadan or the sixth, or he travelled in the last few days of the month of Ramadan and returned after the month of Ramadan but does not know whether he travelled on the twenty-fifth or the twenty-sixth, in both cases, he can keep *qaḍāʾ* fasts for the lower figure – i.e. five days – although the recommended precaution is that he should keep *qaḍāʾ* fasts for the higher figure, i.e. six days.

Ruling 1667. If someone has *qaḍāʾ* fasts left over from a number of previous Ramadans, it does not matter which month of Ramadan he keeps *qaḍāʾ* fasts for first. However, if the time for the *qaḍāʾ* of the last month of Ramadan is short – for example, he has to keep five *qaḍāʾ* fasts from the last month of Ramadan and only five days remain until the beginning of the next month of Ramadan – it is better that he keep the *qaḍāʾ* fasts for the last month of Ramadan first.

Ruling 1668. If a person has to keep *qaḍāʾ* fasts for a number of Ramadans and he does not specify in his intention which month of Ramadan he is keeping a *qaḍāʾ* fast for, it will not be regarded as the *qaḍāʾ* fast for the last year; as a result, the *kaffārah* for delaying its *qaḍāʾ* would not be waived.[11]

Ruling 1669. One can invalidate the *qaḍāʾ* fast of the month of Ramadan before *ẓuhr*. However, if the number of days left for him to keep his *qaḍāʾ* fasts [before the start of the month of Ramadan] are few, it is better that he does not invalidate them.

Ruling 1670. If a person has kept a *qaḍāʾ* fast for a dead person, it is better that he does not invalidate it after *ẓuhr*.

[11] See Ruling 1678.

Ruling 1671. If someone does not fast in the month of Ramadan due to illness, *ḥayḍ*, or *nifās*, and he dies before the passing of a period in which he could have made up those fasts, then those fasts do not have to be made up.

Ruling 1672. If due to illness one does not fast in the month of Ramadan and his illness continues until the month of Ramadan of the following year, it is not obligatory for him to make up the fasts he did not keep; and for each day he must give one *mudd* (approximately 750 grams) of food – i.e. wheat, barley, bread, and suchlike – to a poor person.[12] However, if one does not fast because of another legitimate excuse – for example, he was travelling – and his excuse remains valid until the following month of Ramadan, he must make up the fasts that he did not keep; and the obligatory precaution is that for each day, he must also give one *mudd* of food to a poor person.

Ruling 1673. If due to illness one does not fast in the month of Ramadan, and after the month of Ramadan his illness is cured but another legitimate excuse arises such that he cannot make up the fasts until the following month of Ramadan, he must make up the fasts he did not keep; and based on obligatory precaution, he must also give one *mudd* of food to a poor person for every missed fast. The same applies if in the month of Ramadan one has another legitimate excuse – other than illness – and after the month of Ramadan that excuse expires and until the month of Ramadan of the following year he cannot fast due to illness.

Ruling 1674. If in the month of Ramadan one does not fast due to a legitimate excuse and after the month of Ramadan that excuse expires but he intentionally does not make up the fasts before the following month of Ramadan, he must make them up and give one *mudd* of food to a poor person for each day.

Ruling 1675. If a person is negligent in keeping *qaḍāʾ* fasts until the time [before the next month of Ramadan] becomes short, and in the shortage of time a legitimate excuse arises, he must make them up; and based on obligatory precaution, he must also give one *mudd*

[12] This type of compensative payment is known as *fidyah*.

of food to a poor person for each day. The same applies if after the excuse expires he decides to make up his fasts but before he does so, a legitimate excuse arises in the short time [remaining before the month of Ramadan].

Ruling 1676. If a person's illness continues for some years, he must make up the fasts for the last month of Ramadan after he gets better; and for each missed day of the previous years, he must give one *mudd* of food to a poor person.

Ruling 1677. Someone who must give one *mudd* of food to a poor person for each missed fast can give the *kaffārah* of several days to one poor person.

Ruling 1678. If a person delays keeping the *qaḍāʾ* fasts of the month of Ramadan for a few years, he must make them up. For the first year's delay, he must give one *mudd* of food to a poor person for each missed fast [as *kaffārah*]; however, for the delay in the later years, there is no obligation for him [to give *kaffārah*].[13]

Ruling 1679. If a person intentionally does not keep the fasts of the month of Ramadan, he must make them up; and for each missed fast, he must fast for two months, or give food to sixty poor people, or free one slave. In the event that he does not make them up until the next month of Ramadan, then based on obligatory precaution, he must also give one *mudd* of food as *kaffārah*.

Ruling 1680. If a person intentionally does not keep a fast of the month of Ramadan, and in the day he repeatedly has sexual intercourse or masturbates, the *kaffārah* is not repeated. Similarly, if one does something else that invalidates a fast a number of times – for example, he eats food a number of times – then giving one *kaffārah* is sufficient.

Ruling 1681. After a father's death, the eldest son must, based on

[13] For example, if someone has to make up one fast and he delays making it up for three years, he must give one *kaffārah* [i.e. one *mudd* of food] to a poor person, not three *kaffārahs*.

obligatory precaution, keep his father's *qaḍā'* fasts of the month of Ramadan as per the details mentioned in Ruling 1370 concerning prayer. Instead of fasting each day, he can give 750 grams of food to a poor person even from the deceased's property if the heirs consent to it.

Ruling 1682. If a father had not kept obligatory fasts other than the fasts of the month of Ramadan – for example, he had not kept a fast that had become obligatory on account of a vow – or, if he had been hired to fast on behalf of someone else but had not done so, it is not obligatory for the eldest son to make up such fasts.

LAWS OF FASTING FOR A TRAVELLER

Ruling 1683. A traveller must not fast if his obligation on a journey is to perform the four-unit (*rakʿah*) prayers as two *rakʿah*s [i.e. in *qaṣr* form]. A traveller who performs his prayer in its complete (*tamām*) form – such as someone whose work is travelling or whose journey is sinful – must fast on his journey.

Ruling 1684. Travelling during the month of Ramadan is not forbidden. However, travelling to escape fasting is disapproved. Similarly, travelling in general in the month of Ramadan is disapproved except for *ʿumrah*[14] or because of necessity.

Ruling 1685. If an assigned [i.e. time-specific] fast – other than the fast of the month of Ramadan – is obligatory for a person, then in the event that it has become obligatory because he has been hired by someone to fast and suchlike, or it is the third fast of the days of spiritual retreat (*iʿtikāf*),[15] he cannot travel on that day; and if he is on a journey and it is possible, he must make an intention to stay in a place for ten days and fast on that day. However, if the fast of that day has become obligatory on account of a vow, the apparent

[14] *ʿUmrah* refers to the pilgrimage to Mecca that has fewer rituals than the hajj pilgrimage. It is sometimes referred to as the 'minor pilgrimage'.

[15] *Iʿtikāf* refers to the act of staying in a mosque under particular conditions with the intention of worshipping Allah. The laws of *iʿtikāf* are stated in the next chapter.

(*ẓāhir*)[16] ruling is that travelling is permitted on that day and it is not obligatory to make an intention to stay, although it is better not to travel if one is not obliged to, and if he is on a journey, it is better to make an intention to stay. However, if it has become obligatory on account of an oath (*qasam*) or a covenant (*ʿahd*), then based on obligatory precaution, one must not travel, and if he was on a journey, he must make an intention to stay.

Ruling 1686. If a person makes a vow to keep a recommended fast but does not assign a day for it, he cannot keep that fast on a journey. However, in the event that one makes a vow that he will fast on a particular day on a journey, he must keep that fast on a journey. Furthermore, if one makes a vow to fast on a particular day, whether he is travelling or not, he must fast on that day even if he is travelling.

Ruling 1687. A traveller can keep recommended fasts in Medina for three days for the fulfilment of wishes [i.e. for particular needs (*ḥājāt*) of his to be granted]; and the obligatory precaution is for those three days to be Wednesday, Thursday, and Friday.

Ruling 1688. If someone who does not know that a traveller's fast is invalid fasts on a journey and finds out the ruling during the day, his fast becomes invalid; and if he does not find out until *maghrib*, his fast is valid.

Ruling 1689. If a person forgets that he is a traveller or that a traveller's fast is invalid and fasts on a journey, then based on obligatory precaution, his fast is invalid.

Ruling 1690. If a fasting person travels after *ẓuhr*, he must, based on obligatory precaution, complete his fast; and in such a case, it is not necessary for him to make up that fast. If he travels before *ẓuhr*, then based on obligatory precaution, he cannot fast on that day, particularly if he had made the intention to travel the night before. In any case, he must not do anything that invalidates a fast

[16] For practical purposes in jurisprudential rulings, expressing an 'apparent' ruling equates to giving a fatwa.

before reaching the permitted limit (*ḥadd al-tarakhkhuṣ*);[17] otherwise, *kaffārah* becomes obligatory for him.

Ruling 1691. If a traveller in the month of Ramadan – whether he travelled before sunrise or he was fasting and then travelled – reaches his home town (*waṭan*)[18] or a place where he intends to stay for ten days before *ẓuhr*, in the event that he did not do anything that invalidates a fast before reaching that place, he must, based on obligatory precaution, fast on that day and it is not obligatory for him to make it up. If he did something that invalidates a fast before reaching that place, the fast of that day is not obligatory for him and he must make it up.

Ruling 1692. If a traveller reaches his home town or a place where he intends to stay for ten days after *ẓuhr*, then based on obligatory precaution, his fast is invalid and he must make it up.

Ruling 1693. It is disapproved for a traveller, and indeed anyone who has a legitimate excuse for not fasting, to have sexual intercourse or eat and drink to his full during the day in the month of Ramadan.

THOSE ON WHOM FASTING IS NOT OBLIGATORY (*WĀJIB*)

Ruling 1694.* Fasting is not obligatory for someone who finds fasting excessively difficult due to old age, nor is it necessary for such a person to make up the fasts. However, for each day [that he does not fast], he must give one *mudd* of food – i.e. wheat, barley, bread, and suchlike – to a poor person. If fasting for him is not possible at all [as opposed to being excessively difficult], it is not necessary that he give *fidyah*.[19, 20]

17 The permitted limit is explained in Ruling 1304.

18 Rulings 1314–1318 explain what is legally considered one's home town.

19 *Fidyah* is explained in the footnote pertaining to Ruling 1672.

20 The wording of this ruling in this edition of *Islamic Laws* is clearer than it was previously. If someone finds fasting excessively difficult due to old age, they do not have to fast nor make up the fasts later. But they have to give *fidyah* (i.e. 750 grams

Ruling 1695. If someone who has not fasted on account of old age is able to fast after the month of Ramadan, the recommended precaution is that he should make up the fasts that he did not keep.

Ruling 1696. If someone has an illness that makes him very thirsty and he cannot bear being thirsty, or it is excessively difficult for him to bear it, then fasting is not obligatory for him. However, in the second case, he must give one *mudd* of food to a poor person for each missed fast; and in the event that he is able to fast afterwards, it is not obligatory for him to make them up.

Ruling 1697. Fasting is not obligatory for a pregnant woman approaching the time of delivery if it is harmful for her or the unborn child. Such a woman must give one *mudd* of food to a poor person for each missed fast, and she must make up the fasts she did not keep.

Ruling 1698. If fasting is harmful for a woman who is breastfeeding her child and who has little milk – whether she is the child's mother or wet nurse, or someone who is breastfeeding the child without getting paid – or, if fasting is harmful for the child that she is breastfeeding, it is not obligatory for her to fast and she must give one *mudd* of food to a poor person for each missed fast and she must make up the fasts she did not keep. However, based on obligatory precaution, this rule only applies to the case where giving milk to the child is limited to this way. Therefore, if there is another way of giving milk to the child – for example, a number of women participate in breastfeeding the child, or the child is fed with the aid of a bottle – then affirming this rule is problematic (*maḥall al-ishkāl*) [i.e. based on obligatory precaution, it is not permitted for such a woman to not fast].[21]

---

of wheat, barley, bread, or other staple food) to a poor person for each missed fast.

If a person cannot fast at all due to old age – i.e. their position is such that it goes beyond finding fasting excessively difficult – then they do not even have to give *fidyah*.

Note: It is permissible to give *fidyah* payments to an agent or representative (*wakīl*), such as a trusted charity, who will buy the required food and distribute it on the person's behalf.

[21] As mentioned in Ruling 6, the term 'problematic' (*maḥall al-ishkāl*) amounts to saying the ruling is based on obligatory precaution.

WAYS OF ESTABLISHING THE FIRST OF THE MONTH

Ruling 1699.* The first of the month is established in four ways:[22]

1. a person sees the moon himself. The seeing must be done with the naked eye, i.e. without any equipment. Therefore, in the event that the crescent moon cannot be sighted with the naked eye, seeing it with the aid of a telescope is not sufficient;
2. a group of people from whose statement one derives certainty or confidence say that they have seen the moon. Similarly, [the first of the month is established] by means of anything that one derives certainty from, or a rational source that one derives confidence from;
3. two dutiful (*ʿādil*) men say they have seen the moon at night. However, if they describe attributes of the crescent that contradict one another, the first of the month is not established. Similarly, the first of the month is not established by the testimony of two dutiful men if one is certain or confident about them having made a mistake, or if their testimony is affected by a countervailing argument (*muʿāriḍ*), or by something that comes under the rule of a countervailing argument. For example, if a large group of the city's people go to sight the moon but no more than two dutiful people claim to have sighted the moon; or, if a group of people go to sight the moon and two dutiful people from among them claim to have sighted the moon and others do not sight it, while amongst those others there are two other dutiful people who are as good in knowing the position of the crescent and are as sharp-sighted as the first two dutiful people, and furthermore, the sky is clear and for those two there is no probable obstacle to seeing the moon; in these cases, the first of the month is not established by the testimony of two dutiful people;
4. thirty days from the first of the month of Shaʿbān pass, by means of which the first of the month of Ramadan is established; and thirty days from the first of the month of Ramadan

[22] The underlined words are new to this edition of *Islamic Laws*.

pass, by means of which the first of the month of Shawwāl is established.

Ruling 1700. The first of the month is not established by the ruling of a fully qualified jurist (*al-ḥākim al-sharʿī*) unless by means of his ruling, or the first of the month being established in his view, one derives confidence in the moon having been sighted.

Ruling 1701. The first of the month is not established by the predictions of astronomers unless one derives certainty or confidence from their statements.

Ruling 1702. The moon being high or setting late is no evidence that the night before was the first night of the month. Similarly, if the moon has a halo, it is no evidence that it is the second night.

Ruling 1703. If the month of Ramadan is not established for someone and he does not fast, and afterwards it is established that the previous night was the first of the month, he must make up the fast for that day.

Ruling 1704. If the first of the month is established in a city, the first of the month will also be established in other cities that are united with it on the horizon. The meaning of 'unity of horizon' here is that if the moon is seen in the first city, it would also be seen in the second city if there were no obstacles, such as clouds and dust. This brings about confidence in the case where the second city – if it is to the west of the first city – has a latitudinal position close to that of the first city; and if it is to the east of the first city, then in addition to closeness in latitudinal position, there must not be a large difference in the longitudinal position either.

Ruling 1705. If a person does not know whether it is the last day of the month of Ramadan or the first of Shawwāl, he must fast on that day. However, if during the day he finds out that it is the first of Shawwāl, he must break his fast.

Ruling 1706. If a prisoner cannot be certain about whether or not it is the month of Ramadan, he must act according to his supposition; and if he can find a stronger supposition, he cannot act on the weaker supposition. Furthermore, he must endeavour to attain the strongest probability; if there is no other way, he must as a final resort draw lots (*qurʿah*) if this results in strengthening his inclination. If acting according to supposition is not possible, he must fast a month that he deems is probably the month of Ramadan. Moreover, he must bear that month in mind and if he finds out afterwards that the month he fasted was after the month of Ramadan, there is no obligation for him; however, if it becomes known that it was before the month of Ramadan, he must make up the fasts of the month of Ramadan.

UNLAWFUL (*ḤARĀM*) AND DISAPPROVED (*MAKRŪH*) FASTS

Ruling 1707. Fasting on Eid al-Fiṭr[23] and Eid al-Aḍḥā[24] is unlawful. Furthermore, if one does not know whether it is the last day of Shaʿbān or the first day of the month of Ramadan and fasts with the intention of it being the first day of the month of Ramadan, it is unlawful.

Ruling 1708. If a recommended fast of a woman conflicts with her husband's conjugal rights, it is unlawful for her to keep it. Similarly, with regard to a fast that is obligatory but the day on which it must be kept has not been assigned – for example, a vow that [has been made to keep a fast, but the day of the fast] has not been assigned – if it conflicts with the conjugal rights of her husband, then based on obligatory precaution, the fast is invalid and it does not fulfil the vow. Based on obligatory precaution, the same applies if her husband forbids her to keep a recommended fast or an obligatory fast for which a day has not been assigned, even if it does not conflict with his rights. And the recommended precaution is that she should not keep a recommended fast without his consent.

Ruling 1709. If a recommended fast kept by a child is a source of annoyance for his father or mother due to their compassion for him, it is unlawful for the child to keep it.

[23] The 1st of Shawwāl.

[24] The 10th Dhū al-Ḥijjah.

Ruling 1710. If a child keeps a recommended fast without the consent of his father or mother and during the day his father or mother forbid him to continue keeping his fast, in the event that the child's opposition may annoy the parent due to the parent's compassion for his or her child, the child must break his fast.

Ruling 1711. Someone who knows fasting will not cause him significant harm – even though a doctor says it is harmful for him to fast – must fast. And someone who is certain or supposes that fasting will cause him significant harm – even though a doctor says it will not harm him – is not obliged to fast.

Ruling 1712. If a person is certain or confident that fasting will cause him significant harm or he deems this probable, and the probability creates fear in him, in the event that his deeming it probable would be considered by rational people to be reasonable, it is not obligatory for him to fast. In fact, if that harm would result in him dying or losing a limb, fasting is unlawful; otherwise, if he fasts with the intention of *rajāʾ* and afterwards he realises that it did not cause him any significant harm, his fast is valid.

Ruling 1713. If someone who believes that fasting does not harm him fasts and after *maghrib* he finds out that fasting has caused him significant harm, then based on obligatory precaution, he must make it up.

Ruling 1714. Apart from the fasts mentioned here, there are other unlawful fasts mentioned in more detailed books.

Ruling 1715. Fasting is disapproved on the Day of ʿĀshūrāʾ[25] and on the day that one doubts is the Day of ʿArafah[26] or Eid al-Aḍḥā.[27]

RECOMMENDED (*MUSTAḤABB*) FASTS

Ruling 1716. Fasting on any day of the year – apart from the days

[25] The 10th of Muḥarram. [26] The 9th of Dhū al-Ḥijjah. [27] The 10th of Dhū al-Ḥijjah.

on which fasting is unlawful or disapproved, which were mentioned previously – is recommended; and it has been recommended more to fast on some days, such as:

1. the first and last Thursday of each month, and the first Wednesday after the tenth of the month. If someone does not fast on these days, it is recommended that he make them up. In the event that one cannot fast at all [on these days], it is recommended that he give for each day one *mudd* of food or 12.6 *nukhuds*[28] of minted silver[29] to a poor person;
2. the 13th, 14th, and 15th of each month;
3. the entire month of Rajab and Shaʿbān, or at least some days of these two months, even if only one day;
4. the Eid of Nawrūz;[30]
5. from the 4th to the 9th of Shawwāl;
6. the 25th and 29th of Dhū al-Qaʿdah;
7. from the 1st to the 9th of Dhū al-Ḥijjah (until and including the Day of ʿArafah); however, if due to weakness from fasting one cannot recite the supplications (*duʿā'*s) of the Day of ʿArafah, then fasting on that day is disapproved;
8. the auspicious day of Eid al-Ghadīr (the 18th of Dhū al-Ḥijjah);
9. the day of Mubāhalah (the 24th of Dhū al-Ḥijjah);
10. the 1st, 3rd, and 7th of Muḥarram;
11. the joyous birthday of the Most Noble Messenger (Ṣ) (the 17th of Rabīʿ al-Awwal);
12. the 15th of Jumādā al-Ūlā;
13. the day of Mabaʿth of His Eminence, the Most Noble Messenger (Ṣ) (the 27th of Rajab).

If someone keeps a recommended fast, it is not obligatory for him to complete it. In fact, if a fellow believer invites him to eat, it is recommended for him to accept the invitation and break his fast during the day, even if it is after *ẓuhr*.

[28] A *nukhud* is a measure of weight equal to 0.192 grams. Therefore, 12.6 *nukhuds* is equivalent to 2.419 grams.

[29] In the present time, when minted silver is not prevalent, the silver does not have to be minted (*Tawḍīḥ al-Masāʾil-i Jāmiʿ*, vol. 1, p. 587, Ruling 2122).

[30] The day of the spring equinox.

TIMES WHEN IT IS RECOMMENDED (*MUSTAḤABB*) FOR ONE TO ABSTAIN FROM THINGS THAT INVALIDATE A FAST

Ruling 1717. It is recommended for five types of people – even if they are not fasting – to abstain from things that invalidate a fast in the month of Ramadan:

1. a traveller who has done something that invalidates a fast and who reaches his home town or a place where he intends to stay for ten days before *ẓuhr*;
2. a traveller who after *ẓuhr* reaches his home town or a place where he intends to stay for ten days;
3. a sick person who gets better after *ẓuhr*; similarly, if he gets better before *ẓuhr* and has done something that invalidates a fast. In case he has not done anything that invalidates a fast, then based on obligatory precaution, he must fast on that day;
4. a woman whose *ḥayḍ* or *nifās* stops during the day;
5. a disbeliever who becomes a Muslim and who had done something that invalidates a fast before becoming a Muslim.

Ruling 1718. It is recommended for a fasting person to perform *maghrib* and *ʿishāʾ* prayers before breaking his fast. However, if someone is waiting for him or he is very drawn to food – such that he cannot pray with presence of heart – it is better that he first break his fast. However, as much as he possibly can, he should perform the prayers within their prime time (*waqt al-faḍīlah*).[31]

[31] This refers to the early period of the prescribed time for a prayer during which there is more reward for performing it.

CHAPTER FIVE

Spiritual Retreat (*Iʿtikāf*)

Ruling 1719. *Iʿtikāf* is one of the recommended (*mustaḥabb*) ritual acts of worship (*ʿibādāt*) that becomes obligatory (*wājib*) by means of a vow (*nadhr*), covenant (*ʿahd*), oath (*qasam*), and suchlike. A valid *iʿtikāf* is when one stays in a mosque with the intention of attaining proximity to Allah (*qaṣd al-qurbah*). And the recommended precaution (*al-iḥtiyāṭ al-mustaḥabb*) is that the stay should take place with the intention of performing ritual acts of worship, such as prayers (*ṣalāh*) and supplications (*duʿā*'s).

Ruling 1720. There is no particular time for performing *iʿtikāf*; rather, whenever it is correct (*ṣaḥiḥ*) to keep a fast (*ṣawm*) during the year, performing *iʿtikāf* at that time is also correct. The best time for performing *iʿtikāf* is the blessed month of Ramadan, more so during the last ten nights of the month of Ramadan.

Ruling 1721. The minimum length of time for *iʿtikāf* is two nights and three days; less than that is not correct. There is no maximum limit. There is no problem in including the first or the fourth night in the intention of *iʿtikāf*. If a person is a *muʿtakif* [the term given to someone who is performing *iʿtikāf*] for five full days, he must also be a *muʿtakif* on the sixth day.

Ruling 1722. The starting time for *iʿtikāf* is the time of morning (*ṣubḥ*) prayers on the first day, and, based on obligatory precaution (*al-iḥtiyāṭ al-wājib*), the finishing time for *iʿtikāf* is the time of *maghrib* prayers on the third day. For a valid *iʿtikāf* to take place, a period equivalent to three days will not suffice; i.e. one cannot be a *muʿtakif* after the time of *ṣubḥ* prayers on the first day [and stay in the mosque until the same time on the fourth day] even if he compensates the time lost from the first day on the fourth day; for example, he stays in the mosque from the time of afternoon prayers (*ẓuhr*) of the first day until the time of afternoon prayers on the fourth day.

CONDITIONS FOR THE VALIDITY OF *IʿTIKĀF*

Ruling 1723. The following are the conditions for a valid *iʿtikāf*.

i. The *muʿtakif* must be a Muslim.

ii. The *muʿtakif* must be sane (*ʿāqil*).
iii. *Iʿtikāf* must be performed with the intention of attaining proximity to Allah.

Ruling 1724. A *muʿtakif* must have the intention of attaining proximity to Allah in the same manner that was mentioned regarding ablution (*wuḍūʾ*).[1] *Iʿtikāf* must be performed from start to finish with a sincere intention to attain proximity to Allah.

iv. The duration of the *iʿtikāf* must be a minimum of three days.

Ruling 1725. The minimum duration of *iʿtikāf* is three days; less than three days is incorrect. However, there is no maximum limit, as mentioned in Ruling 1721.

v. A *muʿtakif* must fast during the days of *iʿtikāf*.

Ruling 1726. A *muʿtakif* must fast during the days of *iʿtikāf*. Therefore, *iʿtikāf* performed by someone who cannot [legally] fast [during those days] – such as a traveller who does not intend to stay somewhere for ten days, a sick person, a woman in menstruation (i.e. a *ḥāʾiḍ*), and a woman who is experiencing lochia (*nifās*) – is not correct. Furthermore, on the days of *iʿtikāf*, it is not necessary to fast *especially* for performing *iʿtikāf*; rather, it is acceptable for one to keep any fast during *iʿtikāf*, even a fast that one has been hired to keep (*istījārī*), or a recommended fast, or a lapsed (*qaḍāʾ*) fast.

Ruling 1727. While a *muʿtakif* is fasting – i.e. from the time of *ṣubḥ* prayers until the time of *maghrib* prayers – everything that invalidates (i.e. makes *bāṭil*) a fast also invalidates *iʿtikāf*. Therefore, a *muʿtakif* must refrain from intentionally (*ʿamdan*) doing the things that invalidate a fast.[2]

vi. *Iʿtikāf* must be performed in one of 'the four mosques' or a *jāmiʿ* mosque.

[1] See the sixth condition for the validity of *wuḍūʾ* and Ruling 281.
[2] See Ruling 1551 for a list of things that invalidate a fast.

Ruling 1728. It is correct to perform *iʿtikāf* in Masjid al-Ḥarām, Masjid al-Nabī (Ṣ), Masjid al-Kūfah, and Masjid al-Baṣrah. Similarly, it is correct to perform *iʿtikāf* in the *jāmiʿ* mosque of every town, except when the religious leadership (*imāmah*) of that mosque is in the hands of a person who is not dutiful (*ʿādil*), in which case, based on obligatory precaution, *iʿtikāf* is not correct. A *jāmiʿ* mosque is one that is not particular to people of a specific locality, area, or group; rather, it is a place where people of different areas and localities of the town gather and frequent. The legality (*mashrūʿiyyah*) of *iʿtikāf* performed in any mosque other than a *jāmiʿ* mosque is not established; however, there is no problem in performing *iʿtikāf* in other mosques with the intention that it being a desirable act is probable. As for performing *iʿtikāf* in a place that is not a mosque – for example, in a place that is a *ḥusayniyyah*[3] or only a prayer room – it is not correct and has no legal basis.

vii. *Iʿtikāf* must take place in one mosque.

Ruling 1729. It is necessary that *iʿtikāf* be performed in one mosque. Therefore, one *iʿtikāf* cannot be performed in two mosques, whether they are separate from each other or joined together, unless they are joined together in a manner that they are commonly considered one mosque.

viii. *Iʿtikāf* must be performed with the permission of one whose permission is legally (*sharʿan*) required.

Ruling 1730. *Iʿtikāf* must be performed with the permission of one whose permission is legally required. Therefore, if a woman's staying in a mosque is unlawful (*ḥarām*) – for example, because she has left her house without the consent of her husband – her *iʿtikāf* is invalid. In case a woman's staying in a mosque is not unlawful but performing *iʿtikāf* conflicts with her husband's rights, the validity of her *iʿtikāf* – if performed without her husband's permission – is problematic (*maḥall al-ishkāl*) [i.e. based on obligatory precaution, it

[3] A *ḥusayniyyah* is a congregation hall used by Shia Muslims for religious ceremonies.

is not valid].[4] Similarly, if *iʿtikāf* disturbs and annoys one's parents due to their compassion and sympathy for him, it is necessary for him to obtain their permission. And if it does not annoy them, the recommended precaution is that he should get their consent.

ix. A *muʿtakif* must refrain from doing the unlawful acts of *iʿtikāf*.

Ruling 1731. Someone who is performing *iʿtikāf* must refrain from doing the unlawful acts of *iʿtikāf*, which are as follows:

1. smelling a pleasant fragrance;
2. having sexual intercourse with one's spouse;
3. masturbating, having sexual contact with one's spouse by means of touching, and lustfully kissing (based on obligatory precaution);
4. disputing (*mumārāh*) and arguing (*mujādalah*) with others;
5. buying and selling.

Doing these things invalidates one's *iʿtikāf*. In the case of an *iʿtikāf* that is not an assigned obligation [i.e. it is not *al-wājib al-muʿayyan*],[5] the obligation to refrain from these things – apart from having sexual intercourse – is based on obligatory precaution.[6]

Ruling 1732. It is not permitted (*jāʾiz*) for a *muʿtakif* to smell perfumes in any circumstance – whether he derives pleasure from smelling them or not – neither is it permitted for him to smell fragrant plants and flowers if he derives pleasure from doing so; however, there is no problem if he does not derive pleasure from smelling them. Similarly, a *muʿtakif* can use perfumed personal cleansing products, such as

[4] As mentioned in Ruling 6, the term 'problematic' (*maḥall al-ishkāl*) amounts to saying the ruling is based on obligatory precaution.

[5] An assigned obligation is an act of worship that must be performed at one distinct time. One way that an *iʿtikāf* could become an assigned obligation is by means of a vow.

[6] This means that, with regard to an *iʿtikāf* that is not an assigned obligation, the obligation to refrain from having sexual intercourse is a fatwa, whereas the obligation to refrain from the other things is based on obligatory precaution (see Ruling 6 for the distinction between a fatwa and a ruling based on obligatory precaution). As for an *iʿtikāf* that is an assigned obligation, the obligation to refrain from these things is a fatwa.

liquid soap or a bar of soap, shampoo, and toothpaste that has a pleasant smell. However, it is not permitted to smell the perfume that people who are not performing *iʿtikāf* usually apply when they come to mosques; but, apparently, merely having a sense of the fragrant smell is not a problem, nor is it necessary for one to hold his nose.

Ruling 1733. While one is performing *iʿtikāf*, it is not permitted for him to have sexual intercourse with his spouse – even if it does not result in ejaculation – and doing so intentionally invalidates *iʿtikāf*.

Ruling 1734. Based on an obligatory precaution, a *muʿtakif* must not intend to ejaculate (even by lawful means); furthermore, he must refrain from having sexual contact with his spouse by means of touching, and he must refrain from lustfully kissing her. Looking lustfully at one's spouse during *iʿtikāf* does not invalidate one's *iʿtikāf*, but the recommended precaution is that one should refrain from doing so.

Ruling 1735. Arguing about worldly or religious matters while one is performing *iʿtikāf* is unlawful if it is done with the intention of defeating the other person or showing off one's virtues and superiority. However, if it is done with the intention of making evident what is right, clarifying what is true, and resolving an error or mistake made by the other party, not only is it not unlawful but it is one of the best forms of worship. Therefore, the criterion [of whether such action is unlawful or not] is the intention of the *muʿtakif*.

Ruling 1736. Buying and selling while one is performing *iʿtikāf* is unlawful. And based on obligatory precaution, any type of business transaction – such as hiring (*ijārah*), sleeping partnership (*muḍārabah*),[7] and exchange (*muʿāwaḍah*) – is also unlawful, although the transaction (*muʿāmalah*) that is conducted is valid.

Ruling 1737. Whenever a *muʿtakif* is compelled to conduct a transaction to procure food and drink or other necessary items, and he

[7] This is a contract between two people in which one of them provides capital to the other so that the latter may trade with it and the profits be divided between them. See Chapter 14.

cannot find someone else who is not a *muʿtakif* to do this on his behalf by way of agency (*wikālah*), and it is not possible for him to procure the items mentioned above without conducting a transaction – for example, by way of receiving them as a gift or borrowing them – in such a case, there is no problem in him conducting the transaction.

Ruling 1738. If a *muʿtakif* intentionally commits an unlawful act of *iʿtikāf* despite knowing the religious law (*al-ḥukm al-sharʿī*), his *iʿtikāf* becomes invalid.

Ruling 1739. If a *muʿtakif* inadvertently (*sahwan*) or forgetfully commits an unlawful act of *iʿtikāf*, it does not invalidate his *iʿtikāf* in any circumstance.

Ruling 1740. If a *muʿtakif* commits an unlawful act of *iʿtikāf* on account of not knowing the ruling about this, in the event that he was culpably ignorant (*al-jāhil al-muqaṣṣir*),[8] his *iʿtikāf* becomes invalid. If he was inculpably ignorant (*al-jāhil al-qāṣir*), his *iʿtikāf* is valid and it will be ruled to be inadvertence [which as mentioned in the previous ruling, does not invalidate one's *iʿtikāf* in any circumstance].

Ruling 1741. If a *muʿtakif* invalidates his *iʿtikāf* by doing one of the things that renders an *iʿtikāf* invalid – which were mentioned in the previous rulings (*masāʾil*) – and if the *iʿtikāf* is an assigned obligation,[9] then based on obligatory precaution, he must make up the *iʿtikāf* [i.e. he must perform it belatedly as *qaḍāʾ*]. If the *iʿtikāf* is not an assigned obligation – for example, one makes a vow to perform *iʿtikāf* without assigning a time for it – it is obligatory that he start the *iʿtikāf* all over again. If it is a recommended *iʿtikāf* and one invalidates his *iʿtikāf* after the completion of the second day, then based on obligatory precaution, he must make up the *iʿtikāf*. And if one invalidates a recommended *iʿtikāf* before the completion of the second day, there is no obligation for him and he does not have to make it up.

[8] The terms 'culpably ignorant' and 'inculpably ignorant' are explained in footnotes pertaining to Ruling 12.

[9] See the first footnote pertaining to Ruling 1731 for an explanation of this term.

x. A *muʿtakif* must remain in the place of *iʿtikāf* and he must not leave it except in cases where leaving is legally permitted.

Ruling 1742. In cases where it is permitted for a *muʿtakif* to leave the mosque, he must not stay outside the mosque for longer than it is necessary for him to attend to the matter in question.

LEAVING THE PLACE OF *IʿTIKĀF*

Ruling 1743. Leaving the place of *iʿtikāf* for necessary and unavoidable matters – such as going to the toilet – is permitted. Leaving the mosque to perform ritual bathing (*ghusl*) for ritual impurity (*janābah*) is also permitted; indeed, it is obligatory. Similarly, women are permitted to leave to perform the *ghusl* for irregular blood discharge (*istiḥāḍah*). If a woman who is experiencing *istiḥāḍah* and who must perform *ghusl* does not do so, the validity of her *iʿtikāf* is not affected.

Ruling 1744. Leaving the place of *iʿtikāf* to perform ablution (*wuḍūʾ*) for an obligatory prayer within its prescribed time (*adāʾ*) is permitted, even if the time for the prayer has not yet set in. Leaving to perform *wuḍūʾ* for an obligatory *qaḍāʾ* prayer – in case there is ample time for performing it – is problematic [i.e. based on obligatory precaution, one must not leave in this case].

Ruling 1745. In the event that there are facilities for performing *wuḍūʾ* inside the mosque, a *muʿtakif* cannot leave the mosque to perform *wuḍūʾ*.

Ruling 1746. If it becomes obligatory for a *muʿtakif* to perform *ghusl*, in case the *ghusl* is one of the *ghusl*s that is not permitted to be performed in a mosque – such as the *ghusl* for *janābah*, which would require staying in the mosque while in the state of *janābah* or would cause the mosque to become impure – then he must leave; otherwise, his *iʿtikāf* becomes invalid. In case there is no problem in performing *ghusl* in the mosque – such as the *ghusl* for touching a corpse (*mass al-mayyit*) – and it is possible to perform *ghusl*, then based on obligatory precaution, it is not permitted to leave the mosque.

Ruling 1747. Leaving the place of *iʿtikāf* to perform recommended *ghusls* – such as the Friday *ghusl* or the *ghusl* for performing the rituals (*aʿmāl*) of Umm Dāwūd[10] – and similarly, leaving to perform a recommended *wuḍūʾ*, is problematic [i.e. based on obligatory precaution, one must not leave to perform them]. Generally speaking, leaving a mosque for supererogatory matters (i.e. those that are religiously preferred to be done rather than not done) – excluding matters that are commonly considered necessary – is problematic, and precaution must be observed [i.e. based on obligatory precaution, one must not leave the mosque for supererogatory matters]. However, a *muʿtakif* can leave the place of *iʿtikāf* for the purposes of attending a funeral procession (*tashyīʿ al-janāzah*), preparing a corpse for *ghusl*, the funeral prayer (*ṣalāt al-mayyit*), burial (*dafn*), and suchlike; [he can also leave for] visiting the sick and attending the Friday prayer (*ṣalāt al-jumuʿah*).

Ruling 1748. Based on obligatory precaution, it is not permitted for a *muʿtakif* to leave the mosque to attend congregational prayers (*ṣalāt al-jamāʿah*) that are being held outside the place of *iʿtikāf* unless one is a *muʿtakif* in the holy city of Mecca, in which case he can leave the mosque to perform congregational prayers or to perform prayers on his own (*furādā*). Furthermore, he can perform these prayers wherever in Mecca he wants.

Ruling 1749. A *muʿtakif* cannot leave the mosque to bring things he needs if he can instruct someone who is not a *muʿtakif* to bring them for him.

Ruling 1750. A *muʿtakif* can leave the place of *iʿtikāf* to sit secondary school, university, or *ḥawzah* (Islamic seminary) examinations in the event that it is commonly considered necessary. However, he must not stay outside the mosque for a long time such that the form of the *iʿtikāf* is lost; up to two hours, for example, is not a problem.

Ruling 1751. If a *muʿtakif* leaves the mosque to attend to some urgent

[10] The rituals of Umm Dāwūd are a recommended set of acts of worship that are usually performed in the middle of the month of Rajab. See, for example, Shaykh ʿAbbās al-Qummī's *Mafātīḥ al-Jinān*, in the section on the recommended acts for Rajab.

matter but stays outside for a long time such that the form of his *iʿtikāf* is lost, his *iʿtikāf* is invalid even if he was compelled or forced to leave, or if he left because of necessity or due to forgetfulness.

Ruling 1752. If a *muʿtakif* leaves the place of *iʿtikāf* – intentionally, of his own choice, and while knowing the religious law – for a matter that is neither necessary nor one for which a *muʿtakif* is permitted to leave, his *iʿtikāf* becomes invalid.

Ruling 1753. If a *muʿtakif* leaves the place of *iʿtikāf* – on account of not knowing the ruling (*masʾalah*) and being ignorant of the religious law – for a matter that is neither necessary nor one for which a *muʿtakif* is permitted to leave, his *iʿtikāf* becomes invalid.

Ruling 1754. If a *muʿtakif* leaves the mosque due to forgetfulness, his *iʿtikāf* becomes invalid. If a *muʿtakif* leaves the mosque because he was compelled or forced to leave, his *iʿtikāf* does not become invalid unless he stays outside for a long time such that the form of *iʿtikāf* is lost, in which case his *iʿtikāf* becomes invalid.

Ruling 1755. If it is obligatory for a *muʿtakif* to leave the place of *iʿtikāf* – for example, to pay a debt that is obligatory for him, and the time to repay it is due, and he has the ability to repay it, and the lender wants it to be repaid; or, to accomplish something else that is obligatory for him and which requires him to leave – then in these cases, if he acts contrary to his duty and does not leave, he commits a sin but his *iʿtikāf* does not become invalid.

Ruling 1756.* A *muʿtakif* must not stay outside the mosque for longer than is necessary; and while he is outside, if possible, he must not sit under a shade. However, if he cannot help sitting under a shade in order to attend to the matter in question, there is no problem. And based on obligatory precaution, after he has attended to the matter, he must not sit at all unless it is necessary for him to do so.

Ruling 1757. A *muʿtakif* can walk under a shade outside the mosque, although the recommended precaution is that he should avoid doing so.

Ruling 1758. Based on obligatory precaution, it is necessary for a *muʿtakif* to take the shortest route when he leaves the place of *iʿtikāf* or returns to it. However, if he would end up staying outside the mosque for a shorter time by using a longer route, he must choose the longer route.

MISCELLANEOUS RULINGS ON *IʿTIKĀF*

Ruling 1759. When one makes the intention to perform an *iʿtikāf* that is not an assigned obligation,[11] he can stipulate a condition from the outset that if a problem arises, he will leave the *iʿtikāf*.[12] Therefore, by stipulating such a condition, one can leave the *iʿtikāf* if a problem arises, and there is no problem in doing so even on the third day. However, if a *muʿtakif* stipulates a condition that he will stop his *iʿtikāf* even if no particular reason arises, the validity of such a condition is problematic [i.e. based on obligatory precaution, it is not a valid condition]. It is worth mentioning that stipulating the aforementioned condition (i.e. the condition of leaving the *iʿtikāf* in the middle of it if a problem arises) before or after the *iʿtikāf* has started is not correct; rather, it must be stipulated at the time of making the intention to perform *iʿtikāf*.

Ruling 1760. A valid *iʿtikāf* is not conditional on one having reached the age of legal responsibility (*bulūgh*), and *iʿtikāf* performed by a child who is able to discern between right and wrong (*mumayyiz*) is also correct.

Ruling 1761. If a *muʿtakif* sits on a usurped (*ghaṣbī*) carpet and he is aware of the fact that it is usurped, he commits a sin but his *iʿtikāf* does not become invalid. If someone gets to a place first and reserves it and a *muʿtakif* takes his place without his consent, then although he commits a sin, his *iʿtikāf* is valid.

Ruling 1762. If at the time of making the intention for an obligatory *iʿtikāf* one stipulates a condition of returning (i.e. a condition of leaving the *iʿtikāf* in the middle of it if a problem arises) – the details

[11] See the first footnote pertaining to Ruling 1731 for an explanation of this term.
[12] Such a condition is known as 'a condition of returning (*rujūʿ*)'.

of which were mentioned in Ruling 1759 – in the event that he does something that is unlawful for one to do during *iʿtikāf*, it is not necessary for him to make up the *iʿtikāf* nor to start it all over again.

Ruling 1763. If a woman who is performing *iʿtikāf* becomes *ḥāʾiḍ* after the completion of the second day of *iʿtikāf*, it is obligatory for her to leave the mosque immediately. And based on obligatory precaution, it is necessary for her to make up the *iʿtikāf* unless from the outset she had stipulated a condition of returning (i.e. a condition of leaving the *iʿtikāf* in the middle of it if a problem arises), the details of which were mentioned in Ruling 1759.

Ruling 1764. Performing an obligatory *qaḍāʾ iʿtikāf* is not an immediate obligation (*al-wājib al-fawrī*).[13] However, making it up must not be delayed to such an extent that it would be regarded as being careless in accomplishing the obligation. And the recommended precaution is that it should be made up immediately.

Ruling 1765. If a *muʿtakif* dies in the middle of an *iʿtikāf* that has become obligatory on account of a vow, oath, covenant, or the passing of two days of *iʿtikāf*, it is not obligatory for his guardian (*walī*) (i.e. the eldest son) to make up the *qaḍāʾ iʿtikāf*, although the recommended precaution is that a *qaḍāʾ iʿtikāf* of a deceased person should be performed. Of course, in the event that a *muʿtakif* had stipulated in his will that in such a case someone must be hired from the one-third of his estate[14] to perform *iʿtikāf* for him, then the deceased *muʿtakif*'s will must be followed.

Ruling 1766. If a *muʿtakif* intentionally invalidates his *iʿtikāf* by having sexual intercourse – be it during the day or at night – it is obligatory for him to give recompense (*kaffārah*). As for [intentionally invalidating one's *iʿtikāf* by performing] other unlawful acts, there is no *kaffārah*, although the recommended precaution is that one should give *kaffārah*.

[13] This is an obligation that must be performed as soon as it is possible to do so, and delaying its performance is not permitted.

[14] This refers to the maximum amount of one's estate over which he has discretion in a will for it to be disposed of in accordance with his wishes after his death.

The *kaffārah* for invalidating an *iʿtikāf* is the same as the *kaffārah* for invalidating a fast of the month of Ramadan – i.e. one has the choice of fasting for sixty days or feeding sixty poor people (*fuqarāʾ*) – although the recommended precaution is that one should observe the sequence in giving *kaffārah*, meaning that one should first fast for sixty days, and if he cannot, he should then feed sixty poor people.

Ruling 1767. It is not permitted to change from one *iʿtikāf* to another, whether both *iʿtikāf*s happen to be obligatory, like when a person has made one of them obligatory on account of a vow and the other on account of an oath; or, both are recommended; or, one is obligatory and the other recommended; or, one is to be performed for himself and the other on behalf of someone else (*niyābah*), or he is being hired to perform it for someone else; or, both are to be performed on behalf of someone else.

CHAPTER SIX

The One-Fifth Tax (*Khums*)

Ruling 1768. *Khums* becomes obligatory (*wājib*) on seven things:

1. surplus income from earnings and gains;
2. mined products;
3. treasure troves;
4. lawful (*ḥalāl*) property that has become mixed with unlawful (*ḥarām*) property;
5. precious stones that are acquired by underwater diving;
6. spoils of war;
7. land that a *dhimmī*[1] purchases from a Muslim, based on the opinion held by most jurists (*mashhūr*).

The laws (*aḥkām*) of these will now be mentioned in detail.

1. SURPLUS INCOME FROM EARNINGS AND GAINS

Ruling 1769. Whenever a person acquires property by means of trade, craftsmanship, or any other form of earning – even if, for example, he performs the prayers (*ṣalāh*) and keeps the fasts (*ṣawm*) of a deceased person, and with the wages he receives from that he acquires some property – then, in the event that it exceeds his and his family's living expenses for the year, he must pay *khums* – i.e. one-fifth – of it in accordance with the instructions that will be mentioned later.

Ruling 1770. If a person acquires property without earning it – for example, he is gifted something – then, with the exception of the cases mentioned in the next ruling, he must pay *khums* on it provided that it exceeds his living expenses for the year.

Ruling 1771. *Khums* is not liable on the dowry (*mahr*) that a wife receives, nor on the property that a husband receives in exchange

[1] *Dhimmīs* are People of the Book (*ahl al-kitāb*) – i.e. Jews, Christians, and Zoroastrians – who have entered into a *dhimmah* treaty, i.e. an agreement that gives them rights as protected subjects in an Islamic state.

for a *khulʿ* divorce,[2] nor on religious blood money (*diyah*) that one receives, whether that be blood money for a limb or for a life (i.e. for someone who has been killed). The same applies to the inheritance that one receives in accordance with those laws of inheritance that are considered valid. Therefore, if a Shia Muslim inherits property in another way, such as by *taʿṣīb*,[3] then the property is considered a gain and *khums* must be paid on it. Similarly, if a person inherits from an unexpected source that is neither from his father nor his son, then based on obligatory precaution (*al-iḥtiyāṭ al-wājib*), he must pay *khums* on the inheritance if it exceeds his living expenses for the year.

Ruling 1772.* If a person inherits some property and knows that the person from whom he inherited it did not pay *khums* on it, he must pay *khums* on it. Similarly, if the property itself is not liable for *khums* but the heir knows that the person he inherited it from owed some *khums*, he must pay *khums* on it from the deceased's estate. However, in both cases, if the person from whom he inherited it did not believe in paying *khums*, or never paid it, and neither stipulated in his will that it be paid from his estate, then it is not necessary for the heir to pay the *khums* owed by the deceased.

Ruling 1773. If a person saves money on his living expenses for the year by being frugal, he must still pay *khums* on it.

Ruling 1774. If a person's entire living expenses are paid by someone else, he must pay *khums* on his entire earnings.

Ruling 1775. If someone gives some property to particular persons – for example, he gives his children some property as a charitable endowment (*waqf*) – in the event that the property is farmed or trees are planted on it, and something is earned from it, and the earnings exceed their living expenses for the year, then those persons must pay *khums* on the extra earnings. Similarly, if they profit from the property in some other way – for example, they give it on hire

[2] This is a divorce of a wife who has an aversion to her husband and gives him her dowry (*mahr*) or some of her other property so that he divorces her. See Rulings 2546–2548.

[3] This is a matter of inheritance that is common among Sunni Muslims but invalid from a Shiʿi perspective. [Author]

(*ijārah*) – they must pay *khums* on the amount that exceeds their living expenses for the year.

Ruling 1776. If the property that a poor person (*faqīr*) has received from obligatory charitable payments (*ṣadaqah*) – such as recompense (*kaffārah*) and *radd al-maẓālim*[4] – or, if he has received it from recommended (*mustaḥabb*) *ṣadaqah*, and if the property exceeds his living expenses for the year or he acquires profit from it – for example, he acquires fruit from a tree that was given to him – and the profit exceeds his living expenses for the year, then based on obligatory precaution, he must pay *khums* on it. However, if he receives some property as *khums* or alms tax (zakat), being someone entitled (*mustaḥiqq*) to receive it, then it is not necessary for him to pay *khums* on the property itself; but if the profit that accrues from it exceeds his living expenses for the year, then the profit is liable for *khums*.

Ruling 1777. If a person purchases something with the actual money on which *khums* has not been paid, i.e. he tells the seller that he is purchasing the item with that money,[5] then, in the event that the seller is a Twelver (Ithnā ʿAsharī) Shia, the entire transaction (*muʿāmalah*) is valid (*ṣaḥīḥ*), and the item that has been purchased with the money is liable for *khums*; and there is no need to get authorisation or approval from a fully qualified jurist (*al-ḥākim al-sharʿī*).

Ruling 1778. If a person purchases something by undertaking to pay for the item later, and after the transaction he pays the seller money on which *khums* has not been paid,[6] the transaction is valid but he will be indebted to those entitled (*mustaḥiqqūn*) to receive *khums* for the *khums* on the money he paid the seller.

Ruling 1779. If a Twelver Shia Muslim purchases something on which *khums* has not been paid, the seller is liable for its *khums*, not the buyer.

[4] *Radd al-maẓālim* refers to giving back property – which has been unrightfully or unknowingly taken – to its rightful owner, or if that is not possible, to the poor as *ṣadaqah* on behalf of the rightful owner.
[5] This is known as a 'specified' (*shakhṣī*) purchase. See the second footnote pertaining to Ruling 807.
[6] This is referring to a type of purchase known as a 'non-specified undertaking'. See the first footnote pertaining to Ruling 807.

Ruling 1780. If a person gifts something to a Twelver Shia Muslim on which *khums* has not been paid, the benefactor is liable for its *khums*, not the beneficiary [but as stated in ruling 1770, if at the end of the year the gift exceeds his living expenses for the year, he must pay *khums* on it at that point].

Ruling 1781. If a person acquires some property from a disbeliever (*kāfir*) or someone who does not believe in paying *khums* or does not pay *khums*, it is not obligatory for him to pay *khums* on it.

Ruling 1782.* If a businessman, merchant, craftsman, clerk, etc., starts trading or working, then after the passing of one year, he must pay *khums* on the amount that exceeds his living expenses for the year. The same applies to a preacher etc., even if his income is earned at certain times of the year, provided that the income is sufficient to meet a significant portion of his living expenses for the year. As for someone who does not have an occupation by which he can earn a living and who receives help from the government or from people, or someone who incidentally acquires some profit, such persons must pay *khums* on the amount that exceeds their living expenses for the year after one year has passed from the time they acquired the profit. Therefore, [for the purposes of *khums*] they can calculate a different year for each amount.

Ruling 1783. During the year, a person can pay *khums* on his profit whenever he acquires it, and it is also permitted (*jāʾiz*) for him to delay paying *khums* until the end of the year. However, if he knows that he will not need it until the end of the year, then based on obligatory precaution, he must pay *khums* on it immediately. Furthermore, there is no problem if one adopts the solar year for the payment of *khums*.

Ruling 1784. If a person makes a profit and he dies during the year, his living expenses until the time of his death must be deducted from the profit, and after that *khums* must be paid immediately on the balance.

Ruling 1785. If the price of a commodity that a person has purchased for the purposes of business rises, and if the person does not sell it and its price falls during the same year [and it is not worth more than the price he paid for it], then *khums* on the amount of increase in the price is not obligatory for him.

Ruling 1786. If the price of a commodity that a person has purchased for the purposes of business rises, and if the person does not sell it until after the year finishes in the hope that the price will rise, and if in actual fact the price falls, then based on obligatory precaution, it is obligatory for him to pay *khums* on the amount of increase in the price.

Ruling 1787. If a person has purchased property that was not for business and he has paid *khums* on it, in the event that its price rises and he sells it, he must pay *khums* on the amount that has increased in price and which exceeds his living expenses for the year. Similarly, if, for example, a tree bears fruit or a sheep that is kept for its meat becomes fat, one must pay *khums* on the excess gain.

Ruling 1788. If a person creates a garden with money on which he has paid *khums* or which is not liable for *khums*, and if he wants to sell it after its price appreciates, he must pay *khums* on the fruits, and on the growth of the trees and shrubs that were already growing or that he planted, and on the dry branches that can be pruned and used, and on the increase in the price of the garden. However, if his intention is to sell the fruit of the trees and to benefit from their value, then *khums* is not obligatory on the increase in price and the rest is liable for *khums*.

Ruling 1789. If a person plants willows, planes, or similar trees, he must pay *khums* every year on their growth. Similarly, with regard to the branches of trees that are usually pruned every year, if [they are sold and the income] exceeds his living expenses for the year, he must pay *khums* on them.

Ruling 1790. A person who has a number of lines of business – for example, with his capital he has bought [and trades in] sugar and rice – in the event that all the lines of his business are the same in business matters such as income and outcome, bookkeeping, and profit and loss, he must pay *khums* on the amount that exceeds his living expenses for the year. In the event that he gains a profit from one line and makes a loss from another, he can offset the loss from that line with the profit from the other. However, if he has two different lines of business – for example, he trades as well as farms – or, if he has one line of business but the profit and loss are calculated separately from each other, then in these two cases, he cannot, based on obligatory precaution, offset the loss of one with the profit of the other.

Ruling 1791. A person can deduct from his profit the expenses he incurs in making the profit – such as brokerage and transportation costs – and the same applies to any damage done to his tools and equipment, and it is not necessary for him to pay *khums* on that amount.

Ruling 1792. The amount a person spends from his profit during the year on food, clothing, furniture, the purchase of a house, the wedding of his son, the trousseau of his daughter, *ziyārah*,[7] and suchlike, is not liable for *khums* provided that the amount spent is not beyond his status [i.e. the expenses are considered reasonable for someone of his status to incur].

Ruling 1793. The amount one spends on a vow (*nadhr*) and *kaffārah* is considered part of his annual living expenses. Similarly, property that one gives to someone as a gift or prize is also considered part of his annual living expenses, provided that it is not beyond his status.

Ruling 1794. If it is common practice [where the person lives] for a person to acquire the trousseau for his daughter gradually over a number of years, and if he does not acquire the trousseau it would be unbefitting of his status – albeit because he was unable to acquire it all at the required time – and if during the year he purchases some of the trousseau from the profit of that year, and his purchases do not exceed his status, and acquiring such a portion of the trousseau in one year would be commonly considered to be part of his normal annual expenditure, then in such a case, it is not obligatory for him to pay *khums* on it. However, if his purchases exceed his status or he acquires the trousseau next year from the current year's profit, he

[7] *Ziyārah* is a visitation to the place of burial of a holy personality or a holy place.

must pay *khums* on it.

Ruling 1795. The expenses incurred for hajj and other *ziyārahs* are considered part of one's living expenses for the year; and if his journey is prolonged until part of the following year, he must pay *khums* on what he spends from the previous year's profits in the second year.

Ruling 1796. With regard to someone who has earned profit from trade, business, or other means, if he owns some other property on which *khums* is not obligatory, he can calculate his living expenses for the year only from the profit he has earned.

Ruling 1797. If the provisions that a person purchases from his profit of the year are surplus to his needs at the end of the year, he must pay *khums* on them. In the event that he wants to pay its monetary value instead, then, if it has increased since the time he bought the provisions, he must calculate the *khums* based on the price at the end of the year.

Ruling 1798.* If before paying *khums* a person purchases household furniture with the profit earned by him and uses the items before the end of his *khums* year, it is not necessary for him to pay *khums* on the items if they are no longer needed after the year end. Similarly, the items are not liable for *khums* if they are not needed during the year, provided that they are things that are usually kept aside for future years, such as winter and summer clothes. Apart from these types of items, if they are not needed at all during the year, the obligatory precaution is that one must pay *khums* on them. As for the jewellery of a woman who no longer uses them for adornment, it is not liable for *khums*.

Ruling 1799. If a person does not make any profit in a year, he cannot deduct his expenses for that year from the profit he makes in the following year.

Ruling 1800. If a person does not make any profit at the beginning of a year and spends out of his capital but then makes some profit before the year's end, he can deduct the amount he had taken from his capital from the profit he earned.

Ruling 1801. If part of one's capital is lost in business and similar activities, he can deduct the lost amount from the profit made in the same year.

Ruling 1802. If some property other than one's capital is lost and he needs that item in the same year, he can acquire it during the year from his profit and it is not liable for *khums*.

Ruling 1803.* If a person does not make a profit at the end of a year and borrows money to meet his living expenses, he cannot deduct the borrowed amount from the profit made by him in future years and thereby not pay *khums* on the profit. However, if he borrows money to pay for [something that is a necessary or reasonable expense], such as a car or a house for his personal use, then while he owes money for the purchase of that item and is using it, he can deduct the borrowed amount from his income in future years provided he has not already deducted that borrowed amount from his income in previous years. If he borrows money during the year to meet his living expenses and makes a profit before the year's end, he can deduct the borrowed amount from his profit. Furthermore, in the first case, he can repay the borrowed amount from the income he receives in future years and that amount will not be liable for *khums*.[8]

Ruling 1804. If a person borrows money to increase his wealth or to purchase something that he does not need, then in the event that he repays the loan from the profit he acquires in that year without paying *khums*, he must pay *khums* on the money he borrowed or the item he purchased with the loan after the arrival of the *khums* year unless the money he borrowed / item he purchased with it perishes during the year.

[8] This ruling marks a change from al-Sayyid al-Sistani's previous opinion on loans. His Eminence now allows the remaining outstanding balance of a loan to be deducted from the surplus income of future years until the time the person's cumulative surplus income reaches the amount of the outstanding loan balance. After that point, only payments of the interest part of the loan will be considered deductible expenses for the purposes of calculating one's *khums* liability; repayments of the capital loan amount will not be deductible. For further information, see *Khums: A Brief Guide* (available on the OneStopFiqh online portal at fiqh.world-federation.org), pp. 8–11; and *Minhāj al-Ṣāliḥīn*, vol. 1, pp. 444–445, Ruling 1231.

Ruling 1805. A person can pay the *khums* of an item that is liable for *khums* from the item itself, or he can pay the monetary value of the *khums* that has become obligatory. However, if he wants to give something else on which *khums* has not become obligatory, then this is problematic (*maḥall al-ishkāl*) [i.e. based on obligatory precaution, he cannot do this],[9] unless he does so with authorisation from a fully qualified jurist.

Ruling 1806. If a person's property becomes liable for *khums* and a year has passed, he does not have disposal over that property until he pays *khums* on it.

Ruling 1807. A person who owes *khums* cannot take responsibility for it – meaning that he cannot regard himself as being indebted to those entitled to receive it – yet still have disposal over his entire wealth. In the event that he uses the wealth and it is lost, [not only will he have committed a sin but he will still be deemed responsible and] he must pay *khums* on it.

Ruling 1808. If a person who owes *khums* makes an interchange settlement[10] with a fully qualified jurist and takes responsibility for it, he has disposal over his entire property; and the profit he earns from it afterwards belongs to him. He must, however, gradually repay the debt in a manner that is not careless.

Ruling 1809. If a person who is a [business] partner with someone else pays *khums* on his profit but his partner does not, and in the following year his partner offers his property on which *khums* has not been paid as capital for the partnership, the first partner – supposing he is a Twelver Shia – has disposal over the joint property.

Ruling 1810.* If a child who is a minor (*ṣaghīr*) acquires some profit, albeit from gifts, and if during the year the profit is not used for the child's living expenses, it becomes liable for *khums* and it is obligatory

[9] As mentioned in Ruling 6, the term 'problematic' (*maḥall al-ishkāl*) amounts to saying the ruling is based on obligatory precaution.

[10] Here, the fully qualified jurist takes the *khums* from the person who owes it and then returns it to him as a loan. In this way, the person who owes *khums* can have disposal over his property.

for the guardian (*walī*) of the child to pay *khums* on it. In the event that the guardian does not pay it, it is obligatory for the child to pay *khums* on it after he reaches the age of legal responsibility (i.e. becomes *bāligh*). However, if a non-*bāligh* child who is *mumayyiz* [i.e. able to discern between right and wrong] follows a jurist [i.e. does *taqlīd* of a *mujtahid*] who believes that the property of a non-*bāligh* child is not liable for *khums*, then the guardian of that child does not have the right to pay *khums* on the child's property from the child's property.

Ruling 1811. If a person who acquires property doubts whether the former owner has paid *khums* on it or not, he still has disposal over the property. In fact, even if the new owner is certain that the former owner has not paid *khums* on it, if the former owner is someone who does not pay *khums* and the new owner is a Twelver Shia, he has disposal over it.

Ruling 1812. If a person purchases something with the profit earned by him during the year, but the item cannot be considered a necessary or reasonable expense [as per his status] for the year, it is obligatory for him to pay *khums* on it at the end of the year. In the event that he does not pay *khums* on it and the value of the property increases, he must pay *khums* on its current value.

Ruling 1813. If a person purchases something with money on which *khums* has not been paid for a year [as a non-specified undertaking, which is explained in the first footnote pertaining to Ruling 807], and if its price increases, then in the event that he did not intend to buy the item as an investment and to sell it when its price increases – for example, he purchases land for farming [rather than to sell it once its price increases] – he must pay *khums* on the purchase price. However, if, for example, he gives the seller the actual money on which *khums* has not been paid and tells him that he is purchasing the item with that money,[11] he must pay *khums* on the current value of the item.

Ruling 1814. If someone has not paid *khums* from the time he became

[11] This is known as a 'specified' (*shakhṣī*) purchase. See the second footnote pertaining to Ruling 807.

legally obliged to fulfil religious duties, or if he has not paid *khums* for a period of time – for example, a number of years – then, if during the year he purchases something that he does not need from the profit made by trading and one year passes from the time he started trading – or, if he is not a trader and one year passes from the time he made the profit – he must pay *khums* on the item. However, if he purchases household furniture and other items that he needs according to his status, it is not necessary for him to pay *khums* on them provided that he knows that he purchased them during the year in which he made a profit, and he purchased them with the same year's profit, and he used them in the same year. If he does not know this, then based on obligatory precaution, he must arrive at a settlement (*muṣālaḥah*) with a fully qualified jurist on an amount that is proportionate to the probability; for example, if he deems it 50% probable that *khums* on the items is obligatory, then he must pay *khums* on that 50%.

2. MINED PRODUCTS

Ruling 1815. Mined products such as gold, silver, lead, copper, iron, oil, coal, turquoise (*fīrūzah*), agate (*ʿaqīq*), alum, salt, and others, are considered to be *anfāl*, i.e. they belong to the Imam (ʿA). However, if someone extracts them and there is no legal obstacle, he can own them; and in the event that the mined product's value reaches the taxable limit (*niṣāb*), he must pay *khums* on it.

Ruling 1816. The *niṣāb* for mined products is fifteen common (*ṣayrafī*) *mithqāls*[12] of coined gold, i.e. if the value of something that is extracted from a mine reaches fifteen common *mithqāls* of coined gold after deducting the costs for extracting it, then the subsequent expenses – such as the costs for purifying it – are subtracted and *khums* must be paid on the remainder.

Ruling 1817. When the value of something that has been extracted from a mine does not reach fifteen common *mithqāls* of coined gold, *khums* on it becomes necessary only when it – either on its own or in combina-

[12] Based on the definitions in Ruling 1912, one common *mithqāl* is equal to 4.608 grams; therefore, fifteen common *mithqāls* is equal to 69.12 grams.

tion with one's other profits – exceeds his living expenses for the year.

Ruling 1818. Based on obligatory precaution, the rules (*aḥkām*) of mined products also apply to chalk and lime. Therefore, if their value reaches the *niṣāb*, one must pay *khums* on them without deducting his living expenses for the year from their value.

Ruling 1819. A person who acquires something from a mine must pay *khums* on it, whether the mine is over the ground or under it, located on land owned by him or in a place that does not have an owner.

Ruling 1820. If a person does not know whether or not the value of the thing he has extracted from a mine reaches fifteen common *mithqāl*s of coined gold, the obligatory precaution is that if it is possible, he must ascertain its value by weighing it or by some other way; and if this is not possible, then *khums* is not obligatory for him.

Ruling 1821. If a few persons extract something from a mine, in the event that its total value reaches fifteen common *mithqāl*s of coined gold but the share of each person does not reach that value, it is not liable for *khums*.

Ruling 1822. If by digging, a person extracts a mined product from under some land that belongs to someone whose consent he did not get, the opinion held by most jurists (*mashhūr*) is that whatever is acquired from that belongs to the owner of the land. However, this is problematic and the obligatory precaution is that they must arrive at a settlement. In the event that they are not willing to arrive at a settlement, they must refer to a fully qualified jurist (*al-ḥākim al-sharʿī*) to settle the dispute.

3. TREASURE TROVES

Ruling 1823. A treasure trove is moveable, concealed property that is not within reach of people. It is hidden underground, in a tree, or on a mountain or wall, and its presence there is not normal.

Ruling 1824. If a person finds a treasure trove on land that does not belong to anyone or which is barren, and he becomes the owner of it by making it fertile, he can take the treasure trove for himself but he must pay *khums* on it.

Ruling 1825. The *niṣāb* for treasure troves is 105 *mithqāl*s of coined silver or fifteen *mithqāl*s of coined gold; i.e. if the value of the treasure trove is equal to either of these two amounts, then *khums* becomes obligatory on it.

Ruling 1826. If a person finds a treasure trove on land that he has purchased from someone or on land over which he has disposal on account of renting it and suchlike, and if that treasure trove does not legally (*sharʿan*) belong to a Muslim or a *dhimmī*, or if it does then it was such a long time ago that he is unable to ascertain whether or not there is an heir for it, in such a case, he can take the treasure trove for himself but he must pay *khums* on it. If he deems it rationally probable that the treasure belongs to the previous owner, then in case the previous owner had disposal over the land, the treasure trove, or its location as a result of owning the land, he must inform him. After that, if the previous owner makes a claim over the treasure trove, he must hand it over to him; and if he does not make a claim over it, he must inform the person who owned the land before the previous owner and who had disposal over it, and so on with regard to all the previous owners who had such disposal. If none of them makes a claim over the treasure trove and the present owner does not know whether or not it once belonged to another Muslim or *dhimmī*, he can take it for himself but he must pay *khums* on it.

Ruling 1827. If a person finds treasure troves in a number of places and their total value is 105 *mithqāl*s of silver or fifteen *mithqāl*s of gold, he must pay *khums* on them. However, if he finds the treasure troves at different times, then, if there was not a long interval between finding them, the value of all of them together must be calculated; but if there was a long interval, then each one must be calculated separately.

Ruling 1828. If two people find a treasure trove that has a total value that reaches 105 *mithqāl*s of silver or fifteen *mithqāl*s of gold but their individual shares do not come to that amount, it is not necessary for them to pay *khums* on it.

Ruling 1829. If a person purchases an animal and finds some property in its stomach, in the event that he deems it probable that it belongs to the seller or the previous owner, and they had disposal over the animal and over the object that was found in the animal's stomach, he must inform them about it. After that, if he does not find an owner for it, in the event that its value reaches the *niṣāb* of a treasure trove, he must pay *khums* on it. In fact, based on obligatory precaution, he must pay *khums* on it even if its value is less than the *niṣāb*; and the rest is his property. This rule also applies to fish etc., provided that it was looked after in a particular place and somebody undertook to feed it. However, if the fish was caught from the sea or a river, it is not necessary to inform anyone.

4. LAWFUL PROPERTY THAT HAS BECOME MIXED WITH UNLAWFUL PROPERTY

Ruling 1830. If lawful property has become mixed with unlawful property in a way that a person cannot distinguish one from the other, and if the owner and the quantity of the unlawful property are not known, and if one does not know whether the quantity of the unlawful property is less or more than one-fifth of the entire property, then by paying *khums* on it, it becomes lawful. And based on obligatory precaution, the *khums* must be given to someone entitled to receive both *khums* and *radd al-maẓālim.*

Ruling 1831. If lawful property becomes mixed with unlawful property and one knows the quantity of the unlawful property – irrespective of whether it is more or less than *khums* – but he does not know who its owner is, he must give away that quantity with the intention of *ṣadaqah* on behalf of its owner. And the obligatory precaution is that he must first obtain permission from a fully qualified jurist.

Ruling 1832. If lawful property becomes mixed with unlawful property and one does not know the quantity of the unlawful property but does know who its owner is, in the event that the person and the owner cannot come to a mutual agreement [as to the quantity of the unlawful property], the person must give the owner a quantity that he is certain is his. In fact, if the person himself was at fault in the two properties – i.e. the lawful and the unlawful – becoming mixed, then as an obligatory precaution, he must give him more than what he deems probable is his property.

Ruling 1833. If a person pays *khums* on lawful property that has become mixed with unlawful property and later realises that the quantity of unlawful property was more than the *khums*, he must give the extra quantity that he knows was more than *khums* as *ṣadaqah* on behalf of its owner.

Ruling 1834. If a person pays *khums* on lawful property that has become mixed with unlawful property, or if he gives some property as *ṣadaqah* on behalf of the owner who is unknown to him and later the owner is found, then in the event that the owner does not agree [to the action taken], based on obligatory precaution, the person must reimburse him his share.

Ruling 1835. If lawful property is mixed with unlawful property and the quantity of the unlawful property is known, and if a person knows that the owner can only be one of a group of people but he does not know which one, then in such a case, he must inform all of them. After that, in the event that one of them says it belongs to him and the others say it is not theirs or they confirm that it belongs to him, the person must give it to him. However, if two or more persons say it belongs to them, in the event that the dispute is not resolved by way of settlement and suchlike, they must refer to a fully qualified jurist to settle the dispute. If all of them claim they did not know or are not prepared to settle, then what is apparent (*ẓāhir*)[13] is that ownership of the property must be determined by drawing lots (*qurʿah*); and as an obligatory precaution, the lots must be drawn by a fully qualified jurist or his representative (*wakīl*).

[13] For practical purposes in jurisprudential rulings, expressing an 'apparent' ruling equates to giving a fatwa.

5. GEMS ACQUIRED BY UNDERWATER DIVING

Ruling 1836. If by means of underwater diving a person acquires pearls, corals, or other gems, whether they be growing things or minerals, in the event that their value reaches eighteen *nukhuds*[14] of gold, he must pay *khums* on them – irrespective of whether they were brought up in a single dive or multiple dives – provided there is not a long interval between them; and if there is – for example, he dives in two different seasons – then, in the event that [the gems found in] each dive do not reach the value of eighteen *nukhud*s of gold, it is not obligatory to pay *khums* on them. Similarly, if the share of each diver taking part in the dive does not reach the value of eighteen *nukhud*s of gold, it is not obligatory to pay *khums* on it.

Ruling 1837. If a person acquires gems from the sea by means other than diving, then based on obligatory precaution, it is obligatory for him to pay *khums* on them. However, if he acquires them from the surface of the sea or the seashore, he must pay *khums* on them only if what he has acquired on its own, or in combination with other profits made by him, exceeds his living expenses for the year.

Ruling 1838. *Khums* on fish and other animals that a person catches without diving into the sea is only obligatory if on its own, or in combination with other profits made by him, it exceeds his living expenses for the year.

Ruling 1839. If a person dives into the sea without the intention of bringing anything out of it, and if he incidentally finds a gem and intends to keep it, he must pay *khums* on it. In fact, the obligatory precaution is that he must pay *khums* on it in any situation.

Ruling 1840. If a person dives into the sea and brings out a creature and finds a gem in its stomach, in the event that the creature is like an oyster that by its nature can contain a gem, he must pay *khums* on it provided that its value reaches the *niṣāb*. If the creature has incidentally swallowed the gem, then the obligatory precaution is that

[14] A *nukhud* is a measure of weight. One *nukhud* is equivalent to 0.192 grams; therefore, eighteen *nukhud*s is equal to 3.456 grams.

one must pay *khums* on it even if its value does not reach the *niṣāb*.

Ruling 1841. If a person dives into big rivers like the Tigris and Euphrates and brings out a gem, he must pay *khums* on it.

Ruling 1842. If a person dives into water and brings out some ambergris with a value equal to eighteen *nukhud*s of gold or more, he must pay *khums* on it. In fact, the same rule applies even if it is obtained from the sea's surface or the seashore.

Ruling 1843. If a person whose profession is diving or extracting minerals pays *khums* on what he finds and the value of these items on which he has paid *khums* exceeds his living expenses for the year, it is not necessary for him to pay *khums* on them again.

Ruling 1844. If a child extracts a mineral, finds a treasure trove, or brings out gems from the sea by diving, his guardian must pay *khums* on them; and in the event that he does not, the child must pay the *khums* after he becomes *bāligh*. Similarly, if the child has lawful property mixed with unlawful property, the guardian must act according to the rules mentioned in the section on lawful property that has become mixed with unlawful property.[15]

6. SPOILS OF WAR

Ruling 1845. If Muslims fight a war against disbelievers (*kuffār*) in compliance with the command of the Imam (ʿA) and they acquire items from the war, those items are called *ghanāʾim* (spoils of war). The items that are exclusively for the Imam (ʿA) from the spoils of war must be put aside and *khums* must be paid on the rest. With regard to the liability of *khums*, there is no difference between movable and immovable things. Land that is not *anfāl* belongs to the general Muslim public even if the war was not fought with the permission of the Imam (ʿA).

Ruling 1846. If Muslims fight in a war against disbelievers without

[15] See Rulings 1830–1835.

authorisation from the Imam (ʿA) and the Muslims acquire spoils of war from them, then everything they acquire as spoils of the war belongs to the Imam (ʿA) and the fighters have no right over them.

Ruling 1847. The rules on spoils of war do not apply to things that are in the hands of disbelievers in the event that the owner is someone whose property is inviolable (*muḥtaram al-māl*), i.e. a Muslim, or a *dhimmī* disbeliever, or a cosignatory with Muslims to a peace or security treaty (*muʿāhad*).

Ruling 1848. Stealing etc. from a *ḥarbī* disbeliever[16] is unlawful in the event that it is considered treachery and a breach of security. And based on obligatory precaution, whatever is taken from him in this way must be returned.

Ruling 1849. The opinion held by most jurists (*mashhūr*) is that a believer can appropriate the property of a *nāṣibī*[17] and pay *khums* on it. However, this rule is problematic [i.e. based on obligatory precaution, one must avoid doing this].[18]

7. LAND THAT A *DHIMMĪ* PURCHASES FROM A MUSLIM

Ruling 1850. If a *dhimmī* disbeliever purchases land from a Muslim, then based on the opinion held by most jurists (*mashhūr*), he [i.e. the Muslim] must pay *khums* on it from the land itself or his other property. However, the obligation to pay *khums* – as it is commonly understood – in this case is problematic [i.e. he must pay *khums* on it as above but this is based on obligatory precaution].

[16] This refers to a disbeliever who is not a *dhimmī* and has not entered into a peace or security treaty with Muslims.

[17] In Ruling 103, *nawāṣib* (pl. of *nāṣibī*) are defined as 'those who show enmity towards the Imams (ʿA)'.

[18] See *Minhāj al-Ṣāliḥīn*, vol. 1, p. 428, Ruling 1190; and *Tawḍīḥ al-Masāʾil-i Jāmiʿ*, vol. 1, p. 700, Ruling 2436.

DISTRIBUTION OF *KHUMS*

Ruling 1851. *Khums* must be divided into two parts: one part is the portion for *sayyids*[19] (*sahm al-sādāt*), which must be given to a poor *sayyid*, an orphan *sayyid*, or a *sayyid* who is stranded on a journey. The second part is the portion for the Imam (ʿA) (*sahm al-imām*), which at present [i.e. during the time of the Imam's (ʿA) occultation] must either be given to a fully qualified jurist or spent for purposes that he authorises. And the obligatory precaution is that the jurist must be the most learned (*aʿlam*) *marjaʿ*[20] and be well aware of public affairs.

Ruling 1852. An orphan *sayyid* to whom *khums* is given must be poor. However, a *sayyid* who is stranded on a journey can be given *khums* even if he is not a poor person in his home town (*waṭan*).

Ruling 1853. If the journey of a *sayyid* who is stranded was for a sinful purpose, then based on obligatory precaution, he must not be given *khums*.

Ruling 1854. A *sayyid* who is not a dutiful person (*ʿādil*) can be given *khums*. However, *khums* must not be given to a *sayyid* who is not a Twelver Shia.

Ruling 1855. A *sayyid* who uses *khums* for sinful purposes cannot be given *khums*. In fact, the obligatory precaution is that *khums* must not be given to him if it assists him to commit sins, even if he does not spend it directly for sinful purposes. Similarly, the obligatory precaution is that a *sayyid* who consumes alcohol, does not perform prayers, or publicly commits sins, must not be given *khums*.

Ruling 1856. If a person claims that he is a *sayyid*, *khums* cannot be given to him unless two dutiful persons confirm it, or one attains certainty or confidence (*iṭmiʾnān*) by some other way that he is a *sayyid*.

[19] A *sayyid* is a male descendant of Hāshim, the great grandfather of Prophet Muḥammad (Ṣ).

[20] A *marjaʿ* is a jurist who has the necessary qualifications to be followed in matters of Islamic jurisprudence (*fiqh*). See Ruling 2.

Ruling 1857. *Khums* can be given to a person who is known to be a *sayyid* in his home town, provided that one is not certain or confident that he is not a *sayyid.*

Ruling 1858. If one's wife is a *sayyidah,*[21] then based on obligatory precaution, he must not give his *khums* to her to spend on her living expenses [that are obligatory for him to provide]. However, if it is obligatory for her to meet the living expenses of others but she cannot do so, it is permitted (*jā'iz*) for him to give his *khums* to her to spend on them. The same applies [i.e. as with the case mentioned at the beginning of this ruling, he must not, based on obligatory precaution,] give his *khums* to her to spend on her maintenance (*nafaqah*) that is not obligatory for him to provide.

Ruling 1859. If it is obligatory for a person to meet the living expenses of a *sayyid* or of a *sayyidah* who is not his wife, then based on obligatory precaution, he cannot provide for their food, clothing, and other obligatory maintenance from *khums.* However, there is no problem if he gives some *khums* to them to spend on things that are not obligatory for him to provide.

Ruling 1860. *Khums* can be given to a poor *sayyid* whose living expenses are obligatory for another person to meet but who cannot, or does not, meet the *sayyid*'s living expenses.

Ruling 1861.* The obligatory precaution is that one must not give a person entitled to receive *khums* an amount of *khums* that is more than his living expenses for the year in one go. And if one gives such a person his living expenses for the year in instalments, then once the amount reaches the level of his living expenses for the year, it is definitely not permitted to give him any more.

Ruling 1862. If there is no one entitled to receive *khums* in a person's town, he can take it to another town. In fact, he can take it to another town even if there is someone entitled to receive it in his town, provided that this act is not considered nonchalance in paying *khums.* In

[21] A *sayyidah* is a female descendant of Hāshim, the great grandfather of Prophet Muḥammad (Ṣ).

either case, if the *khums* perishes, he is responsible (*ḍāmin*) for it even if he was not negligent in looking after it. Furthermore, he cannot deduct the costs for taking it [to the other town] from the *khums*.

Ruling 1863. If a person takes possession of his *khums* by way of agency (*wikālah*) of a fully qualified jurist or his representative, he [is deemed to have paid his *khums* and] is absolved of his responsibility. Furthermore, if he transfers it to another town in compliance with the direction of a fully qualified jurist or his representative, and in the process it perishes without him being negligent, he is not responsible for it.

Ruling 1864. It is not permitted for one to calculate an item as having a higher price than it actually does and then give it in lieu of *khums*. And as stated in Ruling 1805, it is problematic [i.e. based on obligatory precaution, one must not] give something else in lieu of *khums* – apart from money – except with authorisation from a fully qualified jurist or his agent.

Ruling 1865.* If a person is owed money by a *sayyid* who is entitled to receive the portion for *sayyid*s, and the person who is owed wants to calculate the amount he is owed in lieu of the portion for *sayyid*s that he is liable to pay, he must, based on obligatory precaution, first obtain permission from a fully qualified jurist, or he must give the portion for *sayyid*s to the *sayyid* indebted to him who after that returns it to him in lieu of the money he owes him. Alternatively, the person who is owed the money can become an agent for the *sayyid* and take possession of it on his behalf as payment in lieu of what he is owed. As for the portion for the Imam (ʿA), if someone is owed money by a poor person, he cannot calculate the amount he is owed in lieu of the blessed portion for the Imam (ʿA) even if that poor person is unable to repay his debt. However, if the person who owes the money is entitled to receive the portion for the Imam (ʿA), leaving aside the fact that he owes money, then it is possible to give him the portion for the Imam (ʿA) while observing what was mentioned in Ruling 1851, and he can repay his debt with that money.

Ruling 1866. A person who must pay *khums* cannot make it a condition on someone entitled to receive it that he must return the amount to him.

CHAPTER SEVEN

Enjoining Good and Forbidding Evil

Among the most important religious obligations are enjoining good (*al-amr bil-maʿrūf*) and forbidding evil (*al-nahy ʿan al-munkar*). Allah the Exalted states in the Noble Qur'an:

﴿وَلْتَكُنْ مِنْكُمْ أُمَّةٌ يَدْعُونَ إِلَى الْخَيْرِ وَيَأْمُرُونَ بِالْمَعْرُوفِ وَيَنْهَوْنَ عَنِ الْمُنْكَرِ وَأُولَـٰئِكَ هُمُ الْمُفْلِحُونَ﴾

There must be a nation among you summoning to goodness, enjoining good, and forbidding evil. It is they who are felicitous.[1]

It has been reported that the Most Noble Messenger (Ṣ) said:

لَا تَزَالُ أُمَّتِي بِخَيْرٍ مَا أَمَرُوا بِالْمَعْرُوفِ وَنَهَوْا عَنِ الْمُنْكَرِ وَتَعَاوَنُوا عَلَى الْبِرِّ فَإِذَا لَمْ يَفْعَلُوا ذٰلِكَ نُزِعَتْ مِنْهُمُ الْبَرَكَاتُ وَسُلِّطَ بَعْضُهُمْ عَلَىٰ بَعْضٍ وَلَمْ يَكُنْ لَهُمْ نَاصِرٌ فِي الْأَرْضِ وَلَا فِي السَّمَاءِ

My nation will always be with good as long as its people enjoin good and forbid evil and assist one another in righteousness. If they do not do that, then blessings will be taken away from them and some of them will impose their rule over others, and there will be no helper for them on the earth or in the sky.[2]

It has been reported that His Eminence Amīr al-Muʾminīn [Imam ʿAlī] (ʿA) said:

لَا تَتْرُكُوا الْأَمْرَ بِالْمَعْرُوفِ وَالنَّهْيَ عَنِ الْمُنْكَرِ فَيُوَلَّى عَلَيْكُمْ شِرَارُكُمْ ثُمَّ تَدْعُونَ فَلَا يُسْتَجَابُ لَكُمْ

Do not abandon enjoining good and forbidding evil; otherwise, the evil people among you will take charge over you, and then when you supplicate, you will not be answered.[3]

Ruling 1867.* Enjoining good and forbidding evil becomes obligatory

[1] Āl ʿImrān (Chapter 3), verse 104.
[2] M. Ḥ. al-Nūrī, *Mustadrak al-Wasāʾil wa Mustanbaṭ al-Masāʾil*, Qum: Muʾassisah Āl al-Bayt ʿAlayhim al-Salām, 1987, vol. 12, p. 181.
[3] M. Al-Raḍī (compiler), *Nahj al-Balāghah*, Qum: Hijrat, 1993, Letter 47 (Ṣubḥī al-Ṣāliḥ arrangement).

(*wājib*) when performance of the good deed in question is obligatory and performance of the evil deed in question is unlawful (*ḥarām*). In this situation, enjoining good and forbidding evil is a collective obligation (*al-wājib al-kifāʾī*), meaning that if some people act according to this duty, then everyone else is excused from it. However, it is incumbent on everyone to not be indifferent if they encounter something unlawful being done or something obligatory being abandoned, and they express their aversion in their speech and actions. Acting to this extent is an individual obligation (*al-wājib al-ʿaynī*).[4] It has also been reported that His Eminence Amīr al-Muʾminīn [Imam ʿAlī] (ʿA) said:

أَمَرَنَا رَسُوْلُ اللّٰهِ (ص) أَنْ نَلْقَى أَهْلَ الْمَعَاصِيْ بِوُجُوْهٍ مُكْفَهِرَّةٍ

The Messenger of Allah (Ṣ) commanded us to meet people of disobedience with sullen faces.[5]

When the good deed being enjoined is a recommended (*mustaḥabb*) act (and not an obligatory one), or the evil deed being forbidden is a disapproved (*makrūh*) act (and not an unlawful one), enjoining good and forbidding evil is recommended.

Furthermore, when a person enjoins good and forbids evil with respect to recommended and disapproved acts, the status and personality of the other party must be taken into account so that he is not troubled or disrespected. In addition, one must not be so severe and harsh that the wrongdoer becomes averse to the religion and religious activities.

Ruling 1868. The following five conditions must exist for enjoining good and forbidding evil to be obligatory.

1. One must know what is good and what is evil, albeit in a general sense. Therefore, enjoining good and forbidding evil is not obligatory for someone who does not know what good and evil are and does not distinguish between them. Indeed, to enjoin good and forbid evil, it is sometimes obligatory to

[4] This is an obligation that every duty-bound person must perform irrespective of whether others have also performed it or not.

[5] M. al-Kulaynī, *al-Kāfī*, Tehran: Dār al-Kutub al-Islāmiyyah, 1986, vol. 5, p. 59.

learn and know what is good and what is evil as a prerequisite.

2. One must deem it probable that it will have an effect on the wrongdoer. Therefore, if he knows that his speech and words are ineffective, the opinion held by most jurists (*mashhūr*) is that he is under no duty and it is not obligatory for him to enjoin good and forbid evil. However, the obligatory precaution (*al-iḥtiyāṭ al-wājib*) is that he must express in any way possible his disapproval and displeasure with the wrongdoer's improper actions, even if he knows that it will not have any effect on him.
3. The wrongdoer must intend to continue doing the improper and wrong actions. Therefore, in the event that the wrongdoer does not want to repeat his wrong actions, it is not obligatory to enjoin him to good and forbid him from evil.
4. The wrongdoer must not be legally excused (*maʿdhūr*) in his improper and wrong actions; i.e. he must not believe that the improper act he did was permissible (*mubāḥ*), nor must he believe that the good act he abandoned was not obligatory.

   However, if the evil deed is something that the Holy Legislator [Allah] is never pleased with – such as the killing of an innocent person – then it is obligatory to prevent it, even if the perpetrator is legally excused and he is not duty-bound (*mukallaf*).[6]
5. The person enjoining good and forbidding evil must not be in danger of significant harm being inflicted to his person, reputation, or wealth. Furthermore, it must not cause excessive difficulty (*mashaqqah*) or unendurable hardship, except in the case where the good or evil act in question is regarded by the Holy Legislator [Allah] as being so important that one must endure harm and hardship in its cause.

If the person who enjoins good and forbids evil is not in danger of any significant harm being inflicted on himself but other Muslims are – whether that be to their person, reputation, or wealth – then it does not become obligatory for him to enjoin good and forbid evil. In this situation, the level of harm must be compared with the act in question, and sometimes even when harm is caused, he will not be excused from enjoining good and forbidding evil.

[6] A *mukallaf* is someone who is legally obliged to fulfil religious duties.

Ruling 1869.* Enjoining good and forbidding evil is carried out at different levels:

1. displaying heartfelt aversion; for example, by turning away one's face from the wrongdoer, or not speaking to him, or not keeping company with him;
2. verbally advising and guiding;
3. physically enforcing; for example, by hitting or imprisoning the wrongdoer.

It is necessary for one to start at the first or second level and to choose a method that will be the least troublesome and the most effective. If that method does not yield any result, he must gradually increase the severity and harshness of the methods he uses. If displaying heartfelt aversion and verbally advising and guiding – i.e. the first and second levels – prove ineffective, he must progress to the physical level. However, at this level, the obligatory precaution is that he must get authorisation from a fully qualified jurist (*al-ḥākim al-sharʿī*). Furthermore, it is necessary that he start in a way that causes the least displeasure and trouble, and if that does not yield any result, he must increase the severity and force he uses in his methods; however, it must not reach a point where it causes a bone to break or the body to become wounded.

Ruling 1870. The obligation to enjoin good and forbid evil on every *mukallaf* is greater with respect to his family and relatives. Therefore, if with regard to his family and relatives he feels that they are inattentive to, and unconcerned about, religious obligations such as performing prayers (*ṣalāh*), keeping fasts (*ṣawm*), paying the one-fifth tax (*khums*), and suchlike, or if he sees that they are careless and fearless with regard to committing unlawful acts such as backbiting and lying, then he must prevent improper actions being performed by them and invite them to do good deeds with a greater sense of importance while observing the three levels of enjoining good and forbidding evil.

However, with regard to one's mother and father, the obligatory precaution is that he must guide them by adopting a soft and gentle approach, and he must never be harsh with them.

CHAPTER EIGHT

Alms Tax (Zakat)

Ruling 1871. Zakat is obligatory (*wājib*) on ten things:

1. wheat;
2. barley;
3. dates;
4. raisins;
5. gold;
6. silver;
7. camels;
8. cows;
9. sheep [and goats];
10. business goods, based on obligatory precaution (*al-iḥtiyāṭ al-wājib*).

If someone owns one of these ten things, then, given the conditions mentioned below, he must give the specified amount in one of the prescribed ways.

CONDITIONS FOR ZAKAT TO BECOME OBLIGATORY (*WĀJIB*)

Ruling 1872. It becomes obligatory for a person to give zakat on the ten things mentioned above when they reach the taxable limit (*niṣāb*), which will be mentioned later, and they are his personal property, and he is a free person.

Ruling 1873. If someone owns cows, sheep, camels, gold, or silver for eleven months, then even though zakat becomes obligatory for him at the beginning of the twelfth month, he must consider the next year as beginning after the end of the twelfth month.

Ruling 1874. Zakat being obligatory on gold, silver, and business goods is conditional upon its owner being sane (*ʿāqil*) and of the age of legal responsibility (*bāligh*) throughout the year. However, in the case of wheat, barley, dates, raisins, camels, cows, and sheep, it is not a condition that the owner be sane and *bāligh*.

Ruling 1875. Zakat is liable on wheat and barley when they can be called 'wheat' and 'barley'; zakat on raisins is obligatory when they are grapes; and zakat is liable on dates when Arabs call them '*tamr*' [dry dates]. However, the time for determining their *niṣāb* is when they are dry; the time for giving zakat on wheat and barley is when the grain is threshed and separated from the chaff; and the time for giving zakat on dates and raisins is when they are picked. Therefore, if from this time onwards one delays giving zakat without having a legitimate excuse (*ʿudhr*), and there are persons entitled (*mustaḥiqqūn*) to receive zakat, and the item perishes, then the owner is responsible (*ḍāmin*) for it.

Ruling 1876. For zakat to be liable on wheat, barley, raisins, and dates – as defined in the previous ruling – it is not a requirement that they be at the owner's disposal. Therefore, if the goods are not with him or his agent (*wakīl*) – for example, they have been usurped – then it is obligatory for him to give the zakat that is liable on them whenever he gets them back.

Ruling 1877. If the owner of cows, sheep, camels, gold, and silver is intoxicated or unconscious for part of the year, zakat is not waived for him. The same applies if he is intoxicated or unconscious when zakat on wheat, barley, dates, and raisins becomes obligatory.

Ruling 1878. It is a condition for zakat to be liable on things other than wheat, barley, dates, and raisins, that the owner have disposal over them legally and actually. Therefore, if someone usurps them for a significant period during the year [and so he cannot actually have disposal over them], or if the owner is legally forbidden to have disposal over them, then there is no zakat to give.

Ruling 1879. If a person borrows gold or silver or any other thing on which it is obligatory to give zakat and it remains with him for a year, he must give zakat on it and the lender is not liable. However, if the lender gives zakat on it, the borrower is exempt from giving it.

ZAKAT OF WHEAT, BARLEY, AND RAISINS

Ruling 1880. Zakat of wheat, barley, dates, and raisins becomes obligatory when their quantity reaches the *niṣāb*, which is 300 *ṣāʿ*s or approximately 847 kilograms.[1]

Ruling 1881. If before giving zakat that is due on grapes, dates, wheat, and barley, a person and members of his family consume them, or, for example, he gives them to a poor person (*faqīr*) without the intention of giving zakat, he must give zakat on the quantity that was consumed or given.

Ruling 1882. If the owner of some wheat, barley, dates, or grapes dies after zakat on them has become obligatory, the zakat on them must be given from his estate. However, if he dies before zakat on them becomes obligatory, each of the heirs whose share reaches the *niṣāb* must give zakat on their share.

Ruling 1883. A person who has been appointed by a fully qualified jurist (*al-ḥākim al-sharʿī*) to collect zakat can ask for it at the time when grain is threshed and separated from the chaff, and when dates and grapes become dry. If the owner does not give it and the thing on which zakat has become obligatory perishes, the owner must give compensation for it.

Ruling 1884. If zakat becomes obligatory on a date tree, grapevine, or crop of wheat or barley after a person becomes the owner of them, he must give it.

Ruling 1885. After zakat becomes obligatory on wheat, barley, dates, and grapes, if one sells the crop and trees, the seller must give the zakat on them; and in the event that he does so, it is not obligatory for the buyer.

Ruling 1886. If a person buys wheat, barley, dates, or grapes, and he knows that the seller has given zakat on them, or he doubts whether the seller has given zakat on them or not, then zakat is not obligatory

[1] A *ṣāʿ* is a measure of weight equivalent to 2.823 kilograms.

for him; but if he knows that the seller has not given zakat on them, he must give it. However, if the seller has cheated him, he can claim the amount of zakat he gave from the seller after giving the zakat.

Ruling 1887. If the weight of wheat, barley, dates, or grapes when they are wet reaches the *niṣāb* and reduces to below the *niṣāb* when they become dry, then zakat on them is not obligatory.

Ruling 1888. If a person consumes wheat, barley, or dates before the time they become dry, in the event that their weight, when dry, reaches the *niṣāb*, he must give zakat on them.

Ruling 1889. Dates are of three kinds:

1. dates that are dried; the rule (*ḥukm*) of zakat for this type was mentioned earlier;
2. dates that are in the process of becoming edible *ruṭab* [soft, moist dates];
3. dates that are eaten when they are unripe (*khalāl*).

With regard to the second kind, in the event that their weight when dry reaches the *niṣāb*, the recommended precaution (*al-iḥtiyāṭ al-mustaḥabb*) is that one should give zakat on them. As for the third kind, what is apparent (*ẓāhir*)[2] is that zakat is not obligatory on them.

Ruling 1890. Wheat, barley, dates, and raisins on which zakat has been given are not liable for zakat again even if they remain with a person for some years.

Ruling 1891. If wheat, barley, dates, or grapes are irrigated by rain or a stream, or if like in Egypt, crops use the moisture in the earth, the zakat on them is one-tenth [10%] of them. If they are watered by buckets of water or by means of a pump and suchlike, then the zakat on them is one-twentieth [5%].

Ruling 1892. If wheat, barley, dates, or grapes are irrigated by

[2] For practical purposes in jurisprudential rulings, expressing an 'apparent' ruling equates to giving a fatwa.

both rain and buckets of water and suchlike, in the event that it is commonly considered that their irrigation is by means of buckets of water and suchlike, the zakat on them is one-twentieth [5%]. If it is commonly considered that their irrigation is by means of a stream or rain, then the zakat on them is one-tenth [10%]. And if it is such that it is commonly considered that their irrigation is by both means, then the zakat on them is three-fortieths [7.5%].

Ruling 1893. In the event that one doubts whether it would be commonly considered that their irrigation is by both means or, for example, by rain, then it is sufficient if he gives three-fortieths [7.5%].

Ruling 1894. If a person doubts whether it would be commonly considered that their irrigation is by both means or by means of buckets of water and suchlike, it is sufficient to give one-twentieth [5%]. The same applies if he deems it probable that it would be commonly considered that their irrigation is by rain.

Ruling 1895. If wheat, barley, dates, or grapes are watered by rain and by a stream, and if they do not need buckets of water and suchlike but are also irrigated by means of buckets of water nevertheless, and if the buckets of water do not help produce an increase in crop, then the zakat on them is one-tenth [10%]. And if they are irrigated by buckets of water and suchlike and do not need stream or rainwater, but they are also watered by a stream and rainwater nevertheless, and if the stream and rainwater do not help produce an increase in crop, then the zakat on them is one-twentieth [5%].

Ruling 1896. If a crop is irrigated by buckets of water and suchlike and crops on the adjacent land utilise the moisture from that land and do not need to be irrigated, then the zakat on the crops that are irrigated by buckets of water is one-twentieth [5%], and the zakat on the crops on the adjacent land is, based on obligatory precaution, one-tenth [10%].

Ruling 1897. Expenses incurred in the growing of wheat, barley, dates, or grapes cannot be deducted from the produce and then the *niṣāb* calculated. Therefore, if any of them reaches the *niṣāb* before accounting for the expenses, zakat must be given on it.

Ruling 1898. The seeds that a person uses in his farming – irrespective of whether they are his own or he buys them – cannot be deducted from the produce and then the *niṣāb* calculated; instead, he must calculate the *niṣāb* having accounted for the entire produce.

Ruling 1899. It is not obligatory to give zakat on the portion the government takes from the produce itself. For example, if the produce is 2000 kilograms and the government takes 100 kilograms in tax, then zakat is obligatory on only 1900 kilograms.

Ruling 1900. Based on obligatory precaution, a person cannot deduct the expenses he incurs from the produce before or after zakat has become due and give zakat on only what remains.

Ruling 1901. After zakat has become due, a person cannot deduct the expenses he incurs from the produce with respect to the amount of zakat that must be given. And based on obligatory precaution, [he cannot do this] even if he has obtained authorisation from a fully qualified jurist or his representative (*wakīl*) to incur those expenses.

Ruling 1902. It is not obligatory to wait until wheat and barley are ready for threshing, or until grapes and dates become dry, and then give zakat; rather, once zakat becomes obligatory, it is permitted (*jāʾiz*) to calculate the value of zakat and give the value of it with the intention of zakat.

Ruling 1903. After zakat becomes due, a person can submit the actual crop, dates, or grapes, before it is harvested or picked, to someone entitled to receive it or a fully qualified jurist, or a representative of theirs, in the form of joint ownership (*mushāʿ*) and after that share the expenses.

Ruling 1904. In case the owner submits the actual crop, dates, or grapes to a fully qualified jurist or to someone entitled to receive it, or to their representative, it is not necessary for him to look after it by way of joint ownership for free; rather, he can charge rent for it staying on his land until the time of their harvest or until they have become dry.

Ruling 1905. If a person owns wheat, barley, dates, or grapes in various towns which have harvesting times that differ, and if the crops or fruits are not acquired simultaneously but are nevertheless considered to be the produce of one year, then in the event that the first thing to ripen reaches the *niṣāb*, he must give zakat on it when it ripens and on the rest whenever they are acquired. However, if what ripens first does not reach the *niṣāb*, he must wait until the rest ripens; if the combined produce reaches the *niṣāb*, zakat is obligatory on it, and if it does not reach the *niṣāb*, zakat is not obligatory on it.

Ruling 1906. If a date tree or grapevine bears fruit twice a year, and if the combined total of the fruit reaches the *niṣāb*, then based on obligatory precaution, zakat is obligatory on it.

Ruling 1907. If a person possesses a quantity of fresh dates or grapes that would reach the *niṣāb* if they were dry, there is no problem if he gives – with the intention of zakat – an amount of the fresh dates or grapes that were they to be dry would equal the amount of zakat obligatory for him.

Ruling 1908. If the zakat on dried dates or raisins is obligatory for a person, he cannot give their zakat in the form of fresh dates or grapes. In fact, even if he calculates the value of the produce that he must give as zakat and then gives grapes, fresh dates, raisins, or even other dried dates equal to that value in payment for the zakat, it is problematic (*maḥall al-ishkāl*) [i.e. based on obligatory precaution, he cannot do this].[3] Similarly, if the zakat on fresh dates or grapes is obligatory for him, he cannot give their zakat in the form of dried dates or raisins. And even if he gives other dates or grapes, albeit fresh ones, in payment for the value of the produce, it is also problematic [i.e. based on obligatory precaution, he cannot do this either].

Ruling 1909. With regard to someone who has a debt and possesses the actual property on which zakat has become obligatory, if he dies, the entire zakat must be given from the property on which zakat has become obligatory, and then the debt must be repaid. However, if

[3] As mentioned in Ruling 6, the term 'problematic' (*maḥall al-ishkāl*) amounts to saying the ruling is based on obligatory precaution.

he is liable to pay a debt of zakat [as opposed to his actual property having become liable for zakat], then this debt is like his other debts.[4]

Ruling 1910. With regard to someone who has a debt but possesses wheat, barley, dates, or grapes, if he dies and his inheritors pay his debt from some other wealth before zakat on these items becomes obligatory, then the inheritor whose share reaches the *niṣāb* must give zakat on it. If the debt is not paid before zakat on these items becomes obligatory, in the event that the property of the deceased is sufficient only to repay his debt, it is not obligatory to give zakat. However, if the property of the deceased is more than his debt, in the event that his debt is such that if they wanted to repay it they would need to pay the creditor an amount from the wheat, barley, dates and grapes, then what they give to the creditor is not liable for zakat. As for the rest of the property, the inheritor whose share reaches the *niṣāb* must give zakat on it.

Ruling 1911. If some of the wheat, barley, dates, and raisins on which zakat has become obligatory is of superior quality and some of it is of inferior quality, the obligatory precaution is that one must not use inferior quality produce to give zakat that is due on the superior quality produce.

THE TAXABLE LIMIT (*NIṢĀB*) FOR GOLD

Ruling 1912. There are two *niṣāb*s for gold.

1. Twenty legal (*sharʿī*) *mithqāl*s.[5] A legal *mithqāl* is eighteen *nukhuds*.[6] Therefore, when gold reaches the weight of twenty legal *mithqāl*s – which is equivalent to fifteen common (*ṣayrafī*)

[4] This means that if the combined total of his zakat debt and his other debts is equal to or less than his estate, his zakat debt and his other debts must be repaid. However, if the combined total of his zakat debt and his other debts is more than his estate, his estate must be proportionally divided between those entitled to receive zakat and his creditors.

[5] One legal *mithqāl* is equivalent to 3.456 grams; therefore, twenty legal *mithqāl*s is equal to 69.12 grams.

[6] A *nukhud* is a measure of weight. One *nukhud* is equivalent to 0.192 grams.

mithqāls – and if the other conditions that were mentioned are fulfilled, one must give one-fortieth [2.5%] – which is equivalent to nine *nukhuds* – as zakat. As long as gold does not reach this amount, zakat is not obligatory on it.

2. Four legal *mithqāls*, which is equivalent to three common *mithqāls*, meaning that if three [common] *mithqāls* are added to fifteen [common] *mithqāls*, one must give zakat on the entire eighteen *mithqāls*, which is equivalent to one-fortieth [2.5%]; and if less than three *mithqāls* is added, he must give zakat on only fifteen *mithqāls* [which was the first *niṣāb* mentioned above], and the extra is not liable for zakat. The same applies to every other addition, meaning that if three *mithqāls* are added, one must give zakat on the entire amount; and if less than three *mithqāls* is added, the added amount is not liable for zakat.

THE *NIṢĀB* FOR SILVER

Ruling 1913. There are two *niṣāb*s for silver.

1. 105 common *mithqāls*. Therefore, if silver reaches 105 *mithqāls* and the other conditions that were mentioned are fulfilled, one must give one-fortieth [2.5%] – which is equivalent to two *mithqāls* and fifteen *nukhuds* – as zakat. As long as silver does not reach this amount, zakat is not obligatory on it.
2. Twenty-one *mithqāls*, meaning that if twenty-one *mithqāls* are added to 105 *mithqāls*, one must give zakat on the entire 126 *mithqāls* in a manner that was previously mentioned; and if less than twenty-one *mithqāls* are added, he must give zakat on only 105 *mithqāls* [which was the first *niṣāb* mentioned above], and the extra is not liable for zakat. The same applies to every other addition, meaning that if twenty-one *mithqāls* are added, one must give zakat on the entire amount; and if less than twenty-one *mithqāls* are added, the added amount is not liable for zakat. If a person doubts whether or not silver has reached the *niṣāb*, then based on obligatory precaution, he must investigate further.

Ruling 1914. If the gold or silver that someone owns has reached the *niṣāb*, then even if he has given zakat on it he must continue giving zakat on it every year as long as it does not fall below the *niṣāb*.

Ruling 1915. Zakat on gold and silver becomes obligatory in the event that the gold or silver is minted and used prevalently in transactions (*muʿāmalāt*) [as money]. If the stamped effects [on the gold or silver money] have been effaced but it is still used prevalently in transactions, then zakat must be given on it. However, if it is no longer used prevalently, it is not liable for zakat even if the stamped effects remain on it. Therefore, at present, when gold and silver are not used in transactions as money, notes and coins that are not made of gold or silver, such as nickel coins, do not come under the rules of gold and silver and it is not obligatory to give zakat on them.

Ruling 1916. In the event that minted gold and silver coins that are used by women as ornaments are used prevalently in transactions – meaning that gold and silver are used as money in transactions – then based on obligatory precaution, zakat is obligatory on them. However, if they are not used prevalently in transactions, then zakat is not obligatory on them.

Ruling 1917. If a person owns gold and silver and neither of them is equal to the first *niṣāb* – for example, he owns 104 *mithqāl*s of silver and fourteen *mithqāl*s of gold – then zakat is not obligatory on them.

Ruling 1918. As stated earlier, zakat on gold and silver becomes obligatory when a person maintains ownership of their *niṣāb* for eleven months, and if during those eleven months the amount of gold and silver falls below the first *niṣāb* for each of them, then zakat is not obligatory on them.

Ruling 1919. If during the period of eleven months a person exchanges the gold or silver that he owns with something else, or he melts them, then zakat is not obligatory for him. However, if to escape giving zakat he exchanges them for gold and silver – meaning that he exchanges gold for gold or silver, or he exchanges silver for silver or gold – then the obligatory precaution is that he must give zakat on them.

Ruling 1920. If a person melts gold and silver coins in the twelfth month, he must give zakat on them. If as a result of melting the coins their weight or value decreases, he must give the amount of zakat that was obligatory for him prior to melting them.

Ruling 1921. If gold or silver coins contain a more than usual quantity of alloy, then, if they can be called gold and silver coins and they reach the *niṣāb*, zakat on them is obligatory even if the pure quantity does not reach the *niṣāb*. However, if they can no longer be called gold and silver coins, then zakat is not obligatory on them even if the quantity that is pure reaches the *niṣāb*.

Ruling 1922. If a person owns gold or silver coins that are mixed with a usual amount of alloy, there is no problem if he gives zakat on them in gold and silver coins that contain more than the usual amount of alloy in them, or in coins that are not of gold or silver. However, in such a case, the value of the coins he pays in must be equal to the value of the zakat that is obligatory for him.

ZAKAT OF CAMELS, COWS, AND SHEEP

Ruling 1923. In addition to the conditions mentioned previously, the zakat of camels, cows, and sheep has one more condition: the animal must graze in open fields for the entire year. Therefore, if it grazes on pre-cut grass during the entire year or part of the year, or it grazes on crops belonging to its owner or someone else, it is not liable for zakat. However, if during the entire year the animal grazes on only a small amount of the owner's grass such that it can be commonly said that the animal has grazed the entire year in open fields, zakat on it becomes obligatory. Furthermore, with regard to camels, cows, and sheep, it is not a condition that they must not have worked during the entire year; rather, zakat on them is obligatory if they are used [a little] for irrigation, ploughing, and similar work, as long as it can be commonly said that they have not worked [significantly]. In fact, even if this cannot be said, based on obligatory precaution, zakat on them must be given.

Ruling 1924. If a person buys or rents for his camels, cows, and sheep pastureland which has not been cultivated by anyone, the obligatory precaution is that zakat must be given. If he pays tax for grazing his animals there, he must give zakat.

The *niṣāb* for camels

Ruling 1925. There are twelve *niṣāb*s for camels.

1. Five camels, and the zakat on them is one sheep. As long as the number of camels does not reach this amount, zakat is not liable on them.
2. Ten camels, and the zakat on them is two sheep.
3. Fifteen camels, and the zakat on them is three sheep.
4. Twenty camels, and the zakat on them is four sheep.
5. Twenty-five camels, and the zakat on them is five sheep.
6. Twenty-six camels, and the zakat on them is one camel that is in its second year.
7. Thirty-six camels, and the zakat on them is one camel that is in its third year.
8. Forty-six camels, and the zakat on them is one camel that is in its fourth year.
9. Sixty-one camels, and the zakat on them is one camel that is in its fifth year.
10. Seventy-six camels, and the zakat on them is two camels that are in their third year.
11. Ninety-one camels, and the zakat on them is two camels that are in their fourth year.
12. 121 camels and above, and the zakat on every forty camels is one camel that is in its third year; and on every fifty camels, one camel that is in its fourth year. A person can also calculate the zakat based on groups of forty-five; and in some cases, such as 200 camels, he has the choice of calculating them in groups of forty or fifty.

However, in every case, he must calculate the zakat in a way that there is no remainder, or if there is, then it must not exceed nine camels. For example, if he owns 140 camels, for 100 of them, he must give two camels that are in their fourth year, and for the remaining forty, he must give one camel that is in its third year.

Camels that are given as zakat must be female. However, if in the sixth *niṣāb* one does not own a female camel that is in its second year, it is sufficient to give a male camel in its third year. If a person does not own one of these either, he has a choice in what he purchases [i.e. he can purchase either a female camel that is in its second year, or a male camel that is in its third year, and give that as zakat].

Ruling 1926. Giving zakat is not obligatory on the number of camels between two *niṣāb*s. Therefore, if the number of camels that a person owns is more than the first *niṣāb*, which is five camels, but it does not reach the second *niṣāb*, which is ten camels, he must give zakat on only five camels. The same applies to all the other *niṣāb*s.

The *niṣāb* for cows

Ruling 1927. There are two *niṣāb*s for cows.

1. Thirty cows; when the number of cows a person owns reaches thirty – and if the other conditions that were mentioned are fulfilled as well – he must give one calf that is in its second year as zakat; and the obligatory precaution is that it must be a male calf.
2. Forty cows, and the zakat on them is one female calf that is in its third year. Giving zakat is not obligatory on the number of cows between thirty and forty. For example, if someone has thirty-nine cows, he must give zakat on only thirty cows; and if he has more than forty cows, then as long as the number does not reach sixty, he must give zakat on only forty cows; and after reaching sixty, as it is twice the number of the first *niṣāb*, he must give two calves that are in their second year. The same applies if the number of cows increases; i.e. he must either calculate in groups of thirty, forty, or both, and he must give zakat according to the rule explained earlier. However, he must calculate the zakat in a way that there is no remainder, or if there is, it must not exceed nine cows. For example, if he owns seventy cows, he must calculate them in groups of thirty and forty because if he calculates only in groups of thirty, there will be ten cows remaining on which he will not give zakat. In some cases, such as 120, he has the choice.

The *niṣāb* for sheep

Ruling 1928. There are five *niṣāb*s for sheep.

1. Forty sheep, and the zakat on them is one sheep. As long as the number of sheep does not reach this amount, zakat is not liable on them.
2. 121 sheep, and the zakat on them is two sheep.
3. 201 sheep, and the zakat on them is three sheep.
4. 301 sheep, and the zakat on them is four sheep.
5. 400 sheep and above, and the zakat on every 100 sheep is one sheep. It is not necessary that zakat be given from the same sheep; rather, it is sufficient if some other sheep or the monetary value of the sheep is given.

Ruling 1929. Giving zakat is not obligatory on the number of sheep between two *niṣāb*s. Therefore, if the number of sheep that a person owns is more than the first *niṣāb*, which is forty sheep, but it does not reach the second *niṣāb*, which is 121 sheep, he must give zakat on only forty sheep, not on more than that. The same applies to all the other *niṣāb*s.

Ruling 1930. Zakat is obligatory on camels, cows, and sheep that reach the *niṣāb*, irrespective of whether all of them are male, or all of them are female, or some of them are male and others are female.

Ruling 1931. In matters of zakat, cows and buffaloes are counted as one species, and Arabian and non-Arabian camels are counted as one species. Similarly, goats, ewes, and year-old lambs are not considered differently for the purposes of zakat.

Ruling 1932. If a person gives one sheep as zakat, then based on obligatory precaution, it must be at least in its second year; and if one gives a goat, then as an obligatory precaution, it must be in its third year.

Ruling 1933. There is no problem if the value of the sheep that is given as zakat is slightly lower than his other sheep. However, it is better that he give a sheep whose value is higher than his other sheep. The same applies to cows and camels.

Ruling 1934. If a few people are partners, the one whose share reaches the first *niṣāb* must give zakat. Zakat is not obligatory for those whose shares are less than the first *niṣāb*.

Ruling 1935. If a person owns cows, camels, or sheep in various places and their combined total reaches the *niṣāb*, he must give zakat on them.

Ruling 1936. If the cows, sheep, and camels that a person owns are sick or have a defect, they are still liable for zakat.

Ruling 1937. If all the cows, sheep, and camels that a person owns are sick, have a defect, or are old, he can give the zakat on them from them. However, if they are all healthy, have no defect, and are young, he cannot give the zakat on them from sick animals, those that have a defect, or are old. In fact, if some of them are healthy and others sick, or some have a defect and others do not, or some are old and others young, then the obligatory precaution is that for their zakat he must give those animals that are healthy, do not have a defect, and are young.

Ruling 1938. If before the eleventh month is complete one exchanges the cows, sheep, and camels that he owns with something else, or he exchanges the *niṣāb* he owns with a *niṣāb* of the same species – for example, he gives forty sheep and procures another forty sheep in return – then zakat is not obligatory for him as long as this is not done with the intention to escape giving zakat. However, if it is done with such an intention, then in case both sets of animals confer the same type of benefit – for example, both sets of sheep are milk-giving sheep – then the obligatory precaution is that he must give zakat on them.

Ruling 1939. If a person who must give zakat on cows, sheep, and camels gives it from other wealth that he owns, he must give zakat on the animals every year as long as their number does not fall below the *niṣāb*. If he gives the animals themselves as zakat and their number falls below the first *niṣāb*, then zakat is not obligatory for him. For example, if someone who owns forty sheep gives zakat on them from his other wealth, then as long as the number of sheep does not fall below forty, he must give one sheep every year; and if he gives sheep as zakat, then zakat is not obligatory for him until the number of sheep reaches forty.

ZAKAT ON BUSINESS GOODS*

Goods which a person comes to own through a contract of exchange (*ʿaqd al-muʿāwaḍah*)[7] and which he keeps for business and profit earning is, based on obligatory precaution, liable for zakat if certain conditions are fulfilled. The zakat on such property is one-fortieth [2.5%]. The conditions are listed below.

1. The owner must be *bāligh* and sane.
2. The goods must have a value of at least fifteen *mithqāl*s of coined gold or 105 *mithqāl*s of coined silver.
3. One year must have passed from the time the owner intended to make a profit from the goods.
4. The intention to make a profit must remain throughout the year; therefore, if the owner changes his mind during the year and, for example, decides to spend it on his living expenses, then zakat is not obligatory.
5. The owner must have right of disposal over them throughout the year.
6. Throughout the year, the goods must be saleable for an amount equal to, or more than, the capital outlay. Therefore, if during a period of the year the goods are not saleable for the amount that is [at least] equal to the capital outlay, it is not obligatory for him to give zakat on them.

DISTRIBUTION OF ZAKAT

Ruling 1940. Zakat can be distributed in eight ways.

[7] This is a contract in which something is given in exchange for something else.

1. It can be given to a poor person (*faqīr*). A poor person is defined as someone who does not possess the means to meet his and his family's expenses for one year. Therefore, someone who has a trade, property, or capital by means of which he can meet these expenses for a year, is not a poor person.
2. It can be given to a needy person (*miskīn*). A needy person is defined as someone whose living conditions are worse than those of a poor person.
3. It can be given to a person who has been appointed by the Imam (ʿA) or his representative (*nāʾib*) to collect and safeguard zakat, maintain its accounts, and deliver it to the Imam (ʿA) or his representative, or to the poor (*fuqarāʾ*) and those entitled (*mustaḥiqq*) to receive it.
4. It can be given to disbelievers (*kuffār*) who will be inclined to the religion of Islam if zakat is given to them, or who will assist Muslims in battle or some other matter. Zakat can also be given to Muslims whose faith in some of the Most Noble Messenger's (Ṣ) teachings is weak but which will be strengthened as a result of giving zakat to them. Furthermore, zakat can be given to a Muslim who does not believe in the vicegerency (*wilāyah*) of the Commander of the Faithful [Imam ʿAlī] (ʿA) but who will be inclined to believe in it if zakat is given to him.
5. It can be used to buy and free slaves, the details of which are mentioned in their appropriate place.
6. It can be given to a person who is in debt but is unable to repay his debt.
7. It can be given in the way of Allah (*fī sabīl allāh*), i.e. acts that benefit the general Muslim public, such as building mosques and religious schools, keeping the town clean, tarmacking and expanding roads, and suchlike.
8. It can be given to a stranded traveller (*ibn al-sabīl*).

These are the ways in which zakat can be spent. However, in the third and fourth cases, the receiver of the zakat cannot spend zakat without the permission of the Imam (ʿA) or his representative. And based on obligatory precaution, in the seventh case, the receiver of the zakat must obtain permission from a fully qualified jurist. The laws (*aḥkām*) concerning these ways will be explained in the following rulings (*masāʾil*).

Ruling 1941. The obligatory precaution is that a poor or needy person must not receive zakat that is more than his and his family's expenses for one year. If he has some money or goods, he must only receive an amount of zakat that makes up the shortfall for what he needs to meet his expenses for a year.

Ruling 1942. If a person has sufficient means to meet his expenses for a year and spends part of it, and then he doubts whether or not the remaining amount will be sufficient to meet his expenses for one year, he cannot receive zakat.

Ruling 1943. A craftsman, proprietor, or a businessman whose income is less than his expenses for one year can receive zakat to meet his shortfall, and it is not necessary for him to sell his tools or property or to spend his capital to meet his expenses.

Ruling 1944. A poor person who does not possess the means to meet his and his family's expenses for one year can receive zakat even if he owns a house in which he lives, or he possesses a vehicle without which he cannot lead his life or uphold his respect. The same applies to household furniture, utensils, summer and winter clothes, and other things needed by him. If a poor person does not have such things but needs them, he can purchase them from zakat.

Ruling 1945. A poor person who can work and thereby meet his and his family's expenses but does not do so due to laziness is not permitted to receive zakat. A poor student for whom working will be an obstacle to him continuing with his studies cannot in any case receive the portion of zakat that is for poor people unless studying for him is an individual obligation (*al-wājib al-ʿaynī*).[8] As for receiving it from the 'in the way of Allah' portion of zakat, it is permitted if his education will benefit the general public and, based on obligatory precaution, it is given with the authorisation of a fully qualified jurist. A poor person for whom it is not difficult to learn a trade cannot, based on obligatory precaution, live on zakat, although he can receive zakat while he is learning the trade.

[8] This is an obligation that every duty-bound person must perform irrespective of whether others have also performed it or not.

Ruling 1946. One can give zakat to a person who was previously poor and who says he is poor now even if he does not attain confidence (*iṭmiʾnān*) in his statement. However, based on obligatory precaution, one cannot give zakat to a person about whom it is not known whether he was previously poor [and who says he continues to be poor] until he attains confidence about him being poor.

Ruling 1947. If a person who was not poor previously says he is poor now, in the event that confidence cannot be derived from what he says, zakat cannot be given to him.

Ruling 1948. If a person who must give zakat is owed some amount by a poor person, he can count the amount he is owed by the poor person towards his zakat.

Ruling 1949. If a poor person dies and his estate is insufficient to repay his debt, one may count the amount he is owed by the deceased towards his zakat. In fact, if his property is sufficient to repay his debt but his inheritors do not settle his debt, or if for some other reason he cannot reclaim the money he loaned the deceased, he can count the amount he is owed towards his zakat in this case as well.

Ruling 1950. If a person gives something to a poor person with the intention of zakat, it is not necessary for him to tell him it is zakat. In fact, if the poor person is ashamed by taking zakat, it is recommended (*mustaḥabb*) that he give it to him with the intention of zakat but without disclosing to him that it is zakat.

Ruling 1951. If a person gives someone zakat thinking that he is poor and later realises that he was not poor, or if on account of not knowing the ruling he gives zakat to someone whom he knows is not poor, it is not sufficient [and he will not have discharged his duty]. Therefore, in the event that the item he gave the beneficiary still exists, he must take it back from him and give it to someone entitled to receive zakat. However, if the item does not exist and the beneficiary knew it was given to him as zakat, then he can claim its replacement from the beneficiary and give it to someone entitled to receive zakat; but, if the beneficiary did not know it was zakat, he cannot take anything from him and he must give zakat again from his own property to someone entitled to receive it, even if, based on obligatory precaution, he investigated about the beneficiary or he relied upon something that was legally authoritative (*al-ḥujjah al-sharʿiyyah*) [such as the statement of a reliable person].

Ruling 1952. A person who is in debt but is unable to repay his debt – even if he has the means to meet his expenses for one year – can receive zakat to repay his debt. However, he must not have spent the loan for a sinful purpose.

Ruling 1953. If a person gives zakat to someone who is in debt but is unable to repay his debt and he later realises that the debtor spent the loan for a sinful purpose, in the event that the debtor is poor, the person can count what he gave him as the portion of zakat that is given to poor people.

Ruling 1954. With regard to a person who is in debt but is unable to repay his debt, the lender can count the amount owed to him by the person as zakat even if the person is not poor.

Ruling 1955. If a traveller runs out of funds or his means of transportation stops functioning, in the event that the purpose of his journey is not sinful and he cannot reach his destination by borrowing or selling something, he can receive zakat even if he is not a poor person in his home town (*waṭan*). However, if he can procure funds for his journey at another place by borrowing money or selling something, he can receive zakat up to the amount that will enable him to get to that place. And based on obligatory precaution, if he can raise money by selling or renting some property in his home town for the expenses of his journey, he must not receive zakat.

Ruling 1956. If a stranded traveller has received zakat and after reaching his home town finds that some of the zakat has remained unspent, in the event that he cannot return it to the benefactor, he must return it to a fully qualified jurist stating it is zakat.

CRITERIA FOR BEING ENTITLED (*MUSTAḤIQQ*) TO RECEIVE ZAKAT

Ruling 1957. The receiver of zakat must be a Twelver (Ithnā ʿAsharī) Shia. If one gives zakat to a person he believes to be a Shia and later realises that he was not a Shia, then based on obligatory precaution, he must give zakat again even if he had made investigations about the person or he had relied upon something that was legally authoritative.

Ruling 1958. If a poor Shia individual is a non-*bāligh* child or an insane person, one may give zakat to his guardian (*walī*) with the intention that what he gives is the property of the child or the insane person. Furthermore, either by himself or through a trustworthy person (*amīn*), he can spend zakat on the child or on the insane person, in which case he must make the intention of zakat when he does so.

Ruling 1959. A person can give zakat to a poor person who begs provided that the fact of his poverty is established. However, one must not give zakat to a person who spends it for sinful purposes. In fact, the obligatory precaution is that zakat must not be given to someone who, as a result of receiving it, will be encouraged to commit sins even if he does not spend it directly for sinful purposes.

Ruling 1960. The obligatory precaution is that one must not give zakat to a person who consumes alcohol, does not perform prayers, or publicly commits major sins.

Ruling 1961. If a person is in debt but is unable to repay his debt, one can repay it for him from zakat even if his expenses are obligatory for him.

Ruling 1962. A person cannot pay the living expenses of those whose expenses are obligatory for him – such as his children, father and mother, and permanent wife – from the portion of zakat for poor people. However, if he does not pay for their living expenses, others can give zakat to them. If he is unable to give obligatory maintenance (*nafaqah*) for those whom it is obligatory for him to give obligatory maintenance, and if zakat is obligatory for him, he can give their obligatory maintenance from zakat.

Ruling 1963. There is no problem if one gives zakat to his son so that he can pay for the living expenses of his wife, domestic worker, or maid, or so that he can repay his loan, provided that his son satisfies all the other criteria for being entitled to receive zakat.

Ruling 1964. A father cannot buy educational and religious books that are required by his son from the 'in the way of Allah' portion of zakat and make them available to him unless the general public interest necessitates it, and, based on obligatory precaution, he gets authorisation from a fully qualified jurist.

Ruling 1965. A father can use zakat to get his poor son married, and the same applies to the son with respect to his father.

Ruling 1966. Zakat cannot be given to a woman whose husband provides for her living expenses, nor to a woman whose husband does not provide for her living expenses but has the power to compel him to give them to her, albeit by referring to an unjust ruler (*al-ḥākim al-jāʾir*).

Ruling 1967. If a woman who has contracted a temporary marriage (*mutʿah*) is poor, her husband and others can give her zakat. However, if she had stipulated a condition in the contract that her husband must pay for her living expenses, or if paying for her living expenses is obligatory for him for some other reason and he does pay for her living expenses, then zakat cannot be given to her.

Ruling 1968. A woman can give zakat to her husband who is poor, even if the husband spends that zakat on her living expenses.

Ruling 1969. A *sayyid*[9] cannot accept zakat from someone who is not a *sayyid* except in case of necessity; and based on obligatory precaution, the necessity must be to the extent that he cannot meet his living

[9] A *sayyid* is a male descendant of Hāshim, the great grandfather of Prophet Muḥammad (Ṣ).

expenses from *khums* or other religious funds. Furthermore, based on obligatory precaution, if it is possible, he must on a daily basis take only an amount that is sufficient to meet his necessary living expenses for that day.

Ruling 1970. Zakat can be given to a person whom one does not know whether he is a *sayyid* or not. However, if that person himself claims that he is a *sayyid* [it is not permitted to give him zakat], and if one does give him zakat he will not be exempted from the obligation.

INTENTION (*NIYYAH*) FOR GIVING ZAKAT

Ruling 1971. A person must give zakat with the intention of *qurbah*, i.e. in humility to Allah the Exalted. If he gives zakat without the intention of *qurbah*, it is sufficient [in the sense that he will be deemed as having given the zakat that was obligatory for him], although he will have sinned. Furthermore, he must specify in his intention whether what he is giving is zakat on property or *zakāt al-fiṭrah*.[10] In fact, if, for example, zakat on wheat and barley is obligatory for him and he wants to pay a sum of money equal to the value of the zakat on them, he must specify whether he is giving zakat that is due on the wheat or barley.

Ruling 1972. If it is obligatory for a person to give zakat on various items and he gives some zakat without specifying in his intention which item it relates to, in the event that the thing he has given is of the same type as one of the items, it will be counted as zakat of that particular thing. For example, if it is obligatory for him to give zakat on forty sheep and fifteen *mithqāl*s of gold, and he gives one sheep as zakat without specifying in his intention if it is zakat of the sheep or the gold, then it will be counted as zakat of the sheep. However, if he gives some silver coins or notes of money (i.e. a different type of commodity to sheep and gold), then, according to some [jurists], it must be divided between both of them [i.e. for giving the zakat on both the sheep and the gold]. However, this is problematic [i.e. based on obligatory precaution, it does not suffice], and it is probable

[10] The rules concerning *zakāt al-fiṭrah* are mentioned in Ruling 2003 and onwards.

that it cannot be counted as zakat for any of them and remains the owner's property.

Ruling 1973. If a person appoints someone as his agent to give away the zakat of his property, he must make the intention when he hands over the zakat to him. And the recommended precaution is that he should maintain that intention until the zakat reaches the poor.

MISCELLANEOUS RULINGS ON ZAKAT

Ruling 1974. When wheat and barley are separated from the chaff, and when dates and grapes become dry, one must give zakat to the poor or separate it from his property. The zakat on gold, silver, cows, sheep, and camels must be given to the poor or separated from one's property after the eleventh month is complete.

Ruling 1975. After separating zakat [from one's property], it is not necessary that he immediately gives it to someone who is entitled to receive it, and there is no problem if it is delayed because of a rationally acceptable reason.

Ruling 1976. If a person can deliver zakat to someone entitled to receive it but does not, and the zakat perishes due to his negligence, he must give it again in replacement.

Ruling 1977. If a person can deliver zakat to someone who is entitled to receive it but does not, and it perishes without him being negligent in looking after it, in the event that he did not have a valid reason for the delay, he must give zakat again in replacement. In fact, even if he had a good reason for the delay – for example, he had intended to give it to a poor person in particular, or he wanted to distribute it to poor people gradually – then based on obligatory precaution, he is responsible for it.

Ruling 1978. If a person puts aside zakat from the things on which it had become due, he still has right of disposal over the rest of those things; and if he puts aside zakat from some other property of his, he still has right of disposal over the entire property.

Ruling 1979. A person cannot use for himself zakat that he has set aside and replace it with something else.

Ruling 1980. If some profit accrues from the zakat that a person has set aside – for example, a sheep that has been kept aside for zakat gives birth to a lamb – then the profit is subject to the same rules as the zakat.

Ruling 1981. If someone who is entitled to receive zakat is present when a person sets aside zakat, it is better that he give the zakat to him unless he has someone else in mind and for some reason it is better to give it to that other person instead.

Ruling 1982. If a person transacts with the property that he has set aside as zakat without the authorisation of a fully qualified jurist and incurs a loss, he must not deduct anything from the zakat. However, if he makes a profit, then based on obligatory precaution, he must give it to someone who is entitled to receive zakat.

Ruling 1983. If before zakat becomes obligatory for a person he gives something to the poor as zakat, he cannot count it as zakat. However, if afterwards when zakat becomes obligatory for him the thing that he gave to the poor has not perished and the poor person has remained poor, he can count the thing that he gave him as zakat.

Ruling 1984. If a poor person knows that zakat has not become obligatory for someone and yet accepts something from him as zakat and it perishes while it is with him, he [the poor person] is responsible for it. However, when zakat becomes obligatory for the person, if the poor person has remained poor, the one on whom zakat is obligatory can count the thing he had given the poor person as zakat.

Ruling 1985. If a poor person does not know that zakat has not become obligatory for someone and he accepts something from him as zakat and it perishes while it is with him, he [the poor person] is not responsible for it; and the person who gave the thing cannot count it as zakat.

Ruling 1986. It is recommended for one to give zakat on cows, sheep, and camels to poor persons who are respectable. In giving zakat, one should prefer his relatives, learned, and virtuous persons over others, and those who do not beg over those who beg. However, it might be that giving zakat to a poor person is better for some other reason [in which case, it should be given to that poor person].

Ruling 1987. It is better that zakat be given openly and recommended alms to the poor (*ṣadaqah*) be given secretly.

Ruling 1988. If in the town of the person who wants to give zakat there is no one entitled to receive it and he cannot spend it in any other legally justified way, he can transfer the zakat to another place. In this case, if he is not negligent in looking after it but it still perishes, he is not responsible for it. Furthermore, he can obtain agency (*wikālah*) from a fully qualified jurist to take possession of it, and with the authorisation of a fully qualified jurist he can transfer it to another place. In this case too, he is not responsible for any loss, and he can take the transportation costs from the zakat as well.

Ruling 1989. If someone entitled to receive zakat is found in one's town, he can still take it to another town but he must pay the expenses for transferring it to that town himself. If the zakat perishes, he is responsible for it unless he took it in compliance with the command of a fully qualified jurist.

Ruling 1990. The charges for weighing and measuring wheat, barley, raisins, and dates that one gives as zakat must be paid by himself.

Ruling 1991. It is disapproved (*makrūh*) for a person to request someone entitled to receive zakat to sell him the zakat he gave him. However, if the person entitled to receive zakat wants to sell the thing he received, then after its price has been determined, the person who gave him the zakat has the first option to buy it.

Ruling 1992. If a person doubts whether or not he gave the zakat that was obligatory for him, and the property that was subject to zakat still exists, he must give zakat even if his doubt is about the zakat of previous years. However, if the property has perished, then zakat is not liable on it even if it relates to the current year.

Ruling 1993. A poor person cannot settle for a lesser amount of zakat before receiving it, nor can he accept something more expensive than the value of the zakat. Furthermore, the giver of zakat cannot give it to someone entitled to receive it on condition that he must return it to him. However, there is no problem if the entitled person consents to return it to him after receiving it. For example, if someone who owes a lot of zakat but has become poor and cannot give it, and he has repented, and a poor person consents to take his zakat from him and gift it back to him, there is no problem.

Ruling 1994. A person cannot purchase the Qur'an, religious books, or books of supplications (*duʿā's*) from the 'in the way of Allah' portion of zakat and give them as a charitable endowment (*waqf*) unless the general public benefit necessitates it, and, based on obligatory precaution, he gets authorisation from a fully qualified jurist.

Ruling 1995. A person cannot buy property from zakat and give it as a charitable endowment to his children or to those whose living expenses are obligatory for him in order that they spend the income generated from that property on their living expenses.

Ruling 1996. A person can take from the 'in the way of Allah' portion of zakat for hajj, *ziyārah*,[11] and suchlike, even if he is not poor or has already taken an amount of zakat that is equal to his annual living expenses, provided that going for hajj, *ziyārah*, and suchlike is in the general public interest, and, based on obligatory precaution, he has obtained permission from a fully qualified jurist for using zakat in this way.

Ruling 1997. If the owner of some wealth makes a poor person his representative for distributing the zakat of that wealth, in the event that the poor person deems it probable that the owner did not intend for him to take zakat for himself as well, he cannot take anything from it for himself; but, if he has certainty (*yaqīn*) that this was not the intention of the owner, then he can take from it for himself.

Ruling 1998. If a poor person takes camels, cows, sheep, gold, or

[11] *Ziyārah* is a visitation to the place of burial of a holy personality or a holy place.

silver as zakat, in the event that the conditions for zakat to become obligatory for him are fulfilled with regard to those items, he must give zakat on them.

Ruling 1999. If two people jointly own a property on which zakat is obligatory and one of them gives zakat for his share, and after that they divide the property, then even if he knows that his partner has not given zakat on his share and is not going to give it afterwards, there is no problem in him using his own share of the property.

Ruling 2000. If a person owes the one-fifth tax (*khums*) or zakat, and recompense (*kaffārah*), vow (*nadhr*), and suchlike are also obligatory for him, and he has debt as well, in the event that he cannot pay all of these obligations and the wealth on which *khums* and zakat are obligatory has not perished, he must pay the *khums* and zakat. If it has perished, then paying zakat, *khums*, and settling his debt has priority over *kaffārah* and *nadhr*.

Ruling 2001. If a person owes *khums* or zakat, and *ḥajjat al-islām*[12] is obligatory for him, and he has debt as well, then, if he dies and his estate is not sufficient for all of these obligations, in the event that the wealth on which *khums* and zakat is obligatory has not perished, the *khums* and zakat must be paid and the rest of his estate must be used to settle his debt. However, if the property on which *khums* and zakat is obligatory has perished, his estate must be used to settle his debt. If after this anything is left, it must be spent for [hiring someone to perform] hajj [on the deceased's behalf]; and if after this anything remains, it must be divided between the *khums* and zakat debts.

Ruling 2002. If a person is engaged in acquiring knowledge and were he not acquiring knowledge he would be working for a living, in the event that acquiring that knowledge is an individual obligation, the portion of zakat for the poor can be given to him. If acquiring that knowledge is in the public interest, it is permitted to give zakat to him from the 'in the way of Allah' portion with the authorisation of

[12] *Ḥajjat al-islām* is the term used for the hajj that is obligatory on a Muslim to perform once in his lifetime, as opposed to a hajj that is obligatory on a Muslim by means of a vow and suchlike.

a fully qualified jurist, based on obligatory precaution. In cases other than these two, it is not permitted to give zakat to him.

THE *FIṬRAH* ALMS TAX (*ZAKĀT AL-FIṬRAH*)

Ruling 2003. A person who at the time of sunset (*ghurūb*) on the eve of Eid al-Fiṭr[13] is *bāligh* and sane, and not unconscious, poor, or a slave, must give on his behalf and on behalf of those who are dependent on him, one *ṣāʿ* – which is approximately three kilograms – of food per head to someone who is entitled to receive zakat. The food that he gives must be considered a staple food in his town, such as wheat, barley, dates, raisins, rice, millet, or something similar, and it suffices if he gives the food's monetary value instead. The obligatory precaution is that food that is not considered a staple in his town must not be given as zakat, even if what he gives is wheat, barley, dates, or raisins.

Ruling 2004. If a person cannot meet his and his family's living expenses for one year and does not have an occupation by which he can meet his and his family's expenses for one year, then such a person is a poor person and it is not obligatory for him to give *zakāt al-fiṭrah*.

Ruling 2005. A person must give *fiṭrah* on behalf of all those who are considered his dependants at the time of sunset on the eve of Eid al-Fiṭr, irrespective of whether they are young or old, Muslims or disbelievers, whether it is obligatory for him to pay for their living expenses or not, and whether they are in his town or another town.

Ruling 2006. If a person appoints his dependant, who happens to be in another town, to be his agent in giving his [i.e. the dependant's] *fiṭrah* from that person's property, in the event that he is confident he will give the *fiṭrah*, it is not necessary for the person to give his dependant's *fiṭrah* himself.

Ruling 2007. It is obligatory for one to give the *fiṭrah* of a guest who

[13] The 1st of Shawwāl.

arrives at his house before sunset on the eve of Eid al-Fiṭr and spends the night at his place and is considered his dependant, albeit only temporarily.

Ruling 2008. The *fiṭrah* of a guest who arrives at one's house after sunset on the eve of Eid al-Fiṭr is, based on precaution, obligatory for the host provided that the guest is considered the host's dependant; otherwise, it is not. If a person is invited to break his fast (*ifṭār*) on the eve of Eid al-Fiṭr, he is not considered the host's dependant and the guest's *fiṭrah* is not the responsibility of the owner of the house.

Ruling 2009. If a person is insane at the time of sunset on the eve of Eid al-Fiṭr and his insanity continues until the time for *ẓuhr* prayers on the day Eid al-Fiṭr, *zakāt al-fiṭrah* is not obligatory for him; otherwise, based on obligatory precaution, it is necessary for him to give *fiṭrah*.

Ruling 2010. If before sunset a child becomes *bāligh*, or an insane person becomes sane, or a poor person becomes rich, and if that person meets the conditions that make it obligatory for one to give *fiṭrah*, he must give *fiṭrah*.

Ruling 2011. If at the time of sunset on the eve of Eid al-Fiṭr a person does not meet the conditions that make it obligatory for one to give *fiṭrah* but before the time for *ẓuhr* prayers on the day of Eid he does meet the conditions, then the obligatory precaution is that he must give *fiṭrah*.

Ruling 2012. If a disbeliever becomes Muslim after sunset on the eve of Eid al-Fiṭr, it is not obligatory for him to give *zakāt al-fiṭrah*. However, if a Muslim who was not a Shia becomes a Shia after the moon is sighted, he must give *fiṭrah*.

Ruling 2013. If someone possesses only one *ṣāʿ* of wheat and suchlike, it is recommended that he give *zakāt al-fiṭrah*. In the event that he has dependants and he wants to give their *fiṭrah* as well, he can give that one *ṣāʿ* to one of them with the intention of giving *fiṭrah*, and the recipient can in turn give it to another dependant with the same intention, and so on until it reaches the last person; and it is better that the last recipient give the item to someone who is not a member of their family. If one of them is a minor (*ṣaghīr*) or insane, his guardian can take it on his behalf; and the recommended precaution is that the guardian should not take it with the intention of taking it for the minor or insane person but for himself.

Ruling 2014. If after sunset on the eve of Eid al-Fiṭr a woman gives birth to a child, it is not obligatory to give *fiṭrah* for the child. However, if before sunset a woman gives birth or marries and the mother or wife are considered dependants of the father or husband, he must give their *fiṭrah*; but if they are dependants of someone else, then it is not obligatory for him. If they are not dependants of anyone, then the *fiṭrah* of the woman is obligatory for herself and there is no obligation to give *fiṭrah* for the child.

Ruling 2015. If a person is a dependant of someone and before sunset he becomes a dependant of someone else, his *fiṭrah* becomes obligatory for the person he became a dependant of. For example, if a girl moves to her husband's house before sunset, her husband must give her *fiṭrah*.

Ruling 2016.* A person whose *fiṭrah* is obligatory for another person is not obligated to give his *fiṭrah* himself. However, if the other person, without any legitimate excuse or due to forgetfulness, does not give his *fiṭrah*, then based on precaution, it becomes obligatory for the person to give his own *fiṭrah* provided the conditions mentioned in Ruling 2003 are fulfilled. If a well-off person is a dependant of a poor person, it is not obligatory for the poor person to give *fiṭrah*, but if the well-off person meets the conditions that make it obligatory for one to give *fiṭrah*, then he must give *fiṭrah*.

Ruling 2017. If a person whose *fiṭrah* is obligatory for another person gives his own *fiṭrah*, the obligation for the one who must give it is not exempted.

Ruling 2018. A person who is not a *sayyid* cannot give *fiṭrah* to a *sayyid*, and if that *sayyid* is his dependant, he cannot give that *sayyid*'s *fiṭrah* to another *sayyid*.

Ruling 2019. The *fiṭrah* of a child who is breastfed by its mother or a wet nurse is obligatory for the person who pays for the living expenses of the mother or the wet nurse. However, if the mother or the wet nurse takes her living expenses from the child's property, then the *fiṭrah* of that child is not obligatory for anyone.

Ruling 2020. Even if a person pays for the living expenses of his dependants with property that he has acquired unlawfully, he must give their *fiṭrah* from property that he has acquired lawfully.

Ruling 2021. If a person hires someone like a builder, carpenter, or domestic worker, and pays for his living expenses in a manner that the hired person is considered his dependant, he must give the hired person's *fiṭrah* as well. However, if he only pays him for his work, it is not obligatory for him to give his *fiṭrah*.

Ruling 2022. If a person dies before sunset on the eve of Eid al-Fiṭr, it is not obligatory to give his and his dependants' *fiṭrah* from his estate. However, if a person dies after sunset, then based on the opinion held by most jurists (*mashhūr*), his and his dependants' *fiṭrah* must be given from his estate. However, this rule is problematic, and the requisite precautionary action must not be abandoned.

DISTRIBUTION OF *ZAKĀT AL-FIṬRAH*

Ruling 2023. Based on obligatory precaution, *zakāt al-fiṭrah* must only be given to the poor, and this means poor Shias who satisfy the criteria mentioned previously regarding those who are entitled to receive zakat.[14] In the event that there are no poor Shias in one's town, he can give it to other Muslims who are poor, but in any case, *fiṭrah* must not be given to a *nāṣibī*.[15]

Ruling 2024. If a Shia child is poor, one can spend *fiṭrah* on him or make it his property by entrusting it to his guardian.

[14] See Ruling 1957 and onwards.

[15] In Ruling 103, *nawāṣib* (pl. of *nāṣibī*) are defined as 'those who show enmity towards the Imams ('A)'.

Ruling 2025. It is not necessary that the poor person to whom *fiṭrah* is given be a dutiful person (*ʿādil*); however, the obligatory precaution is that *fiṭrah* must not be given to someone who consumes alcohol, does not perform prayers, or publicly commits sins.

Ruling 2026. *Fiṭrah* must not be given to someone who spends it for sinful purposes.

Ruling 2027. The recommended precaution is that a poor person should not be given *fiṭrah* that is less than one *ṣāʿ* unless the total amount of *fiṭrah* is not sufficient for all the poor people. However, there is no problem if more than one *ṣāʿ* is given.

Ruling 2028. If a person gives half a *ṣāʿ* of an item on account of it being double the price – for example, if a particular type of wheat is double the price of ordinary wheat and one gives only half a *ṣāʿ* – it is not sufficient. In fact, even if he gives half a *ṣāʿ* with the intention of paying the value of the *fiṭrah* [as opposed to giving the quantity of the item], it is not sufficient.

Ruling 2029. A person cannot give as *fiṭrah* half a *ṣāʿ* of one item, such as wheat, and half a *ṣāʿ* of another item, such as barley. In fact, even if he gives half a *ṣāʿ* with the intention of paying the value of the *fiṭrah* [as opposed to giving the quantity of the item], it is not sufficient.

Ruling 2030. It is recommended that in giving *zakāt al-fiṭrah* one should prefer his poor relatives and neighbours over others, and it is befitting that he also give preference to learned, religious, and virtuous persons over others.

Ruling 2031. If a person gives *fiṭrah* to someone thinking that he is poor but later realises that he was not poor, in the event that the item he gave him has not perished, he must take it back and give it to someone who is entitled to receive it; and if he is unable to take it back, he must replace the *fiṭrah* from his own property. If the item has perished, in the event that the beneficiary knew the item was given as *fiṭrah*, the beneficiary must replace it; however, if the beneficiary did not know, then replacing it is not obligatory for him and the benefactor must replace it.

Ruling 2032. A person cannot give *fiṭrah* to someone who says he is poor unless he is confident that what he says is the truth or knows that he was poor previously.

MISCELLANEOUS RULINGS ON *ZAKĀT AL-FIṬRAH*

Ruling 2033. A person must give *zakāt al-fiṭrah* with the intention of *qurbah* – i.e. in humility to the Lord of the worlds – and he must make the intention of giving *fiṭrah* at the time of giving it.

Ruling 2034. It is not permitted for one to give *fiṭrah* before the month of Ramadan, and it is better that he does not give it during the month of Ramadan either. However, there is no problem if one gives a loan to a poor person before the month of Ramadan and then counts the loan as *fiṭrah* once *fiṭrah* has become obligatory for him.

Ruling 2035. Wheat or any other thing that a person gives as *fiṭrah* must not be mixed with soil or any other thing. In the event that it is mixed and the item itself is equal to one *ṣāʿ* and it is usable without having to separate it from the other thing, or if separating it does not require extraordinary effort, or the amount that has been mixed is negligible, then there is no problem.

Ruling 2036. If a person gives *fiṭrah* from a defective thing, then based on obligatory precaution, it is not sufficient.

Ruling 2037. If a person gives *fiṭrah* on behalf of a number of persons, it is not necessary for him to give it all from the same item. For example, it is sufficient if he gives the *fiṭrah* of some in wheat and the *fiṭrah* of others in barley.

Ruling 2038. If a person performs Eid prayers, then based on obligatory precaution, he must give *fiṭrah* before Eid prayers. However, if he does not perform Eid prayers, he can delay giving *fiṭrah* until the time of *ẓuhr* prayers [on the day of Eid al-Fiṭr].

Ruling 2039. If a person puts aside some of his property with the intention of *fiṭrah* but does not give it to someone who is entitled to receive it until the time of *ẓuhr* prayers on the day of Eid al-Fiṭr, he must make the intention of *fiṭrah* whenever he gives it, and there is no problem if there was a rationally acceptable reason for the delay.

Ruling 2040. If a person does not give *fiṭrah* until the time of *ẓuhr* prayers on the day Eid al-Fiṭr and does not set it aside either, then based on obligatory precaution, he must give *fiṭrah* afterwards without making the intention of giving it within its prescribed time (*adāʾ*) or belatedly (*qaḍāʾ*).

Ruling 2041. If a person sets aside *fiṭrah*, he cannot take it for his own use and replace it with something else without the permission of a fully qualified jurist.

Ruling 2042. If a person possesses something that has a value greater than *fiṭrah*, in the event that he does not give *fiṭrah* and makes the intention that some of that item is for *fiṭrah*, then based on obligatory precaution, it will not be sufficient.

Ruling 2043. If the property that one has set aside for *fiṭrah* perishes, in the event that he had access to a poor person but delayed in giving the *fiṭrah*, or he was negligent in looking after it, he must replace it. However, if he did not have access to a poor person and was not negligent in looking after it, he is not responsible for it.

Ruling 2044. If a person entitled to receive *fiṭrah* is found in one's area, the obligatory precaution is that he must not transfer the *fiṭrah* to another place. However, if he does transfer it and delivers it to someone who is entitled to receive it, it is sufficient; but if he transfers it to another place and it perishes, he must replace it.

CHAPTER NINE

Hajj[1]

[1] This chapter contains only a selection of al-Sayyid al-Sistani's rulings on hajj. A separate work, titled *Manāsik al-Ḥajj wa Mulḥaqātuhā*, contains all his rulings on hajj.

Ruling 2045. Hajj means visiting the House of Allah [the Kaʿbah in Mecca] and performing the prescribed rituals there. It is obligatory (*wājib*) on someone who fulfils the following conditions to perform hajj once in his lifetime:

1. being of the age of legal responsibility (*bāligh*);
2. being sane (*ʿāqil*) and a free person;
3. on account of going for hajj, one must not be compelled to commit an unlawful (*ḥarām*) act which is more important to avoid than performing hajj; nor must he be compelled to abandon an obligatory act which is more important than performing hajj. However, if such a situation transpires and he goes for hajj, his hajj is valid (*ṣaḥīḥ*) although he will have sinned;
4. being able (*mustaṭīʿ*). This is determined by the following criteria:
    a. he must possess the provisions, and – in the event that he requires it – the means of transportation for the journey; or, he must have the wealth to procure them;
    b. he must be healthy and able to travel to Mecca and perform hajj without having to experience excessive difficulty (*mashaqqah*). This condition is a requirement for the obligation of hajj when a person is performing it himself. As for someone who has the financial capacity but not the physical ability to perform it himself, or performing it himself would cause him hardship (*ḥaraj*) and he is not hopeful of his physical condition improving, such a person must appoint a representative (*nāʾib*) [to perform hajj on his behalf];
    c. during any stage of his journey, there must not be an obstruction to going further. If the route is closed or a person fears he will lose his life or honour on the journey or his property will be taken, it is not obligatory for him to perform hajj. However, if he is able to go by another route, he must do so even if it is a longer route unless that route is so much longer and so unusual that it can be said the road for hajj is closed;
    d. he must have sufficient time to perform the rituals of hajj;
    e. he must be able to meet the living expenses of those whose maintenance is obligatory for him, such as his

wife and children, and those who, if he were to stop spending on them, it would cause him hardship;

f. upon returning, he must have a business, a farm, an income from a property, or some other means of earning his livelihood, i.e. it must not be such that because of the expenses he incurs for hajj, he is compelled to live in difficulty when he comes back.

Ruling 2046. With regard to someone who, on account of not owning a house experiences hardship, hajj only becomes obligatory for him when he has money for a house as well.

Ruling 2047. With regard to a woman who is able to go to Mecca, if upon her return she will not possess any wealth and her husband is, for example, a poor person (*faqīr*) who does not meet her living expenses, and if therefore she would have to live in difficulty, then it is not obligatory for her to go for hajj.

Ruling 2048. If someone does not possess the provisions and the means of transportation for the journey, and if someone else tells him to go for hajj and that he will pay for his living expenses and the living expenses of his dependants during his trip for hajj, then in the event that he is confident (i.e. he has *iṭmi'nān*) that the person will pay for his expenses, hajj is obligatory for him.

Ruling 2049. If for a person to perform hajj some people gift him the expenses for going to and returning from Mecca, and they also gift him the living expenses of his dependants during the time he is on his journey to Mecca, then hajj is obligatory for him even if he has a debt to pay off and even if he does not possess wealth that he can live on when he returns. However, if the journey for hajj falls on the days when he earns a living and were he to go for hajj he would not be able to repay his debt on time, or he would not be able to pay for his living expenses for the rest of the year, then hajj is not obligatory for him.

Ruling 2050. If some people provide one's travel expenses and the living expenses of his dependants for the period he is in Mecca, and they tell him to go for hajj but the money will not be his own, [rather, it will only be permissible for him to use it,] then, in the event that he is confident that they will not take it back from him, hajj is obligatory for him.

Ruling 2051. If some people provide someone with an amount of money that is sufficient for performing hajj, but they make it a condition that during the journey to Mecca he must serve someone who is giving him the money, hajj is not obligatory for him.

Ruling 2052. If some people gift an amount of money to someone, making hajj obligatory for him, in the event that he performs hajj and later acquires wealth himself, hajj is not obligatory for him again.

Ruling 2053. If a person goes on a business trip to Jeddah, for example, and there he acquires some wealth that would enable him to go to Mecca if he wanted to go there, then he must go for hajj. In the event that he performs hajj and later acquires wealth that enables him to go to Mecca from his home town (*waṭan*), hajj is not obligatory for him again.

Ruling 2054. If a person is hired to personally go for hajj on behalf of another person, in the event that he is unable to go himself and wants to send someone else on his behalf, he must get authorisation from the person who hired him.

Ruling 2055. If someone becomes able to go to Mecca but does not reach the plains of ʿArafāt and Mashʿar al-Ḥarām at the prescribed time, in the event that he is unable to go for hajj in subsequent years, hajj will not be obligatory for him. However, if he was able to go for some years but did not, he must go for hajj even if it entails difficulty.

Ruling 2056. If a person who has become able does not go for hajj, and afterwards due to old age, illness, or incapacitation he is unable to perform hajj, or it entails hardship, and if he loses hope in being able to perform hajj himself in subsequent years, then he must send someone to perform hajj on his behalf; and if in subsequent years he is able to perform hajj himself, he must do so. The same applies if a person cannot perform hajj due to old age, illness, or incapacitation in the first year that he acquires a sufficient amount of wealth for performing hajj, and he loses hope in being able to perform it in subsequent years. In all of these cases, the recommended precaution (*al-iḥtiyāṭ al-mustaḥabb*) is that if the person being represented (*al-manūb ʿanhu*) is a man, then the representative (*nāʾib*) should be someone who will go for hajj for the first time (*ṣarūrah*).

Ruling 2057. A person who has been hired to perform hajj on behalf of someone else must perform *ṭawāf al-nisāʾ*[2] on behalf of that other person, and if he does not, then sexual relations are unlawful for the person who has been hired.

Ruling 2058. If a person does not perform *ṭawāf al-nisāʾ* correctly or forgets to perform it, in the event that he remembers this after a few days, goes back, and then performs it, it is valid. However, in the event that returning causes him excessive difficulty, he can appoint a representative [to perform it on his behalf].

[2] This is an obligatory circumambulation (*ṭawāf*) of the Kaʿbah that is performed as part of the hajj rituals.

CHAPTER TEN

Buying and Selling

Ruling 2059. It is befitting for a trader to learn the laws (*aḥkām*) of buying and selling concerning issues he commonly encounters. In fact, if he would be at risk of committing an unlawful (*ḥarām*) act or abandoning an obligatory (*wājib*) act as a result of not learning the laws, then it would be necessary [not just befitting] for him to learn them. It is reported that His Eminence Imam al-Ṣādiq (ʿA) said, 'One who wishes to engage in buying and selling must learn its laws. If he were to buy and sell before learning its laws, he would fall into ruin by means of invalid (*bāṭil*) and dubious transactions (*muʿāmalāt*).'

Ruling 2060. If a person does not know whether a transaction (*muʿāmalah*) he has conducted is valid (*ṣaḥīḥ*) or invalid due to him not knowing the ruling (*masʾalah*), he cannot have disposal over what he received in the transaction nor what he handed over; rather, he must learn the ruling or exercise precaution (*iḥtiyāṭ*), albeit by means of a settlement (*muṣālaḥah*). However, if he knows that the other party consents to him having disposal over the item even though the transaction is invalid, then having disposal over it is permitted (*jāʾiz*).

Ruling 2061. If a person does not have any wealth but certain expenses are obligatory for him – such as providing for his wife and children – he must earn his living. As for recommended (*mustaḥabb*) matters – such as providing a better livelihood for one's family and helping the poor (*fuqarāʾ*) – for such matters, earning is recommended.

RECOMMENDED (*MUSTAḤABB*) ACTS OF BUYING AND SELLING

Some things are considered recommended when buying and selling, including:

1. one should not discriminate between buyers with respect to the price of goods except when taking into account the buyer's impoverished situation and suchlike;
2. at the start of business proceedings, one should say the *shahā-*

datayn (two testimonies),[1] and at the time of the transaction, one should say *takbīr*;[2]

3. one should give more of what is being sold and take less of what is being bought;
4. if the other party involved in the transaction regrets making the transaction and requests to annul (*faskh*) it, one should accept his request.

DISAPPROVED (*MAKRŪH*) TRANSACTIONS

Ruling 2062. Some disapproved transactions are as follows:

1. selling real estate, unless one buys another real estate with the money acquired from the transaction;
2. to be a butcher;
3. selling shrouds (*kafans*);
4. transactions with people of low character;
5. transactions between the start of the time for the morning (*ṣubḥ*) prayer and sunrise;
6. making one's profession the buying and selling of wheat, barley, and suchlike;
7. intervening in someone else's transaction in order to buy the goods that the other person wishes to buy.

UNLAWFUL (*ḤARĀM*) TRANSACTIONS

Ruling 2063. There are many unlawful transactions; some of them are as follows:

1.* buying and selling intoxicating drinks, non-hunting dogs, pigs, and – based on obligatory precaution (*al-iḥtiyāṭ al-wājib*) – impure (*najis*) carcasses, except for what is removed from a living human body to be transplanted into another body. Apart

[1] That is, testifying to the oneness of Allah and the prophethood of Prophet Muḥammad (Ṣ).

[2] *Takbīr* is a proclamation of Allah's greatness by saying '*allāhu akbar*'.

from these, buying and selling an intrinsic impurity (*ʿayn al-najāsah*) is permitted if it is for some significant and lawful use, such as buying and selling impure animal waste for use as fertilisers;
2. buying and selling usurped (*ghaṣbī*) property, if this necessitates having disposal over it, such as handing it over and taking possession of it;
3.* transactions with money that is no longer legal tender or with counterfeit money, if the other party is unaware of this. If he is aware, the transaction is permitted if that money has a significant value;
4. transactions of unlawful objects; that is, things that have been made in a form that is usually utilised in an unlawful manner and its value is due to its unlawful utilisation, such as idols, crucifixes, gambling implements, and instruments of unlawful entertainment;
5. transactions in which there is deceit. It is reported that the Most Noble Messenger (Ṣ) said, 'One who deceives Muslims in his transactions is not one of us. Allah takes away the blessing of his sustenance, closes the path of his livelihood, and leaves him to himself.' Deceit can take place in different ways, such as:
    a. mixing a good item with a bad one or with something else; for example, mixing milk with water;
    b. making an item appear better than it really is; for example, spraying water onto old vegetables to make them appear fresh;
    c. feigning an item as something else; for example, gold-plating an item without informing the buyer [that it is not solid gold];
    d. concealing a defect in an item when a buyer trusts the seller not to conceal defects.

Ruling 2064. There is no problem in selling an item that has become impure but is washable and may become pure (*ṭāhir*), such as a rug or utensil. The same applies if the item is not washable but the lawful and usual use of it is not dependent on it being pure, such as crude oil. In fact, even if its lawful and usual use is dependent on it being pure, in the event that it has a lawful and significant benefit, it is permitted to sell it.

Ruling 2065. If a person wishes to sell something impure, he must tell the buyer that it is impure in the event that were he not to tell him, the buyer would be at risk of committing an unlawful act or abandoning an obligatory act; for example, the buyer would use impure water to perform ablution (*wuḍūʾ*) or ritual bathing (*ghusl*) and then perform obligatory prayers (*ṣalāh*); or he would use the impure item for eating or drinking. Of course, if one knows that telling the buyer would be of no avail – for example, he is unconcerned about religious matters – then it is not necessary to tell him.

Ruling 2066. Buying and selling impure consumable and non-consumable medicine is permitted; however, the seller must inform the buyer of it being impure in the situation mentioned in the previous ruling.

Ruling 2067. There is no problem in buying and selling oil that has been imported from non-Muslim countries if one does not know it is impure. As for oil and other things that are acquired after the animal has died, such as gelatine, in the event that one acquires them from a disbeliever (*kāfir*) or they are imported from non-Muslim countries, they are pure and it is permitted to buy and sell them as long as one deems it probable that they have been acquired from an animal which was slaughtered according to Islamic law; however, it is unlawful to consume these things. Furthermore, it is necessary for the seller to tell the buyer how it was acquired in the event that were he not to tell him, the buyer would be at risk of committing an unlawful act or abandoning an obligatory one, similar to what was mentioned in Ruling 2065.

Ruling 2068. If a fox or similar animal is not slaughtered according to Islamic law or dies by itself, then based on obligatory precaution, buying and selling its skin is not permitted; however, if it is doubtful [as to how the animal died], there is no problem.

Ruling 2069. It is permitted to buy and sell leather that is imported from non-Muslim countries or acquired from a disbeliever in the event that one deems it probable that it is from an animal which was slaughtered according to Islamic law. Moreover, it is correct (*ṣaḥīḥ*) to perform prayers with it [if one deems it probable that it is from an animal which was slaughtered according to Islamic law].

Ruling 2070. Oil and other products acquired from an animal after it has died are considered pure, and buying and selling them is permitted. The same applies to leather acquired from a Muslim whom a person knows to have acquired it from a disbeliever without investigating whether or not the leather was acquired from an animal that was slaughtered according to Islamic law. However, consuming such oil and the like is not permitted.

Ruling 2071. A transaction of wine and other intoxicating drinks is unlawful and invalid.

Ruling 2072. The sale of usurped property is invalid unless the owner subsequently consents to it; and [if the owner does not,] the seller must return to the buyer the money he received from him.

Ruling 2073. If a buyer seriously intends to engage in a transaction but his intention (*qaṣd*) is to not pay for the item that he is buying, this intention does not affect the validity of the transaction. However, it is necessary for him to pay the seller for the item.

Ruling 2074. If a buyer purchases an item undertaking to pay for it later, but he wishes to pay for it with unlawful wealth, the transaction is valid. However, he must pay the amount he owes from lawful wealth to be absolved of his responsibility [to pay the seller].

Ruling 2075. The buying and selling of unlawful instruments of entertainment is not permitted. As for instruments that can be used for lawful or unlawful purposes, such as radios, recorders, and video players, there is no problem in buying and selling them, and it is permitted to keep them when one is confident (i.e. has *iṭmiʾnān*) that he and his family will not use them in unlawful ways.

Ruling 2076. If something that can be used in a lawful manner is sold so that it is used in an unlawful way – for example, a person sells grapes so that wine can be produced from them – then, irrespective of whether it was decided to sell that thing for the unlawful use at the time of the transaction or before it, if the transaction takes place on the basis of the unlawful use, it is unlawful. However, if a person does not sell it for that reason but knows that the buyer will produce wine from the grapes, there is no problem with the transaction.

Ruling 2077. Based on obligatory precaution, it is unlawful to make sculptures of living things; however, there is no problem in buying and selling such sculptures. As for illustrating living things, this is permitted.

Ruling 2078. Buying items that have been acquired through gambling, theft, or void (*bāṭil*) transactions is unlawful if this amounts to having disposal over them. If someone buys such an item and receives it from the buyer, he must return it to its original owner.

Ruling 2079. If a person sells ghee that is mixed with suet and he specifies it – for example, he says, 'I am selling 1 kilogram of this ghee' – then in case the amount of suet is a lot, i.e. to the extent that the product could not be said to be ghee, the transaction is void. But if the amount of suet is a little, i.e. to the extent that the product could be said to be 'ghee mixed with suet', then the transaction is valid. However, in this case, the buyer has the right to annul due to a defect (*khiyār al-ʿayb*),[3] i.e. he can annul the transaction and take back his money. Furthermore, if the ghee is distinguishable from the suet, the transaction in relation to the amount of suet mixed in the ghee is void, and the money that the seller takes for the suet belongs to the buyer and the suet belongs to the seller. The buyer can also annul the transaction with respect to the pure ghee within the product. However, if the seller does not specify it and sells 1 kilogram of ghee, undertaking to give it later, and he later gives ghee mixed with suet, the buyer can return the mixed ghee and demand pure ghee.

Ruling 2080. If a commodity that is sold by weight or measure is sold for a greater weight or measure of the same commodity – for example, 1 kilogram of wheat is sold for 1.5 kilograms of wheat – it is usury (*ribā*) and unlawful. In fact, if one of two commodities is without defect and the other is defective, or the quality of one of them

[3] See Ruling 2134, case 6.

is good and the other is bad, or they are different to one another in price – then, in the event that the seller receives more than he gives, it is still usury and unlawful. Therefore, if a person gives unbroken copper and receives a greater amount of broken copper, or he gives rice of superior quality and receives a greater amount of inferior quality rice, or he gives gold that has been crafted [such as a piece of jewellery] and receives a greater amount of gold that has not been crafted, it is usury and unlawful.

Ruling 2081. If the extra thing that a seller receives is different to what he sells – for example, he sells 1 kilogram of wheat for 1 kilogram of wheat and 10 pence – it is still usury and unlawful. In fact, even if the seller does not receive any extra goods but makes it a condition that the buyer must do something for him, it is also usury and unlawful.

Ruling 2082.* If a person gives a lesser amount but adds something else – for example, he sells 1 kilogram of wheat and one handkerchief for 1.5 kilograms of wheat – there is no problem as long as he intends the handkerchief to be the item for which he is receiving the extra amount [i.e. the extra half kilogram of wheat,] and as long as the transaction is an immediate exchange (*naqd*) transaction.[4] Similarly, there is no problem if both sides add something extra – for example, one of them sells 1 kilogram of wheat and one handkerchief to the other person for 1.5 kilograms of wheat and one handkerchief – as long as they intend the handkerchief on the one side, and the handkerchief and half kilogram of wheat on the other, to be the items of exchange.

Ruling 2083. If a person sells a commodity that is sold in metres or yards, such as cloth, or a commodity that is sold by count, such as eggs and walnuts, and he takes more in return, there is no problem except if both [the commodity being sold and the payment in exchange (*ʿiwaḍ*)] are of the same commodity and the transaction has a period, in which case its validity is problematic (*maḥall al-ishkāl*) [i.e.

[4] That is, a transaction in which there is no lapse of time between the buyer paying for the item and receiving it. This is in contrast to credit (*nasīʾah*) and prepayment (*salaf*) transactions.

based on obligatory precaution, it is not valid].[5] An example [of such a problematic transaction] is when a person gives ten walnuts at present to receive twelve walnuts after one month. The same applies to selling currency. Therefore, there is no problem if, for example, a person sells British pounds sterling for another currency such as dinars or dollars, whether that be at present or at another time. However, if the person wishes to sell some currency for the same currency and receive more in return, then that transaction must not have a period; otherwise, its validity is problematic [i.e. based on obligatory precaution, it is not valid]. An example [of such a problematic transaction] is when a person sells £100 at present to receive £110 after six months.

Ruling 2084. With regard to commodities that are sold by weight or measure in one city or most cities, and by count in other cities, it is permitted to sell that commodity for more in the city in which it is sold by count.

Ruling 2085. With regard to things that are sold by weight or measure, if the thing that is sold and the payment in exchange for it are not of the same commodity and the transaction does not have a period, there is no problem in taking more. However, if the transaction has a period, it is problematic [i.e. based on obligatory precaution, it is not valid]. Therefore, if 1 kilogram of rice is sold for 2 kilograms of wheat after one month, the validity of the transaction is problematic [i.e. based on obligatory precaution, it is not valid].

Ruling 2086. Selling ripe fruit for unripe fruit with extra is not permitted. If there is no extra and the transaction does not have a period, it is disapproved (*makrūh*), and if it is on credit, it is problematic [i.e. based on obligatory precaution, it is not permitted].

Ruling 2087. With regard to usury-based transactions, barley and wheat are considered to be the same commodity. Therefore, if, for example, a person gives 1 kilogram of wheat and receives 1.5 kilograms of barley in return for it, it is usury and unlawful. Also, if, for example, a person buys 10 kilograms of barley in return for

[5] As mentioned in Ruling 6, the term 'problematic' (*maḥall al-ishkāl*) amounts to saying the ruling is based on obligatory precaution.

10 kilograms of wheat at the beginning of the harvest, then because he acquires the barley immediately but will give the wheat after some time, it is as if he has acquired something extra, rendering the transaction unlawful.

Ruling 2088. A father and his child, and a wife and husband, can take interest from one another. Similarly, a Muslim can take interest from a disbeliever (*kāfir*) who is not under the protection of Islam. However, an interest-based transaction with a disbeliever who is under the protection of Islam is unlawful. Of course, after the transaction has taken place, one can take more from him if giving interest is permitted in his religion.

Ruling 2089. Shaving one's beard and taking a fee for doing so is not permitted, based on obligatory precaution. The exception to this rule is if it is done out of necessity, or it would result in harm or hardship (*ḥaraj*) that cannot normally be endured, even if that hardship amounts to being mocked or insulted.

Ruling 2090. Singing (*ghinā*) is unlawful. The meaning of 'singing' here is void (*bāṭil*) speech that is articulated in a tune appropriate to gatherings of entertainment and amusement. Similarly, it is not permitted to recite the Qur'an, supplications (*duʿāʾs*), and the like in such a tune. And based on obligatory precaution, other forms of speech, apart from the ones already mentioned, must not be articulated in such a tune either. Similarly, listening to singing is unlawful, and taking a fee for singing is also unlawful, and the fee does not become the property of the person who took it. Learning and teaching to sing is also not permitted. Music, i.e. playing instruments that are specially designed for music, is also unlawful if it is in a way that is appropriate to gatherings of entertainment and amusement [and listening to such music is unlawful as well]; other than that, it is not unlawful. Taking a fee for playing unlawful music is unlawful, and the fee taken does not become the property of the person who took it. Teaching and learning it is also unlawful.

CONDITIONS RELATING TO THE SELLER AND THE BUYER

Ruling 2091. Six conditions must be fulfilled by the seller and the buyer [for the transaction to be valid]:

1. they must be of the age of legal responsibility (*bāligh*);
2. they must be sane (*ʿāqil*);
3. they must not be foolish with finances (*safīh*); i.e. they must not spend their wealth in futile ways;
4. they must have an intention to buy and sell. Therefore, if, for example, someone jokingly says, 'I sell my property', the transaction is void;
5. they must not be compelled by anyone [to carry out the transaction];
6. they must, respectively, be the owners of the commodity being sold and the payment made in exchange.

The rulings about these conditions will be explained below.

Ruling 2092.* A transaction carried out with a non-*bāligh* child who acts independently in the transaction is void even if it is carried out with the permission of his guardian. The exception to this is a transaction of things that have little value and with which it is normal to transact with a non-*bāligh* child who is able to discern between right and wrong (*mumayyiz*); such a transaction is valid if the child has permission from his guardian. If the transaction is carried out with his guardian (*walī*) and the non-*bāligh mumayyiz* child only says the formula (*ṣīghah*)[6] for the transaction, it is valid in each case. In fact, if the commodity or the money belongs to someone else and the child sells the commodity as the agent (*wakīl*) of the owner or buys something with the money, the apparent (*ẓāhir*)[7] ruling is that the transaction is valid even though the *mumayyiz* child may be independent in having disposal over the commodity/money. Similarly,

[6] See Rulings 2107 and 2108.

[7] For practical purposes in jurisprudential rulings, expressing an 'apparent' ruling equates to giving a fatwa.

if the child merely acts as an intermediary for delivering the money to the seller, the transaction is valid even if the child is not *mumayyiz* because in reality, two *bāligh* people will have transacted with one another.

Ruling 2093. If a person buys something from or sells something to a non-*bāligh* child when transactions with such a child are not valid, he must return the commodity or the money that was taken from the child – in the event that it was the property of the child – to his guardian. If, however, it belonged to someone else, he must return it to its owner or obtain the owner's consent. In the event that he does not know who the owner is and does not possess any means of identifying him, he must give the thing he acquired from the child to the poor on behalf of the owner as *radd al-maẓālim*.[8] And the obligatory precaution is that to do this, he must obtain permission from a fully qualified jurist (*al-ḥākim al-sharʿī*).

Ruling 2094. If a person carries out a transaction with a *mumayyiz* child when transactions with such a child are not valid, and the child destroys the commodity or the money he gave him, he can claim it from the child's guardian or the child himself after he becomes *bāligh*. If the child is not *mumayyiz* or he is *mumayyiz* but does not destroy the property himself but it is destroyed while it is with him, albeit as a result of his negligence or dissipation, he is not responsible (*ḍāmin*) for it.

Ruling 2095. If a buyer or a seller is compelled to carry out a transaction but then consents to it after the transaction – for example, he says, 'I consent' – the transaction is valid. However, the recommended precaution (*al-iḥtiyāṭ al-mustaḥabb*) is that the two parties should repeat the transaction formula.

Ruling 2096. If a person sells someone's property without his authorisation, the transaction is void if the owner does not consent to its sale and does not subsequently authorise it.

[8] *Radd al-maẓālim* refers to giving back property – which has been unrightfully or unknowingly taken – to its rightful owner, or if that is not possible, to the poor as *ṣadaqah* on behalf of the rightful owner.

Ruling 2097. The father and paternal grandfather of a child, and the executor (*waṣī*) of the father or the executor of the paternal grandfather of a child, can sell the property belonging to the child. In case none of them is alive, a dutiful (*ʿādil*) jurist (*mujtahid*)[9] can also sell the property of an insane person, an orphan child, or a missing person if a matter of primary importance necessitates it.

Ruling 2098. If a person usurps some property and sells it, and after that the owner of the property authorises the transaction, the transaction is valid. From the time of the transaction, the property that the usurper sells to the buyer and its usufruct belong to the buyer. And from the time of the transaction, the thing that the buyer gives and its usufruct belong to the person whose property was usurped.

Ruling 2099. If a person usurps some property and then sells it with the intention that the money acquired in return belongs to him, in the event that the owner of the usurped property authorises the transaction, the transaction is valid. However, the money belongs to the owner, not the usurper.

CONDITIONS RELATING TO THE COMMODITY AND THE PAYMENT IN EXCHANGE

Ruling 2100. The commodity that is sold and the thing that is taken as payment in exchange for it must fulfil the following five conditions [for the transaction to be valid]:

1. the amount must be known, either by weight, measure, number, or another similar method;
2. the person must be able to hand over the item; otherwise, the transaction is not valid unless he sells the thing with something else that he can hand over, in which case the transaction is valid. However, if the buyer can acquire the thing that he

[9] A *mujtahid* is a person who has attained the level of *ijtihād*, qualifying him to be an authority in Islamic law. *Ijtihād* is the process of deriving Islamic laws from authentic sources.

has bought even though the seller is unable to hand it over to him, the transaction is valid. For example, if someone sells a horse that has run away and the buyer is able to find it, there is no problem with the transaction; it is valid and there is no need to include something that he can deliver;
3. the particulars of the commodity and the payment in exchange must be known. 'Particulars' here are those things that affect one's decision concerning the transaction [as opposed to inconsequential things];
4. there must not be any other right attached to the commodity or the payment in exchange in that once it ceases to be owned by the owner, he no longer has any right over it;
5. the commodity itself must be sold, not its usufruct. Therefore, if, for example, someone sells the usufruct of a house, the transaction is not valid. However, in the event that the buyer offers the usufruct of his own property instead of money, there is no problem; for example, he buys a rug from someone and in exchange he gives him the usufruct of his house for a year.

The rulings about these conditions will be explained below.

Ruling 2101. A commodity that is sold by weight or measure in a particular city must be purchased by weight or measure in that city. However, he can purchase the same commodity by viewing it in another city where it is sold by viewing it.

Ruling 2102. Something that is bought and sold by weight can also be transacted by measure; for example, a person wishes to sell 10 kilograms of wheat and uses a measuring vessel that has the capacity to hold 1 kilogram of wheat and sells ten of these measures.

Ruling 2103. If a transaction is void due to one of the conditions that were mentioned earlier – apart from the fourth condition – not being fulfilled, but the buyer and seller consent for the other to have disposal over their property, there is no problem in them having this disposal.

Ruling 2104. The transaction of something that has been given as a charitable endowment (*waqf*) is invalid. However, if the thing is damaged to the extent that it can no longer be used for the purpose for which it was endowed, or it is close to reaching this stage – for example, the *ḥaṣīr*[10] of a mosque is so torn that one cannot perform prayers on it – then there is no problem if the trustee (*mutawallī*) or someone who is ruled to be in his position sells it. But wherever possible, the money acquired should – based on recommended precaution – be used in the same mosque in a manner that is most congruous with the aims of the endower (*wāqif*).

Ruling 2105. If a dispute arises between the beneficiaries of a charitable endowment to the extent that it is supposed that not selling the endowment may result in the loss of property or the loss of life, then selling the endowment is problematic [i.e. based on obligatory precaution, it must not be sold]. However, if the endower makes a condition that it must be sold if it is advisable, then there is no problem in selling it in this case.

Ruling 2106. There is no problem in buying or selling a property that has been rented to someone else. However, the use of the property during the rental period belongs to the tenant/hiree (*mustaʾjir*). If the buyer does not know that the property has been given on rent or he bought the property supposing that the rental period is short, he can annul his transaction after discovering the situation.

THE TRANSACTION FORMULA (*ṢĪGHAH*)

Ruling 2107. When buying and selling, it is not necessary to say a particular formula [or for it to be] in Arabic. For example, if a seller says in English, 'I sell this property in exchange for this money', and the buyer says, 'I accept', the transaction is valid. However, the buyer and the seller must have an intention to establish (*qaṣd al-inshāʾ*) [a contract of sale]; i.e. when they say these sentences, they must intend to buy/sell.

Ruling 2108. If at the time of the transaction the formula is not said

[10] A *ḥaṣīr* is a mat that is made by plaiting or weaving straw, reed, or similar materials of plant origin.

but the seller, in exchange for the property that he takes from the buyer, makes the buyer the owner of his own property, the transaction is valid and both become owners [of the exchanged items].

BUYING AND SELLING FRUIT

Ruling 2109. The sale of fruit that has shed its flower and developed buds, and about which it is known whether it has been saved from disease or not, such that the quantity of that tree's produce can be estimated, is valid even before it is picked. In fact, even if it is not yet known whether it has been saved from disease or not, in the event that the sale is of two years or more of fruit, or the sale is of the quantity that has grown at the moment, the transaction is valid on condition that the fruit has a significant value. Similarly, if a produce of the earth or something else is sold with it, the transaction is valid. However, the obligatory precaution in this case is that the other produce must be incorporated into the transaction in a way that if the buds do not form into fruit, the buyer's capital is protected.

Ruling 2110. The sale of fruit that is on trees before the fruit forms buds and sheds its flower is permitted, but it must be sold with something else in the way described in the previous ruling; or, the sale must be for one year or more of fruit.

Ruling 2111. There is no problem in the sale of the fruit of date palms which are on the trees, whether they be ripe or unripe. However, the payment in exchange must not be dates, whether they be from the same tree or another. However, there is no problem if the fruit is sold for ripe *ruṭab* [soft, moist dates] or unripe ones that have not yet become dates. If someone owns one date palm in the house of another person and getting to it is difficult for him, then, in case the quantity is estimated and the owner of the date palm sells it to the owner of the house and receives dates in exchange, there is no problem.

Ruling 2112.* There is no problem in selling cucumbers, aubergines, vegetables, and the like which are picked a number of times a year as long as the produce has become apparent and is visible and the number of times the buyer will pick and purchase the produce has been specified. However, if the produce has not become apparent and visible, selling it is not permitted based on obligatory precaution.

Ruling 2113. If wheatears are sold after they have formed grains, for wheat acquired from those or other wheatears, the transaction is not valid.

IMMEDIATE EXCHANGE (*NAQD*) AND CREDIT (*NASĪʾAH*) TRANSACTIONS

Ruling 2114. If a commodity is sold in an immediate exchange transaction, both the buyer and the seller can claim the commodity and the payment from each other after the transaction and take possession of them. The handing over of a moveable commodity, such as a rug or clothes, and an immoveable commodity, such as a house or land, is realised by relinquishing the item and making it available to the other party in a way that he could have disposal over it if he wanted. This would be different in different cases.

Ruling 2115. In a credit transaction, the deferment period must be precisely defined. Therefore, if a person sells a commodity with the understanding that he would get the payment at the beginning of harvest, the transaction is invalid because the deferment period is not precisely defined.

Ruling 2116. If a commodity is sold on credit, the seller cannot claim payment for it from the buyer before the completion of the agreed deferment period. However, if the buyer dies and leaves behind an estate, the seller can claim payment from the heirs before the completion of the deferment period.

Ruling 2117. If a commodity is sold on credit, the seller can claim the payment for it from the buyer after the completion of the agreed deferment period. However, if the buyer is unable to pay, the seller must give him respite or annul the transaction and take back the commodity if it still exists.

Ruling 2118. If a person sells a commodity on credit to someone who does not know its price and the seller does not tell him the price, the transaction is invalid. However, if he sells the commodity for a higher price to someone who knows its immediate exchange transaction price – for example, he says, 'The commodity I am selling to you on credit is £10 more than its immediate exchange transaction price', and the buyer accepts, there is no problem.

Ruling 2119. With regard to a person who has sold a commodity on credit and has specified a time for receiving the payment, if he, for example, reduces the amount he is owed after half of the deferment period has passed and takes the rest immediately, there is no problem.

PREPAYMENT (*SALAF*) TRANSACTION AND ITS CONDITIONS

Ruling 2120. A prepayment transaction is when a person sells a commodity that has been defined in general terms for an amount that is paid immediately, and the seller hands over the commodity after some time. Therefore, if the buyer says, for example, 'I give you this money so that after six months I take such and such commodity', and the seller responds by saying, 'I accept'; or if the seller takes the money and says, 'I sell such and such commodity and I will hand it over after six months', the transaction is valid.

Ruling 2121. If a person sells by way of a prepayment transaction a commodity made of gold or silver and accepts gold or silver money in exchange, the transaction is invalid. However, if a person sells a commodity or currency which is not made of gold or silver and takes another commodity or gold or silver money in exchange, the transaction is valid as per the details that will be mentioned in the seventh condition in the next ruling. And the recommended precaution is that in exchange for the commodity one sells, he should receive money, not another commodity.

Ruling 2122. A prepayment transaction must fulfil the following seven conditions [for it to be valid]:

1. the particulars which determine differences in the commodity's price must be specified. A lot of precision is not necessary; it is sufficient if people would say its particulars are known;
2. before the buyer and the seller depart from each other, the buyer must pay the entire price to the seller; or, he must be owed an amount by the seller to be paid immediately, which he offsets against the commodity's price which the seller accepts. In the event that the buyer pays only part of the price, although the transaction is valid with respect to that part, the seller can annul the transaction;
3. the period [within which the commodity must be handed over] must be precisely defined. If the seller says, 'I will hand over the commodity by the beginning of the harvest', the transaction is invalid because the period is not precisely defined;
4. the time for handing over the commodity must be specified such that the seller is able to hand over the commodity in that time, whether the item is scarce or abundant;
5. based on obligatory precaution, the place where the commodity will be handed over must be precisely specified. If the place is clear from the discussions of the two parties, it is not necessary to mention the name of the place;
6. the weight, measure, or number of items of the commodity must be specified. If commodities that are usually sold by viewing are sold by prepayment, there is no problem. However, as is the case with certain walnuts and eggs, the difference between the individual items of the commodity must be so small that people would not give it importance;
7. if the commodity being sold is usually sold by weight or measure, the thing that is received in exchange for it must not be of the same commodity; in fact, based on obligatory precaution, neither must it be a commodity that is sold by weight or measure. If the thing that is being sold is a commodity that is sold by number, then based on obligatory precaution, the thing that is received in exchange for it must not be an extra amount of the same commodity.

LAWS RELATING TO PREPAYMENT (*SALAF*) TRANSACTIONS

Ruling 2123. A person cannot sell a commodity that has been acquired by prepayment to a person other than its seller before the end of the stipulated period. However, there is no problem in selling it after the period has expired, even if he has not yet taken possession of it. But selling a commodity that is sold by weight or measure – apart from fruit – to a person other than its seller before taking possession of it is not permitted unless it is sold for a price equal to or less than the price paid for it.

Ruling 2124. In a prepayment transaction, if the seller delivers the agreed commodity on its due date, the buyer must accept it if it is in the same condition that was stipulated. If the commodity is in a better condition, again he must accept it unless there was a stipulation that allowed for a rejection of a better condition.

Ruling 2125. If the commodity delivered by the seller is of a lower quality than what was agreed, the buyer can choose not to accept it.

Ruling 2126. If the seller delivers a commodity that is different from the commodity that was agreed, there is no problem as long as the buyer consents.

Ruling 2127. If a seller who has sold a commodity by prepayment is unable to obtain it at the time when he must hand it over, the buyer can wait until he obtains it, or he can annul the transaction and take back what he had given in exchange, or he can take something else instead [of what he had given in exchange]. And based on obligatory precaution, he cannot sell it to the seller at a higher price.

Ruling 2128. If a person sells a commodity and agrees to hand it over after some time and take the payment after some time, the transaction is invalid.

SELLING GOLD AND SILVER FOR GOLD AND SILVER

Ruling 2129. If gold is sold for gold or silver is sold for silver, irrespective of whether the gold and silver are minted coins or not, then in the event that the weight of one of them is more than the weight of the other, the transaction is unlawful and invalid.

Ruling 2130. If gold is sold for silver or silver is sold for gold in an immediate exchange transaction, the transaction is valid and it is not necessary for their weight to be the same. However, if the transaction has a period, it is invalid.

Ruling 2131. If gold or silver is sold for gold or silver, the seller and buyer must hand over the commodity and the payment in exchange to each other before they depart from each other. If they do not hand over any amount of the thing that they had agreed on, the transaction is invalid. If they hand over part of it, the transaction relating to that part is valid.

Ruling 2132. If the seller or the buyer hands over everything that was agreed but the other party hands over only a part of what he agreed and they depart from each other, the transaction is in order with respect to the part that was handed over. However, the party that did not receive the whole amount can annul the transaction.

Ruling 2133. If silver dust from a mine is sold for pure silver, or gold dust from a mine is sold for pure gold, the transaction is invalid unless it is known that, for example, the amount of silver dust is equivalent to the amount of pure silver. However, as explained previously, there is no problem in selling silver dust for gold, or gold dust for silver.

CASES WHEN A PERSON CAN ANNUL A TRANSACTION

Ruling 2134. The right to annul a transaction is referred to as a *khiyār* (option). A buyer or a seller can annul a transaction in one of the following eleven cases:

1. when the buyer and the seller have not departed from each other, even though they may have left the meeting place of the transaction. This option is known as 'the option while meeting' (*khiyār al-majlis*);
2. when either the buyer or the seller in the case of a sale, or one of the two parties of a transaction in the case of other transactions, has been cheated. This is referred to as 'the option due to cheating' (*khiyār al-ghabn*). The establishment of this type of option stems from something that is rooted in common custom, namely, that in every transaction each party in the transaction has in his mind that the property he receives should not be drastically lower in value than the property he gives in return; and if it is drastically lower, he should have the right to annul the transaction. However, in the event that in some cases something else is rooted in a particular custom – for example, if someone receives a property that is lower in value than the property he gives in return, he can claim the difference between the two from the other party, and if this is not possible he can annul the transaction – then in such cases, that particular custom must be observed;
3. when the parties stipulate in the contract that either one of them or both of them can annul the transaction within a specified period. This option is referred to as 'the option due to a stipulated condition' (*khiyār al-sharṭ*);
4. when one of the parties of the transaction displays his property in a way that it looks better than it truly is, and this makes the other party desirous of it or increases his desire for it. This is referred to as 'the option due to deceit' (*khiyār al-tadlīs*);
5. when one of the parties of the transaction makes a condition with the other that he will do something, but he does not fulfil that condition; or, he makes it a condition that the specified property which is to be given by the other party must be of a special type but he discovers that it is not of that type. In these cases, the person who makes the condition can annul the transaction. This is known as 'the option due to a breach of condition' (*khiyār takhalluf al-sharṭ*);

6. when there is a defect in the commodity or the payment exchanged for it. This is referred to as 'the option due to a defect' (*khiyār al-ʿayb*);
7. when it is later discovered that part of the commodity that was transacted belonged to someone else. In this case, if the owner does not consent to the transaction, the receiver of the commodity can annul the transaction or take back what he paid in exchange for it if he had already paid for it. This is referred to as 'the option due to a partnership' (*khiyār al-shirkah*);
8. when the owner describes to the other party the particulars of a specific commodity which the other party has not seen, and it is later discovered that the commodity is not as it was described; or, the other party had previously seen the commodity and thought that it still possessed the qualities he had seen in the past, and it is later discovered that it no longer has those qualities. In this case, the other party can annul the transaction. This is referred to as 'the option pertaining to seeing' (*khiyār al-ruʾyah*);
9. when the buyer fails to hand over the payment for the commodity he purchased within three days, and the seller has not yet handed over the commodity. In this case, the seller can annul the transaction. This applies when the seller gives the buyer a respite for paying the money but does not specify the period. However, if he does not give him any respite at all, he can annul the transaction after a short delay in paying the money. If he gives a respite of more than three days, he cannot annul the transaction until the respite period is over. Furthermore, if the commodity he sold is something like vegetables or fruit which deteriorates before three days, the respite period is less. This option is referred to as 'the option due to delay' (*khiyār al-taʾkhīr*);
10. when a person purchases an animal, he can annul the transaction within three days. If he acquires an animal in exchange for something that he sells, the seller can annul the transaction within three days of the sale. This is referred to as 'the option pertaining to animals' (*khiyār al-ḥayawān*);
11. when the seller is unable to hand over the commodity he sold; for example, the horse that he sold runs away. In this case, the buyer can annul the transaction. This is referred to as 'the

option due to an inability to hand over' (*khiyār taʿadhdhur al-taslīm*).

Ruling 2135. If the buyer does not know the price of the commodity or is unmindful of it at the time of the transaction and buys it for a price that is higher than its normal price, then in the event that he buys it for a significantly inflated price, he can annul the transaction. Of course, this is on condition that he is still being cheated at the time of annulling the transaction; otherwise, the right to annul is problematic [i.e. based on obligatory precaution, he does not have the right to annul]. Similarly, if the seller does not know the commodity's price or is unmindful of it at the time of the transaction and sells it for a price that is lower than its normal price, then, in case he sells it for a significantly deflated price, he can annul the transaction on the same condition mentioned previously.

Ruling 2136. In a transaction involving a conditional sale, wherein, for example, a house worth £100,000 is sold for £50,000 with an agreement that if the seller returns the money within a stipulated period he can annul the transaction, the transaction is valid provided the buyer and the seller have a genuine intention to buy and sell.

Ruling 2137. In a transaction involving a conditional sale, even if the seller is confident that should he fail to return the money within the stipulated period the buyer will give him the property, the transaction is valid. However, if he fails to return the money within the stipulated period, he does not have the right to claim the property from the buyer. Furthermore, if the buyer dies, he cannot claim the property from his inheritors.

Ruling 2138. If a person mixes high-grade tea with low-grade tea and sells it under the label of high-grade tea, the buyer can annul the transaction.

Ruling 2139. If a buyer realises that a specified item has a defect – for example, he buys an animal and realises that it is blind in one eye – then, in the event that the defect was present in the item before the transaction and the buyer did not know about it, he can annul the transaction and return the item to the seller. In the event that returning the item is not possible – for instance, the item has changed in some way; for example, it has become defective; or, it has been utilised in a manner that prevents it from being returned; for example, the buyer sold it or hired it out; or, [the item was a piece of cloth and] the buyer cut the cloth or stitched it – then in such cases, the difference in price between a non-defective and defective item must be determined, and in proportion to the difference between the two, the buyer can take back part of the money he paid to the seller. For example, if he realises that an item he bought for £4 is defective, in the event that the price of a non-defective item is £8 and a defective one is £6, then since the difference in price between the non-defective item and the defective one is 25%, he can take back 25% of the money he paid to the seller, that is, £1.

Ruling 2140. If a seller realises that there is a defect in the specified payment of exchange for the item that he sold, in the event that the defect was present before the transaction and he did not know about it, he can annul the transaction and return the payment of exchange to its owner. In the event that he is unable to return it due to a change in it or it having been utilised, he can claim back the difference in price between a non-defective and a defective item as per the instructions mentioned in the previous ruling.

Ruling 2141. If a defect is discovered in an item after the transaction but before it is handed over, the buyer can annul the transaction. Also, if a defect is discovered in the payment of exchange for the item after the transaction but before it is handed over, the seller can annul the transaction. And if they wish to take the difference in price, this is permitted if returning the item is not possible.

Ruling 2142. If after a transaction a person realises that the item has a defect, in the event that he wishes to annul the transaction, he must do so immediately. If he delays in annulling for more than a normal amount of time – taking into account the type of case it is – he cannot annul the transaction.

Ruling 2143. If at any time after buying a commodity a person realises that it has a defect, he can annul the transaction even if the seller is not prepared to accept it. The same rule applies to the other options for annulling a transaction.

Ruling 2144.* In the following four cases, a buyer cannot annul a transaction due to a defect in the item nor claim the difference in price:

1. before buying, he knows about the defect in the item;
2. after buying, he accepts the defect;
3. at the time of the sale, he waives his right to annul and take the difference in price;
4. at the time of the transaction, the seller says, 'I am selling this item with all the defects it has'. However, if he specifies a particular defect and says, 'I am selling this item with this defect', and later another defect is discovered, the buyer can return the item owing to the defect that the seller did not specify. And in case he cannot return it, he can claim the difference in price.

Ruling 2145. If a buyer realises that an item has a defect and after taking possession of the item another defect is discovered, he cannot annul the transaction. However, he can claim the difference in price between a non-defective item and a defective one. But if he buys a defective animal and discovers another defect before the passage of time for the option with animals, which is three days,[11] he can return it even if he has taken possession of the animal. Also, if [in a particular transaction] only the buyer has the right to annul the transaction until a particular period and during that period another defect is discovered, he can annul the transaction even though he has taken possession of the item.

Ruling 2146. If a person has an item that he has not seen and its particulars are described to him by another person, in the event that he describes the same particulars to a buyer and sells it to him, and after the sale he realises that it was in fact better than what he had described, he can annul the transaction.

[11] See Ruling 2134, case 10.

MISCELLANEOUS RULINGS

Ruling 2147. If a seller informs a buyer of the price of a commodity, he must inform him of all the things that cause the commodity to appreciate or depreciate in value, even if he sells it to him for that price or less than it. For example, he must inform him if he bought it by immediate payment or on credit. In the event that he does not inform him of some of those particulars and afterwards the buyer comes to know them, the buyer can annul the transaction.

Ruling 2148. If a person gives a commodity to someone and specifies its price and says to him, 'Sell this commodity for this price, and the more you sell the more your commission will be', then whatever he gets above that price belongs to the owner of the commodity and the seller can only take his commission from the owner. However, if this is done in the form of a reward (*juʿālah*)[12] and the owner says, 'If you sell this commodity for a price that is higher than that price, the extra amount belongs to you', there is no problem.

Ruling 2149. If a butcher sells the meat of a male animal but gives the meat of a female animal instead, he will have sinned. Therefore, if he specifies the meat and says, 'I am selling this meat of a male animal' [but gives the meat of a female animal], the buyer can annul the transaction. However, if he does not specify it, then in case the buyer is not pleased with the meat he has received, the butcher must give him the meat of a male animal.

Ruling 2150. If a buyer tells a draper, 'I want to buy a cloth that is colourfast', and the draper sells him a cloth that is not colourfast, the buyer can annul the transaction.

Ruling 2151. If a seller cannot hand over a commodity he has sold – for example, the horse he sold has run away – the transaction is invalid and the buyer can claim his money back.

[12] The laws of *juʿālah* are stated in Chapter 15.

CHAPTER ELEVEN

Partnership (*Shirkah*)

Ruling 2152. If two people form an agreement to trade with property jointly owned by them and to divide the profits between them, and they say a formula (*ṣīghah*) for establishing a partnership – in Arabic or any other language – or they do something that makes it understood that they want to be each other's partner (*sharīk*), their partnership will be valid (*ṣaḥīḥ*).

Ruling 2153. If some people form a partnership with respect to the wages they receive for their work – for example, some masseurs agree to divide whatever wages they earn between them – their partnership is not valid. However, if they reach a settlement (*muṣālahah*) that, for example, half of each of their wages will belong to the other for a specified period in return for half of the other's wages, then the settlement is valid and each of them will be a partner in the wages of the other.

Ruling 2154. If two people form a partnership and [make an agreement that] each of them will purchase a commodity with his own credit, and that person will be responsible for paying off the debt for it, but they will share the profits arising from the commodities each one has purchased, such an agreement is not valid. However, if each one makes the other his agent (*wakīl*) to be his partner in whatever he purchases on credit (*nasī'ah*) – i.e. he purchases a commodity for himself and for his partner with both of them being responsible for paying off the debt – then both of them become partners in the commodity.

Ruling 2155. Individuals who become partners of each other by means of a partnership contract must be of the age of legal responsibility (*bāligh*) and sane (*ʿāqil*). They must also have an intention (*qaṣd*) to enter into the partnership and enter it of their own volition (*ikhtiyār*). Furthermore, they must be able to have disposal over their own property. Therefore, if a person who is foolish with finances (*safīh*) – i.e. someone who spends his wealth in futile ways – enters into a partnership, then because he does not have right of disposal over his own property, the partnership is not valid.

Ruling 2156. If in the partnership contract the partners stipulate a condition that the one who does the work, or who does more work than the other partners, or whose work is of greater importance than that of the others, will take a greater share of the profits, then they must give him whatever they stipulated. Similarly, if they stipulate a condition that the one who does not do any work, or who does not work more than the others, or whose work is not of greater importance than that of the others, will take a greater share of the profits, again the condition is valid and they must give him whatever they stipulated.

Ruling 2157. If the partners agree that one person will take all the profits or that one of them will bear all the losses, the validity of such a partnership is problematic (*maḥall al-ishkāl*) [i.e. based on obligatory precaution (*al-iḥtiyāṭ al-wājib*), it is not valid].[1]

Ruling 2158. If the partners do not stipulate a condition that one of the partners will take a larger share of the profits, in the event that the capital invested by each partner is the same amount, they must enjoy the profits and bear the losses equally. But if the capital invested by each of them is not the same amount, they must divide the profits and losses in proportion to their capital. For example, if two people form a partnership and the capital invested by one is twice that of the other, his share of the profits and losses will also be twice that of the other's, regardless of whether they both work equally or one works less than the other or one does not do any work at all.

Ruling 2159. If in the partnership contract the partners stipulate a condition that both will buy and sell together, or each one of them on their own will conduct transactions (*muʿāmalāt*), or only one of them will conduct transactions, or a third party will be hired to conduct transactions, then in such cases, they must act according to the contract.

Ruling 2160. A partnership can be of two types: [i] a permission-based partnership (*al-shirkah al-idhniyyah*); in this type, before the partnership conducts a transaction (*muʿāmalah*), the trade property is owned by the partners (*shurakāʾ*) in the form of joint ownership (*mushāʿ*).

[1] As mentioned in Ruling 6, the term 'problematic' (*maḥall al-ishkāl*) amounts to saying the ruling is based on obligatory precaution.

And [ii] exchange-based partnership (*al-shirkah al-muʿāwaḍiyyah*); in this type, each partner presents his own property to the partnership, and as a result, each of them exchanges half of their own property with half of the other's property. Therefore, if they do not specify which one of them will buy and sell with the capital, then, if it is a permission-based partnership, none of them can conduct a transaction with the capital without the consent of the others. However, if it is an exchange-based partnership, each partner can conduct a transaction in a way that does not harm the partnership.

Ruling 2161. A partner who has been vested with the right of discretion over the capital must act according to the partnership contract. For example, if it has been agreed with him that he will buy on credit or sell by immediate payment or buy the commodity from a particular place, he must act according to these agreements. However, if no agreement has been made with him, he must conduct transactions in a normal manner and do business in a way that will not harm the partnership.

Ruling 2162. If the partner who conducts transactions with the partnership capital buys and sells in a manner that is contrary to the contract made with him, or if no contract was made with him and he conducts transactions in a manner that is not normal, then in these two cases, even though the transaction is valid based on a stronger opinion (*aqwā*),[2] if the transaction is detrimental to the partnership or part of the partnership's property perishes, the partner who acted contrary to the contract or acted in a manner that was not normal is responsible (*ḍāmin*).

Ruling 2163. If the partner who conducts transactions with the partnership capital is neither excessive nor negligent in safeguarding the capital, but it so happens that part of the capital or all of it perishes, he is not responsible.

Ruling 2164. If the partner who conducts transactions with the partnership capital says that the capital has perished, in the event

[2] For practical purposes, where an opinion is stated to be 'stronger', a fatwa is being given.

that he is trusted by the other partners, they must accept his word. But if this is not the case, they can complain against him to a fully qualified jurist (*al-ḥākim al-sharʿī*) for the dispute to be settled in accordance with adjudication standards.

Ruling 2165. In a permission-based partnership [as defined in Ruling 2160], if all the partners withdraw the consent they gave each other for them to have disposal over their property, then none of them can have disposal over the partnership property. If one of them withdraws his consent, then the other partners do not have right of disposal. However, the one who withdraws his consent can have disposal over the partnership property. In each case, their partnership with respect to the capital remains in place.

Ruling 2166.* In an exchange-based partnership, a period must be specified, and it is necessary that the partnership continue until the end of the period. If the partnership is a permission-based one, it is not necessary that a period be specified, and whenever one of the partners requests that the partnership capital be divided, the others must accept his request even if a period has been specified for the partnership unless dividing it would require some of the partners to spend money, or it would result in a significant loss for the partners.

Ruling 2167. If one of the partners of a permission-based partnership dies or becomes insane or unconscious, the other partners cannot have disposal over the property. The same applies if one of them becomes foolish with finances, i.e. he spends his wealth in futile ways.

Ruling 2168. If a partner buys something on credit for himself, then any profit or loss resulting from this is his. However, if he buys it for the partnership and the partnership agreement allows for credit transactions, then any resulting profit or loss is his and theirs.

Ruling 2169. If one of the partners conducts a transaction with the partnership capital and later realises that the partnership was invalid, in the event that permission for the transaction was not contingent on the validity of the partnership in the sense that had they known that the partnership was not valid they would still have consented for the others to have disposal over the property, the transaction is valid. In such a case, whatever is acquired from the transaction belongs to all of them. However, if it was not such [i.e. permission for the transaction was contingent on the validity of the partnership], then, if those who did not consent for the others to have disposal say, 'We consent to the transaction', the transaction is valid; otherwise, it is void. In each case, whoever from among them worked for the partnership and did so without an intention to work for free can take wages for his efforts at the standard rate, taking into consideration the shares of the other partners. However, in the event that the standard rate is more than the amount of profit he would take on the assumption that the partnership was valid, then he can only take that amount of the profit.

CHAPTER TWELVE

Settlement (*Ṣulḥ*)

Ruling 2170. A settlement is when a person compromises with someone to make the latter the owner of part of his property or the usufruct of his property or to relinquish a claim or right he has. In return, the other person gives him part of his property or the usufruct of his property or relinquishes a claim or right he has. In fact, even if a person compromises with someone to give him part of his property or the usufruct of his property or to relinquish a claim or a right of his without taking anything in return, the settlement is valid (*ṣaḥīḥ*).

Ruling 2171. A person who settles his property with someone must be of the age of legal responsibility (*bāligh*), sane (*ʿāqil*), and he must have an intention (*qaṣd*) to settle. Furthermore, no one must have compelled him [to settle], and he must not be foolish with finances (*safīh*)[1] nor be prohibited from having disposal over that property because of bankruptcy.

Ruling 2172. It is not necessary for a formula (*ṣīghah*) to be said [for a settlement to be valid, nor does it have to be] in Arabic; rather, it is valid by means of any words or actions that make it understood that the parties have concluded a settlement and have compromised with each other.

Ruling 2173. If a person gives his sheep to a shepherd so that, for example, he takes care of them for one year and uses their milk, and in return, he gives that person an amount of oil, then in the event that the person concludes a settlement for the sheep's milk to be given in return for the shepherd's labour and the oil, the settlement is valid. In fact, if he hires the sheep to the shepherd for one year for him to use their milk, and in return, the shepherd gives him an amount of oil, and it is not stipulated that the oil or milk must be from only those sheep, the hire (*ijārah*) contract is valid.

Ruling 2174. If a person wishes to settle a claim or right with someone, it will be valid only if the latter accepts. However, if he wishes to relinquish a claim or a right of his, the acceptance of the other party is not necessary.

Ruling 2175. If a person is aware of the amount he owes but his

[1] Ruling 2091 provides further clarification of this term: it refers to someone who spends his wealth in futile ways.

creditor is not aware of it, then in the event that the creditor settles the debt for an amount that is less than the actual amount – for example, he is owed £500 and settles the debt for £100 – the extra amount [i.e. £400 in this example] is not lawful (*ḥalāl*) for the debtor unless he informs the creditor of the actual amount he owes him and seeks his consent. Alternatively, the situation must be such that had the creditor known the actual amount of the debt, he would still have settled for the same [lesser] amount.

Ruling 2176. If two people have property that is in the hands of the other, or they owe each other some property and they know that one of the two properties is worth more than the other, in the event that selling the two properties to each other would amount to usury (*ribā*) and be unlawful (*ḥarām*), then concluding a settlement with respect to the properties would also be unlawful. In fact, if it is not known that one of the two properties is worth more than the other but there is a probability that it is, they cannot, based on obligatory precaution (*al-iḥtiyāṭ al-wājib*), conclude a settlement with each other with respect to the two properties.

Ruling 2177. If two people are owed by one person or by two persons and the creditors wish to arrive at a settlement between themselves with respect to the debts, in the event that it does not amount to usury as explained in the previous ruling, there is no problem. For example, if both are owed 10 kilograms of wheat, with one of them being owed high quality wheat and the other medium quality, and it is time for both debts to be paid, their settlement is valid.

Ruling 2178. If someone is owed something that he can claim after a certain period, in the event that he settles the debt for a lower amount with the intention of relinquishing his claim to part of the debt and getting the rest immediately, there is no problem. This rule applies when the claim is for gold or silver or for a commodity sold by weight or measure. As for other commodities, it is permitted (*jāʾiz*) for a creditor to settle his claim with a debtor or with someone else for less than the claim, or to sell the debt, as will be explained in Ruling 2307.

Ruling 2179. If two people conclude a settlement with each other with respect to something, they can annul the settlement with each other's consent. Also, if in the transaction (*muʿāmalah*) they stipulate a right for both or one of them to annul the transaction, the person who has that right can annul the settlement.

Ruling 2180. Until the time a buyer and a seller do not depart from each other, they can annul the transaction. Also, if a buyer purchases an animal, he has the right to annul the transaction within three days. If for three days a buyer does not pay for a commodity he has bought and does not take possession of the commodity, then just as it was mentioned in Ruling 2134, the seller can annul the transaction. However, a person who concludes a settlement with respect to something does not have the right to annul the settlement in these three cases. But, in case the other party to the settlement delays paying for the property over which the settlement was reached for a period that exceeds conventional norms, or if a condition is stipulated that, for example, the item will be given immediately but the other party does not fulfil this condition, then one can annul the settlement. Similarly, in the other cases that were mentioned in the rulings (*aḥkām*) pertaining to buying and selling, one can also annul a settlement. Furthermore, in a case where one of the parties to a settlement has been cheated, if the settlement is concluded to resolve the dispute, he cannot annul the settlement. In fact, in settlements other than this, based on obligatory precaution, someone who has been cheated must not annul the transaction.

Ruling 2181. If the thing that one acquires from a settlement is defective, one can annul the settlement. However, if he wishes to take the difference between the price of a non-defective and defective item, it is problematic (*maḥall al-ishkāl*) [i.e. based on obligatory precaution, he cannot do so].[2]

Ruling 2182. Whenever a person concludes a settlement with someone with respect to his own property and makes a condition saying, 'After my death, the property that I settled with you must (for example) be given as a charitable endowment (*waqf*)', and the other person accepts this condition, he must act according to the condition.

[2] As mentioned in Ruling 6, the term 'problematic' (*maḥall al-ishkāl*) amounts to saying the ruling is based on obligatory precaution.

CHAPTER THIRTEEN

Hiring/Renting (*Ijārah*)[1]

[1] The term '*ijārah*' and its derivatives are translated in different ways in English depending on the context. For example, when '*ijārah*' is used in the context of a property transaction, it is usually translated as 'renting' or 'leasing' and the parties involved are termed 'landlord' and 'tenant' or 'lessor' and 'lessee'. But when '*ijārah*' is used for the services of people, it is usually translated as 'hiring' and the two parties are termed 'hirer' and 'hiree' or 'hired'.

Ruling 2183. A person who gives something on rent (*muʾjir*) and a person who takes something on rent (*mustaʾjir*) must be of the age of legal responsibility (*bāligh*) and sane (*ʿāqil*). They must also enter into the rental agreement of their own volition (*ikhtiyār*) and have right of disposal over their property. Therefore, someone who is foolish with finances (*safīh*)[2] cannot rent anything nor give anything on rent as he does not have right of disposal over his property. Similarly, someone who has been proclaimed bankrupt (*mufallas*) cannot give on rent any property over which he does not have disposal, nor can he rent anything with that property. However, he can give himself on hire [as a worker].

Ruling 2184. A person may be an agent (*wakīl*) for another party to give property on rent for him or to rent property for him.

Ruling 2185. If the guardian (*walī*) or custodian of a child gives the child's property on rent or hires the child [as a worker] to another person, there is no problem. If the hire agreement includes a period wherein the child is *bāligh*, the child can annul the remaining period of the hire agreement once he becomes *bāligh*, even though had the hire agreement not included a period wherein the child was *bāligh*, it would not have been in the child's interest. However, if annulling the remaining period is contrary to interests that are required by Islamic law to be protected – i.e. interests which we know the Holy Legislator [Allah] would not be pleased with were they to be disregarded – then, if the hiring was done with the permission of a fully qualified jurist (*al-ḥākim al-sharʿī*), the child cannot annul the contract once he reaches the age of legal responsibility (*bulūgh*).

Ruling 2186. It is not allowed to give on hire a minor (*ṣaghīr*) who does not have a guardian without authorisation from a jurist (*mujtahid*).[3] As for someone who does not have access to a jurist, he can obtain authorisation from a dutiful (*ʿādil*) believer and give the child on hire.

[2] Ruling 2091 provides further clarification of this term: it refers to someone who spends his wealth in futile ways.

[3] A *mujtahid* is a person who has attained the level of *ijtihād*, qualifying him to be an authority in Islamic law. *Ijtihād* is the process of deriving Islamic laws from authentic sources.

Ruling 2187. It is not necessary for the lessor and the lessee to say a particular formula (*ṣīghah*) [for a rental agreement to be valid (*ṣaḥīḥ*), nor does it have to be] in Arabic; rather, if the owner says to someone [in English, for example], 'I rent my property to you', and the other person says, 'I accept', the rental agreement is valid. In fact, even if they do not say anything and the owner simply hands over the property to the lessee with the intention (*qaṣd*) of giving his property on rent to him, and the lessee accepts it with the intention of renting it, the rental agreement is valid.

Ruling 2188. If a person wishes to be hired for a particular task without saying a formula, the hire agreement is valid the moment he engages himself in that task.

Ruling 2189. If a person who is unable to speak conveys by sign that he has given some property on rent or he has rented some property, the rental agreement is valid.

Ruling 2190.* If a person leases a house, shop, or anything else, and the owner stipulates a condition that only he can use it, the lessee cannot sublet it to anyone else to use unless the new rental agreement is such that the use of the property is especially for the lessee, such as when a woman rents a house or a room and later gets married and gives the house or room on rent to her husband for her own residence there. But, if the owner does not stipulate a condition [that only the lessee can make use of it], then the lessee can sublet it to another person. When handing the property over to the second lessee, the first lessee must, based on obligatory precaution (*al-iḥtiyāṭ al-wājib*), obtain authorisation from the owner. However, if the first lessee wishes to give it on rent for a higher rental fee than what he has rented it for, then even though the payment may be in a different commodity, in the event that the property is a house, shop, or ship, he must do some work on it, such as making some repairs or doing some plastering, or he must have suffered a loss in looking after the property. And based on obligatory precaution, the additional rental fee must be commensurate with the work done or the loss suffered.

Ruling 2191. If a person who is hired to do something (*ajīr*) stipulates a condition that he will only work for the person who has hired him, he cannot be hired to someone else except in the way mentioned in the previous ruling. However, if he does not stipulate a condition [that he will only work for the person who has hired him], then the hirer can hire him to another person. However, what he gets for hiring him out must not be more than what he has agreed with him. The same applies if he himself is hired by someone and he then hires someone else to do the work for a lesser amount. However, if he does some of the work himself, he can hire someone else for a lesser amount.

Ruling 2192. If a person rents something other than a house, shop, or ship – for example, he rents some land – and the owner does not stipulate a condition that only he must use it, then, if he gives it on rent for an amount that is higher than what he has rented it for, the validity of the rental agreement is problematic (*maḥall al-ishkāl*) [i.e. based on obligatory precaution, it is not valid].[4]

Ruling 2193. If a person rents a house or a shop for one year for £10,000, for example, and he makes use of half of it himself, he can give the other half on rent for £10,000. However, if he wishes to give the other half on rent for an amount higher than what he rented it for, for example £12,000, he must do some work on it, such as making some repairs.

CONDITIONS FOR PROPERTY GIVEN ON RENT

Ruling 2194. Property that is given on rent must fulfil the following conditions [for the rental agreement to be valid]:

1. it must be specified. Therefore, if a person says, 'I rent one of my houses to you', it is not correct;
2. the person taking it on rent must see it. If it is not ready or it is described in general terms, the person giving it on rent must describe those particulars that affect one's decision to rent it;
3. it must be possible to hand over. Therefore, giving on rent a horse that has run away is invalid (*bāṭil*) if the person taking

[4] As mentioned in Ruling 6, the term 'problematic' (*maḥall al-ishkāl*) amounts to saying the ruling is based on obligatory precaution.

it on rent cannot get hold of it. However, if he can get hold of it, it is valid;

4. using the property must not result in it perishing or being destroyed. Therefore, giving on rent bread, fruit, or other food for eating is not valid;
5. the use for which the property is being hired must be possible. Therefore, it is not valid to give land on rent for farming when neither rainwater is sufficient for farming on that land nor is it irrigated by water from a river;
6. the lessor must own the usufruct for which the property is being given on rent. If he is neither the owner, the agent, nor the guardian (*walī*), it will only be valid if the owner consents to it.

Ruling 2195. Giving a tree on hire so that others can use its fruit when the tree is not currently bearing any fruit is valid. The same applies to giving an animal on hire for its milk.

Ruling 2196. A woman can be hired for wet nursing, and it is not necessary for her to obtain her husband's consent. However, if the act of wet nursing infringes on his rights, she cannot be hired without his consent.

CONDITIONS RELATING TO THE USE OF THE PROPERTY WHICH IS GIVEN ON RENT

Ruling 2197. The use of the property which is given on rent must fulfil the following four conditions [for the rental agreement to be valid]:

1. the use must be lawful (*ḥalāl*). Therefore, if a property has only an unlawful (*ḥarām*) use, or if a condition is stipulated that the property must be used for an unlawful purpose, or if before the transaction (*muʿāmalah*) an unlawful use is specified and the transaction is carried out based on that, then in these cases, the transaction is invalid. Therefore, giving a shop on rent for the sale of wine or for storing wine, or hiring an animal for the transportation of wine, is invalid;

2. [in the case of hiring someone for a service,] the service must not be something that Islamic law deems obligatory (*wājib*) to perform free of charge. An example of this is, based on obligatory precaution, teaching rulings (*masāʾil*) on what is lawful and unlawful, if they concern matters that are commonly encountered. The same applies to the obligatory rituals of preparing a corpse for burial. And, based on obligatory precaution, it is a requirement that people must not consider paying for the service futile;
3. if the item given on rent is multi-purpose, the use that the lessee makes of it must be specified. For example, if an animal that is used for riding and transporting goods is given on rent, it must be specified at the time of the rental agreement whether the lessee will use the animal for riding, transporting goods, or both;
4. the extent of the use must be specified. This will either be in terms of length of time, as with renting a house and a shop, or in terms of action, as with agreeing with a tailor to stitch certain clothing in a particular manner.

Ruling 2198. If the beginning of the rental period is not specified, it will begin the moment the rental contract has concluded.

Ruling 2199. If a house is given on rent for a year, for example, and the beginning of the rental period is set to a month after the rental contract has concluded, the rental agreement is valid even if the house is being rented by someone else at the time of concluding the contract.

Ruling 2200. If the rental period is unknown and the lessor says, 'Whenever you reside in the house its rent will be £1000 a month', the rental agreement is not valid.

Ruling 2201. If a person says to a lessee, 'I have given the house on rent to you for £1000 a month', or he says to him, 'I have given the house on rent to you for one month for £1000; after that, for as long as you reside in the house, the rent will be £1000 a month', then, as long as the beginning of the rental period is known, the rental agreement is in order for the first month.

Ruling 2202. With regard to a house in which travellers and pilgrims take residence and the length of their stay there is not known, if it is agreed that, for example, they will pay £50 a night and the owner of the house consents to this, there is no problem in their use of that house. However, as the rental period is unknown, the rental agreement is only valid with respect to the first night, and the owner can ask them to vacate the premises whenever he wishes.

MISCELLANEOUS RULINGS ON HIRING/RENTING

Ruling 2203. The property by which the lessee pays rent must be known. Therefore, if the property is something that is transacted by weight, such as wheat, then its weight must be known. If it is something that is transacted by count, such as modern currencies, its count must be known. And if it is something like horses and sheep, the lessor must see them for himself or the lessee must describe their particulars to him.

Ruling 2204. If a person gives some land on rent for farming and sets its rent to be the produce of the very same land or another land, but the produce is non-existent at that moment, the rental agreement is not valid. The same applies [i.e. the rental agreement is not valid] if he sets the rent to be a general responsibility [on the lessee to pay] on condition that the rent is paid from the produce of the very same land. However, there is no objection if the produce is existent.

Ruling 2205. A person who has given something on rent cannot claim the rental payment before handing over the rented item. Similarly, if a person has been hired to perform a particular task, he cannot claim his fee before performing the task except when it is normal for the fee to be paid in advance, such as when one is hired to perform hajj.

Ruling 2206. Whenever a lessor hands over the leased item, the lessee must pay its rent even if he does not take possession of it [because, for example, he had gone away at that time,] or he takes possession of it but does not use it to the end of the rental period.

Ruling 2207. If a person is hired to perform a task on a particular day and he shows up to perform that task on that day, the person who hired him must pay him even if he chooses not to give that task to him. For example, if a person hires a tailor to stitch some clothes on a particular day and on that day the tailor is ready to perform that task, he must pay him his fee even if he does not give him the cloth from which to tailor the clothes, or the tailor remains without work that day, or he does his own or somebody else's work.

Ruling 2208. If after the end of the rental period it becomes apparent that the rental agreement was invalid, the lessee must pay the owner of the property the standard rate for that property (*ujrat al-mithl*). For example, if a person gives a house on rent for a year for £10,000 and later finds out that the rental agreement was invalid, in the event that the rent for that house is normally £5,000, the lessee must pay him £5,000. And if the standard rate is £20,000, in the event that the lessor was the owner of the property or an agent who had the authority to specify the rent and knew the normal price of the house, it is not necessary for the lessee to pay more than £10,000; otherwise, he must pay £20,000. Furthermore, if after the passing of some of the rental period it becomes apparent that the rental agreement was invalid, the same rule (*ḥukm*) applies to the fee in relation to the period that has passed.

Ruling 2209. If the rented item is destroyed, the lessee is not responsible (*ḍāmin*) for it as long as he was neither negligent in safeguarding it nor excessive in using it. Similarly, if, for example, the cloth given to a tailor is destroyed, the tailor is not responsible for it as long as he was neither negligent in taking care of it nor excessive in using it.

Ruling 2210. Whenever a hired person, such as a tailor or craftsman, wants to perform a task with the property of the hirer, and he destroys the property that he takes, he is responsible for it.

Ruling 2211. If a butcher slaughters an animal in a manner that renders it unlawful [to consume], he must pay its value to the owner, regardless of whether he has taken a fee for slaughtering it or did it free of charge.

Ruling 2212. If a person hires an animal or vehicle and specifies how much load he will place on it, in the event that he loads more than that amount and the animal or vehicle perishes or becomes defective, he is responsible for it. The same applies if he does not specify the load but places a load on it that is more than normal. In both cases, he must also pay a greater rental fee than normal.

Ruling 2213. If a person gives an animal on hire to carry fragile goods, in the event that the animal slips or stampedes, causing the load to break, the owner of the animal is not responsible for it. However, if the owner of the animal causes the animal to fall by beating it excessively or something similar, and this results in the goods breaking, then he is responsible.

Ruling 2214. If a person is negligent in circumcising a baby or makes a mistake – for example, he cuts more than the normal amount – and the baby dies or is harmed, then that person is responsible. However, if he is neither negligent nor makes a mistake and the baby dies or is harmed as a result of the act of circumcision itself, then he is not responsible as long as he was not consulted to determine whether the baby would be harmed or not, and he did not know that the baby would be harmed.

Ruling 2215. If a doctor gives some medicine to a patient, or he recommends some medicine for him, and the patient suffers harm or dies as a result of taking the medicine, the doctor is responsible even though he was not negligent in trying to cure the patient.

Ruling 2216. If a doctor says to a patient, 'If you are harmed [by this medicine], I am not responsible', in the event that he exercises due care and caution and the patient suffers harm or dies, the doctor is not responsible.

Ruling 2217. A lessee and a lessor can annul the lease agreement with each other's consent. Moreover, if they stipulate a condition in the lease agreement that both of them, or one of them, has the right to annul the lease, they can annul the lease according to their agreement.

Ruling 2218. If a lessor or a lessee realises that he has been cheated, in the event that at the time of concluding the rental agreement he was not aware of being cheated, he can annul the rental agreement as per the details mentioned in Ruling 2134. However, if they had stipulated a condition within the rental agreement that even if they are cheated they do not reserve the right to annul the transaction, then they cannot annul the rental agreement.

Ruling 2219. If a person gives something on rent and someone usurps it before he can hand it over, the lessee can annul the rental agreement and claim back the payment he gave to the lessor. He can also choose not to annul the rental agreement and instead claim back the rental fee from the usurper, based on the standard rate, for the period wherein the leased item was at the disposal of the usurper. Therefore, if he hires an animal for a month for £100, and someone usurps it for ten days, and the usual hire fee for ten days is £150, he can claim £150 from the usurper.

Ruling 2220. If someone does not allow a lessee to take possession of the item he has leased, or if after the lessee has taken possession of the item someone usurps it or prevents him from using it, the lessee cannot annul the rental agreement. Instead, he only reserves the right to claim the rental fee for the item from the usurper based on the standard rate.

Ruling 2221. If a lessor sells the property to the lessee before completion of the rental period, the lease is not nullified and the lessee must pay the rental fee. The same applies if he sells it to someone else.

Ruling 2222. If prior to the commencement of the rental period the rented item becomes unusable for the purpose for which it was rented, the rental agreement is rendered void (*bāṭil*) and the money that the lessee had paid the lessor must be refunded. If the item's state is such that the lessee can make use of only some of it, he can annul the rental agreement.

Ruling 2223. If a person hires something, and after the passage of part of the lease period the item becomes unusable for the purpose for which it was hired, the lease for the remaining period is rendered void. The tenant can also annul the lease pertaining to the preceding period and pay for that period at the standard rate.

Ruling 2224. If a house that contains two rooms, for example, is given on rent and one of the rooms is destroyed, and if it were to be rebuilt in a normal manner it would be very different to the previous building, then the rule in this case is the same as was mentioned in the previous ruling. Otherwise, if the landlord immediately rebuilds it and none of its usability is lost, the rental agreement does not become invalid. Furthermore, the tenant cannot annul the rental agreement. However, if the rebuilding takes so long that a period of the tenant's use of the property is lost, the rental agreement is void for that period. Additionally, the tenant can annul the rental agreement for the entire rental period and pay the standard rate for the period he has used the property.

Ruling 2225. If the lessor or lessee dies, the rental agreement does not become void. However, if [the house does not belong to the lessor but] only its usufruct while he is alive belongs to him – such as when the owner of a house states in his will (*waṣiyyah*) that as long as the lessor is alive, the usufruct of the house will belong to him – then, in the event that the lessor gives the house on rent and dies before the end of the rental period, the lease is void from the time he dies. If the owner of the house endorses the rental agreement [for its remaining period], it is valid, and the rental fee for the period remaining after the death of the lessor belongs to the owner.

Ruling 2226. If an employer appoints a contractor to recruit workers for him, in the event that the contractor pays the workers less than what he receives from the employer, it is unlawful for him to take the difference and he must return it to the employer. However, if he is hired to construct a building and he reserves the right to construct it himself or to subcontract the work to someone else, then in case he constructs part of it himself and subcontracts the rest to someone else for less than what he was hired for, it is lawful for him to take the difference.

Ruling 2227. If a person who dyes clothes agrees to dye a cloth with indigo, for example, then in the event that he dyes it another colour, he does not reserve the right to claim any payment.

CHAPTER FOURTEEN

Sleeping Partnership (*Muḍārabah*)

Ruling 2228. A sleeping partnership is a contract between two people: one of them, the 'owner' (*mālik*), provides capital to the other, the 'worker' (*ʿāmil*). The worker trades with the capital and the profits are divided between him and the owner.

The validity of such a transaction (*muʿāmalah*) is conditional upon the following matters:

1. offer and acceptance. In expressing these, any word or action that conveys their meaning is sufficient;
2. the parties must have reached the age of legal responsibility (*bulūgh*), be sane (*ʿāqil*), and have the ability to take care of and use their wealth in a correct way (*rushd*). They must also enter into the agreement of their own volition (*ikhtiyār*). With regard to the owner specifically, it is a condition that he must not be prohibited from having disposal over his property (*al-maḥjūr ʿalayh*) by a fully qualified jurist (*al-ḥākim al-sharʿī*) due to bankruptcy. This condition does not apply to the worker except in the case where the agreement requires him to have disposal over property that belongs to him but over which he is prohibited from having disposal;
3. the share of the owner and the worker from the profit must be specified in terms of a fraction, such as a third, a half, or any other fraction. But this condition does not apply when the share of each is customarily determined in the market, such that it is commonly understood that there is no need to state this condition. Furthermore, determining each share by stating an amount of the capital, such as £10,000, is not sufficient. However, once the profits become evident, one of them can reach a settlement (*ṣulḥ*) with the other with respect to his share for an amount of the capital;
4. the profits must only be shared between the owner and the worker. Therefore, if a condition is stipulated that some of the profits are to be given to another person, the sleeping partnership is invalid (*bāṭil*) except if it is in exchange for some work relating to the sleeping partnership;
5. the worker himself must be able to trade, in the event that a restriction is mentioned in the contract that he must conduct the trade himself. For example, if it is said, 'I give you this money so that you personally trade with it yourself' and the

worker is unable to do so, the contract is void (*bāṭil*). But if conducting the trade himself is mentioned as a condition [as opposed to a restriction] in the contract – for example, it is said, 'I give you this money so that you trade with it on condition that you do it yourself' – and the worker is unable to do so, the transaction is not void. However, the owner has the option (*khiyār*) to annul (*faskh*) the contract in case the worker does not conduct the trade himself. Furthermore, if the contract mentions neither a restriction nor a condition but the worker is unable to trade even by appointing someone else, the contract is void. If he is able to trade at the beginning but not later, the contract is void from the time he cannot trade.

Ruling 2229. A worker is considered to be non-liable (*amīn*). Therefore, in case the property perishes or becomes defective, he is not responsible (*ḍāmin*) unless he acts beyond the boundaries of the contract or is negligent in safeguarding the property. Similarly, he is not responsible if a loss is incurred; in fact, all losses are borne by the owner. If the owner wishes to stipulate a condition that any loss incurred is not to be borne only by him, then this condition can be expressed in three ways:

1. he stipulates as part of the contract that the worker will be partner to any losses incurred just as he is partner to any profits made. In this case, the condition is invalid but the transaction is valid (*ṣaḥīḥ*);
2. it is stipulated that all losses are to be borne by the worker. In this case, the condition is valid but all profits will also be his, and none of them will belong to the owner;
3. it is stipulated that if there is a loss to the capital, the worker will recompense all or a specified portion of it from his own wealth and will give it to the owner. This condition is valid, and the worker is obliged to act according to it.

Ruling 2230. A sleeping partnership that is based on the owner giving the worker permission to trade with his property (*al-muḍārabah al-idhniyyah*) is not one of the irrevocable (*lāzim*) contracts [in Islamic law], meaning that the owner can revoke the permission he gave to the worker to use his property. Similarly, the worker is not obliged to continue doing the work with the owner's capital. Whenever he wishes, he can refrain from doing the work; this may be before starting the work or after it, or it may be before profits become evident or after it. Furthermore, the worker can do this whether the contract is non-specific about its duration or it specifies the duration. However, if the two parties stipulate a condition that they will not annul the contract until a specified time, then the condition is valid and it is obligatory (*wājib*) on them to act according to it. But, in case one of them does annul, the contract will be considered annulled even though the person will have committed a sin by acting contrary to his undertaking.

Ruling 2231. If a sleeping partnership contract is non-specific and does not mention any particular restrictions, the worker can buy, sell, and decide on the type of goods according to what he thinks is in the best interest [of the partnership]. However, it is not permitted (*jā'iz*) for him to take the goods from that city to another city unless this is something normal, such that the non-specific nature of the contract would be commonly understood to include it or the owner authorises him [to take the goods to another city]. If he transfers the goods to another place without authorisation from the owner and the goods perish or a loss is incurred, he is responsible.

Ruling 2232. With a sleeping partnership based on the owner giving the worker permission to trade with his property, the contract becomes void if the owner or the worker dies. This is because if the owner dies, his property is transferred to his heirs, and a new sleeping partnership agreement is needed for the property to remain in the worker's possession. If the worker dies, the permission is cancelled because the owner's permission was given exclusively to him.

Ruling 2233. In a sleeping partnership contract, both the owner and the worker can stipulate a condition that the other must do something for him or pay him something. As long as the contract continues and is not annulled, it is obligatory for them to act according to this condition whether profit is made or not.

Ruling 2234. Any loss to or destruction of the sleeping partnership property – for example, it is burnt, stolen, or suchlike – is recompensed by any profits made, whether the profit is made before the loss or after it. Therefore, the worker's ownership of his share of the profit depends on there not being any loss or destruction, and only when the sleeping partnership period is over or the contract is annulled will it be definite. However, if the worker stipulates a condition in the contract that any loss will not be recompensed by any prior or subsequent profit, the condition is valid and must be acted on.

Ruling 2235. An owner can invest in things that are sanctioned in Islamic law (*mashrūʿ*) by way of a 'reward' (*juʿālah*)[1] to achieve the same result he would achieve in a sleeping partnership; i.e. he can entrust someone with some property and say, for example, 'Use it for trading or any other operation, and the equivalent of half the profits will be for you'.

[1] The laws of *juʿālah* are stated in the next chapter.

CHAPTER FIFTEEN

Reward (*Juʿālah*)

Ruling 2236. A reward is when a person offers to give something in return for a task performed for him. For example, he says, 'Whoever finds my lost property, I will give him £100'. The person who makes such an offer is called the 'offeror' (*jāʿil*), and the one who performs the task is called the 'worker' (*ʿāmil*). There are a number of differences between a reward and hiring/renting (*ijārah*). Among these differences is that with hiring/renting, once the contract has been concluded, the hired person (*ajīr*) must perform the specified task, and the person who hired him owes him payment. However, with a reward, even though the worker may be a specific person, he can choose not to perform the task, and until he does not perform it, the offeror does not owe him anything.

Ruling 2237. The offeror must be of the age of legal responsibility (*bāligh*), sane (*ʿāqil*), have an intention (*qaṣd*) to make the offer, and make it of his own volition (*ikhtiyār*). He must also legally (*sharʿan*) have disposal over his property. Therefore, the reward of a person who is foolish with finances (*safīh*) – i.e. someone who spends his wealth in futile ways – is not valid (*ṣaḥīḥ*). Similarly, the reward of someone who has been proclaimed bankrupt (*mufallas*) is not valid with respect to that part of his wealth over which he does not have right of disposal.

Ruling 2238. The task that the offeror wishes to be performed for him must not be unlawful (*ḥarām*), pointless, or an obligatory (*wājib*) task that must legally be performed free of charge. Therefore, if a person offers £100 to whoever drinks wine, wanders into a dark place at night without any rational purpose, or performs his obligatory prayers (*ṣalāh*), the reward is not valid.

Ruling 2239. It is not necessary that the property being offered be specified with all its particulars; rather, it is sufficient if it is understood by the worker, such that him taking steps to perform the task would not be considered foolish. For example, if the offeror says, 'For whatever amount above £100 you sell this property, the extra is for you', the reward is valid. Similarly, if he says, 'Whoever finds my horse, I will give him half of its value or 10 kilograms of wheat', again the reward is valid.

Ruling 2240. If the fee for the work is completely vague – for example, the offeror says, 'Whoever finds my child, I will give him some money', and he does not specify the amount – then, in the event that someone performs the task, the offeror must give him a fee equivalent to the value of his work in the eyes of the people.

Ruling 2241. If a worker performs the task before or after the contract is concluded with the intention of not taking any money, he does not have the right to claim any fee.

Ruling 2242. The offeror can annul the reward before the worker starts performing the task.

Ruling 2243. If the offeror wishes to annul the reward after the worker has started to perform the task, it is problematic unless he and the worker come to an agreement.

Ruling 2244. The worker can choose to leave the task unfinished. However, if leaving the task unfinished would cause harm to the offeror or someone for whom the task is being performed, he must complete it. For example, if someone says, 'Whoever operates on my eye, I will give him such and such amount', and a surgeon starts operating on his eye, in the event that were he to leave the operation unfinished it would lead to the offeror having a defective eye, he must complete the operation.

Ruling 2245. If the worker leaves the task unfinished, he cannot claim any fee if the offeror had offered the fee for completing the task; for example, he said, 'Whoever stitches my clothes, I will give him £100'. However, if he had intended to give an amount of money proportional to the amount of work completed, then he must give the worker the fee for the amount of work he has done.

CHAPTER SIXTEEN

Sharecropping (*Muzāraʿah*)

Ruling 2246. Sharecropping is when an owner of land forms an agreement with a farmer to place the land at his disposal so that the farmer may farm the land and give part of the crop to the owner.

Ruling 2247. A number of conditions must be fulfilled for sharecropping to be valid:

1. there must be a contract between the two parties. For example, the owner of the land says to the farmer, 'I place the land at your disposal', and the farmer responds by saying, 'I accept'; or, without uttering a word, the owner places the land at the disposal of the farmer with the intention (*qaṣd*) of farming and the farmer accepts;
2. the owner of the land and the farmer must both be of the age of legal responsibility (*bāligh*), sane (*ʿāqil*), have the intention to make a sharecropping agreement, and enter into the agreement of their own volition (*ikhtiyār*). Furthermore, they must not be foolish with finances (*safīh*) – i.e. they must not spend their wealth in futile ways – and the owner must not have been proclaimed bankrupt (*mufallas*). However, if the farmer has been proclaimed bankrupt, there is no problem as long as the sharecropping agreement does not require him to have disposal over that part of his wealth over which he has been prohibited to have disposal;
3. the share of the land's produce that the owner and the farmer receive must be in the form of a fraction, such as a half or a third and suchlike. Therefore, if they do not fix the share for either of them, or, for example, the owner says, 'Farm this land and in return give me whatever you wish', it is not valid (*ṣaḥīḥ*). Similarly, [it is not valid] if a specific amount of the produce, such as 10 kilograms, is fixed for the owner or the farmer. It is not necessary to determine the share in the whole crop as joint ownership (*mushāʿ*); instead, they can allocate the share of one of them as one part of the crop and the share of the other as the rest of the crop. For example, the owner says, 'Farm the land, and only half of the crop that is harvested earlier is for you'; or he says, 'Only half the crop of that piece of land is for you'.
4. the period for which the land is to be at the farmer's disposal must be specified, and the length of the period must be such

that it is possible to harvest the crop in that time. If a specific day is fixed as the start of the period, and the end of the period is fixed as the time of harvest, it is sufficient;

5. the land must be cultivable. If it is not possible to farm the land at present but it can be worked on so that it becomes possible to farm it, the sharecropping is valid;
6. the crop that the farmer must cultivate must be specified. For example, it must be specified whether it is rice or wheat, and if it is rice, then the type of rice must be specified. However, if the parties do not have a particular crop in mind, it is not necessary for them to specify it. Similarly, if the crop they have in mind is known, it is not necessary to expressly state it;
7. the owner must specify the land if he has a number of pieces of land which are different in terms of their agricultural qualities. However, if there is no difference between them, specifying the land is not necessary. Therefore, [in the latter case,] if the owner says to the farmer, 'Farm one of these pieces of land' and he does not specify which piece, the sharecropping is valid, and after the conclusion of the contract the owner can specify which piece of land [he would like the farmer to farm];
8. the expenses that each of them must pay for – such as the cost of the seeds, fertilisers, farming equipment, and suchlike – must be specified. However, if the expenses that each of them must pay for are such that they are usually known, it is not necessary to expressly state them.

Ruling 2248. If an owner has an agreement with a farmer that an amount of the produce will belong to one of them and the rest of it will be divided between themselves, the sharecropping is invalid (*bāṭil*), even if they know that after taking away that amount there will still be something left over. But, if they have an agreement to the effect that some of the seeds that have been planted or some of the tax that is taken by the government will be excepted from the produce and the rest of it will be divided between themselves, the sharecropping is valid.

Ruling 2249. If a period has been specified for the sharecropping and the period is such that usually produce is harvested by the end of it, but it so happens that the period comes to an end and no produce is harvested, then, in the event that the specified period included this scenario as well – that is, the intention of both parties was that when the period comes to an end, the sharecropping will also come to an end even if no produce is harvested – in this case, if the owner consents – either by taking rent (*ijārah*) or not taking rent – to the crops remaining on his land, and the farmer also consents to it, there is no problem. However, if the owner does not consent to it, he can make the farmer remove the crop. If by removing the crop the farmer suffers a loss, it is not necessary for the owner to give him something in return. However, even if the farmer consents to give the owner something, he cannot compel the owner to keep the crop on the land.

Ruling 2250. If farming the land is not possible due to certain circumstances, such as the land being cut off from a water supply, the sharecropping is nullified. If the farmer does not farm the land without a legitimate excuse (*ʿudhr*), then, if the land was at his disposal and the owner had no disposal over it, the farmer must pay the owner a rental fee for that period at the standard rate.

Ruling 2251. An owner and a farmer cannot annul the sharecropping contract without the consent of the other. However, if they stipulate a condition in the sharecropping agreement that both or one of them reserves the right to annul the agreement, they can annul the agreement according to their agreement. Similarly, if one of them acts contrary to what was stipulated, the other can annul the agreement.

Ruling 2252. If the owner or the farmer dies after the sharecropping contract has been concluded, the sharecropping is not nullified and their heirs take their place. However, if the farmer dies and a restriction had been made in the sharecropping agreement that the farmer would farm the land himself, then the sharecropping agreement is nullified unless the work that was the responsibility of the farmer has been completed, in which case the sharecropping agreement is not nullified and his share must be given to his heirs. Furthermore, his heirs inherit other rights that belonged to him, and they can compel the owner to keep the crops on the land until the end of the sharecropping period.

Ruling 2253. If after farming the land the parties realise that the sharecropping agreement was invalid (*bāṭil*), in the event that the seeds belonged to the owner, the produce also belongs to him. The owner must pay the farmer his wages and all the expenses he incurred. He must also pay him a rental fee for using the cow or other animal that belonged to him and was used to work on the land. If the seeds belonged to the farmer, the crops also belong to him. The farmer must pay the owner a rental fee for his land. He must also pay for all the expenses he incurred and a rental fee for using the cow or other animal that belonged to him and was used to work on the land. In both cases, if the sum of the claim, based on standard rates, is greater than the amount agreed to in the contract and the other party is aware of this, it is not obligatory (*wājib*) to give the extra amount.

Ruling 2254. If the seeds belonged to the farmer and after farming the land the parties realise that the sharecropping agreement was invalid, in the event that the owner and the farmer both consent to letting the crops remain on the land, whether that be for a rental fee or not, there is no problem. However, if the owner does not consent to this, then based on obligatory precaution (*al-iḥtiyāṭ al-wājib*), he must not compel the farmer to remove the crops. Similarly, the owner cannot compel the farmer to keep the crops on his land, whether that be by claiming rent from him for the land or not.

Ruling 2255. If after harvesting the crops and the completion of the sharecropping period, the roots of the crop remain in the ground and they produce crops again in the following year, then in the event that the owner and the farmer had not stipulated a condition that they would own the roots jointly, the following year's crops will belong to the owner of the seeds.

CHAPTER SEVENTEEN

Tree Tending Contract (*Musāqāh*) and Tree Planting Contract (*Mughārasah*)

Ruling 2256. If a person forms an agreement with someone to, for example, hand over some fruit trees – the fruits of which either belong to him or are at his disposal – for a specific period so that he may tend to and water them, and in return take an agreed portion of the fruits for himself, then such a transaction (*muʿāmalah*) is called a 'tree tending contract'.

Ruling 2257. A tree tending transaction with trees that do not yield fruit but have, for example, leaves and flowers of significant value – such as the henna tree whose leaves are used – is valid (*ṣaḥīḥ*).

Ruling 2258. In a tree tending contract, it is not necessary to say a particular formula (*ṣīghah*) [for it to be valid]; rather, if the owner of the trees hands them over with the intention (*qaṣd*) of a tree tending contract and someone who does such work starts doing the work, the transaction is valid.

Ruling 2259. Both the owner and the person who takes on the responsibility of tending to the trees must be of the age of legal responsibility (*bāligh*), sane (*ʿāqil*), and no one must have compelled them [to enter into the tree tending contract]. Furthermore, they must not be foolish with finances (*safīh*) – i.e. they must not spend their wealth in futile ways – and the owner must not have been proclaimed bankrupt (*mufallas*). However, if the gardener has been proclaimed bankrupt, there is no problem as long as the tree tending contract does not require him to have disposal over that part of his wealth over which he has been prohibited to have disposal.

Ruling 2260. The period of the tree tending contract must be known, and the length of the period must be such that it is possible to harvest the crop in that time. If the start of the period is specified and the end of the period is fixed as the time of harvest, it is valid.

Ruling 2261. The share of each party must be a half, a third, and suchlike, of the produce. If they agree that, for example, 10 kilograms will belong to the owner and the rest will belong to the person who does the work, the transaction is not valid.

Ruling 2262. It is not necessary that the tree tending contract be concluded before the produce becomes apparent; rather, if it is concluded after it becomes apparent, in the event that some necessary task remains to be performed to increase the produce, make it better, or safeguard it from disease, the transaction is valid. However, if no such task remains to be performed, then even if there remains some necessary task to be performed for tending to the trees, picking the fruit, or looking after the fruit, the validity of such a transaction is problematic (*maḥall al-ishkāl*) [i.e. based on obligatory precaution (*al-iḥtiyāṭ al-wājib*), the transaction is not valid].[1]

Ruling 2263. Based on the more apparent (*aẓhar*)[2] juristic opinion, a tree tending transaction for honeydew melon and cucumber plants and suchlike is valid.

Ruling 2264. If a tree uses rainwater or moisture from the earth and does not require any additional irrigation, then as long as it requires other tasks – such as those mentioned in Ruling 2262 – a tree tending contract concerning it is valid.

Ruling 2265. The two parties to a tree tending contract can annul it with the other party's consent. If they stipulate a condition in the tree tending contract that both or one of them reserves the right to annul the agreement, there is no problem in annulling it according to their agreement. If they stipulate a particular condition in the tree tending contract and the condition is not fulfilled, the party in whose benefit the condition was made can annul the agreement.

Ruling 2266. If the owner dies, the tree tending contract is not nullified. Instead, his heirs take his place.

Ruling 2267. If the person who has been tasked with tending to the trees dies, his heirs take his place as long as there is no restriction or condition in the contract to the effect that the person [who died] had to tend to the trees himself. If the heirs do not perform the task

[1] As mentioned in Ruling 6, the term 'problematic' (*maḥall al-ishkāl*) amounts to saying the ruling is based on obligatory precaution.

[2] For practical purposes in jurisprudential rulings, an opinion that is termed 'more apparent' equates to a fatwa.

themselves nor hire someone to do it, a fully qualified jurist (*al-ḥākim al-sharʿī*) will hire someone using the deceased's estate and will divide the produce between the heirs and the owner. If there is a restriction in the contract that the person had to tend to the trees himself, the contract is nullified upon his death.

Ruling 2268. If a condition is stipulated that the entire produce belongs to the owner, the tree tending contract is invalid (*bāṭil*) but the produce nevertheless belongs to the owner. Furthermore, the person who does the work on the trees cannot claim any wages. However, if the tree tending contract is invalidated due to another reason, the owner must pay wages at the standard rate to the person who tended to the trees by watering them and performing other tasks. In the event that the standard rate is more than the amount in the contract and the owner is aware of this, it is not necessary for him to pay the additional amount.

Ruling 2269. A tree planting contract is when a person places some land at the disposal of another person to plant trees on it, and they share the proceeds between them. This is a valid transaction, although the recommended precaution is to refrain from it. In fact, the same result can be achieved through a transaction that is valid without any problem. For example, the two parties can arrive at a settlement (*ṣulḥ*) and reach a compromise to the same effect; or, they can be each other's partner (*sharīk*) with respect to the saplings, and after that the gardener can hire (*ijārah*) himself to the owner of the land for planting, tending to, and irrigating the saplings for a specified period in return for half of the proceeds resulting from the land during that period.

CHAPTER EIGHTEEN

Those Prohibited from having Disposal over their Property

Ruling 2270.* A child who is not of the age of legal responsibility (*bāligh*) cannot legally (*sharʿan*) exercise discretion over his liabilities,[1] nor can he have disposal over his property. This is the case even though the child may be perfectly able to discern between right and wrong (*tamyīz*), take care of his wealth, and use it in a correct way (*rushd*). In this regard, neither prior permission nor subsequent authorisation from his guardian (*walī*) is sufficient. However, in certain cases, a child's disposal over his property is valid (*ṣaḥīḥ*), such as his buying and selling of things that have a little value, as was mentioned in Ruling 2092, and his will (*waṣiyyah*) to his close relatives, as will be mentioned in Ruling 2714.

The sign of having reached the age of legal responsibility (*bulūgh*) for a girl is the completion of nine lunar years. For boys, it is one of three things:

1. growth of thick hair below the navel and above the genitalia, [and on the face and above the lips (see next ruling)];
2. ejaculation of semen;
3. completion of fifteen lunar years.

Ruling 2271.* The growth of thick hair on the face and above the lips are signs of *bulūgh*. However, the growth of hair on the chest and under the armpits, and the deepening of a boy's voice and suchlike, are not signs of *bulūgh*.

Ruling 2272. An insane person cannot have disposal over his property. Similarly, a person who has been proclaimed bankrupt (*mufallas*) – i.e. someone who is prohibited by a fully qualified jurist (*al-ḥākim al-sharʿī*) from having disposal over his wealth due to the claims on him by his creditors – cannot have disposal over his property without authorisation from his creditors. Similarly, a person who is foolish with finances (*safīh*) – i.e. someone who spends his wealth in futile ways – cannot have disposal over his property without authorisation from his guardian.

Ruling 2273. If a person is sometimes sane (*ʿāqil*) and sometimes

[1] Therefore, a minor cannot, for example, become a guarantor or take out a loan.

insane, any disposal he exercises over his property during his moments of insanity is not valid.

Ruling 2274. A person can use any amount of his wealth during a terminal illness for himself, his family, guests, and anything that is not considered wasteful. There is no problem if he sells his property at the normal price or gives it on rent (*ijārah*). However, if, for example, he gifts his wealth to someone or sells it for a price that is lower than normal, in the event that the amount he has given or sold cheaply is equivalent to or less than one-third of his property, his disposal is valid. If it is more than one-third, it is valid as long as his heirs authorise it, but if they do not, his disposal over more than one-third is invalid (*bāṭil*).

CHAPTER NINETEEN

Agency (*Wikālah*)

Agency is the act of delegating a transaction (*muʿāmalah*) that a person has the right to perform himself to someone else so that he may perform the task on his behalf. The transaction may be a contract (*ʿaqd*) or a unilateral instigation (*īqāʿ*)[1] or something related to these, such as handing over and taking possession of something. For example, a person may appoint an agent (*wakīl*) to sell his house for him or marry him to a woman. Therefore, someone who is foolish with finances (*safīh*)[2] cannot appoint an agent to sell his house for him as he does not have right of disposal over his property.

Ruling 2275. To form an agency agreement, it is not necessary to say a particular formula (*ṣīghah*). Therefore, if a person conveys to someone that he has made him his agent and the other individual, in turn, conveys to him that he has accepted it – as when a person gives his property to someone to sell it for him and the latter takes it – the agency is valid (*ṣaḥīḥ*).

Ruling 2276. If a person appoints someone in another city to be his agent and sends him a letter of agency and the latter accepts, the agency is valid even if the letter of agency reaches him a while after it was sent.

Ruling 2277. Both the principal (*muwakkil*) – i.e. the person who appoints someone to be his agent – and the agent must be sane (*ʿāqil*). Furthermore, both must have an intention (*qaṣd*) to enter into the agreement and do so of their own volition (*ikhtiyār*). The principal must have reached the age of legal responsibility (*bulūgh*), except in those cases where it is valid for a child who is able to discern between right and wrong (*mumayyiz*) [to carry out the transaction].

Ruling 2278. A person must not become an agent to perform a task that he is not capable of performing or is legally (*sharʿan*) prohibited

[1] The difference between a 'contract' and a 'unilateral instigation' is as follows: with a contract, two parties are required – one to make the offer and the other to accept it. Marriage, therefore, is an example of a contract. In contrast, in a unilateral instigation, one party alone executes the transaction, as is the case with divorce.
[2] Ruling 2091 provides further clarification of this term: it refers to someone who spends his wealth in futile ways.

from performing. For example, a person who is in the state of *iḥrām*[3] for hajj and is therefore not permitted to say the formula for a marriage contract cannot become an agent for someone to say the formula for him.

Ruling 2279. If a person appoints someone to be his agent to perform all his tasks for him, it is valid. However, if he appoints him to be his agent to perform one of his tasks for him but does not specify which task, the agency is not valid. But, if he appoints him to be his agent to perform one of a number of tasks at the agent's discretion – for example, he appoints him as his agent to either sell his house or give it on rent (*ijārah*) – the agency is valid.

Ruling 2280. If a person deposes his agent – i.e. he discharges him from his duty – then once news of this reaches the agent, he cannot perform the task for which he was appointed. However, it is valid if he performs the task before the news reaches him.

Ruling 2281. An agent can discharge himself from the agency, even if the principal is absent.

Ruling 2282. An agent cannot appoint someone else to be his agent to perform the task that was delegated to him to perform. If the principal authorises him to appoint an agent, he must act in the manner that he was instructed. Therefore, if the principal states, 'Appoint an agent for me', he must appoint an agent who will act on behalf of the principal and cannot appoint someone who will act on behalf of himself.

Ruling 2283. If with the authorisation of the principal an agent appoints someone to be an agent for the principal, the agent cannot depose him. If the first agent dies or the principal deposes him, the second agency does not become void (*bāṭil*).

Ruling 2284. If with the authorisation of the principal an agent appoints someone to be an agent for himself, both the principal and the first agent can depose him. If the first agent dies or is deposed, the second agency becomes void.

[3] *Iḥrām* here refers to the state of ritual consecration of pilgrims during hajj and *ʿumrah*.

Ruling 2285. If a person appoints a number of people to be his agents to perform a task and authorises each of them to act solitarily in the performance of that task, then any one of them can perform that task. In the event that one of them dies, the agency of the others does not become void. However, if it was said that they must perform the task together, or it was said in a general way, 'You two are my agents', they cannot act solitarily. In the event that one of them dies, the agency of the others becomes void.

Ruling 2286. If the agent or the principal dies, the agency becomes void. If the item over which the person was appointed to have disposal perishes – for example, the sheep that the person was appointed to sell dies – the agency becomes void. Similarly, if one of them becomes permanently insane or loses consciousness, the agency becomes void. However, if one of them intermittently becomes insane or loses consciousness, then to say the agency becomes void while he is insane or unconscious, let alone when he is in neither of these states, is problematic (*maḥall al-ishkāl*) [i.e. based on obligatory precaution (*al-iḥtiyāṭ al-wājib*), the agency does not become void].[4]

Ruling 2287. If a person appoints someone to be his agent to perform a task and agrees on a remuneration, then upon completion of the task, he must remunerate him according to the agreement.

Ruling 2288. If an agent is not negligent in safeguarding the property that has been placed in his possession and does not use it in any manner except in the way he was authorised, and it so happens the property is destroyed, he is not responsible (*ḍāmin*) for it.

Ruling 2289. If an agent is negligent in safeguarding the property that has been placed in his possession or uses it in a manner that was not authorised, and the property is destroyed, he is responsible for it. Therefore, if he wears a piece of clothing that he was told to sell and that clothing is ruined, he must replace it.

[4] As mentioned in Ruling 6, the term 'problematic' (*maḥall al-ishkāl*) amounts to saying the ruling is based on obligatory precaution.

Ruling 2290. If an agent uses the property in a manner that was not authorised – for example, he wears a piece of clothing that he was told to sell – and afterwards disposes of it as he was authorised, that disposal is valid.

CHAPTER TWENTY

Loan (*Qarḍ*)

Giving a loan to believers, especially the needy among them, is one of the recommended (*mustaḥabb*) acts that has been highly advised in traditions. For example, it has been reported that the Most Noble Messenger (Ṣ) said, 'Whoever gives a loan to his brother in faith and gives him respite until he is financially able to repay it, his wealth will increase and angels will send mercy upon him until the time he takes his money back.' And it is reported that Imam al-Ṣādiq (ʿA) said, 'Every believer who gives another believer a loan with the intention of attaining proximity to Allah, Allah will record for him the reward of giving alms to the poor (*ṣadaqah*) until he takes his property back.'

Ruling 2291. It is not necessary to say a particular formula (*ṣīghah*) when giving a loan; rather, if one gives something to someone with the intention (*niyyah*) of giving a loan and the latter takes it with the same intention, it is valid (*ṣaḥīḥ*).

Ruling 2292. Whenever a borrower repays his loan, the lender must accept it. However, if a period for repaying it at the request of the lender or both parties was agreed upon, then the lender can refuse to receive what he is owed before the period expires.

Ruling 2293. If a period for repaying the loan is agreed upon in the loan agreement, in the event that specifying the period was done at the request of the borrower or both parties, the lender cannot claim what he is owed before the period expires. However, if specifying the period was done at the request of the lender or no period was specified at all, the lender can claim what he is owed whenever he wishes.

Ruling 2294. If a lender claims what he is owed and there is no time [period specified in the loan agreement] or the time for repayment is due, in the event that the borrower can repay his loan, he must do so immediately. If he delays in doing so, he will have sinned.

Ruling 2295. If a borrower owns nothing besides a house that he resides in and some household furniture and some other things which, taking into consideration his status and social position, he needs and without which he would fall into difficulty, the lender cannot claim what he is owed from him. Instead, he must wait until the borrower can repay his loan.

Ruling 2296. If a borrower cannot repay his loan but it is easy for him to trade, or if his job is trading, then it is obligatory (*wājib*) on him to earn and repay his loan. In fact, if none of the above apply to him but he can earn by doing something worthy of his status, the obligatory precaution (*al-iḥtiyāṭ al-wājib*) is that he must earn and repay his loan.

Ruling 2297. If a person has no access to his lender and has no hope of finding him or his heirs in the future, he must give what he owes to a poor person (*faqīr*) on behalf of the lender. The obligatory precaution here is that he must obtain authorisation from a fully qualified jurist (*al-ḥākim al-sharʿī*). However, if he has hope of finding his lender or his heirs, he must wait and search for him/them. In the event that he does not find him/them, he must make a will (*waṣiyyah*) to the effect that if he dies and his lender or his heirs are found, he/they must be paid from his estate what he/they are owed.

Ruling 2298. If the estate of a deceased person is not greater than the costs of his obligatory shroud (*kafan*), burial (*dafn*), and debts, his estate must be spent on these items and his heirs do not inherit anything.

Ruling 2299. If a person borrows an amount of money, wheat, barley, or something else that is fungible and its value depreciates or appreciates, he must return the same amount of those items with the same qualities and particulars that affect the desirability of those items. There is no problem if the borrower and the lender are content with receiving something else instead. However, if he borrows something that is non-fungible, such as sheep, he must give back an amount that is equivalent to the item's value on the day he took it on loan.

Ruling 2300. If the property that someone has borrowed is not destroyed and the owner claims it, it is not obligatory for the borrower to return the same property to him. Likewise, if the borrower wishes to return it, the lender can refuse to accept it.

Ruling 2301. If the lender stipulates a condition that he will take back more than he gives – for example, he gives 10 kilograms of wheat and stipulates that he will take back 11 kilograms, or he gives ten eggs and stipulates that he will take back eleven eggs – this is usury (*ribā*) and unlawful (*ḥarām*). In fact, if it is agreed that the lender will perform a task for him or will return the loan along with some other commodity – for example, he stipulates that the £10 he has given on loan must be returned along with one matchstick – this is also usury and unlawful. Furthermore, if he stipulates a condition that the item being taken on loan must be returned in a particular manner – for example, he gives an amount of gold that has not been crafted and stipulates that gold that has been crafted [such as a piece of jewellery] must be returned – again, this is usury and unlawful. However, if the borrower himself returns the loaned item with an extra amount without such a thing being stipulated, there is no problem; in fact, it is recommended.

Ruling 2302. Giving interest (*ribā*), just like taking interest, is unlawful, but the loan itself is valid. Someone who takes a usurious loan becomes the owner of it but the lender does not become the owner of the extra that he takes, and any use he makes of it is unlawful. Furthermore, if the lender purchases something with the same item [i.e. the extra item he received in the usurious loan], he does not become the owner of it. In the event that had he not made an agreement of usury, the borrower would have consented for the lender to use the money, then his use of it is permitted (*jā'iz*). Similarly, if due to not knowing the ruling (*mas'alah*) the lender takes interest and after finding out the ruling he repents, then what he took when he did not know the ruling is lawful (*ḥalāl*) for him.

Ruling 2303. If a person acquires wheat or something similar through a usurious loan and cultivates it, he becomes the owner of the resulting produce.

Ruling 2304. If a person purchases some clothing and afterwards pays for it with money acquired through usury or with lawful money mixed with such money, he becomes the owner of it and there is no problem in him wearing it and performing prayers in it. However, if he says to the seller, 'I am purchasing this clothing with this money', then he does not become the owner of it and wearing it is unlawful.

Ruling 2305. If a person gives an amount of money to someone so that someone else in another city takes a lesser amount on his behalf, there is no problem. This is called '*ṣarf al-barāt*' [a type of bill of exchange].

Ruling 2306.* If a person gives something to someone so that he may take a greater amount in another city, and if the item is gold, silver, wheat, or barley which can be weighed or measured, it is usury and unlawful. However, if the party taking the extra amount gives or does something in return, there is no problem. If banknotes are given on loan, it is not permitted to take back more even though the amount of debt has decreased due to high prices. However, if the value of the loan goes down too much due to inflation and the like, it is an obligatory precaution to reach a settlement (*ṣulḥ*). If banknotes are sold for banknotes, and the sale is an immediate exchange (*naqd*)[1] or credit (*nasī'ah*) transaction but the money is in two currencies, such as pounds sterling and dollars, then there is no problem with any extra received. However, if it is a credit sale and the money is in one currency only, then receiving an extra amount is problematic (*maḥall al-ishkāl*) [i.e. based on obligatory precaution, one must not receive an extra amount].[2]

Ruling 2307. If a person is owed by someone a commodity that is neither weighed nor measured, he can sell it to the borrower or someone else for a lower price and take the sum immediately. Therefore, in present times, a lender can take a cheque or promissory note from the borrower and sell it to a bank or another person for less than what he is owed – which is commonly known as 'cheque cashing' – and he can take the sum immediately.

[1] In an immediate exchange transaction, there is no lapse of time between the buyer paying for the item and receiving it.

[2] As mentioned in Ruling 6, the term 'problematic' (*maḥall al-ishkāl*) amounts to saying the ruling is based on obligatory precaution.

CHAPTER TWENTY-ONE

Transfer of Debt (*Ḥawālah*)

Ruling 2308. If a person refers his creditor to someone to get the money he is owed, and the creditor accepts to do this, then, if the transfer agreement is concluded according to the conditions that will be mentioned later, the person to whom the debt is transferred becomes indebted to the creditor. After that, the creditor cannot claim what he is owed from the first debtor.

Ruling 2309. The debtor, creditor, and transferee must be of the age of legal responsibility (*bāligh*), sane (*ʿāqil*), and no one must have compelled them [to enter into the transfer of debt agreement]. Furthermore, they must not be foolish with finances (*safīh*); i.e. they must not spend their wealth in futile ways. It is also a requirement that the debtor and the creditor must not have been proclaimed bankrupt (*mufallas*) except if the transfer is to a person who is not indebted to the transferor, in which case if the transferor has been proclaimed bankrupt, there is no problem.

Ruling 2310. In all cases of transfer of debt, [for the transfer to be valid (*ṣaḥīḥ*),] the transferee must be willing to accept the transfer, whether he is indebted or not.

Ruling 2311. When a person makes the transfer, he must be indebted. Therefore, if he wishes to obtain a loan (*qarḍ*) from someone, then until he does not obtain the loan from him, he cannot refer him to someone else to get the sum that he later wishes to borrow from him.

Ruling 2312. The type and amount of the debt being transferred must be specified. Therefore, if a person owes a quantity of wheat (say, 10 kilograms) and an amount of money (say, £10), and he says to the creditor, 'Get one of the two things you are owed from so-and-so' without specifying which item, the transfer is not correct.

Ruling 2313. If the debt is specified but at the time of making the transfer the debtor and the creditor do not know the amount or type, the transfer is valid. For example, if someone's debt is recorded in a document and he makes the transfer before referring to the document, and after that he refers to it and informs the creditor of the amount of the debt, the transfer is valid.

Ruling 2314. A creditor reserves the right to refuse a transfer of debt, even if the [proposed] transferee is wealthy and would not be negligent in paying the debt.

Ruling 2315. If a person who is not indebted to the transferor accepts the transfer of debt to himself, he can claim the amount of the debt from him before paying it. This is unless the debt that has been transferred to him has a period, and the period has not yet expired. In such a case, he cannot claim the amount of the debt from the transferor before the period expires, even if he has already paid it. If the creditor settles what he is owed for a lower amount with the transferee, the latter can only claim that amount from the transferor.

Ruling 2316. Once a transfer of debt has taken place, the transferor and the transferee cannot annul (*faskh*) the transfer. If the transferee is not poor (*faqīr*) at the time of the transfer, even though he may have become so afterwards, the creditor cannot annul the transfer. The same applies if he is poor at the time of the transfer and the creditor is aware that he is poor. However, if the creditor does not know he is poor and realises this afterwards, then, if at that time he is not financially stable, the creditor can annul the transfer and claim what he is owed from the transferor. But if he is financially stable, then for him to have the right to annul is problematic (*maḥall al-ishkāl*) [i.e. based on obligatory precaution (*al-iḥtiyāṭ al-wājib*), he does not have the right to annul the transfer].[1]

Ruling 2317. If a debtor, creditor, and transferee, or one of them, reserves the right to annul the transfer of debt, he/they can annul the transfer according to their agreement.

Ruling 2318. If a transferor himself pays his debt to the creditor, then, if the transferee was indebted to the transferor and he had requested the transferor to pay the creditor, the transferor can claim what he paid to the creditor from the transferee. But, if the transferor paid the creditor without the transferee requesting this, or if the transferee was not indebted to the transferor, then the transferor cannot claim what he paid the creditor from the transferee.

[1] As mentioned in Ruling 6, the term 'problematic' (*maḥall al-ishkāl*) amounts to saying the ruling is based on obligatory precaution.

CHAPTER TWENTY-TWO

Security (*Rahn*)[1]

[1] It is necessary to note that at present, what is commonly known as '*rahn*' among people [in some places] is not, in reality, '*rahn*' [in its jurisprudential sense]. *Rahn* [in its jurisprudential sense] refers to the money that is given to the owner of a house as a loan (*qarḍ*) in return for use of the house as a place of residence. This act, if it takes place without rent (*ijārah*), is usury (*ribā*) and unlawful (*ḥarām*), and the person does not have the right to live in that house. If it takes place with rent, then, if giving the loan is conditional on the rent, it is again unlawful; and if the rent is on condition of the loan, then based on obligatory precaution (*al-iḥtiyāṭ al-wājib*) it is not permitted (*jā'iz*). [Author]

Ruling 2319. In a security agreement, a person deposits some property with another person as collateral for a debt or some property that he is responsible (*ḍāmin*) for so that in the event that he fails to pay off his debt or property, the other party can be compensated from the deposited property.

Ruling 2320. In a security agreement, it is not necessary to say a particular formula (*ṣīghah*). In fact, if the depositor gives his property to the depositee with the intention (*qaṣd*) of a security deposit and the depositee accepts it with the same intention, it is valid (*ṣaḥīḥ*).

Ruling 2321. The depositor and the depositee must be of the age of legal responsibility (*bāligh*), sane (*ʿāqil*), and no one must have compelled them [to enter into the security agreement]. Furthermore, the depositor must not have been proclaimed bankrupt (*mufallas*), nor must he be foolish with finances (*safīh*) (the meaning of these terms was explained in Ruling 2272). However, if a bankrupt person deposits as security property that is not his or property over which he has not been prohibited to have disposal, there is no problem.

Ruling 2322. A person can only deposit as security property over which he can legally (*sharʿan*) have disposal. If he deposits as security another person's property with his consent, it is valid.

Ruling 2323. The property that is deposited as security must be valid to buy and sell. Therefore, it is not correct if wine or suchlike is deposited as security.

Ruling 2324. The profits from the deposited item belong to its owner, whether the owner is the depositor or another person.

Ruling 2325. A depositee cannot give or sell the deposited property without the owner's consent, whether the owner is the depositor or another person. If the owner consents afterwards, there is no problem.

Ruling 2326. If a depositee sells the deposited property with the owner's consent, the proceeds of the sale are not considered security, as the property itself [was considered security]. The same applies if he sells it without the owner's consent but the latter consents afterwards.

However, if the depositor sells that property with the depositee's consent so that the proceeds be deposited as security, then in case he violates this agreement, the transaction (*muʿāmalah*) is void (*bāṭil*) unless the depositee consents to it.

Ruling 2327. If the time arrives for a debtor to pay his debt and the creditor demands it but the debtor does not pay him, in the event that the creditor has agency (*wikālah*) to sell the property that has been deposited as security and take what he is owed from the proceeds, he can sell it and take what he is owed. In case he does not have agency, it is necessary for him to obtain the owner's consent. If he does not have access to him, then based on obligatory precaution (*al-iḥtiyāṭ al-wājib*), he must get authorisation from a fully qualified jurist (*al-ḥākim al-sharʿī*). In both cases, if he acquires an additional amount [from the sale], he must give that additional amount to the owner.

Ruling 2328. If a debtor owns nothing besides the house in which he resides and some things such as household furniture which he needs, a creditor cannot claim what he is owed from him. However, if the property that has been deposited as security is something like a house and household furniture, then the creditor can sell it and take what he is owed in accordance with what was said in the previous ruling.

CHAPTER TWENTY-THREE

Suretyship (*Ḍamān*)

Ruling 2329. If a person wishes to act as guarantor (*ḍāmin*)[1] for paying off someone's debt, it is valid (*ṣaḥīḥ*) only if he conveys to the creditor – by means of any words, even if they are not in Arabic, or actions – that he is acting as guarantor for paying him what he is owed. Furthermore, the creditor must convey his consent to this, but the consent of the debtor is not a condition [for the validity of the person to act as guarantor]. This transaction (*muʿāmalah*) is of two types:

1. the guarantor transfers the debt (*dayn*) that was a liability on the debtor to himself. With this type of transaction, if the guarantor were to die before paying off the debt, then as is the case with other debts, the debt takes priority over inheritance (*irth*) [i.e. the debt first needs to be paid off before anything from his estate is inherited]. Usually, jurists (*fuqahāʾ*) intend this meaning when they discuss 'suretyship';
2. the guarantor is committed to paying off the debt but is not liable to do so. With this type of transaction, if he does not make a will (*waṣiyyah*), the debt is not paid from his estate after his death.

Ruling 2330. The guarantor and the creditor must be of the age of legal responsibility (*bāligh*), sane (*ʿāqil*), and no one must have compelled them [to enter into the suretyship agreement]. Furthermore, they must not be foolish with finances (*safīh*),[2] and the creditor must not have been proclaimed bankrupt (*mufallas*). However, these conditions do not apply to a debtor; for example, if a person acts as guarantor for paying off the debt of a child, an insane person, or someone who is foolish with finances, it is valid.

Ruling 2331. Whenever a person places a condition for himself to act as guarantor – for example, he says, 'If the debtor does not pay back your loan (*qarḍ*), I will pay it', then him acting as guarantor in the first type of suretyship mentioned in Ruling 2329 is problematic (*maḥall al-ishkāl*) [i.e. based on obligatory precaution (*al-iḥtiyāṭ al-wājib*), it is

[1] Sometimes, the guarantor in a suretyship is called the 'surety'.

[2] Ruling 2091 provides further clarification of this term: it refers to someone who spends his wealth in futile ways.

not valid].[3] However, there is no problem [in him acting as guarantor in] the second type mentioned in that ruling (*mas'alah*).

Ruling 2332. The person for whom an individual acts as guarantor must be in debt. Therefore, if a person wishes to acquire a loan from someone, one cannot act as guarantor for him until he acquires the loan. This condition does not apply to the second type of suretyship [mentioned in Ruling 2329].

Ruling 2333. A person can only act as guarantor if the creditor, debtor, and type of debt are specified. Therefore, if two people are owed by someone and another person says, 'I act as guarantor for paying the debt owed to one of you', then him acting as guarantor in this case is invalid (*bāṭil*) as he did not specify whose debt he is acting as guarantor for. Also, if someone is owed by two people and another person says, 'I act as guarantor for paying you the debt owed by one of them', then him acting as guarantor here is invalid as well as he too did not specify whose debt he is acting as guarantor for. Similarly, if someone is owed, for example, a quantity of wheat (say, 10 kilograms) and a quantity of money (say, £10), and another person says, 'I act as guarantor for one of the two items you are owed' and does not specify whether he is acting as guarantor for the wheat or money, it is not valid.

Ruling 2334. If a person acts as guarantor for paying off someone's debt without the debtor's consent, he cannot claim anything from him.

Ruling 2335. If a person acts as guarantor for paying off someone's debt with the debtor's consent, he can claim the suretyship amount from him even before he has paid it. However, if he pays the creditor with a commodity that is different to the commodity owed by the debtor, he cannot claim anything that he gave from the debtor. For example, if the debtor owes 10 kilograms of wheat and the guarantor pays 10 kilograms of rice, the latter cannot claim rice from the debtor. However, there is no problem if the debtor consents to rice being paid.

[3] As mentioned in Ruling 6, the term 'problematic' (*maḥall al-ishkāl*) amounts to saying the ruling is based on obligatory precaution.

Ruling 2336. If a creditor pardons the guarantor of what he is owed, the guarantor cannot claim anything from the debtor. Similarly, if the creditor pardons some of it, he cannot claim that amount. However, if the creditor gives all or some of it as a gift (*hibah*), or calculates it as one-fifth tax (*khums*), alms tax (zakat), alms to the poor (*ṣadaqah*), or something similar, the guarantor can claim it from the debtor.

Ruling 2337. If a person acts as guarantor for paying off someone's debt, he cannot revert from acting as guarantor.

Ruling 2338. A guarantor and debtor cannot, based on obligatory precaution, stipulate a condition that permits them to annul the suretyship agreement whenever they wish.

Ruling 2339. If a person is able to pay off the debt owed to a creditor at the time of the suretyship agreement, even if he were to become poor (*faqīr*) afterwards, the creditor cannot annul (*faskh*) the suretyship agreement and recover the debt from the original debtor. The same applies if he is unable to pay off the debt at that time, but the creditor knows this and consents to him acting as guarantor nevertheless.

Ruling 2340. If a person is unable to pay off the debt owed to the creditor at the time of acting as guarantor and the creditor was not aware of this but now wishes to annul him acting as a guarantor, it is problematic [i.e. based on obligatory precaution, he cannot do this]. This is especially so if the guarantor acquires the ability to pay off the debt before the creditor becomes aware [that he is unable to pay off the debt].

CHAPTER TWENTY-FOUR

Surety for the Appearance of a Debtor (*Kafālah*)

Ruling 2341. *Kafālah* is when a person undertakes to present a debtor whenever the creditor seeks him. Someone who takes on such an undertaking is called a 'surety' (*kafīl*).

Ruling 2342. A *kafālah* is valid (*ṣaḥīḥ*) only if the surety conveys to the creditor – by means of any words, even if they are not in Arabic, or actions – that he undertakes to present the debtor whenever he wishes, and the creditor accepts. And based on obligatory precaution (*al-iḥtiyāṭ al-wājib*), the debtor's consent is also a requirement for the validity of the *kafālah*. In fact, the obligatory precaution is that he must be a party to the contract as well, i.e. both the debtor and the creditor must accept the *kafālah*.

Ruling 2343. The surety must be of the age of legal responsibility (*bāligh*), sane (*'āqil*), and no one must have compelled him [to enter into the *kafālah* agreement]. In addition, he must be able to make the person for whom he is the surety appear, and he must not be foolish with finances (*safīh*).[1] Furthermore, he must not have been proclaimed bankrupt (*mufallas*) in the event that making the debtor appear requires him to have disposal over his property.

Ruling 2344. One of five things annuls a *kafālah* agreement:

1. the surety presents the debtor to the creditor, or the debtor submits himself to the creditor;
2. the debt owed to the creditor is paid;
3. the creditor pardons the debt he is owed or transfers it to another person;
4. the debtor or the surety dies;
5. the creditor releases the surety from the *kafālah*.

Ruling 2345. If a person forcefully frees a debtor from the hands of the creditor, in the event that the creditor does not have access to the debtor, the person who freed the debtor must present him to the creditor or pay off his debts.

[1] Ruling 2091 provides further clarification of this term: it refers to someone who spends his wealth in futile ways.

CHAPTER TWENTY-FIVE

Deposit (*Wadīʿah*) and Trust (*Amānah*)

Ruling 2346. If a person gives some property to someone, saying, 'Let it be trusted to you', and the latter accepts, or if without uttering a word a person conveys to someone that he is giving him some property for safeguarding and the latter accepts in a way that makes it clear he has committed to safeguarding it, then in these cases, the parties must act according to the laws (*aḥkām*) of deposit and trust, which will be mentioned below.

Ruling 2347. The depositor and the safe keeper must both be of the age of legal responsibility (*bāligh*), sane (*ʿāqil*), and no one must have compelled them [to enter into the deposit agreement]. Therefore, if a person entrusts some property to an insane person or a child, or if an insane person or a child entrusts some property to someone, it is not valid (*ṣaḥīḥ*). However, it is permitted (*jāʾiz*) for a child who is able to discern between right and wrong (*mumayyiz*) to entrust another person's property to someone with the owner's consent. Furthermore, the depositor must not be foolish with finances (*safīh*)[1] nor have been proclaimed bankrupt (*mufallas*). However, there is no problem if a person who has been proclaimed bankrupt entrusts property over which he has not been prohibited from having disposal. Also, the safe keeper must not be foolish with finances nor have been proclaimed bankrupt; this is in the event that protecting and safeguarding the deposit would require him to have disposal over his own property in a way that ownership of the property would transfer from him or be destroyed.

Ruling 2348. If a person accepts a deposit from a child without the permission of its owner, he must return it to its owner. If the deposited item belongs to the child, it is necessary to return it to the child's guardian (*walī*). In the event that it perishes before it is returned to them, the safe keeper must replace it. However, if the deposit is at risk of perishing and it is taken from the child to protect and return it to the guardian, then as long as the safe keeper was not negligent in safeguarding or returning it, and he did not use it in an unpermitted manner, he is not responsible (*ḍāmin*) for it. The same applies if the depositor is an insane person.

[1] Ruling 2091 provides further clarification of this term: it refers to someone who spends his wealth in futile ways.

Ruling 2349. A person who is not capable of safeguarding a deposit must not accept it if the depositor is unaware of his incapability. If he does accept it and it perishes, he is responsible for it.

Ruling 2350. If a person conveys to the owner of the property that he is not prepared to safeguard his property, and he does not take the property from him but the owner nevertheless places it with him and leaves, and the property perishes, then the safe keeper is not responsible for it. However, the recommended precaution (*al-iḥtiyāṭ al-mustaḥabb*) is that he should, if possible, safeguard it.

Ruling 2351. A depositor may annul the deposit agreement whenever he likes. Similarly, a safe keeper can also annul the deposit agreement whenever he likes.

Ruling 2352. If a person changes his mind about safeguarding a deposit and annuls the deposit agreement, he must return the deposit to the owner, his agent (*wakīl*), or guardian as soon as he can, or he must inform them that he is no longer prepared to safeguard it. If he fails to return the deposit to them without a legitimate excuse (*ʿudhr*) and does not inform them either, he must replace it in the event that the deposit perishes.

Ruling 2353. A person who accepts a deposit but does not have an appropriate place for it must acquire a suitable place for it. Furthermore, he must safeguard it in such a manner that it could not be said he was negligent in safeguarding it. If he is negligent in this matter and the deposit perishes, he must replace it.

Ruling 2354. If a safe keeper of a deposit is not negligent in safeguarding it nor excessive with it, i.e. he does not use it in an unpermitted manner, but it so happens that it perishes, he is not responsible for it. However, if he is negligent in safeguarding it – for example, he keeps it in a place that is not secure from being found and taken by an unjust person – or he is excessive – for example, he wears the clothing or rides the horse [that he was entrusted with] – then in the event that it perishes, he must replace it for the owner.

Ruling 2355. If the owner of the property specifies a place for safeguarding it and says to the safe keeper, 'You must look after the property here even if you deem it probable that it will be destroyed', the safe keeper cannot take it to another place. If he does [take the property to another place] and it perishes, he is responsible for it unless he is certain (i.e. he has *yaqīn*) that the property would perish there [i.e. in the first location], in which case it is permitted for him to transfer it to a safe place.

Ruling 2356. If the owner of the property specifies a place for safeguarding it, and it is understood from what he says that the place is not of any particular significance to him [i.e. the owner], the safe keeper can take it to another place where it would be safer or just as safe as the first place. In the event that the property perishes there [i.e. in the new location], he is not responsible for it.

Ruling 2357. If the owner of the property becomes permanently insane or unconscious, the deposit agreement becomes void (*bāṭil*) and the safe keeper must immediately return it to the owner's guardian or inform him of the deposit. If he does not do this and the property perishes, he must replace it. If the insanity or unconsciousness of the owner is intermittent, the obligatory precaution (*al-iḥtiyāṭ al-wājib*) is that the safe keeper must do exactly the same.

Ruling 2358. If the owner of the property dies, the deposit agreement becomes void. Therefore, if there are no other rights on the property and it is to be transferred to his heir, then the safe keeper must return it to him or inform him of it. If he does not do this and the property perishes, he is responsible for it. However, if he holds on to the property in order to find out about the heirs or whether they are the only heirs of the deceased and the property perishes, he is not responsible for it.

Ruling 2359. If the owner of the property dies and the property transfers to his heirs, the safe keeper must hand over the property to all of them or their agent. Therefore, if he hands over the entire property to one of the heirs without the consent of the others, he is responsible for their shares.

Ruling 2360. If the safe keeper dies or permanently becomes insane or unconscious, the deposit agreement becomes void and his heirs or guardian must inform the owner of the property as soon as possible or return the deposit to him. If the insanity or unconsciousness of the safe keeper is intermittent, then based on obligatory precaution, his guardian must do exactly the same.

Ruling 2361. If the safe keeper realises that he is nearing death, then based on obligatory precaution, he must, if possible, return the deposit to its owner, the owner's guardian, or the owner's agent, or he must inform them. If this is not possible, he must act in a way that he becomes confident (i.e. he attains *iṭmiʾnān*) that the property will return to its owner after his death. For example, he must write a will (*waṣiyyah*), obtain a witness, and inform the executor (*waṣī*) and the witness about the name of the property's owner, the type of property it is, its particulars, and its location.

Ruling 2362. If the safe keeper has to travel, he can keep the deposit with his family unless safeguarding the deposit is dependent on him being with it. In that case, he must not travel, or he must return the deposit to its owner, the owner's executor (*waṣī*), or the owner's agent, or he must inform them [about his travel].

CHAPTER TWENTY-SIX

Gratuitous Loan (*ʿĀriyah*)

Ruling 2363. A gratuitous loan is when a person gives his property to someone to use without taking anything in return.

Ruling 2364. It is not necessary that the parties say a particular formula (*ṣīghah*) [for a gratuitous loan agreement to be valid (*ṣaḥīḥ*)]. For example, if a person gives clothing to someone with the intention (*qaṣd*) of a gratuitous loan and the latter accepts it with the same intention, it is valid.

Ruling 2365. Lending a usurped (*ghaṣbī*) item or an item that belongs to the lender but its usufruct has been granted to someone else – such as property that has been given on rent (*ijārah*) – is valid only if the [rightful] owner [in the case where the item has been usurped], or the lessee [in the case where the lessee has been granted the item's usufruct], consents to the loan.

Ruling 2366. If the usufruct of a property belongs to a particular individual – because he has rented it, for example – then that individual is allowed to loan it to someone else unless a condition is stipulated in the rental contract that only he can use it. If no such condition is stipulated in the rental contract, then based on obligatory precaution (*al-iḥtiyāṭ al-wājib*), he cannot hand it over without the owner's permission.

Ruling 2367. It is not valid if a child, insane person, or someone who has been proclaimed bankrupt (*mufallas*) or is foolish with finances (*safīh*)[1] lends out his property. However, it is not a problem if the guardian (*walī*) deems it a matter of primary importance and lends out property belonging to someone over whom he has guardianship (*wilāyah*). Similarly, there is no problem in a child merely being an intermediary for delivering the property to the borrower.

Ruling 2368. If a person is neither negligent in safeguarding the loaned property nor excessive in using it, but it so happens that the property perishes, he is not responsible (*ḍāmin*) for it. However, if a condition is stipulated that in the event that the property perishes

[1] Ruling 2091 provides further clarification of this term: it refers to someone who spends his wealth in futile ways.

the borrower will be responsible for it, or if the loaned item is gold or silver, the property must be replaced.

Ruling 2369. If a person borrows gold or silver and stipulates a condition that if it perishes he will not be responsible for it, then in the event that it does perish, he is not responsible for it.

Ruling 2370. If the lender dies, the borrower must act according to the sequence of steps mentioned in Ruling 2358 concerning the death of an owner in a deposit agreement.

Ruling 2371. If the lender can no longer legally (*sharʿan*) have disposal over his property – for example, he becomes insane or unconscious – the borrower must act according to the sequence of steps mentioned in Ruling 2357 concerning deposits.

Ruling 2372. The lender and the borrower can annul the gratuitous loan agreement whenever they like.

Ruling 2373. Lending an item that has no lawful (*ḥalāl*) use – such as instruments of amusement and gambling – is invalid (*bāṭil*). The same applies to lending gold or silver utensils to eat and drink from. In fact, based on obligatory precaution, using these utensils in general is unlawful. However, it is permitted (*jāʾiz*) to lend them for decoration.[2]

Ruling 2374. Lending a sheep to use its milk and wool, and lending a male animal to mate with a female one, is valid.

Ruling 2375. If a borrower returns the loaned item to its owner, the owner's agent (*wakīl*), or the owner's guardian, and afterwards the item perishes, the borrower is not responsible for it. However, if the borrower takes the property to another location without the permission of its owner, the owner's agent, or the owner's guardian, he is responsible for it, even if the location is one to where the owner would usually take the property. For example, if [without permission] the borrower ties a horse in a stable that was built by the owner for

[2] See Ruling 227.

that very purpose, and afterwards the horse perishes or someone causes it to perish, he is responsible for it.

Ruling 2376. If a person lends an impure (*najis*) item, he must inform the borrower of this according to the instructions mentioned in Ruling 2065.

Ruling 2377. A person cannot give on rent or lend an item he has borrowed without the owner's consent.

Ruling 2378. If a person lends some property he has borrowed to someone without the owner's consent, in the event that the person who first borrowed it dies or becomes insane, the second person's loan does not become invalid.

Ruling 2379. If a person knows that the property he has borrowed is usurped, he must return it to its owner; he cannot return it to the lender.

Ruling 2380. If a person borrows some property he knows is usurped and uses it, and it perishes in his possession, the owner can claim compensation for the property and its use from the borrower or the usurper. If the owner acquires compensation from the borrower, the latter cannot claim from the lender anything he has given to the owner.

Ruling 2381. If a borrower does not know that the property he has borrowed is usurped, and it perishes in his possession, in the event that the owner acquires compensation from him, he in turn can claim from the lender what he gave to the owner. However, if the borrowed item is gold or silver, or if the lender stipulates a condition that in the event that the item is destroyed the borrower must replace it, then the latter cannot claim from the lender what he gave to the owner. However, if the owner takes something from him for using the property, he can claim that from the lender.

CHAPTER TWENTY-SEVEN

Marriage

By means of a marriage contract, a man and woman become lawful (*ḥalāl*) for each other. A marriage contract is of two types: permanent (*dāʾim*) and temporary (*munqaṭiʿ*) [also known as '*mutʿah*']. A permanent marriage contract is one in which no period is specified for the marriage. A woman married by such a contract is called a 'permanent wife' (*dāʾimah*). A temporary marriage contract is one in which a period is specified for the marriage, such as a marriage contract that is concluded with a woman for one hour, one day, one month, one year, or longer. However, the period specified for such a marriage must not exceed the lifespan of the husband and wife or one of them; otherwise, the contract is invalid (*bāṭil*). A woman married by such a contract is called a 'temporary wife' (*mutʿah*).[1]

THE MARRIAGE CONTRACT

Ruling 2382. To conclude a marriage contract, whether that be for a permanent marriage or a temporary one, a formula (*ṣīghah*) must be said; the mere consent of the man and the woman is not sufficient, nor is a written contract, based on obligatory precaution (*al-iḥtiyāṭ al-wājib*). The man and the woman can say the formula themselves, or they can appoint an agent (*wakīl*) to say it on their behalf.

Ruling 2383. The agent does not have to be a man; a woman can also be an agent on behalf of a party to say the formula of the marriage contract.

Ruling 2384. As long as the man and the woman are not confident (i.e. they do not have *iṭmiʾnān*) that their agent has said the formula, they cannot consider themselves legally married. Merely supposing (i.e. having *ẓann*) that the agent has said the formula does not suffice. In fact, if an agent says that he has said the formula but they do not have confidence in what he says, the obligatory precaution is that they must not heed what he says.

[1] In the Persian original, the terms '*mutʿah*' and '*ṣīghah*' are used to refer to both temporary marriage and a temporary wife. In his Arabic work *Minhāj al-Ṣāliḥīn*, al-Sayyid al-Sistani refers to a temporary wife as '*mutʿah*', '*al-mutamattaʿ bi-hā*', and '*munqaṭiʿah*' (vol. 3, p. 23).

Ruling 2385. If a woman appoints an agent to marry her to a man for ten days, for example, but she does not specify a starting date for those ten days, the agent can marry her to the man for ten days starting from whenever he likes. However, if it is known that the woman has intended a specific date or time, the agent must say the formula according to her intention (*qaṣd*).

Ruling 2386. One individual can be an agent for both parties to say the formula of the marriage contract, be it temporary or permanent. A man can be an agent for the woman to marry her to himself, both in a temporary marriage and a permanent one. However, the recommended precaution (*al-iḥtiyāṭ al-mustaḥabb*) is that the formula should be said by two individuals.

METHOD OF SAYING THE MARRIAGE CONTRACT FORMULA (*ṢĪGHAH*)

Ruling 2387. If the man and the woman are to say the formula of a permanent marriage themselves, then after specifying the amount of dowry (*mahr*), the woman commences by saying:

زَوَّجْتُكَ نَفْسِيْ عَلَى الصِّدَاقِ الْمَعْلُوْمِ

zawwajtuka nafsī ʿalaṣ ṣidāqil maʿlūm

I wed myself to you with the agreed-upon dowry.

After that, without there being any significant gap, the man says:

قَبِلْتُ التَّزْوِيْجَ

qabiltut tazwīj

I accept the marriage.

If this is done, the marriage contract is valid (*ṣaḥīḥ*). The marriage contract is also valid if the man simply says:

قَبِلْتُ

qabiltu

I accept.

If the man and the woman each appoint an agent to say the marriage contract formula on their behalf, and if, for example, the name of the man is Aḥmad and the name of the woman is Fāṭimah, the woman's agent says:

زَوَّجْتُ مُوَكِّلَكَ أَحْمَدَ مُوَكِّلَتِيْ فَاطِمَةَ عَلَى الصِّدَاقِ الْمَعْلُوْمِ

zawwajtu muwakkilaka aḥmad muwakkilatī fāṭimah ʿalaṣ ṣidāqil maʿlūm

I wed your client Aḥmad to my client Fāṭimah with the agreed-upon dowry.

After that, without there being any significant gap, the man's agent says:

قَبِلْتُ التَّزْوِيْجَ لِمُوَكِّلِيْ أَحْمَدَ عَلَى الصِّدَاقِ الْمَعْلُوْمِ

qabiltut tazwīja limuwakkilī aḥmad ʿalaṣ ṣidāqil maʿlūm

I accept the marriage on behalf of my client Aḥmad with the agreed-upon dowry.

If this is done, the marriage contract is valid. The recommended precaution (*al-iḥtiyāṭ al-mustaḥabb*) is that the words said by the man should be consistent with the words said by the woman. For example, if the woman uses the expression زَوَّجْتُ [*zawwajtu*], the man should respond with قَبِلْتُ التَّزْوِيجَ [*qabiltut tazwīj*] instead of قَبِلْتُ النِّكَاحَ [*qabiltun nikāḥ*].

Ruling 2388. If the man and the woman are to say the formula of a temporary marriage themselves, then after specifying the period and the amount of dowry, the woman says:

زَوَّجْتُكَ نَفْسِيْ فِي الْمُدَّةِ الْمَعْلُوْمَةِ عَلَى الْمَهْرِ الْمَعْلُوْمِ

zawwajtuka nafsī fil muddatil maʿlūmah ʿalal mahril maʿlūm

I wed myself to you for the agreed-upon period with the agreed-upon dowry.

After that, without there being any significant gap, the man says:

قَبِلْتُ

qabiltu

I accept.

If this is done, the marriage contract is valid. If the man and the woman each appoint an agent [to say the marriage contract formula on their behalf], then first the woman's agent says to the man's agent:

زَوَّجْتُ مُوَكِّلَتِيْ مُوَكِّلَكَ فِي الْمُدَّةِ الْمَعْلُوْمَةِ عَلَى الْمَهْرِ الْمَعْلُوْمِ

zawwajtu muwakkilatī muwakkilaka fil muddatil maʿlūmah ʿalal mahril maʿlūm

I wed my client to your client for the agreed-upon period with the agreed-upon dowry.

After that, without there being any significant gap, the man's agent says:

قَبِلْتُ التَّزْوِيْجَ لِمُوَكِّلِيْ هٰكَذَا

qabiltut tazwīja limuwakkilī hākadhā

I accept the marriage on behalf of my client accordingly.

If this is done, the marriage contract is valid.[2]

CONDITIONS OF A MARRIAGE CONTRACT

Ruling 2389. A marriage contract must fulfil the following conditions [for it to be valid]:

1. based on obligatory precaution, the formula must be said in Arabic. If the man or the woman is unable to say the formula

[2] Variations of the marriage formula are mentioned in *Minhāj al-Ṣāliḥīn* (vol. 3, pp. 24–26).

in Arabic, they can say it in a language other than Arabic, and it is not necessary that they appoint an agent; however, they must use words that convey the meaning of زَوَّجْتُ [*zawwajtu*] and قَبِلْتُ [*qabiltu*];

2. the man and the woman, or their agents who say the formula, must have an intention to establish (*qaṣd al-inshāʾ*) [a marriage contract], meaning that if the man and the woman say the formula themselves, when the woman says زَوَّجْتُكَ نَفْسِي [*zawwajtuka nafsī*], she must intend to make herself his wife. Similarly, when the man says قَبِلْتُ التَّزْوِيْجَ [*qabiltut tazwīj*], he must intend to accept her as his wife. If their agents say the formula, then when they say زَوَّجْتُ [*zawwajtu*] and قَبِلْتُ [*qabiltu*], they must intend for the man and the woman who have appointed them as their agents to become husband and wife;
3. the person saying the formula must be sane (*ʿāqil*). If the person is saying it for himself or herself, he/she must also be of the age of legal responsibility (*bāligh*). In fact, based on obligatory precaution, if a non-*bāligh* child who is able to discern between right and wrong (*mumayyiz*) says the formula for someone else, it is not sufficient, and the couple must get a divorce or repeat the formula;
4. if the agent of the man and woman, or their guardians (*walīs*), say the formula, then at the time of the contract, they must specify the husband and wife. For example, they must mention their names or indicate to them. Therefore, if someone who has a number of daughters says to a man, زَوَّجْتُكَ إِحْدَىٰ بَنَاتِي [*zawwajtuka iḥdā banātī*], meaning 'I wed one of my daughters to you', and the man responds by saying, قَبِلْتُ [*qabiltu*], meaning 'I accept', the marriage contract is invalid as they did not specify a particular daughter at the time of the contract;
5. the man and the woman must consent to the marriage. However, if they appear to disapprove but it is known that in their hearts they consent, the marriage contract is valid.

Ruling 2390. If one or more letters is wrongly said in the marriage contract but the meaning does not change, the contract is valid.

Ruling 2391. If a person who says the formula knows its meaning, albeit in a general way, and he intends to bring its meaning into effect, the contract is valid and it is not necessary for him to know the meaning of the formula in detail. For example, [it is not necessary for him to know] which word is a verb and which word is the subject of a verb according to the rules of Arabic grammar.

Ruling 2392. If a woman is wedded to a man without their consent and afterwards the man and the woman consent to the marriage, the marriage contract is valid. Furthermore, for their consent [to be understood], it is sufficient that they say something or do something that conveys their consent.

Ruling 2393. If a man and a woman, or one of them, is compelled to marry, and after the marriage contract has been concluded they consent to it in the manner mentioned in the previous ruling, the contract is valid. It is better, however, that the contract is concluded again.

Ruling 2394. A father or paternal grandfather can wed to someone his non-*bāligh* child/grandchild or his insane child/grandchild who has become *bāligh* while in the state of insanity. After the child becomes *bāligh* or the insane individual becomes sane, if the marriage is detrimental for them, he/she can either approve or reject it. But if such a marriage is not detrimental and he/she annuls the marriage after they become *bāligh* [or after the insane individual becomes sane], the obligatory precaution is that they must either get a divorce or conclude another marriage contract.[3]

Ruling 2395. If a girl wishes to get married and she has reached the age of legal responsibility (*bulūgh*) and is mature (*rashīdah*) – meaning that she is able to determine what is in her interest – and she is a virgin, and she is not in charge of her life's affairs, then such a girl must obtain the consent of her father or grandfather. In fact, based on obligatory precaution, even if she is in charge of her life's affairs, she must still obtain their consent. The consent of her mother or brother is not necessary.

[3] The interpretation of this ruling is based on Ruling 980 of *al-Masā'il al-Muntakhabah* (p. 362).

Ruling 2396.* If a girl is not a virgin, or if she is a virgin but her father or paternal grandfather totally prevent her from marrying every individual who is legally (*sharʿan*) and commonly considered appropriate for her, then it is not necessary for her to obtain their consent. Furthermore, if they are not at all prepared to participate in her getting married, or if they are not competent to give their consent because of insanity and suchlike, then in these cases, their consent is not necessary. Similarly, if it is not possible to get their consent because they are absent for a long time or some other reason, and if the girl has a great need to get married at that time, the consent of her father or paternal grandfather is not necessary. It is worth mentioning that this ruling is related to permanent marriage, and based on obligatory precaution, it does not include temporary marriage.

Ruling 2397. If a father or a paternal grandfather marries his non-*bāligh* son/grandson to a girl, then once he becomes *bāligh* he will have to pay for his wife's living expenses. In fact, even before he reaches *bulūgh*, if he is of an age when he is able to derive sexual pleasure and his wife is not so young that her husband cannot derive sexual pleasure from her, then in such a case, her maintenance (*nafaqah*) is his responsibility. Otherwise, maintenance is not obligatory (*wājib*) on him.

Ruling 2398. If a father or paternal grandfather marries his non-*bāligh* son/grandson to a girl, in the event that the son/grandson does not own any property at the time of the marriage contract, the father or paternal grandfather must provide his wife's dowry. The same applies if he does own some property but his father or grandfather acts as guarantor (*ḍāmin*) for the dowry. Apart from these two cases, if the dowry is not more than the standard amount given for a dowry (*mahr al-mithl*), or if a matter of primary importance necessitates that the dowry be more than the standard amount, then his father or grandfather can pay the dowry from the property of the son/grandson. Otherwise, they cannot pay more than the standard amount from his property, and it would only be valid if he accepts this after he reaches *bulūgh*.

SITUATIONS IN WHICH A MAN AND A WOMAN CAN ANNUL THE MARRIAGE CONTRACT

Ruling 2399.* If a man realises after the conclusion of the marriage contract that his wife had one of the following six defects at the time of the marriage contract, he can annul the contract:

1. insanity, albeit intermittent;
2. leprosy;
3. vitiligo;
4. blindness;
5. paralysis, albeit not to the extent of immobility;
6. the presence of flesh or bone in her uterus, whether or not that prevents sexual intercourse or becoming pregnant, or the vagina itself being sufficiently closed so as to prevent sexual intercourse. If the man realises that at the time of the contract the woman had a cloacal abnormality, meaning that her urethral opening and vagina had become one [vesicovaginal fistula], or her vagina and anus had become one [rectovaginal fistula], or all three had become one [persistent cloaca], then for the man to be able to annul the marriage contract is problematic (*maḥall al-ishkāl*) [i.e. based on obligatory precaution, he cannot annul it].[4] But in the event that he does annul it, the obligatory precaution is that he must also divorce her.

Ruling 2400. If a wife realises after the conclusion of the marriage contract that her husband does not possess a penis, or if after the conclusion of the marriage contract but before having sexual intercourse, or after it, his penis is cut off, or if he has a dysfunction whereby he is unable to have sexual intercourse even if the dysfunction develops after the marriage contract and before having sexual intercourse, or after it, then in all of these cases, the wife can annul the marriage contract without getting a divorce.

If a wife realises after the conclusion of the marriage contract that her husband was insane before the marriage contract, or if after the

[4] As mentioned in Ruling 6, the term 'problematic' (*maḥall al-ishkāl*) amounts to saying the ruling is based on obligatory precaution

conclusion of the marriage contract he becomes insane, irrespective of whether this happens after sexual intercourse or before it, or if she realises that at the time of the marriage contract his testicles had been removed or they had been crushed, or that at the time of the marriage contract he had leprosy, vitiligo, or blindness, then in all of these cases, the obligatory precaution is that she must not annul the marriage contract. But if she does, then the obligatory precaution is that if they wish to continue with their married life, they must conclude another marriage contract; and if they wish to separate, they must get a divorce.

In case a husband cannot have sexual intercourse and his wife wishes to annul the marriage contract, it is necessary that she first refer to a fully qualified jurist (*al-ḥākim al-sharʿī*) or his agent. The jurist will give the husband a one-year respite; if he is unable to have sexual intercourse with his wife or another woman during this period, his wife can annul the marriage contract once the respite period is over.

Ruling 2401. If a wife annuls the marriage contract owing to her husband's inability to have sexual intercourse, the husband must pay her half of the dowry. However, if owing to any of the other aforementioned defects the husband or the wife annul the marriage contract, in the event that they have not had sexual intercourse, the husband does not have to pay her anything. If they have had sexual intercourse, he must pay her the entire dowry.

Ruling 2402. If a woman or a man is described to the other as being better than she/he really is so that the other desires to marry her/him – irrespective of whether this happens at the time of the marriage contract or before it – then in case the marriage contract is concluded on that basis and this matter was realised by the other party after the contract, she/he can annul the marriage contract. The detailed laws (*aḥkām*) of this ruling (*masʾalah*) are explained in *Minhāj al-Ṣāliḥīn*.[5]

[5] This is al-Sayyid al-Sistani's more detailed work on Islamic law.

WOMEN WITH WHOM MARRIAGE IS UNLAWFUL (*ḤARĀM*)

Ruling 2403. It is unlawful for a man to marry women who are his *maḥram*,[6] such as his mother, sister, daughter, paternal aunt, maternal aunt, nieces, and mother-in-law.

Ruling 2404. If a person marries a woman, then even though they may not have had sexual intercourse, her mother, maternal grandmother, and paternal grandmother, however many generations they go back, become *maḥram* to him.

Ruling 2405. If a person marries a woman and has sexual intercourse with her, her daughters and granddaughters, however many generations they go forward, become *maḥram* to him, irrespective of whether they are alive at the time of the marriage contract or are born after it.

Ruling 2406. Even if a person has not had sexual intercourse with the woman he has married, as long as he is married to her, he must not marry her daughter based on obligatory precaution.

Ruling 2407. The paternal and maternal aunts of a person, and the paternal and maternal aunts of his father, and the paternal aunts of his paternal grandfather or paternal grandmother, however many generations they go back, are *maḥram* to him. Similarly, the paternal and maternal aunts of one's mother, and the paternal and maternal aunts of his maternal grandmother or maternal grandfather, however many generations they go back, are *maḥram* to him.

Ruling 2408. The father and grandfather of one's husband, however many generations they go back, and his sons and grandsons, however many generations they go forward, are all *maḥram* to her, irrespective of whether they are alive at the time of the marriage contract or are born after it.

[6] A *maḥram* is a person one is never permitted to marry on account of being related to them in a particular way, such as being their parent or sibling.

Ruling 2409. If a person marries a woman, be it in a permanent or temporary marriage, he cannot marry her sister as long as she is married to him.

Ruling 2410. If a man gives his wife a revocable divorce (*al-ṭalāq al-rijʿī*) in the manner that will be explained in the laws on divorce, he cannot marry her sister during the prescribed waiting period (*ʿiddah*). However, he can marry her sister if she is observing *ʿiddah* of an irrevocable divorce (*al-ṭalāq al-bāʾin*). And the obligatory precaution is that a man must not marry a woman who is observing *ʿiddah* of a temporary marriage.

Ruling 2411. A person cannot marry his wife's niece without her consent. However, if he contracts a marriage with his wife's niece without her consent and afterwards his wife consents to it, there is no problem.

Ruling 2412. If a woman realises that her husband has married her niece and she does not say anything about this, in the event that she consents afterwards, the marriage is valid. But if she does not consent, it is invalid.

Ruling 2413. If a person fornicates with his maternal aunt or paternal aunt before marrying the daughter of either of them, then based on obligatory precaution, he can no longer marry the daughter.

Ruling 2414. If a person marries the daughter of his paternal aunt or maternal aunt and after sexual intercourse or before it, he fornicates with her mother, it does not annul their marriage.

Ruling 2415. If a person fornicates with a woman other than his maternal or paternal aunt, the recommended precaution is that he should not marry her daughter.

Ruling 2416. A Muslim woman cannot marry a man who is a disbeliever (*kāfir*), be it in a permanent marriage or a temporary one. It makes no difference whether the man is from among the People of the

Book (*ahl al-kitāb*)[7] or not. A Muslim man cannot marry women who are disbelievers other than those from among the People of the Book. However, there is no problem if a Muslim man contracts a temporary marriage with Jewish or Christian women but, based on obligatory precaution, he must not contract a permanent marriage with them. As for Zoroastrian women, based on obligatory precaution, a Muslim man must not contract marriage with them, not even a temporary one.

A man who has a Muslim wife cannot contract marriage with women who are from among the People of the Book without his wife's permission; rather, even with her permission, it is not permitted (*jā'iz*) for him to marry them. As for those who consider themselves Muslims but are subject to the rules applicable to disbelievers, such as *nawāṣib*,[8] a Muslim man or woman cannot marry them in a permanent or temporary marriage. The same applies to marrying an apostate (*murtadd*).

Ruling 2417. If a person fornicates with a woman who is observing the *ʿiddah* of a revocable divorce, then based on obligatory precaution, that woman becomes unlawful for him [to marry]. However, if a person fornicates with a woman who is observing the *ʿiddah* of a temporary marriage, the *ʿiddah* of an irrevocable divorce, the *ʿiddah* of a widow (*wafāt*), or the *ʿiddah* of intercourse that has ensued from a mistake (*waṭ' al-shubhah*), then in all of these cases, he can marry her afterwards. The meaning of 'revocable divorce', 'irrevocable divorce', '*ʿiddah* of a temporary marriage', '*ʿiddah* of a widow', and '*ʿiddah* of intercourse that has ensued from a mistake' will be explained in the laws on divorce.

Ruling 2418. If a person fornicates with an unmarried woman who is not observing *ʿiddah*, then based on obligatory precaution, he cannot marry her before she repents. However, there is no problem if another man wishes to marry her before she repents unless she is known for fornicating, in which case, based on obligatory precaution, it is not permitted to marry her before she repents. The same applies to

[7] As mentioned in Ruling 103, the 'People of the Book' are Jews, Christians, and Zoroastrians.

[8] In Ruling 103, *nawāṣib* (pl. of *nāṣibī*) are defined as 'those who show enmity towards the Imams (ʿA)'.

a man known for fornicating [i.e. based on obligatory precaution, it is not permitted to marry him] before he repents. Furthermore, the recommended precaution is that if a man wishes to marry a woman who commits fornication, whether he fornicated with her or not, he should wait until she menstruates and then marry her.

Ruling 2419. If a man marries a woman who is observing the *ʿiddah* of her marriage to another man, in the event that both or one of them knew that her *ʿiddah* was not yet over and they knew that marrying a woman who is observing *ʿiddah* is unlawful, the woman becomes unlawful for him forever even if they did not have sexual intercourse after getting married. If they were ignorant about what *ʿiddah* is or it being unlawful to marry a woman who is observing *ʿiddah*, then the marriage contract is invalid. Furthermore, if they have had sexual intercourse, it is forever unlawful [for them to get married to each other]; otherwise, it is not unlawful and they can get married again once the *ʿiddah* is over.

Ruling 2420.* If it is established for a man that a woman is married, and he knows it is unlawful to marry a married woman but marries her anyway, he must separate from her and not ever marry her again. If he was ignorant of either matter – i.e. the subject (*mawḍūʿ*) [the woman being married] or the rule (*ḥukm*) [of it being unlawful to marry a married woman] – then the marriage contract is invalid but the woman does not become unlawful for him forever, provided they did not have sexual intercourse. If he did not know she was married and had sexual intercourse with her after getting married to her, then based on obligatory precaution, she becomes unlawful for him forever.

Ruling 2421. If a married woman commits adultery, then based on obligatory precaution, she becomes unlawful forever for the adulterous man. However, she does not become unlawful for her husband. In the event that she does not repent and persists in committing adultery, it is better for her husband to divorce her, although he still has to give her dowry to her.

Ruling 2422. If a woman who is divorced – or if a woman who was a temporary wife and who was given the remaining marriage period by her husband, or whose marriage period came to an end – marries again after some time but then doubts whether or not the *ʿiddah* of her first husband had finished when she married her second husband, such a woman must not heed her doubt.

Ruling 2423. The mother, sister, and daughter of a boy who has been sodomised are unlawful for the one who sodomised him if the latter was *bāligh*, even if the extent of penetration was less than the circumcised part of the penis. The same applies, based on obligatory precaution, if the one who was sodomised was a man [i.e. *bāligh*] or the one who sodomised him was not *bāligh*. However, if he merely supposes (i.e. has *ẓann*) that penetration occurred, or he doubts whether or not penetration occurred, then they are not unlawful for him. Furthermore, the mother, sister, and daughter of the one who sodomised are not unlawful for the one who was sodomised.

Ruling 2424. If a person marries a woman and after marrying her sodomises her father, brother, or son, then based on obligatory precaution, she becomes unlawful for him.

Ruling 2425. If a person marries a woman while he is in the state of *iḥrām* (*iḥrām* is one of the requirements of hajj),[9] the marriage contract is invalid even if the woman is not in the state of *iḥrām* herself. In the event that he knew that marrying a woman [in the state of *iḥrām*] was unlawful for him, he can never marry that woman.

Ruling 2426. If a woman marries a man while she is in the state of *iḥrām*, the marriage contract is invalid even if the man is not in the state of *iḥrām* himself. In the event that the woman knew that getting married while in the state of *iḥrām* is unlawful, the obligatory precaution is that she must never marry that man.

Ruling 2427. If a man or a woman does not perform *ṭawāf al-nisāʾ*,[10] which is one of the rituals of hajj and *al-ʿumrah al-mufradah*,[11] then

[9] *Iḥrām* here refers to the state of ritual consecration of pilgrims during hajj and *ʿumrah*.

[10] This is an obligatory circumambulation (*ṭawāf*) of the Kaʿbah that is performed as part of the hajj rituals.

[11] *Al-ʿumrah al-mufradah* refers to the recommended pilgrimage to Mecca that is performed independently of hajj at any time of the year.

sexual activity is not lawful for them until they perform *ṭawāf al-nisāʾ*. However, if they marry, then in the event that they had performed *ḥalq*[12] or *taqṣīr*[13] and come out of the state of *iḥrām*, their marriage is valid even if they have not performed *ṭawāf al-nisāʾ*.

Ruling 2428. If a person marries a non-*bālighah* girl, it is unlawful for him to have sexual intercourse with her until she has completed nine lunar years. However, if he does have sexual intercourse with her before then, it will not be unlawful for him to have sexual intercourse with her after she reaches *bulūgh* even if she has developed a cloacal abnormality (the meaning of which was explained in Ruling 2399). If she has developed a cloacal abnormality, he must pay her blood money (*diyah*), which is equivalent to the blood money for killing a human being. He must also pay for her living expenses forever, even after divorce. In fact, based on obligatory precaution, even if that girl marries someone else after getting divorced [he must still pay for her living expenses].

Ruling 2429. A woman who has been divorced three times – having returned to her husband twice or having again contracted marriage with him twice in between those three divorces – becomes unlawful for her husband. However, if she marries another man according to the conditions that will be mentioned in the laws on divorce, her first husband can marry her again after the second husband dies or divorces her and after her *ʿiddah* finishes.

LAWS OF PERMANENT MARRIAGE

Ruling 2430. It is unlawful for a woman in a permanent marriage to leave the house without the permission of her husband even if this does not infringe on his rights, except in the following cases: [i] a necessity requires her to; [ii] staying in the house causes her hardship (*ḥaraj*); [iii] the house is not appropriate for her. Also, she must submit to giving her husband sexual pleasure, which is his

[12] *Ḥalq* is the shaving of the head performed by men as part of the hajj rituals.

[13] *Taqṣīr* refers to snipping one's hair or trimming one's beard or moustache as part of the hajj and *ʿumrah* rituals.

right, whenever he wishes, and she must not prevent him from having sexual intercourse with her without a legitimate excuse (*ʿudhr*). It is obligatory for a husband to provide his wife with food, clothing, housing, and other things she needs. If he does not provide these for her, irrespective of whether he is able to or not, he will be indebted to her. Furthermore, one of the rights of a wife is that her husband must not subject her to harassment or abuse, and he must not treat her harshly or roughly without a legitimate reason.

Ruling 2431. If a woman does not perform any of her marital duties towards her husband, she has no right over him for food, clothing, and housing, even if she continues to live with him. If she sometimes refuses to submit to her husband's legitimate sexual wants, then based on obligatory precaution, he is not exempted from providing her with her maintenance. As for her dowry, if she does not perform her duties, he is in no way exempted [from owing it to her].

Ruling 2432. A man has no right to compel his wife to do housework.

Ruling 2433. If a wife's living expenses when she is outside her home town (*waṭan*) are more than when she is in her home town, in the event that she travels to that place with the permission of her husband, her living expenses must be borne by her husband. However, the costs of travelling by car, plane, and suchlike, and other expenses necessary for her travel, must be borne by herself. If a husband wants his wife to travel, he must pay for her travel expenses. The same applies if travelling is necessary for her, such as travelling for medical treatment.

Ruling 2434. If a wife's living expenses are borne by her husband but he does not pay for them, she can take her living expenses from his property without his consent. If this is not possible, in the event that she cannot complain to a fully qualified jurist about this and has no option but to work to meet her living expenses, then while she is working to meet her living expenses, it is not obligatory for her to obey her husband [in those matters that are normally obligatory for her to obey him].

Ruling 2435. If, for example, a man has two permanent wives and he stays with one of them one night, it is obligatory for him to also stay with his other wife one in every four nights. Apart from this case, it is not obligatory for him to stay with his wife. However, it is necessary that he does not totally abandon her, and the more precautious and more preferred (*al-aḥwaṭ al-awlā*) [juristic opinion][14] is that a husband should stay with his permanent wife one in every four nights.

Ruling 2436. A husband cannot refrain from having sexual intercourse with a young wife of his for more than four months unless sexual intercourse is harmful or excessively difficult (*mashaqqah*) for him, or the wife consents to it, or he had stipulated a condition in the marriage contract regarding this. There is no difference in this rule, based on obligatory precaution, whether the husband is in his home town or not. Therefore, based on obligatory precaution, it is not permitted for a husband to continue on a non-essential trip for more than four months without a legitimate excuse and without his wife's permission.

Ruling 2437. If in a permanent marriage contract the parties do not specify the dowry, the contract is valid. [If the dowry is not specified, then] in the event that the husband has sexual intercourse with his wife, he must pay her a dowry that women like her usually receive. As for temporary marriage, in the event that the parties do not specify the dowry – even if that be due to ignorance, negligence, or forgetfulness – the marriage contract is invalid.

Ruling 2438. If at the time of concluding a permanent marriage contract a period is not specified for giving the dowry, the wife can refuse to have sexual intercourse with her husband before receiving the dowry, irrespective of whether her husband is able to pay the dowry or not. However, if she consents to have sexual intercourse before receiving the dowry and her husband has sexual intercourse with her, she can no longer refuse to have sexual intercourse with him without a legitimate excuse.

[14] For practical purposes, a 'more precautious and more preferred' juristic opinion is equivalent to recommended precaution.

LAWS OF TEMPORARY MARRIAGE (*MUTʿAH*)

Ruling 2439. A temporary marriage that is not for the purpose of deriving sexual pleasure is valid. However, the woman cannot stipulate a condition that the man must not derive any sexual pleasure.

Ruling 2440. The obligatory precaution is that a husband must not avoid having sexual intercourse for more than four months with his temporary wife if she is young.

Ruling 2441. If a woman in a temporary marriage stipulates a condition in the marriage contract that her husband must not have sexual intercourse with her, the contract and the condition are valid. In such a case, the husband can only derive other forms of sexual pleasure from her. However, if she later consents to have sexual intercourse, her husband can have sexual intercourse with her. The same rule applies in a permanent marriage.

Ruling 2442. A temporary wife is not entitled to living expenses [to be paid for by the husband] even if she becomes pregnant.

Ruling 2443. A temporary wife is not entitled to the right of sleeping together [i.e. the right that was mentioned in Ruling 2435]. She does not inherit from her husband, nor does her husband inherit from her. In the event that one or both of them stipulate a condition [in the marriage contract] that they will inherit [from the other/each other], then the validity of this condition is problematic, but observing precaution (*iḥtiyāṭ*) here must not be abandoned.

Ruling 2444. Even if a woman in a temporary marriage does not know she is not entitled to the right of having her living expenses paid for and the right of sleeping together, the marriage contract is valid. Her ignorance of this does not grant her a right over her husband.

Ruling 2445. A woman in a temporary marriage can leave the house without her husband's permission. However, if the act of leaving the house violates her husband's right, then it is unlawful for her to leave the house. And based on recommended precaution, in case the husband's right is not violated, she should not leave the house without his permission.

Ruling 2446. If a woman appoints a man to be her agent for marrying her to himself for a specified period and a specified amount, and the man marries her to himself in a permanent marriage, or he marries her for a period or an amount that is different to what was specified, then, if the woman consents upon realising this, the marriage contract is valid; otherwise, it is invalid.

Ruling 2447. If in order to become *maḥram*, a father or a paternal grandfather marries his non-*bāligh* daughter/granddaughter or son/grandson to someone for a short period, the marriage contract is valid as long as it is not detrimental. However, if during the period of the marriage the boy is totally unable to derive sexual pleasure, or no sexual pleasure can be derived from the girl, then the validity of the marriage contract is problematic [i.e. based on obligatory precaution, it is not valid].

Ruling 2448. If a father or paternal grandfather of a child who resides in a different place marries the child to someone to become *maḥram* [to that person], not knowing whether the child is alive or not, then, if the marriage period is such that it is possible for the boy to derive sexual pleasure from the girl during it, what is apparent (*ẓāhir*)[15] is that they become *maḥram*. However, if it is later realised that the girl was in fact dead at the time of the marriage contract, then the contract is void and the persons who had apparently become *maḥram* will be non-*maḥram*.

Ruling 2449. If a man gives his wife the remaining period of the marriage, in the event that he had sexual intercourse with her, he must give her all the dowry that he had agreed to give her. However, if he did not have sexual intercourse with her, it is obligatory for him to give her half of it.

Ruling 2450. If a man has a temporary wife whose *ʿiddah* has not

[15] For practical purposes in jurisprudential rulings, expressing an 'apparent' ruling equates to giving a fatwa.

yet finished, he can contract a permanent marriage with her or marry her again in a temporary marriage. However, if the period of the temporary marriage has not yet finished and he contracts a permanent marriage, the marriage contract is invalid unless he first gives her the remaining period and then contracts the permanent marriage.

LOOKING AT NON-*MAḤRAM*

Ruling 2451. It is unlawful for a man to look at the body or hair of non-*maḥram* [Muslim] women, be it with lust or without lust, with fear of sinning or without such a fear. As for looking at the face and hands up to the wrists of non-*maḥram* women, if it is with lust or there is a fear of sinning, it too is unlawful. In fact, the recommended precaution is that a man should not look at these areas even if it is not with lust and there is no fear of sinning. Furthermore, it is unlawful for a woman to look at the body of a non-*maḥram* man with lust or if there is a fear of sinning. In fact, based on obligatory precaution, a woman must not look at these areas even if it is not with lust and there is no fear of sinning. However, there is no problem for a woman to look at those areas of the body that men usually do not cover – such as the head, hands, and feet – if it is not with lust and there is no fear of sinning.

Ruling 2452. With regard to a *mubtadhilah*[16] woman who does not take heed if someone enjoins her to observe hijab, there is no problem in looking at her on condition that it is not with lust and there is no fear of sinning. In this rule, there is no difference between disbelieving women and other women. Likewise, there is no difference between looking at their hands and face and other areas of their body which they usually do not cover.

Ruling 2453. A woman must cover her hair and body, apart from her face and hands, from a non-*maḥram* man. And the obligatory

[16] *Mubtadhilah* is a term used to refer to a woman who does not observe hijab in front of non-*maḥram* men and does not take heed when she is forbidden from continuing with this behaviour.

precaution is that she must also cover her body and hair from a non-*bāligh* boy who understands good and bad if she deems it probable that him looking at the body of a woman would arouse lustful desires. However, a woman can keep her face and hands up to the wrists uncovered from a non-*maḥram* man unless she fears he would fall into sin or she has the intention of making him look at something unlawful; in these two cases, covering those areas as well is obligatory for her.

Ruling 2454. Looking at the private parts of a Muslim who is *bāligh* is unlawful even from behind glass, in a mirror, in clear water, and suchlike. The same applies to looking at the private parts of a disbeliever and a non-*bāligh* child who understands good and bad. However, a husband and wife can look at each other's entire body.

Ruling 2455. A man and a woman who are *maḥram* to each other can look at each other's entire body, except the private parts, if they do not have the intention of deriving pleasure and there is no fear of sinning.

Ruling 2456. A man must not look at the body of another man with the intention of deriving pleasure. It is also unlawful for a woman to look at another woman's body with the intention of deriving pleasure. The same applies [i.e. it is unlawful for a man/woman to look at the body of another man/woman] if there is fear of sinning.

Ruling 2457. If a man knows a non-*maḥram* woman and that woman is not *mubtadhilah*, then based on obligatory precaution, he must not look at a photo of her. However, it is permitted for him to look at her face and hands without the intention of deriving pleasure and there is no fear of sinning.

Ruling 2458. If it becomes necessary for a woman to administer an enema to another woman or a man other than her husband, or to wash her/his private parts, she must wear something on her hands so that they do not come into direct contact with her/his private parts. The same applies if it becomes necessary for a man to administer an enema to another man or a woman other than his wife, or to wash his/her private parts.

Ruling 2459. If a woman is compelled to have medical treatment and a non-*maḥram* man is better placed to administer the treatment, she can refer to a non-*maḥram* man for the treatment. In the event that the man is compelled to look at her and touch her body for administering the treatment, there is no problem. However, if he is able to treat her by only looking at her [and not touch her body], he must not touch her body. Similarly, if he is able to treat her by only touching her, then he must not look at her.

Ruling 2460. If a person is compelled to look at someone's private parts to treat him, then based on obligatory precaution, he must place a mirror opposite [the person's private parts] and look [at his private parts] through the mirror. However, if there is no other way but to look directly at his private parts, there is no problem. The same applies [i.e. there is no problem] if it would be quicker to look directly at the private parts rather than look at them through a mirror.

MISCELLANEOUS RULINGS ON MARRIAGE

Ruling 2461. It is obligatory for someone who falls into sin on account of not having a wife to get married.

Ruling 2462. If a husband stipulates a condition in the marriage contract that his wife must be a virgin but after concluding the marriage he realises that she is not a virgin, he can annul the marriage contract. However, if he does not annul it or he did not make such a stipulation in the marriage contract but married her on the belief that she was a virgin, he can take into account the percentage difference between the standard amount given for a dowry (*mahr al-mithl*) of a virgin woman and that of a non-virgin woman and deduct that percentage difference from the dowry agreed by them; and if he has already given the dowry to her, he can take it back. For example, if her dowry is £1,000 and the dowry of a woman like her, if she is a virgin, is [usually] £800, and if she is not a virgin, it is [usually] £600, which is a difference of 25%, this percentage difference can be deducted from the £1,000 dowry of the woman [and so her dowry would be £750].

Ruling 2463. It is unlawful for a man and a non-*maḥram* woman to remain together in a secluded place where no one else is present in the event that an immoral act taking place is deemed probable, even if the place is such that someone else could enter. However, if an immoral act taking place is not deemed probable, then there is no problem.

Ruling 2464. If a man specifies a woman's dowry in the marriage contract but he does not have the intention to give it, the marriage contract is valid. However, the man must give the dowry.

Ruling 2465. A Muslim who leaves the religion of Islam and chooses to be a disbeliever is called an 'apostate' (*murtadd*). There are two types of apostates:

1. '*fiṭrī*': this is someone whose father and mother, or one of them, were Muslim when he was born, and after he was able to discern between right and wrong (*tamyīz*), he remained a Muslim, and after that he became a disbeliever.
2. '*millī*': this is someone who is the opposite [of a *fiṭrī* apostate; i.e. it refers to someone whose father and mother were disbelievers when he was born, and after he was able to discern between right and wrong, he became a Muslim, and after that he became a disbeliever].

Ruling 2466. If after the conclusion of a marriage contract a woman becomes apostate, whether that be *millī* or *fiṭrī*, her marriage contract becomes void. In the event that her husband has not had sexual intercourse with her, she does not have to observe *ʿiddah*. The same applies if she becomes apostate after sexual intercourse but she is postmenopausal (*yāʾisah*) [as defined below] or a minor (*ṣaghīrah*). However, if she is of the age of women who experience menstruation (*ḥayḍ*), she must observe *ʿiddah* according to the instructions that will be mentioned in the laws on divorce. If she reverts to Islam within the *ʿiddah* period, the marriage contract will remain as it is, although it is better that if the couple wish to live together they should contract a marriage again, and if they wish to separate they should get a divorce. A postmenopausal woman in this ruling is a woman who has reached the age of fifty, and due to her advanced age, she does not experience *ḥayḍ* and has no expectation of experiencing it again.

Ruling 2467. If a man becomes a *fiṭrī* apostate after marriage, his wife becomes unlawful for him. If they have had sexual intercourse and she is neither postmenopausal nor a minor, she must observe the *ʿiddah* of a widow, which will be explained in the rulings on divorce. In fact, based on obligatory precaution, if they have not had sexual intercourse or she is postmenopausal or a minor, she must still observe the *ʿiddah* of a widow. If the man repents within the *ʿiddah* period, then based on obligatory precaution, if the couple wish to live together, they must contract a marriage again, and if they wish to separate, they must get a divorce.

Ruling 2468. If after the conclusion of a marriage contract a man becomes a *millī* apostate, in the event that he has not had sexual intercourse with his wife or his wife is postmenopausal or a minor, the marriage contract becomes void and the woman does not have to observe *ʿiddah*. If he becomes apostate after sexual intercourse and his wife is the age of women who experience *ḥayḍ*, the woman must observe the *ʿiddah* of a divorce, which will be explained in the laws on divorce. Furthermore, if the man reverts to Islam before the completion of the *ʿiddah*, the marriage contract remains as it is.

Ruling 2469. If a woman stipulates a condition in the marriage contract that the man must not take her out of a particular city and the man accepts the condition, then he must not take her out of the city without her consent.

Ruling 2470. If a woman has a daughter from her previous husband, her subsequent husband may marry his son – if he was not born to the same woman – to that daughter. Also, if a man marries his son to a girl, he can marry the girl's mother.

Ruling 2471. It is not permitted to abort a foetus even if a woman becomes pregnant through fornication unless the foetus remaining [in the mother's womb] causes the mother harm or excessive difficulty. In such a case, it is permitted to abort the foetus before the soul has entered it, but [if this is done, then] blood money (*diyah*) must be paid. Aborting a foetus after the soul has entered it is not permitted even if, based on obligatory precaution, it causes the mother excessive difficulty or harm.

Ruling 2472. If a person fornicates with a woman who is neither married nor observing the *ʿiddah* of her marriage to another man, in the event that he marries her afterwards and a child is born to them and they do not know if the child was conceived out of legal wedlock or not, the child is regarded as being of legitimate birth.

Ruling 2473. If a man does not know that a woman is observing *ʿiddah* and he marries her, in the event that the woman did not know either and a child is born to them, he is regarded as being of legitimate birth and is legally the child of both of them. However, if the woman knew that she was observing *ʿiddah* and that marrying while observing *ʿiddah* is not legally permitted, then he is the child of the father. In each case, the marriage contract is void, and as previously explained, the man and the woman are forever unlawful for each other.

Ruling 2474. If a woman says she is postmenopausal, her word must not be accepted. However, if she says she does not have a husband, her word is to be accepted unless she is suspected to be someone whose word in this case cannot be accepted, in which case the obligatory precaution is that investigations must be made about her situation.

Ruling 2475. If a woman says she is not married and subsequently a man marries her, and after that someone claims that the woman is his wife, in the event that the person's claim is not legally established to be correct (*ṣaḥīḥ*), his word must not be accepted.

Ruling 2476.* A father cannot separate a son or daughter from his/her mother before he/she completes two years of age, because looking after a child [up to the age of two] is a right that is shared between the father and the mother. The recommended precaution is that a child should not be separated from his mother until he completes seven years of age; in fact, if separating the child would be harmful for him, it is not permitted.

Ruling 2477. If a marriage proposal is received from a person whose religiosity and morals are approved, it is better not to reject it. It has been reported from the Most Noble Messenger (Ṣ) that he said, 'Whenever a proposal for your daughter arrives from a person whose morals and religiosity you approve, then marry your daughter to him. If you do not do this, great discord and immorality will arise on the earth.'

Ruling 2478. If a wife arrives at a settlement (*ṣulḥ*) with her husband that she renounces her dowry in exchange for him not marrying another woman, it is obligatory for him not to marry another woman. Furthermore, the wife has no right to claim her dowry back.

Ruling 2479. If a person is born from fornication, later marries, and has a child, the child is considered to be of legitimate birth.

Ruling 2480. If a man has sexual intercourse with his wife [while fasting] in the month of Ramadan or when she is in the state of *ḥayḍ*, he will have sinned. However, if a child is born to them, the child is considered to be of legitimate birth.

Ruling 2481. If a wife is certain (i.e. she has *yaqīn*) that her husband has died on a journey, and after the completion of the *ʿiddah* of a widow – the duration of which will be explained in the rulings on divorce – she marries another man, and then her first husband returns from his journey, then in such a case, she must separate from her second husband and she will be considered lawful for her first husband. However, if her second husband had sexual intercourse with her, she must observe the *ʿiddah* of intercourse that has ensued from a mistake, which is the same length of time as the *ʿiddah* of divorce. During her *ʿiddah*, her first husband must not have sexual intercourse with her but he is permitted to derive other forms of sexual pleasure from her. Furthermore, her maintenance is the responsibility of her first husband, and her second husband must give her a dowry that is accordant with the dowry of women like her.

CHAPTER TWENTY-EIGHT

Breastfeeding

Ruling 2482. If a woman breastfeeds a child and fulfils the conditions that will be stated in Ruling 2492, the child becomes *maḥram*[1] to the women mentioned below if the child is a boy, or to the men mentioned below if the child is a girl:

1. the woman herself; she is called the 'nursing mother' (*murḍiʿah*);
2. the nursing mother's husband to whom the milk is related;[2] he is called the 'nursing father' (*ṣāḥib al-laban*);
3. the father and mother of the nursing mother [and her grandparents], however many generations they go back, even if they are her nursing mother and father [or her nursing grandparents];
4. the children who have been born to the nursing mother or who will be born in the future;
5. the offspring of the woman's biological children, however many generations they go forward, whether they [i.e. the offspring of the other generations] are their biological children or their nursing children;
6. the sisters and brothers of the nursing mother, even if they are nursing sisters and brothers, meaning that they have become sisters and brothers of the nursing mother due to having been breastfed by the same woman;
7. the paternal uncles and the paternal aunts of the nursing mother, even if they are nursing paternal uncles and paternal aunts;
8. the maternal uncles and the maternal aunts of the nursing mother, even if they are nursing maternal uncles and maternal aunts;
9. the offspring of the nursing mother's husband to whom the milk is related [i.e. the nursing father], however many generations they go forward, even if they are his nursing offspring;
10. the father and mother of the nursing father [and his grandparents], however many generations they go back;
11. the sisters and brothers of the nursing father, even if they are his nursing sisters and brothers;

[1] A *maḥram* is a person one is never permitted to marry on account of being related to them in a particular way, such as being their parent or sibling.

[2] The phrase 'to whom the milk is related' and its variations refer to the man with whom the woman had sexual intercourse which resulted in her having milk.

12. the paternal uncles and the paternal aunts and the maternal uncles and the maternal aunts of the nursing father, however many generations they go back, even if they are his nursing uncles and aunts.

Some other people also become *maḥram* on account of breastfeeding, as will be explained in the subsequent rulings.

Ruling 2483. If a woman breastfeeds a child and fulfils the conditions that will be mentioned in Ruling 2492, the father of that child cannot marry the woman's biological daughters. In the event that one of them is presently his wife, the marriage contract becomes invalid (*bāṭil*). However, it is permitted (*jā'iz*) for him to marry her nursing daughters, although the recommended precaution (*al-iḥtiyāṭ al-mustaḥabb*) is that he should not marry them. Furthermore, he cannot, based on obligatory precaution (*al-iḥtiyāṭ al-wājib*), marry the biological and nursing daughters of the nursing father. In the event that one of them is presently his wife, then based on obligatory precaution, the marriage contract becomes invalid.

Ruling 2484. If a woman breastfeeds a child and fulfils the conditions that will be mentioned in Ruling 2492, the nursing father does not become *maḥram* to the sisters of that child. Furthermore, the nursing father's relatives do not become *maḥram* to the child's sisters and brothers.

Ruling 2485. If a woman breastfeeds a child, she does not become *maḥram* to the child's brothers. Furthermore, the woman's relatives do not become *maḥram* to the breastfed child's sisters and brothers.

Ruling 2486. If a man marries a woman who has fully breastfed a girl and has sexual intercourse with the woman, he can no longer marry the girl.

Ruling 2487. If a man marries a girl, he can no longer marry the woman who fully breastfed her as a girl.

Ruling 2488. A man cannot marry a girl who has been fully breastfed by his mother or grandmother. And if his father's wife nurses a girl from the milk that is related to his father, he cannot marry that girl. Furthermore, in the event that a man contracts a marriage with a breastfeeding girl and after that his mother, his grandmother, or his father's wife breastfeeds the girl, the marriage contract becomes void (*bāṭil*).

Ruling 2489. A man cannot marry a girl who has been fully breastfed by his sister or his brother's wife from the milk that is related to his brother. The same applies if the girl is breastfed by the man's niece, his sister's granddaughter, or his brother's granddaughter.

Ruling 2490. If a woman fully breastfeeds her daughter's child, the daughter becomes unlawful (*ḥarām*) for her own husband. The same applies if she breastfeeds the child of her daughter's husband from another woman. However, if a woman breastfeeds her son's child, her son's wife – who is the mother of that breastfeeding child – does not become unlawful for her husband.

Ruling 2491. If the wife of the father of a girl breastfeeds the child of the girl's husband with the milk that is related to the girl's father, then based on the precaution mentioned in Ruling 2483, the girl becomes unlawful for her husband, irrespective of whether the child is the child of the same girl or some other woman.

CONDITIONS FOR BREASTFEEDING TO CAUSE SOMEONE TO BECOME *MAḤRAM*

Ruling 2492. Eight conditions must be fulfilled for breastfeeding to cause someone to become *maḥram*:

1. a child must breastfeed the milk of a woman who is alive. Therefore, if a child breastfeeds some of the required amount of milk from the breasts of a dead woman, it is of no use [i.e. the child does not become *maḥram*];
2. The woman's milk must be from a legitimate birth, even if [the conception of the child was] from intercourse that ensued from a mistake (*waṭ' al-shubhah*). Therefore, if, supposedly, a woman

produces milk without giving birth, or the milk of a child that was born from fornication is given to another child, the latter does not become *maḥram* to anyone;

3. the child suckles the milk from the breasts of the woman. Therefore, if the milk is poured into the child's mouth, it has no effect;
4. the milk must be pure and not be mixed with anything;
5. the amount of milk required for someone to become *maḥram* must all be related to one husband. Therefore, if a nursing mother is divorced and then marries another man and becomes pregnant by him, and until she gives birth the milk that she has from her first husband remains [in her body], and, for example, before giving birth she breastfeeds the child eight times with the milk that is related to the first husband, and after giving birth she breastfeeds the child seven times with the milk that is related to the second husband, then in such a case, the child does not become *maḥram* to anyone;
6. the child must not vomit the milk. If he does, it has no effect;
7. the child must be breastfed to the extent that his bones become firm by the milk, and the milk has made the flesh of his body grow. If it is not known whether the child has been breastfed to this extent or not, in the event that the child breastfeeds to his fill for one day and one night or fifteen times in accordance with the next ruling, it is sufficient. However, if it is known that the milk has not had an effect on making the bones firm and growing the flesh of the child's body, even though the child breastfed for one day and one night or fifteen times, then obligatory precaution must be observed; i.e. in such a case, the child must not marry [those who would become *maḥram* to him by means of breastfeeding], nor must he look at them as *maḥrams* would;
8. the child has not completed two years of age. If he is breastfed after he completes two years, he does not become *maḥram* to anyone. In fact, if, for example, before he completes two years he is breastfed eight times and after that he is breastfed seven times, he does not become *maḥram* to anyone. However, in the event that more than two years pass from the time a woman gives birth and she still carries milk, then, if she breastfeeds a child, this child becomes *maḥram* to those who were mentioned above.

Ruling 2493. It is clear from the previous ruling that the amount of milk that causes someone to become *maḥram* is based on three possible criteria:

1. [based on the amount that is suckled if] it is to the extent that it can commonly be said to have caused the flesh to grow and the bones to become firm. The condition here is that [the flesh growing and bones becoming firm] is based on the milk, not on food that is fed with the milk. However, a small amount of food that does not have an effect is no problem. If the child breastfeeds from two women and [a particular] amount of the growth of flesh or firming of bones is based on the milk of one of them and [a particular] amount based on [the milk of] the other, then both of them will be the child's nursing mothers. But if the growth of flesh or firming of bones [in general] is based on the milk of both of them together, then it does not result in the child becoming *maḥram*;
2. based on time. The condition here is that the child does not breastfeed from another woman or eat any food during the one day and night period. However, there is no problem if the child drinks water, takes some medicine, or eats some food to the extent that he cannot be said to have 'eaten food within [the one day and night period]'. Furthermore, the child must have regularly drank milk during the day and night when he needed or wanted to and was not delayed in doing so. In fact, based on obligatory precaution, the start of the day and night period must be counted from the time the child was hungry, and the end of the period must be considered the time he became full;
3. based on number. The condition here is that the child must suckle the milk of one woman fifteen times, and between those times he must not suckle from another woman. However, there is no problem if he eats some food or an interval occurs in between those fifteen times. Furthermore, each time the child breastfeeds, he must do so fully, meaning that he must go from being hungry to becoming completely full without an interval. However, there is no problem if while the child suckles he takes new breaths or stops a little such that from the time he puts the nipple in his mouth to when he becomes full, it can be counted as one go.

Ruling 2494. If a woman breastfeeds a child from the milk that is related to her husband and later marries another man and then breastfeeds another child from the milk that is related to her second husband, the two children do not become *maḥram* to each other.

Ruling 2495. If a woman breastfeeds a number of children with the milk that is related to one husband, all of them become *maḥram* to one another as well as to the husband and the woman who breastfed them.

Ruling 2496. If a person has a number of wives and all of them breastfeed a child and fulfil the conditions mentioned previously, then all of the children become *maḥram* to one another as well as to the man and all the women.

Ruling 2497. If a person has two nursing mothers and, for example, one of them breastfeeds a child eight times and the other breastfeeds him seven times, the child does not become *maḥram* to anyone.

Ruling 2498. If a woman fully breastfeeds a boy and a girl from the milk that is related to one husband, then the brothers and sisters of the girl do not become *maḥram* to the brothers and sisters of the boy.

Ruling 2499. A man cannot marry women who have become his wife's nieces through breastfeeding without his wife's permission. Furthermore, if a man sodomises a boy who is not of the age of legal responsibility (*bāligh*), he cannot marry the boy's nursing daughter, sister, mother, or grandmother, i.e. those who are his daughter, sister, mother, or grandmother through breastfeeding. The same applies, based on obligatory precaution, if the sodomiser is not *bāligh* or the sodomised individual is *bāligh*.

Ruling 2500. A woman who has breastfed a man's brother does not become *maḥram* to that man.

Ruling 2501. A man cannot marry two sisters, even if they are nursing sisters, meaning that they are sisters to each other through breastfeeding. In the event that he marries two sisters and later realises that they are sisters, then, if the marriage contracts were concluded at the same time, both marriage contracts are void. However, if they were not concluded at the same time, the marriage contract of the first is valid (*ṣaḥīḥ*) and the marriage contract of the second is void.

Ruling 2502. If a woman breastfeeds any of the people listed below with the milk that is related to her husband, her husband does not become unlawful for the woman:

1. her brothers and sisters;
2. her paternal and maternal uncles and aunts and their offspring;
3. her grandchildren, although if she were to breastfeed her daughter's child, it would cause her daughter to become unlawful for her own husband;[3]
4. her nephews and nieces;
5. her husband's brothers and sisters;
6. her husband's nephews and nieces;
7. her husband's paternal and maternal uncles and aunts;
8. her husband's grandchildren from his other wives.

Ruling 2503. If a woman breastfeeds the daughter of a man's paternal or maternal aunt, she does not become *maḥram* to him.

Ruling 2504. If a man has two wives and one of them breastfeeds the child of the other wife's paternal uncle, then the wife whose paternal uncle's child breastfed the milk does not become unlawful for her husband.

ETIQUETTES OF BREASTFEEDING

Ruling 2505. The initial right to breastfeed a child belongs to the child's mother. The father does not have the right to give the child to another woman [to breastfeed him] unless the mother wants a wage for breastfeeding the child and the father finds a wet nurse who does it free of charge or for a lower wage. In this case, the father can entrust the child to the wet nurse [to breastfeed him]. Afterwards, if the mother does not accept this and wishes to breastfeed the child herself, she cannot claim a wage from him.

[3] See Ruling 2490.

Ruling 2506. It is recommended (*mustaḥabb*) that a wet nurse who is chosen to breastfeed a child be Muslim, sane (*ʿāqilah*), and possess admirable physical, mental, and moral qualities. It is not befitting to choose a wet nurse who is a disbeliever (*kāfirah*), feeble-minded, aged, or bad looking. And it is disapproved (*makrūh*) to choose a wet nurse of illegitimate birth or whose milk is the result of a child born from fornication.

MISCELLANEOUS RULINGS ON BREASTFEEDING

Ruling 2507. It is better that a woman does not breastfeed every child because it is possible that she may forget whom she has breastfed, and afterwards, [as a result,] two persons who are *maḥram* to each other may get married to each other.

Ruling 2508. It is recommended to breastfeed a child for twenty-one complete months, and it is not befitting to breastfeed a child for more than two years.

Ruling 2509. If a man's rights are violated due to his wife breastfeeding someone else's child, his wife cannot breastfeed the child without his permission.

Ruling 2510. If a woman's husband marries a girl who is being breastfed and his [first] wife breastfeeds the girl, then based on obligatory precaution, the woman becomes forever unlawful for him, and as a precautionary measure, he must divorce the woman and never marry her again. If the milk is related to him, the girl who is being breastfed also becomes forever unlawful for him. If the milk is related to the woman's previous husband, then the marriage contract is invalid based on obligatory precaution.

Ruling 2511. If someone wants his brother's wife to become *maḥram* to him, some [jurists (*fuqahāʾ*)] have said that he must contract a temporary marriage (*mutʿah*) with a breastfeeding girl for two days, for example, and in those two days – while fulfilling the conditions that were mentioned in Ruling 2492 – his brother's wife must breastfeed the girl so that she becomes the nursing mother of his wife. However, if the brother's wife breastfeeds the girl with the milk that is related to the brother, this rule (*ḥukm*) is problematic (*maḥall al-ishkāl*) [i.e. based on obligatory precaution, the rule is not established in this case].[4]

Ruling 2512. If before a man marries a woman he says that through breastfeeding she is unlawful for him – for example, he says he has breastfed the milk of her mother – then in the event that it is possible to substantiate his statement, he cannot marry the woman. If he says this after the conclusion of the marriage contract and the woman accepts his statement, the marriage contract is void. Therefore, if the man has not had sexual intercourse with her, or he has but at the time of intercourse the woman knew that she was unlawful for him, she is not entitled to any dowry (*mahr*). However, if she realises after sexual intercourse that she was unlawful for him, then the husband must pay her a dowry that matches the dowry usually given to women like her.

Ruling 2513. If before the marriage contract is concluded a woman says that through breastfeeding a child she is unlawful for a particular man, in the event that it is possible to substantiate her statement, she cannot marry the man. If she says this after the conclusion of the marriage contract, it is just like the case where a man says after the conclusion of the marriage contract that the woman is unlawful for him; the rule for such a case was mentioned in the previous ruling (*mas'alah*).

Ruling 2514. Being *maḥram* through breastfeeding is established in two ways:

1. by the report of someone, or some people, from whom one attains certainty (*yaqīn*) or confidence (*iṭmi'nān*);
2. the testimony of two dutiful (*'ādil*) men; however, they must describe the circumstances in which the child was breastfed. For example, they must say, 'We have seen such and such child breastfeeding from the breasts of such and such woman for twenty-four hours, and the child did not eat anything during

[4] As mentioned in Ruling 6, the term 'problematic' (*maḥall al-ishkāl*) amounts to saying the ruling is based on obligatory precaution

that period'. Similarly, they must also explain the other conditions that were mentioned in Ruling 2492. As for establishing that a child was breastfed by the testimony of one man and two women, or four women, all of whom are dutiful, this is problematic; therefore, precaution must be exercised here.

Ruling 2515. If one doubts whether or not a child has breastfed a quantity of milk that causes someone to become *maḥram*, or if one merely supposes (i.e. has *ẓann*) that a child has breastfed that amount, the child does not become *maḥram* to anyone. However, it is better to exercise precaution.

CHAPTER TWENTY-NINE

Divorce

Ruling 2516. A man who divorces his wife must be of the age of legal responsibility (*bāligh*) and sane (*ʿāqil*). If a ten-year-old child divorces his wife, then observing precaution (*iḥtiyāṭ*) in this case must not be abandoned. A man must also divorce his wife of his own volition (*ikhtiyār*); if he is compelled to divorce his wife, the divorce is invalid (*bāṭil*). Furthermore, he must have an intention (*qaṣd*) to divorce his wife; therefore, if, for example, a person says the divorce formula (*ṣīghah*) jokingly or while intoxicated, it is not valid.

Ruling 2517. At the time of divorce, the wife must be clear of menstruation (*ḥayḍ*) and lochia (*nifās*), and her husband must not have had sexual intercourse with her in the period she was clear [of *ḥayḍ* and *nifās*]. The details of these two conditions will be mentioned in subsequent rulings (*masāʾil*).

Ruling 2518. The divorce of a woman who is in the state of *ḥayḍ* and *nifās* is valid in the following three cases:

1. since getting married, her husband has not had sexual intercourse with her;
2. she is known to be pregnant. If she is not known to be pregnant and her husband divorces her while she is in the state of *ḥayḍ* and she later realises she was in fact pregnant, the divorce is void (*bāṭil*). However, it is better that precaution be observed here, albeit by means of another divorce.
3. the man is unable to determine whether or not his wife is clear of *ḥayḍ* or *nifās* owing to his absence or some other reason, even if that be because his wife is hiding. However, in such a situation, based on obligatory precaution (*al-iḥtiyāṭ al-wājib*), the man must wait at least one month from the time of separation from his wife and then divorce her.

Ruling 2519. If a man knows his wife to be clear of *ḥayḍ* and divorces her but later realises that she was in the state of *ḥayḍ* at the time of the divorce, the divorce is void except in the scenario mentioned above. If he knows her to be in the state of *ḥayḍ* but divorces her nonetheless and it later becomes known that she was not in the state of *ḥayḍ*, the divorce is valid.

Ruling 2520. If a person knows that his wife is in the state of *ḥayḍ* or *nifās* and he separates from her – for example, he goes on a journey – and he wishes to divorce her, he must wait until he attains certainty (*yaqīn*) or confidence (*iṭmiʾnān*) that she is clear of *ḥayḍ* or *nifās* and then divorce her. The same applies if he doubts [that she is clear of *ḥayḍ* or *nifās*] as long as he observes what was said in Ruling 2518 about divorce by an absent man.

Ruling 2521. If a man who has separated from his wife wishes to divorce her and he is able to find out whether or not his wife is in the state of *ḥayḍ* or *nifās*, albeit by means of her menstrual habit or other signs that have been specified in Islamic law, then, if he divorces her and it later becomes known that she was in the state of *ḥayḍ* or *nifās*, the divorce is not valid.

Ruling 2522. If a man has sexual intercourse with his wife, irrespective of whether or not she was in the state of *ḥayḍ* or *nifās*, and he wishes to divorce her, he must wait until she experiences *ḥayḍ* again and she becomes clear of it. However, if a man divorces a girl who has not completed nine lunar years or a woman who is known to be pregnant after having sexual intercourse with her, there is no problem. The same applies if she is postmenopausal (*yāʾisah*) (the meaning of which was explained in Ruling 2466).

Ruling 2523. If a man has sexual intercourse with a woman who is clear of *ḥayḍ* and *nifās* and he divorces her during the period of her being clear, in the event that it later becomes known that she was pregnant at the time of the divorce, the divorce is invalid. However, it is better that precaution be observed, albeit by means of another divorce.

Ruling 2524. If a man has sexual intercourse with a woman who is clear of *ḥayḍ* and *nifās* and he then separates from her – for example, he goes on a journey – then, in the event that he wishes to divorce her while he is away but is unable to find out about her state, he must wait long enough for her to experience *ḥayḍ* once more and become clear of it. And the obligatory precaution is that the period [he waits] must not be less than one month. Furthermore, if he divorces her, having observed what was said, and it then becomes known that the divorce took place during the first period of her being clear, there is no problem.

Ruling 2525. Regarding a woman who does not menstruate – whether that be because she has always been like that or because of a complication arising from an illness, breastfeeding, taking medication, and suchlike – even though it is normal for women her age to menstruate, if her husband wants to divorce her, he must do so three months after the last intercourse he had with her.

Ruling 2526. The divorce formula must be said in correct Arabic, and it must employ the word '*ṭāliq*' (divorced). Furthermore, two dutiful (*ʿādil*) men must hear it. If the husband wishes to say the divorce formula himself and the name of his wife is Fāṭimah, for example, he must say:

زَوْجَتِيْ فَاطِمَةُ طَالِقٌ

zawjatī fāṭimah ṭāliq

My wife Fāṭimah is divorced.

If he appoints an agent (*wakīl*) [to say the divorce formula on his behalf], the agent must say:

زَوْجَةُ مُوَكِّلِيْ فَاطِمَةُ طَالِقٌ

zawjatu muwakkilī fāṭimah ṭāliq

Fāṭimah, the wife of my client, is divorced.

In the event that the wife is specified, it is not necessary to mention her name. If she is present, it is sufficient for him to say the following while indicating her:

هٰذِهِ طَالِقٌ

hādhihi ṭāliq

This woman is divorced.

Or, he must say the following while addressing her:

أَنْتِ طَالِقٌ

anti ṭāliq

You are divorced.

In the event that a man can neither say the divorce formula in Arabic nor appoint an agent, he can divorce his wife using any words that are synonymous with the Arabic formula in any language.

Ruling 2527. There is no divorce in a temporary marriage (*mutʿah*). Instead, the woman is released when the marriage period ends or when the man gives the remaining period to her; for example, he says, 'I give the marriage period to you'. Furthermore, it is not necessary to have any witnesses, nor is it necessary for the woman to be clear of *ḥayḍ*.

THE PRESCRIBED WAITING PERIOD (*ʿIDDAH*) OF A DIVORCE

Ruling 2528. There is no *ʿiddah* for a girl who has not completed nine lunar years nor for a postmenopausal woman. This means that even if their husbands have had sexual intercourse with them, they can marry immediately after divorce.

Ruling 2529. If a husband divorces his wife with whom he has had sexual intercourse and has completed nine lunar years and is not postmenopausal, she must observe *ʿiddah* after the divorce. The *ʿiddah* of a woman for whom there is a gap of fewer than three months between two of her menstruation cycles is as follows: after her husband has divorced her during a time when she was clear of [of *ḥayḍ* and *nifās*], she must wait long enough to experience *ḥayḍ* once more and become clear of it, and when she experiences *ḥayḍ* for the third time, her *ʿiddah* comes to an end and she can marry again. However, if her husband divorces her before having sexual intercourse with her, there is no *ʿiddah*, meaning that she can marry immediately after her divorce unless the semen of her husband has entered her vagina, in which case she must observe *ʿiddah*.

Ruling 2530. If a woman does not menstruate even though it is usual for women of her age to menstruate, or if a woman menstruates but the gap between two of her menstruation cycles is three months or more, then in the event that her husband divorces her after having had sexual intercourse with her, she must observe *ʿiddah* for three lunar months after the divorce.

Ruling 2531. If a woman whose *ʿiddah* is three months is divorced at the beginning of the lunar month, she must observe *ʿiddah* for three complete months. However, if she is divorced in the middle of the month, she must observe *ʿiddah* for the rest of that month and for the two months after that, and then in the fourth month, she must observe *ʿiddah* for the number of days that had passed in the first month before she started to observe *ʿiddah* so that three complete months are observed. For example, if she was divorced at the time of sunset on the twentieth of the month and that month had thirty days, then her *ʿiddah* would come to an end at sunset on the twentieth of the fourth month. If the first month had twenty-nine days, the obligatory precaution is that she must observe *ʿiddah* for twenty-one days in the fourth month so that the number of days for which she observed *ʿiddah* in the first month equals thirty days [with the addition of the days from the fourth month].

Ruling 2532. If a pregnant woman is divorced, her *ʿiddah* comes to an end when the child is born or miscarried. Therefore, if, for example, her child is born one hour after her divorce, her *ʿiddah* will have ended. However, this applies when the child is the legal offspring of the husband; therefore, if a woman becomes pregnant from adultery and her husband divorces her, her *ʿiddah* does not end with the birth of her child.

Ruling 2533. If a woman who has completed nine lunar years and is not postmenopausal is married in a temporary marriage, and her husband has sexual intercourse with her, and the period of the temporary marriage comes to an end, or the husband gives the remaining time to her, then she must observe *ʿiddah*. Therefore, if she experiences *ḥayḍ*, she must observe *ʿiddah* for two menstruation cycles and not marry during this period. And based on obligatory precaution, [observing *ʿiddah* for only] one menstruation cycle is not sufficient.

However, if she does not experience *ḥayḍ*, she must observe *ʿiddah* for forty-five days before getting married. Furthermore, in the event that she is pregnant, her *ʿiddah* comes to an end when her child is born or miscarried, although the recommended precaution (*al-iḥtiyāṭ al-mustaḥabb*) is that she should observe *ʿiddah* for whichever is the longer period between giving birth and forty-five days.

Ruling 2534. The *ʿiddah* of a divorce begins from the moment the formula for divorce is said, irrespective of whether the woman knows she has been divorced or not. Therefore, if she finds out after the *ʿiddah* period has ended that she has been divorced, she does not have to observe another *ʿiddah*.

THE *ʿIDDAH* OF A WOMAN WHOSE HUSBAND HAS DIED

Ruling 2535. If a woman whose husband has died is not pregnant, she must observe *ʿiddah* for four lunar months and ten days. This means that she must refrain from marrying another man during this period, even if she is a minor (*ṣaghīrah*), postmenopausal, a temporary wife (*mutʿah*), a disbeliever (*kāfirah*), a woman who has been given a revocable divorce (*al-muṭallaqah al-rijʿiyyah*) and is observing *ʿiddah*, or her husband had not had sexual intercourse with her, even if her husband is a child or insane. If she is pregnant, she must observe *ʿiddah* until she gives birth. However, if the child is born before the passing of four lunar months and ten days, then she must wait until four lunar months and ten days have passed after the death of her husband. This *ʿiddah* is known as 'the *ʿiddah* of a widow' (*ʿiddat al-wafāt*).

Ruling 2536. It is unlawful (*ḥarām*) for a woman who is observing the *ʿiddah* of a widow to wear clothes that are an adornment (*zīnah*), apply kohl, or do something that would be considered an adornment. However, leaving the house is not unlawful for her.

Ruling 2537. If a woman is certain that her husband has died, and after she has observed the *ʿiddah* of a widow she marries again, in the event that it becomes known that her husband died at a later time and the second marriage contract was in fact concluded while her first husband was still alive or while she was observing the *ʿiddah* of a widow, then in such a case, she must separate from her second husband and, based on obligatory precaution, she must observe two *ʿiddahs*. This means that if she has become pregnant by her second husband, she must observe *ʿiddah* until childbirth; this *ʿiddah* is for intercourse that has ensued from a mistake (*waṭʾ al-shubhah*). The duration of this *ʿiddah* is the same as that of the *ʿiddah* of a divorce. Then, she must observe the *ʿiddah* of a widow or complete her previous *ʿiddah*. If she is not pregnant and her first husband died before she had sexual intercourse with her second husband, she must first observe the *ʿiddah* of a widow and then observe the *ʿiddah* of intercourse that has ensued from a mistake. But if she had sexual intercourse before her first husband died, then the *ʿiddah* of intercourse that has ensued from a mistake must be observed first.

Ruling 2538. If a husband is absent or comes under the rule (*ḥukm*) of being absent, the *ʿiddah* of a widow begins the moment the wife becomes aware of her husband's death, not from the time of her husband's death. However, with regard to a girl that has not reached the age of legal responsibility (*bulūgh*) or is insane, this rule is problematic (*maḥall al-ishkāl*),[1] and it is obligatory (*wājib*) to observe precaution in such a case.

Ruling 2539. If a woman says, 'My *ʿiddah* has come to an end', her word is to be accepted unless she is suspected to be someone whose word in this case cannot be accepted. If that is so, then based on obligatory precaution, her word is not to be accepted. For example, if she claims that she experienced bleeding three times in one month, her claim is not to be accepted unless her female relatives substantiate that her menstrual habit was like that.

[1] As mentioned in Ruling 6, the term 'problematic' (*maḥall al-ishkāl*) amounts to saying the ruling is based on obligatory precaution.

IRREVOCABLE (*BĀʾIN*) AND REVOCABLE (*RIJʿĪ*) DIVORCE

Ruling 2540.* An irrevocable divorce is when the husband does not have the right to return to his wife after the divorce, meaning that he cannot remarry her without a new marriage contract. This divorce is of six types:

1. the divorce of a girl who has not completed nine lunar years;
2. the divorce of a postmenopausal woman;
3. the divorce of a woman who did not have sexual intercourse with her husband after the conclusion of the marriage contract;
4. the third divorce, which will be explained in Ruling 2545;
5. a *khulʿ* or *mubārāh* divorce, the laws (*aḥkām*) of which will be mentioned later;
6. a divorce given by a fully qualified jurist (*al-ḥākim al-sharʿī*) to a woman whose husband is neither prepared to pay her living expenses nor divorce her, and the divorce which the husband gives as per the instruction of a fully qualified jurist in such a case.

Apart from these, divorce is revocable, meaning that as long as the wife is observing *ʿiddah*, her husband can return to her.

Ruling 2541. It is unlawful for a man who has given his wife a revocable divorce to expel his wife from the house in which she resided at the time of the divorce. However, in some instances, such as when a wife has committed adultery, there is no problem in expelling her from the house. It is also unlawful for the wife to leave the house for non-essential tasks without her husband's permission Furthermore, it is obligatory for the husband to pay for her living expenses during her *ʿiddah*.

LAWS OF RETURNING TO ONE'S WIFE

Ruling 2542. In a revocable divorce, a man can return to his wife in two ways:

1. he says something that means he has re-established the marriage with her;
2. he does something with the intention of returning to her. Having sexual intercourse ascertains this even if he does not have the intention of returning to her. As for kissing and touching with lust, this is problematic, and based on obligatory precaution, if he does not intend to return to her, he must divorce her again.

Ruling 2543. In order to return to his wife, it is not necessary for a man to have a witness or to inform his wife; in fact, even if he returns to her without anyone knowing, his return is valid. However, after completion of the *'iddah*, if the man says, 'I returned to her during her *'iddah*', but the wife does not substantiate his claim, then the man has to prove his claim.

Ruling 2544. If a man who has given his wife a revocable divorce takes some property from her and arrives at a settlement (*ṣulḥ*) with her that he will not return to her, then although this settlement is valid and it is obligatory for him to not return to her, his right to return to her is not abolished. Therefore, if he does return to her, the marriage will be re-established.

Ruling 2545. If a man divorces his wife twice and returns to her, or he divorces her twice and after each divorce he concludes a marriage contract with her, or he returns to her after one divorce and concludes a marriage contract with her after the other divorce, then, after the third divorce, the woman becomes unlawful for him. However, if she marries another man after the third divorce, she becomes lawful for the first husband – meaning that he can marry her again – on fulfilment of five conditions:

1. the marriage to the second husband is a permanent one. If it is a temporary marriage, then after her second husband separates from her, the first husband cannot marry her;
2. the second husband has had sexual intercourse with her. And the obligatory precaution is that it must be vaginal intercourse, not anal;
3. the second husband divorces her or dies;

4. the *ʿiddah* of divorce or the *ʿiddah* of a widow concerning the second husband comes to an end;
5. based on obligatory precaution, the second husband is *bāligh* when they have sexual intercourse.

KHULʿ DIVORCE

Ruling 2546. The divorce of a wife who is not fond of her husband and has an aversion to him, and gives him her dowry (*mahr*) or some of her other property so that he divorces her, is known as a '*khulʿ*' divorce. In a *khulʿ* divorce, it is a requirement that the wife's aversion to her husband be at such a level that it is a threat to her fulfilling her marital duties.

Ruling 2547. If the husband wishes to say the formula of a *khulʿ* divorce himself, then, if the name of his wife is Fāṭimah, for example, he must say the following after the property has been given:

زَوْجَتِيْ فَاطِمَةُ خَلَعْتُهَا عَلَىٰ مَا بَذَلَتْ

zawjatī fāṭimah khalaʿtuhā ʿalā mā badhalat

I give my wife Fāṭimah a *khulʿ* divorce upon accepting what she has given.

And based on recommended precaution, he should also say:

فَهِيَ طَالِقٌ

fahiya ṭāliq

And so she is divorced.

In case the wife is specified, it is not necessary to mention her name. The same applies in a *mubārāh* divorce [the laws of which will be mentioned later].

Ruling 2548. If a wife appoints an agent to give her dowry to her husband, and the husband appoints the same person to divorce his wife, in the event that the name of the husband is Muḥammad, and the name of the wife is Fāṭimah, for example, the agent must say the formula of the divorce in the following manner:

عَنْ مُوَكِّلَتِيْ فَاطِمَةَ بَذَلْتُ مَهْرَهَا لِمُوَكِّلِيْ مُحَمَّدٍ لِيَخْلَعَهَا عَلَيْهِ

ʿan muwakkilatī fāṭimah badhaltu mahrahā limuwakkilī muḥammad liyakhlaʿahā ʿalayh

On behalf of my client Fāṭimah, I give her dowry to my client Muḥammad so that he gives her a *khulʿ* divorce upon accepting it.

After that, the agent says:

زَوْجَةُ مُوَكِّلِيْ خَلَعْتُهَا عَلَىٰ مَا بَذَلَتْ فَهِيَ طَالِقٌ

zawjatu muwakkilī khalaʿtuhā ʿalā mā badhalat fahiya ṭāliq

I give my client's wife a *khulʿ* divorce upon accepting what she has given, and so she is divorced.

If the wife appoints an agent to give something other than her dowry to her husband so that he divorces her, then instead of saying مَهْرَها [*mahrahā*], he must mention the property. For example, if she has given £100, he must say: بَذَلْتُ مِائَةَ جُنَيْهٍ إِسْتَرْلِيْنِي [*badhaltu miʾata junayhin istarlīnī*] ('I give £100').

MUBĀRĀH DIVORCE

Ruling 2549. If a husband and wife do not want each other and have an aversion to each other, and the wife gives some property to her husband so that he divorces her, this is known as a '*mubārāh*' divorce.

Ruling 2550. If the husband wishes to say the formula, in the event that the name of his wife is Fāṭimah, for example, he must say:

بَارَأْتُ زَوْجَتِيْ فَاطِمَةَ عَلَىٰ مَا بَذَلَتْ

bāraʾtu zawjatī fāṭimah ʿalā mā badhalat

I give my wife Fāṭimah a *mubārāh* divorce upon accepting what she has given.

And based on obligatory precaution, he must also say:

فَهِيَ طَالِقٌ

fahiya ṭāliq

And so she is divorced.

If the man appoints an agent, the agent must say:

عَنْ قِبَلِ مُوَكِّلِيْ بَارَأْتُ زَوْجَتَهُ فَاطِمَةَ عَلَىٰ مَا بَذَلَتْ فَهِيَ طَالِقٌ

ʿan qibali muwakkilī bāraʾtu zawjatahu fāṭimah ʿalā mā badhalat fahiya ṭāliq

On behalf of my client, I give his wife Fāṭimah a *mubārāh* divorce upon accepting what she has given, and so she is divorced.

In both cases, there is no problem if instead of عَلَىٰ مَا بَذَلَتْ [*alā mā badhalat*] he says بِمَا بَذَلَتْ [*bimā badhalat*].

Ruling 2551. If possible, the formula of the *khulʿ* and *mubārāh* divorce must be said in correct Arabic. In the event that it is not possible, the rule is the same as that for divorce, which was mentioned in Ruling 2526. However, there is no problem if the wife says the following in English, for example, for giving her property to her husband: 'I give such and such property to you for divorce'.

Ruling 2552.* If during the *ʿiddah* of a *khulʿ* or *mubārāh* divorce, a wife declines to give the property, or part of it, to her husband, her husband can return to her and re-establish the marriage without a new marriage contract.

Ruling 2553.* The property that a husband acquires in a *mubārāh* divorce must not be greater than the dowry; in fact, it is better if it is less than the dowry. However, in a *khulʿ* divorce, there is no problem if it is greater than the dowry.

MISCELLANEOUS RULINGS ON DIVORCE

Ruling 2554. If a man has sexual intercourse with a woman who is not his wife, supposing that she was his wife, the woman must observe *ʿiddah*, irrespective of whether she knew that he was not her husband or supposed that he was her husband.

Ruling 2555. If a man fornicates with a woman he knows is not his wife, and the woman knows that he is not her husband, it is not necessary for her to observe *ʿiddah*. However, if she supposes that he is her husband, then the obligatory precaution is that she must observe *ʿiddah*.

Ruling 2556. If a man deceives a woman into not fulfilling her marital duties towards her husband so that her husband is led into divorcing her and she marries the man, the divorce and the marriage are valid. However, both of them will have committed a grave sin.

Ruling 2557. If a woman stipulates a condition in the marriage contract that she has the right to divorce in certain circumstances – for example, if her husband travels for a long time, or does not pay her expenses for six months, or is sentenced to a long imprisonment – then such a condition is invalid. However, if she stipulates a condition that in certain circumstances, or without any restriction or condition, she is to be his agent in being able to divorce herself, then such a condition is valid and her husband cannot later depose her of her agency (*wikālah*), and if she divorces herself the divorce is valid.

Ruling 2558. If a wife's husband has disappeared and she wishes to marry another man, she must refer to a dutiful jurist (*mujtahid*).[2] In certain circumstances, which are mentioned *Minhāj al-Ṣāliḥīn*,[3] the jurist can divorce her.

Ruling 2559. The father and paternal grandfather of a man who is permanently insane can divorce his wife if that is in his interests.

Ruling 2560. If the father or paternal grandfather of a child marries

[2] A *mujtahid* is a person who has attained the level of *ijtihād*, qualifying him to be an authority in Islamic law. *Ijtihād* is the process of deriving Islamic laws from authentic sources.

[3] This is al-Sayyid al-Sistani's more detailed work on Islamic law.

him to a girl in a temporary marriage, he can give the remaining period of the marriage to the girl if it is in the child's interests. This applies even if part of the period includes a time when the boy is *bāligh*; for example, a father marries his fourteen-year-old son to a girl for two years. However, the father or paternal grandfather cannot divorce the child's permanent wife.

Ruling 2561. If a person considers two people to be dutiful on the basis of something that is legally authoritative (*al-ḥujjah al-sharʿiyyah*) [such as the statement of a reliable person], and he divorces his wife in their presence, then in such a situation, another man can marry that woman himself, or he can marry her to another man after her *ʿiddah* comes to an end even if he doubts in the two witnesses being dutiful but deems it probable that the man who divorced the woman considered them dutiful. However, he cannot marry the woman if he is certain about the two witnesses not being dutiful.

Ruling 2562. If a man gives his wife a revocable divorce, she is still considered his legal wife until her *ʿiddah* comes to an end. Therefore, she must not prevent her husband from deriving any sexual pleasure that is his right. Also, it is permitted (*jāʾiz*) – rather, it is recommended (*mustaḥabb*) – for her to make herself look attractive to him, and it is not permitted for her to leave the house without his permission. As for the husband, it is obligatory for him to pay for her maintenance (*nafaqah*) if she is not recalcitrant (*nāshizah*),[4] and her shroud (*kafan*) and *fiṭrah* alms tax (*zakāt al-fiṭrah*) are also his responsibility. In the event of death of one of them, the other inherits from the deceased. Furthermore, the man cannot marry the woman's sister while the former is observing *ʿiddah*.

[4] A recalcitrant wife is one who does not perform her obligatory marital duties, which are explained in Ruling 2430.

CHAPTER THIRTY

Usurpation (*Ghaṣb*)

Usurpation is when a person unjustly takes control over the property or right of someone else. It is something that the intellect, Qur'an, and traditions all judge to be unlawful (*ḥarām*). It has been reported that the Most Noble Messenger (Ṣ) said, 'Whosoever usurps one span of land from another, seven layers of that land will be hung around his neck like a collar on the Day of Resurrection.'

Ruling 2563. If a person does not allow people to make use of a mosque, school, bridge, or any other place that has been built for public use, he will have usurped their right. If a person reserves a place for himself in a mosque and someone drives him out of that place and does not allow him to make use of it, he will have sinned.

Ruling 2564. If a depositor and a depositee agree that the item deposited [as security] will be in the possession of the depositee or a third party, the depositor cannot take back the item before paying off his debt. If he does, he must return it immediately.

Ruling 2565. If an item that has been deposited with someone is usurped by a third party, both the owner of the property and the depositee can claim the usurped item from the usurper. In the event that they take the item back, it will be considered a deposited item once again.

Ruling 2566. If a person usurps something, he must return it to its owner. If the item is destroyed and it was of some value, he must replace it for the owner as per the explanation in Rulings 2576 and 2577.

Ruling 2567. If some gain is acquired from an item that has been usurped – for example, a usurped sheep gives birth to a lamb – it will belong to the owner. Similarly, if a person usurps a house, for example, he must pay its rent (*ijārah*) even if he does not reside in it.

Ruling 2568. If a person usurps property that belongs to a child or insane person, he must return it to their guardian (*walī*). If the property is destroyed, he must replace it.

Ruling 2569. If two people usurp something together and each of them has complete control over it, they are both responsible (*ḍāmin*) for it, even if neither of them could have usurped the property on his own.

Ruling 2570. If a person mixes something that he has usurped with something else – for example, he mixes wheat that he has usurped with barley – then, in the event that it is possible to separate the two items, even if it requires some effort, he must separate them and return the usurped item to the owner.

Ruling 2571. If a person usurps a piece of gold that has been crafted, such as an earring, and melts it, he must return it to the owner along with the difference in its value before and after it was melted. If he does not pay the difference in value but says, 'I will make it like it was', the owner does not have to accept his offer. Also, the owner cannot compel him to make it like it was.

Ruling 2572. If a person changes something that he has usurped into something better – for example, he makes an earring from gold that he has usurped – then, in the event that the owner says, 'Give me the item as it is', the usurper must give it to him and he cannot claim any wages for his efforts. Also, a person does not have the right to revert an item to its original form without the owner's consent. However, if he reverts the item to its original form or changes it to another form without the owner's consent, then it is not known whether he is responsible for the difference in value between the two states.

Ruling 2573. If a person changes something that he has usurped into something better and the owner says, 'You must revert it to its original form', then, if the owner has a purpose for saying that, it is obligatory (*wājib*) on the usurper to revert it to its original form. In the event that its value depreciates due to the changes made to it, he must pay the difference to the owner. Therefore, if he makes an earring from gold that he has usurped and the owner says, 'You must revert it to its original form', in the event that its value after he has melted it is lower than what it was before he made it into an earring, he must pay the difference.

Ruling 2574. If someone farms on land that he has usurped or plants trees on it, the crops he cultivates, the trees, and their fruits belong to him. However, if the owner of the land does not consent to the crops or trees remaining on his land, the usurper must immediately remove them. He must also pay rent to the owner for the time the crops and trees are there. Furthermore, he must repair any damage done to the land; for example, he must fill in any holes caused by removing the trees. If the value of the land depreciates due to the damage, he must pay the difference, and he cannot compel the owner of the land to sell or rent it to him. Similarly, the owner of the land cannot compel the person to sell the trees or the crops to him.

Ruling 2575. If an owner of some land consents to crops and trees remaining on his land, it is not necessary for the usurper of the land to remove them. However, he must pay rent for using the land from the time he usurped it until the time the owner gave his consent.

Ruling 2576. If an item that has been usurped is destroyed, and it was a non-fungible item, such as cows and sheep, the usurper must pay its value. An item is considered 'non-fungible' when there are not many other items like it in terms of those particulars that affect its desirability. In the event that its market value varies according to supply and demand, the usurper must pay for the item's value at the time it was destroyed.

Ruling 2577. If an item that has been usurped is destroyed and it was a fungible item, such as wheat and barley, the usurper must replace it with another item like it. An item is considered 'fungible' when there are many other items like it in terms of those particulars that affect its desirability. However, the thing that the usurper gives must have the same type of particulars that affect the item's desirability as that of the usurped and destroyed item. For example, if a person usurps high grade rice, he cannot replace it with lower grade rice.

Ruling 2578. If a person usurps a non-fungible item and it is destroyed, in the event that it acquired a quality that increased its value while it was with the usurper – for example, [it was an animal and] it gained weight before it was destroyed – he must pay the amount it was worth when it had gained weight. This applies as long as the gain in weight was not a result of him better tending to it. If it was a result of him better tending to it, then it is not necessary for him to pay the increase in value.

Ruling 2579. If a person usurps an item and another individual usurps it from him and it is destroyed, the owner can claim its replacement from either of the two usurpers, or he can claim some of it from each of them. In the event that he takes its replacement from the first usurper, the first usurper can claim what he gives him from the second usurper. However, if the owner takes the replacement from the second usurper, the second usurper cannot claim what he gave him from the first usurper.

Ruling 2580. If one of the conditions of a valid transaction (*muʿāmalah*) is not fulfilled in a sale – for example, an item that must be bought and sold by weight is sold without weighing it – the transaction is invalid (*bāṭil*). Despite this, in the event that the seller and the buyer consent to the other having disposal over the property, there is no problem. Otherwise [i.e. if they do not consent], the thing they have taken from each other is like usurped property and must be returned to the other. In case the property of one of them perishes while it is in the possession of the other, the latter must replace it, whether he knows the transaction was invalid or not.

Ruling 2581. If a person takes some property from a seller to have a look at it or to keep it for a while so that if he likes it, he will buy it, and if that property perishes, then based on the opinion held by most jurists (*mashhūr*), he must give its replacement to the owner.

CHAPTER THIRTY-ONE

Found Property

Ruling 2582. If a person finds some lost property, other than an animal, and the property does not possess any identifying features by which the owner can be known – irrespective of whether or not its value is less than one dirham (12.6 *nukhud*[1] of minted silver) – he can take the property for himself. However, the recommended precaution (*al-iḥtiyāṭ al-mustaḥabb*) is that he should give it to the poor (*fuqarāʾ*) as alms (*ṣadaqah*) on behalf of the owner. This is also the case with money that does not bear any signs [as to whom it belongs]. However, if the amount and the particulars of the time and place [where it was found] give an indication, then the person must announce it, as will be explained in the next ruling (*masʾalah*).

Ruling 2583. If a person finds some property that possesses identifying features by which the owner can be known, then even if he knows that the owner is a disbeliever (*kāfir*) whose property is inviolable, he must announce it in a public place for one year from the day he found it if its value is one dirham or more. But if its value is less than one dirham, then based on obligatory precaution (*al-iḥtiyāṭ al-wājib*), he must give it to the poor as alms on behalf of the owner. If the owner is found [after the property has been given as alms], in the event that the owner does not consent to him having given the property to the poor as alms, he must replace it.

Ruling 2584. If a person does not wish to make an announcement [about finding some property] himself, he can ask someone he trusts to announce on his behalf.

Ruling 2585. If a person makes an announcement for one year and the owner of the property is not found, then in case the property was found in a place other than the sacred precinct (*ḥaram*) of Mecca, he can safeguard it for the owner [with the intention of] returning it to him whenever he is found. During this period, there is no problem in him using the property while looking after it. Alternatively, he can give it to the poor as alms on behalf of the owner. The obligatory precaution is that he must not take it for himself. If the property is found in the sacred precinct of Mecca, the obligatory precaution

[1] A *nukhud* is a measure of weight equal to 0.192 grams. Therefore, 12.6 *nukhuds* is equivalent to 2.4192 grams.

is that he must give it to the poor as alms on behalf of its owner.

Ruling 2586. If after a person has announced for one year the owner is not found, and the finder safeguards the property for the owner but it is destroyed nonetheless, in the event that he was not negligent in safeguarding it and did not transgress – i.e. he was not excessive – he is not responsible (*ḍāmin*). However, if he has given it to the poor as alms on behalf of the owner [and afterwards the owner is found], the owner can choose to consent to the act of charity or claim for the item to be replaced; if he chooses the latter, the reward for the act of charity will belong to the person who gave the alms.

Ruling 2587. If a person who finds some property intentionally (*ʿamdan*) does not announce it as per the instructions that were mentioned, he will have sinned. In the event that he deems it probable that announcing it will be beneficial, it is obligatory (*wājib*) on him to announce it.

Ruling 2588. If an insane person or a child who is not of the age of legal responsibility (*bāligh*) finds something that possesses identifying features and its value is at least one dirham, then his guardian (*walī*) can announce it. In fact, it is obligatory for him to announce it if he has taken the item from the child or the insane person. If he announces it for one year and the owner is not found, he must act according to what was mentioned in Ruling 2585.

Ruling 2589. If a person loses hope in finding the owner during the year in which he makes the announcement, he must – with the permission of a fully qualified jurist (*al-ḥākim al-sharʿī*), based on obligatory precaution – give it to the poor as alms.

Ruling 2590. If the item is destroyed during the year in which a person announces [that he has found the property], in the event that he was negligent in safeguarding it or made use of it, he is responsible for replacing it for the owner, and he must continue to announce it. However, if he was neither negligent nor made use of it, nothing is obligatory for him [concerning this matter].

Ruling 2591. If a person finds some property that possesses identifying features and it has a value of one dirham or more, and if the place where the property was found is such that were he to announce [that he has found the property], the owner would still not be found, then in such a case, he must give the property to the poor as alms on behalf of the owner from the day he found it. Based on obligatory precaution, this must be done with the permission of a fully qualified jurist, and the finder must not wait until the year ends.

Ruling 2592. If a person finds some property and takes it thinking that it belongs to him but afterwards realises that it is not his property, then the laws (*aḥkām*) that were mentioned in the previous rulings (*masāʾil*) will apply to him.

Ruling 2593. A person who finds some property must announce it in such a way that were the owner to hear it, he would deem it probable that the property belongs to him. This is something that will vary from case to case. For example, sometimes, it will be sufficient for the person to say, 'I have found something'. However, in other cases, the person must also specify the type of thing he has found; for example, he must say, 'I have found a piece of gold'. And still in other cases, he must add some particulars; for example, he must say, 'I have found a gold earring'. In any case, he must not mention all the particulars of the property in case it becomes individuated. Furthermore, he must announce it in a place where he deems it probable that news of it will reach the owner.

Ruling 2594. If a person finds something and another individual says, 'It belongs to me' and describes some of its identifying features, the finder must only give it to him if he is confident (i.e. he has *iṭmiʾnān*) that it belongs to him. In this case, it is not necessary for the claimant to describe those features of it that an owner would not usually notice.

Ruling 2595. If a person finds something that has a value of one or more dirhams, in the event that he does not announce it and places it in a mosque or some other public place and the item is destroyed or is taken by another person, the person who found it is responsible for it.

Ruling 2596. If a person finds something that cannot remain for a year, he must take care of it for as long as it remains while protecting all those particulars that affect its price. And the obligatory precaution is that he must announce [that he has found the property] during this period. In the event that the owner is not found, the finder can specify a value for it and take it for himself, or he can sell it and keep the money. In both cases, he must continue to announce it. If the owner is found, he must give him its value. But if the owner is not found for one year, he must act according to what was said in Ruling 2585.

Ruling 2597. If at the time of performing ablution (*wuḍūʾ*) or prayers (*ṣalāh*) a person has with him something that he has found, his ablution or prayers does not become invalid (*bāṭil*) even if he does not wish to hand the property over to the owner.

Ruling 2598. If a person takes someone else's shoes and replaces them with another pair, then in the event that the person whose shoes were taken knows that the shoes that are left with him belong to the person who took his shoes, and he consents to take those shoes in lieu of his own shoes that were taken, he can take those shoes in lieu of his own. The same applies if he knows that his shoes were unrightfully and unjustly taken. However, in this case, the value of the shoes he takes must not be more than the value of his own shoes. If it is, the law (*ḥukm*) of an item whose owner is unknown (*majhūl al-mālik*) applies to the extra amount. In cases other than these two, the law of items whose owner is unknown applies to the shoes.

Ruling 2599. If a person possesses some property that belongs to an unknown owner, and it is not regarded as being 'lost property', then in case he is confident that the owner would consent to him using the property, it is permitted (*jāʾiz*) for him to use the property in any way to which he knows the owner would consent. Otherwise, he must look for the owner for as long as he deems it probable that he will be found. If he loses hope in finding him, he must give the property to the poor as alms, and the obligatory precaution is that he must do this with the permission of a fully qualified jurist. Furthermore, with the permission of a fully qualified jurist, he can give the property's value to the poor as alms. If the owner is found afterwards but he does not consent to the person giving it to the poor as alms, then based on obligatory precaution, the person must replace the property for the owner.

CHAPTER THIRTY-TWO

Slaughtering and Hunting Animals

Ruling 2600. If either a wild or domesticated animal whose meat is lawful (*ḥalāl*) to eat is slaughtered according to the instructions that will be mentioned later, then after it dies, its meat is lawful to eat and its body is pure (*ṭāhir*). There are other ways for a camel, fish, and locust to become lawful to eat; these will be mentioned in the following rulings (*masāʾil*).

Ruling 2601. If a wild animal whose meat is lawful to eat, such as a deer, partridge, or mountain goat, is killed by hunting according to the instructions that will be mentioned later, it becomes pure and lawful to eat. The same applies to a domesticated animal whose meat is lawful to eat and has turned wild, such as a domesticated cow or camel that fled and has become wild or unyielding and cannot be caught. However, a domesticated animal whose meat is lawful to eat, such as a sheep or hen, and a wild animal whose meat is lawful to eat and has been domesticated through training, does not become pure nor lawful to eat if it is killed by hunting.

Ruling 2602. A wild animal whose meat is lawful to eat can only become pure and lawful to eat by hunting it if it is able to flee or fly away. Therefore, a fawn [a baby deer] that cannot flee, or a cheeper [a baby partridge] that cannot fly away, does not become pure and lawful to eat if it is killed by hunting. If a person kills a deer and its fawn that is unable to flee using one arrow, the deer is lawful to eat but the fawn is unlawful (*ḥarām*).

Ruling 2603. If an animal whose meat is lawful to eat and whose blood does not gush out [when its jugular vein is cut], such as a fish, dies on its own accord, it is pure but its meat cannot be eaten.

Ruling 2604. An animal whose meat is unlawful to eat and whose blood does not gush out, such as a snake and lizard, is pure when it is dead; therefore, killing it by hunting or slaughtering does not change this.

Ruling 2605. Slaughtering a dog or a pig or killing it by hunting does not make it pure, as these animals cannot be made pure. Furthermore, it is unlawful to eat their meat. Similarly, the flesh and skin of small animals that live in nests in the ground and have blood that gushes out, such as mice and ferrets, do not become pure if such animals are killed by hunting.

Ruling 2606. The flesh and skin of animals whose meat is unlawful to eat – except those mentioned in the previous ruling (*mas'alah*) – become pure if they are slaughtered or killed by hunting with a weapon, whether the animal is a predatory one or not. This applies even to elephants, bears, and apes (about which there is a difference of opinion from a jurisprudential perspective). However, if animals whose meat cannot be eaten are killed by hunting dogs, then to consider them pure is problematic (*maḥall al-ishkāl*) [i.e. based on obligatory precaution (*al-iḥtiyāṭ al-wājib*), they are not considered pure].[1]

Ruling 2607. If a dead baby animal is delivered or taken out from the womb of a live animal, it is unlawful to eat its meat.

METHOD OF SLAUGHTERING AN ANIMAL

Ruling 2608. The method of slaughtering an animal is that four ducts must be severed completely:

1. the windpipe (trachea);
2. the food pipe (oesophagus);

3–4. the two thick arteries on the two sides of the oesophagus and trachea. Based on obligatory precaution, simply making an incision in them or severing only the trachea is not sufficient. Severing these four ducts can only happen by severing from below the protrusion from which the trachea and oesophagus separate.

Ruling 2609. It is not sufficient to sever some of these four ducts, wait for the animal to die, and then sever the remaining ducts. However, if the four ducts are severed before the animal dies, the animal is pure and lawful to eat even if all the ducts were not severed in continuous succession.

[1] As mentioned in Ruling 6, the term 'problematic' (*maḥall al-ishkāl*) amounts to saying the ruling is based on obligatory precaution.

Ruling 2610. If a wolf tears apart a sheep's throat such that none of the four ducts remains, the sheep becomes unlawful to eat. The same applies if nothing of the windpipe remains. In fact, if a wolf tears apart some of a sheep's throat and the four ducts are left hanging from the head or connected to the body, then based on obligatory precaution, the sheep is unlawful to eat. However, if another part of its body is torn apart and the sheep remains alive and it is then slaughtered according to the instructions that will be mentioned later, it is lawful to eat and pure. This rule (*ḥukm*) is not exclusive to wolves and sheep.

CONDITIONS OF SLAUGHTERING AN ANIMAL

Ruling 2611. Slaughtering an animal has the following conditions:

1. the person slaughtering the animal must be a Muslim man or woman. The child of a Muslim who is *mumayyiz* – i.e. able to discern between right and wrong – can also slaughter an animal. If an animal is slaughtered by a disbeliever (*kāfir*) who is not from among the People of the Book (*ahl al-kitāb*),[2] or by someone who is subject to the rules applicable to disbelievers, such as a *nāṣibī*,[3] the animal does not become lawful to eat. In fact, if an animal is slaughtered by a disbeliever from among the People of the Book, even if he says '*bismillāh*', the animal does not become lawful based on obligatory precaution;
2. as far as possible, the animal must be slaughtered with something made of iron; and based on obligatory precaution, a steel knife is not sufficient. However, if an item made of iron is not available, the animal can be slaughtered using something sharp enough to sever the four ducts, such as a piece of glass or a stone, even if it is not urgent to slaughter the animal;
3. the animal must face the qibla[4] when being slaughtered. Therefore, if the animal is sitting or standing, it must face qibla

[2] As mentioned in Ruling 103, the 'People of the Book' are Jews, Christians, and Zoroastrians.

[3] In Ruling 103, *nawāṣib* (pl. of *nāṣibī*) are defined as 'those who show enmity towards the Imams (ʿA)'.

[4] Qibla is the direction towards the Kaʿbah in Mecca.

in the same way a person faces qibla in prayers (*ṣalāh*). If the animal is lying on its right or left side, the point where it is cut and its stomach must face qibla, but it is not necessary for its hands, feet, and face to face qibla. If someone knows that an animal must be slaughtered facing qibla and intentionally (*ʿamdan*) does not make it face qibla, the animal is unlawful to eat. However, there is no problem if he forgets or does not know the ruling about this or mistakes the direction of qibla. If a person does not know the direction of qibla or cannot make the animal face qibla even with the help of someone else, then in case the animal is unruly or is in a well or has fallen into a pit and one is compelled to slaughter it, there is no problem in slaughtering it in any direction. The same applies if one fears that the delay caused by making it face qibla will result in its death. If a Muslim does not believe that an animal must be slaughtered while facing qibla, the slaughter is still correct (*ṣaḥīḥ*) even if he does not make it face qibla. The recommended precaution (*al-iḥtiyāṭ al-mustaḥabb*) is for the person slaughtering the animal to also face qibla;

4. at the time of slaughtering the animal, or before that but at a time connected to the act of slaughtering the animal, the person slaughtering the animal must mention the name of Allah the Exalted; it is not sufficient for someone else to mention it. It is sufficient to say '*bismillāh*' or '*allāhu akbar*'; in fact, if he only says '*allāh*', it is sufficient, although this goes against precaution (*iḥtiyāṭ*). If he mentions the name of Allah the Exalted without an intention (*qaṣd*) to slaughter the animal, or if due to not knowing the ruling he does not mention the name of Allah the Exalted, the animal is not lawful to eat. However, there is no problem if he does not mention the name of Allah the Exalted due to forgetfulness;
5. the animal must make some movement after it has been slaughtered, even by moving its eyes or tail or striking its foot against the ground. Fulfilment of this condition is necessary only when there is a doubt as to whether the animal is alive or not at the time of being slaughtered; otherwise, it is not necessary;
6. a normal amount of blood must drain out of the animal's body. Therefore, if its blood congeals in its veins and does not drain

out, or if the amount of blood that drains out is relatively little for an animal of its type, the animal is not lawful to eat. However, if the amount of blood that drains out is relatively little due to the animal having bled before it was slaughtered, there is no problem;

7. a person must sever the animal's throat with the intention of an Islamic slaughter. Therefore, the animal is not lawful to eat if a knife falls from someone's hand and happens to sever the throat of the animal, or if the person who is slaughtering the animal is asleep, intoxicated, or unconscious, or he is a non-*mumayyiz* child or an insane person, or if the knife draws against the throat of the animal for some other reason and it happens to sever its throat.

Ruling 2612. Based on obligatory precaution, the head of an animal must not be separated from its body before the spirit (*rūḥ*) has left its body, although this does not make the animal unlawful to eat. However, there is no problem if the animal's head is accidentally separated from its body or due to the knife's sharpness. Similarly, [it is not permitted,] based on obligatory precaution, to break the animal's neck or cut its spinal cord before the spirit has left its body. The spinal cord is like a white thread that runs between the lumbar vertebrae and extends from the animal's neck to its tail.

METHOD OF SLAUGHTERING A CAMEL

Ruling 2613. For a camel to become lawful to eat and pure, it must be slaughtered [in a specific way, which is termed '*naḥr*']. The instructions for this are as follows: while fulfilling the aforementioned conditions of slaughtering an animal, the person slaughtering the camel must thrust a knife – or something else made of iron and sharp – into the hollow area between the camel's neck and chest. It is better that the camel be standing when it is slaughtered.

Ruling 2614. If a person severs the four ducts [as mentioned Ruling 2608] of a camel instead of performing *naḥr* [as described in the previous ruling], or if a person performs *naḥr* on a sheep, cow, or similar animal, then their meat is unlawful to eat and their body is impure (*najis*). However, if a person slaughters a camel according to Islamic law (*dhabḥ*) and before the camel dies he performs *naḥr*, its meat is lawful to eat and its body is pure. Also, if *naḥr* is performed on a cow, sheep, or similar animal and before the animal dies a person severs the four ducts, its meat is lawful to eat and its body is pure.

Ruling 2615. If an animal becomes unruly and cannot be slaughtered according to the instructions of Islamic law, or, for example, it falls into a well and it is deemed probable that it will die in the well and killing it according to the instructions of Islamic law is not possible, then wherever a wound is inflicted on its body and it dies on account of that wound, it becomes lawful to eat. In such a case, it is not necessary to make it face qibla. However, the other conditions that were mentioned with regard to slaughtering an animal must be fulfilled.

RECOMMENDED (*MUSTAḤABB*) ACTS WHEN SLAUGHTERING AN ANIMAL

Ruling 2616. Jurists (*fuqahāʾ*) – may Allah's pleasure be with them – have considered a number of things to be recommended when slaughtering an animal:

1. when slaughtering a sheep, both its front legs and one of its back legs should be tied together, and the other leg should be left free. When slaughtering a cow, all its front and back legs should be tied, and its tail should be left free. When slaughtering a camel, if it is sitting, its front legs should be tied together from the lower part of its leg up to its knees or below the top of its leg, and its back legs should be left free. If it is standing, its left leg should be tied. It is recommended that a chicken be let free after it is slaughtered so that it can flap its wings;
2. before slaughtering the animal, water should be placed in front of it;
3. the animal should be slaughtered in a manner that reduces its suffering. For example, the knife should be well sharpened, and the animal should be slaughtered swiftly.

DISAPPROVED (*MAKRŪH*) ACTS WHEN SLAUGHTERING AN ANIMAL

Ruling 2617. In some traditions, a number of things are considered to be disapproved when slaughtering an animal:

1. to remove the hide of an animal before the spirit (*rūḥ*) has left its body;
2. to slaughter an animal in a place where a similar animal can see it being slaughtered;
3. to slaughter an animal at night or before midday (*ẓuhr*) on Friday. However, it is not disapproved in case of necessity;
4. for a person to slaughter a quadruped he has raised himself.

LAWS RELATING TO HUNTING WITH WEAPONS

Ruling 2618. If a wild animal whose meat is lawful to eat is hunted with a weapon and it dies, its meat is lawful to eat and its body is pure on the fulfilment of five conditions:

1. the hunting weapon must be sharp, like a knife or a sword, or it must be like a spear or an arrow that can pierce an animal's body. With regard to the latter [i.e. hunting weapons that pierce an animal's body,] if the weapon does not have a spearhead, then for the animal to be lawful to eat, it is a condition that the weapon wound and pierce the animal's body. But if the weapon does have a spearhead, it is sufficient that it kills the animal even though it does not wound it. If an animal is hunted using a trap, piece of wood, stone, or something similar, and it dies, the animal does not become pure and it is unlawful to eat. The same applies, based on obligatory precaution, if the animal is hunted using something sharp that is not a weapon, such as a knitting needle, fork, skewer, or something similar. If an animal is hunted using a gun, in the event that the bullet sinks into and tears the animal's body, it is pure and lawful to eat, irrespective of whether or not the bullet is sharp and conical in shape. It is not necessary that the bullet be made of iron.

However, if the bullet does not sink into the animal's body but the striking force of it kills the animal, or the heat of it burns the animal's body and the animal dies, then it being pure and lawful to eat is problematic;

2. the person hunting the animal must be a Muslim or the child of a Muslim on condition that the child can discern good from evil. If he is a disbeliever who is not from among the People of the Book, or he is subject to the rules applicable to disbelievers, such as a *nāṣibī*, the hunted animal is not lawful. In fact, even if a disbeliever who is from among the People of the Book hunts an animal and mentions the name of Allah the Exalted, the hunted animal is not lawful to eat based on obligatory precaution;
3. the weapon must be used for hunting an animal. Therefore, if, for example, a person aims at a particular target and incidentally kills an animal, the animal is not pure and eating it is unlawful. However, if he shoots an arrow intending to hunt a particular animal but kills another animal instead, that animal is lawful to eat;
4. at the time of using the weapon, the person must mention the name of Allah the Exalted. In the event that he mentions the name of Allah the Exalted before the animal is hit, it is sufficient. If he intentionally does not mention the name of Allah the Exalted, the animal does not become lawful; but there is no problem if he forgets to do so;
5. the hunter must reach the animal after it has died, or if it is still alive, there must not be enough time to slaughter it. In the event that there is enough time to slaughter it but he does not do so before it dies, it is unlawful to eat.

Ruling 2619. If two people hunt an animal and one of them fulfils the conditions mentioned above but the other does not – for example, one of them mentions the name of Allah the Exalted but the other intentionally does not – the animal is not lawful to eat.

Ruling 2620. If, for example, an animal falls into some water after it is hit by an arrow, and one knows that the animal has died due to being hit by both the arrow and falling into the water, the animal is not lawful to eat. In fact, if he does not know that the animal died solely due to the arrow, it is not lawful to eat.

Ruling 2621. If a person hunts an animal with a dog or a weapon that is usurped (*ghaṣbī*), the animal is lawful to eat and belongs to him. However, in addition to the fact that he has sinned, he must pay a fee to the owner for using the weapon or the dog.

Ruling 2622. If a person uses a sword or some other hunting weapon to cut off some parts of an animal's body, such as its front and back legs, those parts are unlawful to eat. However, if the animal is slaughtered having fulfilled the conditions mentioned in Ruling 2618, then the rest of its body is lawful to eat. If the hunting weapon cuts the animal's body in two, and the conditions mentioned above are fulfilled, and its head and neck remain on one part, and the hunter reaches the animal after it has died, then both parts of the body are lawful to eat. The same applies if the animal is alive but there is insufficient time to slaughter it. However, if there is sufficient time to slaughter it and it is possible that it may live for some time, then the part that does not have the head and neck is unlawful to eat. As for the part that has the head and neck, it is lawful to eat if the animal is slaughtered according to the instructions mentioned earlier; otherwise, that part is also unlawful to eat.

Ruling 2623. If an animal is cut in two with some wood, stone, or something else with which it is not correct to hunt an animal, the part that does not have the head and neck is unlawful to eat. As for the part that has the head and neck, it is lawful to eat if the animal is alive and it may stay alive for a while and it is slaughtered according to the instructions mentioned earlier; otherwise, that part is also unlawful to eat.

Ruling 2624. If an animal is killed by hunting or is slaughtered and a live offspring is taken out of its womb, in the event that the offspring is slaughtered according to the instructions mentioned earlier, it is lawful to eat; otherwise, it is unlawful to eat.

Ruling 2625. If an animal is killed by hunting or is slaughtered and a dead offspring is taken out of its womb, it is pure and lawful to eat in the event that it did not die before its mother was killed or due to a delay in taking it out of its mother's womb, and its development is complete and hair or wool has grown on its body.

HUNTING WITH A HUNTING DOG

Ruling 2626. If a hunting dog hunts a wild animal that is lawful to eat, the hunted animal is pure and lawful to eat if six conditions are fulfilled:

1. the dog must be trained in a manner that whenever it is sent to hunt, it goes, and whenever it is restrained, it stays. However, there is no problem if it cannot be restrained once it is has drawn close to the prey and seen it. There is also no problem if it has a habit of eating the prey before its owner reaches it. Similarly, there is no problem if it has a habit of drinking the prey's blood. However, based on obligatory precaution, the condition is that if its owner wishes to take the prey from it, it must not have a habit of preventing its owner and opposing him;
2. its owner must have sent it [to hunt the prey]. Therefore, if the dog hunts the prey of its own accord and kills it, it is unlawful to eat it. In fact, if it hunts the prey of its own accord and after that its owner calls it to catch the prey quicker, then even if the dog hastens to the prey on account of its owner's call, one must refrain from eating the prey based on obligatory precaution;
3. the person who sends the dog must be a Muslim as per the details mentioned in the conditions relating to hunting with a weapon;
4. when the hunter sends the dog, or before the dog reaches the prey, the hunter must mention the name of Allah the Exalted. If he intentionally does not mention the name of Allah the Exalted, the prey is unlawful to eat. However, there is no problem if he forgets;
5. the prey must die due to the wound inflicted by the dog's teeth. Therefore, if the dog suffocates the prey or if the prey dies as a result of running or fear, it is not lawful to eat;
6. the person who sent the dog must reach the prey after it has

died, or if it is still alive, there should not be enough time to slaughter it as long as he has not delayed in reaching the prey for an abnormal length of time. If when he reaches the prey there is enough time to slaughter it but he does not, it is not lawful to eat.

Ruling 2627. If the person who sent the dog reaches the prey when there is enough time for him to slaughter it, in the event that some time passes while he does some things that are preliminary to slaughtering it, such as taking out his knife, and the prey dies, it is lawful to eat it. However, if he does not have anything with him to slaughter the prey with and it dies, then based on obligatory precaution, it is not lawful to eat it. Of course, if he lets the prey go in this situation so that the dog kills it, it becomes lawful to eat.

Ruling 2628. If a person sends a number of dogs to hunt a prey together and all of them fulfil the conditions mentioned in Ruling 2626, the prey is lawful to eat. But if one of the dogs does not fulfil those conditions, the prey is unlawful to eat.

Ruling 2629. If a person sends a dog to hunt an animal and the dog hunts another animal instead, that animal is lawful to eat and pure. Also, if the dog hunts that animal and another animal, both of them are lawful to eat and are pure.

Ruling 2630. If a number of people together send a dog for hunting and one of them intentionally does not mention the name of Allah the Exalted, the prey is unlawful to eat. If one of the dogs that are sent has not been trained in the manner described in Ruling 2626, the prey is unlawful to eat.

Ruling 2631. If a hawk or animal other than a hunting dog hunts an animal, that animal is not lawful to eat. However, if the hunter reaches the animal while it is still alive and slaughters it in the manner mentioned earlier, it is lawful to eat.

FISHING AND HUNTING LOCUSTS

Ruling 2632. If a fish is commonly considered to have scales – even though its scales may have fallen off due to some incident – and it is caught alive in the water and dies out of the water, it is pure and lawful to eat. In the event that it dies in the water, it is pure but it is unlawful to eat even if it dies by means of something, such as poison; however, if it dies in a fishing net in the water, it is lawful to eat. As for fish that are commonly considered not to have scales, they are unlawful to eat even if they are caught alive in the water and die out of the water.

Ruling 2633. If a fish springs out of the water, or a wave throws it out, or the water recedes and the fish is left stranded on dry land, then in the event that someone catches it with his hands or by some other means before it dies, it is lawful to eat after it dies. But if it dies before it is caught, it is unlawful to eat.

Ruling 2634. It is not necessary for a fisherman to be a Muslim [for the fish to be lawful to eat], nor does he have to mention the name of Allah the Exalted at the time of catching the fish. However, a Muslim must witness – or attain confidence (*iṭmiʾnān*) in some other way – that the fish was caught alive in the water or that it died in the net in the water.

Ruling 2635. If it is not known whether a dead fish was caught alive or dead in the water, in the event that it is in the hands of a Muslim who has disposal over it, which is proof of it being lawful to eat – for example, he sells or buys it – it is lawful. However, if the fish is in the hands of a disbeliever, then even if he says, 'I caught it alive', it is unlawful to eat unless one is confident that he caught it alive in the water or that it died in the net in the water.

Ruling 2636. It is permitted (*jāʾiz*) to eat a live fish.

Ruling 2637. If a fish is roasted alive or killed out of the water before it dies [by itself], it is permitted to eat it.

Ruling 2638. If a fish is cut in two out of the water and one part falls in the water while still alive, it is permitted to eat the part that is out of the water.

Ruling 2639. If a person catches a locust alive in his hands or by other means, it is lawful to eat it after it dies. It is not necessary that the person who catches it be a Muslim, nor does he have to mention the name of Allah the Exalted at the time of catching it. However, if a dead locust is in the hands of a disbeliever and it is not known whether he caught it alive or not, it is unlawful to eat it even if he says, 'I caught it alive'.

Ruling 2640. It is unlawful to eat a locust that has not developed wings and cannot fly.

CHAPTER THIRTY-THREE

Eating and Drinking

Ruling 2641. It is unlawful (*ḥarām*) to eat all birds of prey that have talons, such as falcons, eagles, hawks, and vultures. Similarly, all types of crows, even choughs, are unlawful to eat, based on obligatory precaution (*al-iḥtiyāṭ al-wājib*). Also, every bird that flaps its wings less than it glides while flying and has talons is unlawful to eat. However, every bird that flaps its wings more than it glides while flying is lawful (*ḥalāl*) to eat. Therefore, birds that are unlawful to eat can be distinguished from those that are lawful to eat by considering how they fly. However, if it is not known how a particular bird flies, then, if that bird has a crop, gizzard, or a spur at the back of its feet, it is lawful to eat, and if it does not have any of these, it is unlawful to eat. As for other birds, apart from the ones that have been mentioned, such as chickens, pigeons, sparrows, and even ostriches and peacocks, they are all lawful to eat. However, killing some birds is disapproved (*makrūh*), such as hoopoes and swallows. As for animals that fly but do not have feathers, such as bats, they are unlawful to eat, so too are bees, mosquitoes, and flying insects, based on obligatory precaution.

Ruling 2642. If something [from an animal's body] that contains life is separated from the animal – for example, a person cuts off the tail fat or some flesh from a living sheep – it is impure (*najis*) and unlawful to eat.

Ruling 2643. Even from those animals that are lawful to eat, some parts must not be eaten. These things are fourteen in number:

1. blood;
2. droppings;
3. penis;
4. vagina;
5. uterus;
6. glands;
7. testicles;
8. pituitary gland;
9. spinal cord;
10. the two nerves that are on either side of the vertebral column, based on obligatory precaution;
11. gallbladder;
12. spleen;

13. urinary bladder;
14. iris of the eye.

All these things are from animals whose meat is lawful to eat, excluding birds, fish, and locusts. With regard to birds, their blood and droppings are definitely unlawful; apart from these two things, in the case of birds, all the other things mentioned in the list above are unlawful based on obligatory precaution. Similarly, based on obligatory precaution, the blood and droppings of fish and the droppings of locusts are unlawful; apart from these, nothing else of them is unlawful.

Ruling 2644. It is unlawful to drink the urine of animals whose meat is unlawful to eat. The same applies to the urine of animals whose meat is lawful to eat, even that of camels, based on obligatory precaution. However, there is no problem in drinking the urine of camels, cows, and sheep for medical treatment.

Ruling 2645. It is unlawful to eat mud. The same applies to soil and sand, based on obligatory precaution. If one is compelled to, there is no problem in eating Daghistani or Armenian mud, or other mud, for medical treatment. It is permitted (*jāʾiz*) to eat a little – i.e. up to the size of an average chickpea – of the *turbah*[1] of His Eminence Sayyid al-Shuhadāʾ [Imam al-Ḥusayn] (ʿA) for medicinal purposes. If the *turbah* is not taken from the sacred grave itself or from around it, then even if it can be called '*turbah* of Imam al-Ḥusayn (ʿA)', based on obligatory precaution, it must be dissolved in some water and suchlike until it becomes diluted and then drunk. Similarly, this precaution (*iḥtiyāṭ*) must be observed when one does not have confidence (*iṭmiʾnān*) that the *turbah* is from the sacred grave of His Eminence and there is no proof to verify it.

Ruling 2646. It is not unlawful to swallow nasal mucus or phlegm that has gathered in the mouth. Similarly, there is no problem in swallowing food particles that become dislodged from between the teeth when using a toothpick.

[1] A *turbah* is a piece of earth or clay on which one places his forehead when prostrating.

Ruling 2647. It is unlawful to eat or drink anything that would cause death or inflict significant harm to a person.

Ruling 2648. It is disapproved to eat the meat of a horse, mule, or donkey. If someone has sexual intercourse with these animals, their meat becomes unlawful. Similarly, their milk and offspring after intercourse with them become unlawful to consume, based on obligatory precaution, and their urine and dung become impure. Such animals must be taken out of the city and sold elsewhere. If the person who had sexual intercourse with the animal is not its owner, he must pay the value of the animal to its owner. The money received from the sale of the animal belongs to the person who had sexual intercourse with it. If a person has sexual intercourse with an animal whose meat is usually eaten, such as a cow, sheep, and camel, their urine and dung become impure and it is unlawful to eat their meat. Similarly, based on obligatory precaution, drinking their milk and the milk of their offspring is unlawful. Furthermore, the animal must be killed and burnt, and if the person who had sexual intercourse with it is not its owner, he must pay its value to its owner.

Ruling 2649. If a kid [i.e. a baby goat] suckles milk from a pig to the extent that the milk strengthens its flesh and bones, the kid and its offspring become unlawful to eat and their milk becomes unlawful to drink. In case a kid suckles milk to a lesser extent, then based on obligatory precaution, it must undergo a process of *istibrāʾ*, and after that it becomes lawful to eat. The process of *istibrāʾ* for a kid is that it must suckle pure milk for seven days. If it does not need milk, it must eat grass for seven days. Based on obligatory precaution, a suckling calf, lamb, and the young of other animals whose meat is lawful to eat fall under the same rule (*ḥukm*) as a kid. It is unlawful to eat the meat of an excrement-eating animal, but in the event that it undergoes the process of *istibrāʾ*, it becomes lawful to eat. The process of *istibrāʾ* for such animals was explained in Ruling 219.

Ruling 2650. Drinking wine [and other alcoholic beverages] is unlawful. In some traditions, it is considered one of the gravest sins. It has been reported from Imam al-Ṣādiq (ʿA) that he said, 'Wine is the root of evil and the origin of sins. A person who drinks wine loses his intellect, and at that moment, he does not know Allah, fear any sin, keep the respect of anyone, observe the rights of his near relatives, or turn away from openly obscene acts. If he takes a sip of it, Allah the Exalted, the angels, the Prophets, and the believers curse him. And if he drinks until he becomes intoxicated, the spirit of belief and the ability to know Allah leave him and the spirit of filthy evil takes their place. His prayers (*ṣalāh*) are not accepted for forty days (even though it is obligatory (*wājib*) on him to perform his prayers and his prayers are valid (*ṣaḥīḥ*)).'

Ruling 2651. It is unlawful to eat something from a table on which wine is consumed. Similarly, [it is unlawful,] based on obligatory precaution, to sit at such a table.

Ruling 2652. It is obligatory for every Muslim to give food and water to another Muslim who is on the verge of dying from hunger or thirst and save him from death if his own life is not in danger. The same applies if the person is not a Muslim and is someone whom it is not permitted to kill.

ETIQUETTES OF EATING

Ruling 2653. With regard to eating and drinking, the following things are recommended (*mustaḥabb*) for one to do:

1. to wash both hands before eating;
2. to wash both hands after eating and dry them with a piece of cloth;
3. the host should start eating before everyone else and stop eating after everyone else. Before eating, the host should wash his hands first, then the person seated to his right [should wash his], and so on until the turn comes to the person seated to the left of the host. After eating, the person seated to the left of the host should wash his hands first, and so on until the turn comes to the host;
4. to say '*bismillāh*' at the beginning of the meal. If there is a variety of dishes on the table, one should say '*bismillāh*' before eating each of them;
5. to eat with the right hand;

6. to eat with three or more fingers and to avoid eating with two fingers;
7. if a number of people are seated at a table, each person should eat the food that is in front of him;
8. to eat small morsels;
9. to sit for a long time at the table and to prolong the meal;
10. to chew the food properly;
11. to praise the Lord of the worlds after the meal;
12. to lick one's fingers;
13. to use a toothpick after the meal. However, one should not pick his teeth with a toothpick made from a sweet basil plant, pomegranate tree, reed, or the leaf of a date palm;
14. to gather and eat the pieces of food that have fallen on the table cloth. However, if one is having a meal outdoors, it is recommended to leave the pieces of food for birds and animals;
15. to eat at the start of the day and the start of the night, and to avoid eating during the day and during the night;
16. to lie on one's back after a meal and place the right foot over the left foot;
17. to eat salt at the start of the meal and the end of it;
18. to wash fruit before eating it.

THINGS THAT ARE DISCOURAGED (*MADHMŪM*) WHEN EATING

Ruling 2654. The following things are discouraged when eating:

1. to eat when one is full;
2. to eat until one is full. It is reported that the Lord of the worlds detests a full stomach more than anything else;
3. to look at the faces of other people while [they are] eating;
4. to eat [very] hot food;
5. to blow on something that one is eating or drinking;
6. to wait for another dish after bread has been placed on the table;
7. to cut bread with a knife;
8. to place bread under a utensil for food;

9. to clean the meat off a bone to the extent that nothing remains on it;
10. to peel the skin of fruit that is eaten with its skin;
11. to throw away fruit before it is completely eaten.

ETIQUETTES OF DRINKING

Ruling 2655. A number of things are considered to be etiquettes of drinking:

1. to drink water by sipping it;
2. to drink water during the day while standing;
3. to say '*bismillāh*' before drinking water and '*alḥamdu lillāh*' after drinking it;
4. to drink water in three gulps;
5. to drink water when one desires it;
6. after drinking water, to remember His Eminence Abā ʿAbdillāh [Imam al-Ḥusayn] (ʿA) and his household, and to curse his killers.

THINGS THAT ARE DISCOURAGED (*MADHMŪM*) WHEN DRINKING

Ruling 2656. It is discouraged to drink a lot of water, to drink water after eating fatty food, and to drink water at night while standing. It is also discouraged to drink water with the left hand, from a broken side of the vessel, and from the place of its handle.

CHAPTER THIRTY-FOUR

Vow (*Nadhr*) and Covenant (*ʿAhd*)

Ruling 2657. A vow is when a person makes it obligatory (*wājib*) on himself, for the sake of Allah the Exalted, to perform a good deed or refrain from doing something that is better not to do.

Ruling 2658. In a vow, a formula (*ṣīghah*) must be said. It is not necessary that the formula be said in Arabic; therefore, if a person says [in English, for example], 'Should such and such sick person get better, it is incumbent upon me to give £100 to a poor person (*faqīr*) for the sake of Allah', his vow is valid (*ṣaḥīḥ*). And if he says, 'For the sake of Allah, I vow to do such and such a thing', then based on obligatory precaution (*al-iḥtiyāṭ al-wājib*), he must do that thing. However, if he does not mention the name of Allah the Exalted and only says, 'I make a vow', or if he mentions the name of one of the Friends (*awliyāʾ*) of Allah the Exalted, the vow is not valid. If a vow is valid and a duty-bound person (*mukallaf*)[1] intentionally (*ʿamdan*) does not act according to it, he will have sinned and he must give recompense (*kaffārah*). The *kaffārah* for not fulfilling one's vow is the same as the *kaffārah* for not fulfilling one's oath (*qasam*), which will be mentioned later.[2]

Ruling 2659. A person who makes a vow must be of the age of legal responsibility (*bāligh*) and sane (*ʿāqil*). He must also make the vow of his own volition (*ikhtiyār*) and have the intention (*qaṣd*) to make it. Therefore, a vow is not valid if it is made by someone who has been compelled to make it, or who in his anger made it unintentionally or did not make it of his own volition.

Ruling 2660. With regard to a person who is foolish with finances (*safīh*) – i.e. someone who spends his wealth on futile tasks – if, for example, he vows to give something to the poor (*fuqarāʾ*), it is not valid. The same applies to someone who has been proclaimed bankrupt (*mufallas*); therefore, if he vows to, for example, give something to the poor from his property over which he has been prohibited from having disposal, it is not valid.

Ruling 2661. The vow made by a wife without prior permission from

[1] A *mukallaf* is someone who is legally obliged to fulfil religious duties.

[2] See Ruling 2687.

or subsequent consent of her husband on a matter that infringes on his conjugal rights is not valid, even if she made the vow before getting married. As for the validity of a wife's vow made with respect to her own wealth without her husband's consent, this is problematic (*maḥall al-ishkāl*) [i.e. based on obligatory precaution, it is not valid].[3] Therefore, in such a case, precaution (*iḥtiyāṭ*) must be observed except for [a vow made for] performing hajj, giving alms tax (zakat), giving alms to the poor (*ṣadaqah*), being benevolent to her mother and father, and maintaining good family ties (*ṣilat al-arḥām*).

Ruling 2662. If a wife makes a vow with her husband's consent, he cannot annul her vow or prevent her from fulfilling it.

Ruling 2663. The vow of a son/daughter is not conditional on the father's consent. However, if the father or mother prohibits him/her from doing what he/she has vowed to do, and their prohibition is due to their compassion for him/her, and his/her opposition would annoy them, then his/her vow becomes invalid (*bāṭil*).

Ruling 2664. A person can only vow to perform something that is possible for him to perform. Therefore, if a person who, for example, is unable to walk to Karbala vows to do so, his vow is not valid. If at the time of making a vow one is able to perform it but later becomes unable to do so, his vow becomes void (*bāṭil*) and nothing is obligatory for him [concerning this matter]. The exception to this is if he vows to keep a fast, in which case if he cannot do so, the obligatory precaution is that he must give 750 grams of food to the poor for every day [that he had vowed to fast but was unable to], or he must give 1.5 kilograms of food to someone to fast on his behalf.

Ruling 2665. If a person vows to do something unlawful (*ḥarām*) or disapproved (*makrūh*), or to refrain from doing something obligatory (*wājib*) or recommended (*mustaḥabb*), his vow is not valid.

Ruling 2666. If a person vows to do – or refrain from doing – something permissible (*mubāḥ*), in the event that doing it and refraining

[3] As mentioned in Ruling 6, the term 'problematic' (*maḥall al-ishkāl*) amounts to saying the ruling is based on obligatory precaution.

from doing it are legally (*sharʿan*) the same from all aspects, his vow is not valid. However, if doing it is legally better from some aspect, and a person makes a vow intending that aspect – for example, he vows to eat something that would give him the strength to worship (*ʿibādah*) – his vow is valid. Similarly, if refraining from doing it is legally better from some aspect and a person makes a vow to refrain from doing that thing and intends that aspect – for example, he vows to refrain from smoking as it is harmful and an obstacle to performing religious duties in the best way – his vow is valid. However, if refraining from smoking becomes harmful for him, his vow becomes invalid.

Ruling 2667. If a person vows to perform his obligatory prayers (*ṣalāh*) in a place where there is no particular reason for one to receive more reward for performing prayers there – for example, he vows to perform prayers in an ordinary room – then, in the event that performing prayers there is legally better from some aspect – for example, due to the solitude there one is able to perform prayers with presence of heart – in such a case, if he makes a vow concerning this aspect, his vow is valid.

Ruling 2668. If a person vows to do something, he must do it in the manner he vowed to do it. Therefore, if he vows to give alms to the poor on the first day of the month, or to fast on that day, or to perform the prayer for the first of the month, in the event that he does the vowed act before or after that day, it does not suffice. Also, if he vows to give alms to the poor once a particular sick person gets better, in the event that he gives the alms before the sick person gets better, it is not sufficient.

Ruling 2669. If a person vows to keep a fast but does not specify when and for how long, in the event that he fasts for one day, it is sufficient. If he vows to perform prayers but does not specify how many prayers or their particulars, in the event that he performs a single two-unit (*rakʿah*) prayer or the *witr* prayer,[4] it is also sufficient. If he vows to give alms to the poor but does not specify the type of thing he

[4] This is the one *rakʿah* prayer that is performed as part of the night prayer. See Ruling 752.

will give or its quantity, in the event that he gives something about which it could be said, 'He has given alms to the poor', he will have fulfilled his vow. If he vows to do something for the sake of Allah the Exalted, then in case he performs one prayer, fasts for one day, or gives something to the poor as alms, he will have fulfilled his vow.

Ruling 2670. If a person vows to fast on a specific day, he must fast on that day. In case he intentionally does not fast on that day, he must not only make it up [i.e. keep a *qaḍā'* fast] but give *kaffārah* as well. However, he can choose to travel on that day and not fast, and in the event that he is already on a journey, it is not necessary for him to make an intention to stay [for ten or more days] and fast. In case a person does not fast due to travelling or some other legitimate excuse (*ʿudhr*), such as sickness or menstruation (*ḥayḍ*), it is necessary for that person to keep a *qaḍā'* fast, but there is no *kaffārah*.

Ruling 2671. If a person volitionally does not fulfil his vow, he must give *kaffārah*.

Ruling 2672. If a person vows to refrain from an act for a specific period, then once the period comes to an end, he can do the act. If before the period comes to an end he does the act owing to forgetfulness or necessity, then nothing is obligatory for him [concerning this matter]; however, he must still not do the act [again] until the period comes to an end. In the event that he does the act again without a legitimate excuse before the period comes to an end, he must give *kaffārah*.

Ruling 2673. If a person vows to refrain from an act but does not specify a period for it, in the event that he does the act owing to forgetfulness, necessity, negligence, error, or because someone compelled him, or he was inculpably ignorant (*al-jāhil al-qāṣir*),[5] then in any of these cases, it is not obligatory for him to give *kaffārah*. However, the vow remains in place; therefore, if he does the act volitionally from then onwards, he must give *kaffārah*.

[5] 'Inculpably ignorant' is a term used to refer to someone who has a valid excuse for not knowing; for example, he relied upon something that he thought was authoritative but in fact was not.

Ruling 2674. If a person vows to fast on a specific day every week, such as Friday, in the event that Eid al-Fiṭr or Eid al-Aḍḥā[6] falls on a Friday, or if on Friday the person has another legitimate excuse to not fast, such as travelling or *ḥayḍ*, he/she must not fast on that day but must keep a *qaḍāʾ* fast.

Ruling 2675. If a person vows to give a specific amount of alms to the poor, in the event that he dies before he is able to give the alms, it is not necessary for that amount to be given as alms to the poor from his estate. However, it is better that his *bāligh* heirs give the amount on behalf of the deceased from their share [of the inheritance].

Ruling 2676. If a person vows to give alms to a specific poor person, he cannot then give it to another poor person. If the specified poor person dies, it is not necessary for the person who made the vow to give the alms to his heirs.

Ruling 2677. If a person vows to visit [i.e. go for *ziyārah* to] the burial place of a specific Imam (ʿA), such as His Eminence Abā ʿAbdillāh [Imam al-Ḥusayn] (ʿA), in the event that he goes for *ziyārah* of another Imam (ʿA), it is not sufficient. If he is unable to go for *ziyārah* of that particular Imam (ʿA) owing to a legitimate excuse, then nothing is obligatory for him [concerning this matter].

Ruling 2678. If a person vows to go for *ziyārah* but does not vow to perform the ritual bathing (*ghusl*) for *ziyārah* nor to perform the prayer for *ziyārah*, it is not necessary for him to perform them.

Ruling 2679. If a person vows to give something to the shrine (*ḥaram*) of one of the Infallible Imams (ʿA) or one of the children of the Infallible Imams (ʿA) but does not have a specific intention in mind as to how it should be spent, then it must be spent for constructing, illuminating, and carpeting the shrine, or for any similar use. If this is not possible or the shrine is totally needless of the vowed item, it must be used in helping needy visitors to the shrine.

[6] Eid al-Fiṭr is on the 1st of Shawwāl and Eid al-Aḍḥā is on the 10th of Dhū al-Ḥijjah. It is unlawful to fast on these days. See Ruling 1707.

Ruling 2680. If a person vows to give something in the name of the Most Noble Messenger of Allah (Ṣ), one of the Infallible Imams (ʿA), one of the children of the Infallible Imams (ʿA), or one of the past scholars, etc., then in the event that he intends for it to be spent in a specific manner, he must give it to be spent in that manner. However, if he does not intend for it to be spent in any specific way, he must give it to be spent on something that is associated with that distinguished personality, such as helping poor visitors to his shrine, or he must give it to be spent on his shrine or in a way that would elevate his name.

Ruling 2681. If a person vows to give a sheep to the poor as alms, or to give it in the name of one of the Infallible Imams (ʿA), then in the event that it gives milk or gives birth before it is given to fulfil the vow, the milk/lamb belongs to the person who made the vow unless his intention [when he made the vow] included the milk/lamb. However, the sheep's wool and the amount of weight it gains are part of the vow.

Ruling 2682. If a person vows that if a sick person gets better or a traveller returns [safely from his journey], he will do some act, then in the event that it becomes known that before he made the vow the sick person had got better, or the traveller had returned, it is not necessary for him to fulfil the vow.

Ruling 2683. If a father or mother vows to marry his/her daughter to a *sayyid*[7] or someone else, their vow with respect to their daughter is not valid, and it does not place any responsibility (*taklīf*) on her.

Ruling 2684. If a person makes a covenant with Allah the Exalted that he will do some act if a particular legitimate need is fulfilled, he must do the act once his need is fulfilled. If he makes a covenant to do something without mentioning any need, it becomes obligatory for him to do the act.

Ruling 2685. As with a vow, a formula must be said in a covenant. For

[7] A *sayyid* is a male descendant of Hāshim, the great grandfather of Prophet Muḥammad (Ṣ).

example, a person says, 'I make a covenant with Allah the Exalted to do such and such act'. The act the person covenants to do does not need to be legally better; rather, it is sufficient that it is not something that has been legally prohibited and would be preferred in the opinion of rational people, or it is in the person's interest that it be done. If the act is no longer in the person's interest after the covenant is made or is no longer legally preferred, even though it may not have become disapproved, it is not necessary to fulfil the covenant.

Ruling 2686. If a person does not fulfil his covenant, he will have sinned and must give *kaffārah*. The *kaffārah* is feeding sixty poor people, fasting two consecutive months, or freeing a slave.

CHAPTER THIRTY-FIVE

Oath (*Qasam*)

Ruling 2687. If a person takes an oath to do something or to refrain from doing something – for example, he takes an oath to keep a fast or to stop smoking – then in the event that he intentionally (*ʿamdan*) does not fulfil his oath, he will have sinned and he must give recompense (*kaffārah*). That is, he must free a slave, feed ten poor people (*fuqarāʾ*), or clothe them. If he cannot do any of these, he must fast for three consecutive days.

Ruling 2688. An oath must fulfil the following conditions [for it to be valid (*ṣaḥīḥ*)]:

1. the person taking the oath must be of the age of legal responsibility (*bāligh*) and sane (*ʿāqil*). He must also have an intention (*qaṣd*) to take the oath and to take it of his own volition (*ikhtiyār*). Therefore, an oath taken by a child, an insane or intoxicated person, or someone who has been compelled, is not valid. The same applies [i.e. an oath is not valid] if it is taken by someone who in his anger took it unintentionally or did not take it of his own volition;
2. the act for which one takes an oath must not be unlawful (*ḥarām*) or disapproved (*makrūh*). And the act that one takes an oath to refrain from must not be an obligatory (*wājib*) or recommended (*mustaḥabb*) act. If a person takes an oath to do – or refrain from doing – something that is permissible (*mubāḥ*), in the event that doing it or refraining from doing it is something that would be preferred in the opinion of rational people or it is in the person's worldly interest, the oath is valid;
3. a person must swear by one of the names of the Lord of the worlds that are reserved exclusively for His Holy Essence, such as 'God' and 'Allah'. Alternatively, Allah the Exalted may be invoked using words that describe attributes and actions exclusive to Him; for example, one can say, 'I swear by the one who created the heavens and the earth'. If one swears by a name that is also used for a being other than Allah the Exalted, but it is used so frequently to refer to Allah the Exalted that whenever someone mentions it, the Holy Essence of the Lord comes to mind – such as swearing by 'the Creator' (al-Khāliq) or 'the Sustainer' (al-Rāziq) – this too is valid. In fact, if one swears by a name that only comes to mind when one is taking

an oath – such as 'the All-Hearing' (al-Samīʿ) and 'the All-Seeing' (al-Baṣīr) – then again the oath is valid;

4. one must verbally say the oath. However, it is valid if a dumb person takes an oath using sign language. If a person who is unable to speak writes it down and intends it in his heart, it is sufficient. In fact, if a person who is able to speak writes it down, then based on obligatory precaution (*al-iḥtiyāṭ al-wājib*), he must fulfil it;
5. it must be possible for one to fulfil the oath. If at the time of taking the oath it is not possible for one to fulfil it but afterwards it becomes possible, it is sufficient. If at the time of taking the oath it is possible for one to fulfil it but afterwards he becomes unable to fulfil it, then his oath becomes annulled from the time he became unable to fulfil it. The same applies if fulfilling the oath becomes so excessively difficult (*mashaqqah*) for him that he cannot endure what it takes to fulfil it. If him not being able to fulfil the oath was due to his own free actions, or it was not due to his own free actions but he did not have a legitimate excuse (*ʿudhr*) for delaying the fulfilment of the oath when he was able to fulfil it, then he will have sinned and *kaffārah* is obligatory for him.

Ruling 2689. If a father prevents his son from taking an oath, or if a husband prevents his wife from taking an oath, then any oaths they take are not valid.

Ruling 2690. If a son takes an oath without his father's permission, or a wife takes an oath without her husband's permission, the father and the husband can annul their oaths.

Ruling 2691. If a person does not fulfil his oath owing to forgetfulness, necessity, or negligence, it is not obligatory for him to give *kaffārah*. The same applies if someone forces him not to fulfil his oath. Furthermore, if an obsessively doubtful person (*muwaswis*) takes an oath – for example, he says, 'By Allah! I will engage in performing prayers now', and due to his obsessive doubting (*waswās*) he does not engage in performing his prayers, in the event that his obsessive doubting was such that he did not act of his own volition when he did not fulfil his oath, *kaffārah* is not obligatory for him.

Ruling 2692. If a person takes an oath to establish that what he is saying is the truth, in the event that his words are indeed true, the act of taking such an oath is disapproved; and if his words are false, it is unlawful. In fact, a false oath taken to resolve a dispute is one of the major sins. However, if one takes such an oath to save himself or another Muslim from the evil of an unjust person, there is no problem; rather, it sometimes becomes obligatory to do so. Furthermore, if someone is able to employ equivocation (*tawriyah*) while being aware of doing so, then the obligatory precaution is that he must do so. *Tawriyah* is when a person intends a meaning that is contrary to the apparent meaning of what he says, i.e. what he says does not indicate what he intends [but at the same time, it is not, strictly speaking, a lie]. For example, an unjust person wishes to harass a particular individual, and he asks someone, 'Have you seen him?' Now, even though the person being asked saw him an hour ago, he replies, 'I have not seen him', and by that he means he has not seen him in the last five minutes.

CHAPTER THIRTY-SIX

Charitable Endowment (*Waqf*)

Ruling 2693. If a person endows some property, it no longer belongs to him. Neither he nor anyone else can gift or sell the item, nor can anyone inherit it. However, in some cases mentioned in Rulings 2104 and 2105, there is no problem in selling it.

Ruling 2694. It is not necessary for the formula (*ṣīghah*) of an endowment to be said in Arabic; rather, if a person says [in English], for example, 'I endow this book to students of the religious sciences', the endowment is valid (*ṣaḥīḥ*). In fact, an endowment can also be realised by an act. For example, an endowment is realised if a person places a *haṣīr*[1] in a mosque with the intention (*qaṣd*) of making an endowment to the mosque, or if he builds a building in the way that mosques are built with the intention of making a mosque. However, an endowment is not realised by only making an intention. Also, acceptance is not necessary in an endowment, be it a public charitable endowment (*al-waqf al-ʿāmm*) or a private charitable endowment (*al-waqf al-khāṣṣ*).[2] Furthermore, an intention to attain proximity to Allah (*qaṣd al-qurbah*) is not necessary.

Ruling 2695. If a person specifies some property for an endowment but changes his mind or dies before he gives it as an endowment, then an endowment is not realised. The same applies if, in a private charitable endowment, the beneficiary of the endowment (*al-mawqūf ʿalayh*) dies before he takes possession.

Ruling 2696. An endower (*wāqif*) of some property must endow it forever from the moment he makes the charitable endowment. Therefore, if, for example, he says, 'This property is to be a charitable endowment after my death', it is not valid because it is not an endowment from the moment he says the formula until his death. Similarly, if he says, 'This is a charitable endowment for ten years but not after that', or if he says, 'This is a charitable endowment for ten years; after that, it will not be a charitable endowment for five years, and after

[1] A *ḥaṣīr* is a mat that is made by plaiting or weaving straw, reed, or similar materials of plant origin.

[2] A 'public' charitable endowment is one that is made for a public interest – such as an endowment to a school – or to a general category of people, such as the poor. A 'private' charitable endowment, on the other hand, is one that is made to a particular individual or individuals, such as an endowment to one's children.

that, it will be a charitable endowment again', the endowment is not valid. However, in this case, if he makes the intention of a bequest (*ḥubs*),[3] then a bequest is realised.

Ruling 2697. A private charitable endowment is valid only if the endowed property (*al-ʿayn al-mawqūfah*) is placed at the disposal of the individuals to whom it has been endowed or their agent (*wakīl*) or guardian (*walī*); possession of it by the trustee (*mutawallī*) will not suffice. It is sufficient if those who are alive from the first generation of beneficiaries have disposal over it; and if some of them have disposal over it, then the endowment is valid only with respect to them. If a person makes an endowment to his offspring who are minors (*ṣaghīr*s), then as long as the actual property is in his possession, it is sufficient and the endowment is valid.

Ruling 2698. In the case of public charitable endowments, such as those made to schools, mosques, and suchlike, possession is not a requirement and the endowment is realised merely by making the endowment.

Ruling 2699. An endower must be of the age of legal responsibility (*bāligh*), sane (*ʿāqil*), have an intention to make the endowment, and make it of his own volition (*ikhtiyār*). He must also legally (*sharʿan*) have disposal over his own property. Therefore, if a person who is foolish with finances (*safīh*) – i.e. someone who spends his wealth in futile ways – endows something, it is not valid because he does not have right of disposal over his own property.

Ruling 2700. If some property is endowed to a child that is still in the womb of its mother, the validity of it is problematic (*maḥall al-ishkāl*),[4] and it is necessary to observe precaution (*iḥtiyāṭ*) here. However, if some property is endowed for persons who are currently

[3] There are two main differences between a 'bequest' and a 'charitable endowment': firstly, in a bequest, the bequeathed property still belongs to the person who made the bequest, whereas in a charitable endowment, the endowed property no longer belongs to the person who made the endowment. Secondly, a bequest can be made for a temporary period, whereas a charitable endowment must be made forever.

[4] As mentioned in Ruling 6, the term 'problematic' (*maḥall al-ishkāl*) amounts to saying the ruling is based on obligatory precaution.

alive, and after them for those who will be born in the future, then the endowment is valid even if the latter are not in the wombs of their mothers at the time of making the endowment. For example, it is valid if a person endows something to his children, and after them to his grandchildren, and to each generation to use the endowment after the previous generation.

Ruling 2701. If a person endows something to himself – for example, he endows a shop to himself so that after his death the income from it would be spent on paying off his debts or hiring someone to perform his lapsed (*qaḍāʾ*) ritual acts of worship (*ʿibādāt*) – then such an endowment is not valid. However, if, for example, he endows a house to accommodate poor people (*fuqarāʾ*) and he himself becomes poor, he can reside in that house. But if he endows the property so that its rental income is to be distributed among the poor and he himself becomes poor, then for him to take from the rental income is problematic [i.e. based on obligatory precaution (*al-iḥtiyāṭ al-wājib*), he must not take from it].

Ruling 2702. If a person appoints a trustee for the property that he has endowed, the trustee must act according to the endowment. If a person does not appoint anyone, in the event that he has endowed the property to specific individuals, such as his children, the authority (*ikhtiyār*) to use the property lies with them. But if they are not *bāligh*, the authority lies with their guardian. Furthermore, it is not necessary to obtain permission from a fully qualified jurist (*al-ḥākim al-sharʿī*) to use the endowment. However, for matters pertaining to the interest of the endowment or the interest of future generations – such as making repairs to the endowed property and giving it on rent (*ijārah*) for the benefit of subsequent generations – the authority for it lies with a fully qualified jurist.

Ruling 2703. If a person endows some property to the poor or *sādāt*[5] or for its profits to be used for charitable causes, in the event that he does not appoint a trustee for the property, the authority over it lies with a fully qualified jurist.

[5] *Sādāt* (pl. of *sayyid*) are descendants of Hāshim, the great grandfather of Prophet Muḥammad (Ṣ).

Ruling 2704. If a person endows some property to specific individuals, such as his children, so that each generation uses it after the previous generation, in the event that the trustee of the endowment gives it on rent and dies after that, the rental agreement does not become void (*bāṭil*). However, if there is no trustee for the endowment and those from one of the generations for whom the property was endowed give it on rent and after that they die during the rental period, then in the event that those from the next generation do not endorse the rental agreement, it will become void. If the lessee of the rented property has paid the rent for the entire rental period, he can take back the amount he has paid from the time the agreement became void.

Ruling 2705. If the endowed property is ruined, it does not cease to be an endowment unless the endowment is conditional on a particular subject and that subject ceases to exist. For example, a person endows a garden on condition that it remains a garden; if the garden is ruined, the endowment becomes void and reverts to the endower's heirs.

Ruling 2706. If part of a property has been endowed and part of it has not been endowed and the property has not been divided, the trustee of the endowment and the owner of the part that has not been endowed can separate the endowed part.

Ruling 2707. If the trustee of an endowment acts disloyally – for example, he does not spend the income from it in a specified way – then a fully qualified jurist can appoint a trustworthy individual (*amīn*) to join up with him to prevent him from acting disloyally. If this is not possible, a fully qualified jurist can depose him and appoint a trustworthy person as trustee in his place.

Ruling 2708. A rug that has been endowed to a *ḥusayniyyah*[6] cannot be taken to a mosque to be used for prayers (*ṣalāh*) even if the mosque is situated close to the *ḥusayniyyah*. However, if it is the property of the *ḥusayniyyah*, it can be taken to another place with the trustee's consent.

[6] A *ḥusayniyyah* is a congregation hall used by Shia Muslims for religious ceremonies.

Ruling 2709. If some property is endowed for repairing a mosque but the mosque does not need any repairs and neither is it expected that it will need some repair work in the not too distant future, and if it is not possible to collect the income from the property and keep it so that it can be spent on repairing the mosque later on, then in such a case, the obligatory precaution is that the income from the property must be spent on a cause that is close to what the endower had in mind, such as securing items that are required by the mosque or repairing another mosque.

Ruling 2710. If a person endows some property so that the income from it can be used to repair a mosque and be given to the imam of the congregation (*jamāʿah*) and to the person who says the call to prayer (*adhān*) at the mosque, in the event that the endower has specified an amount for each one of them, the income must be spent in that way. But if the endower has not specified the amounts, then the income must first be spent on repairing the mosque. If anything is left over, the trustee must divide it, as he sees fit, between the imam of the congregation and the person who says the *adhān*. However, it is better that these two people arrive at a settlement (*ṣulḥ*) on the division of the income.

CHAPTER THIRTY-SEVEN

Will (*Waṣiyyah*)

Ruling 2711. A will is an instruction by a person for certain tasks to be performed for him after his death. In a will, a person may state that after his death something from his property is to be owned by someone, or that something from his property is to be transferred to someone or be spent on charitable and good causes. In a will, a person may also appoint someone to be the custodian and guardian of his children and dependants. A person who gives effect to a will is called an 'executor' (*waṣī*).

Ruling 2712. If a person who is unable to speak conveys his intentions by indicating, he can make a will for any task. In fact, a will made by a person who is able to speak but conveys his intentions by indicating is also valid (*ṣaḥīḥ*).

Ruling 2713. If a document is found with the signature or seal of the deceased, in the event that there are contextual indicators that make it appear to be the deceased's will, it must be acted upon.

Ruling 2714. A testator (*mūṣī*) [i.e. a person who makes a will] must be of the age of legal responsibility (*bāligh*) and sane (*ʿāqil*); he must not be foolish with finances (*safīh*)[1] and must voluntarily make the will. Therefore, the will of a child who is not *bāligh* is not valid unless the child is ten years old and his will is for his close relatives or for spending on general charitable causes; in these two cases, the will is valid. However, if he makes a will for other than close relatives, or if the child is seven years old and he makes a will that pertains to a small part of his estate, then the validity of such a will is problematic (*maḥall al-ishkāl*);[2] therefore, precaution (*iḥtiyāṭ*) must be observed here. If the person is foolish with finances, his will pertaining to his wealth is ineffective but it is effective with regard to other matters, such as preparing his body for burial.

Ruling 2715. If a person injures himself with the intention of committing suicide or consumes deadly poison and then makes a will

[1] Ruling 2091 provides further clarification of this term: it refers to someone who spends his wealth in futile ways.

[2] As mentioned in Ruling 6, the term 'problematic' (*maḥall al-ishkāl*) amounts to saying the ruling is based on obligatory precaution.

for part of his estate to be spent in a particular way and then dies, his will is not valid unless he was performing jihad in the way of Allah the Exalted. His will with respect to non-financial matters, however, is valid.

Ruling 2716. If a person makes a will that something from his property is to be owned by someone, and if the latter accepts the will – irrespective of whether he accepts it during the lifetime of the testator or after his death – then, as long as the item is not more than a third of the testator's estate, he becomes the owner of the item upon the testator's death.

Ruling 2717. Whenever a person notices the signs of his approaching death, he must immediately return those things he was holding on trust (*amānah*) to their owners or inform them as per the details mentioned in Ruling 2361. If he is indebted to someone and the date for repaying the debt is not yet due, or it is due but the creditor does not ask for it, or the creditor asks for it but he is unable to pay him, then in such cases, he must make arrangements such that he is confident (i.e. he has *iṭmiʾnān*) that his debt will be paid to the creditor after his death. For example, if his debt is unknown to others, he must make a will [regarding this debt] and get someone to witness it. However, if he is able to pay the debt and its date is due and the creditor asks for it, he must immediately pay it even if he does not notice the signs of his approaching death.

Ruling 2718. If a person who notices the signs of his approaching death owes the one-fifth tax (*khums*), alms tax (zakat), or *maẓālim*[3] but is unable to pay it at present, in the event that he has sufficient wealth to pay it, or he deems it probable that someone else will pay it, he must make arrangements such that he is confident that his debt will be paid after his death. For example, he must make a will for a trusted individual [to pay it]. The same applies if hajj is obligatory for him and he is unable to get a representative (*nāʾib*) [to perform hajj on his behalf] at present. However, if he is able to pay the debt of his religious dues at present, he must pay it without delay even if he does not notice the signs of his approaching death.

[3] *Maẓālim* refers to property which has been unrightfully or unknowingly taken.

Ruling 2719. If a person notices the signs of his approaching death and has lapsed (*qaḍāʾ*) prayers (*ṣalāh*) and fasts (*ṣawm*), he must make arrangements such that he is confident that they will be made up on his behalf after his death. For example, he must make a will that someone is to be hired from his estate to perform them. In fact, if he does not have an estate but deems it probable that someone may perform them free of charge, again it is obligatory (*wājib*) on him to make a will [regarding this]. However, if there is someone, such as his eldest son, whom he knows would perform his lapsed prayers and fasts were that person to be informed of them, then it is sufficient for that person to be informed and it is not necessary to make a will [regarding this].

Ruling 2720. If a person who notices the signs of his approaching death has kept some property with someone, or he has hidden it in a place not known to his heirs, the obligatory precaution (*al-iḥtiyāṭ al-wājib*) is that he must inform them of it. Furthermore, it is not necessary for him to appoint a custodian and guardian for his children who are minors (*ṣaghīr*). However, in the event that their property would perish or they would be ruined, he must appoint a trustworthy (*amīn*) custodian for them.

Ruling 2721. An executor must be sane. An executor must also be trustworthy regarding matters concerning the testator and, based on obligatory precaution, matters concerning others. Furthermore, based on obligatory precaution, the executor of a Muslim must be Muslim. To appoint a minor to be an executor on his own is not correct (*ṣaḥīḥ*), based on obligatory precaution, if the testator intends the minor to have disposal over the estate while he is still a minor and without the permission of his guardian (*walī*). The minor's disposal over the estate must have the permission of a fully qualified jurist (*al-ḥākim al-sharʿī*). But, if the testator intends the minor to have disposal over the estate after he has reached the age of legal responsibility (*bulūgh*) or with the permission of his guardian, then there is no problem.

Ruling 2722. If a person appoints a number of executors for his will and gives permission for each to execute the will independently, it is not necessary for them to attain each other's permission in executing the will. However, if the testator does not give such permission, irrespective of whether or not he has stated that they should jointly execute the will, they must execute the will in consultation with each other. If they are not prepared to execute the will jointly and there is no legal impediment that prevents each of them from doing so, then a fully qualified jurist may compel them to execute the will jointly. If they fail to comply or have a legal impediment that prevents each of them from doing so, then the fully qualified jurist may appoint another person in place of any one of them.

Ruling 2723. If a person retracts his will – for example, he states that the one-third of his estate[4] is to be given to someone but then states that it must not be given to him – such a will becomes void (*bāṭil*). If he changes his will – for example, he appoints a custodian for his children but then appoints someone else in his place – his first will becomes void and his second will must be acted upon.

Ruling 2724. If a person does something that demonstrates he has retracted his will – for example, he sells the house that he had left to someone in his will, or he appoints an agent (*wakīl*) to sell the house, contrary to what he had stated in his will – such a will becomes void.

Ruling 2725. If a person makes a will that a particular item is to be given to someone and after that makes a will that half of it is to be given to someone else, then half of that thing must be given to each of them.

Ruling 2726. If a person gifts part of his wealth to someone during the period of his terminal illness [but does not actually hand it over it while he is alive] and makes a will that after his death some of his estate is to be given to someone else, in the event that one-third of his estate is insufficient to cover both [i.e. the gift and what was bequeathed in the will] and the heirs are not prepared to give permission for more than one-third to be given from the estate, then first the property that was gifted must be taken out of the one-third, and then the remaining property must be dealt with according to the will.

[4] This refers to the maximum amount of one's estate over which he has discretion in a will for it to be disposed of in accordance with his wishes after his death.

Ruling 2727. If a person makes a will that the one-third of his estate must be sold and the proceeds from it must be spent in a particular way, his words must be acted upon.

Ruling 2728. If a person states during his terminal illness that he owes an amount to someone, in the event that he is believed to have a vested interest in saying this, namely to inflict a loss on his heirs, they must give the specified amount from the one-third of his estate. However, if he is not believed to have such a vested interest, his avowal (*iqrār*)[5] is effective and they must pay the amount from his main estate.

Ruling 2729. If a person makes a will that something is to be given to a particular beneficiary, it is not necessary that the beneficiary be alive at the time the will was made. Therefore, if the beneficiary is alive after the testator's death, it is necessary to give the thing to him. If, however, the beneficiary is not alive after the death of the testator, then, if it can be construed from the will that the thing can be used in other ways, it must be used in a way that is nearest to the testator's original intention; otherwise, the heirs can share it among themselves. However, if a person makes a will that something from his property is to be owned by a particular beneficiary after his death and that beneficiary is alive at the time of the testator's death – albeit as a foetus into which the soul has not yet entered – the will is valid; otherwise, it is void, and the heirs will share what was bequeathed among themselves.

Ruling 2730. If a person comes to know that someone has appointed him as his executor and he informs the testator that he is not prepared to execute his will, it is not necessary for him to execute the will after the testator's death. However, if he does not come to know before the testator's death that the testator had appointed him as his executor, or he comes to know this but does not inform the testator that he is not prepared to execute his will, then as long as it does not cause him excessive difficulty (*mashaqqah*), he must execute his will. If the executor becomes aware before the testator's death but at a time

[5] An avowal in Islamic law is when someone admits to a right to his own detriment or denies a right for himself over someone else.

when the testator is unable to appoint another executor due to the severity of his illness or some other reason, then based on obligatory precaution, he must accept to execute the will.

Ruling 2731. If a testator dies, his executor cannot appoint another person to execute the will and excuse himself from doing it. However, if the executor knows that the testator did not intend for him to perform the task himself, rather his intention was simply that the task be performed, he can appoint another person on his behalf.

Ruling 2732. If a person appoints two individuals as his executors and one of them dies or becomes insane or a disbeliever (*kāfir*), then, if it can be understood from the wording of the will that in such a situation the other person is to act as executor on his own, the will must be executed in this way; otherwise, a fully qualified jurist will appoint another person in his place. If both die or become insane or apostate, the fully qualified jurist will appoint two people. However, if one person is able to execute the will, it will not be necessary for him to appoint two people.

Ruling 2733. If an executor cannot carry out the deceased's will by himself, albeit by appointing an agent or hiring someone, a fully qualified jurist will appoint another person to assist him.

Ruling 2734. If some of the deceased's estate perishes in the possession of the executor, in the event that he is negligent in safeguarding it or excessive – for example, the testator had specified that a particular amount be given to the poor (*fuqarāʾ*) in a particular city but the executor takes the property to a different city and it perishes on the way – in such a case, the executor is responsible (*ḍāmin*). However, he is not responsible if he was neither negligent nor excessive.

Ruling 2735. If a person appoints someone as his executor and says, 'Should this executor die, so-and-so is to be my executor', the second executor must execute the will after the first executor dies.

Ruling 2736. Hajj that had become obligatory for a deceased person on account of him being able (*mustaṭīʿ*)[6] to perform it, and the debts and religious dues that are obligatory to pay – such as *khums*, zakat, and *maẓālim* – must be paid from his entire estate even if he has not made provision for these in his will. As for dues pertaining to recompense (*kaffārah*) and vow (*nadhr*), including hajj that had become obligatory on account of a vow, these are paid from the one-third of his estate if they have been mentioned in a will.

Ruling 2737. If the deceased's estate exceeds the amount required to pay for his debts, his obligatory hajj, and his obligatory religious dues like *khums*, zakat, and *maẓālim*, then in the event that he has made a will that the one-third of his estate or part of the one-third of his estate must be spent for a particular purpose, his will must be executed accordingly. If he has not made a will, the remaining amount belongs to his heirs.

Ruling 2738. If the dispensation specified by a testator is more than one-third of his estate, his will concerning the amount exceeding one-third will be valid only if his heirs give permission by words or action; heartfelt consent is not sufficient. If they give permission some time after his death, the will is valid. In the event that some of his heirs give permission and others do not, the will is valid and effective only with regard to the shares of those who give permission.

Ruling 2739. If the dispensation specified by a testator is more than one-third of his estate and his heirs give permission for it, they cannot retract their permission. If they deny permission during the testator's lifetime, they can give permission after his death. However, if they deny permission after his death, then permission given afterwards is ineffectual.

Ruling 2740. If a person makes a will that his *khums*, zakat, or other debts must be paid from the one-third of his estate and that someone should be hired to perform his lapsed prayers, fasts, and recommended acts such as feeding the poor, then, first his debts must be paid from the one-third of his estate, and if anything remains after that, it must be used for hiring someone to perform his lapsed

[6] See Ruling 2045, condition 4.

prayers and fasts. If anything remains after that, it must be used for the recommended acts specified by the deceased. In the event that one-third of his estate is adequate only to pay for his debts and the heirs do not give permission for more than a third of his estate to be spent, then his will with regard to his lapsed prayers, fasts, and recommend acts is invalid (*bāṭil*).

Ruling 2741. If a person makes a will that his debts are to be paid off, that someone is to be hired to perform his lapsed prayers and fasts, and that recommended acts are to be performed on his behalf, then in the event that he does not stipulate in his will that these are to be paid from the one-third of his estate, his debts must be paid from his entire estate. If anything remains after that, one-third of it must be spent on the lapsed prayers, fasts, and the recommended acts that he had specified. In case one-third of the remaining wealth is not sufficient, then, if his heirs give permission, his wishes in his will must be executed. If they do not give permission, the lapsed prayers and fasts must be paid for from one-third of the remainder. If anything remains after that, it must be used for the recommended acts that he had specified.

Ruling 2742. If a person says, 'The deceased had willed for such and such amount to be given to me', then what is claimed by him must be given to him in the following cases:

1. two dutiful (*ʿādil*) men verify his claim;
2. he takes an oath (*qasam*) and one dutiful man verifies his claim;
3. one dutiful man and two dutiful women testify to his claim;
4. or four dutiful women testify to his claim.

If one dutiful woman testifies to his claim, then one-quarter of what he claims must be given to him. If two dutiful women testify, half of it must be given to him. And if three dutiful women testify, three-quarters of it must be given to him. If his claim is verified by two men from the People of the Book (*ahl al-kitāb*)[7] who are *dhimmīs*[8]

[7] As mentioned in Ruling 103, the 'People of the Book' are Jews, Christians, and Zoroastrians.

[8] *Dhimmīs* are People of the Book who have entered into a *dhimmah* treaty, i.e.

and considered dutiful according to their own religion, and there is no Muslim to testify, then what is claimed by him must be given to him.

Ruling 2743. If a person says, 'I am the executor of the deceased in disposing of his estate', his claim will be established if two dutiful men verify it, or if there is no Muslim to testify, two *dhimmī* men who are considered dutiful according to their own religion verify his claim. Similarly, his claim will be established by the avowal (*iqrār*) of the heirs.

Ruling 2744. If a person makes a will that something from his estate is to be given to an individual and the latter dies before he can accept or reject it, his heirs can accept the property as long as they have not rejected the will. However, this rule (*ḥukm*) applies when the testator does not retract his will; if he does retract it, they will have no right over the property.

---

an agreement that gives them rights as protected subjects in an Islamic state.

CHAPTER THIRTY-EIGHT

Inheritance (*Irth*)

Ruling 2745. There are three groups of people who inherit from a deceased person on the basis of kinship.

The first group consists of the deceased's father, mother, and offspring, and in the absence of offspring, the grandchildren, however many generations they go forward. Whoever from among them is nearer to the deceased inherits from him. As long as there is even one person from this group, those in the second group do not inherit.

The second group consists of the deceased's grandfathers, grandmothers, sisters, and brothers, and in the absence of sisters and brothers, their offspring. Whoever from among them is nearer to the deceased inherits from him. As long as there is even one person from this group, those in the third group do not inherit.

The third group consists of the deceased's paternal uncles and paternal aunts, maternal uncles and maternal aunts, and their offspring. As long as even one person from the paternal uncles and paternal aunts and maternal uncles and maternal aunts of the deceased is alive, their offspring do not inherit. However, if there is one paternal half-uncle from the father's side[1] and one full paternal cousin, and there are no maternal uncles or maternal aunts, then the paternal cousin inherits from him to the exclusion of the paternal half-uncle. If there are a number of paternal uncles or paternal cousins, or if the deceased's widow is alive, then this rule (*ḥukm*) is problematic (*maḥall al-ishkāl*) [i.e. based on obligatory precaution (*al-iḥtiyāṭ al-wājib*), the rule is not established in this case].[2]

Ruling 2746. If there are no paternal uncles, paternal aunts, maternal uncles, or maternal aunts, nor any of their offspring or grandchildren, then the deceased is inherited by the paternal uncles and paternal aunts and maternal uncles and maternal aunts of the deceased's parents. If they are not alive, their offspring inherit. If they are not alive, the paternal uncles and paternal aunts and maternal uncles and maternal aunts of the deceased's paternal grandparents inherit. If they are not alive, their offspring inherit.

[1] That is, a paternal half-brother of his father (*al-Masā'il al-Muntakhabah*, p. 477, Ruling 1344).

[2] As mentioned in Ruling 6, the term 'problematic' (*maḥall al-ishkāl*) amounts to saying the ruling is based on obligatory precaution.

Ruling 2747. A husband and wife inherit from one another as per the details that will be mentioned later.

INHERITANCE OF THE FIRST GROUP

Ruling 2748. If there is only one heir of the deceased from the first group – for example, his father or mother, or one son or one daughter – then that person inherits the deceased's entire estate. If there is one son and one daughter, then the estate is divided among them in such a way that the son receives twice the share of the daughter.

Ruling 2749. If the only heirs of the deceased are his father and his mother, the estate is divided into three parts: two parts are inherited by his father and one part by his mother. However, if the deceased has two brothers or four sisters, or one brother and two sisters, and they are all Muslims and free [i.e. not slaves], and their father is also the father of the deceased even though their mothers may be different, and they have been born, then they do not inherit anything while the deceased's father and mother are alive. In such a case, his mother inherits one-sixth of the estate and his father inherits the rest.

Ruling 2750. If the only heirs of the deceased are his father, mother, and one daughter, in the event that the deceased does not have a brother or sister who fulfils the conditions mentioned in the previous ruling, the estate is divided into five parts: his father and mother inherit one part each and his daughter inherits three parts. If the deceased has a brother or sister who fulfils the conditions mentioned previously, then his father inherits one-fifth, his mother one-sixth, and his daughter three-fifths. With regard to the one-thirtieth that remains – which is probably the share of the mother, just as it is probable that three-quarters of it are the share of his daughter and one-quarter is the share of his father – based on obligatory precaution, they must arrive at a settlement (*muṣālaḥah*).

Ruling 2751. If the only heirs of the deceased are his father, mother, and one son, the estate is divided into six parts: his father and mother inherit one part each and his son inherits four parts. If the deceased has a number of sons or daughters, then the four parts must be divided equally among them. If he has a son and a daughter, then the four parts must be divided among them in a way that each son receives twice the share of each daughter.

Ruling 2752. If the only heirs of the deceased are his father or mother and one or a number of sons, the estate is divided into six parts: one part is inherited by his father or mother and five parts are inherited by his son. If there are a number of sons, then the five parts are divided equally among them.

Ruling 2753. If the only heirs of the deceased are his father or mother and a number of his sons and daughters, the estate is divided into six parts: one part is inherited by his father or mother and the remainder is divided among his sons and daughters in a way that each son receives twice the share of each daughter.

Ruling 2754. If the only heirs of the deceased are his father or mother and one daughter, his estate is divided into four parts: one part is inherited by his father or mother and the rest is inherited by his daughter.

Ruling 2755. If the only heirs of the deceased are his father or mother and a number of daughters, the estate is divided into five parts: one part is inherited by his father or mother and four parts are divided equally among his daughters.

Ruling 2756. If the deceased has no offspring, the child of his son receives the share of the deceased's son even if she is a girl, and the child of his daughter receives the share of the deceased's daughter's share even if he is a boy. For example, if the deceased has a grandson from his daughter and a granddaughter from his son, the estate is divided into three parts: one part is inherited by the grandson from his daughter and two parts are inherited by the granddaughter from his son. With regard to grandchildren inheriting, it is not a condition that their father and mother be deceased.

INHERITANCE OF THE SECOND GROUP

Ruling 2757. The second group of persons who inherit on the basis of kinship consists of the deceased's grandfathers, grandmothers, brothers, and sisters. If the deceased does not have any brothers or sisters, their offspring inherit.

Ruling 2758. If the only heir of the deceased is one brother or one sister, he or she inherits the entire estate. If he has more than one full brother or more than one full sister, the estate is divided equally between them. If he has both full brothers and full sisters, then every brother receives twice the share of every sister. For example, if he has two full brothers and one full sister, the estate is divided into five parts: each brother receives two parts while the sister receives one part.

Ruling 2759. If the deceased has full brothers and full sisters, his half-brothers and half-sisters who have the same father as the deceased but a different mother do not inherit from him. If he has no full brothers or full sisters and has only one paternal half-sister or only one paternal half-brother, then the entire estate is inherited by him or her. If he has more than one paternal half-brother or more than one paternal half-sister, then the estate is divided equally between them. If he has paternal half-brothers as well as paternal half-sisters, then every half-brother receives twice the share of every half-sister.

Ruling 2760. If the only heir of the deceased is one maternal half-sister or one maternal half-brother, their father being different to the father of the deceased, he or she inherits the entire estate. If he has more than one maternal half-brother or more than one maternal half-sister, or more than one of both [i.e. more than one maternal half-brother and more than one maternal half-sister], then the estate is divided equally between them.

Ruling 2761. If the deceased has full brothers and full sisters as well as paternal half-brothers and paternal half-sisters and one maternal half-brother or one maternal half-sister, the paternal half-brothers and paternal half-sisters do not inherit. In this case, the estate is divided into six parts: one part is received by the maternal half-brother or maternal half-sister, and the remainder is divided among the full brothers and full sisters, with every brother receiving twice the share of every sister.

Ruling 2762. If the deceased has full brothers and full sisters as well as paternal half-brothers and paternal half-sisters and more than one maternal half-brother and maternal half-sister, the paternal half-brothers and paternal half-sisters do not inherit. In this case, the estate is divided into three parts: one part is divided equally between the maternal half-brothers and maternal half-sisters, and the remainder is divided between the full brothers and full sisters, with every brother receiving twice the share of every sister.

Ruling 2763. If the only heirs of the deceased are his paternal half-brothers and paternal half-sisters and one maternal half-brother or one maternal half-sister, the estate is divided into six parts: one part is received by the maternal half-brother or maternal half-sister, and the remainder is divided between the paternal half-brothers and paternal half-sisters, with every brother receiving twice the share of every sister.

Ruling 2764. If the only heirs of the deceased are his paternal half-brother and paternal half-sister and more than one maternal half-brother and maternal half-sister, the estate is divided into three parts: one part is shared equally between the maternal half-brothers and maternal half-sisters, and the remainder is received by the paternal half-brother and paternal half-sister, with every brother receiving twice the share of every sister.

Ruling 2765. If the only heirs of the deceased are his brother, sister, and wife, the wife inherits as per the details that will be mentioned later, and the sister and brother inherit as stated in the previous rulings. Furthermore, if a woman dies and her only heirs are her sister, brother, and husband, the husband inherits half of the estate and the sister and the brother inherit as stated in the previous rulings. For the wife or husband to inherit, nothing is deducted from the share of the maternal half-brother and maternal half-sister, but there is a deduction from the share of the full brother and full sister or paternal half-brother and paternal half-sister. For example, if the heirs of the deceased are her husband, maternal half-brother and maternal half-sister, and full brother and full sister, then half of the estate is received by the husband, and one-third of the estate is received by the maternal half-brother and maternal half-sister; whatever remains is the property of the full brother and full sister. Therefore, if the total estate of the deceased is £6000, £3000 goes to the husband, £2000 goes to the maternal half-brother and maternal half-sister, and £1000 is the share of the full brother and full sister.

Ruling 2766. If the deceased does not have a sister or a brother, their share of the inheritance is given to their offspring, and the share of the maternal half-brother's child and maternal half-sister's child is divided equally among them. As for the share of the paternal half-brother's child and paternal half-sister's child, or the child of the full sibling, based on the opinion held by most jurists (*mashhūr*), every son receives twice the share of the daughter. However, it is not farfetched (*baʿīd*)[3] that the estate must be divided equally between them and, based on obligatory precaution, they must arrive at a settlement.

Ruling 2767. If the only heir of the deceased is one grandfather or one grandmother, irrespective of whether they are paternal or maternal, the entire estate is inherited by him/her. The great grandfather of the deceased does not inherit as long as the grandfather is alive. If the only heirs of the deceased are his paternal grandfather and paternal grandmother, the estate is divided into three parts: two parts are inherited by the grandfather and one part by the grandmother. If the heirs are his maternal grandfather and maternal grandmother, the estate is divided equally between them.

Ruling 2768. If the only heir of the deceased is one paternal grandfather or paternal grandmother as well as one maternal grandfather or maternal grandmother, the estate is divided into three parts: two parts are inherited by the paternal grandfather or paternal grandmother and one part by the maternal grandfather or maternal grandmother.

[3] For practical purposes, a legal opinion that is termed 'not farfetched' equates to a fatwa.

Ruling 2769. If the heirs of the deceased are paternal grandparents and maternal grandparents, the estate is divided into three parts: one part is divided equally between the maternal grandfather and the maternal grandmother, and the remaining two parts are inherited by the paternal grandfather and the paternal grandmother, with the paternal grandfather receiving twice the share of the paternal grandmother.

Ruling 2770. If the only heirs of the deceased are his wife, paternal grandparents, and maternal grandparents, his wife inherits as per the details that will be mentioned later. One-third of the deceased's estate is received by the maternal grandparents, divided equally between them. The remainder is received by the paternal grandparents, with the paternal grandfather receiving twice the share of the paternal grandmother. If the heirs of the deceased are her husband and paternal and maternal grandparents, the husband receives half of the estate and the grandparents inherit in accordance with the instructions that were mentioned in the previous rulings.

Ruling 2771. When there is a combination of one brother or sister, or some brothers or sisters with grandparents, there are a number of scenarios, as follows.

1. Each of the grandparents and brother or sister is from the deceased's mother's side. In this case, the estate is divided equally between them even though some of them may be male and others female.
2. All of them are from the father's side. In this case, the estate is also divided equally between them, provided that all of them are male or all of them are female. If they are of different genders, every male receives twice as much as every female.
3. The grandfather or grandmother is from the deceased's father's side, and the brother or sister are siblings of the deceased. The rule (*ḥukm*) in this case is the same as the one in the previous case. It has previously been established that if the paternal half-brother or paternal half-sister of the deceased combines with a full brother or full sister, the paternal half-siblings do not inherit.
4. The grandfathers or grandmothers, or both, paternal and

maternal, are combined with brothers or sisters, or both, who are also paternal and maternal. In this case, one-third of the estate is received by the maternal relatives comprising the brothers and sisters, grandfather and grandmother; this is to be divided equally between the males and the females. Two-thirds of the estate are received by the paternal relatives, with every male receiving twice as much as every female. If all of them are male or all of them are female, then it must be divided equally between them.

5. A paternal grandfather or grandmother combines with a maternal half-brother or maternal half-sister. In this case, if there is only one maternal half-brother or maternal half-sister, he/she receives one-sixth of the estate. If there are more than one, they receive one-third of the estate divided equally among them. The remainder is inherited by the paternal grandfather or paternal grandmother, and if both the paternal grandfather and the paternal grandmother are alive, the paternal grandfather receives twice as much as the paternal grandmother.
6. The maternal grandfather or maternal grandmother, or both, combine with one or more paternal half-brothers. In this case, one-third is for the maternal grandfather or maternal grandmother, and if both are alive, then that one-third is divided equally between them. Two-thirds is for the brother or brothers. If one paternal half-sister combines with those maternal grandparents, she receives half, and if there are more than one, they receive two-thirds. In all cases, the share of the maternal grandfather and maternal grandmother is one-third. Based on this, one-sixth of the estate will be left over if there is only one sister. It is doubtful whether she inherits this or it is divided between her and the maternal grandfather and maternal grandmother; in this case, as an obligatory precaution, they must arrive at a settlement [concerning that remaining one-sixth].
7. The grandfathers or grandmothers, or both, paternal and maternal, are combined with one or more paternal half-brother or paternal half-sister. In this case, one-third is for the maternal grandfather or maternal grandmother. If there are more, it is divided equally among them even if some of them are male and others female. The remaining two-thirds of the estate are

for the paternal grandfather or paternal grandmother and the paternal half-brother or paternal half-sister, with each male receiving twice the share of each female. If those grandfathers or grandmothers are combined with a maternal half-brother or maternal half-sister, then the share of the maternal grandfather or maternal grandmother and the maternal half-brother or maternal half-sister is one-third, to be divided equally among them even if some of them are male and others female. The share of the paternal grandfather or paternal grandmother is two-thirds, with the paternal grandfather receiving twice the share of the paternal grandmother.

8. There are brothers or sisters, some of whom are paternal half-siblings and others maternal half-siblings, as well as the paternal grandfather or paternal grandmother. In this case, one-sixth of the estate is for the maternal half-brother or maternal half-sister if there is only one of them, and one-third if there are more than one, to be divided equally among them. The remainder of the estate is for the paternal half-brother or paternal half-sister and the paternal grandfather or paternal grandmother, with each male receiving twice the share of each female. If those brothers or sisters are combined with a maternal grandfather or maternal grandmother, the total share of the maternal grandfather or maternal grandmother and the maternal half-brother or maternal half-sister is one-third, to be divided equally among them. The share of the paternal half-brother or paternal half-sister is two-thirds, the male receiving twice the share of the female.

Ruling 2772. If the deceased has a brother or sister, their children do not inherit. However, this rule does not apply when the inheritance of a brother's child or sister's child does not clash with that of the brother or sister. For example, if the deceased has a paternal half-brother and maternal grandfather, the paternal half-brother inherits two-thirds and the maternal grandfather inherits one-third of the estate. In this case, if the maternal half-brother of the deceased has a son, then the maternal half-brother's son shares one-third of the estate with the maternal grandfather.

INHERITANCE OF THE THIRD GROUP

Ruling 2773. The third group of heirs consists of paternal uncles, paternal aunts, maternal uncles, maternal aunts, their offspring, and grandchildren. The persons in this group inherit when none of the persons belonging to the first two groups is alive.

Ruling 2774. If the only heir of the deceased is one paternal uncle or one paternal aunt, irrespective of whether he or she is the full paternal uncle/aunt – i.e. he or she is from the same father and mother as the deceased's father – or he or she is the paternal half-uncle or paternal half-aunt from the father's side [i.e. a paternal half-brother/sister of the deceased's father] or the paternal half-uncle or paternal half-aunt from the mother's side [i.e. a maternal half-brother/sister of the deceased's father], he or she inherits the entire estate. If there is more than one paternal uncle, or more than one paternal aunt, and all of them are full paternal uncles/aunts, or all are paternal half-uncles/aunts from the father's side or all are paternal half-uncles/aunts from the mother's side, the estate is divided equally among them. If there is both a paternal uncle and a paternal aunt, each paternal uncle receives twice the share of each paternal aunt.

Ruling 2775. If the heirs of the deceased are paternal uncles and paternal aunts, some of them being paternal half-uncles/aunts from the father's or mother's side and others being full paternal uncles/aunts, then the paternal half-uncles/aunts from the father's side do not inherit. Therefore, if the deceased has one paternal half-uncle or one paternal half-aunt from the mother's side, the estate is divided into six parts: one part is given to the paternal half-uncle/aunt from the mother's side, and the rest is given to the full paternal uncles/aunts. If they are not alive, it is given to the paternal half-uncles/aunts from the father's side. If the deceased has both a paternal half-uncle and a paternal half-aunt from the mother's side, then the estate is divided into three parts: two parts are given to the full paternal uncles/aunts, and if they are not alive, they are given to the paternal half-uncles/aunts from the father's side, and one part is given to the paternal half-uncles/aunts from the mother's side. In each case, the paternal uncle receives twice the share of the paternal aunt.

Ruling 2776. If the deceased has only one maternal uncle or only one maternal aunt, he or she inherits the entire estate. If he has both a maternal uncle and a maternal aunt, whether they are full – i.e. they share the same father and mother with the deceased's mother – or they are half-maternal uncles/aunts from either the father's or mother's side, then it is not farfetched that the maternal uncle inherits twice the share of the maternal aunt. It is also probable that they inherit equally. Therefore, they must arrive at a settlement on the extra amount based on obligatory precaution.

Ruling 2777. If the only heirs of the deceased are one or more maternal half-uncles and maternal half-aunts from the mother's side, and full maternal uncles and maternal aunts, and maternal half-uncles and maternal half-aunts from the father's side, then for the maternal half-uncles and maternal half-aunts from the father's side not to inherit is problematic. In any case, the maternal half-uncle or maternal half-aunt from the mother's side, if there is only one of them, receives one-sixth, and if there are more than one, they receive one-third of the estate. The remainder is given to the maternal half-uncle or maternal half-aunt from the father's side or the full maternal uncle and maternal aunt. In each case, it is probable that the maternal uncle inherits twice the share of the maternal aunt; however, based on obligatory precaution, they must arrive at a settlement.

Ruling 2778. If the heirs of the deceased are one or more maternal uncles, or one or more maternal aunts, or a maternal uncle and a maternal aunt with one or more paternal uncles or paternal aunts, or a paternal uncle and a paternal aunt, then the estate is divided into three parts: one part is given to the maternal uncle or maternal aunt or both of them, and the remainder is given to the paternal uncle or paternal aunt or both of them. The method of distribution among each group has already been mentioned.

Ruling 2779. If the deceased does not have any living paternal uncles or paternal aunts, or maternal uncles or maternal aunts, then their shares pass on to their offspring. Therefore, if the deceased has one female cousin from his paternal aunt and some male cousins from his maternal uncle, the female cousin receives two-thirds, and the male cousins receive one-third to be divided equally among them.

This group – i.e. the children of paternal and maternal uncles and aunts – have priority over the deceased's father's and mother's paternal and maternal uncles and aunts.

Ruling 2780. If the heirs of the deceased are his father's and mother's paternal and maternal uncles and aunts, the estate is divided into three parts: one part is inherited by the deceased's mother's paternal and maternal uncles and aunts; in this regard, whether each of them receives an equal share or the males receive twice the share of the females is a matter of disagreement [amongst jurists]. Therefore, the obligatory precaution is that they must arrive at a settlement. The remaining two parts are divided into three parts: one part is received by the deceased's father's maternal uncle and maternal aunt to be divided between them in the same manner that was mentioned, and the remaining two parts are received by the deceased's father's paternal uncle and paternal aunt to be divided between them in the same manner that was mentioned.

INHERITANCE OF HUSBAND AND WIFE

Ruling 2781. If a woman dies without any offspring, half of her estate is inherited by her husband and the remainder by her other heirs. If she has offspring from that husband or another husband, her husband inherits one-quarter of the estate and the remainder is inherited by her other heirs.

Ruling 2782.* If a man dies without any offspring, a quarter of his estate is inherited by his wife and the remainder by his other heirs. If he has offspring from that wife or from another wife, his wife inherits one-eighth of the estate and the remainder is inherited by his other heirs. A wife does not inherit anything from the land of a house, garden, plantation, or any other land, neither from the land itself nor from the value of it. Furthermore, she does not inherit from what stands on the land, such as buildings and trees. She does, however, inherit from their value, and the heirs can give her their value from other wealth. The same applies to the trees, crops, and buildings on the land of a garden, plantation, or any other land. However, she does inherit from the actual fruit that was present on the trees at the time of her husband's death.

Ruling 2783.* If the wife wishes to have right of usage over things that she does not inherit, such as the land of a residential house, she must obtain permission from the other heirs. It is not permitted (*jāʾiz*) for the other heirs – as long as they have not given the wife her share – to have disposal over those things of which she inherits the value, such as buildings and trees, which would cause their price to decrease, nor can they sell such things, without the wife's permission.

Ruling 2784. If the heirs wish to undertake the valuation of the buildings, trees, and similar things, they must do so in the way experts usually undertake valuations. That is, they must disregard the particulars of the land it is situated on and not base their valuation on how much it would be worth if it were [*per impossibile*] uprooted from the land or it remained unrented on the land.

Ruling 2785. The watercourses for subterranean canals and suchlike have the same rule as land, and the bricks and other things used for their construction have the same rule as buildings. As for the water itself, the actual water is inherited.

Ruling 2786. If the deceased has more than one wife and no offspring, one-quarter of the estate must be divided equally among his wives. If he has offspring, one-eighth of the estate as per the explanation given previously must be divided equally among his wives. This rule applies even if the husband did not have sexual intercourse with all or some of them. However, if he married a woman during his terminal illness and did not have sexual intercourse with her, that woman does not inherit from him, nor is she entitled to a dowry.

Ruling 2787. If a woman marries a man while she is ill and subsequently dies from that illness, her husband inherits from her even if he did not have sexual intercourse with her.

Ruling 2788. If a woman is given a revocable divorce (*al-ṭalāq al-rijʿī*) in the manner explained in the rulings on divorce, and she dies during the prescribed waiting period (*ʿiddah*), her husband inherits from her.

Furthermore, if her husband dies during that *ʿiddah* period, his wife inherits from him. However, if one of them dies after the expiry of the *ʿiddah* period or during the *ʿiddah* period of an irrevocable divorce (*al-ṭalāq al-bāʾin*), then the other does not inherit from him/her.

Ruling 2789. If a husband divorces his wife while he is ill and dies before the expiry of twelve lunar months, his wife inherits from him on fulfilment of three conditions [as below], irrespective of whether the divorce was revocable or irrevocable.

1. During this time, she has not married another man. If she has married another man, she does not inherit. However, the recommended precaution (*al-iḥtiyāṭ al-mustaḥabb*) is that they [the ex-wife and the heirs] arrive at a settlement.
2. The divorce has not taken place at the request of the wife; otherwise, she does not inherit, irrespective of whether she paid her husband something to divorce her or not.
3. The husband died with the same illness he had when he divorced her, and he died due to that illness or some other cause. Therefore, if the husband recovers from that illness and dies later due to another cause, the divorced wife does not inherit from him unless his death happened during the *ʿiddah* period of a revocable divorce.

Ruling 2790. The clothes that a husband buys for his wife to wear are treated as part of his estate after his death even though she may have worn them, unless he gave her ownership. A wife is entitled to seek ownership of clothes from her husband as part of his obligations to provide maintenance (*nafaqah*) for her.

MISCELLANEOUS RULES OF INHERITANCE

Ruling 2791. The deceased's Qur'an, ring, sword, and clothes that he had worn or kept to wear belong to the eldest son. If the deceased had more than one of the first three things – for example, he left two copies of the Qur'an or two rings – the obligatory precaution is that the eldest son must arrive at a settlement with the other heirs regarding those things. The same applies to the reading stand (*riḥāl*) for the Qur'an and the gun, dagger, or other weapons. The sheath of the sword and bookmark for the Qur'an are considered part of those items.

Ruling 2792. If the deceased has more than one eldest son – for example, two sons are born of two wives at the same time – the items mentioned earlier must be divided equally among them. This rule is specific to the eldest son even though there may be daughters older than him.

Ruling 2793. If the deceased has a debt equal to his estate or more, the eldest son must give those things mentioned earlier that belong to him to settle the debt, or he must pay their equivalent worth from his own wealth. If the deceased's debt is less than his estate but his estate without those items that belong to the eldest son is not sufficient to settle his debt, then the eldest son must give from those items or from his own wealth to settle the debt. However, if the rest of his estate is adequate to clear the debt, the obligatory precaution is that the eldest son must still participate in clearing the debt in the manner mentioned previously. For example, if the estate of the deceased is worth £600 and the items that belong to the eldest son are worth £200 and the deceased has a debt of £300, the eldest son must pay £100 from the items he received to pay off the debt.

Ruling 2794. A Muslim inherits from a disbeliever (*kāfir*), but a disbeliever does not inherit from a deceased Muslim, even if he is the deceased's father or son.

Ruling 2795.* If a person kills one of his relatives intentionally (*ʿamdan*) and unjustly, he does not inherit from him. However, if the killing was justified – for example, it was a retributory punishment (*qiṣāṣ*) [as sanctioned by a judge], or the legal execution of a punishment, or in self-defence – then he does inherit from him. The same applies if the killing was due to some error. For example, if he threw a stone in the air and by chance it hit one of his relatives and killed him, he inherits from him; however, he does not inherit from the blood money (*diyah*) that his relatives pay for the killing. As for manslaughter – i.e. killing someone without intending to, by intentionally doing something to the person that would not usually result in death – this does not prevent him from inheriting, but he does not have a share in the blood money that he must pay to the heirs.

Ruling 2796. Whenever it is proposed to divide the inheritance, the share of a child who is in his mother's womb and will inherit if he is born alive must be kept safe. This is on condition that it is known whether there is one child or more in the womb and whether the child is male or female, even if this is discovered using scientific instruments. If it is not known but a reliable probability exists that there is more than one child in the womb, the share of one son multiplied by the probable number of children must be put aside. In the event that, for example, one son or one daughter is born, the extra amount must be divided between the heirs.

Glossary

adāʾ accomplishment of a religious duty within its prescribed time, as opposed to *qaḍāʾ*

adhān call to prayer

ʿādil a dutiful person, i.e. someone who does the things that are obligatory for him and refrains from doing the things that are unlawful for him; just; possessing moral probity

ʿahd covenant

aḥkām (pl. of *ḥukm*) laws; rules

ahl al-khibrah expert(s)

ahl al-kitāb People of the Book, i.e. Jews, Christians, and Zoroastrians

al-aḥwaṭ al-awlā more precautious and more preferred (for practical purposes, a 'more precautious and more preferred' juristic opinion is equivalent to recommended precaution)

aʿlam the most learned *mujtahid*, i.e. the *mujtahid* who is most capable of understanding the law of Allah from among all the *mujtahids* of his time

ʿalaqah clot of blood

ajīr a person who is hired to do something

aʿmāl rituals; acts of worship

aʿmāl Umm Dāwūd a recommended set of ritual acts of worship that are usually performed in the middle of the month of Rajab

amānah trust

ʿamdan intentionally

ʿāmil worker

amīn (1) a trustworthy person (2) non-liable

al-amr bil-maʿrūf enjoining good

anfāl property belonging to the Imam (ʿA)

al-ʿaqd al-dāʾim permanent marriage contract

al-ʿaqd al-lāzim irrevocable contract

ʿaqd al-muʿāwaḍah contract of exchange; a contract in which something is given in exchange for something else

al-ʿaqd al-munqaṭiʿ temporary marriage contract

ʿāqil sane

aqwā stronger opinion (for practical purposes, where an opinion is stated to be 'stronger', a fatwa is being given)

ʿāriyah gratuitous loan; commodate

arkān (pl. of *rukn*) elemental components of an act of worship

ʿaṣr afternoon

awliyāʾ Friends (of Allah)

awwal al-waqt start of the prescribed time for prayers

al-ʿayn al-mawqūfah charitable endowed property

ʿayn al-najāsah intrinsic impurity; actual source of impurity

aẓhar more apparent ruling (for practical purposes in jurisprudential rulings, an opinion that is termed 'more apparent' equates to a fatwa)

baʿīd farfetched; unlikely (for practical purposes, a legal opinion that is termed 'not farfetched' equates to a fatwa)

bāligh someone who is of the age of legal responsibility; a major

bāṭil (1) invalid (2) void

bulūgh age of legal responsibility
dafn burial
dāʾimah permanent wife
ḍamān suretyship
ḍāmin (1) responsible (2) guarantor; surety
ḍarīḥ lattice encloser of a tomb
dayn debt
dhabḥ slaughtering of an animal according to Islamic law
dhikr (1) remembering Allah (2) declaring in *rukūʿ* and *sujūd* that Allah is free from imperfections
dhimmī People of the Book (*ahl al-kitāb*) – i.e. Jews, Christians, and Zoroastrians – who have entered into a *dhimmah* treaty, i.e. an agreement that gives them rights as protected subjects in an Islamic state
diyah blood money
duʿāʾ supplication
al-fajr al-kādhib the false dawn, also known as 'the first dawn'
al-fajr al-ṣādiq the true dawn, also known as 'the second dawn'
faqīh (sing. of *fuqahāʾ*) jurist
faqīr (sing. of *fuqarāʾ*) a poor person, i.e. someone who does not possess the means to meet his and his family's expenses for one year
faskh annulment
fatwa edict issued by a *mujtahid*
fidyah compensative payment of one *mudd* (approximately 750 grams) of staple food to a poor person for a fast of the month of Ramadan that is missed under certain circumstances
fiqh Islamic jurisprudence
fuqahāʾ (pl. of *faqīh*) jurists
fuqarāʾ (pl. of *faqīr*) poor people, i.e. those who do not possess the means to meet their and their family's expenses for one year
fuqqāʿ beer
furādā performing an act of worship on one's own, as opposed to in *jamāʿah*
ghanāʾim (pl. of *ghanīmah*) spoils of war
ghanīmah (sing. of *ghanāʾim*) spoil of war
ghaṣbī usurped
ghasl washing
ghaybah occultation
ghinā singing
ghurūb sunset
ghusālah waste water, i.e. *qalīl* water that separates from an impure object when that object is washed or after it has been washed
ghusl ritual bathing
al-ghusl al-irtimāsī immersive ritual bathing
al-ghusl al-irtimāsī al-dafʿī instantaneous immersive ritual bathing
al-ghusl al-irtimāsī al-tadrījī gradual immersive ritual bathing
ghusl mass al-mayyit the *ghusl* for touching a corpse
al-ghusl al-tartībī sequential ritual bathing
ḥadath occurrence, i.e. something that invalidates *wuḍūʾ*
al-ḥadath al-akbar major occurrence, i.e. something that requires one to perform *ghusl* in order to perform an act of worship that requires *wuḍūʾ*
al-ḥadath al-aṣghar minor occurrence, i.e. something that requires one to perform *wuḍūʾ* in order to perform an act of worship that requires *wuḍūʾ*
ḥadd al-tarakhkhuṣ permitted limit

ḥāʾiḍ a woman in menstruation
ḥāʾir an area of approximately 11.5 metres around the sacred grave of Imam al-Ḥusayn (ʿA) in Karbala
hajj visiting the House of Allah, i.e. the Kaʿbah in Mecca, and performing the prescribed rituals there
ḥajj al-ifrād pilgrimage to Mecca performed by Muslims who reside within 88 kilometres of Mecca (see also *ḥajj al-qirān*)
ḥajjat al-islām the hajj that is obligatory for a Muslim to perform once in his lifetime, as opposed to a hajj that is obligatory for a Muslim by means of a vow and suchlike
ḥajj al-qirān pilgrimage to Mecca performed by Muslims who reside within 88 kilometres of Mecca. Unlike *ḥajj al-ifrād*, *ḥajj al-qirān* requires one to have his sacrificial animal with him when he enters the state of *iḥrām*.
hajj al-tamattuʿ pilgrimage to Mecca performed by Muslims who reside further than 88 kilometres from Mecca
al-ḥākim al-jāʾir unjust ruler
al-ḥākim al-sharʿī fully qualified jurist
ḥalāl lawful
ḥalq shaving of the head performed by men as part of the hajj rituals
ḥaraj hardship
ḥaram (1) shrine (2) sacred precinct
ḥarām unlawful; prohibited
ḥawālah transfer of debt
ḥawzah Islamic seminary
ḥayḍ menstruation; period
hibah gift
ḥubs bequest
al-ḥujjah al-sharʿiyyah legally authoritative; legal proof
ḥukm (sing. of *aḥkām*) law; rule
al-ḥukm al-sharʿī religious law
ḥulūl immanence
ḥusayniyyah congregation hall used by Shia Muslims for religious ceremonies
ʿibādah (sing. of *ʿibādāt*) ritual act of worship
ʿibādāt (pl. of *ʿibādah*) ritual acts of worship
ibn al-sabīl a stranded traveller
ʿiddah prescribed waiting period for a woman before she can remarry
ʿiddat al-wafāt the *ʿiddah* of a widow, i.e. the prescribed waiting period for a woman whose husband has died
ifṭār breaking a fast
iḥrām state of ritual consecration of pilgrims during hajj and *ʿumrah*
iḥtiyāṭ precaution
al-iḥtiyāṭ al-lāzim necessary precaution (this is the same as *al-iḥtiyāṭ al-wājib*)
al-iḥtiyāṭ al-mustaḥabb recommended precaution
al-iḥtiyāṭ al-wājib obligatory precaution
ijārah hiring; renting; leasing
ijtihād (1) the process of deriving Islamic laws from authentic sources (2) the level of someone who is a jurist
ikhfāt whispering the recitation (*qirāʾah*) of prayers, as opposed to pronouncing it aloud (*jahr*)
ikhtiyār volition; authority
al-ʿilm al-ijmālī non-specific knowledge
imāmah religious leadership
inqilāb change
intiqāl transfer
īqāʿ unilateral instigation

iqāmah call to stand up for prayer

iqrār (1) avowal (2) admitting to a right to one's own detriment or denying a right for oneself over someone else

irth inheritance

ʿishāʾ evening

istibrāʾ (1) the process of clearing the male urethra of urine after urinating (2) preventing an excrement-eating animal from eating impurity for some time and feeding it pure food so that after that period, it is no longer considered to be an excrement-eating animal (3) the method of checking whether or not menstruation has stopped

istiḥāḍah irregular blood discharge

al-istiḥāḍah al-kathīrah excessive irregular blood discharge

al-istiḥāḍah al-mutawassiṭah medium irregular blood discharge

al-istiḥāḍah al-qalīlah slight irregular blood discharge

istiḥālah transformation

istījārī a ritual act of worship that a person is hired to perform on behalf of someone else

istikhārah the practice of seeking from Allah the best choice between two or more options

istinjāʾ purification of the anus and the urinary outlet

istisqāʾ invocation for rain

Ithnā ʿAsharī Twelver

iʿtikāf spiritual retreat; the act of staying in a mosque under particular conditions with the intention of worshipping Allah

iṭmiʾnān confidence

ʿiwaḍ payment in exchange

jabīrah something with which a wound or a break in a bone is bandaged, or the medication that is applied to a wound

al-jāhil al-muqaṣṣir culpably ignorant person

al-jāhil al-qāṣir inculpably ignorant person

al-jahl al-quṣūrī inculpable ignorance

al-jahl al-taqṣīrī culpable ignorance

jahr pronouncing the recitation (*qirāʾah*) of prayers aloud, as opposed to whispering it (*ikhfāt*)

jāʿil offeror

jāʾiz permitted; lawful

jamāʿah congregation

janābah ritual impurity

juʿālah reward

junub someone in the state of *janābah*

kafālah surety for the appearance of a debtor

kafan shroud

kaffārah recompense

kafīl surety, i.e. a person who undertakes to present a debtor whenever the creditor seeks him

kāfir (sing. of *kuffār*) disbeliever

al-kāfir al-ḥarbī a disbeliever who is not a *dhimmī* and has not entered into a peace or security treaty with Muslims

kāfūr camphor

kathīr al-safar frequent traveller

kathīr al-shakk excessive doubter

khiyār option; the right to annul a transaction

khiyār al-ʿayb option due to a defect

khiyār al-ghabn option due to cheating

khiyār al-ḥayawān option pertaining to animals
khiyār al-majlis option while meeting
khiyār al-ru'yah option pertaining to seeing
khiyār al-sharṭ option due to a stipulated condition
khiyār al-shirkah option due to a partnership
khiyār ta'adhdhur al-taslīm option due to an inability to hand over
khiyār al-tadlīs option due to deceit
khiyār takhalluf al-sharṭ option due to a breach of condition
khiyār al-ta'khīr option due to delay
khul' the divorce of a wife who has an aversion to her husband and gives him her dowry or some of her other property so that he divorces her
khums the one-fifth tax
kitābī one who is among the People of the Book, i.e. Jews, Christians, and Zoroastrians
kuffār (pl. of *kāfir*) disbelievers
kufr disbelief
al-kullī fī al-dhimmah non-specified undertaking
kunyah an appellation given to someone as the father or mother of someone
kurr a quantity of water greater or equal to approximately 384 litres
laqab epithet; title
madhhab religious denomination
madhī fluid that sometimes comes out of the penis as a result of sexual arousal
ma'dhūr someone who is legally excused
mā fī al-dhimmah intention to fulfil whatever one's obligation happens to be with regard to a particular act
maghrib the time shortly after sunset (*ghurūb*) when the redness of the sky in the east has passed overhead
maḥall al-ishkāl problematic (for practical purposes, if a matter is said to be 'problematic' it amounts to saying the ruling is based on obligatory precaution)
maḥall al-ta'ammul a matter of deliberation (for practical purposes, if a matter is said to be one of 'deliberation', it amounts to saying the ruling is based on obligatory precaution)
al-maḥjūr 'alayh someone who is prohibited from having disposal over his property
mahr dowry
mahr al-mithl the standard amount for a dowry
maḥram a person one is never permitted to marry on account of being related to them in a particular way, such as being their parent or sibling.
majhūl al-mālik unknown owner
makrūh (sing. of *makrūhāt*) disapproved
makrūhāt (pl. of *makrūh*) disapproved acts
mālik owner
ma'mūm someone who follows an imam in congregational prayers
al-manūb 'anhu someone who is represented
marāji' (pl. of *marja'*) jurists who have the necessary qualifications to be followed in matters of Islamic jurisprudence; sources of emulation in these matters

marjaʿ (sing. of *marājiʿ*) a jurist who has the necessary qualifications to be followed in matters of Islamic jurisprudence; a source of emulation in these matters

masāʾil (pl. of *masʾalah*) rulings

masʾalah (sing. of *masāʾil*) ruling

masḥ wiping

mashaqqah excessive difficulty

mashhūr opinion held by most jurists

mashrūʿ sanctioned in Islamic law

mashrūʿiyyah legality

al-masjid al-jāmiʿ a mosque that is not particular to a specific group of people but is frequented by people from different areas of the city

maʿṣūm (sing. of *maʿṣūmīn*) Infallible

maʿṣūmīn (pl. of *maʿṣūm*) Infallibles

al-mawqūf ʿalayh beneficiary of an endowment

maẓālim property that has been unrightfully or unknowingly taken

miḥrāb niche, chamber, or slab in a mosque facing the direction of Mecca and where the imam usually stands for congregational prayers

miskīn a needy person; someone whose living conditions are worse than that of a poor person (*faqīr*)

muʿāhad a cosignatory with Muslims to a peace or security treaty

muʿāmalah (sing. of *muʿāmalāt*) transaction

muʿāmalāt (pl. of *muʿāmalah*) transactions

muʿāriḍ countervailing argument

muʿāwaḍah exchange

mubāḥ (1) permissible (2) not usurped

mubāhalah mutual imprecation

al-mubāḥāt al-aṣliyyah property that does not belong to anyone in particular and can be used by people in general

mubārāh a divorce that takes place when a husband and wife have an aversion to each other and the wife gives some property to her husband so that he divorces her

mubtadhilah a woman who does not observe hijab in front of non-*maḥram* men and does not take heed when she is forbidden from continuing with this behaviour

mubtadiʾah a menarcheal woman, i.e. a woman who has her period for the first time

mubṭilāt things that invalidate

muḍāf mixed water

muḍārabah sleeping partnership; silent partnership

al-muḍārabah al-idhniyyah sleeping partnership that is based on the owner giving the worker permission to trade with his property

muḍghah embryo

muḍṭaribah a woman with a disordered menstruation habit

mufallas someone who has been proclaimed bankrupt

mughārasah tree planting contract

muḥtaḍar a dying person; moribund

muḥtalim someone who has had a 'wet dream', i.e. semen has been ejaculated in his sleep

muḥtaram al-māl someone whose property is inviolable, i.e. a Muslim, or a *dhimmī* disbeliever, or a cosignatory with Muslims to a peace or security treaty (*muʿāhad*)

mujādalah disputing with others
mu'jir a person who gives something on rent; lessor
mujtahid jurist; someone who has attained the level of *ijtihād*, qualifying him to be an authority in Islamic law
mukallaf a duty-bound person; someone who is legally obliged to fulfil religious duties
mumārah altercating with others
mumayyiz someone who is able to discern between right and wrong; a discerning minor
munqaṭiʿah temporary wife
muqallid a follower of a jurist in matters of Islamic law
murḍiʿah nursing mother
murtadd apostate
al-murtadd al-fiṭrī someone who was born to one or both Muslim parents and later became a disbeliever
al-murtadd al-millī someone who was born to one or both disbelieving parents and later became a disbeliever
muṣālaḥah arriving at a settlement with someone
musāqāh tree tending contract
mushāʿ joint ownership
mūṣī testator
mustaḥabb (sing. of *mustaḥabbāt*) recommended
mustaḥabbāt (pl. of *mustaḥabb*) recommended acts
mustaḥāḍah a woman who is experiencing *istiḥāḍah*
mustaḥiqq (sing. of *mustaḥiqqūn*) a person who is entitled (mostly used with regard to someone who is entitled to receive *khums* or zakat)
mustaḥiqqūn (pl. of *mustaḥiqq*) those who are entitled (mostly used with regard to persons who are entitled to receive *khums* or zakat)
musta'jir a person who takes something on rent; tenant; hirer; lessee
mustaṭīʿ someone who is able to go for hajj
mutʿah temporary marriage; fixed-term marriage; a temporary wife
muṭahhirāt things that purify an impure object
muʿtakif someone who is in the act of performing *iʿtikāf*
al-muṭallaqah al-rijʿiyyah a woman who has been given a revocable divorce
al-mutamattaʿ bihā temporary wife
mutanajjis something that has become impure by secondary means, as opposed to being an intrinsic impurity (*ʿayn al-najāsah*)
mutawallī trustee
muṭlaq unmixed water
muwakkil principal (used with regard to agency)
muwālāh close succession
muwaswis an obsessively doubtful person
muzāraʿah sharecropping
nadhr vow
nafaqah maintenance; alimony
nāfilah the supererogatory prayer
naḥr slaughtering of a camel according to Islamic law
al-nahy ʿan al-munkar forbidding evil
nā'ib representative
najāsah (sing. of *najāsāt*) an impurity
najāsāt (pl. of *najāsah*) impurities
najis impure
naqd immediate exchange transaction;

a transaction in which there is no lapse of time between a buyer paying for an item and receiving it

nāshizah a recalcitrant wife, i.e. a wife who does not perform her obligatory marital duties

nasī'ah credit

nāṣibī (sing. of *nawāṣib*) someone who shows enmity towards the Imams (ʿA)

nāsiyah a woman who has forgotten the habit of her period

nawāṣib (pl. of *nāṣibī*) those who show enmity towards the Imams (ʿA)

al-nāẓir al-muḥtaram 'a respected onlooker', i.e. someone who is sane (*ʿāqil*), able to discern between right and wrong (*mumayyiz*), of the age of legal responsibility (*bāligh*), and not married to the person being seen

nifās lochia, i.e. blood discharge after childbirth

niṣāb taxable limit

niyābah doing something on behalf of someone else; by proxy

niyyah intention

nufasā' a woman who is experiencing *nifās*

qaḍā' (1) making up a religious duty that was not performed in its prescribed time, as opposed to *adā'* (2) a lapsed ritual act of worship

qā'idat al-tasāmuḥ fī adillat al-sunan principle of leniency in evidence for recommended acts

qalīl water that does not gush from the earth and is less than *kurr*

qasam oath

qaṣd intention

qaṣd al-inshā' intention to establish

qaṣd al-qurbah intention to attain proximity to Allah, i.e. to humbly obey Allah

qaṣd al-qurbah al-muṭlaqah a general intention to attain proximity to Allah / humbly obey Allah, i.e. an intention to perform a ritual act of worship in order to attain proximity to Allah / humbly obey Allah without specifying any particulars about that act

qaṣr shortened prayers of a traveller

qibla direction towards the Kaʿbah in Mecca

qirā'ah recitation

qiṣāṣ retributory punishment

qiyām standing position in prayers

qunūt the act of supplicating in prayers with the hands placed in front of the face

qurʿah lot (as in *to draw lots*)

radd al-maẓālim giving back property – which has been unrightfully or unknowingly taken – to its rightful owner, or if that is not possible, to the poor as *ṣadaqah* on behalf of the rightful owner

rahn security; deposit; collateral

rakʿah a unit of the prayer

rajā' (shorter form of *rajā' al-maṭlūbiyyah*) intention to perform/avoid something in the hope that it is desired by Allah

rashīdah a mature female who has reached *bulūgh* and is able to determine what is in her interest

ribā usury; interest

risālah manual of Islamic rulings

rūḥ spirit

rujūʿ (1) acting on the fatwa of the next

most learned *mujtahid* when one's *marjaʿ* has stated that a ruling is based on obligatory precaution (2) returning (used to refer to a condition made in *iʿtikāf* to leave in the middle of it if a problem arises)

rukn (sing. of *arkān*) elemental component of an act of worship

rukūʿ bowing position in the prayer

rushd ability to take care of one's wealth and use it in a correct way

ṣadaqah alms given to the poor; charity

sādāt (pl. of *sayyid*) descendants of Hāshim, the great grandfather of Prophet Muḥammad (Ṣ)

safīh someone who is foolish with finances, i.e. someone who spends his wealth in futile ways

ṣaghīr a minor; a child who is not of the age of legal responsibility (*bāligh*)

ṣāḥib al-laban nursing father

ṣaḥīḥ (1) valid (2) correct

sahm al-imām the portion of khums for the Imam (ʿA)

sahm al-sādāt the portion of khums for *sayyids*

sahwan inadvertently

sahwiyyāt acts that are inadvertently left out in prayers

sajdah prostration

sajdatā al-sahw the two prostrations for inadvertence

sajdat al-shukr the prostration for offering thanks

salaf prepayment transaction

ṣalāh (1) prayer; ritual prayer (2) sing. of *ṣalawāt*

salām salutation

ṣalāt al-āyāt the prayer of signs

ṣalāt al-ghufaylah a recommended prayer that is performed between *maghrib* and *ʿishā'* prayers

ṣalāt al-iḥtiyāṭ the precautionary prayer

ṣalāt al-istisqā' the prayer for invoking rain

ṣalāt Jaʿfar al-Ṭayyār the Prayer of Jaʿfar al-Ṭayyār; a four *rakʿah* recommended prayer taught by the Holy Prophet (Ṣ) to his cousin, Jaʿfar al-Ṭayyār

ṣalāt al-jamāʿah congregational prayers

ṣalāt al-jumuʿah the Friday prayer

ṣalāt al-layl the night prayer; also known as '*ṣalāt al-tahajjud*' (the night vigil prayer)

ṣalāt al-mayyit the funeral prayer

ṣalāt al-waḥshah the prayer of loneliness (in the grave)

ṣalawāt (1) invocation of blessings upon Prophet Muḥammad (Ṣ) and his progeny (2) pl. of *ṣalāh*

ṣarūrah someone going for hajj for the first time

ṣawm fasting

saʿy hajj and *ʿumrah* ritual of traversing to and from the mountains of Ṣafā and Marwah

sayyid (sing. of *sādāt*) a male descendant of Hāshim, the great grandfather of Prophet Muḥammad (Ṣ)

sayyidah a female descendant of Hāshim, the great grandfather of Prophet Muḥammad (Ṣ)

shahādatayn the two testimonies, i.e. the testimony to the oneness of Allah and the prophethood of Prophet Muḥammad (Ṣ)

shākhiṣ an indicator, such as an upright rod, used to determine the timing of certain prayers by examining the length of its shadow

shakhṣī specified (used with regard to purchases)

shakk doubt

shakkiyyāt doubts that arise in prayers

sharʿan legally

sharīk partner

al-sharṭ al-wāqiʿī absolute condition, i.e. a condition that must be fulfilled for an action to be valid irrespective of the performer's state of knowledge with regard to that condition

shirkah partnership

al-shirkah al-idhniyyah permission based partnership

al-shirkah al-muʿāwaḍiyyah exchange based partnership

shurakāʾ partners

sidr lote tree leaves

ṣīghah formula

ṣilat al-arḥām maintaining good family ties

ṣubḥ morning

sujūd prostrating

ṣulḥ settlement

surah chapter of the Qur'an

tabaʿiyyah subsequence

ṭahārah (1) purification (2) being in a state of ritual purity, i.e. having *wuḍūʾ*, *ghusl*, or *tayammum*

ṭāhir pure

taḥnīṭ camphorating

tajwīd the discipline of reciting the Qur'an correctly

takbīr proclamation of Allah's greatness by saying '*allāhu akbar*'

takbīrat al-iḥrām saying '*allāhu akbar*' at the beginning of the prayer

takfīn shrouding

taklīf responsibility

al-ṭalāq al-bāʾin irrevocable divorce

al-ṭalāq al-rijʿī revocable divorce

talqīn inculcation of principle beliefs to a dying person or a corpse

tamām complete form of the prayer

taʿqībāt supplications after prayers

taqiyyah dissimulation or concealment of one's beliefs in the face of danger

taqlīd following a jurist

taqwā God-wariness

tamyīz ability to discern between right and wrong

taqṣīr snipping one's hair or trimming one's beard or moustache as part of the hajj and *ʿumrah* rituals

tartīb sequence

al-tasbīḥāt al-arbaʿah the four glorifications, i.e. '*subḥānal lāhi wal ḥamdu lillāhi wa lā ilāha illal lāhu wal lāhu akbar*'

tashahhud testifying

tashyīʿ al-janāzah funeral procession

taʿṣīb a matter of inheritance that is common among Sunni Muslims but invalid from a Shiʿi perspective

ṭawāf circumambulation of the Kaʿbah

ṭawāf al-nisāʾ an obligatory circumambulation of the Kaʿbah that is performed as part of the hajj rituals

tawriyah equivocation

tayammum dry ablution

turbah a piece of earth or clay on which one places his forehead when prostrating

ʿudhr legitimate excuse

ujrat al-mithl standard rate paid for the hired property or work *al-ujrah al-musammāh* agreed rate paid for the hired property or work

ʿumrah pilgrimage to Mecca that has fewer rituals than the hajj pilgrimage; the minor pilgrimage

al-ʿumrah al-mufradah recommended pilgrimage to Mecca that is performed independently of hajj at any time of the year

uṣūl al-dīn fundamentals of religion

uṣūl al-fiqh principles of jurisprudence; legal theory

wadhī fluid that sometimes comes out of the penis after the ejaculation of semen

wadī fluid that sometimes comes out of the penis after urinating

wadīʿah deposit

wājib obligatory

al-wājib al-ʿaynī individual obligation, i.e. an obligation that every duty-bound person must perform irrespective of whether or not others have also performed it

al-wājib al-fawrī immediate obligation, i.e. an obligation that must be performed as soon as it is possible to do so, and delaying its performance is not permitted

al-wājib al-kifāʾī collective obligation, i.e. an act of worship that is obligatory for all duty-bound persons in the first instance but is lifted from them all if it is discharged by someone or some people

al-wājib al-muʿayyan assigned obligation; time-specific obligation, i.e. an act of worship that must be performed at one distinct time

al-wājib al-takhyīrī optional obligation, i.e. an act of worship for which a *mukallaf* has the choice to either perform that act itself or some other particular act

al-wājib al-taʿyīnī fixed obligation, i.e. an act of worship for which there is no alternative act that a *mukallaf* can perform instead

wakīl agent; representative

walī guardian

waqf charitable endowment

al-waqf al-ʿāmm public charitable endowment

al-waqf al-khāṣṣ private charitable endowment

wāqif endower

waqt al-faḍīlah prime time for performing prayers, i.e. the early period of the prescribed time for a prayer in which there is more reward for performing it

waṣī executor of the bequest of a deceased person

waṣiyyah will

waswās obsessive doubting

waṭʾ al-shubhah sexual intercourse ensuing from a mistake

waṭan home town

wikālah agency

wilāyah (1) guardianship (2) vicegerency

wuḍūʾ ablution

al-wuḍūʾ al-irtimāsī immersive ablution

yāʾisah a postmenopausal woman; in rulings pertaining to marriage and divorce, a woman who has reached the age of fifty (in rulings pertaining to menstruation, the age is sixty), and due to her advanced age she does not experience menstruation and has no expectation of experiencing it again

yaqīn certainty

yawm al-shakk day of doubt, i.e. the day regarding which someone doubts whether it is the last day of Shaʿbān or the first day of the month of Ramadan

ẓāhir apparent ruling (for practical purposes in jurisprudential rulings, expressing an 'apparent' ruling equates to giving a fatwa)

zakat alms tax

zakāt al-fiṭrah *fiṭrah* alms tax

ẓann supposition; conjecture

zawāl the time after midday when the sun begins to decline

ziyārah visitation to the place of burial of a holy personality or a holy place

ẓuhr midday

al-ẓuhr al-sharʿī legal midday, i.e. after the midway point of the day

Appendix 1: Table of Weights, Measures, Values, and Quantities

Weight/Measure/ Value/Quantity	Explanation
dhirāʿ	cubit, i.e. the length from the elbow to the tip of the middle finger of the hand, equivalent to approximately 46 centimetres
dirham	value equivalent to 2.4192 grams of minted silver; also, measure of size equivalent to the upper joint of the thumb
farsakh	measure of distance equivalent to approximately 5.5 kilometres, or 3.4 miles
kurr	quantity of water greater or equal to approximately 384 litres
al-mithqāl al-ṣayrafī	common *mithqāl*, i.e. a measure of weight equivalent to 4.608 grams
al-mithqāl al-sharʿī	legal *mithqāl*, i.e. a measure of weight equivalent to 3.456 grams
mudd	measure of weight equivalent to approximately 750 grams
nukhud	measure of weight equivalent to 0.192 grams
ṣāʿ	measure of weight equivalent to 2.823 kilograms

Appendix 2: Biography of His Eminence al-Sayyid Ali al-Husayni al-Sistani

In the name of Allah, the All-Beneficent, the Ever-Merciful.

All praise belongs to Allah, who elevated the stations of the scholars, until He endowed upon them the station of the Prophets and gave preference to their ink over the blood of the martyrs. And may the choicest of His blessings and salutations descend upon the one He chose from amongst all the former and latter generations, and whom He sent as a mercy to all the worlds. And [similarly upon] his noble and pure family.

Indeed, the honour of knowledge is not hidden, and its merits cannot be enumerated. Those worthy of it have inherited it from the Prophets, and thereby attained the position of representing the Seal of Successors, for as long as the earth and sky remain.

And from amongst those who – in pursuit of it – traversed the path of the righteous predecessors, is the honourable scholar, who acts according to his knowledge, is eminent and distinguished, is relied upon by the magnificent jurists, is the authoritative source on Islam, al-Sayyid Ali al-Sistani. May Allah perpetuate the days of his abundant contributions and conferring of benefit to others; and may He increase the likes of him, [those] scholars who act according to their knowledge...[1]

These beautiful words are the beginning of an official letter of recognition of *ijtihād*, given to Sayyid al-Sistani by his teacher the late Sayyid Abu al-Qasim al-Khoei (may Allah have mercy upon him) in 1380 AH. In this letter, Sayyid al-Khoei attests that Sayyid al-Sistani – who at that time was only thirty-one years of age – is a

[1] *Al-Sīrat al-Dhātiyyah*, Official Website of the Office of His Eminence al-Sayyid Ali al-Husseini al-Sistani. https://www.sistani.org/arabic/data/1 (accessed 8 July 2022).

qualified jurist who must act in accordance with his own deduction of Islamic law (that is, he must exercise his own *ijtihād*). In his letter, Sayyid al-Khoei also authorises Sayyid al-Sistani to narrate hadiths from him.

Sayyid al-Sistani is a distinguished scholar who has been a guardian of the Twelver Shia faith for a period of over thirty years. The following lines amount to a short biography of His Eminence, focussing on his family, seminary studies, and *marjaʿiyyah.*

HIS LINEAGE

'They were descendants one of another.' (Qur'an 3:34)

Sayyid al-Sistani is the son of Sayyid Muḥammad Bāqir, the son of Sayyid ʿAlī, the son of Sayyid Muḥammad Riḍā. His father, Sayyid Muḥammad Bāqir al-Sistani (d. 1370 AH), was one of the well-known pious scholars of the city of Mashhad, and his noble mother was the daughter of the scholar Sayyid Riḍā al-Mihrabānī al-Sarābī.

The noble family of His Eminence is one that is well-known for both knowledge and piety. In the eleventh century AH, the family lived in Isfahan, the then capital of Safavid Iran. Later on, one of the forefathers of His Eminence, named Sayyid Muḥammad, was appointed to the official position of *shaykh al-islām* in the province of Sistan, located in eastern Iran. From then on, the family came to be known as al-Sistani.

One of the outstanding scholars of this family was Muḥammad Bāqir Astarābādī (d. 1041 AH), more famously known as Mīr Dāmād (may Allah have mercy upon him). Remembered primarily as a philosopher, Mīr Dāmād was a polymath, who from a very young age had mastered various intellectual and traditional sciences. Moreover, he was a teacher of spirituality and ethics who reared eminent students such as Ṣadr al-Dīn Muḥammad ibn Ibrāhīm al-Shīrāzī (d. 1050 AH), known as Mullā Ṣadrā (may Allah have mercy upon him). In many places, Mullā Ṣadrā refers to this teacher of his with amazing words. For example, in his commentary on *Uṣūl al-Kāfī*, Mullā Ṣadrā writes:

> My master, support, teacher...the most sublime and illuminated *sayyid*, the most radiant and holy scholar, the godly philosopher, the godly

jurist, the master of his age and the choicest of his era...whose name is Muḥammad and whose title is Bāqir al-Dāmād al-Ḥusaynī, may Allah sanctify his intellect with godly light.[2]

A few generations thereafter, we come across the grandfather of His Eminence and his namesake. Sayyid ʿAlī al-Sistani (d. 1340 AH), the grandfather, was one of the students of Mīrzā Muḥammad Ḥasan al-Shīrāzī and Sayyid Ismāʿīl al-Ṣadr in the early fourteenth century AH. Mīrzā al-Shīrāzī was the *marjaʿ* at that time and had established a seminary in the city of Samarra. He is famously known for the edict he issued in 1309 AH that forbade the smoking of tobacco. Sayyid Ismāʿīl al-Ṣadr was also a well-known jurist and seminary teacher of his time, who intentionally avoided becoming the *marjaʿ* after Mīrzā's death. He was one of the earlier figures of the Ṣadr family; both Imam Mūsā al-Ṣadr and the martyr Muḥammad Bāqir al-Ṣadr are amongst his grandsons (may Allah have mercy upon them all). Āghā Buzurg Tihrānī (d. 1389 AH), one of the teachers of His Eminence, narrates the following about Sayyid ʿAlī al-Sistani the grandfather, 'Verily he attained a lofty status, and obtained an abundant share of knowledge along with piety and righteousness. His conduct was excellent, his character outstanding, and his personality was flawless.'[3]

HIS STUDIES

'And [He] made her grow up in a worthy fashion.' (Qur'an 3:37)

Sayyid al-Sistani was born in Mashhad on 9 Rabīʿ al-Awwal 1349 AH. At the age of five he began learning the Noble Qur'an. Thereafter, he went to a religious school where he learnt to read and write, along with other elementary studies, including calligraphy. At the age of eleven, upon his father's advice, he commenced his studies in the Islamic seminary. He quickly progressed through the introductory and intermediary levels, to reach the *baḥth al-khārij* in less than nine years, while still in his teens. *Baḥth al-khārij* refers to the highest level of classes in the Islamic seminary, where the teacher does not limit

[2] Ṣadr al-Dīn Muḥammad ibn Ibrāhīm al-Shīrāzī, *Sharḥ al-Kāfī*, vol. 1, p. 214.

[3] Āghā Buzurg Tihrānī, *Ṭabaqāt Aʿlām al-Shīʿah*, vol. 16, p. 1434.

themselves to a specific textbook, but rather they present their own research on the subject by referring to the views of various jurists and then presenting their own view with its own evidence and justification.

In addition to studying the traditional subjects of Arabic grammar, jurisprudence, and the principals of jurisprudence, during this time Sayyid al-Sistani also studied the intellectual sciences of philosophy and *ʿirfān*.

In 1368 AH, before the age of twenty, Sayyid al-Sistani moved to the holy city of Qum. There, he continued *baḥth al-khārij* studies under great jurists such as the late *marjaʿ*, Sayyid Ḥusayn Burūjardī. In a telling incident during this time, Sayyid al-Sistani once engaged in a jurisprudential discussion about rulings pertaining to the qibla. In a series of letters that he wrote to a well-known jurist named Sayyid ʿAlī al-Bahbahānī of Ahwaz, he discussed and challenged the understanding of Sayyid al-Bahbahānī and his teacher. In one responding letter, Sayyid al-Bahbahānī lauded the scholarly level of the young Sayyid al-Sistani, addressing him as, 'the pillar of those scholars who investigate and examine, and the choicest of the jurists who are precise and closely scrutinise.'[4]

In 1371 AH, Sayyid al-Sistani then moved to the holy city of Najaf. There, he remained focussed on his *baḥth al-khārij* studies under the leading jurists of Najaf such as Sayyid Muḥsin al-Ḥakīm, Sayyid Maḥmūd al-Shāhrūdī, Sayyid al-Khoei, and Shaykh Ḥusayn al-Ḥillī. In the words of Sayyid al-Khoei, the presence of Sayyid al-Sistani in his class was not like that of other students. Rather, it was of one of 'comprehension, meticulous investigation, deep immersion, and careful precision.'[5] It is worth noting that throughout his studies – whether in Mashhad, Qum, or Najaf – all his teachers were among the greatest scholars of their time.

In 1380 AH, at the age of thirty-one, Sayyid al-Sistani was given an official recognition of *ijtihād* from his teachers Sayyid al-Khoei and Shaykh Ḥusayn al-Ḥillī. Such an open recognition is an age-old tradition of the Islamic seminary, and while many who reach the level of *ijtihād* may not receive such written recognition, for those who do

[4] An image of this letter is available in the biography on the official website of Sayyid al-Sistani, previously cited.

[5] Refer to the same recognition of *ijtihād* that was quoted in the beginning of this article.

receive it, the acknowledgement serves to act as a proof to others.

From 1381 AH onwards, Sayyid al-Sistani began to teach *baḥth al-khārij*. In the subject of Islamic jurisprudence, he taught various topics such as transactions, purification, prayers, fasting, and *khums*. In the principles of jurisprudence, he completed three entire courses, the last of which ended in 1411 AH. In the words of his famous student Sayyid Munīr al-Khabbāz, the courses of His Eminence in jurisprudence were 'the most brilliant' in all of Najaf, and his method in the principles of jurisprudence was 'the most comprehensive' of all.[6] While initially these courses were offered in Persian, His Eminence later taught in Arabic as well.

In the past few decades, however, Sayyid al-Sistani's public classes have stopped for security reasons, as he has been forced to remain at his home. Despite these difficulties, and along with the many meetings he holds with visitors, Sayyid Munīr al-Khabbāz narrates that His Eminence continues to teach his sons at home.[7] Those who visit him are pleasantly surprised with how he, despite his age, enthusiastically engages in academic discourse. Visitors are also taken by surprise upon witnessing his remarkable memory.

HIS *MARJAʿIYYAH*

'Scholars are the inheritors of the Prophets.' (Imam al-Ṣādiq (ʿA))[8]

Sayyid al-Sistani's life and legacy are not limited to his scholarly contributions. Rather, he has played an active and fundamental role in navigating the political turmoil that has engulfed the noble and oppressed nation of Iraq. When he moved to Iraq in 1371 AH, the country was still a monarchy under King Faisal II. Over the decades which ensued, His Eminence would be witness to revolution and war. First, a revolution toppled the monarchy and established a republic in 1377 AH. Later, the Baʿath party came to power, and ruled for over twenty years, led by the ruthless dictator Saddam Hussein.

[6] Refer to an interview with Sayyid Munīr al-Khabbāz published in the Iranian journal *Andīshih*: Ali Teymoori, 'Ayatollah Sistani's Doctrine Differs from Ayatollah Khoei's One', *Itjihad Network*, 26 September 2020. http://ijtihadnet.com/ayatollah-sistanis-doctrine-differs-ayatollah-khoeis-one (accessed 8 July 2022). [7] Ibid.

[8] Abū Jaʿfar Muḥammad ibn Yaʿqūb al-Kulaynī, *al-Kāfī*, vol. 1, p. 32, narration 2.

Perhaps no period was harder for Sayyid al-Sistani than during the rule of Saddam Hussein, lasting from 1399 AH until the American invasion in 1424 AH. Saddam limited the mourning ceremonies of Imam al-Ḥusayn (ʿA), forbade the Shias from walking to Karbala in commemoration of Arbaʿīn, and sought to weaken the Islamic seminary. Saddam launched an eight-year war against the nascent Islamic Republic of Iran that led to hundreds of thousands of people losing their lives. He brutally suppressed uprisings and executed his opponents.

In 1411 AH, Saddam invaded and annexed neighbouring Kuwait. In response, the United States led a coalition of countries that fought what is known as the First Gulf War, seeking to expel Iraqi forces from Kuwait. When the objective of this war was quickly achieved and a ceasefire was declared, Iraq itself exploded into uprisings. Various groups in Iraq, united in their desire to oust Saddam, began to rebel. Encouraged by Saddam's defeat in Kuwait, the uprisings made quick progress. Within two weeks, most of the country had fallen to the revolutionaries. However, this victory was not to last. Despite the UN establishing no-fly zones in the Shiʿi areas of southern Iraq, Saddam used his helicopters to crush the opposition. A bloodbath ensued. Many people were killed and millions were forced to flee. Even the blessed shrines in Najaf and Karbala were attacked by Saddam's army. Many Islamic seminaries and mosques were destroyed and priceless original manuscripts were lost. The foremost *marjaʿ* of the Shiʿi world, Sayyid al-Khoei, was arrested and taken to Baghdad where he was forced to meet with Saddam on national television in an attempt to humiliate him and seek legitimacy for the Baʿath party. During this chaotic period, Sayyid al-Sistani was arrested along with other Iranian nationals living in the city of Najaf and suffered physical torture at the hands of his jailers.

In 1413 AH, Sayyid al-Khoei, the eminent *marjaʿ* and teacher of Sayyid al-Sistani, passed away, having led a long life dedicated to spreading the teachings of the school of the Ahl al-Bayt (ʿA). Prior to Sayyid al-Khoei's demise, scholars in Najaf had already begun to consider who would be the most suitable jurist to succeed him, and who would be the most qualified *mujtahid* to take up the position of *marjaʿiyyah* and uphold the strength of the Islamic seminary of Najaf. The answer was clear: Sayyid al-Sistani was considered amongst the most prominent *mujtahids* for this role. In addition to his own outstanding and compelling scholarly credentials, there were even indications that this was the desire of the late Sayyid al-Khoei. For example, some years earlier, Sayyid al-Khoei appointed Sayyid al-Sistani to lead congregational prayers in his place when he was too sick to lead.[9] Within a short span of time, Sayyid al-Sistani, who hitherto was only known in the seminary circles of Najaf, began to be recognised as the foremost *marjaʿ* of the Shia world. It was not long before a three volume Arabic manual of Islamic laws titled *Minhāj al-Ṣāliḥīn* (*The Path of the Righteous*) was published in accordance with the edicts of His Eminence. In the Introduction to this work, Sayyid al-Sistani writes:

> I have responded to the request that a group of believers have made – may Allah the Exalted give them success in attaining His pleasure – [asking me] to change the differing rulings [where Sayyid al-Khoei's fatwas were different, and replace them with the new fatwas that are] in accordance with my own opinion.[10]

With the death of other outstanding and widely followed *marājiʿ* in successive years, the position of Sayyid al-Sistani as the most prominent *marjaʿ* gained more following and popularity. For example, both Sayyid ʿAbd al-Aʿlā Sabzawārī in Iraq and Sayyid Muḥammad Riḍā Gulpaygānī in Iran, passed away in 1414 AH. Within a few years, English copies of the book *Islamic Laws*, in accordance with Sayyid al-Sistani's fatwas, were widely available in the West.

In 1424 AH, the United States again invaded Iraq and this time toppled Saddam, stating that Iraq had failed to abandon its weapons of mass destruction. Allah says, 'And the wrongdoers will soon know to what place of turning they shall turn back' (Qur'an 26:227).

In the two decades that have passed since the fall of Saddam, Sayyid al-Sistani's role in Iraq has been crucial. In the beginning, he started by encouraging people to be involved in the post-Saddam political process by calling for democratic elections. In this manner, he was guiding the Iraqi society to the fact that their political rights need to be acquired through modern methods and that it was necessary to draft a majority endorsed constitution that recognises the rights

[9] Refer to Sayyid al-Sistani's biography on the website of his office, previously cited. [10] Sayyid Ali al-Husayni al-Sistani, *Minhāj al-Ṣāliḥīn*, vol. 1, p. 4.

of all citizens equally. In 1425 AH, His Eminence quickly rushed back from a heart operation in the United Kingdom to peacefully end a fierce battle that had broken out between Iraqi and US forces against Muqtadā al-Ṣadr, sacrificing his personal health to return to Basra to save Iraq from unnecessary bloodshed. Moreover, he spearheaded the multi-million people's march from Basra to Najaf, protesting the American-led war, despite risks to his life, and even against the warning of the Iraqi Minister of Security. In 1435 AH, he issued a call for all those who were able to help the Iraqi security forces in their fight against ISIS.

At the same time, Sayyid al-Sistani called for Shias to refrain from revenge attacks on Sunnis after explosions in holy shrines, such as in Samarra. He called for Shias to understand that Sunnis are not only 'our brethren' but rather 'ourselves'. In addition, the team of His Eminence worked effortlessly to accommodate displaced non-Muslim Iraqis, including Christians and Yezidis, as refugees in the Shia shrine cities, until they could return to their homes safely. As a result, scholars of the Islamic world, especially in Iraq, together with many international figures, continue to depict His Eminence's *marjaᶜiyyah* as one of moderation (*wasaṭiyyah*) and wisdom, in whose fatherly compassion all seek refuge. The moderation of His Eminence is seen also in his ruling that Muslims who reside in countries as minorities must respect the national laws that apply to them insofar as there is no contravention with Islamic law.

On another note, in striving to serve the community while understanding its challenges more scientifically, the office of Sayyid al-Sistani established multiple humanitarian and academic institutions, such as the Al Ayn Foundation, the Astronomical Research Centre, and the Theological Research Centre. These organisations, as well as others of their like, ensure that His Eminence is up to date with the latest social developments, including moon sighting issues, economic and intellectual challenges, and even matters relating to the COVID-19 pandemic.

The foregoing paragraphs outline but a few of the outstanding achievements and different dimensions of the life and personality of our noble *marjaᶜ*, Sayyid Ali al-Husayni al-Sistani. May Allah lengthen his blessed life and elevate his lofty rank in both this world and the Hereafter.

Appendix 3: List of Updated Rulings

The following rulings have been revised since the publication of the previous edition of this work. They are marked in the text with an asterisk [*]. The rulings that contain the most important changes are highlighted in bold.

8, 12, 25, 35

100, 104, 105, 107, 109, 111, 112, 133, 134, 152, 172, 178

220, 223, 267, after 281 (7th cond.), 292

307, 336, 338, 341, 342, 343, 355 no. 3, 383, 393, 394

403, 419, 466, 467

503, 505, 537, 560, 566, 585, **597**

611, 612, 617 no. 1, 617 no. 7, 632, 633, 686

712, 719, 757, 790, 799

807, 820, 829, 858

974, 976, 988

1220, 1222, 1266, 1287, 1288, 1294

1370, 1387

1419, 1459, 1489, **1498**

1500, 1537, 1542, **1562,** 1584

1694, 1699

1756, 1772, 1782, 1798

1803, 1810, 1861, 1865, 1867, 1869

after 1939 (Zakat on Business Goods, 2nd cond.)

2016, 2063 no. 1, 2063 no. 3, 2082, 2092

2112, 2144, 2166, 2190

2247 no. 3, 2270, 2271

2306, 2396, 2399

2420, 2476

2540, 2552, 2553

2782, 2783, 2795

Works Consulted

The following is a list of the works on Islamic law by His Eminence al-Sayyid Ali al-Husayni al-Sistani which were consulted during the course of this translation.

Al-Fiqh lil-Mughtaribīn, compiled by ʿAbd al-Hādī Muḥammad Taqī al-Ḥakīm, Qum: Bāqiyāt, 2006.

Manāsik al-Ḥajj wa Mulḥaqātuhā, Qum: Dār al-Badhrah, 2012.

Al-Masāʾil al-Muntakhabah, Qum: Bāqiyāt, 2006.

Minhāj al-Ṣāliḥīn, Mashhad: Mashhad Office of Ayatollah al-Sayyid al-Sistani, 2018.

Taʿlīqāt ʿalā al-ʿUrwah al-Wuthqā li-Muḥammad Kāẓim al-Yazdī, Qum: Qum Office of Ayatollah al-Sayyid al-Sistani, 2004.

Tawḍīḥ al-Masāʾil-i Jāmiʿ, Mashhad: Mashhad Office of Ayatollah al-Sayyid al-Sistani, 2014.

Printed in Poland
by Amazon Fulfillment
Poland Sp. z o.o., Wrocław

25631225R00460